# The Right to Exclude

# The Right to Exclude

*A Critical Race Approach to Sovereignty, Borders, and International Law*

JUSTIN DESAUTELS-STEIN

# OXFORD
UNIVERSITY PRESS

Great Clarendon Street, Oxford, OX2 6DP,
United Kingdom

Oxford University Press is a department of the University of Oxford.
It furthers the University's objective of excellence in research, scholarship,
and education by publishing worldwide. Oxford is a registered trade mark of
Oxford University Press in the UK and in certain other countries

© Justin Desautels-Stein 2023

The moral rights of the author have been asserted

First Edition published in 2023

All rights reserved. No part of this publication may be reproduced, stored in
a retrieval system, or transmitted, in any form or by any means, without the
prior permission in writing of Oxford University Press, or as expressly permitted
by law, by licence or under terms agreed with the appropriate reprographics
rights organization. Enquiries concerning reproduction outside the scope of the
above should be sent to the Rights Department, Oxford University Press, at the
address above

You must not circulate this work in any other form
and you must impose this same condition on any acquirer

Public sector information reproduced under Open Government Licence v3.0
(http://www.nationalarchives.gov.uk/doc/open-government-licence/open-government-licence.htm)

Published in the United States of America by Oxford University Press
198 Madison Avenue, New York, NY 10016, United States of America

British Library Cataloguing in Publication Data

Data available

Library of Congress Control Number: 2022940211

ISBN 978–0–19–886216–1

DOI: 10.1093/oso/9780198862161.001.0001

Printed and bound in the UK by
Clays Ltd, Elcograf S.p.A.

Links to third party websites are provided by Oxford in good faith and
for information only. Oxford disclaims any responsibility for the materials
contained in any third party website referenced in this work.

*For that Night at Villa Ridge in the Summer of 1981*

# Acknowledgements

It's a strange thing, deciding how to backdate a project like this. I'm tempted to say that it began with my first publication as a professional academic from about ten years ago, an article titled *Race as a Legal Concept*. My effort to analyze racism as a structure of legal argument, which is key to the book you might be holding in your hands, certainly has its origins in that article—an article for which I received a great deal of valuable assistance. Neil Gotanda, Adrienne Davis, and Duncan Kennedy probably sit at the top of the list of people that offered indispensable advice and critique. Nevertheless, the roots of the project surely go further back, into my school days and deep engagements with David Kennedy, Martti Koskenniemi, Susan Marks, and Tony Anghie. Their insights were as invaluable then as they are today. Nevertheless, I can't help but date the project earlier still, and point to seminal classes and discussions in my teens with Dwight Mullen and Ed Katz. Mullen and Katz opened my eyes to the power of beliefs and ideas in exactly the way a college experience should, and I owe them the deepest of gratitude. But truth be told, this book is rooted in my childhood. Growing up in a biracial family in the American South, as the older member of a mixed-race pair of siblings, my greatest debts are to the two people that first helped me understand how and why to fight racism, my mother and my brother, Alex. I have no doubt that my commitments as a critical philosopher would be of a very different sort today, but for them.

With respect to the arguments laid out in these pages, I have been the fortunate repository of a vast commentary. It is difficult to catalogue all of the helpful criticisms I have logged along the way, but thanks are certainly due to many, many generous thinkers that I am failing to list here. Among the many readers, co-panelists, and interlocutors I have had the pleasure to engage over the past several years as the book has progressed, and that I would like to single out for appreciation, include Tendayi Achiume, Jim Anaya, Paulo Barrozo, Devon Carbado, Kristen Carpenter, Nahum Demetri Chandler, Ming Hsu Chen, Kim Crenshaw, Michael Fakhri, Sharon Jacobs, Arnulf Becker Lorca, Fred Megret, Sam Moyn, Aziz Rana, Akbar Rasulov, Pierre Schlag, Natsu Taylor Saito, Mohammad Shahabuddin, Chantal Thomas, Ntina Tzouvala, and Adrien Wing. I also must acknowledge the very generous support I have received from the University of Colorado Law School, the University of Colorado's Center for Critical Thought, and the Gordon Gamm Prize for Social Justice. Finally, I thank my Dad for his unwavering interest and encouragement, Dakota and Noah for their hugs, their laughter, and their being, and Amy for her love and kindness and patience…for her everything.

# Contents

Introduction     1

### PART I: LIBERALISM AND THE RACIAL SUBJECT

1. *Imperium* and *Dominium*     25
   - I THE THREE THESES OF LIBERAL LEGALISM     30
     - A Medieval Aristotelianism     30
     - B Hobbes     34
     - C Locke     37
   - II THE SOVEREIGN'S RIGHT TO EXCLUDE     41
     - A *Pomerium, Dominium, Imperium*     43
     - B The Domestic Analogy and the Global *Demos*     49

2. The Racial *Xenos*     62
   - I THE LOGIC OF EXCLUSION AND ITS LIMITS     63
   - II THE BIOPOLITICS OF RACIAL SUBJECTION     68
   - III THE GLOBAL CONTEXT OF RACIAL XENOPHOBIA     76
     - A From Environment to Evolution     80
     - B Eugenics     84
     - C From Raciality to Ethnocultures     87

3. Nations of Daylight, Children of the Night     95
   - I ON RACIAL IDEOLOGY     97
   - II CLASSIC RACIAL IDEOLOGY IN INTERNATIONAL LAW     103
     - A Property, Sovereignty, and Territory     103
     - B Articulating Racial Ideology in the Classic Style     113

### PART II: MODERN RACIAL IDEOLOGY IN INTERNATIONAL LEGAL THOUGHT

4. Modern Racial Ideology as Naturalizing Juridical Science     135
   - I THE RISE OF LEGAL FUNCTIONALISM     138
   - II FUNCTIONALISM IN INTERNATIONAL LEGAL THOUGHT     150
   - III THE LOGIC OF INCLUSION     156

5. The Promise of International Migration Law     161
   - I MIGRATION LAW IN THE FAMILY OF NATIONS AND THE UNITED STATES     164
   - II CLASSICAL RACIAL IDEOLOGY FROM BELOW     166

X  CONTENTS

III  CLASSICAL RACIAL IDEOLOGY FROM ABOVE — 169
IV  RACIAL IDEOLOGY AND *DOMINIUM* IN THE SUPREME
COURT — 175
V  THE TRANSFORMATION OF MIGRATION LAW AFTER
WORLD WAR I — 181

6. Decolonization and the Ambivalence of Self-Determination — 189
I  THE INTERWAR ALLIANCE BETWEEN ANTIRACIST AND
ANTICOLONIAL STRATEGY — 193
A  The Universal Races Congress — 193
B  Pan-Africanism, The League Against Imperialism, and the Black
Radical Tradition — 199
C  Decolonizing the United Nations — 205
II  FROM ANTICOLONIAL SELF-DETERMINATION TO HUMAN
RIGHTS — 210
A  *Western Sahara* — 211
B  Case Concerning the Frontier Dispute — 215
C  The Acquired Rights Debate — 218
D  *Imperium* and the New International Economic Order — 220
E  After Apartheid — 222

7. On the Ideological Threshold — 229
I  THE ANTICLASSIFICATION/ANTISUBORDINATION DEBATE — 233
II  TOWARD NEOLIBERALISM AND NEOFORMALISM — 238
III  TOWARD THE UN'S DISCRIMINATION CONVENTION — 245
IV  RACIAL EQUALITY, REFUGEES, AND THE RIGHT TO
EXCLUDE — 253

## PART III: POSTRACIAL XENOPHOBIA

8. Multiculturalism, Nationalism, Pragmatism — 265
I  THE CRITIQUE OF NEOFORMALISM: POSTRACIAL
MULTICULTURALISM — 267
A  LatCrit and TWAIL — 272
B  Postracial Self-Determination — 275
C  An Analytics of Raciality — 281
II  THE CRITIQUE OF FUNCTIONALISM: POSTRACIAL
NATIONALISM — 286
III  THE CRITIQUE OF STRUCTURE: POSTRACIAL PRAGMATISM — 298

9. On the Inevitability of Racial Borders — 313
I  GLOBAL GOVERNANCE AND DEMOCRATIC DEFICITS — 316
II  THE *DEMOS* UNBOUND — 322
III  ARE RACIAL BORDERS AN IRON CAGE? — 331

*Index* — 339

# Introduction

This book applies critical race theory to the law of sovereignty. Curiously, while there exists a rich literature on the figure of the sovereign in the space of international law, as well as a vast and interdisciplinary discourse on critical race theory, there is a relatively small amount of work that has aimed at the space connecting the two.[1] Why might that be? In an intellectual terrain already drenched in theory, what accounts for the lack of a critical race approach on the global plane?[2] In the pages ahead, I suggest that the challenges we face in the effort to conceptualize race and racism in the global context of sovereign rights is due to a tangled knot of ideological transformation, a situation in which it has become increasingly difficult to ask, much less answer, questions about how the concept of sovereignty itself assists in the production of racial hierarchy.[3] Or, to put that another way, the point is not that because there has been a relative lack of work applying critical race theory to international law, that international law has had nothing to say about racism. It

---

[1] For a sample of that twilight literature, *see* CHANTAL THOMAS, DISORDERLY BORDERS: HOW INTERNATIONAL LAW SHAPES IRREGULAR MIGRATION (2022); NATSU SAITO TAYLOR, SETTLER COLONIALISM, RACE, AND THE LAW: WHY STRUCTURAL RACISM PERSISTS (2020); E. Tendayi Achiume, *Beyond Prejudice: Structural Xenophobic Discrimination Against Refugees*, 45 GEO. J. INT'L L. 323 (2014); Robert Knox, *Valuing Race? Stretched Marxism and the Logic of Imperialism*, 4 LONDON REV. INT'L L. 81 (2016); Celina Romany & Joon-Beom Chu, *Affirmative Action in International Human Rights Law: A Critical Perspective of its Normative Assumptions*, 36 CONN. L. REV. 831 (2004); Kim Benita Vera, *From Papal Bull to Racial Rule: Indians of the Americas, Race, and the Foundations of International Law*, 42 CAL. W. INT'L L.J. 453 (2012); Adrien Katherine Wing, *Global Critical Race Feminism: A Perspective on Gender, War, and Peace in the Age of the War on Terror*, 15 MICH. ST. J. INT'L L. 1 (2007); Ruth Gordon, *Critical Race Theory and International Law: Convergence and Divergence*, 45 VILL. L. REV. 827 (2000).

[2] My focus here is on race and international law. For global perspectives on race without that focus, *see, e.g.*, DENISE FERREIRA DA SILVA, TOWARD A GLOBAL IDEA OF RACE (2007); SRDJAN VUCETIC, THE ANGLOSPHERE: A GENEALOGY OF RACIALIZED IDENTITY IN INTERNATIONAL RELATIONS (2011); EMPIRE, RACE, AND GLOBAL JUSTICE (Duncan Bell ed., 2019); Paul Ortiz, *Anti-Imperialism as a Way of Life: Emancipatory Internationalism and the Black Radical Tradition in the Americas*, *in* FUTURES OF BLACK RADICALISM (Gaye Theresa Johnson & Alex Lubin eds., 2017); PAUL ORTIZ, AN AFRICAN AMERICAN AND LATINX HISTORY OF THE UNITED STATES (2018); ALEXANDER DAVIS ET AL., THE IMPERIAL DISCIPLINE: RACE AND THE FOUNDING OF INTERNATIONAL RELATIONS (2020); ROBERT VITALIS, WHITE WORLD ORDER, BLACK POWER POLITICS (2015); PATRICIA HILL COLLINS, INTERSECTIONALITY AS CRITICAL SOCIAL THEORY 123 (2019) (placing Crenshaw's theory of intersectionality in larger context); MARY DUDZIAK, COLD WAR CIVIL RIGHTS: RACE AND THE IMAGE OF AMERICAN DEMOCRACY (2000); BRENNA BHANDAR, COLONIAL LIVES OF PROPERTY: LAW, LAND, AND RACIAL REGIMES OF OWNERSHIP (2018).

[3] My focus on ideological transformation builds off of my prior work in JUSTIN DESAUTELS-STEIN, THE JURISPRUDENCE OF STYLE: A STRUCTURALIST HISTORY OF AMERICAN PRAGMATISM AND LIBERAL LEGAL THOUGHT (2018).

---

*The Right to Exclude.* Justin Desautels-Stein, Oxford University Press. © Justin Desautels-Stein 2023.
DOI: 10.1093/oso/9780198862161.003.0001

## 2 THE RIGHT TO EXCLUDE

surely does.[4] Indeed, a regular feature of human rights discourse is reference to the International Convention on the Elimination of Racial Discrimination (ICERD) and related instruments, as well as to the office of the United Nations' (UN) Special Rapporteur on Contemporary Forms of Racism, and it is true that, for better or worse, the machinery of international institutions has been directed against racism for generations.[5] The issue, therefore, is not about international law's effort to regulate racial discrimination. It is rather about a strange silence surrounding the willingness to interrogate the functions of racial ideology in international law, and more specifically, how a xenophobic theory of sovereign rights contributes to and sustains racial inequities.[6]

I believe that there are at least four reasons for the languid character of racial critique in international law, all of which speak to what we can characterize as the growing influence of a contemporary and global structure of racial ideology. These include related ideas about the lapse of colonialism and the rise of a human rights framework buoyed by an antidiscrimination principle, an analytical separation between racism and xenophobia, a sense that "neoliberal colorblindness" has been displaced by a return to older modes of racial ideology, and a general disinclination to think about raciality in structural terms.

With respect to the notion that with the end of decolonization racism has ceased to be a problem for international law, the place to begin is with a traditional narrative about the ways in which international law has historically served the interests of Eurocentrism.[7] Indeed, throughout the nineteenth century, international

---

[4] *See, e.g.*, HENRY RICHARD III, THE ORIGINS OF AFRICAN-AMERICAN INTERESTS IN INTERNATIONAL LAW (2008); MICHAEL BANTON, INTERNATIONAL ACTION AGAINST RACIAL DISCRIMINATION (1996).

[5] The current Rapporteur, Tendayi Achiume, has led the way here in a series of pathbreaking interventions. *See, e.g.*, E. Tendayi Achiume, *Racial Borders*, 110 GEO. L.J. 445 (2022); E. Tendayi Achiume, *Migration as Decolonization*, 71 STAN. L. REV. 1509 (2019).

[6] As I argue later in Chapter 8, I do not see the movement known as Third World Approaches to International Law (TWAIL) as synonymous with critical race theory. For general discussion, *see* James Thuo Gathii, *Writing Race and Identity in a Global Context: What CRT and TWAIL Can Learn From Each Other*, 67 UCLA L. REV. 1610 (2021); Chantal Thomas, *Critical Race Theory and Postcolonial Development Theory: Observations on Methodology*, 45 VILL. L. REV. 1195 (2000). TWAIL has consistently developed a series of brilliant critiques of the international legal order, but they have only rarely focused on race, such as Makau Matua, *Why Redraw the Map of Africa? A Moral and Legal Inquiry*, 16 MICH. J. INT'L L. 1113 (1995). More so than with critical race theory, TWAIL has a stronger genealogical tie with the international application of LatCrit studies. *See, e.g.*, Berta Esperanza Hernandez-Truyol, *Building Bridges: Bringing International Human Rights Home*, 9 LA RAZA L.J. 69 (1996). On TWAIL generally, *see, e.g.*, Makau Mutua, *What is TWAIL?* 94 PROC. ANN. MEET. AM. SOC. INT'L L. 31 (2000); Antony Anghie & B.S. Chimni, *Third World Approaches to International Law and Individual Responsibility in Internal Conflicts*, 2 CHI. J. INT'L L. 77 (2003); Luis Eslava & Sundhya Pahuja, *Beyond the Postcolonial: TWAIL and the Everyday Life of International Law*, 45 LAW & POL. IN AFR., ASIA & LATIN AM. 195 (2012); RATNA KAPUR, GENDER, ALTERITY, AND HUMAN RIGHTS: FREEDOM IN A FISHBOWL (2018); Upendra Baxi, *What May the Third World Expect from International Law?* 27 THIRD WORLD Q. 713 (2006).

[7] For powerful critiques of eurocentrism in international law, *see* B.S. CHIMNI, INTERNATIONAL LAW AND WORLD ORDER (2017); ARNULF BECKER LORCA, MESTIZO INTERNATIONAL LAW (2014); BALAKRISHNAN RAJAGOPAL, INTERNATIONAL LAW FROM BELOW: DEVELOPMENT, SOCIAL MOVEMENTS AND THIRD WORLD RESISTANCE (2009); ANTONY ANGHIE, IMPERIALISM, SOVEREIGNTY, AND THE MAKING OF INTERNATIONAL LAW (2007).

INTRODUCTION    3

lawyers, diplomats, and philosophers worked tirelessly to justify an imperial conception of world order, a conception that justified the exclusion of racially "inferior" peoples from full participation as free and equal members of international society.[8] As the traditional narrative has it, in the wake of World War I certain portions of these colonized peoples were funneled into the League of Nations' "mandate system."[9] The road to freedom was both sluggish and weird, but as the colonized world travelled through the mandates scheme, into the Trusteeship and Non-Self-Governing Territories (NSGT) systems of the UN, and through the global movement that was decolonization, international law's campaign against racial hierarchy went into recession.[10] By the 1960s, human rights instruments like the ICERD had been adopted by a diverse international society, and by the end of the century, a genuinely multicultural ethos had assisted in the elimination of the last remnant of a vulgar history of racial discrimination: South African apartheid.[11] It is a story of progress, triumph, independence, and in many ways, it is a story worth celebrating.

It is also a story that makes it increasingly difficult to talk about how international law might continue to produce systems of racial disadvantage, *today*.[12] As the narrative suggests, if the history of sovereignty has an unsavory backstory, the path forward seems rather clear: Don't repeat it. If peoples continue to be excluded, include them. If peoples continue to suffer discrimination, make it stop. If there is racism, eliminate it. These path-dependent avenues for reform are certainly alluring, and indeed, it is easy to feel as if there's no other way to even think about antiracist strategy on the international plane, other than through the lens of the exclusion/inclusion rubric of human rights and multiculturalism, through the elimination of racial discrimination and the celebration of cultural difference. As critical race theory has long taught, however, it is precisely in the space of a broad convergence of interest about the value of the antidiscrimination principle and arguments

---

[8] *See infra* Chapter 3.

[9] *See* MOHAMMAD SHAHABUDDIN, MINORITIES AND THE MAKING OF POSTCOLONIAL STATES IN INTERNATIONAL LAW (2021).

[10] For discussion, *see* ADOM GETACHEW, WORLDMAKING AFTER EMPIRE: THE RISE AND FALL OF SELF-DETERMINATION (2020).

[11] For discussion of a series of antiracism campaigns that culminates with the defeat of apartheid, *see* DAVID THEO GOLDBERG, THE THREAT OF RACE: REFLECTIONS ON RACIAL NEOLIBERALISM (2008). On multiculturalism, *see, e.g.*, DAVID HOLLINGER, POSTETHNIC AMERICA: BEYOND MULTICULTURALISM (1995); Charles Taylor, *The Politics of Recognition, in* MULTICULTURALISM (Amy Guttman ed., 1994), Avishai Margalit & Joseph Raz, *National Self-Determination, in* THE RIGHTS OF MINORITY CULTURES (Will Kymlicka ed., 1995); Paul Gilroy, *The End of Antiracism*, in RACE, CULTURE, AND DIFFERENCE 50 (James Donald & Ali Rattansi eds., 1992) ("the common sense ideology of antiracism has also drifted towards a belief in the absolute nature of ethnic categories and a strong sense of the insurmountable cultural and experiential divisions which, it is argued, are a feature of racial difference").

[12] On the use of history in this way, *see* David Kennedy, *The Disciplines of International Law*, 12 LEIDEN J. INT'L L. 9, 88–101 (1999).

# 4    THE RIGHT TO EXCLUDE

that prioritize culture over race that we should be alert to the ideology of white supremacy.[13]

Beyond the sense in which human rights and multiculturalism have come to own the field of racial justice reform, there is a separate analytical effect in their historical confluence. At the end of the nineteenth century, the question of racial justice in international society was caught up in debates about global migration and, in particular, migration between "white" and "nonwhite" populations.[14] The possibility of an international migration law had surfaced, in which international rules might govern national decisions about admission, citizenship, deportation, and so on, but as became clear, for example, in Japan's unsuccessful attempt to insert a racial equality clause in the Covenant of the League of Nations, decisions about border controls would be given over to a sovereign's right to exclude. Fueled by the increasingly influential field of eugenics, the sovereign's right to exclude entered a phase of intense racialization, and with it came international law's definitive statement on race and borders: these were matters of sovereign right.[15]

Just as the process of excluding nations from participation in international society on the basis of race—a process that had been so prevalent in the nineteenth century—became increasingly suspect, so too did the process of excluding individual human beings eventually conform to the antidiscrimination principle.[16] What was left entirely intact, however, was the sense that sovereigns enjoyed a "plenary" power in the space of migration, and that when it came to questions about defending and protecting national identities, these were questions largely beyond the pale of human rights law. To be sure, to the extent a sovereign might violate a human rights norm with respect to a protected class, that sovereign was, at least in theory, on the hook. But more critically for present purposes, what for more than a hundred years international law has left to the sovereign's discretion is the entire space of the border regime, and not only in terms of territorial boundaries.[17] This is

---

[13] *See, e.g.*, Derrick Bell, *Brown v. Board of Education and the Interest-Convergence Dilemma*, 93 HARV. L. REV. 518 (1980); Kimberle Crenshaw, *Race, Reform, and Retrenchment: Transformation and Legitimation in Antidiscrimination Law*, 101 HARV. L. REV. 1331 (1988); Kimberle Crenshaw, *Mapping the Margins: Intersectionality, Identity Politics, and Violence against Women of Color*, 43 STAN. L. REV. 1241 (1991); Devon Carbado, *Critical What What?* 43 CONN. L. REV. 1595 (2011); CRITICAL RACE THEORY: THE KEY WRITINGS THAT FORMED THE MOVEMENT (Kimberle Crenshaw et al. eds., 1996).

[14] LUCY MAYBLIN & JOE TURNER, MIGRATION STUDIES AND COLONIALISM (2021); MARILYN LAKE & HENRY REYNOLDS, DRAWING THE GLOBAL COLOUR LINE: WHITE MEN'S COUNTRIES AND THE INTERNATIONAL CHALLENGE OF RACIAL EQUALITY (2008); VINCENT CHETAIL, INTERNATIONAL MIGRATION LAW (2019).

[15] *See infra* Chapter 5.

[16] Hiroshi Motomura, *The New Migration Law: Migrants, Refugees, and Citizens in an Anxious Age*, 105 CORNELL L. REV. 457 (2020).

[17] There is, of course, the field of refugee law. It is a field, however, that does little more than prove the primacy of the sovereign's right to exclude. For discussion, *see* E. Tendayi Achiume, *Race, Refugees, and International Refugee Law, in* THE OXFORD HANDBOOK OF INTERNATIONAL REFUGEE LAW (Cathryn Costello et al. eds., 2021).

the space of national, and relatedly, cultural identity, and the right of the sovereign to produce and enforce that identity through the naming of ethnocultural *others*.[18]

Inherent to the sovereign's right to exclude is an insider/outsider dynamic, or what Patrick Wolfe called a "xenology," a means for distinguishing between human collectivities.[19] That is, the right to exclude demands borders.[20] And in this exclusionary role for borders, there is the supplemental demand that insiders and outsiders *exist*—and if they don't, then they must be produced.[21] In this light, the right to exclude is unavoidably coercive. It draws lines and interpellates subjects,[22] and it is precisely through the bounding of subjection that the right to exclude is definitively committed to the production of foreignness, to the *xenos*, and relatedly, xenophobia.[23] Even if what is defined as the foreign is not necessarily an object of vilification—as what is "foreign" can certainly be loved—what is foreign is also what is excludable, and this much inheres in the sovereign's right to exclude. This line of reasoning suggests that if the right to exclude constitutes the liberal conception of sovereignty, then sovereignty requires the production of a *xenos*, a foreigner, an outsider. Or, as Carl Schmitt had put it in a different context, "The ability to recognize a just enemy is the beginning of all international law."[24] It is in this sense that I argue for a structural linkage between sovereignty and xenophobia,

---

[18] Influential treatments here include Arash Abizadeh, *Democratic Theory and Border Coercion: No Right to Unilaterally Control Your Own Borders*, 36 POL. THEORY 37 (2008); Arash Abizadeh, *Does Collective Identity Presuppose an Other?*, 99 AM. POL. SCI. REV. 45 (2005); HOMI BHABA, THE LOCATION OF CULTURE (1994); STUART HALL, ESSENTIAL ESSAYS, VOLUME 2: IDENTITY AND DIASPORA (David Morley ed., 2019); ROBERT J.C. YOUNG, WHITE MYTHOLOGIES (1990); GAYATRI CHAKRAVORTY SPIVAK, A CRITIQUE OF POSTCOLONIAL REASON: TOWARD A HISTORY OF THE VANISHING PRESENT (1999).

[19] PATRICK WOLFE, TRACES OF HISTORY: ELEMENTARY STRUCTURES OF RACE 7 (2016).

[20] *See infra* Chapter 2.

[21] On the "constitutive outside," *see* Ernesto LACLAU, NEW REFLECTIONS ON THE REVOLUTION OF OUR TIME 18 (1990); CHANTAL MOUFFE, THE DEMOCRATIC PARADOX 21 (2005); Hannah Richter, *Beyond the "Other" as Constitutive Outside: The Politics of Immunity in Robert Esposito and Niklas Luhmann*, 18 EUR. J. POL. THEORY 216 (2019). *See also* SEYLA BENHABIB, THE RIGHTS OF OTHERS: ALIENS, RESIDENTS, AND CITIZENS (2004); WENDY BROWN, WALLED STATES, WANING SOVEREIGNTY (2010); MATHEW LONGO, THE POLITICS OF BORDERS: SOVEREIGNTY, SECURITY, AND THE CITIZEN AFTER 9/11 (2018); PHILLIP COLE, PHILOSOPHIES OF EXCLUSION: LIBERAL POLITICAL THEORY AND EXCLUSION (2000).

[22] On interpellation in general, *see* LOUIS ALTHUSSER, LENIN AND PHILOSOPHY AND OTHER ESSAYS 64–68 (2001); LOUIS ALTHUSSER, FOR MARX 161–218 (1969).

[23] David Haekwon Kim and Robert Sundstrom explain that, as a term of art, the "phobic" aspect of xenophobia does not necessitate a sense of "fear." *See* David Haekwon Kim & Robert Sundstrom, *Xenophobia and Racism*, 2 CRIT. PHIL. RACE 20 (2014). *See also* Robert Bernasconi, *Where is Xenophobia in the Fight against Racism?* 2 CRITICAL PHIL. RACE 5, 6 (2014). Natsu Saito Taylor has suggested that in international law we define xenophobia to reference "both attitudes and actions that construct individuals and peoples as outsiders—often racialized outsiders—and then use that construction (i) to exclude them from benefits associated with an insider status that is often correlated, accurately or not, with a national or statist identity; (ii) to incite or excuse ideological or physical attacks on those deemed outsiders; or (iii) to facilitate the otherwise unlawful exclusion or removal of these groups or individuals from particular physical locations." Natsu Taylor Saito, *Why Xenophobia?* LA RAZA L. REV. 1 (2021). For more general treatments, *see* ERIKA LEE, AMERICA FOR AMERICANS: A HISTORY OF XENOPHOBIA IN THE UNITED STATES (2021); GREG GRANDIN, THE END OF THE MYTH: FROM THE FRONTIER TO THE BORDER WALL IN THE MIND OF AMERICA (2020).

[24] CARL SCHMITT, THE NOMOS OF THE EARTH 52 (2006).

## 6 THE RIGHT TO EXCLUDE

a generalized alertness to, if not anxiety about, the perennial outsider, the foreign mass, the barbarian horde.[25]

The contemporary effect of this historical separation between a foregrounded effort to tame racial discrimination through human rights law, and a backgrounded sovereign right of exclusion, has been to isolate both theorizing and efforts at reform with respect to racism and xenophobia.[26] And it is this isolation which has further hampered the ability to interrogate international law's complicity in the reproduction of contemporary forms of racial hierarchy. Indeed, and despite the fact that xenophobia and racism are certainly not the same (xenophobia, for one thing, is much older than racism), it has been a mistake to analyze prejudice against foreigners and prejudice on the basis of color as neatly separated into the problematics of ethnocultural xenophobia on the one side, and racism on the other.[27]

In some ways, these older and deeper tendencies to mark off xenophobic harms for ethnocultures find reflection in the legacy of important and much more recent debates from the turn of the century about concerns with essentialism in the study of race and racism.[28] In a word, the issue was whether racial approaches to law and society had made the mistake of masquerading a particular variable as a universal explanation. For example, an anti-essentialist critique might suggest that seeing racism as *the* explanation for a given society's experiences with domination and exploitation essentializes race at the expense of the economy or other metrics that are necessarily implicated.[29] Or the critique might be that in its study of racism, critical race theory made the mistake of reflecting white racism against Blacks as also and at the same time an analysis of racism against all people of color.[30] Or yet again, the critique might be that in its presentation of an analysis of racial dynamics in the United States (US), critical race theory promotes a disciplinary imperialism

---

[25] To be sure, anxiety about the "foreign" predates the liberal concept of sovereignty by a great deal, as does xenophobia arrive in human history *much* earlier than racism, which only enters the scene in the eighteenth century. As I discuss in Chapter 3, it was in the nineteenth century that the *xenos* was first racialized in the context of international law—sovereignty's home field. It was through the direct importation of racial ideology into the structure of international law that the figure of the *racial xenos* was produced, and along with it, racial xenophobia: fears, anxieties, and bigotries produced through the racialization of the foreign. For discussion, *see* ANN LAURA STOLER, RACE AND THE EDUCATION OF DESIRE: FOUCAULT'S HISTORY OF SEXUALITY AND THE COLONIAL ORDER OF THINGS (1995).

[26] Neil Gotanda, *The Racialization of Islam in American Law*, 637 ANN. AM. AC. POL. & SOC. SCI. 184 (2011); Robert Chang, *A Meditation on Borders, in* IMMIGRANTS OUT! THE NEW NATIVISM AND THE ANTI-IMMIGRANT IMPULSE IN THE UNITED STATES (Juan Perea ed., 1996).

[27] *See, e.g.,* LAURA GOMEZ, INVENTING LATINOS: A NEW STORY OF AMERICAN RACISM (2020).

[28] On essentialism in legal scholarship, *see* Angela Harris, *Race and Essentialism in Feminist Legal Theory*, 42 STAN. L. REV. 581 (1990); Devon Carbado & Cheryl Harris, *Intersectionality at 30: Mapping the Margins of Anti-Essentialism, Intersectionality, and Dominance Theory*, 132 HARV. L. REV. 2193 (2019).

[29] This is the view that is sometimes attributed to the complaint with critical race theory issued by critical legal studies. *See* Kimberle Crenshaw, *Twenty Years of Critical Race Theory: Looking Back to Move Forward*, 43 CONN. L. REV. 1253, 1288–89 (2011).

[30] Juan Perea, *The Black/White Paradigm of Race: The Normal Science of American Racial Thought*, 85 CAL. L. REV. 1213 (1997); Rachel Moran, *Neither Black Nor White*, 2 HARV. LAT. L. REV. 61 (1997).

INTRODUCTION 7

in the suggestion that these "parochial" explanations are relevant worldwide.[31] The result was a tendency to localize racism—and indeed, *racisms*—into as many particularized contexts as possible. In this way, the actual lived experiences of racism could find their way toward fruitful recognition.[32]

These are crucial considerations in the development of critical race theory, LatCrit studies, Asian-American Jurisprudence, ClassCrits, and so much else.[33] It is also important to note that anti-essentialism helped foster racism as a necessarily *local* problem of personal animus and experience, and a view of xenophobia as a necessarily *global* problem the result of inescapable collisions of cultural difference. At the same time, the local irrationality of racism becomes stylized as an anomaly that ought to be eliminated, while a global phenomenon of xenophobia is characterized as lamentable but natural, shameful but inevitable.[34] The upshot: international law's concern is with ensuring that sovereigns are alive to the presence of racial discrimination within their borders, and with characterizing xenophobia as a natural occurrence best addressed in the language of pluralism, diversity, and difference. All of this tends to obscure the contemporary structure of international law's racial ideology, a structure that has always operated as an ideology of *othering*, as a type of racial xenophobia. The founding position in racial ideology, I suggest, is the figure of the *racial xenos*.

There is a third reason that hinders a grappling with racial ideology in the space of the sovereign, and it concerns the way in which global discourses of racial and ethnic division have evolved in these early decades of the twenty-first century. Critical race theorists have argued that after the 1960s a new racism replaced Jim Crow, a racism that was "colorblind."[35] At the same time, political theorists have similarly suggested that the last third of the twentieth century came under the spell of "neoliberalism."[36] I discuss these concepts at length later on, but for the moment it worth noting the mutually reinforcing tendencies between colorblindness and neoliberalism.[37] As Eduardo Bonilla-Silva has written, colorblindness is a form of racial ideology that "explains contemporary racial inequality as the outcome of

---

[31] For discussion, *see* Keith Aoki, *Space Invaders: Critical Geography, The 'Third World' in International Law and Critical Race Theory*, 45 VILL. L. REV. 913 (2000).

[32] *See, e.g.*, George Frederickson, "Reflections on the Comparative History and Sociology of Racism," *in* RACIAL CLASSIFICATION AND HISTORY (E. Nathaniel Gates ed., 1997); ANTONIO DARDER & RODOLFO TORRES, AFTER RACE: RACISM AFTER MULTICULTURALISM (2004).

[33] *See* Athena Mutua, *The Rise, Development, and Future Directions of Critical Race Theory and Related Scholarship,* 84 DEN. U. L. REV. 329 (2006); Richard Delgado, *Crossroads and Blind Alleys: A Critical Examination of Recent Writing about Race*, 82 TEX. L. REV. 121 (2003); FRANCISCO VALDEZ & STEVEN BENDER, LATCRIT: FROM CRITICAL LEGAL THEORY TO ACADEMIC ACTIVISM (2021).

[34] YAEL TAMIR, WHY NATIONALISM? (2020).

[35] Neil Gotanda, *A Critique of "Our Constitution is Colorblind,"* 44 STAN. L. REV. 1 (1991); IAN HANEY LOPEZ, WHITE BY LAW: THE LEGAL CONSTRUCTION OF RACE (1996).

[36] *See* QUINN SLOBODIAN, GLOBALISTS: THE END OF EMPIRE AND THE BIRTH OF NEOLIBERALISM (2018); FOUCAULT AND NEOLIBERALISM (Daniel Zamora & Michael Behrent eds., 2015).

[37] *See infra* Chapters 7 and 8.

## 8  THE RIGHT TO EXCLUDE

nonracial dynamics."[38] From the perspective of the colorblind, people needn't be treated differently on the basis of race. The key to prohibiting racial discrimination, on this view, is prohibiting racial discrimination, plain and simple. To the extent racial groups face varying challenges in their life circumstances, colorblindness points to ineffective performance in a competitive marketplace, ostensibly due either to individual weakness or cultural difference. As for neoliberalism, this is an ideology of the market in which persons and states came to be analogized as both members of firms and as themselves firms, "and in both cases as appropriately conducted by the governance practices appropriate to firms."[39] As Wendy Brown says, in neoliberalism "both persons and states are expected to comport themselves in ways that maximize their capital value in the present and enhance their future value, and both persons and states do so through practices of entrepreneurialism, self-investment, and/or attracting investors."[40] Neoliberalism in its racial register yields the ideology of neoliberal colorblindness: a view of racism as the anomalous effect of persons, firms, and sovereigns competing and exchanging in a world ripped from its historical and political contexts. The warrant for this relentlessly colorblind decontextualization of race and racism is the claim that there is simply no value added in judging anything on the basis of race. Besides, the champions of neoliberal colorblindness knew they weren't racist. After all, they were well aware of their intellectual bedfellows in human rights law.[41]

Until recently, neoliberal colorblindness was a useful target for critique. The trouble now is the rising sense that both neoliberalism and colorblindness have in their own ways ran their respective courses, and that the world has arrived . . . somewhere else. If that's right, and neoliberal colorblindness is exhausted, has racial ideology returned to its more vulgar manifestations? With ethnic divisions in Europe as raw as they have been in generations, with racial discourse shriller than it has been in recent memory, and with overarching dynamics like global pandemics and sovereigns invading sovereigns, is it wrong to think that our political and racial ideologies are moving backward in time? I *do* think that it is wrong to think as much, and that in our tendencies for nostalgia we misunderstand what neoliberal colorblindness has become. In a word, my argument is that neoliberal colorblindness has morphed into a new phase of racial ideology, what I outline in the book's final chapters as postracial xenophobia.

As I have already noted, it is useful to characterize the figures of raciality in the context of sovereignty as racial *xenophobia*. What, then, of *postracial*

---

[38] Eduardo Bonilla-Silva, Racism without Racists: Color-blind Racism and the Persistence of Racial Inequality in America 2 (2018).

[39] Wendy Brown, Undoing the Demos: Neoliberalism's Stealth Revolution 34 (2015).

[40] *Id.* at 22.

[41] For discussion, *see* Richard Ford, Racial Culture: A Critique (2005). On the latter, *see* Samuel Moyn, Not Enough: Human Rights in an Unequal World (2019).

INTRODUCTION 9

xenophobia?[42]" The first thing to note about a transformation from neoliberal colorblindness and into postracialism is that it is *not* a transition away from racism, away from xenophobia, or in any way the marking of a moment of triumph over bigotry and exploitation. Indeed, it was colorblindness that taught its adherents the value of seeing race without history, as *after* history. Postracial ideology, in contrast, suggests a more nimble posture, an approach to race and racism that is as comfortable with neoliberalism as it is with moderate progressives. It is ad hoc, pragmatic, postmodern, grassroots, local, quotidian. As Kimberle Crenshaw has argued:

> While colorblindness declared racism as a closed chapter in our history, post-racialism now provides reassurance to those who weren't fully convinced that this history had ceased to cast its long shadow over contemporary affairs. Post-racialism offers a gentler escape, an appeal to the possibility that racial power can be side-stepped, finessed and ultimately overcome by regarding dominance as merely circumstance that need not get in the way of social progress.[43]

The ideological shift from neoliberal colorblindness and into postracial xenophobia relies upon four premises. First, *race is fictive nonfiction*. It is now a commonplace to conceive race entirely in sociohistorical terms, which is to say that race is only rarely considered as a biological concept or a meaningful term for physical anthropologists.[44] As it is, however, entirely typical for non-specialists (which is practically everyone) to believe that raciality remains a biological aspect of human identity, the result is a bifurcated situation in which race is at once regarded as unreal and real, a social construction as well as an unalterable part of human identity. We believe that race is a product of social engineering, and that race is as natural as nature gets. In this respect, the physical anthropology of racial identity combines with everyday common sense to produce a curiously "postracial" image of the human being.

Second, *while racism is real, the best way to eliminate it is by shifting the analysis to the ethnocultural forms of difference that have underwritten the older forms*

---

[42] *See generally* DAVID THEO GOLDBERG, ARE WE ALL POSTRACIAL YET? (2015); Crenshaw, *supra* note 29, at 1253; Sumi Cho, *Post-Racialism*, 94 IOWA L. REV. 1589 (2009). Wendy Brown has explained that the "prefix 'post' signifies a formation that is *temporally after but not over* that to which it is affixed. 'Post' indicates a very particular condition of afterness in which what is past is not left behind, but, on the contrary, relentlessly conditions, even dominates a present that nevertheless also breaks in some way with its past. In other words, we use the term 'post' only for a present whose past continues to capture and structure it." WENDY BROWN, WALLED STATES, WANING SOVEREIGNTY 33 (2010).

[43] *Id.* at 1326–27.

[44] *See, e.g.,* ROBERT WALD SUSSMAN, THE MYTH OF RACE: THE TROUBLING PERSISTENCE OF AN UNSCIENTIFIC IDEA (2014); MICHAEL YUDELL, RACE UNMASKED: BIOLOGY AND RACE IN THE TWENTIETH CENTURY (2014); THE CONCEPT OF RACE IN NATURAL AND SOCIAL SCIENCE (E. Nathaniel Gates ed., 1997); ANTHONY APPIAH, IN MY FATHER'S HOUSE: AFRICA IN THE PHILOSOPHY OF CULTURE 35–36 (1993).

10 THE RIGHT TO EXCLUDE

*of racism all along.* Following from this idea that we are postracial in the sense that in the register of the natural sciences race is a fiction, the ideal has shifted into inclusion as cultural diversity, where we promote *ethnic* and *cultural* difference in ways that are almost always oblivious to race—all the while refusing the language of colorblindness. The way forward is to leave raciality behind, without really leaving it, since the reality of ethnocultural identities, and the unavoidable differences between these identities, are what racial xenophobia has been hiding all along. Postraciality, in a word, denotes an abandonment of racial analysis for the analysis of ethnocultural difference and diversity, and promotes minimalism and the quotidian as the appropriate modes for understanding and addressing racism. Despite its status as an overarching worldview, postracialism pushes antiracism into nooks and crannies, determined to define racial hierarchy as only and ever and always local.

Third, *emphases on ethnocultural integrity as the engine for self-determination, whether at the level of subnational cultural groupings, or national identity, reinforce the sovereign's right to exclude—and as a result, reproduce the demand for a xenos, as well as the staying power of xenophobia.* If postracialism promotes cultural difference and cultural diversity as the vehicles for self-determination, it simultaneously promotes ancient distinctions between insiders and outsiders, certainly at the level of subnational ethnocultures, but also between a national self and an outer world of foreigners. And just as liberal theory has shouldered the task of defending multiculturalism, so too has it defended nationalism, a liberal theory of national identity meant to ground a functional political community—the nation. This liberal vision of the national community, just like the subnational ethnocultural communities against which it is pitted, is imagined as coming *after* race, as ethnocultural and entirely postracial. The *xenos* hasn't gone anywhere, but it has become a postracial *xenos*.

Fourth, *the ideology of postracial xenophobia has moved beyond colorblindness, neoformalism, and neoliberalism, and into pragmatism.* Whereas a considerable degree of the multicultural and nationalist planks feature neoliberal colorblindness, we can see both within the multicultural and nationalist discourses, and between them, a pragmatic preference for ad hoc divergence from the strictures of a neoliberal emphasis on individualism and diversity. The postracial pragmatist, in other words, has lost faith both in neoliberalism and in colorblindness, but feels compelled to use them anyway, as the situation demands. Strategies of legal argument (or what I call naturalizing juridical science), such as functionalism or formalism, may persuade here and there, but in the end what matters for the postracial pragmatist is a workable pastiche of cultural diversity over racial justice that is small-scale, grass-roots, trial-and-error. To be sure, the effects of pragmatic postracialism can certainly be positive—this is not the return of Bull Connor, the rise of the Proud Boys, or whatever else is being cooked up in the fringes of white

INTRODUCTION    11

supremacy radicalism. But they can just as easily turn bizarre, if not racist in their own right.[45]

The book's latter chapters explore these features of postracial xenophobia (antiracialism, the priority of ethnocultural difference, the reproduction of xenophobic discourse, and minimalist pragmatism) in the context of the contemporary situation for international human rights, self-determination, globalization, and global governance and, more specifically, the evaporation of race and racism from the general terrain of international legal thought. They conclude by situating postracial xenophobia in the argumentative context of what I have elsewhere defined as "pragmatic liberalism."[46] As legal ideology in the space of argumentative practice, pragmatic liberalism encourages precisely the kind of tensions and oscillations that appear to define postracialism. Postracial ideology, Crenshaw continued,

> [J]ettisons the liberal ambivalence about race consciousness to embrace a colorblind stance even as it foregrounds and celebrates the achievement of particular racial outcomes. In the new post-racial moment, the pragmatist may be agnostic about the conservative erasure of race as a contemporary phenomenon but may still march under the same premise that significant progress can be made without race consciousness. This realignment brings liberals and some civil rights activists on board so that a variety of individuals and groups who may have been staunch opponents of colorblindness can be loosely allied in post-racialism.[47]

Postracial pragmatism is not merely the extension of neoliberal colorblindness into the governance toolkit of depoliticized problem-solving. It is a way of reconceiving colorblindness as somehow at once utterly cognizant of race and racism, and at the same time utterly oblivious as to why race and racism warrant further discussion. The contemporary discourse of "Diversity, Equity, and Inclusion" is emblematic, with its warm assurances that white privileged males needn't worry about racial hierarchy so long as they are marching to the drumbeat of properly authorized propaganda.

Thus far I have referenced three roadblocks on the road toward a critical race approach to international law. They are: (1) the sense that racism has largely been eliminated as a problem in international legal thought, and that a cultural pluralist/

---

[45] By way of example, consider the brave new world of "Diversity, Equity, and Inclusion" (DEI) training. Without a doubt, these education initiatives battle entrenched prejudices and provide opportunities for advancement where they otherwise might have floundered. And yet, it is the ideology of DEI that both allows and encourages the white and the privileged to disparage and alienate people of color when those racial minorities talk about racism in ways that disturb the facile jargon of "diversity." Indeed, (and I have seen this personally), when a white man of privilege calls a Black man "offensive" and "inadequate" because the Black man deems his chronic experiences with and lifetime explorations of racism as relevant for understanding the needs and demands of "diversity," the project of racial justice has surely gone off the rails.

[46] DESAUTELS-STEIN, *supra* note 3.

[47] *Id.*

## 12 THE RIGHT TO EXCLUDE

human rights toolkit offers an appropriate response to bigotries and prejudices that remain in domestic society; (2) the sense that racism and xenophobia are analytically distinct categories and phenomena, and that as a result, warrant very different treatments; and (3) the sense that neoliberal colorblindness has been displaced by a retrograde form of racism. As I have argued, each of these ideas is ripe for critique. First, it is well worth asking how the antidiscrimination principle might foster blind spots in which the sovereign right to exclude flourishes. Second, the analytical separation of racial and xenophobic harm encourages a study of racism as increasingly local, multiple, and contingent, and a view of xenophobia as a global phenomenon that is natural and unfortunately necessary. As a result, it is useful to collapse this distinction and conceptualize racial xenophobia as a means for interrogating the racial ideology of sovereigns and their borders. Third, rather than characterize neoliberal colorblindness as retreating in the face of a retro-fascism reminiscent of the early decades of the twentieth century, my suggestion is that we trace the morphing of colorblindness into the "postracial," and neoliberalism into "pragmatic liberalism." The result is a contemporary form of racial ideology, *postracial xenophobia*.

It is here that I want to highlight a fourth roadblock, and it concerns the way in which the ideology of postracial xenophobia tends to insulate itself. Taken together, postracialism's antiracialism, culturalism, xenophobia, and pragmatism systematically redirect attention away from the structural and the global, and always toward the dispersed and multivalent terrain of the "grassroots" and the "everyday." The problem, in other words, is that precisely at the moment we might want to expose "structural racism," a form of *antistructural* racial ideology has emerged. On this view, the way to understand racism is *not* as a structure, but as fragment and debris. David Theo Goldberg hit the nail on the head when he wrote:

> Postraciality seeks to avoid completely the questions of structural differentiation. The postracial is the racial condition in denial of the structural. It avoids the fact that the structural forms and fashions the racial, and so too the social advantages, losses, and limits racially ordered. And in these denials and evasions the structural conditions of racial reproduction and racist articulation don't so much lie dormant as persist unattended. For the postracial, race is (to be) racially erased, racisms are thus rendered illegible, disparate impact is reduced to merely unfortunate happenstance.[48]

In this book, I take up the challenge of constructing the ideological structure of postracial xenophobia. There are, of course, many ways in which one might analyze "structure."[49] I define structuralism in the context of semiotics, in the tradition

---

[48] GOLDBERG, POSTRACIAL, *supra* note 42, at 35.

[49] *See infra* Chapter 1. For works at the intersection of critical theory and race and which tend to speak of racism in structural terms, *see* CHARLES MILLS, FROM CLASS TO RACE: ESSAYS IN WHITE

INTRODUCTION    13

of what I have elsewhere defined as "the Harvard School" of legal structuralism.[50] To view a legal domain as a "structure," in this sense, is to view it as a language-system, a language espoused by jurists and laymen—a language that makes the jurist just as much as the jurist makes it. Frantz Fanon has remarked in a related context, "To speak means to be in a position to use a certain syntax, to grasp the morphology of this or that language, but it means above all to assume a culture, to support the weight of a civilization."[51] As for the "domain," my object of analysis is what I call "liberal legal thought."[52] This is a language of legal argument generated out of foundational, or grammatical, postulates associated with liberal political theory. Out from the grammar of the system we move into an array of legal concepts. These concepts are shaped by two directives. First, they are governed by the system's grammar. Think here, if you like, about how the rules of a haiku shape the poem's content. Second, the rules immanent in a legal concept—what we can refer to as the sub-system's lexicon—are largely indeterminate, and the rules take on greater or lesser degrees of "closure" as a function of the style in which the rules are articulated. Consequently, in the structure of liberal legal thought ideology has three basic locations: in the grammar, in the lexical plane, and in the articulation of style.[53] The relation between grammar, lexicon, and style is not transcendental, not analytical. It is what Stuart Hall, following Louis Althusser, called "structuralist causality—a logic of arrangement, of internal relations, of articulation of parts within a structure."[54]

There is no shortage of work on the critique of what I am calling the "grammar" of liberal legal thought.[55] As I discuss below, the grammar is centrally constituted through a contest between ideas of individual right and free competition on the one side, and ideas of ordered liberty and social control on the other. My focus is much less on the grammatical theses themselves and much more on the articulation of style, of argumentative practice—those techniques through which the indeterminate spaces of legal concepts become "decontested," "naturalized," and shaped

---

MARXISM AND BLACK RADICALISM (2003); W.J.T. MITCHELL, SEEING THROUGH RACE (2012); ETIENNE BALIBAR & IMMANUEL WALLERSTEIN, RACE, NATION, CLASS: AMBIGUOUS IDENTITIES (1991); ACHILLE MBEMBE, CRITIQUE OF BLACK REASON (2017); ACHILLE MBEMBE, NECROPOLITICS (2019); REILAND RABAKA, AFRICANA CRITICAL THEORY: RECONSTRUCTING THE BLACK RADICAL TRADITION, FROM W.E.B. DU BOIS AND C.L.R. JAMES TO FRANTZ FANON AND AMILCAR CABRAL (2010); KEHINDE ANDREWS, BACK TO BLACK: BLACK RADICALISM FOR THE 21ST CENTURY (2019); FRED MOTEN, IN THE BREAK: THE AESTHETICS OF THE BLACK RADICAL TRADITION (2003); CHRISTINA SHARPE, IN THE WAKE: ON BLACKNESS AND BEING (2016).

[50] DESAUTELS-STEIN, *supra* note 3, at 35–70.

[51] FRANTZ FANON, BLACK SKIN, WHITE MASKS 17–18 (1986).

[52] DESAUTELS-STEIN, *supra* note 3, at 3–18.

[53] On legal ideology, *see* Justin Desautels-Stein & Akbar Rasulov, *Deep Cuts: Four Critiques of Legal Ideology*, 31 YALE J. L. & HUMAN. 435 (2021).

[54] HALL, *supra* note 18, at 59.

[55] I limit myself here to two canonical examples. *See* ROBERTO UNGER, KNOWLEDGE AND POLITICS (1975); DUNCAN KENNEDY, A CRITIQUE OF ADJUDICATION: FIN DE SIÈCLE (1999).

## 14 THE RIGHT TO EXCLUDE

in ways that lead the observer to conclude that certain interpretations of concepts are neutral, natural, the way things always have been, and will likely continue to be.

This focus on the structure of liberal legalism suggests the orientation of the present study—it is not on US law, or international law, or the law of any geographic space, per se. The focus is rather on the structure of a legal language, and it is a structure that could be operating anywhere. For just as the language-system known as Japanese can operate anywhere in the world, it is also true that we can talk meaningfully about the philology of that language, the locations in which it is spoken the most, the dialects that emerge in this place here, and why. Generally speaking, this sort of approach to liberal legalism might be an intellectual history, concerned with its origins and the like, or a social history focused on liberal political economy, or a cultural history of freedom and restraint. My interest, however, is with the history of the legal structure, the structure's causality, and the structure's transformations. That said, it isn't the entire structure of liberal legal thought that I'm after here. The critical race approach I develop is more specific, in two ways. First, I am interested in a very particular style of articulation. Second, I am interested in the legal concept, or the lexical terrain, of sovereignty, and to a lesser extent, its sister concept of property. The style of articulation is what I call "racial ideology."[56]

Let me expand for a moment on each of these layers in the structural analysis— on racial ideology (the style of articulation) on the one side, and sovereignty and property (the lexical terrain) on the other. Roland Barthes explained that ideology shoulders the "task of giving a historical intention a natural justification, and making contingency appear eternal."[57] We can say that ideology is a pattern of argumentative practice, where these practices squeeze and bleed the insides of a political idea out into every nook and cranny of a culture, to the point that you can't see the political anymore and are left with the cultural remains. This is what Barthes refers to as the ideological tendency to encourage a movement from the historical to the natural, a movement of "unceasing hemorrhage," the flowing of political content out from some historical moment of contest and into a commonplace recognition of "just the way things are." Barthes observed that the "world enters languages as a dialectical relation between activities, between human actions … " When the ideological maneuver succeeds, this dialectical relation in

---

[56] My development of the concept of racial ideology has been largely influenced by NAHUM CHANDLER, X: THE PROBLEM OF THE NEGRO AS A PROBLEM OF THOUGHT (2013); DENISE FERREIRA DA SILVA, TOWARD A GLOBAL IDEA OF RACE (2007); SAIDIYA HARTMAN, SCENES OF SUBJECTION: TERROR, SLAVERY, AND SELF-MAKING IN NINETEENTH-CENTURY AMERICA (1997); GIORGIO AGAMBEN, THE OMNIBUS HOMO SACER (2017); MICHEL FOUCAULT, THE BIRTH OF BIOPOLITICS: LECTURES AT THE COLLEGE DE FRANCE, 1978–1979 (2010); ROLAND BARTHES, MYTHOLOGIES (Richard Howard & Annette Lavers trans., 2013); ANTONIO GRAMSCI, SELECTIONS FROM THE PRISON NOTEBOOKS 328 (1989); STUART HALL, ESSENTIAL ESSAYS, VOLUME 1: FOUNDATIONS OF CULTURAL STUDIES 60 (David Morley ed., 2019). For discussion of how the phrase "racial ideology" has been used in the past, see ROBERT MILES & MALCOLM BROWN, RACISM 7 (2d ed. 2003).

[57] BARTHES, *supra* note 56, at 254.

language comes out *"as a harmonious display of essences."*[58] Moving now into the context of *racial* ideology, we examine argumentative structures justified through the use of racial conceptions of the human being. As Hall has observed, "Racism has its own logic. It claims to ground the social and cultural differences which legitimate racialized exclusion in genetic and biological differences: i.e., in Nature. This 'naturalizing effect' appears to make racial difference a fixed, scientific 'fact', unresponsive to change or reformist social engineering."[59] Wolfe has similarly written, "In systematically harnessing social hierarchies to natural essences and recruiting physical characteristics to underwrite the scheme, race constitutes an ideology in the purest of senses."[60]

With respect to the lexical terrain, if our starting point is the structure of liberal legal thought (i.e., grammar, lexicon, style of articulation), and if we urge a *global* critical race perspective on that structure which orients the analysis toward the entanglement of (post)colonial and racial forms of xenophobia, the path of least resistance leads toward the legal concept of sovereignty.[61] More than any other legal concept in the language-system of liberal legalism, sovereignty stands in a pivotal position with respect to the relation between the domestic and global orders. The reason for this is what international theorists have long termed "the domestic analogy."[62] I say more on this below, but for now the basic idea is that just as liberal political theory imagines the human being as a rights-bearing individual in a state of nature, so too is the sovereign imagined as a rights-bearing individual in a *global* state of nature. The result is that, in the context of liberal legalism, the concept of sovereignty stands as the generative material for the legal characterization of the political community—the *demos*—in both its national and international manifestations.[63]

In liberal legal thought, the concept of sovereignty does its heaviest lifting in the field of international law. Indeed, in this liberal register sovereignty has been the central organizing idea for international law for centuries. A principle technique

---

[58] *Id.* at 255.

[59] HALL, *supra* note 18, at 52–53 (David Morley ed., 2019) ("Racism has critical ideological dimensions, and "the analysis has been foreshortened by a homogenous, noncontradictory conception of consciousness and of ideology.").

[60] WOLFE, *supra* note 19, at 7.

[61] DANIEL LEE, THE RIGHT OF SOVEREIGNTY: JEAN BODIN ON THE SOVEREIGN STATE AND THE LAW OF NATIONS (2021); BEN HOLLAND, THE MORAL PERSON OF THE STATE: PUFENDORF, SOVEREIGNTY, AND COMPOSITE POLITIES (2017); CARL SCHMITT, POLITICAL THEOLOGY: FOUR CHAPTERS ON THE CONCEPT OF SOVEREIGNTY (1985); F.H. HINSLEY, SOVEREIGNTY (1986); JENS BARTELSON, A GENEALOGY OF SOVEREIGNTY (1995).

[62] *See, e.g.,* David Singh Grewal, *The Domestic Analogy Revisited: Hobbes on International Order*, 125 YALE L.J. 618 (2016).

[63] On democratic theory and the conceptualization of borders, *see* ADAM DAHL, EMPIRE OF THE PEOPLE: SETTLER COLONIALISM AND THE FOUNDATIONS OF MODERN DEMOCRATIC THOUGHT (2018); MICHAEL WALZER, SPHERES OF JUSTICE: A DEFENSE OF PLURALISM AND EQUALITY 31 (1983); DAVID MILLER, STRANGERS IN OUR MIDST: THE POLITICAL PHILOSOPHY OF IMMIGRATION (2016); CHANTAL MOUFFE, THE DEMOCRATIC PARADOX (2005); SARAH SONG, IMMIGRATION AND DEMOCRACY (2019).

## 16 THE RIGHT TO EXCLUDE

in doing so, and indeed, a defining characteristic of sovereignty, has been the sovereign's "right to exclude."[64] To be sure, we are more familiar with this particular right in the contexts of individual ownership, personal integrity, and self-determination. In the field of property law, for example, law students learn about the individual owner's right to exclude the world from their things and their lands, as well as from their persons. Structurally, the sovereign's right to exclude is similar, but it is not identical. While the sovereign possesses a right to exclude the world from its territory (in something like the right enjoyed by the individual property owner), it also has the right to exclude the world from international society (and this is a right the property owner does *not* have). From this structuralist vantage, I refer to the sovereign's right to exclude, understood in the context of territorial independence and self-determination, as a *right of dominium*.[65] In contrast, I refer to the sovereign's right to exclude, understood in the context of the boundaries of the international, as a *right of imperium*.[66]

This leads us to the central questions at the heart of this book: What is the connection between the sovereign's right to exclude and the ideology of the racial *xenos*, of racial xenophobia? What has that connection been, and crucially, what is the contemporary structure of racial ideology—postracial xenophobia? The discussion unfolds in three Parts. Part I details the structuralist approach to liberal legalism, the sovereign's right to exclude, the figure of the *racial xenos*, and the development of racial ideology in the context of a physical science of xenophobia. It concludes with a look at what I call a "classic" style of racial ideology in international law. Recall from above my reference to the domestic analogy, the metaphor that treats sovereign states as if they are rights-bearing individuals surviving, maybe thriving, in a global state of nature.[67] Hobbes famously suggested an image

---

[64] Arash Abizadeh, *Democratic Theory and Border Coercion: No Right to Unilaterally Control Your Own Borders*, 36 POL. THEORY 37 (2008); Arash Abizadeh, *Does Collective Identity Presuppose an Other?* 99 AM. POL. SCI. REV. 45 (2005); ANNA STILZ, TERRITORIAL SOVEREIGNTY: A PHILOSOPHICAL EXPLORATION 187 (2019); E. Tendayi Achiume, *Migration as Decolonization*, 71 STAN. L. REV. 1509 (2019).

[65] On self-determination in international law, *see, e.g.*, THE THEORY OF SELF-DETERMINATION (Fernando Teson ed., 2016); KAREN KNOP, DIVERSITY AND SELF-DETERMINATION IN INTERNATIONAL LAW (2002); SIBA N'ZATIOULA GROVOGUI, SOVEREIGNS, QUASI SOVEREIGNS, AND AFRICANS: RACE AND SELF-DETERMINATION IN INTERNATIONAL LAW (1996); JORG FISCH, THE RIGHT OF SELF-DETERMINATION OF PEOPLES: THE DOMESTICATION OF AN ILLUSION (2015).

[66] *See* ROBERT C.J. YOUNG, EMPIRE, COLONY, POSTCOLONY 17 (2015). For discussions of *imperium* in international law in ways other than how I'm using the term here, *see* MARTTI KOSKENNIEMI, TO THE UTTERMOST PARTS OF THE EARTH: LEGAL IMAGINATION AND INTERNATIONAL POWER, 1300–1870 (2021); ANTHONY CARTY, THE DECAY OF INTERNATIONAL LAW: A REAPPRAISAL OF THE LIMITS OF LEGAL IMAGINATION IN INTERNATIONAL AFFAIRS 50–64 (1988); JOHN WESTLAKE, CHAPTERS ON THE PRINCIPLES OF INTERNATIONAL LAW 129 (1894).

[67] *See, e.g.*, EMER DE VATTEL, THE LAW OF NATIONS 8 (2008); SAMUEL PUFENDORF, DE OFFICIO HOMINIS ET CIVIS JUXTA LEGEM NATURALEM LIBRI DUO 17–21 (1927); DAVID ARMITAGE, FOUNDATIONS OF MODERN INTERNATIONAL THOUGHT (2013). This canon is unmistakably "European," and should not be understood as universal in any sense. *See* T.J. LAWRENCE, THE PRINCIPLES OF INTERNATIONAL LAW 4–5 (1895) ("[T]he notions of classical antiquity differ immensely from those of modern Europe, and in our own day there is a great gulf fixed between the views of European and American statesmen on the one hand and those of the potentates of Central Africa on the other. But though there are several

INTRODUCTION 17

of humanity's natural condition, in which there existed a permanent state, whether latent or patent, of a war of all against all.[68] If there was no such thing as a natural community, and if there were no natural constraints on what an individual might define as a threat to their right of self-preservation, everyone, Hobbes explained, had a right to everything: other people's property, other people's bodies, everything. Obviously, this was an unhappy world. In it there existed a constant state of war, where all reprisals and measures deployed in anticipation of future reprisals were justified. After all, there was no higher authority capable of determining *a priori* when a threat was insufficient to trigger a deadly response. In this natural condition, justice was a matter of individual discretion.[69]

Sovereigns had no need to agree to a global social contract, but the voluntary law of the "great society" functioned to supply something of a stand-in. And conceptualizing the domestic analogy in this way—where sovereigns were like individuals in a state of nature that needn't renounce their full rights of self-preservation, and yet at the same time, were still governed by a global society's "voluntary law of nations," had some long-lasting effects. Sovereigns emerged as both subjects and objects of the international legal order, both the makers of the law and the law's citizenry. What this means is that we can imagine—in international law—sovereigns as *both/either* leviathans *and/or* rights-bearing individuals. And this is why the sovereign's right of *imperium* has such a curious cast: sovereigns are conceptualized as possessing the rational, self-determining mind of an individual citizen, and also the power to decide both the identity of the planet's foreign—killable—human bodies, as well as the geographic spaces inhabited by these killable bodies. The classic liberal domestic analogy yielded a global *demos* of sovereigns in which each sovereign at once enjoyed the equal right to determine the boundaries of that *demos*, as well as an equal right to determine the content of the voluntary law of nations—those rights binding throughout that sovereign *demos*.[70]

Part II elaborates on the ideological structure of the "modern" style. In the context of this modern structure, I trace the transformation of racial ideology through the rise of the first international race conferences, debates about eugenics and migration, the shift into the UN framework of decolonization and self-determination, and the eclipse of a formalistic mode of legal argument by a functionalist one. In

---

systems of international law, there is but one important system ... it grew up in Christian Europe, though some of its roots may be traced back to ancient Greece and ancient Rome. It has been adopted by all the civilized states of the earth .... We have, therefore, in our definition, spoken of it as "the rules which determine the conduct of the general body of *civilized* states.").

[68] THOMAS HOBBES, LEVIATHAN 183 (C.B. Macpherson ed., 1968).

[69] ARASH ABIZADEH, HOBBES AND THE TWO FACES OF ETHICS (2018). This relates to the distinction between reasons of the right, enforceable through the sovereign's law, and reasons of the good, which were matters of conscience.

[70] This should not be mistaken for the idea that international law promotes democracy for nation-states. *See, e.g.*, James Crawford & Susan Marks, *The Global Democracy Deficit: An Essay on International Law and its Limits, in* RE-IMAGINING POLITICAL COMMUNITY (Daniele Archibugi et al. eds., 1998); Thomas Franck, *The Emerging Right to Democratic Governance*, 86 AM. J. INT'L L. 46 (1992).

## 18 THE RIGHT TO EXCLUDE

contrast with the demand to make international society more inclusive, these were claims for self-determination and nonintervention regarding a people's national territory. These were freedom claims, freedom from the colonizers, from apartheid, from racial discrimination, as well as freedoms to *become*, to realize the cultural destiny of the nation. There is, however, a "doubled" aspect of self-determination as it was developing in the 1960s and 1970s that is worth emphasizing. On the one hand, in the early decades of the twentieth century it had become utterly "natural" to conceptualize sovereignty as including a right to exclude individual migrants from the territory of the *demos*. Self-determination was about a particular community defining itself, and if eugenics was the north star, so be it. On the other hand, the anticolonial use of *dominium* viewed the "plenary power" of self-definition, of the right to determine the life-story of the *demos*, as the central pillar in a global strategy that was as antiracist as it was anticolonialist. Indeed, for many of these thinkers and activists, the sovereign's right of *dominium* (i.e., self-determination) was a necessary condition for decolonization, as well as the elimination of racial hierarchy. The right of *dominium*, in other words, was configured as both a means for entrenching and eliminating racial hierarchy, all at the same time.

What, however, did the "elimination of racial hierarchy" mean in this decolonizing space? What it did not mean is as important as what it did. In international law the rights of self-determination and nonintervention had become deeply inflected with processes of racial subjection. The result was that by the time the formerly colonized states were reaching out for the new rights of sovereignty, what they were reaching for included a naturalizing right to exclude that sequestered questions about the raciality of migration, borders, and the identity of the foreign. Questions about how the right to exclude and the consolidation of borders might *themselves* reproduce structures of racial hierarchy had been removed from the international legal agenda, as the naturalization of the sovereign's plenary rights regarding the boundaries of the *demos* had already been accomplished. To underline the point, the anticolonial use of self-determination as antiracism never even fathomed something called "international migration law," a field of norms that might constrain the new sovereigns in their choices about how to identify their political communities, define their outsiders, and control their borders.

Another thing that the "elimination of racial hierarchy" did not mean at this point was the "elimination of racial discrimination." That is, while there was certainly talk of human rights and antidiscrimination in this decolonial context, that talk signaled something quite different than what was yet to come. To assist in making this distinction clear, I will refer at times to early and late phases in international law's modern racial ideology. Through the middle decades of the twentieth century, international legal discourse about decolonization typically referenced human rights as an *effect* of national self-determination. Once the formerly colonized people took control of their "house," and emerged as a full participant in the global order, then (and only then) could individual citizens enjoy their rights. But if the sovereign was crippled, so too would be the individual human being. This is what Adom Getachew has called the "worldmaking" manifestation of anticolonial self-determination,[71] and what I refer to as an aspect of "early modern" racial ideology. Of course, it was already in the early 1960s that work was under way to adopt the ICERD. And the twin human rights covenants were right behind it. But it was not until this "worldmaking" class of self-determination claims had exhausted themselves that the way really opened up for thinking about "the elimination of racial discrimination" in the way we do today.

Part II concludes with this transition away from direct engagements with international law's complicity with "racial hierarchy" and toward the more tepid focus on "racial discrimination." This shift into "late modern" racial ideology is above all about the capture of the sovereign's right to exclude by a logic of inclusion on the side of *imperium*, and by the antidiscrimination principle on the side of *dominium*. It is also a moment when the right of self-determination dislocates from antiracism altogether. This process in which the antidiscrimination principle becomes the lodestar for a hegemonic human rights movement is marshaled forward by several interrelated ideas: colorblindness, neoformalism, and neoliberalism. By the last decades of the twentieth century, international law's modern racial ideology had largely matured to a point where neoliberal colorblindness and international human rights law had together emerged as the singular points of entry for analyzing racism in the space of international law.

Part III examines the transformation of the modern style into the contemporary structure of racial ideology, "postracial xenophobia." As I mentioned above, we can target the transition into postracialism by way of the transformation from neoliberalism into pragmatic liberalism. As Wendy Brown has noted, by the turn of the new century, whatever neoliberalism had initially been, by the 2000s it had turned "monstrous." Brown explained:

Democracy has been throttled and demeaned, yes. However, the effect has been the opposite of neoliberal aims. Instead of being insulated from and thus capable of steering the economy, the state is increasingly instrumentalized by big capital— all the big industries, from agriculture and oil to pharmaceuticals and finance, have their hands on the legislative wheels. Instead of being politically pacified, citizenries have become vulnerable to demagogic nationalistic mobilization decrying limited state sovereignty and supranational facilitation of global competition and capital accumulation. And instead of spontaneously ordering and disciplining populations, traditional morality has become a battle screech, often emptied of substance as it is instrumentalized for other ends. As antidemocratic

---

[71] ADOM GETACHEW, WORLDMAKING AFTER EMPIRE: THE RISE AND FALL OF SELF-DETERMINATION (2020).

## 20 THE RIGHT TO EXCLUDE

political powers and energies in constitutional democracies have swollen in magnitude and intensity, they have yielded a monstrous form of political life ... [72]

My claim is that neoliberalism's "Frankenstein Monster" is pragmatic liberalism. The question with which the book concludes, however, is whether Frankenstein is now an irrelevant bogeyman? For if the ideology of postracial xenophobia is a blend of postracial multiculturalism, postracial nationalism, and postracial pragmatism, and if this is a fair picture of international law's "contemporary" articulation of racial ideology, then what of the fact of "globalization"?[73] If the literature on globalization has it right, and sovereignty is a far more peripheral category than it once was, does international law's ideology of postracial xenophobia even matter? Predictably, my argument is that of course that it matters, and quite a great deal.

For more than 20 years now, the response to globalization has been characterized as "global governance." As opposed to global *government*, global governance is the international version of Brown's neoliberalism-gone-mad. "[G]overnance reconceives the political as a field of management or administration ... Thus, when governance becomes a substitution for government, it carries with it a very specific model of public life and politics." Brown continues, "Note what does *not* appear in [the governance] account of the public realm: deliberation about justice and other common goods, contestation over values and purposes, struggles over power, pursuit of visions for the good of the whole. Rather, public life is reduced to problem solving and program implementation ... "[74] The result is a governing framework in which the political bleeds out, incessantly. Indeed, this is the dynamic Barthes had described as ideological hemorrhage, in which the historical and the contingent drains away, leaving the natural and the necessary in its stead. "Indeed," Brown explains, "when this narrowing of public life is combined with the strong emphasis of governance on consensus, a hostility to politics becomes palpable. As problem solving replaces deliberation about social conditions and possible political futures, as consensus replaces contestation among diverse perspectives, political life is emptied ... "[75] Paulo Barrozo has argued similarly, criticizing the effects of global governance on the political lifeblood of the democratic body.

*The political* is both a forum and a mode of participation in it. As a forum, *the political* is ideal-typically characterized by equal shared access, equal recognition of participants, focus on collective life, and engagement with the future in normative terms. As a mode of participation, *the political* calls for cognitive, normative, and attitudinal virtues. It lives out of individuals invested in thinking in deliberative,

[72] WENDY BROWN, IN THE RUINS OF NEOLIBERALISM: THE RISE OF ANTIDEMOCRATIC POLITICS IN THE WEST 84 (2019).
[73] *See infra* Chapter 9.
[74] *Id.* at 127.
[75] *Id.*

reflective, and solidaristic ways about the present and future of the form of collective life they inhabit; its manifestation is that of a political culture and practice that continuously weaves into the present a society's aspirations for its future. Thus defined, *the political* has anthropological as well as institutional bases. And yet, *the political* is not reducible to its bases. No matter how many pre-conditions and component parts *the political* is analyzed into, there always remains an irreducible normative dimension to it; a dimension which from the point of view of the present, is aware of the past as it attempts to bind the future to some of its possible configurations. In relation to its bases, *the political* presents a phenomenological surfeit of self-reflectivity, deliberation, normativity, and futurism. Thus, *the political* transmutes the potentials already present in its bases into an irreducible, future-oriented, normative and ultimately solidarity-enhancing sphere of deliberation and binding choices predicated upon and advancing equality, liberty, dignity and justice as guarantees of access to it and as *the political*'s permanently recommitted ends.[76]

Barrozo and Brown's critiques are versions of the complaint that a consequence of global governance is a democratic deficit—that there is a lack of transparency and accountability between actors doing all of this global governing, and the various peoples of the planet being governed. What to do? Interestingly, what seems to unite many thinkers from across the political spectrum is that for in order for a demos to be effective, we must be able to distinguish one demos from the rest. That is, a major problem for global governance is the unavoidable unavailability of a global demos. It just can't work, so the story goes, because in order for a people to enjoy the rights consequent to political order, there must be people not included—hence the trouble with a political community global in scope. Democracy requires a *xenos*. Or to put that in the language of international legal thought, democracy requires the sovereign's right to exclude.

Which brings us to this. If the ideological history of racial xenophobia explored in this book might at first seem reasonable, doesn't it run out of gas by the first decades of the twenty-first century? After all, if the claim is that there is a structure of racial ideology operating in and throughout the legal concept of sovereignty, but it turns out that sovereignty has become largely irrelevant in the new world order of globalization, then international law's race problem—even from the perspective of critical race theory—isn't a problem at all. But of course there is a problem, as has been plain for decades, and the problem concerns the need to protect democracy from global governance. Put aside the fact that so many treatments of globalization constantly remind of the continued *relevance* of sovereignty; focus instead on way in which the sovereign's right to exclude once again resurfaces as

---

[76] Paulo Barrozo, *What Are Transitions For? Atrocity, International Criminal Justice, and the Political,* 32 QUIN. L. REV. 675, 679–680 (2014).

22    THE RIGHT TO EXCLUDE

the answer to a fundamental difficulty for the global order. The way (we are told) to reinforce democratic legitimacy is to ensure that the borders of a given *demos* are sharply delineated. And this delineation requires a great deal more than clarity about territorial frontiers. It requires more than a shared sense of civic ideals. What the borders actually require, as we have come to understand from liberal theorists of cultural and national identity, is an underlying *ethnos*, and distinguishable from the *ethnos*, a *xenos*.

And what is the *ethnos*?[77] The concept of ethnicity is almost as slippery as the concept of culture, but what appears relatively clear is this: When contrasted with culture, ethnicity looks like race, and when contrasted with race, ethnicity looks like culture.[78] On a spectrum between objectivity and subjectivity, racial identity appears definitively ascriptive, culture appears as a set of beliefs and practices, and ethnicity appears as a liminal concept between the two. The trouble, here in the context of the liberal demand for an *ethnos* to constitute the *demos*, is that ethnicity is a mere proxy for race. And if raciality is indeed the source material for securing democratic legitimacy in the face of a globalizing world, we are deeply mistaken if we think we have moved beyond the sovereign's right to exclude. To the contrary, the postracial production of the *racial xenos* is alive and well. In fact, in some ways it is a process less amenable to critique than ever before.

Given the historical moment in which we find ourselves, we might very well wonder, how did we come to arrive at a point in which racial discourse has gone mad, in which the study of racial history becomes illegal? My argument is not that in order to understand the contemporary wave of postracial animus that you first have to understand the history of international law. The argument is rather that we need a way of understanding how older techniques of racializing the foreign, the outsider, the other, have transformed. We need to better understand what they have become, in and through and after these transformations. Coming to grips with global concepts like sovereignty, exclusion, subjection, and xenophobia might at first glance seem something of a distance from where we are today. Maybe even, quite a very great distance. Nevertheless, I propose that this sense of detachment, of alienation, should in itself be a cause for concern. For as I argue in the pages ahead, the feeling that these are problems for others elsewhere is precisely what makes the ideology of postracial xenophobia so seductive.

---

[77] DAVID HOLLINGER, POSTETHNIC AMERICA: BEYOND MULTICULTURALISM (1995); Charles Taylor, *The Politics of Recognition, in* MULTICULTURALISM (Amy Guttman ed., 1994), Avishai Margalit & Joseph Raz, *National Self-Determination, in* THE RIGHTS OF MINORITY CULTURES (Will Kymlicka ed., 1995); Paul Gilroy, *The End of Antiracism, in* RACE, CULTURE, AND DIFFERENCE 50 (James Donald & Ali Rattansi eds., 1992) ("[T]he common sense ideology of antiracism has also drifted towards a belief in the absolute nature of ethnic categories and a strong sense of the insurmountable cultural and experiential divisions which, it is argued, are a feature of racial difference.").

[78] *See infra* Chapters 2, 3, 8, and 9.

# PART I
# LIBERALISM AND THE RACIAL SUBJECT

# 1

## *Imperium* and *Dominium*

This is a book about raciality in international law, and the story it tells is one of the rise of racialized borders as a central feature of the global legal order. Like most stories, this one too requires some character-building. It is the aim of these first few chapters to lay that groundwork for the arguments to come, situating the parameters for the narrative of international legal thought that begins in Chapter 3. As for the sort of story it will be, this book provides neither an intellectual nor a cultural history of race or racism in the global order, but rather a *structural history of racial ideology*, as deployed in the *global context* of *liberal legal thought*.[1]

So let me say a few brief words at the outset about these italicized characters. The unfolding discussion of liberal legal thought expounds a structure that is grammatical, lexical, and stylized: (1) The structure's grammatical level is composed of three governing theses, or what would be called in structuralist parlance, the *langue*.[2] They are (i) the thesis of individual right and free competition, (ii) the thesis of ordered liberty and social control, and (iii) the thesis of naturalizing juridical science.[3] (2) In the language-system that is liberal legalism, these theses govern the forms in which jurists argue about and derive conclusions from the structure's lexical plane of legal concepts.[4] (3) The syntactical forms, modes, techniques, and

---

[1] This largely follows the schema developed in JUSTIN DESAUTELS-STEIN, THE JURISPRUDENCE OF STYLE: A STRUCTURALIST HISTORY OF AMERICAN PRAGMATISM AND LIBERAL LEGAL THOUGHT (2018). For a sample of expository works on liberal political theory more generally, *see* EDMUND FAWCETT, LIBERALISM: THE LIFE OF AN IDEA (2018); LAURA KALMAN, THE STRANGE CAREER OF LEGAL LIBERALISM (1998); MICHAEL FREEDEN, LIBERAL LANGUAGES: IDEOLOGICAL IMAGINATIONS AND TWENTIETH CENTURY PROGRESSIVE THOUGHT (2005); LIBERALISM: CRITICAL CONCEPTS IN POLITICAL THEORY (G.W. Smith ed., 2002). Most influential on my treatment is ROBERTO UNGER, KNOWLEDGE AND POLITICS (1975); ROBERTO UNGER, LAW IN MODERN SOCIETY (1976). On the notion of globality as context, *see* DENISE FERRERIA DA SILVA, TOWARD A GLOBAL IDEA OF RACE (2007).

[2] On structuralism, *see, e.g.*, EVE TAYLOR BANNET, STRUCTURALISM AND THE LOGIC OF DISSENT (1989); JONATHAN CULLER, STRUCTURALIST POETICS (1975); TERENCE HAWKES, STRUCTURALISM AND SEMIOTICS (2003); FERDINAND DE SAUSSURE, COURSE IN GENERAL LINGUISTICS (1959); THE STRUCTURALISTS: FROM MARX TO LEVI-STRAUSS (Richard T. De George & Fernande M. De George eds., 1972); PETER CAWS, STRUCTURALISM: THE ART OF THE INTELLIGIBLE (1988); ROSALIND COWARD & JOHN ELLIS, LANGUAGE AND MATERIALISM: DEVELOPMENTS IN SEMIOLOGY AND THE THEORY OF THE SUBJECT (1977). Early examples of legal structuralism include MARTTI KOSKENNIEMI, FROM APOLOGY TO UTOPIA: THE STRUCTURE OF INTERNATIONAL LEGAL ARGUMENT (1989); Duncan Kennedy, *Form and Substance in Private Law Adjudication*, 89 HARV. L. REV. 1685 (1976); Duncan Kennedy, *The Structure of Blackstone's Commentaries*, 28 BUFF. L. REV. 205 (1979); Gerald Frug, *The City as a Legal Concept*, 93 HARV. L. REV. 1057 (1980); David Kennedy, *Theses About International Law Discourse*, 23 GERMAN Y.B. INT'L L. 353 (1980).

[3] DESAUTELS-STEIN, *supra* note 1, at 3–10.

[4] These legal conclusions, or juridical utterances, can be likened to *parole*. *See* Duncan Kennedy, *A Semiotics of Legal Argument*, 42 SYRACUSE L. REV. 75 (1991).

---

*The Right to Exclude.* Justin Desautels-Stein, Oxford University Press. © Justin Desautels-Stein 2023.
DOI: 10.1093/oso/9780198862161.003.0002

## 26 THE RIGHT TO EXCLUDE

maneuvers in which jurists go about this task is the point at which phenomenology meets structuralism, and I round it all up in the notion of *style*.[5]

I characterize liberal legal thought as a language-system, and the lexicon of the system as a population of legal concepts. In contrast with the fixed status of the system's grammar, legal concepts tend toward indeterminacy, which I take to mean that these fields or clusters of concepts are largely "open-ended."[6] There is nothing (to take an example of importance to the book as a whole) indigenous to the conceptual terrain of property law that will assist the jurist in deciding between conceptual interpretations of the thesis of individual right, or conceptual interpretations of the thesis of ordered liberty—much less choices between the two theses themselves.[7] What does help the jurist in navigating these concepts, however, is style. Moving "vertically" from the grammar, up through the lexical indeterminacy of the concept, and arriving at a legal conclusion, a style of argumentative practice gives a jurist a set of ready-made tropes for casting certain rules as "mainstreamed" or "normal," and others as more heterodox.[8] Perhaps more powerfully, a style of argumentative practice might foster a sense that certain rules are hardly rules at all, but rather natural fixtures of the world in which we find ourselves. These rules function deep in the background, artifacts of "just the way things are and have been."

If a legal style can "background" a concept's rules, it can similarly situate other rules in the jurist's foreground. Unlike background rules that tuck away out of sight, a legal concept's foreground rules are conspicuous. We tend to see them as pieces of legislation and regulation, through statute or court decision, sometimes through custom. In whatever the case, foreground rules deliver a sense of the coercive, telling us what we can and cannot do with our things. They constrain our uses, and because they take on a more explicit form of management, foreground rules are the rules we most typically see, and as a consequence, target for reform. Background rules, in contrast, are less seldom the aim for projects of social transformation. In the context of property as a legal concept, for example, foreground rules speak to who can use what and where and for which purposes (think zoning or fair housing law), where background rules arise from the very possession of the thing (think prohibitions on trespass or takings without compensation). Background rules are experienced as freedom-enhancing rules, while foreground rules are taken

---

[5] DESAUTELS-STEIN, *supra* note 1, at 71. *See also* HAYDEN WHITE, METAHISTORY: THE HISTORICAL IMAGINATION IN NINETEENTH CENTURY EUROPE (1973).

[6] Kennedy, *supra* note 4.

[7] On legal interpretation generally, *see* STANLEY FISH, DOING WHAT COMES NATURALLY: CHANGE, RHETORIC, AND THE PRACTICE OF THEORY IN LITERARY AND LEGAL STUDIES (1990); RONALD DWORKIN, LAW'S EMPIRE (1986); H.L.A. HART, THE CONCEPT OF LAW (1961). For international law in particular, *see* INGO VENZKE, HOW INTERPRETATION MAKES INTERNATIONAL LAW: ON SEMATIC CHANGE AND NORMATIVE TWISTS (2012); INTERPRETATION IN INTERNATIONAL LAW (Andrea Bianchi et al. eds., 2015).

[8] *See* DAVID KENNEDY, INTERNATIONAL LEGAL STRUCTURES (1987).

as freedom-restricting rules. Background rules set the terms for what "freedom" means. Foreground rules set the terms for how far that freedom can go. This, in any event, is how the pairing of background and foreground presents itself phenomenologically in the broader context of liberal legal thought.

If the three theses (individual right, ordered liberty, and naturalizing juridical science) constitute the grammatical base, or the *langue*, and these theses govern the shape of argumentative practice in the context of particular legal concepts like property, the explanation (if one is provided) of whether a particular rule presents itself in a conceptual field as backgrounded or foregrounded is largely ideological. That is, legal style *is* legal ideology, and a fundamental fixture of this ideology is what is often described as the quintessential feature of property: the owner's right to exclude the world. In saying that the right to exclude is "quintessential," we are saying that it is a background rule, and if we are saying it is a background rule, well there you have it—we are caught up in at least one type of legal ideology.[9] In similar fashion, and as I argue below, as property backgrounds a right of exclusion on the part of the private property owner, so too does international law background a right of exclusion for sovereigns.

With that very cursory statement on grammar, conceptual lexicon, and argumentative style—all of which will be further elaborated in the pages ahead—let me now summarize the argument. In the structure of liberal legal thought, the two theses of individual right (competition) and ordered liberty (control) stand as clashing counterparts. It is the province of the third thesis—naturalizing juridical science—to provide the jurist with styles of argument that might mediate or harmonize the demands of competition and order, casting a sense of legal necessity for some or another legal conclusion. Still in the context of property as a legal concept, a classic liberal style of naturalizing juridical science positions the right to exclude as a background rule, but in various forms. The two that are of interest here are *territorial* and *generative*.

First, the right to exclude is territorial: it is about keeping outsiders out and away from a bounded piece of earth. This first aspect draws on theories of occupation and possession. Second, the right to exclude is generative: it helps define the identity of an organic system through the creation of boundaries, thus constituting the identity of outsiders and insiders in the first place. This second aspect draws on theories of property and personhood. In the conceptual terrain of individual property rights, these two aspects of the right to exclude coalesce as a mastery over things on the one side, and as the production of a legally individuated self (system) on the other.

Switching over to the conceptual terrain of sovereignty, the territorial dimension of the right to exclude generates *both* mastery over things *and* production of

---

[9] *See generally* Justin Desautels-Stein & Akbar Rasulov, *Deep Cuts: Four Critiques of Legal Ideology*, 31 YALE J.L. & HUMAN. 435 (2021).

28   THE RIGHT TO EXCLUDE

the legally individuated self. That is, in the context of sovereignty, the territorial dimension of the right to exclude gives rise to two complementary and overlapping perspectives on possession and personality. The former reflects the sovereign's right of nonintervention, while the latter is the right to self-determination. The generative dimension of the sovereign's right to exclude, however, is a bit of a different beast, for it gives the sovereign the right to reconcile what I will call *international law's boundary problem.*[10] This is the sovereign's right to determine the outer limits of international law's application, to establish the borders of international society, to mark "the *frons* of the *imperium mundi*, which expands to the only limits it can acknowledge, namely, the limits of the world."[11] This is the right to determine the identity of the global *demos* of international persons,[12] which is a matter of geography as much as a matter of power.[13]

In other words, the sovereign's right to exclude is more capacious than the private owner's right of the same name. For both individual owners and sovereigns, the territorial dimension of the right to exclude connects mastery over things with the production of the state's legal personality. It is only for sovereigns, however, that the generative dimension gives a right to set the rules for the international system, and vitally, creating that system through the delimitation of its borders.

For ease of exposition moving forward, and in the effort to avoid confusion about when I am referring to *individual* rights of exclusion or *sovereign* ones, I detail the sovereign's right to exclude in the following manner. Borrowing from Roman law, I call the territorial dimension of the sovereign's right to exclude *dominium*, and the generative dimension *imperium*. The territorial right of *dominium* functions similarly for both private owners and sovereign states: owners and sovereigns enjoy a natural right to exclude the world from their territories. In the parlance of the classic liberal style, sovereign exclusion as *dominium* was a right against all other *sovereigns*. Sovereigns had a natural right to keep other sovereigns out of their occupied territories. What this right of *dominium* did not entail, however, was a sovereign's right to exclude individual migrants from their territories. *Dominium*, in other words, only marginally applied to migration. (In the modern style that emerged in the twentieth century, this would change.)

---

[10] This notion is similar to the one more familiar in democratic theory. *See* Frederick Whelan, *Prologue: Democratic Theory and the Boundary Problem*, 25 Nomos 13 (1983); Charles Taylor, *The Dynamics of Democratic Exclusion*, 9 J. Dem. 143 (1998).

[11] Ladis Kristoff, *The Nature of Frontiers and Boundaries*, 49 Annals Ass'n Am. Geogr. 269, 270 (1959).

[12] For discussion, *see, e.g.*, Global Democracy: Normative and Empirical Perspectives (Daniele Archibugi et al. eds., 2011); Hans Agne, *Why Does Global Democracy Not Inspire Explanatory Research? Removing Conceptual Obstacles Toward a New Research Agenda*, 16 J. Int'l Pol. Theory 68 (2020); Rogers Smith, *The Principle of Constituted Identities and the Obligation to Include*, 1 Ethics & Glob. Pol. 139 (2008).

[13] *See, e.g.*, Edward Soja, Postmodern Geographies: The Reassertion of Space in Critical Social Theory (2011).

As I have said, the generative right functions differently, since it connects in the context of sovereignty with a right to set the rules for the *international* system. I call it a right of *imperium* because it is a right of the sovereign to constitute international society by deciding the point at which its law ends, to mark the line between the world of free and equal subjects of international law, and the world of outlaws, or what Giorgio Agamben calls the plane of "bare life."[14] Unlike the physical boundaries of possession, marking the territorial line between what is mine and thine, here we see the generation of new subjects—a process of interpellation and subjection churned out through the marking of lines between an international community of sovereigns and a world of killable peoples. And the right to mark the line—the legal borderlines for international society—is perhaps *the* most definitive exercise of sovereign, *imperial* power. The question of bounding a *demos* (a community or people), whether it is a *demos* of individuals or a *demos* of sovereigns, cannot be decided by that *demos*, it must *already* be decided, hence the imperial status of the right to mark the border. And what is it that justifies this imperial power, this decision to mark the global? In the global context of liberal legal thought, the right to bound the community through law, whatever the community might be, is the sovereign's right to exclude.

As I discuss below, in liberal legal thought every sovereign's right to exclude cashes out in each of these two often overlapping dimensions, that of *dominium* and *imperium*.

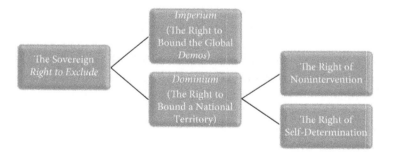

This chapter is presented in two parts. In the first, I explore the three theses of liberal legal thought, and in the second, I move to the sovereign's right to exclude in international law. The issue of how and why the right to exclude is backgrounded in the structure of liberal legal thought is an ideological one, and the introduction of *racial* ideology is the focus of Chapters 2 and 3. It is in the use of racial ideology that we also are introduced to the particularly *global context* of liberal legal thought, for as I discuss later on, racial ideology emerged as a style of naturalizing juridical science which explicitly characterized itself as empirical and anthropological—that

---

[14] GIORGIO AGAMBEN, OMNIBUS: HOMO SACER 61 (2017).

30    THE RIGHT TO EXCLUDE

is, entirely oblivious to political forms of organization and targeted at the human being as a *species*.


# I THE THREE THESES OF LIBERAL LEGALISM

## A  Medieval Aristotelianism

In the effort to ground the three theses of liberal legalism, it is helpful to contrast them first with a set of ideas against which they were first developed: Medieval Aristotelianism.[15] More specifically, given my narrow interest in establishing the grounds of liberal exclusion, the focus here is limited to just two relevant elements in the tradition. As relayed through the work of St. Thomas Aquinas, the first element is this tradition's natural law universalism.[16] In this Thomistic mode of legal argument, jurists derive normative authority for a given rule from a universal hierarchy of objectively ascertainable laws. First in this hierarchy was God's law, the eternal law of the divine realm.[17] As the Dutch Protestant Hugo Grotius explained, citing St. Thomas, "Let us give first place and pre-eminent authority to the following rule: What God has shown to be his Will, that is law ... the act of commanding is a function of power, and primary power over all things pertains to God."[18] And again, "[t]he Will of God is revealed ... in the very design of the Creator; for it is from this last source that the law of nature is derived."[19] Next is the law of revelation, that translation of the divine into scripture. This law of revelation is mirrored in a law of nature—a law that precedes and governs the lives of human beings. For many of the Thomistic writers, the duplication of revelation in the law of nature had the beneficial result of allowing human beings to discern God's will, even without explicit acquaintance with scripture.[20] Finally in this universal hierarchy came the

---

[15] *See* QUENTIN SKINNER, HOBBES AND REPUBLIC LIBERTY (2008); ALISDAIR MACINTYRE, AFTER VIRTUE 62 (2007); BERTRAND RUSSELL, THE HISTORY OF WESTERN PHILOSOPHY (1945); ANNABEL BRETT, LIBERTY, RIGHT, AND NATURE: INDIVIDUAL RIGHTS IN LATER SCHOLASTIC THOUGHT (2003); RICHARD TUCK, NATURAL RIGHTS THEORIES: THEIR ORIGIN AND DEVELOPMENT (1982).

[16] QUENTIN SKINNER, THE FOUNDATIONS OF MODERN POLITICAL THOUGHT, I: THE RENAISSANCE 148–66 (1978). *See, e.g.,* Francisco Vitoria, *On the American Indians, in* POLITICAL WRITINGS 277–92 (A. Pagden & J. Lawrance eds., 2008 [1539]).

[17] SKINNER, FOUNDATIONS, *supra* note 16, at 148.

[18] HUGO GROTIUS, COMMENTARY ON THE LAW OF PRIZE AND BOOTY 8 (1950 [1604]). *See also* E.B.F. MIDGLEY, THE NATURAL LAW TRADITION AND THE THEORY OF INTERNATIONAL RELATIONS 137 (1975).

[19] GROTIUS, PRIZE AND BOOTY, *supra* note 18, at 20. I recognize that there is disagreement about whether Grotius ought to be characterized as a pre-liberal or proto-liberal or some other thing. *See, e.g.,* ARTHUR NUSSBAUM, A CONCISE HISTORY OF THE LAW OF NATIONS 109 (1954); RICHARD TUCK, THE RIGHTS OF WAR AND PEACE: POLITICAL THOUGHT AND THE INTERNATIONAL ORDER FROM GROTIUS TO KANT (2001). I follow David Kennedy and Martti Koskenniemi's characterization of Grotius as a "pre-liberal" due to his consistent tendency to locate legal authority in nature or the divine rather than the sovereign state. David Kennedy, *Primitive International Legal Scholarship*, 27 HARV. INT'L L.J. 1, 8 (1986); KOSKENNIEMI, FROM APOLOGY TO UTOPIA, *supra* note 2.

[20] SKINNER, FOUNDATIONS, *supra* note 16, at 151.

positive law of human action—the law of the prince. These three levels of legal rule were descending in order of primacy. Human law was subject to natural law, and natural law was a reflection of the divine. But whereas there was no concern about natural law diverging from its source in God, it was of course possible for human law to go off the rails. If this happened, and the rule of the prince veered away from its proper source, positive law lost all authority as law per se.[21] As Quentin Skinner has put it,

> The [Dominican Thomists] all insist that if the positive laws which men create for themselves are to embody the character and authority of genuine laws, they must be compatible at all times with the theorems of natural justice supplied by the law of nature. Thus the law of nature provides a moral framework within which all human laws must operate.[22]

Crucially, this hierarchical framework was *universal*. It did not depend on the consent of particular cultures, sovereigns, individuals, or anything else. The law of nature derived its authority from God, not from the character of human nature or the caprice of human will. It applied globally and equally to Emperors, slaves, and every type of human actor in between.[23] Consequently, this mode of legal thought paid no attention to distinctions between national and international law, the public and private, or the moral and legal.[24] The legal was legal *because* it was moral, and there was one single and universal source for all of it, for all.[25] True, the Thomists delineated the *jus gentium*, the law of nations—but this was understood as an aspect of the law of nature, and not a separate and autonomous sphere of sovereign decision.

A second element in this approach is a commitment to eudaimonistic teleology.[26] As is well known, for Aristotle both the human being and the city-state were understood in teleological, or purposive, terms: Everything had its reason for being, and the function of ethics was to assist man in the transition from his immature beginnings to his natural end.[27] Man's *telos*, his purpose, was to find happiness, what Aristotle called *eudaomonia*. But the happiness of the ancients is not the happiness of the moderns, and it was available only through the habitual performance of practical reason in accordance with the virtues.[28] And this habitual performance

---

[21] Vitoria, *supra* note 16, at 279.

[22] Skinner, Foundations, *supra* note 16, at 148–49.

[23] *Id.* at 252–64. *See also* Wilhelm Grewe, The Epochs of International Law 84 (2000).

[24] Kennedy, *supra* note 19.

[25] Hersch Lauterpacht, *The Grotian Tradition in International Law*, 23 Brit. Y.B. Int'l L. 1 (1946).

[26] MacIntyre, *supra* note 15, at 54.

[27] *See, e.g.*, Aristotle, The Nicomachean Ethics 8–9 (2d ed. 1999 [350 BC]); MacIntyre, *supra* note 15, at 148.

[28] *See generally* Benjamin Constant, The Liberty of Ancients Compared with that of Moderns (1819); Martin Thom, Republics, Nations, and Tribes (1995); Monte Ransome Johnson, Aristotle on Teleology (2005).

## 32 THE RIGHT TO EXCLUDE

required society—hence the human being was conceived as an inherently sociable creature, an innately political animal, *homo politicus*.[29] It wasn't "you doing you," as some like to say today. As Alasdair MacIntyre explained, "it is worth remembering Aristotle's insistence that the virtues find their place not just in the life of the individual, but in the life of the city and that the individual is indeed intelligible only as a *zoon politikon*."[30] Of course, happiness meant different things for different people, just as human beings had different functions, and so the social practice of the virtues produced different results for different types of persons. Some were born as natural slaves, some were destined to be philosophers, and *eudaimonia* depended on one's station.[31] As with the universalism of its legal framework, so too is the teleology of happiness a jurisprudence of hierarchy.[32]

This inegalitarianism was not limited to the exclusion of slaves and barbarians from the pursuit of happiness. It was inherent in the system. Consider the teleological structure of the scheme in which human nature is meant to conform to the virtues. Aristotle's ethics presumed that the bare life of the human being begins in a state of ethical dysfunction. We come into the world without virtuous experience, and without moral (political) education, we continue as such. It is only in a sustained and habitualized encounter with the science of virtues that this untutored condition could realize its potentiality, like the acorn growing into the oak. Built-in to Aristotle's ethics, as a result, was a progressive schedule of moral improvement, where the bare life of the human being—as he is—could only become what he ought to be by way of a passage through the ethics. The same scheme held true for the *polis* itself, but whereas the purpose of man was happiness, the purpose of the city was justice. Justice was ostensibly achieved through the codification of certain laws that appropriately channeled the virtuous life.[33] Again, this meant different things depending on the particular regime of the city-state, but in each case the city-state, like the human being, was understood first as a creature with a purpose. Knowing how to realize that purpose meant knowing how to configure the city's laws from their vulgar nature in the original bare condition and into a regime in accordance with an objective and universal body of ethics.[34] Thankfully, those beings at the top of the food chain knew just how to do it, and these were the philosophers.

We can see the same structure of thought at work in the theologian Francisco Vitoria's scholastic approach to the question of the Spanish conquest. Tasked by

---

[29] SKINNER, FOUNDATIONS, *supra* note 16, at 158.

[30] *Id.* at 150.

[31] ARISTOTLE, THE POLITICS AND THE CONSTITUTION OF ATHENS 15–19 (Stephen Everson ed., 1996). *See also* IVAN HANNAFORD, RACE: THE HISTORY OF AN IDEA 45 (1996).

[32] ARISTOTLE, THE POLITICS 6 (Benjamin Jowett trans., 2017). Consider also Robert Schlaifer, *Greek Theories of Slavery from Homer to Aristotle*, 47 HARV. STUD. CLASS. PHIL. 165 (1936). In the context of international law, *see generally* ANTONY ANGHIE, IMPERIALISM, SOVEREIGNTY AND THE MAKING OF INTERNATIONAL LAW (2004); Benedict Kingsbury, *Sovereignty and Inequality*, 9 EUR. J. INT'L L. 599 (1998).

[33] ARISTOTLE, THE POLITICS, *supra* note 32, at 168.

[34] MACINTYRE, *supra* note 15, at 147.

the Habsburg Emperor, Charles V, with the question of whether the Spanish held legitimate title to the lands of the New World, Vitoria argued that the Indians enjoyed the rights of *dominium*, mastery over their persons and possessions.[35] For if the Jews and Saracens, those "continual enemies of the Christian religion," were not "natural slaves" in the Aristotelian sense, why say the same of the Indians?[36] The Indians were by nature neither slaves nor barbarians, and as result, Vitoria explained that they were subject to the same natural rights as any other nation of barbarians. The Indians, like the vulgar masses in any Christian community, had as their purpose—limited and inchoate as it was—the pursuit of *eudaimonia*. That said, Vitoria emphasized again and again the "cowardly, foolish, and ignorant" qualities of Indian life.[37] Their feral culture had yet to encounter the disciplining effects of the ethics, or a city capable of educating the people through ethical laws. And without that ethical discipline, the Indians could never realize their true potential, could never be what they ought to be.

Vitoria explained that the provision of the ethics—that necessary bridge between an untutored human nature and a virtuous human nature—was supplied by the *jus gentium*, what we now call international law.[38] Through adherence to this "law of nations," the Indians would find their *telos*, and transform into what they were to "naturally" become. And if the Indians failed to adhere to the norms of international law, to practice the virtues, Vitoria concluded that the Spanish would consequently have rights of war against them.[39] The trouble is, as Antony Anghie has demonstrated, Vitoria's *jus gentium* was plainly a table of qualities Vitoria believed were best exemplified in the life of the idealized Spaniard.[40] Thus, in order for the Indians to "realize" their natural potential, what international law apparently required was for the Indian to no longer be Indian, but to become *Spanish*. Of course, Vitoria didn't put it this way. Rather, following the basic Thomistic scheme he claimed that international law derived from natural law, and owing its ultimate normative authority to the divine, the *jus gentium* represented "the common consent of mankind." By following these natural dictates, the whole of humankind might achieve its own grand telos, namely, the practice of virtuous sociability. A first question was, virtuous sociability according to whom? And a second: if "Indian" itself designated a kind of life excluded from the ambit of legal protection, what were the legal implications for the Spanish killings in the New World?

---

[35] Vitoria, *supra* note 16, at 250.

[36] *Id.* at 251.

[37] *Id.* at 282.

[38] BENEDICT KINGSBURY & BENJAMIN STRAUSSMAN, THE ROMAN FOUNDATIONS OF THE LAW OF NATIONS (2010); Stanislaw Wielgus, *The Genesis and History of* Ius Gentium *in the Ancient World and Middle Ages*, 47 ANNALS PHIL. 335 (1999); NUSSBAUM, *supra* note 19, at 14–15; MIDGLEY, *supra* note 18, at 136.

[39] Vitoria, *supra* note 16, at 281.

[40] For a critique, *see* ANTONY ANGHIE, IMPERIALISM, SOVEREIGNTY, AND THE MAKING OF INTERNATIONAL LAW (2005).

# 34 THE RIGHT TO EXCLUDE

## B Hobbes

I will return to these implications shortly, but first, it is against this image of universal teleology that I contrast the three theses of liberal legalism. In liberal theory it became impermissible to imagine human beings as predetermined in some way to fulfill a particular purpose, or become any certain thing.[41] People were not acorns, holding within themselves the latent potential to transform in just one, singularly determined way. In this system, human beings were now to be regarded as independent, equal, autonomous creatures, and the only justifiable claim on what a person ought to become could come from the subject himself.[42] Aristotelian teleology became *illiberal* by definition since it depended on the existence of some "theory of intelligible essences," a conception of what a human being's essential function might be.[43] It is in opposition with this theory of intelligible essence that the first thesis of liberal legalism surfaces: human beings are naturally entitled to determine for themselves what they will become. *This is the liberal thesis of individual right and free competition.* The role of law, in the classic liberal view, was precisely to assist the individual person in his efforts at self-determination.[44] Through the exercise of individualized right, the human agent might chart his course.

The work of Thomas Hobbes is illustrative. In Hobbes' version of the state of nature, the *homo politicus* was recharacterized, to use C.B. Macpherson's (in)famous phrase, as a "possessive individual."[45] These new individuals were morally autonomous, rights-bearing actors constrained only by figures of authority to which they had given their consent.[46] Individuals were sources of subjective value, and no other source of value was defensible as legal constraint. Values could never be objective, in the sense of preexisting the individual, and this is why Hobbes suggested that in the state of nature, there was no morality.[47] Individuals could do no right or

---

[41] ARASH ABIZADEH, HOBBES AND THE TWO FACES OF ETHICS 100 (2018) (Abizadeh's point is more specifically about Hobbes, not "liberalism" per se.).

[42] PIERRE MANENT, AN INTELLECTUAL HISTORY OF LIBERALISM 25 (1995).

[43] UNGER, KNOWLEDGE, *supra* note 1, at 66–90. For discussion of these two senses of natural law, *see* LEO STRAUSS, NATURAL RIGHT AND HISTORY 7 (1965): "Natural right in its classic [Aristotelian] form is connected with a teleological view of the universe. All natural beings have a natural end, a natural destiny, which determines what kind of operation is good for them."

[44] This idea is at work in Henry Sumner Maine's famous thought about the shift from "status to contract." *See* HENRY MAINE, ANCIENT LAW (1870). *See also* FRIEDRICH HAYEK, THE CONSTITUTION OF LIBERTY (1978); Duncan Kennedy has framed the idea in his "will theory" of law, where "[t]he state ought to and largely did in fact define the rules of law so as to guarantee the free exercise of individual will, subject to the constraint that willing actors respect the like rights of other willing actors." *See* Duncan Kennedy, *From the Will Theory to the Principle of Private Autonomy: Lon Fuller's "Consideration and Form,"* 100 COLUM. L. REV. 94, 96 (2000).

[45] A now-classic statement is available in C.B. MACPHERSON, THE POLITICAL THEORY OF POSSESSIVE INDIVIDUALISM: HOBBES TO LOCKE (2011). For more recent discussions of Hobbes' thought, *see* ABIZADEH, *supra* note 41; JOANNE WRIGHT, ORIGIN STORIES IN POLITICAL THOUGHT (2004).

[46] THOMAS HOBBES, LEVIATHAN 189 (C.B. Macpherson ed., 1968).

[47] UNGER, KNOWLEDGE, *supra* note 1, at 76. *See also* CAROLE PATEMAN, THE SEXUAL CONTRACT (1988).

wrong—everything was allowable so long as the individual's efforts were directed toward the promotion of their self-preservation.[48] And only the individual was the judge of what promoted such self-preservation, and what did not. Nevertheless, Hobbes' argument in *Leviathan* was certainly not that individuals were always supreme in their subjectivity. Rather, it was that there was nothing in human nature which provided any particular person with natural authority over any other. There was no such thing as a person whose natural purpose was to be enslaved or to enslave.[49]

If value could only be sourced in individual will, no individual had a natural right of authority over anyone else. The concept of equality was inextricably linked to the principle of individualism, since if any one person had a right of independence and self-preservation, then *all* people had them.[50] This right of self-preservation was enjoyed by all, and if any one single individual was barred from the enjoyment of the right, the concept of subjective value seemed incoherent. But now, in the context of imperial ambition, servitude, coverture, and class, consider the problem lurking everywhere: If some individuals decided that other individuals had *less* of a right than they, the first group would be forced to appeal to something *other* than subjective value in order to defend the idea that the second group had been treated with liberal justice. Otherwise, liberalism might collapse back into a theory of intelligible essences. Equality in the state of nature was axiomatic—to deny absolute equality was to deny individualism. If equality were to be restricted, the restrictions would need to come from within liberalism itself.

Though Hobbes emphasized that in this natural condition, human beings were individual and equal, he did not, however, believe in the existence of natural community.[51] But due to the brutal quality of life that raged in the world of subjective value, individuals felt it in their interests to renounce and surrender the total right of self-preservation—*the right to all*—in exchange for order.[52] By giving up their full rights to a single, arbitrarily chosen individual, Hobbes identified the transition from a natural condition of chaotic individualism to a political community through the creation—via a "social contract"—of a political sovereign.[53] In this new political society, individuals would no longer be the sole source of value and authority, and the community could be ordered through the legitimizing power of the one, political authority.[54] As in Scholastic tradition, this is of course a theory of natural law. However, and crucially, this is a *liberal* natural law, whereby the natural

---

[48] HOBBES, *supra* note 46, at 189.

[49] *Id.* at 183: "Nature has made men so equal, in the faculties of the body, and mind; as that though there can be found one man sometimes manifestly stronger in body, or quicker of mind than another; yet when all is reckoned together, the difference between man and man is not so considerable."

[50] KOSKENNIEMI, FROM APOLOGY TO UTOPIA, *supra* note 2, at 58–69.

[51] HOBBES, *supra* note 46, at 185.

[52] *Id.* at 227.

[53] *Id.* at 228.

[54] *Id.* at 229.

## 36 THE RIGHT TO EXCLUDE

rules for political society and ultimately law creation are not derived from some universal divinity, but instead from Hobbes' image of human nature.[55] And it is this vision of human nature which also produces the second thesis in liberal legal thought: *the liberal thesis of ordered liberty and social control.*

A question that emerged with increasing importance for later writers turned on the apparent difficulties implicated in the subordination of individual freedoms to the new and coercive power of the sovereign.[56] One could ask, for example: "In solving the problem of order, have we done violence to the thesis of individual right? How could the sovereign's order be achieved without substituting the interests of one particular group for those of everyone else?"[57] According to Hobbes' initial premise, no single theory of the "good life" could trump any other—this is part and parcel of the liberal critique of universal teleology. But wasn't such a trumping precisely the consequence of raising the sovereign in the first place?[58] It is here in the conflict between liberal individualism and liberal authority that we witness the perennial specter of a "fundamental contradiction."[59]

To emphasize a particular slant on this tension between these two theses in liberal legal thought, let me re-state it. First, Hobbes derived the rules of his new political art from an image of human nature.[60] In this image, all people have common needs.[61] We want to be happy, we want to be admired, and we want to live in peace.[62] These are universal characteristics of the species. Aware of these natural and apparently uncontroversial features of human personality, Hobbes argued against Aristotle in an effort to build government precisely out of respect for these features—rather than in an effort to use government to transform them.[63] This is the rise of the liberal thesis of individual right. Second, thinkers who followed Hobbes but were unsatisfied with the way his system threatened the core principles of individualism and equality through absolute rule, pushed for the elaboration of objective rules that would better constrain the sovereign in its dealings with the citizenry.[64] This is the thesis of ordered liberty.

In crucial ways, the subsequent history of liberal legalism has been precisely about the way in which *law* might somehow resolve the conflict between the theses of individual right and ordered liberty, perhaps in a Hegelian synthesis. After all, it was "illiberal" merely to substitute a single, arbitrary will in the place of an incessant contest of individual wills.[65] The only way to better reconcile the apparent tension

---

[55] *See* STRAUSS, NATURAL LAW, *supra* note 43; MACPHERSON, POSSESSIVE THEORY, *supra* note 45.
[56] *See, e.g.,* JEAN-JACQUE ROUSSEAU, THE DISCOURSES AND OTHER EARLY WRITINGS (V. Gourevitch ed., 1997).
[57] UNGER, KNOWLEDGE, *supra* note 1, at 67.
[58] *Id.*
[59] KARL MARX, THE GERMAN IDEOLOGY (1998); MACINTYRE, *supra* note 15, at 8–9.
[60] HOBBES, *supra* note 46, at 183.
[61] Describing human nature is the role of Pt I of Hobbes's LEVIATHAN, "Of Man."
[62] *Id.* at 184–85.
[63] *Id.* at 227–28; MANENT, *supra* note 42, at 19.
[64] For a "recent" example, *see* JOHN RAWLS, A THEORY OF JUSTICE (1980).
[65] UNGER, KNOWLEDGE, *supra* note 1, at 84–88.

between the demands of personal freedom and the need for an ordered society, liberalism counseled, involved the translation of our inevitably subjective interests into a legal code of impersonal purposes and policies.[66] Perhaps liberalism had rejected universal forms of authority in favor of individualist conceptions of the good life, but it still required a sense of order, and so the trick was to secure a form of government that simultaneously respected notions of equal rights and provided laws that were justifiably objective. The *rule of law* would emerge as the answer. Hence the third thesis of naturalizing juridical science in liberal legal thought: *it is the task of the rule of law to justifiably resolve tensions between the theses of individual right and ordered liberty.*

As Hobbes famously explained, living in a world of self-preserving, rights-bearing individuals was no piece of cake. Despite the radical form of freedom enjoyed in that so-called natural condition, it was a place well worth exiting, nasty as it was (i.e., the thesis of individual right). In a world of sovereign individuals, we are at constant war. And so liberal legalism directs itself towards the limitation of individual freedom in the name of social control (i.e., the thesis of ordered liberty). But liberal legalism cannot be arbitrary. It must govern in an impersonal, neutral, objective, universal language (i.e., the thesis of the rule of law). The rule of law must be something *other* than political rule, even liberal democratic rule. But once liberal legalism heads down this road, hoping to transform the political beliefs of our legislators into the objective maneuvers of our courts, it finds itself in a tangle. Tasked with the satisfaction of two apparently contradictory goals, liberal legalism must first establish a form of government that is in the service of individual freedoms on an equal basis. It then must establish a form of government that brings order through the rule of law, that is to say, a legal system capable of producing impersonal resolutions to legal conflict without doing violence to the principle of individualism. The task of liberal legal thought, and in particular, the task of naturalizing juridical science, is to *harmonize* the demands of freedom and order.

## C  Locke

Let us now turn from 1651 to 1689, and from Hobbes to John Locke. Like Hobbes, Locke begins with the so-called natural condition: the "state all men are naturally in, and that is a state of perfect freedom to order their actions and dispose of their possessions and persons as they think fit, within the bounds of the law of nature, without asking leave, or depending upon the will of any other man."[67] As a consequence of this natural freedom, all men naturally have an equal right to the exercise

---

[66] *Id.* at 89.
[67] John Locke, The Second Treatise on Government and a Letter Concerning Toleration 2 (Paul Negri & Tom Crawford eds., 2002 [1689]).

38   THE RIGHT TO EXCLUDE

of that freedom. These free and equal men are found in the state of nature so long as they live together "according to reason, without a common superior on earth with authority to judge between them."[68] If they have no common superior, and yet disregard reason, Locke tells us that men have left the state of nature and have entered the state of war.

It is this "Rule of Reason" which therefore serves as the measure of natural law. It is reason which prohibits human beings from destroying themselves, and not to (unless justice so demands) "harm another in his life, health, liberty, or possessions."[69] The only compulsion to constrain oneself, and the only available form of enforcement, exists in the reasoned heart of man himself. As the sole judge of what constitutes "harm," every man has the right to enforce the law of nature and punish its offenders in a reasonable manner. All men have a right to compensation for harm done to them—punishment for wrongdoing is insufficient. These two rights of punishment and compensation function independently, in that while any man may punish an offense of the natural law, only the injured man can demand compensation. This flows from the injured man's primal right of self-preservation.

Locke emphasized how in this natural condition men possessed the right of ownership, first and foremost, to their own physical bodies. As Hobbes pushed against Aristotle in his elaboration of sovereign right, so did Locke set himself against medieval notions of common ownership.[70] While men were given the land in common with others, Locke explained that men were given land (in the beginning) so as to use it "to the best advantage of life and convenience."[71] Or, as Locke wrote a few pages on, God did not actually provide the commons for the use of all men: "He gave it to the use of the industrious and rational (and labour was to be his title to it), not to the fancy or the covetousness of the quarrelsome and contentious."[72] This qualification sets up the rest of the picture: "The fruit or venison which nourishes the wild Indian, who knows no enclosure, and is still a tenant in common, must be his, and so his, i.e., a part of him, that another can no longer have any right to it."[73]

The fact that something nourishes does not make that thing a man's property, however. In order to transform something into a property, one must appropriate it—that is, he must pour his labor into the thing. There are therefore two "unquestionable" postulates at work: men own their bodies, and they own the labor their

---

[68] *Id.* at 9.

[69] *Id.* at 3.

[70] For discussion, *see, e.g.,* JAMES TULLY, A DISCOURSE ON PROPERTY: JOHN LOCKE AND HIS ADVERSARIES (1980); ETIENNE BALIBAR, IDENTITY AND DIFFERENCE: JOHN LOCKE AND THE INVENTION OF CONSCIOUSNESS (2013); MATTHEW KRAMER, JOHN LOCKE AND THE ORIGINS OF PRIVATE PROPERTY (1997); JOHN DUNN, POLITICAL THOUGHT OF JOHN LOCKE: AN HISTORICAL ACCOUNT OF THE ARGUMENT OF THE "TWO TREATIES OF GOVERNMENT" (1969); LOUIS HARTZ, THE LIBERAL TRADITION IN AMERICA (1991).

[71] LOCKE, *supra* note 67, at 12.

[72] *Id.* at 15.

[73] *Id.* at 12.

bodies produce. By the force of a kind of transitive property, when one mixes his labor with a piece of land, that land is inevitably fenced in, and properly becomes his own. But just as soon as Locke set the idea down, he famously added another layer. It is not simply that the property owner may take possession of the field which he has tilled, or the orchard he has cultivated. There is also a hierarchical relationship immanent in the mechanism, for as Locke wrote, "the grass my horse has bit, *the turfs my servant has cut*, and the ore I have dug in any place where I have a right to them in common with others, become my property without the assignation or consent of anybody."[74] The question here, which is a question equally unanswered in Hobbes, goes to the constitution of *who* gets to be an owner, and *who* gets to be the servant. It is a question about how liberalism generates this community of free and equal owners through the production of its boundaries.

Locke explained that, even before the political community is established, property owners developed an impressive catalogue of *natural* economic practices. Indeed, Locke's private owner was capable of complex commercial transactions, beginning with the right to formalize the manifestations of his independent will in contract. This was a natural right, Locke explained, because "promises and bargains for truck truth and keeping of faith belong to men as men, and not as members of society."[75] Whereas dominion over property may have once been constrained by a natural and universal teleology, in liberalism constraints on use were so often rendered irrelevant, since the improvement of the land could never diminish the goods available to mankind—it only increased them. Here, as Locke suggested, one needed to understand that a single acre of enclosed land benefited the whole of mankind by ten to a hundred times as that of a hundred acres in common possession. Greed wouldn't bar the hoarding of land, so long as that land was being put to use.

Locke distinguished this competitive market society from an anarchical state of war, which forces the question of why it was necessary to establish the political state in the first place. After all, Locke's version of the state of nature isn't all that bad. It would seem that in Locke's understanding, the first thesis of individual right and free competition held primacy. There was no fundamental contradiction, since the pursuit of individual right yielded its own natural form of order. And if that was right, no need for a third thesis (the rule of law) at all. But that was not Locke's story. To be sure, Locke's state of nature is not Hobbes' state of nature. But they agreed on all three points: (1) individuals had the right to determine what they would become, (2) these rights were endangered and therefore necessitated a form of ordered liberty, and (3) this form of order would enjoy legitimation through the rule of law. As Locke explained, even in a society of free and equal men knowing property and contract, without a common authority among them, every man will

---

[74] *Id.* at 13.
[75] *Id.* at 7.

## 40 THE RIGHT TO EXCLUDE

be judge, jury, and executioner in his own case. However, men are never impartial about their own interests, and so the right to enjoy possessions will always be in jeopardy. And so the truth was, market society was actually a place where man lived a life "full of fears," lamenting that his property was "very unsafe, very unsecure."[76] Thus we have Locke's "great and chief end" for establishing a government and political society: "[T]he preservation of the property of all the members of that society as far as is possible."[77] Indeed, Locke goes further, for it is not simply that government has the protection of property as its key purpose, but that the political state cannot even exist "without having in itself the power to preserve the property, and in order thereunto, punish the offenses of all those of that society."[78]

The force of this shift should not be lost. For Locke, there was a strong notion of a natural freedom that consisted almost entirely of a right to private ownership. But before the creation of the state, this freedom was constantly under siege. In order to establish a "real" and meaningful freedom, Locke explained the need to codify property as a political and positive right in addition to that of a natural right. This may at first seem odd, given Locke's insistence that property is a natural, and not an artificially political freedom. Nevertheless, he also insisted that politics was in fact a pre-requisite for the true enjoyment of a market society. Thus, while the political state takes the market as a precondition, and was substantively obliged by those private principles, those principles in turn required the existence of government. The sovereign's territorial rights, as a consequence, sat on a naturally preexisting edifice of private property rights. As C.B. Macpherson explained:

> The wholesale transfer of individual rights was necessary to get sufficient collective force for the protection of property. In these circumstances individualism must be, and could safely be, left to the collective supremacy of the state. The notion that individualism and "collectivism" are the opposite ends of a scale along which states can be arranged, regardless of the stage of social development in which they appear, is superficial and misleading. Locke's individualism, that of an emerging capitalist society, does not exclude but on the contrary demands the supremacy of the state over the individual.[79]

The resulting image of liberal legal thought is straightforward, even if two-faced. On the one side is Locke's argument about possession of things as the foundation of ownership. At the center of human personality lies mastery over possessions and the capacity to independently and equally buy and sell goods and services: property and contract. In order to properly realize these individual rights, the state

---

[76] *Id.* at 57.
[77] *Id.* at 39.
[78] *Id.*
[79] *Id.* at 256.

promulgates and protects them not only against private transgressors, but from the sovereign itself. The mechanism for this promulgation and protection is free market competition guaranteed by the rule of law, quite literally grounded in private title over territory. On the other side is Hobbes' argument about authority over the community as the foundation of sovereignty. At the center of political order lies the right of the sovereign to dictate the terms of a social contract, a contract between members of the political community and the state. Fundamentally, the state *is* a membership, a people united through surrender, and at the same time, it is a Mortal God, a Leviathan, the last true bearer of natural right. It is the task of the rule of law to determine to which people the rights of jurisdictional authority flow, founded upon a right to decide who shall be members, and who shall not. At the center of the picture is a deep analogy between property and sovereignty, between rights of individual owners and rights of sovereign rulers.

## II THE SOVEREIGN'S RIGHT TO EXCLUDE

My claim is that, in the context of the liberal structure of these legal concepts of property and sovereignty, a central task in liberal legal thought has been to elaborate and justify a *right of exclusion* consistent with the rule of law. This right to exclude operates differently in the contexts of varying legal concepts, and differently as well in its synchronic and diachronic registers. The remainder of this chapter will focus, however, on the legal concepts of property and sovereignty, and the way in which a right to exclude functions there as a *background rule*, and in particular, how that right connects up with the discussion of liberal legal thought from above. My purpose in discussing the individual's right to exclude in property is to set up the sovereign's right to exclude as it has matured in the liberal context of international legal thought.

The right to exclude is most well-known in the context of Anglo-American property law: the right of an owner, with respect to some thing, to exclude the world from his possession. The right to exclude, in this property context, therefore depends on a particular view of the concept's core: (1) individualism, (2) possession, and (3) things.[80] First, the rights at issue are entitlement claims belonging to individuals, and not groups.[81] As we have already seen, Locke's argument for individual ownership begins with an inalienable right of ownership over one's body.

---

[80] Henry Smith, *Property as the Law of Things*, 125 HARV. L. REV. 1691 (2012); Henry Smith, *The Elements of Possession, in* LAW AND ECONOMICS OF POSSESSION 96 (Yun-Chien Change ed., 2015); Thomas Merrill & Henry Smith, *The Property/Contract Interface*, 101 COLUM. L. REV. 773, 786–87 (2001).

[81] *See, e.g.*, Richard Epstein, *Possession as the Root of Title*, 13 GEO. L. REV. 1221 (1979); Carol Rose, *Possession as the Origin of Property*, 52 U. CHI. L. REV. 73 (1985); JEDEDIAH PURDY, THE MEANING OF PROPERTY: FREEDOM, COMMUNITY, AND THE LEGAL IMAGINATION (2010); RICHARD SCHLATTER, PRIVATE PROPERTY: THE HISTORY OF AN IDEA (1951).

## 42  THE RIGHT TO EXCLUDE

As a consequence, when a person mixes their labor-power with a thing, that thing therefore becomes that person's property. It is the magic of human cultivation that transforms what had once belonged to the commons into a thing of individual ownership. And once this transformation has taken place, Locke explained, we bear witness to a single owner's rights over that thing.[82] Second, these are individual rights of possession. Possession happens when an individual has exercised a certain authority over the thing in question, an unquestionable control demonstrable through labor and cultivation. Erecting a simple fence, for example, is insufficient to make out a claim of good possession. The inchoate owner must show that he is working the land, improving it, turning "the sand to gold."[83] Third, these are individual claims of possession to *things,* to territories and goods. That there is a legal relationship between an individual and a thing is the basic idea, for as the property scholar Henry Smith has suggested, a focus on the individual right to a thing "promotes the decontextualization needed in order to extend norms of possession into *legal* norms."[84] "Decontextualization" is a terrific word here, as it suggests exactly what it is essential from this perspective about the owner–thing relationship: the fact that no other context is required, or even desired. In the classic liberal style of property argument, *individual rights of possession over things is the basis of property ownership.*[85]

With this conceptual base in place, on the part of the owner there emerges a right of exclusion. We can say that a right to exclude *emerges* because, in this classic liberal style of argument, it is unnecessary for positive law to enact such a right. It simply happens, naturally. Once an owner has proved mastery over a thing, *nature* generates the owner's right to exclude the world from his possession; if there is no right to exclude, "possession" is defective, meaningless.[86] Nature's characterization of this right sends an unmistakable message: "Keep Out!" This is the *in rem* aspect of the person's possessory rights over the thing.[87] Unlike personal rights, *in rem* rights "create duties of noninterference with things marked in conventional ways as being owned, which duties apply as a matter of law to all persons ... This duty applies without regard to who the owner of Blackacre happens to be, or the form of

---

[82] LOCKE, *supra* note 67, at 22–23. *See generally* Ian Shapiro, *Resources, Capacities, and Ownership: The Workmanship Ideal and Distributive Justice, in* EARLY MODERN CONCEPTIONS OF PROPERTY (John Brewer & Susan Staves eds., 1995).

[83] John Dillon, *Property—Its Rights and Duties in our Legal and Social Systems,* 29 AM. L. REV. 161, 167 (1895).

[84] Smith, *Elements, supra* note 80, at 89.

[85] Henry E. Smith, *The Persistence of System in Property Law,* 163 U. PENN. L. REV. 2055, 2065–66 (2015).

[86] Henry E. Smith, *Property and Property Rules,* 79 N.Y.U. L. REV. 1719, 1753 (2004). *See also* Eric Hirsch, *Property and Persons: New Forms and Contests in the Era of Neoliberalism,* 39 ANNALS REV. ANTHRO. 347 (2010).

[87] Thomas Merrill & Henry E. Smith, *What Happened to Property in Law and Economics?* 111 YALE L.J. 357, 360–64 (2001).

ownership in which it is held, or what uses the owner has in mind for Blackacre."[88] Rights of exclusion, in other words, are neither arbitrary nor relational. They are architecturally *basic*, worn into the legal background, triggered by our possessory interests over things. They are unrelated to any particular duty on the part of any particular people in the context of any particular adjudication. They exist against the known world, prior to adjudication, prior to any given legal controversy.[89]

There is considerable debate in the contemporary literature on questions about the "actual" primacy of the right to exclude, about its relations to other "sticks" in the bundle of property rights, about the political, moral, economic, and social implications of the right to exclude, and much more. Truly, it is a robust and lively conversation about how best to conceptualize the heart and soul of property today.[90] What I want to pursue, however, is an examination of the way in which this classic framing of the right to exclude—so familiar to students of property law—not only manifests in the legal concept of property, but in the legal concept of sovereignty as well. The question, however, is not a constitutional one about the extent of state power via the individual citizen. It is also not an argument in political theory, about whether we can ground the sovereign's territorial rights in the property rights of individual owners.[91] Mine is a rather a question for international law, and the rights of sovereigns in the international community. What is the structure of the sovereign's right to exclude, what does it do, and how is it justified?

## A *Pomerium, Dominium, Imperium*

The answer that will do some considerable work throughout this book begins with the ancient distinction between *dominium* and *imperium*. Dating back to the early years of the Roman Republic, Roman law specified distinct capabilities with respect to mastery over a given object.[92] On the one side were the powers of the rulers (*imperium*), and on the other side were the powers of the private citizens (*dominium*). *Imperium* was a power typically held by a local official, such as a

---

[88] Thomas Merrill & Henry E. Smith, *Making Coasean Property More Coasean*, 54 J.L. & Econ. S77, S81 (2011).

[89] Henry E. Smith, *The Language of Property: Form, Context, and Audience*, 55 Stan. L. Rev. 1105, 1108 (2003).

[90] For discussion in the context of property law, *see, e.g.*, Laura Underkuffler, The Idea of Property (2003); Thomas Merrill, *Property and the Right to Exclude II*, 3 Brigham-Kanner Prop. Rts. Conf. J. 1 (2014); Ezra Rosser, *Destabilizing Property*, 48 Conn. L. Rev. 397 (2015); Joseph Singer, *Property as the Law of Democracy*, 63 Duke L.J. 1287 (2014); Gregory Alexander, *Governance Property*, 160 U. Pa. L. Rev. 1853 (2012); Gregory Alexander, *The Complex Core of Property*, 94 Cornell L. Rev. 1063 (2009); Hanoch Dagan, *Remedies, Rights, and Properties*, 4 J. Tort L. 1 (2011). *See also* Shyam Balganesh, *Demystifying the Right to Exclude: Of Property, Inviolability, and Automatic Injunctions*, 31 Harv. J.L.& Pub. Pol'y 593 (2008).

[91] Anna Stilz, *Why Do States Have Territorial Rights?* 1 Int'l Theory 185 (2009); Hillel Steiner, *Territorial Justice*, in National Rights, International Obligations (Simon Caney et al. eds, 1996).

[92] Max Radin, *Fundamental Concepts of the Roman Law*, 13 Cal. L. Rev. 207 (1925).

## 44 THE RIGHT TO EXCLUDE

magistrate. It involved a power to command the Roman legions outside the sacred boundaries of the city of Rome itself.[93] Within the confines of Rome proper, the citizens' power of *dominium* sat in tandem with the official use of *potestas*, the power to govern held by praetors (consuls), magistrates, lictors, and other governing officers.[94] Historians often frame the *potestas* as a subordinated type of administrative power, called the *imperium domi*, whereas the power to exercise military command was called the *imperium militiae*.[95] But regardless of where one falls in the debate over the proper name for the ruling power in Rome (*potestas* vs. *imperium domi*), what is clear is how vital to the early Republic was the *pomerium* to the full exercise of total, imperial power. On one side of the *pomerium* the power of *imperium* was civil; outside the *pomerium* the power of *imperium* was total.

The *pomerium* was an exclusion, what literally became a wall outlining the borders of Rome but developed over time into a metaphysical boundary laden with heavily conceptual and religious overtones. And it was only outside of these borders that Rome exercised its war powers, its conquering, terrorizing power over the non-Roman world—it was only in a state of exception that dictatorial rule eliminated this borderland, welcoming *imperium militia* within the civil boundaries of the *pomerium*. As Michael Koortbojian has recently explained, the borders themselves were highly ritualized, where the rituals served as justification for the magistrate's use of imperial power beyond the *pomerium*, and his duty to relinquish that power upon reentry:[96]

> It was a fundamental tenet of the Republican constitution that, as magistrates moved between the spheres of *domi* and *militiae*, it was required that the power to command be renewed. One took the auspices to acknowledge the passing of this fundamental boundary in either direction in order to inquire of Jupiter if the *imperium* about to be exercised in action—in either sphere of that authority—was unobstructed and might legitimately proceed. The import of these rituals is clear: without religious sanction, the power to command (*imperium*), whether exercised "at home" or "in the field," lost its legal foundation. So one readily understands how, for Roman magistrates and commanders, to "cross the *pomerium*" was a highly significant act.[97]

---

[93] "Imperium was the supreme military power in the state and empowered a magistrate with absolute regal authority, including the power of life and death, over citizen-soldiers, allies, and enemies assigned to him by the state." *See* Fred Drogula, *Imperium, Potestas, and Pomerium in the Roman Republic*, 56 HISTORIA 419, 451 (2007); Andrew Lintott, *What was the Imperium Romanum?* 28 GREECE & ROME 53 (1981).

[94] Drogula, *supra* note 93, at 435.

[95] J.S. Richardson, *Imperium Romanum: Empire and the Language of Power*, 81 J. ROM. STUD. 3 (2012) ("In the early stages of the growth of Roman power in the Mediterranean region, [imperium] will have applied to all the activity of a holder of imperium outside the boundaries of the city itself, and thus all that work which we normally call 'provincial administration.'") *Id.* at 7–8.

[96] MICHAEL KOORTBOJIAN, CROSSING THE POMERIUM: THE BOUNDARIES OF POLITICAL, RELIGIOUS, AND MILITARY INSTITUTIONS FROM CAESAR TO CONSTANTINE (2020).

[97] *Id.* at 11.

For its part, *dominium* was a power enjoyed by private citizens within the bounds of the *pomerium*.[98] To be sure, it was not the case that a private citizen would lose his status as a *dominus* upon leaving the city, as indeed was the case of a magistrate that would lose the power of *imperium militiae* when crossing the *pomerium* back into the city. But *dominium* was a creature of the civil law, and the civil law was a creature of Rome. In its ancient Republican sense, *dominium* indicated mastery, a total control over the possession, whether it was land, cattle, or people. In contrast, *dominium* did not entail a Hohfeldian bundle of various rights enjoyed by the *dominus*.[99] *Dominium* wasn't about rights at all, but was rather an assortment of capabilities, gifts bestowed on men by gods, to be used in the service of a particular *telos*. It was the master's ultimate, foundational power over his physical things,[100] but a power that was nevertheless disciplined by a universal teleology, a morally correct order for all people and objects.[101] This is property with its preliberal, Aristotelian face.[102]

The distinction between an *imperium* exercised outside of a city and a power of the same name exercised within began to erode with the growth of the Roman Empire. And much later, powers of command over city and society and powers of control over property were increasingly blurred in the feudal era, where lords of estate tended to blend rights of *dominium* and *imperium* in the rule over vassal. Further, whereas in the early Republican tradition *dominium* indicated mastery over a human slave, in the feudal period *dominium* increasingly associated itself with the ritualized handing of multiple and overlapping property rights (*feudum*) from lords to tenants.[103] As for the heritage of *imperium*, as David Armitage has argued, "the Roman legacy of *imperium* to medieval and early modern Europe" offered rulers justifications for territorial authority.[104] Armitage explained:

> *Imperium* in the sense of independent and self-sufficient authority offered a more generally applicable precedent for later polities and, especially, their rulers. To claim *imperium* was to assert independence, whether from external powers or from internal competitors ... According to this reformulation, the sovereign— whether collective or individual—within each polity could claim the same independence of authority that had been enjoyed by the Roman emperors at the

---

[98] For general discussion, *see* Annabel Brett, Liberty, Right and Nature: Individual Rights in Later Scholastic Thought 20–22 (2003).

[99] *See, e.g.*, Wesley Hohfeld, *Fundamental Legal Conceptions as Applied in Judicial Reasoning*, 26 Yale L.J. 710 (1917).

[100] William Buckland, A Textbook of Roman Law from Augustus to Justinian 188 (1963).

[101] Brian Tierney, The Idea of Natural Rights: Studies on Natural Rights, Natural Law, and Church Law, 1150–1625 17 (1997).

[102] *See, e.g.*, Jeremy Waldron, *Property and Ownership, in* Stanford Encyclopedia of Philosophy (2020).

[103] Andrew Fitzmaurice, Sovereignty, Property, and Empire 38 (2017).

[104] David Armitage, The Ideological Origins of the British Empire 30 (2000).

## 46 THE RIGHT TO EXCLUDE

height of their power ... All of these conceptions of *imperium* were territorially static.[105]

As Morris Cohen famously put it, "The essence of feudal law—a system not confined to Europe—is the inseparable connection between land tenure and personal homage involving often rather menial services on the part of the tenant and always genuine sovereignty by the landlord."[106] Cohen's argument from 1925 was that, in the climate of a peaking laissez-faire, liberalism had replaced the feudal image with a common sense view of property as private and sovereignty as public, in some ways hearkening back to the Roman distinction between personal *dominium* and official *imperium*. The trouble was that, in its generation of a new kind of public-private distinction, Cohen accused classic liberalism of cheating. Or rather, in its use of the "so-called labor contract as a free bargain," market economies masked the real relation between *dominium* and *imperium*, between property and sovereignty, obscuring the "character of property as sovereign power compelling service and obedience."[107] "The essence of private property," Cohen observed, "is always the right to exclude others."[108] This is a right of nonintervention, a right on the part of the private owner to marshal the power of the state against the world. Thus, if a third party seeks entrance, or desires goods from the territory over which the owner holds dominion, the state gives the owner a compelling power over these excluded people. As Cohen said, "we must not overlook the actual fact that dominion over things is also *imperium* over our fellow human beings."[109]

As Cohen's 100-year old critique makes plain, the Roman and teleological separation between *dominium* and *imperium* travelled through the Middle Ages and the feudal collapse of powers in the figure of the lord, and arrived in the nineteenth century with a host of various uses and meanings. But in the particular context of liberal legal thought (and in the more specific context of classic liberalism that was Cohen's target), the distinction between *dominium* and *imperium* seemed to resonate most clearly in the division between private and public law, a naturalized law of things on the one side and a politicized law of power on the other. Property law covered the owner's dominance over real and personal possession, while constitutional law governed the state's power to command the citizenry. *Dominium* was about private property, and *imperium* was about public sovereignty.

Of course, while the Roman notions of *dominium* and *imperium* continue to cast a shadow, it is important to remember that the Roman understanding of these terms is alien to our Anglo-American structure of public and private law, and the idea that in classic liberalism there had been a return to the Roman meaning of

[105] *Id.* at 30.
[106] Morris Cohen, *Property and Sovereignty*, 13 CORNELL L. REV. 8, 9 (1927).
[107] *Id.* at 12.
[108] *Id.* at 12.
[109] *Id.* at 13.

*dominium* and *imperium* is certainly misleading. Briefly, to the extent we now think of *dominium* as the root of title in property law, we no longer understand *dominium* to enjoy its connotations of master and slave, having exchanged the *dominus* for the contemporary owner of private property, with all the strings attached. And while the Roman notion of *dominium* always existed independently of possession, in classic liberalism property justifications begin with the core rights of possession over a thing.[110] Further, the Roman conception had no connection with our liberal view of property *rights*. *Dominium* was a power or a capability, a substance enjoyed by a citizen with the grace of the gods and in the service of some set of universally ordained functions.

Nevertheless, it is a commonplace today to think of *dominium* as the ancient ancestor of property law's right to exclude, no matter the changes that have necessarily taken place over the millennia. With *dominium* and its attendant right to exclude sequestered in the conceptual space of private property law, *imperium* would seem to now be about little more than the state's authority to make the rules. Perhaps a melding of civil procedure, constitutional law, administrative law, and other public law sectors, the contemporary heir of *imperium* is simply a question of the public use of coercion, when and how and where it is necessary, and why. This is *imperium* in the language of liberal democracy.

My claim about the status of the right to exclude in international law begins with a reorientation of this commonplace way of tracing *dominium* and *imperium* from its Roman roots through feudalism and into the contemporary distinction between private and public law. This reorientation, as I will argue throughout, cuts against the grain of much international law scholarship.[111] James Crawford, for example, provides the baseline when he writes that:

> The analogy between sovereignty over territory and ownership of real property appears more useful than it really is ... The legal competence of a state includes considerable powers in respect of internal organization and the disposal of territory. This general power of government, administration, and disposition is *imperium*, a capacity recognized and delineated by international law. *Imperium* is distinct from *dominium* in the form of public ownership of property within the state; *a fortiori* in the form of private ownership recognized as such by the law.[112]

In contrast, and with all due respect, I will argue that the relation between sovereignty and property is *more* useful than we tend to think, precisely because we tend to link *imperium* with sovereignty and *dominium* with individual right. Rather

---

[110] Friedrich Kratochwil, *Of Systems, Boundaries, and Territoriality: An Inquiry into the Formation of the State System*, 39 WORLD POL. 27 (1986).

[111] *Cf.* MARTTI KOSKENNIEMI, TO THE UTTERMOST PARTS OF THE EARTH: LEGAL IMAGINATION AND INTERNATIONAL POWER, 1300–1870 (2021).

[112] JAMES CRAWFORD, BROWNLIE'S PRINCIPLES OF INTERNATIONAL LAW 193 (2019).

## 48   THE RIGHT TO EXCLUDE

than regard the powers of *dominium* and *imperium* from the perspective of multiple agents and fields, I will explore them from the single structure of the sovereignty concept, characterized as an "international legal person."[113] That is, as a rights-bearing subject in international society, can we conceptualize the sovereign as both *dominus* and *imperator*, an agent of *dominium* and *imperium*? Further, can we conceptualize *dominium* and *imperium* as the natural rights of the sovereign, rather than as teleologies? Finally, is it sensible to follow Morris Cohen's realist lead, and suggest that whereas *dominium* is exclusion and *imperium* is coercion, in international law these two rights are each about both?

My answer to these questions, which I hope by now is rather apparent, is yes. Just as the private property owner enjoys a kind of *dominium* over territories and goods, so too does the sovereign state aspire toward the same. And because of the way in which international jurists have constructed liberal legal thought, sovereigns simultaneously enjoy the right of *imperium*, a right to set the rules for the global order. What is peculiar about international law in this respect is that the rights of *imperium* and *dominium* conflate in the one concept of the sovereign, whereas in Roman law the rights belonged to two persons: *imperium* for the magistrate, *dominium* for the private citizen. This view of the sovereign from the vantage of international law, in which *dominium* is as constitutive of sovereignty as is *imperium*, resonates with Cohen's effort to see the political in the private, and the private in the political. This view is similarly consistent with the recent work of political theorists like Daniel Lee, arguing that at least in Hobbes, the sovereign's *imperium* is itself a "structure of *dominium*."[114]

For some time now international theorists have analyzed the connection between *dominium* and sovereignty.[115] In his 1983 review of Kenneth Waltz' *Theory of International Politics*, John Ruggie offered what Ben Holland has since termed "the Roman Law thesis."[116] Ruggie argued that as the modern concept of sovereignty developed, two ideas came into conversation with one another: the Roman notion of *dominium* as personal mastery over property, and "mutually exclusive territorial state formations" standing in relation to one another much like the owners of private estates.[117] This analogous situation with respect to the sovereign's territory and the private owner's property disclosed "the distinctive feature of the modern system of rule [which] is that it has differentiated its subject

---

[113] *See, e.g.*, Mortimer Sellers, Republican Principles in International Law 89 (2006).

[114] Daniel Lee, *Sovereignty and Dominium: The Foundations of Hobbesian Statehood*, in Hobbes' On the Citizen: A Critical Guide 134 (Robin Douglass & Johann Olsthoorn eds., 2019).

[115] *See, e.g.*, Quinn Slobodian, Globalists: The End of Empire and the Birth of Neoliberalism (2018); Martti Koskenniemi, *Empire and International Law: The Real Spanish Contribution*, 61 U. Toronto L.J. 1 (2011).

[116] Ben Holland, *Sovereignty as Dominium? Reconstructing the Constructivist Roman Law Thesis*, 54 Int'l Stud. Q. 449 (2010).

[117] John Ruggie, *Continuity and Transformation in the World Polity: Toward a Neorealist Synthesis*, 35 World Pol. 261, 276 (1983).

collectivity into territorially defined, fixed, and mutually exclusive enclaves of legitimate dominion."[118] The distinction Ruggie was discussing, here in the context of a new type of sovereign *dominium,* was what we today call the exercise of self-determination: an act of individualized differentiation, distinguishing the world from the "self."[119] This mode of sociopolitical individuation, Ruggie argued, gave rise to our system of possessive individualism, both with respect to the property owner's relation to the political community, and the sovereign's relation to international society.

Ruggie's point was that, as we come to see how this order of sovereign *dominium* is socially constructed, we position ourselves to theorize the elements of social transformation. When, for example, Ruggie's contemporaries argued for the increasing irrelevance of sovereignty in the international order and the coming of the Washington Consensus (as I discuss in Chapter 9), their accounts of the sovereign *episteme* were typically incomplete.[120] For if it was right to see a structural connection between private property rights and sovereign territorial rights, then it was probably also right to craft our theories of social change around this deeper structure of *dominium.*[121] Treating sovereignty as an international concept, divorced from this deeper structure, could only generate partial theories of change in the international order.

I generally agree with Ruggie's basic claim about the structural connections between sovereignty and *dominium.* But whereas Ruggie and others offered the "Roman Law thesis" in order to motivate a constructivist theory of international relations, my focus is on the interplay between the rights of *dominium* and *imperium* in a structure of exclusion in international law. In international law, both sovereign rights are about exclusion, excluding sovereigns from one's territory on the one side, and excluding non-sovereign peoples from the society of sovereigns on the other. Ideologically, the two rights go hand-in-hand. When sovereigns understand themselves as having gained the right of *imperium* (the right to shape international society), they understand just as well that they have gained the right of *dominium* (the right to govern their territory).

## B The Domestic Analogy and the Global *Demos*

The right to exclude constitutes two contrasting sets of boundary—boundaries for a territorial community, and boundaries for international society. In international

---

[118] John Ruggie, *Territoriality and Beyond: Problematizing Modernity in International Relations,* 47 INT'L ORG. 139, 151 (1993).

[119] Anna Stilz, *The Value of Self-Determination, in* 2 OXFORD STUDIES IN POLITICAL PHILOSOPHY (David Sobel et al. eds., 2016).

[120] Ruggie, *Territoriality, supra* note 118, at 157.

[121] Ruggie, *Continuity, supra* note 117, at 280.

## 50  THE RIGHT TO EXCLUDE

law, the twinned right to establish both sets of boundary is a right belonging to the sovereign, but the manifestation of that right relies upon what is known as "the domestic analogy."[122] As we have seen in the discussion of liberal legal thought, the right to exclude has at its founding a basic commitment to a particular vision of the human being, both in the dimensions of sovereignty (Hobbes) and property (Locke).[123] As we saw in Hobbes, that vision of the human being is as a rights-bearing, self-determined individual.[124] The Hobbesian version of the *homo politicus* is alone, self-interested, and beholden to none. Hobbesian man is no political animal; his natural state is independent and autonomous, and the only justice he knows is the justice demanded in the pursuit of self-preservation.[125] No God, no city, no form of natural life holds preexisting authority for this man, for he is the natural equal of each and every other.[126] When the sovereign is conceived as an individual with legal personality in the international legal order, an analogy is drawn between the new sovereign person and the individual human being in the state of nature. That is, just as the individual human being is characterized by Hobbes in the state of nature, in making the domestic analogy we constitute the sovereign in an *international* state of nature. The relevant political society for this international person is a global one, a society of free and equal sovereigns.[127] I do not want to give the wrong impression here, but I think it is useful to describe this international society as a global *demos*, a society of sovereigns who are at once the objects and subjects of the international legal order. Members of the global *demos* are those who are the authors of a law which is also and at the same time somehow binding upon them.

Hobbes, however, was no theorist of the global order. His domain was the realm of domestic politics, not international politics.[128] A bit of a bridge between

---

[122] *See, e.g.*, Hersch Lauterpacht, Private Law Sources and Analogies on International Law (1970); Chiara Bottici, Men and States: Rethinking the Domestic Analogy in a Global Era (2009); Edwin Dickinson, *The Analogy Between Natural Persons and International Persons in the Law of Nations*, 26 Yale L.J. 564 (1917); Ian Hurd, *The International Rule of Law and the Domestic Analogy*, 4 Global Const. 365 (2015); Teemu Ruskola, *Raping Like a State*, 57 UCLA L. Rev. 1477 (2010).

[123] *See, e.g.*, Emer de Vattel, The Law of Nations (Bela Kapossy & Richard Whatmore eds., 2008 [1758)]); Samuel Pufendorf, De officio hominis et civis juxta legem naturalem libri duo 17–21 (1927); Immanuel Kant, Perpetual Peace and Other Essays 29–40 (1983).

[124] Koskenniemi, *supra* note 2, at 58–94.

[125] For discussion of the distinction between these Aristotelian themes and classic liberalism in international legal thought, *see* Justin Desautels-Stein, *Chiastic Law in the Crystal Ball: Exploring Legal Formalism and its Alternative Futures*, 2 Lon. Rev. Int'l L. 263 (2014).

[126] *Id.* at 274–76.

[127] As the eighteenth-century philosopher Christian Wolff put it: "Nations, it is true, can only be considered as so many individual persons living in a state of nature; and for that reason, we must apply to them all the duties and rights which nature prescribes and attributes to men in general, as being naturally born free, and bound to each other by no ties but those of nature alone." *See* Christian Wolff, Ius Naturae et Ius Gentium (1972 [1748]).

[128] Thomas Hobbes, De Cive, ch. 14, Section 4, 5 (2017). "The maxims of each of these laws are precisely the same: but as states once established assume personal properties, that which is termed the natural law when we speak of the duties of individuals, is called the law of nations when applied to whole nations or states."

Hobbesian theory and the global was supplied by the German philosopher Samuel Pufendorf, a natural law theorist and author of the influential *Law of Nature and Nations* of 1672.[129] Writing only a couple decades after Hobbes' publication of *Leviathan*, Pufendorf is sometimes characterized as one of Hobbes' most important early popularizers.[130] As Quentin Skinner has said, Pufendorf was "the first and perhaps most important" among "a group of absolutely crucial European writers on the *jus gentium* to come forward with [Hobbes'] theory."[131] And this theory held the state as a moral *person*, with rights and duties.[132] As Pufendorf wrote, it was through various contractual arrangements that "a multitude of men unite to form a state, which is conceived as a single person with intelligence and will, performing other actions peculiar to itself and separate from those individuals."[133] Once constituted, the sovereign state was itself "a compound moral person, whose will, intertwined and united by the pacts of a number of men, is considered the will of all."[134]

For Pufendorf, the person of the sovereign state holds "supreme" authority over a territorial possession.[135] This authority is supreme in the sense that the sovereign is unaccountable to any other human being, and is the sole source of law. Pufendorf thus joined with Hobbes in the battle against pre-liberal universal teleology, arguing against the view that citizens might justifiably appeal to norms and rules operating beyond the ken of the sovereign. The sovereign, in this proto-liberal view, was the end of the line. Or rather, Pufendorf argued that citizens only had rights and duties when they were "perfect," and perfection indicated a citizen's habitation within and reliance upon a sovereign's territorial jurisdiction.[136] Citizens also enjoyed "imperfect" rights and duties, derived as they were from natural law. But unless these natural rights and obligations were made law by the sovereign, they were unenforceable, i.e., imperfect. "No acts are of themselves obligatory or unlawful, until they have been made so by law."[137] It was because Pufendorf saw sovereigns as moral persons in the Hobbesian sense, and because of the way in which a person's rights and obligations were inextricably connected to the supreme

---

[129] On the political context in which Pufendorf was imagining the idea of sovereignty, *see* R. Friedenberg & M. Seidler, *The Holy Roman Empire of the German Nation*, in EUROPEAN POLITICAL THOUGHT, 1450–1700: RELIGION, LAW AND PHILOSOPHY (H. Lloyd et al. eds., 2008).

[130] FIAMETTA PALLADINI, SAMUEL PUFENDORF DISCIPLE OF HOBBES: FOR A RE-INTERPRETATION OF MODERN NATURAL LAW (David Saunders trans., 2020).

[131] Quentin Skinner, *A Genealogy of Liberty*, available at https://cluelesspoliticalscientist.wordpress.com/2017/05/18/a-genealogy-of-the-state-by-quentin-skinner-lecture-transcript/. *See also* Quentin Skinner, *A Genealogy of the Modern State*, 162 PROC. BRIT. ACAD. 325 (2009).

[132] JEAN-JACQUES ROUSSEAU, THE SOCIAL CONTRACT, bk. 1, ch. 7, 63 (1993). *See also* BEN HOLLAND, THE MORAL PERSON OF THE STATE: PUFENDORF, SOVEREIGNTY AND COMPOSITE POLITICS (2020).

[133] PUFENDORF, *supra* note 123, at 983.

[134] *Id.* at 984.

[135] *Id.* at 1055.

[136] This idea drew in part on Grotius's theory of defective jurisdiction. *See* HUGO GROTIUS, DE IURE PRAEDAE (2006 [1868]).

[137] PUFENDORF, *supra* note 123, at 184.

## 52 THE RIGHT TO EXCLUDE

authority of the sovereign, that Pufendorf regarded the law of nations as natural law.[138] To make the law of nations, or international law, truly *supreme*, it would require a legal provenance superior to that of the sovereign.[139] And from Pufendorf's perspective, neither Christian Aristotelianism nor Imperial fiat could do it. The former was just wrong, and the latter was inadequate. Sovereign states, as persons, were obliged to follow the dictates of natural law—just as any persons were so obliged as a matter of conscience. But these dictates were "imperfect" and unenforceable, and hence, not of the stuff of true law.

Pufendorf's account of the natural law of moral persons helps situate the two dimensions of the sovereign's right to exclude, *dominium* and *imperium*. Natural law was universal and perpetual, binding on all of humankind and unchanging.[140] What this meant for the sovereign, among other things, was a natural right of *dominium* over its territory. As Lee has explained in discussing Hobbes' similar take, "What makes the state distinctive and different from other kinds of association, then, is this *dominium* and the subservience of duty-bound slavish citizens to their common *dominus*."[141] Lee is emphasizing here the classical relation between mastery over persons, but in Pufendorf, sovereignty as *dominium* has a different connotation, that of mastery over territory.[142] Of course, in the classical sense these objects of control amounted to the same thing—mastery over *things*, including people. As Ian Hunter has argued, Pufendorf—largely following Hobbes—proposes a thoroughly *territorial* view of sovereign personhood:

> Given that justice arises from the obligation to obey the laws of a legitimate authority, and considering that the authority of Pufendorf's superior arises from his capacity to protect citizens from each other and from "external" enemies, then Pufendorf's construction of justice is territorial in a dual sense. First, justice or right is spatially restricted to the political territory or jurisdiction in which the superior's subjects reside and over which he can exercise the effective coercive control required to command laws. Second, once the civil state has been entered in accordance with the command of natural law, then justice and right are normatively restricted to the geo-ethical space created by a territorial legislator, losing the global or cosmopolitan reach of scholastic (or Lockean) natural right; for in Pufendorf's Hobbesian construction the legislative decisions of a territorial

---

[138] To be clear, this is not the same as the scholastic sense of characterizing the *jus gentium* as natural law.

[139] PUFENDORF, *supra* note 123, at 226.

[140] *Id.* at 179.

[141] Daniel Lee, *Sovereignty and Dominium: The Foundations of Hobbesian Statehood*, in HOBBES' ON THE CITIZEN: A CRITICAL GUIDE 132 (Robin Douglass & Johann Olsthoorn eds., 2019).

[142] BRIAN TIERNEY, THE IDEA OF NATURAL RIGHTS: STUDIES ON NATURAL RIGHTS, NATURAL LAW, AND CHURCH LAW, 1150–1625 260 (1997); ANTHONY PAGDEN, LORDS OF ALL THE WORLD: IDEOLOGIES OF EMPIRE IN SPAIN, BRITAIN, AND FRANCE 50 (1998).

state are the sole effective determinant of the natural-law norm of sociability or peaceability.[143]

Pufendorf elaborated a comprehensive approach to natural personality, and the theological details need not detain us.[144] But what is worth noting at this point is Pufendorf's insistence on the natural equality of moral persons, "an equality of right, which has its origin in the fact that an obligation to cultivate a social life is equally binding upon all men, since it is an integral part of human nature as such."[145] Here Pufendorf's account of the natural condition is more sociable than that of Hobbes, since for Pufendorf, the natural state of men is peace and friendship.[146] This "natural state of peace" was "founded on the following laws: A man shall not harm one who is not injuring him; he shall allow every one to enjoy his own possessions; he shall faithfully perform whatever has been agreed upon; and he shall willingly advance the interests of others, so far as he is not bound by more pressing obligations."[147] Pufendorf, like Locke, therefore places both property (*dominium*) and contract (*pacta sunt servanda*) in the natural condition, derived from human nature's adaptation to the social world. But how?

Unlike in the work of Emerich Vattel, mentioned below, Pufendorf rejected the idea that the natural rights of sovereigns might be deduced from the either the common consent of mankind, or through evidence of the custom of nations. Deriving natural law from what nations have agreed to do couldn't make any sense, since nations might very well agree to just about anything.[148] And even if it was possible to meaningfully analyze the customs of every people the world over, what one would inevitably find would be a wild variety of conflicting practices.[149] Anticipating an argument that would find more traction in the nineteenth century, might it be possible to exclude the barbarians and find the provenance of natural law in the consent and custom of those civilized states? Nope.

For what people, endowed with enough judgment to preserve its existence, will be willing to acknowledge that it is barbarous? Or what nation will claim so much for itself as to demand that all other nations be measured by its customs, and to adjudge that one barbarous which departs from them? In former days the Greeks, in their pride, looked down upon all other peoples as barbarians, and the Romans succeeded to their arrogance; and today in Europe some of us claim for ourselves

---

[143] Ian Hunter, *The Figure of Man and the Territorialisation of Justice in 'Enlightenment' Natural Law: Puffendorf and Vattel*, 23 INT'L HIST. REV. 289, 293 (2013).

[144] For a discussion of theological aspects, *see* HOLLAND, THE MORAL PERSON OF THE STATE, *supra* note 131.

[145] PUFENDORF, *supra* note 123, at 333.

[146] *Id.* at bk. 2, ch. 2, 168–72.

[147] *Id.* at bk. 2, ch. 2, 172.

[148] *Id.* at 189.

[149] *Id.* at 190–92.

## 54 THE RIGHT TO EXCLUDE

to be superior to others in the development of our culture, while on the other hand, there are peoples who rank themselves far above us.[150]

The true source for natural law, Pufendorf concluded, was "the dictate of right reason in the sense that the mind of man has the faculty of being able to clearly understand, from the observation of his condition, that he must of necessity order his life by that law, and at the same time to search out the principle whereby its commands can be convincingly and clearly demonstrated."[151] These dictates of reason "are true principles that are in accordance with the properly observed and examined nature of things, and are deduced by logical sequence from prime and true principles."[152] Thus, the natural equality of sovereign persons, with their rights of territorial *dominium*, were *true* to the extent that these moral persons were properly analogized to human persons, and *dominium* was consistent with the dictates of right reason.[153]

As I mentioned, neither Hobbes nor Pufendorf were persuaded that the domestic analogy might develop to the end, resulting in sovereign surrender to a global leviathan. Sovereigns were likened to human beings in a state of nature, but they were not *so* like human beings, since they never came together in a social contract. Hence, no international law. At the same time, however, Pufendorf pushed the ball forward, arguing that through the use of reason sovereigns could come to understand the benefits of social cooperation. It wasn't exactly a social contract theory for sovereign states, but it was on the way.

The state of liberal international legal thought made a decisive shift in the work of the extraordinarily influential Swiss diplomat Emerich Vattel. For Vattel, the work of Hobbes, Pufendorf, and above all, Christian Wolff, served as a helpful preface for conceptualizing the international order.[154] The key, as we have seen, was the "domestic analogy," a metaphor in which the sovereign state became a "moral person," analogous to the rights-bearing individual.[155] Further, the "natural condition" to which the sovereign lived was analogized was Hobbes' warring state of nature.[156] The problem for international lawyers like Vattel, however, was

[150] *Id.* at 189.
[151] *Id.* at 202.
[152] *Id.* at 203.
[153] *Id.* at bk. 4, ch. 4, 532.
[154] VATTEL, *supra* note 123, at 8. A helpful summary of Vattel's work is available in STEPHANE BEAULAC, THE POWER OF LANGUAGE IN THE MAKING OF INTERNATIONAL LAW: THE WORD SOVEREIGNTY IN THE BODIN AND VATTEL AND THE MYTH OF WESTPHALIA (2004).
[155] Daniel Dickinson, writing in 1846, citing Georg Friedrich von Marten, citing Vattel, and quoted by Andrew Fitzmaurice, explained: "From the moment a nation has taken possession of a territory in right of first occupier, and with the design to establish themselves for the future, they become the absolute and sole proprietors of it, and that it contains; and have a right to exclude all other nations from it, use it, and dispose of it as they think proper; provided, however, that they do not, in anywise, encroach of the rights of other nations." *See* FITZMAURICE, *supra* note 103, at 213.
[156] VATTEL, *supra* note 123, at 36–37 ("Since men are naturally equal, and a perfect equality prevails in their rights and obligations, as equally proceeding from nature—nations composed of men, and considered as so many free persons living together in the state of nature, are naturally equal, and inherit

IMPERIUM AND DOMINIUM    55

figuring out just what this analogy should mean. Did it mean, for example, that sovereigns ought to renounce their natural rights of self-preservation in the process of creating a global social contract? Would international law be the province of a global leviathan, a world government? It would seem sensible to answer in the affirmative, since for Hobbes, the new art of politics took flight once the individual surrendered some aspect of his natural right in order to legitimate the normative authority of government.[157] And at least for Wolff, Vattel's greatest influence, there was indeed a necessity in imagining international law as the product of a global authority, the *civitatis maximae*. Wolff's project was fundamentally about justifying the meaning and relevance of this great and global republic.[158]

While Vattel followed much of Wolff's lead, he didn't follow it here. Vattel explained, like Hobbes, Pufendorf, and so many others, that the sovereign was a moral person in possession of "an understanding and a will peculiar to herself," with natural obligations and rights.[159] International law, as a result, was the "science which teaches the rights subsisting between nations or states, and the obligations correspondent to those rights."[160] Now, while there is certainly a whiff of Hohfeld in Vattel's treatment of rights as the derivative of duties,[161] Vattel is unquestionably committed to a natural rights approach: "Sovereign states are to be considered as so many free persons living together in the state of nature."[162] But unlike individuals who must surrender their natural rights of self-preservation to the Leviathan under the social contract, Vattel saw no reason for sovereigns in the international state of nature to do the same. Sovereigns retain the natural rights of self-preservation, remaining "absolutely free and independent" in their relations with other nations.[163] While individuals in the natural condition were compelled to renounce some range of their natural rights, "Nothing of this kind can be conceived or supposed to subsist between nations. Each sovereign state claims and actually possesses an absolute independence on all the others."[164]

To be sure, this didn't mean for Vattel that natural law didn't govern sovereigns. Vattel believed that natural law applied to states just as it did to individual human beings, but that in the international context, natural law's application *changed*. The business of international law was precisely to detail the content of those changes.[165]

---

from nature the same obligations and rights. Power or weakness does not in this respect produce any difference. A dwarf is as much a man as a giant; a small republic is no less a sovereign state than the most powerful kingdom.")

[157] *Id*. at 38.

[158] VATTEL, *supra* note 123, at 14. *See also* Nicolas Onuf, *Civitas Maxima: Wolff, Vattel, and the Fate of Republicanism*, 88 AM. J. INT'L L. 280 (1994).

[159] VATTEL, *supra* note 123, at 67.

[160] *Id*. at 67.

[161] *Id*. at 68. *See also* ALFRED RUBIN, ETHICS AND AUTHORITY IN INTERNATIONAL LAW 78 (1997).

[162] VATTEL, *supra* note 123, at 68.

[163] *Id*. "The nation possesses also the same rights which nature conferred upon men in order to enable them to perform their duties."

[164] VATTEL, *supra* note 123, at 14.

[165] *Id*. at 69.

## 56 THE RIGHT TO EXCLUDE

The result was a tripartite structure of international law, what Vattel called the necessary, arbitrary, and voluntary law of nations. The first two forms are of less concern given our immediate object—the necessary law of nations was the direct application of natural law to the sovereign's conscience, ideas about the common good that were incapable of generating binding obligations;[166] the arbitrary law of nations were those rules traceable to state consent, behavior and will, such as treaties and rules of custom. Vattel's explanation for the voluntary law of nations, however, is what we need if we are to visualize international law's boundary problem.

As Martti Koskenniemi explained, Vattel's necessary law is an argument about justice that seems hopelessly irrelevant to the concrete world of state practice. Vattel's arbitrary law, on the other hand, is only normative to the extent that a state agrees to be bound. Its normativity is never anything more than ephemeral. The voluntary law of nations, in contrast, is Vattel's answer to Wolff's *civitatis maximae* and Hobbes' Leviathan. It is a body of rules meant to be simultaneously normative and rooted in sovereign consent. Vattel explained that, following more of a Pufendorfian view of the sociable nature of mankind, nations are "bound to cultivate human society with each other."[167] The object of this "great society" was the "interchange of mutual assistance for their own improvement and that of their condition."[168] At the same time, Vattel stressed the fundamental equality of sovereigns and that while every sovereign was obligated to contribute toward the "happiness and perfection" of every other sovereign, no state could compel another to behave in any particular way.[169] The source of compulsion, consistent with this fundamental commitment to sovereign equality *and* the great society of sovereigns, was the "voluntary law of nations."

> It is therefore necessary, on many occasions, that nations should suffer certain things to be done, though in their own nature unjust and condemnable; because they cannot oppose them by force, without violating the liberty of some particular state, and destroying the foundations of their natural society. And since they are bound to cultivate that society, it is of course *presumed* that all nations have consented to the principle we have just established. The rules that are deduced from it, constitute what Monsieur Wolff calls "the voluntary law of nations."[170]

Unlike treaties and customary rules, which "arbitrarily" trace their origins to sovereign caprice, and the necessary law of nature, which is timeless but binding only

---

[166] *Id.* at 71.

[167] *Id.* at 73.

[168] *Id.*

[169] Compulsion was only available for Vattel when one sovereign enjoyed a perfect right against another. *See* VATTEL, *supra* note 123, at 75.

[170] *Id.* at 76.

upon the sovereign's conscience, the voluntary law was binding on all sovereigns due to its derivation from the demands of the great society of states. The rules of the voluntary law are deduced from concepts of "general welfare and society," obliging states to follow.[171] And importantly, sovereigns have presumably consented to these rules, given their prior natural commitments to safeguard international society.[172] The domestic analogy, in other words, went only halfway. Sovereigns were moral persons, analogized to individuals in the natural condition. However, while sovereigns were not expected to renounce any rights, they were at the same time expected to respect certain rules of conduct. Sovereigns were under binding obligations to respect the territorial integrity of sovereigns, for example, since this was itself a requirement of membership in the great society of sovereigns.[173]

Sovereign states enjoyed equal rights of *dominium*, of territorial integrity, wherein no sovereign was legally justified in using force on the territory of another.[174] As Vattel explained, "The right of making war belongs to nations only as a remedy against injustice: it is the offspring of unhappy necessity."[175] Vattel believed that, unlike in Hobbes' state of nature, states enjoyed a legal warrant to use force only when the use of force was in the service of a "perfect right."[176] Rights to use force, in turn, were only available when another state had violated some prior obligation. As a consequence, in the absence of a legally cognizable injury the use of force between sovereigns was illegal.[177] Indeed, Vattel explained that "Self-defense against unjust violence is not only the right but the duty of a nation, and one of her most sacred duties."[178]

However, this did not mean that wars were only legally justified when they were defensive.[179] "Offensive" wars were legally justifiable as well, but only when their purpose was to compensate for or prevent future injuries.[180] The legal category of offensive war did not, as a consequence, include "conquest, or the desire of invading

---

[171] *Id.* at 17.

[172] *Id.* at 261.

[173] My brief discussion here is focused only on Vattel's view of the *jus ad bellum*. For Vattel's discussion on the rules constraining the modes of warfare, see Chapter VIII, Of the Rights of Nations in War, *supra* note 123.

[174] VATTEL, *supra* note 123, at 74–75. *See also* THEODORE WOOLSEY, INTRODUCTION TO THE STUDY OF INTERNATIONAL LAW 59 (1908) ("All sovereign states stand on the same level in this respect—the and the new the new, the large and small, monarchies and republics—for the conception of a state to be applied to all is the same, and their sovereignty is the same."); TRAVERS TWISS, THE LAW OF NATIONS CONSIDERED AS INDEPENDENT POLITICAL COMMUNITIES 12–13 (1861) ("The independence of a nation is absolute, and not subject to qualification, so that nations in respect of their intercourse under Common Law are Peers or Equals.")

[175] VATTEL, *supra* note 123, at 500.

[176] *Id.* at 483–84 ("The right of employing force, or making war, belongs to nations no farther than is necessary for their own defense and for the maintenance of their rights.")

[177] VATTEL, *supra* note 123, at 484.

[178] *Id.* at 487.

[179] *Id.*

[180] *Id.* at 484 ("We may therefore distinctly point out, as objects of a lawful war, the three following: 1. To recover what belongs or is due to us. 2. To provide for our future safety by punishing the aggressor or offender. 3. To defend ourselves, or to protect ourselves from injury, by repelling unjust violence.")

## 58    THE RIGHT TO EXCLUDE

the property of others: views of that nature, destitute even of any reasonable pretext to countenance them, do not constitute the object of regular warfare, but of robbery."[181] This category did include, however, justifiable acts in the service of preventing future harms. The line between conquest and the prevention of harm, of course, is concededly gray. But unlike Hobbes's view that the line was meaningless since the prevention of harm was always a decision left solely to individual discretion, Vattel suggested that the distinction was made real by those maxims derived from the common interests of mankind.[182] As a result, in this Vattelian model sovereigns did not initially enjoy a right to make war whenever they suspected a threat to their sense of self-preservation, whereas Hobbesian individuals enjoyed exactly that right. There are rules governing *when* and *where* sovereigns can fight, and as these doctrines progressed over time, rules eventually emerged for governing *how* sovereigns could fight as well.[183]

One could follow the analogy to its logical end and theorize the necessary surrender of the sovereign's full rights to some global leviathan, a world government with supreme political authority. From the traditional vantage points of liberal legal thought, however, the analogy stops short. Sovereigns enjoyed all the natural rights that individuals did in the natural condition, but unlike those individuals, sovereigns had no need to give any of them up—or, at least, they could hold on to quite a good number of them. The classic result, founded upon this partial analogy between a surrendering individual human being in a domestic state of nature, and a never-surrendering individual sovereign state in an international state of nature, was that *all* sovereigns were at once holders of both *dominium* and *imperium*. In other words, every sovereign state being the equal of every other, each sovereign

---

[181] *Id.* at 471.

[182] The mechanism by which Vattel believed such maxims to take on a binding character was the "voluntary law." For a summary, *see* VATTEL, *supra* note 123, at 18–20.

[183] This is the distinction between *jus ad bellum* and *jus in bello*. What Vattel described and that I have here very briefly summarized, are the rules governing whether states can justifiably go to war: *jus ad bellum*. The *jus in bello* is a different historical story, concerning those rules governing how states fight. The modern view of the *jus in bello* often begins with the Hague Peace Conferences held at the turn of the twentieth century. Despite the academic usefulness of the distinction between *jus ad bellum* and *jus in bello*, it has nevertheless been questioned. As Ian Brownlie has argued, international law before World War I ceased to have any "limiting effect" on the decisions of states to use violence against one another. *See* IAN BROWNLIE, INTERNATIONAL LAW AND THE USE OF FORCE BY STATES 48 (1963). "The practice and doctrine of the period before 1920 present both a right of self-help and a right of self-preservation, the latter being unfortunately predominant and therefore obscuring the judicial value of the doctrine of self-help. This latter doctrine, which regarded war as a mode of judicial settlement, was nevertheless gaining ground in the period before the First World War. The greatest obstacle to adequate legal regulation of the use of force was the right of self-preservation and related tangle of doctrine concerning necessity and intervention. Categories such as self-preservation and necessity are too vague and susceptible to selfish interpretation to provide a sufficient basis for a legal regime ... Lastly, the attempt to use vague categories of intervention and self-preservation to give a veneer of legality and morality to the exercise of the right of war or to the numerous interventions which occurred in this period obscured the situation and complicated the task of creating an adequate legal regime for the use of force."). *See also* J.H.W. VERZIJL, INTERNATIONAL LAW IN HISTORICAL PERSPECTIVE 215 (1968) ("Never until the twentieth century has the use of force been banned by positive international law, nor would it have even been possible to ban it in a society without any central authority to enforce the ban.").

enjoyed mastery over their bounded territory, as well as a jurisdictional power to make the rules for international society. The trick was that, since it was unnecessary as a matter of natural law for sovereigns to renounce their natural rights, *every* sovereign enjoyed exactly the same rights of *dominium* and *imperium*. Sovereigns therefore serve in the paradoxical position as both *private* and *imperati*, both as subjects and makers of international law. This "paradoxical position" is definitively democratic in the sense that it is a system in which subjects are both the rulers and the ruled.[184]

It is here, when we combine the relation between legitimate rule and boundary on the one side, with the generative right of *imperium* on the other, that the sovereign's right to exclude comes into view. In the domestic sphere, *imperium* is the province of the sovereign state, and at least under a modern positivist theory of lawmaking, rules are valid when they are legitimately traced back to the sovereign will.[185] The legitimacy of the sovereign process may be a function of domestic procedure, but the ultimate right of the state to say what that procedure will be is what we might call a modern take on *imperium*.[186] Does the sovereign state enjoy this same rulemaking power when we switch contexts from domestic society and into international society, from domestic law to international law? Again, from a strictly positivist perspective the answer is basically yes: sovereigns are only bound by those rules that enjoy that sovereign's consent. If the sovereign hasn't agreed to the rule in question, the rule is invalid.[187] The procedures for determining the rules of the global order are determined by sovereign states.

What is missing from this account is a crucial feature of the imperial right to exclude. *Imperium* isn't only about the power to make the rules. It is also about the right to determine the bounds of the collectivity subject to those rules, which is perhaps the most fundamental power of all. Or to put that another way, the supposedly pre-political ground for determining the boundaries of the human collectivity that legitimately exercises power, and for excluding the rest, is a sovereign's natural right of *imperium*. Indeed, before we meaningfully focus on the right of the sovereign to participate in the making of international law, there is the problem of determining the identity of the global *demos* in the first place. As I explore in much of the remainder of the book, the manner in which sovereign rights of *imperium* and *dominium* have gone about "solving" international law's boundary problem has moved through several iterations.

---

[184] *See generally* CHANTAL MOUFFE, THE DEMOCRATIC PARADOX (2000).

[185] *See generally* INTERNATIONAL LEGAL POSITIVISM IN A POSTMODERN WORLD (Jorg Kammerhofer & Jean d'Aspremont eds., 2014).

[186] To some extant this tracks Hart's discussion of primary and secondary rules. *See* HART, *supra* note 7.

[187] The question of whether consent is really the right trigger has come under increasing scrutiny over the years. For two different inquiries on relations of validity, *see, e.g.*, Michael Glennon, *How International Rules Die*, 93 GEO. L.J. 939 (2005); Oona Hathaway & Scott Shapiro, *Outcasting: Enforcement in Domestic and International Law*, 121 YALE L.J. 252 (2011).

60   THE RIGHT TO EXCLUDE

Traditionally, treatises on international law have treated this issue under the headings of "Recognition" or "Subjects of International Law." But the question goes back as far as one cares to look in histories of the law of nations. Vitoria and Grotius each relied upon an Aristotelian scheme for assigning status under international law. By the nineteenth century, a definition of statehood was coming into focus, eventually memorialized in the Montevideo Convention on Rights and Duties of States of 1933. Article 1 of that Convention, which continues as the standard for today, defines a state as a "person of international law" when the aspiring state provides evidence of a permanent population (preferably a *national* community), a stable connection between that community and some defined territory, the capacity for that people to administer an effective government, and for that government to be wholly independent, subject to no higher forms of political or legal authority. A problem that had developed through the nineteenth century, and found its most sustained treatment at the hands of Hersch Lauterpacht by the middle of the twentieth, was whether a political community that could arguably satisfy each of these conditions was therefore an international legal person, a rights-bearing member of the global *demos*.

Lauterpacht surveyed two basic approaches, the "declaratory" and the "constitutive" views of recognition. The former approach suggested that states merely acknowledged a set of facts about the global order when it officially recognized the sovereign status of a state. Recognition could be declared as a political matter, but in terms of international law, a given people's emergence as an international legal person was a legal issue prior to the political determinations of other states. The constitutive approach to recognition, however, held that a people's satisfaction of the criteria of statehood was insufficient to achieve international legal personality. To become a member of international society, an aspiring state required the consent of those sovereigns already in existence. Thus, recognition "constituted" the new state as a rights-bearing, international legal person. It was this constitutive approach that held sway for much of the nineteenth century, and it was Lauterpacht's view as well. What Lauterpacht wanted to claim, however, was that unlike those jurists who believed the act of recognition to be a purely political question about the frontiers of international law's boundary, he saw recognition as a legal duty.[188]

Eventually, it was the declaratory view of recognition that became more popular, though the question of how to solve international law's boundary problem has only become more and more confused. While sovereign states no longer hold a monopoly on the right to international legal personality, they are regularly viewed as the "principal" actors. It was with the advent of international legal functionalism (explored in Chapter 4), that non-state actors began the slow creep toward

---

[188] HERSCH LAUTERPACHT, RECOGNITION IN INTERNATIONAL LAW 2 (1947).

international legal personality, leading up to the current position in which states, international organizations, and even individual human beings, share in the status of international legal personality. But even with the rise of postwar functionalism, international law discourse remains entirely wedded to the view that sovereign states remain the gatekeepers. The question of what the global *demos* is remains a matter for the community of sovereigns.

It is in this way that the entire topic of recognition often seems like a dead end. Sure, it was provocative a couple hundred years ago, but by the 1970s the debate was over. If you were a state, you were a state. But of course, the "full stop" is premature—the debate over recognition turned out to be something of a red herring, since questions and answers about how to mark the frontiers of international law's community remain a mess. And more to the point, they remain a mess as we try to understand the legacy of racial ideology in its work to justify particular configurations of that global community. But why? As I will argue, in my use of liberal legalism as the material of international law's *pomerium*, the starting points are those international theorists that first took Hobbes as ground zero, and founded international law on the domestic analogy. As we have seen, in the works of thinkers like Pufendorf and Vattel, international law's boundary problem was hardly articulated, much less solved, and in this respect international legal theory simply followed liberal political theory: Hobbes never dealt with the boundary problem in the context of the social contract, either.

The result is that much of the writing from this period feels like it has universal application, and international law doesn't actually have a boundary problem. Every sovereign, everywhere, has the same right of *imperium*. It wasn't until the nineteenth century, however, that it became clear that the body of international law had the same boundary problem as any liberal state, and international lawyers looked for criteria to justify limits for who the subject/objects of the international legal order would turn out to be. By the 1850s, a distinctive form of racial ideology emerged as precisely the justification these theorists were searching for, and so a system of racial hierarchy served as the answer to international law's boundary problem. In Chapters 4, 5, and 6 I explain how, by the turn of the twentieth century, vulgar racism was receding as a way of legitimizing the boundaries of international society, and a new, modern racial ideology was coming into view. Aided by a functionalist mode of legal reasoning, a consensus slowly emerged about the need to give nonwhite peoples the rights of sovereignty, and to give legal personality to international institutions, and eventually, to individual human beings. As I discuss in Chapters 7, 8, and 9, in the last decades of the twentieth century international law's modern racial ideology transformed once again, into a *postracial* ideology. It is this postracial approach to international law's boundary problem that is still with us today. This is the argument to come. First, however, must come the more fundamental question of what a racial ideology is.

# 2
# The Racial *Xenos*

In Chapter 1, I introduced a gallery of figures. There is the *structure* of liberal legal thought, and within that structure there is a *grammar*, a *lexical plane of concepts*, and *styles of argumentative practice*. I explored the three theses of liberal legal thought, emphasized a classic style in which to interpret the legal concept of sovereignty, and how therein there emerges a sovereign's *right to exclude*. The sovereign's right to exclude unpacks in two dimensions, the right of *imperium* and the right of *dominium*. The right of *imperium* is the sovereign's right to constitute the boundaries of the global *demos* of rights-bearing subjects. The right of *dominium* is the sovereign's right to exclude other sovereigns from its territory, which itself unfolds in the twin rights of *nonintervention* and *self-determination*. In this chapter, I turn to the province of naturalizing juridical science, and more specifically, the question of how to justify or legitimize the right to exclude. As I discuss below, what emerged in the nineteenth century as the gold standard for justifying the sovereign's rights of *imperium* and *dominium*, was racial ideology. The result: the beginnings of international law's racialized structure of exclusion.

As I briefly mentioned in Chapter 1, it was the *pomerium* that, in a fundamentally sacred way, operationalized the Roman Republican distinction between *imperium* and *dominium*. What began as an actual wall eventually transformed into a conceptual and spiritual boundary between the *urbs* and the *terrae nullius*, between the civilized plane of the Roman citizenry and the barbarous lands of the non-Roman world. What is interesting about the *pomerium*, for present purposes, is how the *pomerium* did more than merely mark a line in the sand. It offered the Republic a *justification* for the mark; it legitimized what the mark was meant to signify. When the wielders of *imperium* departed Rome, it was at the *pomerium* and only through a heavily ritualized practice of prayer, sacrifice, and a taking of the auspices, that these rulers gained the full rights of military power. That is to say, it was in this ritualistic passage that the exercise of political authority was made legitimate. The auspices justified *imperium militiae*, also as they justified the limitation of that power within the bounds of the *pomerium*. Indeed, it was the ideological status of the *pomerium* that legitimized the boundary between the holders of *dominium* on the one side, and an outside and outlaw world in which a raw and absolute authority ran riot.

The focus of this chapter is not on the function of the *pomerium* in the classical law of the Roman Republic, but rather on the need from within liberal theory to duplicate something *like* a *pomerium*, or at least, duplicate its ideological function.

*The Right to Exclude*. Justin Desautels-Stein, Oxford University Press. © Justin Desautels-Stein 2023.
DOI: 10.1093/oso/9780198862161.003.0003

The issue at stake here might be characterized quite broadly, as when Giorgio Agamben refers to this moment as "the decisive event of modernity."[1] My focus, while still moving out from Agamben's point of departure, is, however, more narrow in the sense that I avoid claims about whether and how raciality is itself constitutive of liberal theory. Raciality, sexuality, and other elements surely entwine in manifold ways—but my analysis is less on the lived experiences of intersectional life and more on one style of naturalizing juridical science, what I will call the style of racial ideology—racial ideology as one manifestation of the liberal *pomerium*.

As I mentioned in Chapter 1, "the boundary problem" of liberal democratic states is that there are no apparent means from *within* liberal theory to justifiably limit the relevant *demos*, and the ones that come from beyond liberalism (i.e., Christian/Pagan, Master/Slave) are, simply put, illiberal. However, rather than survey contemporary efforts to solve the boundary problem (i.e., cultural nationalism and territorial right),[2] and with some assistance from Denise Ferreira da Silva, Saidya Hartman, Giorgio Agamben, and Michel Foucault, I discuss how the invention of race science offered one very influential kind of solution. That is, the invention of raciality was entirely compatible with liberal theory, and helpfully provided an answer to the boundary problem. Between the end of the seventeenth century and the early decades of the twentieth, anthropologists, ethnologists, and biologists offered *empirical* justifications for new ways of imagining the racial variations of the human being. If the Roman *pomerium* was legitimized by a practice of ritual and prayer, liberalism's boundaries were legitimized in the same way—only now, these rituals went by the auspices of an empirical practice of race science.

## I  THE LOGIC OF EXCLUSION AND ITS LIMITS

Classic liberal political theory has instructed its listeners for close to half a millennium on the paramount place of equality and freedom in the construction of the state.[3] In Hobbes we imagined a world in which life was so horrible that it was necessary for its inhabitants to leave it, renouncing the natural freedoms they enjoyed there in order to gain artificial freedom in a political elsewhere. In choosing to exit that natural world and enter a political one, these people contracted to constrain their natural rights of equality and freedom in exchange for a political authority

---

[1] GIORGIO AGAMBEN, HOMO SACER: SOVEREIGN POWER AND BARE LIFE 7 (1998).

[2] I discuss this further in Chapter 9.

[3] The literature on liberalism is massive. For illustrative texts, *see* MATTHEW KRAMER, LIBERALISM WITH EXCELLENCE (2017); JAMES KLOPPENBERG, THE VIRTUES OF LIBERALISM (2000); LIBERALISM: CRITICAL CONCEPTS IN POLITICAL THEORY (G.W. Smith ed., 2002); IAN SHAPIRO, THE EVOLUTION OF RIGHTS IN LIBERAL THEORY (1986); QUENTIN SKINNER, LIBERTY BEFORE LIBERALISM (1998).

## 64 THE RIGHT TO EXCLUDE

capable of maintaining order without entirely destroying those natural liberties.[4] Who were the *parties* to this contract? The contract's imagined terms seem open to anyone that might willingly submit. But who was *really* in, who was out, and who was able to decide?[5] Consider Anthony Farley's rendering of the scene:

> We are all flesh and all flesh is common until it is marked. The marking of flesh is accomplished by violence. Some are to have and others are to have not. Those who want to possess must mark the others by dispossession. These haves must come together as one, as Leviathan, because no *one* can rule another alone ... Law begins as the masters come together as one through the mark ... The mark, written or found already-written on the skin, separates those who are to have from those who are to have not. The mark splits the first commons. The first commons is the skin we are all in. Before the mark, we are. After the mark, we are white-over-black.[6]

As Dominico Losurdo has argued, rather than see racial hierarchy as a glitch, it is really a feature of liberalism, where systems of exclusion and domination constitute a theory of freedom and equality.[7] Etienne Balibar and Immanuel Wallerstein have asked in a similar spirit, "[Do racism and sexism] not, however, run against the logic of generalized economy and individual rights? In no way. We both believe that the universalism of bourgeois ideology (and therefore also its humanism) is not incompatible with the system of hierarchies and exclusions which, above all, takes the form of racism and sexism."[8] Referring to seventeenth-century British North America, Barbara Fields has written, "Whatever truths may have appeared to have been self-evident in those days, neither an inalienable right to life and liberty nor the founding of government on the consent of the governed was among them."[9] Similarly, Charles Mills has explained that in his formulation of "racial liberalism," racism penetrates "into liberalism's descriptive and normative apparatus

---

[4] Perhaps the most influential contemporary treatment is JOHN RAWLS, A THEORY OF JUSTICE (1971).

[5] On the topic of the proper bounds of political community from a liberal perspective, *see* WILL KYMLICKA, CONTEMPORARY POLITICAL PHILOSOPHY (1990); Arash Abizadeh, *Does Liberal Democracy Presuppose a Cultural Nation? Four Arguments*, 96 AM. POL. SCI. REV. 495 (2002). For philosophical accounts with a focus on race, *see, e.g.*, CHARLES MILLS, BLACK RIGHTS/WHITE WRONGS: THE CRITIQUE OF RACIAL LIBERALISM (2017); Charles Mills, *Multiculturalism as/and/or Anti-Racism? in* MULTICULTURALISM AND POLITICAL THEORY 89 (Anthony Simon Laden & David Owen eds., 2007); Lucius T. Outlaw, Jr., On Race and Philosophy, in RACISM AND PHILOSOPHY 50 (Susan E. Babbitt & Sue Campbell eds., 1999); THOMAS MCCARTHY, RACE, EMPIRE, AND THE IDEA OF HUMAN DEVELOPMENT (2009); DAVID THEO GOLDBERG, RACIAL SUBJECTS (1997); KWAME ANTHONY APPIAH, IN MY FATHER'S HOUSE: AFRICA IN THE PHILOSOPHY OF CULTURE (1992).

[6] Anthony Farley, *The Colorline as Accumulation*, 56 BUFF. L. REV. 953, 953 (2008).

[7] DOMENICO LOSURDO, LIBERALISM: A COUNTER-HISTORY (2011).

[8] ETIENNE BALIBAR & IMMANUEL WALLERSTEIN, RACE, NATION, CLASS 9 (1991).

[9] Barbara Fields, *Slavery, Race, and Ideology in the United States of America*, 1 NEW LEFT REV. 95, 102 (1990).

so as to produce a more-or-less consistent racialized ideology, albeit one that evolves over time, rather than seeing race as being externally and 'anomalously' related to it."[10] Mills continues:

> Racial liberalism, or white liberalism, is the actual liberalism that has been historically dominant since modernity: a liberal theory whose terms originally restricted full personhood to whites (or, more accurately, white men) and relegated nonwhites to an inferior category, so that its schedule of rights and prescriptions for justice were all color-coded ... So racism is not an anomaly in an unqualified liberal universalism but generally symbiotically related to a qualified and particularistic liberalism.[11]

Such criticisms of liberalism tend to move in more traditional and more radical formations. The traditional critique is concerned with the social and historical *reality* of liberal theory, a reality that most will acknowledge has been thoroughly discriminatory from the start. (Or at least, this was the trend before the Trumpian attack on Critical Race Theory that was still evolving in the early 2020s). On this traditional view, the problem here is not so much the ideal theory of political liberalism. It is rather that liberalism has an originary dynamic of exclusion built-in to its very source material: There are the rights-bearing sovereign individuals of Hobbes and Locke, and the question has always been about excluding various populations from that sovereign sphere. What is potentially racist is the liberal justification for exclusion; but liberal theory in and of itself needn't be understood in racial terms. Denise Ferreira da Silva has dubbed this traditional way of conceiving liberalism's race problem the "sociohistorical logic of exclusion,"[12] the argumentative toolkit used to limit the rights and entitlements of liberal personhood for racially developed human beings.

Obviously, the traditional critique of racial exclusion is indispensable. But as Silva explains, it is insufficient to analyze racism *only* in this way, as a matter of exclusion, for when we do so we tend to underestimate the governing and generative power of raciality.[13] For if raciality only "constitutes a strategy of power when race difference is invoked to justify exclusionary practices,"[14] we find ourselves

---

[10] MILLS, BLACK RIGHTS, *supra* note 5, at xv. I do not mean to imply that there was any single group of Europeans at issue here. As the history of race science itself demonstrates, divisions between European groups were just as common as divisions between Europeans and others. As Charles Gallagher has rightly said: "Missing from the common-sense understanding of white is how an amalgamation of diverse and warring populations from what is now Europe came to see themselves and their own self-interests as whites, place themselves at the top of this hierarchy, and impose a system of racial stratification on rest of the world." *See* Charles Gallagher, *White, in* HANDBOOK ON THE SOCIOLOGY OF RACIAL AND ETHNIC RELATIONS 9, 10 (Hernán Vera & Joe R. Feagin eds., 2007).

[11] MILLS, BLACK RIGHTS, *supra* note 5, at 31.

[12] DENISE FERRERIA DA SILVA, TOWARD A GLOBAL IDEA OF RACE (2007).

[13] Denise Ferreira da Silva, *Toward a Critique of the Socio-Logos of Justice: The Analytics of Raciality and the Production of Universality*, 7 SOC. IDENTITIES 421 (2001).

[14] *Id.* at 423.

## 66 THE RIGHT TO EXCLUDE

misdirected away from the ways in which racial ideology helps *produce* the kinds of beings to be excluded.[15] What Silva illuminates is that the traditional critique of the logic of exclusion only goes so far—yes, it is essential to know how, why, and when racial ideology justifies the exclusion of individuals and groups from equal treatment. But perhaps more importantly, we need to know how raciality creates "modern subjects who can be excluded from (juridical) universality without unleashing an ethical crisis."[16] We know much of how raciality performs as a justification for exclusion, but we know less about how it generates the process of human subjection. How does raciality produce a subject that is naturally—and permissibly—excludable?

Silva's focus on the limits of the sociohistorical logic of exclusion yields an analytical distinction between two ways of conceptualizing liberal racism: (1) the traditional view of racial discrimination, subordination, and exclusion; and (2) a more radical view of "racial subjection." Historically, reform has focused on the first type, involving an assault on subordination through the elimination of racial discrimination. In this mode, we target the logic of exclusion and seek to invert it by way of a logic of inclusion, characteristically categorize the ways in which humans are treated unequally on account of race, raise consciousness about it, and seek social change. The second conceptualization—racial subjection—is something else. For Silva, "racial subjection is not a process of othering, of exclusion, in which an already historic racial or cultural other becomes the site of projection of unwanted attributes that, once specified, reveal the ideological (false or contradictory) basis upon which European particularity has been constructed."[17] Rather, racial subjection entails a fashioning of racial beings, insiders and outsiders, marked flesh of the sort Farley describes. In the study of racial subjection, Silva continues, we

> [D]iscern the ways in which emancipatory discourses of rights, liberty, and equality instigate, transmit, and effect forms of racial domination and liberal narratives of individuality idealize mechanisms of domination and discipline. It is not simply that rights are inseparable from the entitlements of whiteness or that blacks should be recognized as legitimate rights bearers; rather, the issue at hand is the way in which the stipulation of abstract equality produces white entitlement and black subjection in its promulgation of formal equality.[18]

These two modes of raciality—racial discrimination and racial subjection—do not merely work in tandem. Rather, as Silva suggests, the sociohistorical logic of exclusion, and the critical works that have exposed its ins and outs, may inadvertently

---

[15] *Id.*
[16] SILVA, GLOBAL, *supra* note 12, at xxx–xxxi.
[17] *Id.* at 7.
[18] *Id.* at 116.

THE RACIAL *XENOS* 67

suppress our ability to understand the full range of racial subjection, the ways in which the concept of race creatively generates new visions of the human being. The trouble is that we aren't merely dealing with chronic forms of wall-building, which is already trouble enough. It is that we are also dealing with chronic forms of *people*-building, and it is this process of building and rebuilding the human subject that is the business of racial subjection. The problem is not only about discrimination, about including the excluded. The problem, perhaps more worryingly, is also the "socio-logical construction of [raciality] to signify a domain outside the terrain of the legal, while retaining the construction of whiteness as the signifier of universal justice."[19] The human races are not *only* bodies of flesh deployed and manipulated by the levers of power, as we have come to understand through the sociohistorical logic of exclusion. The human races *are* levers of power, a ruling strategy for our "contemporary global configuration."[20]

Saidiya Hartman similarly explains the importance of highlighting the radical critique of racial subjection.[21] Writing in the context of American Reconstruction, Hartman emphasizes the limits of analyzing "partial" entries by freed slaves into the realms of rights-bearing society, since these treatments beg the question "of how race, in general, and blackness, in particular, are produced through mechanisms of domination and subjection that have yoked, harnessed, and infiltrated the apparatus of rights."[22] While Hartman explores the ways in which slave discourses helped produce racial subjects, she argues that in the transition from emancipation to Reconstruction, racial subjection morphed as a matter of degree, not of kind. And the trouble was that in assuming the challenge to be a matter of elevating racial others to a standard of universal self-determination—of including the excluded—the raciality of the subject continued in abeyance. If we are to penetrate the governing realities of racial ideology, the core issue is less about closing the gap between racial discrimination and the universal, but about how the universals of liberal theory became raced. Hartman observes:

> Abstract universality presumes particular forms of embodiment and excludes or marginalizes others. Rather, the excluded, marginalized, and devalued subjects that it engenders, variously contained, trapped, and imprisoned by nature's whimsical appointments, in fact, enable the production of universality, for the denigrated and deprecated, those castigated and saddled by varied corporeal maledictions, are the fleshy substance that enable the universal to achieve its ethereal splendor.[23]

---

[19] *Id.* at 426.
[20] *Id.* at xxiv.
[21] Saidiya Hartman, Scenes of Subjection: Terror, Slavery, and Self-Making in Nineteenth-Century America (1997).
[22] *Id.* at 118.
[23] *Id.* at 122.

I agree with Her and Hartman about the important distinction between traditional critiques of foregrounded racial discrimination and radical critiques of backgrounded racial subjection. Indeed, and as I argue later in the book, the antidiscrimination principle is a powerful source of misdirection in contemporary international law, and a central constituent in the formation of postracial xenophobia. However, I will argue that while it is customary to link sociohistorical processes of exclusion with the "discrimination" side of the analytic, exclusion plays an important role on the side of "subjection" as well, as when Hartman speaks of "the exclusions *constitutive* of liberalism."[24] This link between exclusion and subjection becomes clear once we pass away from the contexts of the social sciences (i.e., sociology and anthropology), for in these contexts exclusion certainly does present itself on the side of discrimination and subordination. And this is why, with respect to the sociological and historical facets of racial exclusion, Silva is correct to say that a focus on exclusion leads us away from the ruling structure of global raciality.

Her concern with the sociohistorical logic of exclusion, and her interest in shifting attention away from the exclusion/inclusion dynamic, seem less applicable however, when we transition away from a *sociohistorical logic of exclusion* and toward a sovereign's *right to exclude* in the context of naturalizing juridical science. That is, if we pass from the contexts of the social sciences and into the context of legal thought, the right to exclude emerges as a constitutive feature of legal concepts likes sovereignty and property. And it is in this transition to legal thought that we see the right to exclude now on the terrain of racial *subjection*, moving away from the association between exclusion and discrimination and into the question of how the right to exclude functions in a legal concept as a background rule. No doubt, we want to know how racial ideology justifies the sociohistorical exclusion of privileged populations from the rest.[25] But we *also* need to know how the right to exclude functions as a constituting feature of sovereignty itself, and here we have a good way still to go.

## II  THE BIOPOLITICS OF RACIAL SUBJECTION

My effort to locate the sovereign's right to exclude in the space of racial subjection begins with a return to the classic liberal presentation of "nature." As we saw in Chapter 1, nature is critical to the distinction between the human being and what we can call the rights-bearing citizen, between the resident of the state of nature

---

[24] *Id.* at 6 (emphasis added).
[25] *See* RACE, RACISM, AND INTERNATIONAL LAW (Devon Carbado et al. eds., forthcoming 2023); EMPIRE, RACE, AND GLOBAL JUSTICE (Duncan Bell ed., 2021); ROUTLEDGE HANDBOOK OF LAW, RACE, AND THE POSTCOLONIAL (Denise Ferriera da Silva & Mark Harris eds., 2018).

and that citizen of political society, *homo politicus*. This is the distinction between what Giorgio Agamben terms *zoe* and *bios*, "bare life" and "politicized life."[26] This crafting of the rights-bearing citizen is also the mold for the rights-bearing sovereign, as we have seen in the interplay between the rights of *dominium* and *imperium*. It is the mold in yet another way as well, however, where the rights and powers of the Leviathan are produced through the making of the mark dividing political society from a prepolitical natural condition. Indeed, without this border between the political and the natural—the liberal *pomerium*—the Hobbesian image of the state does not materialize. Recall that the Leviathan is the last man standing, the last vestige of natural right that has yet to be renounced, leading Agamben to conclude that "the law of nature and the principle of the preservation of one's own life is truly the innermost center of [Hobbes'] political system ... "[27] In consequence, residents of the state of nature who remain political society's outsiders languish in a sort of twilight. Once the political and its sphere of sovereign rights is introduced, these outsiders enjoy rights to the extent they belong to some political society. They no longer possess natural rights in a pre-political "natural condition," and yet they also don't possess legal rights as a result of citizenship. In opposition with the *homo politicus*, these are the *xenoi*, the foreign and the strange.

Agamben refers to this situation of the human being—a being crafted to be abandoned by political society—by way of a double structure.[28] On the one side is the distinction between the political and the natural, wherein the sovereign's law presumptively applies to the former but doesn't to the latter. In its exclusion of the state of nature from political society, however, we can just as well say that what has been "excluded" by the state due to its retention of the prepolitical is also and at the same time "included" as political society's constitutive differential. For without the state of nature, the political society of the Leviathan would be unrecognizable. The political sphere's existence depends on the "inclusive exclusion" of its natural counterpoint. The natural condition, the habitat of those abandoned human beings, is included in political society through a rule proclaiming its exclusion. And because of this, Agamben observes, the sovereign retains a basic right to declare situations of exception—the *imperial* right to declare when rights expire, or the space in which rights no longer exist. That is, the state of nature (and its residents) shows itself within political society at those moments of exception, when the right of the sovereign is to evacuate the rules. Hence the conceptual bleeding between the state of nature and the state of exception. As Agamben puts it:

> [T]he state of nature and the state of exception are nothing but two sides of a single topological process in which what was presupposed as external (the state of

---

[26] AGAMBEN, *supra* note 1, at 36.
[27] *Id.*
[28] *See also* HANNAH ARENDT, THE ORIGINS OF TOTALITARIANISM (1951).

70 THE RIGHT TO EXCLUDE

nature) now reappears ... in the inside (as state of exception), and the sovereign power is this very impossibility of distinguishing between outside and inside, nature and exception, physis and nomos.[29]

If the liberal theory of sovereignty begins with this "inclusive exclusion" regarding a sphere of legal exception always residing within the sphere of legal application, it also begins with another: the distinction between the rights-bearing citizen and that "bare" resident of the state of nature, or what Agamben calls *homo sacer*— sacred man. This sacred man is not sacred in the way we think of the term today, for here it means something like the opposite. For Agamben, *homo sacer* is a being (and here we might anticipate the coming arrival of Du Bois) of double consciousness.[30] In one sense, *home sacer* has been excluded from the political society of the sovereign, and as such, has no rights against the sovereign, and no rights against any rights-bearing citizen. Indeed, *homo sacri* are freely killable, creatures to murder with impunity. In a second sense, in addition to the killing of the sacred man as excusable under the sovereign's law, it is equally excusable under the divine as well. The killing of *homo sacer* cannot be an act of sacrifice, as God has banished him from spiritual society just as has the sovereign banished him from the political. The liminal result is that, as Agamben says, *homo sacer* is a human being that is both legally killable and exempt from spiritual compensation. And yet, *homo sacer* is no animal—he is a human being, a human *of* the kingdoms of heaven and earth, but *in* neither.

The concept of *homo sacer* approaches Silva's notion of the racial subject, a being whose *essence* is excludability from the rights of political society "without unleashing an ethical crisis." *Homo sacer* is built to be excluded, without moral cost. Agamben suggests that just as the state of nature (exception) operates as an inclusive exclusion, so too does the figure of *homo sacer*. *Homo sacer* represents the converse of the rights-bearing individual, and it is that bare human being who constitutes the political order of *homo politicus*, precisely as a result of his exclusion. Agamben writes, *homo sacer* is "included in the community in the form of being able to be killed."[31] At the same time, *homo sacer's* killing is inaudible in the spiritual register as well, now belonging to the community of God and the realm of the moral in the form of his unsacrificability.[32] The sacred man, pointing at once toward the law of the sovereign and the law of the divine, is paradoxically included in these communities through a rule demanding his exclusion. Both the state of

[29] AGAMBEN, *supra* note 1, at 37.
[30] To be clear, Agamben didn't use the phrase "double consciousness." I am using that language here to anticipate the racialization of bare life, the racial *xenos*. On Du Bois, *see* W.E.B. DU BOIS, THE SOULS OF BLACK FOLK (1961); W.E.B. DU BOIS, BLACK RECONSTRUCTION IN AMERICA, 1860–1880 (1998 [1935]); W.E.B. DU BOIS, SELECTIONS FROM HIS WRITINGS (2014); W.E.B. DU BOIS, DARKWATER: VOICES FROM WITHIN THE VEIL (2021).
[31] AGAMBEN, *supra* note 1, at 82.
[32] *Id.*

THE RACIAL *XENOS*    71

nature (exception) and the sacred man are figures *produced* through this inclusive exclusion. They are not chaotic spheres of materiality prior to the moment of exclusion, bodies of flesh discovered by science. They are made *through* it. Emphasizing the point, Agamben explains, citing Carl Schmidt:

> What is at issue in the sovereign exception is not so much the control or neutralization of an excess as the creation and definition of the very space in which the juridico-political order can have validity. In this sense, the sovereign exception is the fundamental localization (ortung), which does not limit itself to distinguishing what is inside from what is outside but instead traces a threshold (the state of exception) between the two, on the basis of which outside and inside, the normal situation and chaos, enter into those complex topological relations that make the validity of the juridical order possible.[33]
>
> The relation of exception is a relation of ban. He who has been banned is not, in fact, simply set outside the law and made indifferent to it but rather abandoned by it, that is, exposed and threatened on the threshold in which life and law, outside and inside, become indistinguishable. It is literally not possible to say whether the one who has been banned is outside or inside the juridical order.[34]

As I mentioned above, Agamben's claim about sovereignty and the "bare life" of the sacred man—as opposed to the political being of the rights-bearing individual—is intended as a key to the entire "Western" tradition, ranging from Aristotle, to Hobbes, to Schmidt. This claim is, in part, a reworking of Michel Foucault's theory of biopower, articulated mostly in fragments toward the end of his career.[35] For Foucault, the notion of biopower begins by contrasting itself with more traditional forms of state power, or a version of what in Chapter 1 I referred to as "foreground" rules. This was the exercise of state power from "above," a "juridical" right to "appropriate a portion of wealth, a tax of products, goods and services, labor and blood, levied on the subjects."[36] Biopower, by comparison, is more like the type I called "background": "a power bent on generating forces, making them grow, and ordering them, making them submit, or destroying them."[37] Rather than a top-down type of regulatory control, biopower concerns itself with population management, with fashioning the contours of the life of the species. Biopower is the exercise of authority aimed at the propagation of a particular vision of how the human species ought to be developing, in biological terms. Emerging at the end

---

[33] *Id.* at 19.

[34] *Id.* at 28–29.

[35] For discussion, *see* BEN GOLDER & PETER FITZPATRICK, FOUCAULT'S LAW (2009).

[36] MICHEL FOUCAULT, THE HISTORY OF SEXUALITY 1, 136 (1990); MICHEL FOUCAULT, THE BIRTH OF BIOPOLITICS: LECTURES AT THE COLLEGE DE FRANCE, 1978–1979 (2004).

[37] FOUCAULT, THE BIRTH OF BIOPOLITICS, *supra* note 36.

# 72  THE RIGHT TO EXCLUDE

of the eighteenth century,[38] Foucault explained that biopower, "is a technology which aims to establish a sort of homeostasis, not by training individuals, but by achieving an overall equilibrium that protects the security of the whole from internal dangers ... a technology in which bodies are replaced by general biological processes."[39]

Population control, the elevation of hygienic and sanitary codes, and the advancement of medicine all portended a new kind of power, a power having less to do with "juridical regulation" than had previously been the case. But was the rise of this new type of control a good thing? To be sure, it certainly could be, and quite often, it was. The arrival of antibiotics and the treatment of previously incurable diseases, not to mention so many more sundry items, all suggested the imminence of better, healthier lives. At the same time, however, biopower had its dark sides, and as Foucault pointed out, when framed in the context of war, biopolitics became racialized.[40] Eugenics and Nazism stand as its most obvious exemplars. Foucault understood racism as racial hierarchy, as a means for separating and subdividing the human species into a mixture of races.[41] But more importantly, racism as biopower reconceptualized the idea of war: "the more the inferior species die out, the fewer degenerates there will be, the stronger will be the species, and me along with it. The death of the bad race, of the inferior race is something that will make life in general healthier and purer. This is a biological relationship. This is biopower."[42] To emphasize the point, Foucault argued that in this context the rise of biopower enabled a new, totalizing kind of violence, where war was no longer about winning a political victory, but rather about exterminating segments of the human population that might otherwise degrade the whole of the species. And it was the idea of raciality that provided the fuel:

> We can understand why racism should have developed in modern societies that function in the biopower mode; we can understand why racism broke out at a number of privileged moments, and why they were precisely the moments when the right to take life was imperative. Racism first develops with colonization, or in other words, with colonizing genocide. If you are functioning in the biopower mode, how can you justify the need to kill people, to kill populations, and to kill civilizations? By using the themes of evolutionism, by appealing to racism.[43]

---

[38] Michel Foucault, Society Must Be Defended: Lectures at the College de France, 1976–1976 245 (Mauro Bertani & Alessandro Fontano eds., 1997).

[39] *Id.* at 249.

[40] *Id.* at 254.

[41] *Id.* at 255.

[42] *Id.*

[43] *Id.* at 257.

As I mentioned, Foucault traced the emergence of biopower to the last decades of the eighteenth century, the Age of Revolutions.[44] For Agamben, in contrast, sovereignty has always been about controlling life, in the biopolitical sense: "[T]he inclusion of bare life in the political realm constitutes the original—if concealed—nucleus of sovereign power. *It can even be said that the production of the biopolitical body is the original activity of sovereign power.* In this sense, biopolitics is at least as old as the sovereign exception."[45] With this maneuver, Agamben works to explain the relation between Foucault's two types of power—the foregrounded power of juridical institutions and the backgrounded power of population control—by locating the inclusion of *homo sacer* in the very center of the sovereign figure. What is lost in Agamben's strategy, however, is the motivation to theorize raciality in the eighteenth and nineteenth centuries as a defining feature of biopower and sovereign rights.[46]

I want to pursue a line of analysis in which we build upon Agamben's conceptualization of an inclusive exclusion productive of sovereignty itself, as well as Foucault's suggestive account of racism's charge to nineteenth century Europeans, that "society must be defended." This suggests that, as Devon Carbado has similarly argued in the context of racializing *homo sacer*, we place Agamben's pregnant phrasing—"Every society—even the most modern—decides who its 'sacred men' will be"—in the context of raciality.[47] The outcome is what I call the racial *xenos*, an outsider marked for killing through processes of racial subjection.[48] Herein lie the seeds of racial xenophobia.

While this is not explicit in the works of scholars like Silva and Hartman, Carbado's through-line from Foucault and Agamben to Hartman and Silva is clear enough: If Agamben is right about an originary distinction in liberalism between a sphere of sovereign right and a space of sacred men, between *homo politicus* and the racial *xenos*, we can reconfigure these sacred men as the world's racially "undeveloped" peoples, and the owner of sovereign right as the apex figure of racial development. As Carbado explained in the context of the United States (US):

> Implicit in Agamben's conception of bare life is the notion that inclusion can be a social vehicle for exclusion and that inclusive exclusions can have constitutive power. This understanding allows us to conceive of blackness itself as a form of bare life. Simply put, the notion is this: blackness has often been included in the

---

[44] *See* Eric Hobsbawn, The Age of Revolution: 1789–1848 (1996).

[45] Agamben, *supra* note 1, at 6.

[46] *See* Agamben and Colonialism (Marcelo Svirsky & Simone Bignall eds., 2012).

[47] Agamben, *supra* note 1, at 139. *See also* Devon Carbado, *Naturalizing Race*, 57 Am. Q. 633, 638 (2005); Enakshi Dua, *Revisiting Genealogies: Theorizing Anti-Racism Beyond the Impasse*, in Theorizing Anti-Racism: Linkages in Marxism and Critical Race Theories (Abigail Bakan & Enakshi Dua eds., 2014).

[48] References to killable bodies in this context can certainly refer to actual death. They can also, however, refer to social configurations of domination, subordination, and exploitation.

## 74 THE RIGHT TO EXCLUDE

juridical order solely in the form of its exclusion (that is, its capacity to be subordinated). This inclusive exclusion historically has positioned black people both inside and outside America's national imagination—as a matter of law, politics, and social life. Blackness, in this sense, might be thought of as an insular identity; like Puerto Rico, blackness is foreign in a domestic sense. This racial liminality— outside and inside the borders of the American body, not quite not American—is precisely what I enlist the term racial naturalization to convey.[49]

And as Silva says in a more global context, "[w]hile the *human body* can be found across the surface of the globe, *man* existed exclusively within the limits of the modern European space."[50] The bare life of the "human body" (the racialized body of color, the body of *homo sacer*) is indeed a human body, to be sure, but a *killable* body, guarded neither by the laws of political society nor the laws of morality. But "Man," in this context, is *homo politicus*, the Hobbesian Man, the Lockean Man, the rational, reasoning, self-determining, Man—and, as I discuss below, the white Man. "Whiteness," Silva explains, "was produced to indicate the form of consciousness able to conceive of universal principles that emerged in the European space—the only raced consciousness able to fulfill the material and moral projects of modernity."[51] But this is no matter of excluding the so-called racially inferior peoples from the realms of white universality and self-determination; the figure of the (white) sovereign is *produced* through the inclusive exclusion of the (nonwhite) figures of bare life, the racial *xenoi*.

Pushing further still, if Foucault is right about how the nineteenth century defined biopower, and how raciality emerged as a kind of background rule, we can leverage the planks of white supremacy and white sovereignty out of the abstractions of liberal theory and into the planetary contexts of race science. What this accomplishes is a movement beyond the assumption that while racial subjection might have produced the figure of bare life/sovereign right, such a production would have been limited to the vulgar excess of slavery and colonialism. And it is this kind of assumption that leads into the pitfalls of the sociohistorical logic of exclusion: If the rights of sovereignty and the rightslessness of bare life have been distributed along a schedule of racial development, then (so the argument goes) redistribute the rights so as to make the global space more inclusive. And indeed, this is the trajectory of the antidiscrimination principle. But the focus on the biopower of nineteenth-century raciality helps illuminate that racial subjection continued on, beyond the aftermath of the US Civil War, beyond late-nineteenth-century imperialism, beyond the arrival of international institutions, beyond anticolonialism, beyond the civil rights and human rights movements, beyond

---

[49] AGAMBEN, *supra* note 1, at 139.
[50] SILVA, GLOBAL, *supra* note 12, at 430.
[51] *Id.* at 431.

the end of apartheid, and right into our so-called "postracial" era. This turn to the biopower of nineteenth-century racial subjection, as Silva suggests, and as I emphasize below, is the key to understanding "how the racial governs the contemporary global configuration."[52] To be sure, racism has been about exclusion, and a great deal of inclusive social reform over the last century has done a tremendous amount of good. But as Hartman has emphasized, "racial inclusion" has obscured the biopolitics of racial subjection: "the abolition of slavery conferred on [freed slaves] the inalienable rights of man and brought them into the fold of liberal individualism ... The civil and political rights bestowed upon the freed dissimulated the encroaching and invasive forms of social control exercised over black bodies through venerations of custom; the regulation, production, and protection of racial and gender inequality in the guise of social rights ... "[53]

In seeking out the biopolitics of racial subjection, in the following section I analyze the emergent raciality of sovereign right and the rightslessness of the racial *xenos* in the context of the natural science of racial development. As this new "science" of race matured, an indigenous form of argumentative practice developed from within liberal theory, providing a far more elegant technique for conceptualizing the nature of bare life than anything that had preceded it.[54] The deployment of racial classifications, whether by scientists or by the jurists relying upon those scientists, was decisively global in its positivist and empirical commitments.[55] By articulating the universality of human equality in the global discourse of science, rather than in the discourse of God, classic liberals could argue in *liberal* terms for the sovereignty of certain peoples, and the killability of the rest. This way of conceptualizing raciality as the liberal production of outsiders, of foreignness, of the *homo sacri*, yields a racial *xenos*, or an ideology of racial xenophobia, which I define as *a structure of legal argument that produces relations of racial subjection on account of a naturalized foreignness.* The idea here was that at the heart of sovereignty is the natural condition of bare life. It resides there through an "inclusive exclusion," the threshold at which rights-bearing citizens (*homo politicus*) in political society are distinguished from the human bodies of nature (the racial *xenos*).

As we will see, what is fascinating about this idea, particularly when we elevate it to the field of international law, is how the dynamic mirrors itself. Recall that in international law sovereigns perform in the domestic analogy, where sovereigns on the global plane are analogized to rights-bearing individuals in a prepolitical

---

[52] *Id.* at 7.

[53] *Id.* at 117–18.

[54] For discussion of similar themes, *see* JENNIFER PITTS, A TURN TO EMPIRE: THE RISE OF IMPERIAL LIBERALISM IN BRITAIN AND FRANCE (2006).

[55] For a helpful discussion of Comte's impact on nineteenth century social science, as well as the relation between Bacon's empiricism and Scottish commonsense philosophy, *see* DOROTHY ROSS, THE ORIGINS OF AMERICAN SOCIAL SCIENCE 27–30 (1991). *See also* MARK MAZOWER, GOVERNING THE WORLD 99–100 (2012).

76  THE RIGHT TO EXCLUDE

state of nature. What this means is that we can imagine—in international law—sovereigns as *both/either* leviathans *and/or* rights-bearing individuals. And this is why the sovereign's right of *imperium* has such a curious cast: sovereigns are imagined as possessing the rational, self-determining mind of an individual citizen, and also the power to decide both the identity of the planet's sacred—killable—human bodies, as well as the geographic spaces inhabited by these killable bodies.


## III  THE GLOBAL CONTEXT OF RACIAL XENOPHOBIA

Thirty years after the arrival of Hobbes' *Leviathan* and just five years before Locke wrote his *Second Treatise*, Francois Bernier published in 1684 the first of many attempts to recast human flesh as racial flesh, to reimagine human beings as racial beings, and offer up a new scientific view of human classification to replace older theological and metaphysical measures.[56] Of course, thinkers since Aristotle had eagerly typologized the human being. What distinguished these new sets of classification was a focus on physically observable characteristics divorced from function and social purpose—of the dichotomies of vice and virtue, Christian and Heathen.[57] Out from the Cartesian baseline of thinking the materiality of human life as a rational system knowable through reason, thinkers like Bernier initially suggested that there were four basic *especes ou races*, and that these varieties were distinguished on the basis of geographic origin and physical appearance: (1) Europeans, South Asians, North Africans, and Americans, all of which shared in similar climates and complexions; (2) Africans (central and south); (3) Asians

---

[56] The account in this chapter draws from Ivan Hannaford, Race: The History of an Idea in the West (1996); Thomas Gossett, Race: The History of an Idea in America (1997); Reginald Horsman, Race and Manifest Destiny: The Origins of American Racial Anglo-Saxonism (1981); Nancy Stepan, The Idea of Race in Science (1982); Kwame Anthony Appiah, Lines of Descent (2014); Peter Baum, The Rise and Fall of the Caucasian Race (2006); Nell Irvin Painter, The History of White People (2010); George Fredrickson, Racism: A Short History (2002); The Concept of Race in Natural and Social Science (E. Nathaniel Gates ed., 1997); Brendan O'Flahtery & Jill S. Shapiro, *Apes, Essences, and Races: What Natural Scientists Believed About Human Variation, 1700–1900*, in Race, Liberalism, and Economics 21 (David Colander et al. eds., 2009); Audrey Smedley, Race in North America (3d ed. 2007). In this chapter, I do not mean to imply that this new style of human classification was either necessitated by classic liberalism, or its cause. Instead, notably, in the second half of the seventeenth century, at exactly the same time that classic liberalism was in its infancy, science became preoccupied with human diversity and physical explanations for cultural phenomena. The projects of liberalism and what would later be called "race science" were conducted in tandem—of that, at least, we can be certain. As for questions of causation and correlation, these may be left for elsewhere. *See generally* Theodore Koditschek, *Capitalism, Race, and Evolution in Imperial Britain, 1850–1900*, in Race Struggles 48 (Theodore Koditschek et al. eds., 2009); Maria Grahn-Farley, *Race and Class: More than a Liberal Paradox*, 56 Buff. L. Rev. 935 (2008); Michael Omi & Howard Winant, Racial Formation in the United States (2d ed. 1994).

[57] Thinkers like Descartes, Hobbes, and Locke had already begun the work of empirical divisions of the human species, but the modern notion of race didn't begin until Bernier. *See* Hannaford, *supra* note 56, at 191.

(central and north); and (4) Lapps, "people who were ugly, squat, small, and animal-like."[58]

More influential in this first phase of characterizing human beings as racial beings was Georges-Louis Leclerc, Comte de Buffon.[59] Buffon believed that far in the past an original human species spread itself over the globe, and in the process was gradually exposed to differences in climate, food, and disease. As a result of these exterior pressures, the human body took on various complexions, sizes, and temperaments. The critical feature of his theory was that these varieties of people were impressionable and historically contingent. All human beings were creatures of reason, to be sure. The impact of exterior stimuli, however, resulted in the production of certain classes of human being, where some were more capable of reason than others. It is here we bear witness to the beginnings of the racial subject, the racial *xenos*. True, Buffon believed that these exterior effects could be modified, and even reversed. But what nature had produced and bequeathed, at least by the 1700s, was white raciality as the "norm" of racial development and "the real and natural color of man."[60] Everything else was *foreign*. The point is that from the very beginning, the empirical effort to classify humans in terms of race was at the same time a philosophical effort to distinguish the genuinely superior characteristics of the scientist's own racial identity from the identities of foreigners. From the start, the science of racial development was an ideology of racial xenophobia, a means for defining whiteness through the racialization of the foreign and the strange.

What was emerging here, in the eighteenth and nineteenth centuries, was the discipline that we today call physical anthropology, a scientific discourse concerned with the evolutionary development of the biological and behavioral qualities of human bodies.[61] As the authors of a popular textbook on physical anthropology explain, theirs is a discourse that "helps us explain what it means to be human and how we came to be the way we are."[62] Indeed, this was precisely the mission of early thinkers like Bernier and Buffon: What does it mean to be human, and how did humans come to be the way that they are? And perhaps most importantly, what explains the "obvious" fact that certain types of humans are superior to others? The concept of raciality was a powerful answer to all of these questions, from what it meant to be a human being, to the provision of a schedule of racially developed human bodies. This is the moment, as anticipated from the discussion from above, of the racialization of bare life. As Silva put it, the emerging discourse of racial

---

[58] About 50 years later, Carlos Linnaeus offered a fifth group: (1) *Homo ferus* (savage), (2) *Europaeus albus* (light-skinned, intelligent, law-abiding), (3) *Americanus rubescus* (tanned, happy-go-lucky, custom-abiding), (4) *Asiaticus luridus* (yellow-skinned and sad), (5) *Afer niger* (dark-skinned, lazy, "governed by the arbitrary will of the master"). *See* HANNAFORD, *supra* note 56, at 204; GOSSETT, *supra* note 56, at 32–33.

[59] HANNAFORD, *supra* note 56, at 203–14.

[60] GOSSETT, *supra* note 56, at 36.

[61] ROBERT JURMAIN ET AL., INTRODUCTION TO PHYSICAL ANTHROPOLOGY (2017).

[62] *Id.* at 5.

## 78 THE RIGHT TO EXCLUDE

development was a mode of "scientific signification [which] deployed the racial to produce modern subjects" which could soon be separated into groups bearing heavy resemblance to the rights-bearing citizens of liberal theory, and to others who would not. "When the racial writes Europeans and the others of Europe" as products of an exterior environment, Silva writes, "it institutes the body, social configurations, and global regions as signifiers of the mind."[63]

The pioneering work of Bernier and Buffon, and the project of creating racial beings, was further developed by Johann Friedrich Blumenbach, later known as the father of anthropology,[64] who published a series of editions of his immensely influential *On the Natural Variety of Mankind* in the midst of the American and French Revolutions.[65] Blumenbach believed in the unity of the human species, but also in the subdivision of the species into five groups: Caucasians, Mongolians, Ethiopians, Americans, and Malays.[66] These new classes of racial subject were of a single species, but the species existed along a continuum of racial development.[67] The "highest" class of racial development was the Caucasian, and the "lowest" were the Mongolian and Ethiopian races. Transitional groups were the American, shading between the Caucasian and Mongolian, and the Malay, shading between the Caucasian and the Ethiopian. Blumenbach agreed with Buffon about the racial superiority of the white racial subject, emphasizing their unparalleled beauty and intelligence.[68] Blumenbach followed Buffon with the claim that the physical differences between humans were mostly a matter of environmental pressures, and denied that humans belonged to the animal kingdom, rejecting the notion that all natural creatures existed on a natural scale of transitional differentiation.[69] As a result, Blumenbach left behind the old notion of the Great Chain of Being, the view that there were several species of humans, linked in a hierarchically arranged system with monsters on one end and European men on the other, followed by primates and other creatures reminiscent of Aristotle's natural scale.[70]

---

[63] *Id.* at 29.

[64] HANNAFORD, *supra* note 56, at 206. Blumenbach explained that human beings were of several types: Caucasians, Mongolians, Ethiopians, Americans, and Malays.

[65] JOHANN FRIEDRICH BLUMENBACH, ON THE NATURAL VARIETY OF MANKIND (1969).

[66] Blumenbach coined the term "Caucasian." *See* PAINTER, *supra* note 56, at 79. Blumenbach offered a helpful explanation as to why this variety of human being would be identified with the Caucuses: "I have taken the name of this variety from Mount Caucasus, both because of its neighborhood, and especially its southern slope, produces the most beautiful race of men, I mean the Georgian." *Id.* at 81.

[67] This view was known as *monogenism*, meaning "one species" or "one people." *See* HANNAFORD, *supra* note 56, at 211 ("For Blumenbach all varieties and differences overlapped and merged into one another and had to be viewed according to the species, which was one and the same—a unity.").

[68] *Id.* at 88 ("The Tartar-Caucasian was first and foremost the beautiful race. The Mongolian was the ugly race, 'weak in body and spirit, bad, and lacking in virtue' ").

[69] As Ivan Hannaford explained: "During the last forty years of [Blumenbach's] long life controversy raged over items he had put squarely on the agenda: degeneration, ... the significance of language and milieu (geography, climate, relief, soil, land), and perhaps most important of all, the capacity of peoples for progressive physical, moral, and political development. *Id.* at 213.

[70] This was Linnaeus' view. *See* HANNAFORD, *supra* note 56, at 203–08. Perhaps the most well-known account is ARTHUR LOVEJOY, THE GREAT CHAIN OF BEING: A STUDY OF THE HISTORY OF AN IDEA (1971). Bruce Baum writes, "All in all, Blumenbach left a paradoxical racial legacy. He was one of the

Johann Gottfied von Herder's writings at the end of the eighteenth century were of apiece with Blumenbach's view of a unified but differentiated human species, but rather than begin with these new racial conceptualizations of the human being, Herder suggested instead the idea of the cultural nation.[71] Herder believed in the importance of a given people's psychological adaptation to a particular environment, which he labeled the culture or the spirit of a people. These varying adaptations led to different senses of the people's spirit, manifested in ways to hunt, to fish, to eat, to pray, to speak, and so on. These habits and customs were what consolidated into the people's spirit, the nation's culture, and what Herder described as essentially a common family.[72] Herder's view of the relation between unity and diversity, between the idea of unity of the human species and the historical realities of cultural difference, aligned nicely with Blumenbach's physical anthropology: each theorist promoted a universal vision of the racial/cultural subject, offset by a geographic distinction between greater and lesser types. Herder also believed in a hierarchy of racial subjects, generating the German Teutons as the masters in all things, and Africans, Asians, and Jews as foreign degenerates.[73]

The proto-racial ideas of Blumenbach and Herder dominated the science of racial xenophobia until the 1850s.[74] Vying for consideration were the minority positions of scientists like Charles White and Peter Camper, who argued respectively for the notion that Africans were the link between Europeans and apes, and that the proof for this theory was the statistical display of facial angle measurements and skull shapes.[75] In early nineteenth-century Britain, the argument that Africans comprised a distinct species, linking "real" humans to apes, was regarded as nonsense.[76] Writers like Thomas Winterbottom, James Prichard, and William Lawrence believed that the evidence overwhelmingly placed humans outside of the animal kingdom, obviating the need to provide any "link" at all. To be sure, practically all writers agreed that it was empirically justifiable to recast human

---

least racist of Enlightenment thinkers but nonetheless reinforced racist ideas by establishing a 'hierarchical ordering of human diversity.' *Id.* at 89.

[71] JOHANN GOTTFIED VON HERDER, IDEAS ON THE PHILOSOPHY OF THE HISTORY OF HUMANKIND (1784); JOHN ZAMMITO, KANT, HERDER, AND THE BIRTH OF ANTHROPOLOGY (2002); David Denby, *Herder: Culture, Anthropology, and the Enlightenment* 18 HIST. HUM. SCI. 55 (2005). A student and adversary of Kant's, Herder developed his theory of the folk spirit against Kant's own racial theory. On Kant's racial theory, *see* IMMANUEL KANT, ANTHROPOLOGY FROM A PRAGMATIC POINT OF VIEW (1798).

[72] In a similarly holistic view of the human species, Herder published an account in the last decades of the eighteenth century suggesting that a new idea—*culture*—was the real organizing principle for the different manifestations of human society. For Herder, these cultures were equal in the sense that they were technically all *human* cultures, produced through a combination of different linguistic, religious, musical, educational, and ritualistic practices. Again, equality was a driver in Herder's thinking, but the very maneuver of classifying difference enabled much of the race science that would develop in the nineteenth century.

[73] *See* Cedric Dover, *The Racial Philosophy of Johan Herder*, 3 BRIT. J. SOC. 124 (1952).

[74] STEPAN, *supra* note 56, at 10.

[75] *Id.* at 9–10.

[76] These arguments were made in France as well, for example, by Georges Cuvier.

80  THE RIGHT TO EXCLUDE

beings as racial beings, that Africans were the least "developed" of the "races," and physically were the least fortunate, but that these differences were not inherent and merely the result of environmental factors. As Lawrence argued:

> That the Negro is more like a monkey than the European cannot be denied as a general observation. But why is the Negro always selected for this comparison? The New Hollander, the Calmuck, the native American, are not superior to the Africans, and are as much like monkeys. Why then is the Negro alone to be depressed to a level with the brute?[77]

## A From Environment to Evolution

The shift that occurred in the science of racial xenophobia around the middle of the nineteenth century involved a series of moves, all revolving around the rebuttal of environmentalism as a coherent explanation for white supremacy, and the rise of biological determinism—the idea that physical attributes determined intellectual and cultural attributes. These shifts were consistent with contemporaneous social and political currents, certainly taking a more conservative turn first with the defeat of Napoleon and the consolidation of power in Vienna, and then after the failed Revolutions of 1848 and the ending of slavery in the US. As Bruce Baum has said, it was during this time that "European intellectuals moved away from Enlightenment egalitarian and environmentalist notions to 'theories of inequality and organicism,' sometimes adopting a naturalistic fatalism about human affairs."[78] More and more, anthropologists and ethnologists turned to ever-advancing methods of quantifying the many dimensions of the human body, with special emphasis on phrenology.[79] The emerging consensus was that cranial shape signified racial subjection, and that racial subjects differed greatly, and inherently, in their moral, intellectual, and cultural capabilities. The racialization of human flesh and bone was changing its character, moving from contingency to necessity. It was becoming increasingly apparent that raciality was a key to the inner workings of the mind, indeed the racial body was what *explained* the human mind—the minds of both *homo politicus* and the racial *xenos*. Critically, these differences were subject to the same value judgments as they had always been—the intellect and culture generated by the European skull was of a different order of magnitude than those spirited out of "foreign" skulls. Regardless of environmental factors, these

[77] STEPAN, *supra* note 56, at 11 (quoting WILLIAM LAWRENCE, LECTURES ON PHYSIOLOGY, ZOOLOGY, AND THE NATIONAL HISTORY OF MAN (1822)).
[78] BAUM, *supra* note 56, at 97.
[79] GOSSETT, *supra* note 56, at 69–70.

THE RACIAL *XENOS*   81

intellectual, moral, and cultural capabilities were fixed—innate and woven into the very structure of what it meant to possess a racial identity.

In the US, where polygenism was quite popular, the anatomist Samuel George Morton was a leading advocate of the view that human races were distinct species with innate differences.[80] Writing in the decades preceding the American Civil War, Morton accepted Blumenbach's classification of five races (Morton swapped the term "variety" out for "race"), but argued that rather than understand the races as the historical results of varying stimuli, we should instead come to terms with the fact that every race had particular qualities that were independent of context and especially adapted to peculiar locations.[81] These qualities were innate and immutable, and were correlated with the average cranial capacity of each race.[82] Fortuitously for Morton, his measured averages tracked exactly the cultural and aesthetic rankings of Blumenbach's global geography.

Though other race scientists were more influential at the time,[83] it is the French "Father of Racism," Count Arthur de Gobineau, and his 1853 publication of *The Inequality of Races*, which is better known today as one of the key wellsprings for what would later become Nazism.[84] Gobineau's racial subjects were white, black, and yellow: "I understand by *white* men the members of those races which are also called Caucasian, Semetic or Japhetic. By *black* men I mean the Hamites; by *yellow* the Altaic, Mongol, Finnish and Tartar branches. These are the three primitive elements of mankind."[85] Gobineau's racial rankings were familiar: "the peoples who are not of white blood approach beauty, but do not attain it."[86] Gobineau continued, "As the [nonwhite] races recede from the white type, their features and limbs become incorrect in form; they acquire defects of proportion which, in the races that are completely foreign to us, end by producing an extreme ugliness."[87]

---

[80] BAUM, *supra* note 56, at 106.

[81] *Id.*

[82] According to Morton's measurements, the Caucasian cranial capacity averaged 87 cubic inches, Mongolians averaged 83 inches, Malays averaged 81 inches, American Indians averaged 80 inches, and Ethiopians averaged 78 inches. *Id.* at 107. In 1840, Anders Retzius introduced the "cranial index," which was notated by the maximum breadth of the head expressed as a percentage of maximum length. He was also the author of the terms "dolichocephalic" (long-headed skull) and "brachycephalic" (broadheaded skull). *See* BAUM, *supra* note 56, at 130–31.

[83] Back in Britain, the anatomist Robert Knox published *The Races of Men* in 1850. Knox began with an attack on Prichard, arguing that there was no evidence for believing in an original human species that had spread throughout the world, and that the species must be studied with anatomical methods—*biologically*, as the term now appeared consistently in the literature. *Id.* at 5–32. In tandem with this biological conception of race, Knox pushed forward the disaggregation of the Caucasian race, emphasizing the purity of the Saxons, and the destiny of that people to conquer the world. *Id.* at 32–54. Importantly, this structural purity of racial stock was immune to degradation, just as the Jewish people could never hope to improve their own. These differences were biological, and therefore unchangeable. The Revolutions of 1848 were the backdrop here.

[84] HANNAFORD, *supra* note 56, at 265. *See also* ARTHUR DE GOBINEAU, THE INEQUALITY OF HUMAN RACES (Adrian Collins trans., 1967).

[85] HANNAFORD, *supra* note 56, at 146.

[86] *Id.*

[87] *Id.*

## 82 THE RIGHT TO EXCLUDE

Gobineau was not suggesting, however, that all whites were equally attractive—Italians were more beautiful than the Germans, Swiss, French, or Spanish.[88] And, just as no race was as physically strong as the whites, "[i]n strength of fist, the English are superior to all other European races; while the French and Spanish have a greater power of resisting fatigue and privation, as well as the inclemency of extreme climates."[89]

In the following decade, arguments for the innate, anatomical basis of distinct human races, and the moral, cultural, and intellectual consequences that followed, increasingly dominated Europe. As Nancy Stepan has argued:

> The new racial biology appealed to the general public because it appeared to agree with the Europeans' sense of themselves in the world, and to be based on a wider set of data, more sophisticated measurements, and a deeper knowledge of biological processes and functions than previous work on human races. In short, by the middle of the century, a new racial science had come into being in which races were indeed, as [Robert] Knox claimed, "everything."[90]

If writers like Gobineau represented the apogee of polygenist thinking in the first half of the nineteenth century, the use of race as an explanation for white supremacy shifted gears in the second half. After 1859, no examination of human genesis and variety could proceed without taking note of Charles Darwin's *On the Origin of the Species*.[91] From this point forward polygenism hit a dead end, as it became universally accepted in the natural sciences that the human species was not a fixed, unchanging, perfect creation, but one that had been undergoing constant and continuous change since its beginning.[92] At first sight, Darwin's insights into the idea of natural selection—that competition for survival favored those attributes most advantageous to keeping an organism alive—seemed to push the science of racial xenophobia back in the direction of environmentalism. What marked this new phase of race science was not, however, a return to older talk of the "unity of the species." Despite what appeared to be the argument that evolutionary theory posed *against* notions of racial development, evolutionary theory turned out to be a highly effective vehicle for the next step in the science of racial subjection.

How did race science square the view that races were fixed and innate with the notion of continuous, evolutionary change? Anthropologists agreed that though human beings may have once had a common, shared identity, racial formation occurred at a similarly distant point in the past. While human beings as a *species* evolved, the evolution of the *races* had ceased. That is, schedules of racial

---

[88] *Id.* at 152.
[89] *Id.*
[90] STEPAN, *supra* note 56, at 46.
[91] BAUM, *supra* note 56, at 129–30.
[92] *Id.*

THE RACIAL *XENOS*   83

development as they existed in the 1860s were then what they had been for a very long time. The rationale for this curious result was that once human beings had become more intelligent, they were able to subvert and even deny the forces of natural selection. Evolutionary struggle would continue to affect the human species, to be sure, but it would leave untouched the basic scheme of racial development.[93] Consequently, the task became the study of these primordial races and the identification of their natural essences. The trouble with the task was that scientists couldn't identify racial essences from the study of particular individuals. Individuals were now simply too varied to be representative of what were believed to be the "original" racial characteristics, and variations between people who were apparently meant to belong to a single race were chalked up as environmentally produced, or mutations from the racial standard. The obvious problem here was that if racial identity could not be constructed from the study of individual human beings, then how to know if race was really *real* at all?[94]

In the debates before Darwin, theories of racial development had produced a new way of conceptualizing human life, one that had written concepts of indigeneity and foreignness right into flesh and bone. As Silva explains, the *living body* that was once the pinnacle of ancient schemes like the Great Chain of Being, had ceased to be the *human body*. The living body that now represented the being of reason and self-determination had become "the body of post-Enlightenment (Caucasian, white) Europeans ... [whose] 'mental functions' are inscribed in its social configuration, that is, 'civilization.'"[95] One could espouse monogenesis and still subscribe to this new equation since nonwhite bodies were regarded as *human* bodies, just not the bodies of *man*; this is the process of racial subjection, reproducing the figures of bare life (the nonwhite bodies of racial *xenoi*) and political consciousness (the white bodies of *homo politicus*). What changed (among other things) after Darwin's *The Origin of Species* was a shift away from the preoccupation with mapping the forms of human life, and toward the global context of raciality.

While Darwin's *Origin* was not in itself a treatment of racial development, the book's turn to the global setting for evolutionary theory—where natural selection did its work throughout the world, without regard for cultural or national boundaries—set the scene for a way of conceptualizing a relation between

---

[93] *See generally* MIKE HAWKINS, SOCIAL DARWINISM IN EUROPEAN AND AMERICAN THOUGHT 1860–1945 (1997).

[94] Both Gobineau and Ripley were of apiece on this point: "It is not essential to our position, that we should actually be able to isolate any considerable number, nor even a single one, of our *perfect* racial types in the life. It matters not to us that never more than a small majority of any given population possesses even two physical characteristics in their proper association; that relatively few of these are able to add a third to the combination; and that almost no individuals show a perfect union of all traits under one head, so to speak, while contradictions and mixed types are everywhere present." *See* WILLIAM Z. RIPLEY, THE RACES OF EUROPE 108 (1899).

[95] SILVA, GLOBAL, *supra* note 12, at 106.

84   THE RIGHT TO EXCLUDE

the human races that by the 1850s had yet to be developed: the struggle for life. Importantly, however, the struggles that defined the workings of natural selection throughout the animal kingdom didn't operate in the same way for the human species. Darwin explained that due to the intellectual capacity of civilized man, Caucasians had emerged outside of the laws of variation and natural selection, while the geographic particularities of the global variation had had their way with the "undeveloped" races. It wasn't just that the white race(s) were exempt from natural selection due to their superior skull shapes—it was that they had defeated nature, leaving the rest of the human species as vulnerable and impressionable to the pressures of struggle and competition. The obvious result, Darwin explained, was the eventual destruction of the savage races at the hands of the more developed ones.[96]

## B   Eugenics

From here it is but a short hop through Social Darwinism and into the emerging field of eugenics, really hitting its stride in the early years of the twentieth century.[97] Relevant for our purposes is the notion that the so-called undeveloped races had, at least to some extent, short-circuited the laws of natural selection through cunning. If, like other animals, the nonwhite races had selectively produced in a way that would have maximized adaptive advantages, these racial subjects would have expired long ago. But the mind of the racial outsider, even in its geographic particularity, refused the ultimate demands of nature that it should die off, insisting instead to keep on procreating. Eugenics was meant to solve this problem, informing how social policy, in the words of Francis Galton, "may improve or impair the racial qualities of future generations either physically or mentally."[98] As Stepan has commented, already in 1869, Galton's publication of *Hereditary Genius* embodied several of the key assumptions of the eugenics movement. First was the belief that intelligence was discrete, quantifiable, and inheritable. A second and related view was that a person's quotient of inherited intelligence was easily knowable. Third, intelligence was believed to be entirely a matter of racial inheritance—in the debate between nature and nurture, nature was all. Fourth, these lessons were leveraged into policy prescriptions. As Galton noted, whereas nature eliminated the sick and the stupid in the rest of the animal kingdom, humanity protected and celebrated

---

[96] *Id.* at 110.

[97] *See* RANDALL HANSEN & DESMOND KING, STERILIZED BY THE STATE: EUGENICS, RACE, AND THE POPULATION SCARE IN TWENTIETH CENTURY NORTH AMERICA (2013); CHLOE CAMPBELL, RACE AND EMPIRE: EUGENICS IN COLONIAL KENYA (2007); Michael Freeden, *Eugenics and Progressive Thought: A Study in Ideological Affinity*, 22 HIST. J. 645 (1979); NANCY STEPAN, "THE HOUR OF EUGENICS": RACE, GENDER, AND NATION IN LATIN AMERICA (1991); Johannes Hendrikus Burgers, *Max Nordau, Madison Grant, and Racialized Theories of Ideology*, 72 J. HIST. IDEAS 119 (2011).

[98] FRANCIS GALTON, HEREDITARY GENIUS: AN INQUIRY INTO ITS LAWS AND CONSEQUENCES (1869).

its impoverished imbeciles. Man's tinkering with the natural order, so Galton believed, had to be stopped.

By the twentieth century, eugenics was doing more than produce a static image of white supremacy; it was also disaggregating it. What was emerging in addition to the older idea of a natural hierarchy of the races was now the idea that within the Caucasian race itself were important grades of development. The "truly" white variation required teasing out, and among the works to attempt it was the American economist William Z. Ripley's 1899 publication of *The Races of Europe*, a turning point in American racial xenophobia.[99] While Blumenbach's idea of the Caucasian race had gained popularity in the US, the scientific study of so-called Caucasians did not really get under way until after Ripley.[100] Ripley's popularity, as Bruce Baum explains, was due to his explicit efforts to examine a crucial political and social issue of the late nineteenth and early twentieth centuries: immigration into the US.[101] Putting aside the question of Asian immigration, what first needed explaining was why those northern Europeans that had migrated to the US in the middle of the nineteenth century were more racially developed than the south-eastern Europeans immigrating in that century's last decades.[102] Ripley believed that while it made sense to distinguish whites from Mongols or Africans, "whiteness" was misleading with respect to the various groups that might arguably fit within the great white tent.[103]

Turns out, Ripley explained, that there were three primary European races,[104] each identifiable by a single range of cranial shape.[105] These were (1) the Teutons from northwestern Europe, with long heads and faces, light hair and eyes, tall, prominent and thin noses; (2) the Alpines spread through France, Spain, Italy, Germany, and Albania, with round heads and broad faces, chestnut colored hair and hazel eyes, broad noses, and medium and stocky builds; and (3) the Mediterraneans from everywhere south of the Pyrenees, with long heads and faces, dark hair and eyes, very broad noses, and medium and slender builds, who also shared affinities with the negro.[106] The Teutonic races were the dominant, and the Mediterraneans shaded off into other, undeveloped races. Ripley emphasized in later work how the Slavic races and Jewish peoples (Jews were not considered a race at all) were a swamp of genetic degeneracy into which, if they weren't careful, the Teutonic peoples of the US might soon disappear.[107]

---

[99] BAUM, *supra* note 56, at 144.
[100] *Id.*
[101] *Id.* at 150.
[102] *Id.*
[103] RIPLEY, *supra* note 94, at 103.
[104] *Id.* at 37–45.
[105] *Id.*
[106] BAUM, *supra* note 56, at 145.
[107] *Id.* at 150.

86    THE RIGHT TO EXCLUDE

The rub was that, as pretty much everyone seemed to understand, the "science" just wasn't there. There were very few, if any, actual living individuals that possessed all the racial traits characteristic of a particular racial group, and so while one had to admit that in 1900 none of the world's original human races existed, Ripley articulated the common view that because the idea of race had become so vital in making sense of the world, race "exists for us nevertheless."[108] If this faith in a theory of racial identity seems bewildering, writers like Houston Stewart Chamberlain, working at the same time as Ripley, provide some insight into the feverish need to believe. An intellectual disciple of Kant's proto-racial theory, Chamberlain conceded how the scientific method was struggling in its effort to establish a firm footing for the idea of human races.[109] However, this kind of struggle was necessary and expected, given the constant state of intermingling and cross-breeding that had occurred over the ages.[110] The worry was that scientific confusion should be taken as evidence that race wasn't real. For thinkers like Chamberlain, to question the existence of the racial subject was to question the existence of man. As Chamberlain explained:

Nothing is so convincing as the consciousness of the possession of Race. The man who belongs to a distinct, pure race, never loses the sense of it ... Weak and erring like all that is human, a man of this stamp recognizes himself, as others recognize him, by the sureness of his character, and by the fact that his actions are marked by a certain simple and peculiar greatness, which finds its explanation in his distinctly typical and super-personal qualities. Race lifts a man above himself: it endows him with extraordinary—I might almost say supernatural—powers, so entirely does it distinguish him from the individual who springs from the chaotic jumble of peoples drawn from all parts of the world: and should this man of pure origin be perchance gifted above his fellows, then the fact of Race strengthens and elevates him on every hand, and he becomes a genius towering over the rest of mankind, not because he has been thrown upon the earth like a flaming meteor by a freak of nature, but because he soars heavenward like some strong and stately tree, nourished by thousands and thousands of roots—no solitary individual, but the living sum of untold souls striving for the same goal.[111]

For thinkers like these, the idea of race was hardly ever in jeopardy of falling out of fashion, since raciality had become the productive engine for human life. It was simply a matter of science catching up with the natural world, with the facts catching up with what human beings *knew*—or, at least, what was surely known

---

[108] *Id.* at 112.
[109] HOUSTON STEWART CHAMBERLAIN, FOUNDATIONS OF THE NINETEENTH CENTURY 1 (John Lees trans., 1994).
[110] *Id.* at 271.
[111] *Id.* at 269.

THE RACIAL *XENOS*    87

by those white minds about the bodies of other lands.[112] That said, Chamberlain thought that the racial *xenoi* knew the truth of human life just as well; Jews knew it just as Teutons knew it:

> It frequently happens that children who have no conception of what "Jew" means, or that there is any such thing in the world, begin to cry as soon as a genuine Jew or Jewess comes near them! The learned cannot frequently tell a Jew from a non-Jew; the child that scarcely knows how to speak notices the difference. Is not that something?[113]
>
> Besides, if we discard the physical distinctions of race, the decisive greatness of the Germanic race distinguishes itself in its moral and intellectual legacies—which is literally everything that is good.[114]


## C  From Raciality to Ethnocultures

It was when the science of racial xenophobia was reaching something of a fever pitch that Julian Huxley and A.C. Haddon's *We Europeans* landed in 1936.[115] With thinkers like Gobineau and Chamberlain in their sights, and the Nazis gaining power, Huxley and Haddon argued that raciality's true function had been to support the political, social, cultural, and economic superiority of some populations over others. As real science, the theory of racial development wasn't biology at all.[116] That said, it wasn't that Huxley and Haddon were suggesting that raciality was a fiction, in the way that many biologists claim today. Their claim was rather that while racial groups were in fact scientifically distinguishable, it just didn't follow that features of the mind were deducible from the racial characteristics of the body.[117] There was simply no evidence that peach-colored skin or certain cranial measurements signified anything about the rational mind.[118] Whereas

---

[112] *Id.* at 317 ("[R]ace, and nationality which renders possible the formation of race, possess a significance which is not only physical and intellectual but also moral. Here there is before us something which we can characterise as sacred law, the sacred law in accordance with which we enter upon the rights and duties of manhood"). As for how to move forward, Chamberlain believed he had found several rules for race-formation. The origin of a pure race necessitated the presence of a strong stock—a material with which to begin to build. Then, the stock needed to be purified over time through the artificial (in contract to "natural") process of sexual selection and inbreeding. In order to strengthen the racial stock, it then needed to be cross-bred, but only in small doses and in the right quarters. Finally, a great race will be heated in the fires of nationalism, as it is only in the house of the nation that racial greatness can be achieved. *Id.* at 317–20. Smith explained that in the articulation of these pre-conditions he had touched "upon a deep scientific fact." *Id.* at 317.

[113] *Id.* at 537.

[114] *Id.* at 542–50.

[115] Julian Huxley & Alfred C. Haddon, We Europeans (1936).

[116] *Id.* at 144–64.

[117] *Id.* at 144.

[118] Criticizing the idea that one could find average degrees of intelligence based on physiognomy—"there will be in every social class or ethnic group a great quantitative range and a great qualitative diversity of mental characters, and different groups will very largely overlap with each other." *Id* at 70.

88   THE RIGHT TO EXCLUDE

race science had previously urged people to believe that "race was everything" in the debate between nature and culture, Huxley and Haddon urged for people to see how surely wrong was the concept of racial development. Gesturing back to Herder's work, Huxley and Haddon emphasized the explanatory importance of culture in the differentiation of human capabilities, and there was simply no way of quantifying how important nurture or nature might be in any given situation. While they agreed that there were innate differences between populations, and therefore kept within the scientific discourse of a biological raciality, Huxley and Haddon believed that "nothing in the nature of 'pure race' in the biological sense has any real existence."[119] Looking to the Latin *ethnos* for some clarity (via Herodotus), they suggested replacing race with "ethnic group" to provide a better way of labeling political, cultural, social, and economic differences between human populations.[120]

Further work preferring "ethnicity" over "race" came with Ashley Montagu's 1942 publication of *Man's Most Dangerous Myth: The Fallacy of Race*, his work on UNESCO's 1951 "Statement on Race," and *The Concept of Race* published in 1964.[121] Montagu challenged the whole notion of racial development as question-begging:

> For nearly two centuries anthropologists have been directing their attention principally toward the task of establishing criteria by whose means races of mankind might be defined. All have taken completely for granted the one thing which required to be proven, namely, that the concept of race corresponded with a reality which could actually be measured and verified and descriptively set out so that it could be seen to be a fact ... The process of averaging the characters of a given group, knocking the individuals together, giving them a good stirring, and the serving the resulting omelet as a "race" is essentially the anthropological process of race-making. It may be good cooking but it is not science, since it serves to confuse rather than clarify ... The omelet called "race" has no existence outside the statistical frying-pan in which it has been reduced by the heat of the anthropological imagination.[122]

Montagu conceded that populations differed in important ways, but argued that to then call these differences "racial" was to inject into the facts a set of beliefs about the cultural and intellectual baggage that had yet to be explained.[123] Like Huxley and Haddon, Montagu favored the term "ethnic group." Rather than the

[119] *Id.* at 14.

[120] *Id.* at 30–31.

[121] Ashley Montagu, *The Concept of Race in the Human Species in the Light of Genetics*, in THE CONCEPT OF RACE 15–27 (Ashley Montagu ed., 1964). Another important voice in this context belonged to the anthropologist Franz Boas. For discussion, *see, e.g.*, Lee Baker, *The Cult of Franz Boas and his 'Conspiracy' to Destroy the White Race*, 154 PROC. AM. PHIL. SOC. 8 (2010).

[122] Montagu, *supra* note 121, at 5–6.

[123] *Id.* at 18–22.

conclusory effects of naming a subpopulation "racial," Montagu saw "ethnicity" as open and vague enough to force the analyst to address "ethnic group" as a "problem to be solved."[124] In other words, when anthropologists identified differences in particular populations as *racial* rather than *ethnic*, Montagu thought this was essentially cheating, presuming the answer to the question of whether race existed in the first place.[125] In contrast, when anthropologists use "ethnic group" instead of racial group, nothing is presumed about human variation other than that certain populations appear to have diverging gene frequencies.

While it is understandable how anthropologists were beginning to see the substitution of ethnicity for race as a way to unwind the knots of racial development, it is important to remember that here in the middle decades of the twentieth century we are still very much in the thick of a biopolitical discourse of raciality. Thinkers like Huxley, Haddon, and Montagu all backed the idea that there were three major groups of racial bodies: mongoloids, negroids, and caucasoids.[126] They also backed the idea, however, that it was possible to take the racism out of racial subjection. If it was possible to produce genuinely empirical racial classifications, fine, but racial classifications had to be divorced from theories of racial development. The result was a new turn in the sciences to empty racial categories of their cultural content.[127]

In the last decades of the twentieth century and in the beginnings of the twenty-first, advances in genetics helped open the door to what we today call "postracialism." I discuss postraciality in detail in the book's later chapters, but here I mention one aspect of the term—the idea that at least in the biological context, we have moved beyond race as a meaningful way of scientifically classifying the human being.[128] Indeed, there is now consensus among physical anthropologists that the older idea of a range of racial development in which the white race functions as the original standard, is completely erroneous. In fact, the first modern human bodies are traced to Ethiopia, and it was from this originary source in Africa that the rest of the human population and its variations first descended.[129] What there is less certainty about is how these first modern humans migrated around the globe, but what is clear is that these modern humans were polytypic, meaning that local populations of the human species came to differ in the expression of

---

[124] *Id.* at 25.

[125] *Id.* at 26–27.

[126] Ashley Montagu, *On Coon's The Origin of Races*, *in* CONCEPT OF RACE, *supra* note 121, at 236–38; HUXLEY & HADDON, *supra* note 115, at 136–37; UNESCO, THE RACE QUESTION (1950), available at http://unesdoc.unesco.org/images/0012/001282/128291eo.pdf.

[127] Probably the best-known example is CARLETON S. COON, RACIAL ADAPTATIONS (1982).

[128] *See, e.g.*, CAROL MUKHOPADHYAY ET AL., HOW REAL IS RACE? (2007); ROBERT WALD SUSSMAN, THE MYTH OF RACE: THE TROUBLING PERSISTENCE OF AN UNSCIENTIFIC IDEA (2014); MICHAEL YUDELL, RACE UNMASKED: BIOLOGY AND RACE IN THE TWENTIETH CENTURY (2014); THE CONCEPT OF RACE IN NATURAL AND SOCIAL SCIENCE (E. Nathaniel Gates ed., 1997); Crain Soudien, *"Race" and its Contemporary Confusions: Toward a Re-Statement*, 60 THEORIA 15 (2013).

[129] JURMAIN, *supra* note 61, at 389–92.

90    THE RIGHT TO EXCLUDE

physical characteristics. Of course, there was tremendous diversity *within* these local populations as well.

In the span of centuries that we have quickly surveyed, the concept of race referred to geographically patterned variation in physical features within the human species. The concept of racial development, or biological determinism, referred to hierarchies built into these patterns. Today, physical anthropologists and biologists focus on human DNA—that is, on the genotypes rather than the phenotypes— and study patterns of gene frequency. True, there is evidence that clusters of gene frequencies exist in discrete populations—populations that track the major geographical regions of the world: Africa, East Asia, Melanesia, the Americas, and Eurasia.[130] And if gene frequencies correlate with populations of human beings in geographical patterns, is this support for the biological existence of race, after all? No. The bottom line is the oft-quoted conclusion that gene variations occur with far more frequency *within* subpopulations than *between* them. As Robert Jurmain et al., explain:

> [Racial] typologies are inherently misleading because any grouping always includes many individuals who don't conform to all aspects of a particular type. In any so-called racial group, there are individuals who fall into the normal range of variation for another group based on one or several characteristics. For example, two people of different ancestry might differ in skin color, but they could share any number of other traits, including height, head shape, hair color, eye color, and ABO blood type. In fact, they could easily share more similarities with each other than they do with many members of their own populations. To blur this picture further, the characteristics that have been traditionally used to define races are polygenic; that is, they're influenced by more than one gene and therefore exhibit a continuous range of expression. So its difficult, if not impossible, to draw distinct boundaries between populations with regard to many traits.[131]

The upshot is that if your game is about isolating genotypes in the effort to prove the existence of "the human races," the classification will necessarily be global, spanning populations across every spectrum of racial development we've canvassed so far. Which, of course, would unwind any connection between the so-called race and some geographical location. To be sure, sexual selection among individuals can and does result in higher frequencies of certain genes among members of local populations. But the mistake is to conflate the frequency of those genes with something called "race," or any other genetic phenomena. As geneticist Keith Cheng has

---

[130] *See, e.g.*, ROBERT MILES & MALCOLM BROWN, RACISM 44–50 (2d ed. 2003); RACISM IN THE 21ST CENTURY (Ronald E. Hall ed., 2008); JANIS FAYE HUTCHINSON, THE COEXISTENCE OF RACE AND RACISM (2005).

[131] JURMAIN, *supra* note 61, at 417.

noted, "such traits [as the African-American susceptibility to heart disease] would be expected, most of the time, to be inherited independently from skin-color genes, making skin color, and therefore race, an unreliable substitute for knowing the real gene variations that correlate with drug responsiveness."[132] The bottom line, for contemporary physical anthropology, is that genetic variation in the human species is certainly real. These variations, however, cut across every traditional form of racial typology: there is more genetic diversity within the so-called human races, than there are between them. And once again upending the basic assumption of racial development, rather than pin Africa as the most degenerate type of human raciality, Africa is now identified by today's physical anthropologists as the host for the world's original, and most diverse, source of genetic variation.[133]

I focus on this issue in Chapters 8 and 9, but it is worth mentioning here that a contemporaneous development to the postracial phase of race science was that of cultural studies. Culture, of course, is pregnant with a plenitude of meanings. There is the distinction between nature and everything that nature is not (i.e., culture), between high culture and the infinitely complex world of everyday practice, "common sense," "sensuous human praxis,"[134] and between the individualist culture of "modernity" and the bounded cultural practices of particular ethnic groups. It is to this latter idea, however, that I wish note as we push on, and that is "the bounded cultural practices of particular ethnic groups." This is the domain of cultural anthropology, and the stuff of what was becoming known, in the last decades of the twentieth century, as multiculturalism.[135]

For present purposes, what is fascinating about the (multi)cultural turn is the shifty quality of the terms of "culture" and "ethnicity." As we have seen, the idea that behind the face of the racial category was the "real" content of culture (i.e., Herder) or ethnicity (i.e., Huxley, Haddon, and Montagu) is certainly nothing new. What was novel about the discourse as it verged on the millennium, however, was the effect of postracial science.[136] For most of the twentieth century, race remained a biological category. As discussed, the debates that gained steam in that century's

[132] Keith Cheng, *Demystifying Skin Color and "Race," in* RACISM IN THE 21ST CENTURY, *supra* note 130, at 15. As Michael Bamshad (geneticist) and Steve Olson (science writer) have explained: "Given that people can be sorted broadly into groups using genetic data, do common notions of race correspond to underlying genetic differences among populations? ... Because traits such as skin color have been strongly affected by natural selection, they do not necessarily reflect the population processes that have shaped the distribution [of real genetic differences]. Therefore, traits or polymorphisms affected by natural selection may be poor predictors of group membership and may imply genetic relatedness where, in fact, little exists." *See* Michael Bamshad & Steve Olson, *Does Race Exist?* SCI. AM. 78, 83 (Dec. 2003). *See also* Masatoshi Nei & Arun Roychoudhury, *Genetic Relationship and Evolution of Human Races*, EVOLUTIONARY BIOLOGY 14 (1983) (reassessing magnitude of genetic differences among three major human races).

[133] JURMAIN, *supra* note 61, at 423.

[134] STUART HALL, ESSENTIAL ESSAYS, VOLUME 1: FOUNDATIONS OF CULTURAL STUDIES 55 (David Morley ed., 2019).

[135] *Id.* at 95.

[136] MARTIN BARKER, NEW RACISM: CONSERVATIVES AND THE IDEOLOGY OF THE TRIBE (1981).

## 92 THE RIGHT TO EXCLUDE

middle decades were largely about the relation between race and culture—the side that emerged as the dominant one argued that the two concepts were utterly distinct: you couldn't derive any knowledge about a person's cultural aptitudes on the basis of their genetic code. Race might have been blood and bone, but there was no reason to think that this actually meant anything about how a human being excels in the world. Race was biology, and culture was society.

What of ethnicity?[137] On its face, defining ethnicity isn't any easier than defining culture. When it was introduced in the 1930s, it was clearly intended as a rival form of identification, one that was superior to race because of its open-endedness. And this open-endedness was meant to supply a kind of link to culture, and perhaps even a synonym for it. As the century wore on, three approaches came into view. First, race and ethnicity were totally distinct, whereas the former was biology and the latter was society. Second, race and ethnicity were largely distinct, but not completely, whereas the former was biology and the latter was geography. That is, while "Blacks" and "Whites" were racial groups, "Italians," "Chinese," and "Nigerians" were ethnic groups. A third approach suggests that racial groups *are* ethnic groups, but that many ethnic groups are not racial. It is therefore possible, on this view, to talk of racialized and non-racialized ethnicity, and the research focus is why certain groups are racialized while others are not. As some commentators have said, this way of subsuming race within ethnicity suggests a particular model of the *ethnos*:

> In the first place, it referred to groups that shared a common history—real or perceived—and with it a sense of a common geographic origin. It also refers to a shared culture, which is a broad term that can include within it traditions, folkways, values, symbols, language, and religion. Moreover, given that ethnicity is a boundary creating construct, it refers to a belief among group members and outsiders alike that it constitutes a distinctive community formation. Finally, and this is key, race can be seen as one other potential component of ethnic identity and group definition.[138]

A similar text defines ethnicity as "Generally a word that refers to different racial or national groups ... [E]thnicity denotes the self-awareness on the part of a particular group of its own cultural distinctiveness."[139] Two points to note about these characterizations of the *ethnos*. First, it continues to have a firm relation to culture, and in that way, ethnic groups remain subjective. That is, an ethnic group must be something relatively open, where the borders are porous, if it is true that it is defined by social practices that can be discarded or mimicked. At the same time,

---

[137] MILES & BROWN, *supra* note 130, at 92–96; THOMAS HYLLAND ERIKSEN, ETHNICITY AND NATIONALISM (1993).

[138] PETER KIVISTO & PAUL CROLL, RACE AND ETHNICITY: THE BASICS 11 (2012).

[139] CULTURAL THEORY: THE KEY CONCEPTS 114 (Andrew Edgar & Peter Sedgwick eds., 2008).

THE RACIAL *XENOS*   93

blood lines and hereditary descent are a part of the picture as well, and indeed, we have to wonder what happens to an ethnic group when it loses this grounding in the blood of the people—what then distinguishes it from culture? This see-saw effect is only exacerbated in the contemporary climate of postracialism, where ethnicity looks more like culture when it is contrasted with race, and where ethnicity looks more like race when it is contrasted with culture.[140] The upshot is, and as we move forward in the analysis of racial ideology, we can speak of a rival account of *ethnoculture*—a concept that veers to and fro between the social and the biological. As Stuart Hall put it:

> Those who are stigmatized on ethnic grounds, because they are 'culturally different' and therefore inferior, are often *also* characterized as physically different in significant ways ... The biological referent is therefore never wholly absent from discourses of ethnicity, though it is more indirect. The more 'ethnicity' matters, the more its characteristics are represented as relatively fixed; inherent within a group; transmitted from generation to generation, not just by culture and education but by biological inheritance; inscribed on the body; and stabilized above all by kinship and endogamous marriage rules, which ensure that the ethnic group remains genetically, and therefore culturally, 'pure.' ... In short, the articulation of difference with nature (biology and the genetic) is present in the discourse of ethnicity but *displaced through kinship and intermarriage*.[141]

The second point is how much in common this way of looking at the *ethnos* has with traditional discussions of the *nation*. As I discuss in Chapters 8 and 9, this is no accident, and indeed, postracialism has only heightened the sense in which both multiculturalism and nationalism, in their different practices, mystify the effects of racial hierarchy in the international legal order.

This chapter picked up where Chapter 1 left off, examining the racialization of exclusion in liberal theory. It did so by first introducing two ways to think about the history of racial xenophobia. The first is a sociohistorical logic of exclusion. This logic of exclusion is racist, discriminatory, and a source for justifying hierarchies among human populations on the basis of race. The logic of exclusion yearns for inversion—a logic of inclusion pressed forward by an antidiscrimination principle. The second way to think about this history is by the lights of racial subjection. With assistance from thinkers like Silva, Hartman, Agamben, and Foucault, I rehearsed the argument that the logic of exclusion paints only a part of the picture. More troubling, processes of racial subjection are what generate images of the human

---

[140] For discussion, *see* Victoria Hattam, *Ethnicity: An American Genealogy, in* NOT JUST BLACK AND WHITE: HISTORICAL AND CONTEMPORARY PERSPECTIVES ON IMMIGRATION, RACE, AND ETHNICITY IN THE UNITED STATES (Nancy Foner & George Frederickson eds., 2004).

[141] STUART HALL, ESSENTIAL ESSAYS, VOLUME 2: IDENTITY AND DIASPORA 110 (David Morley ed., 2019).

being, where certain images are built to look like the rational citizen—home politicus—whereas others are built to be killed—the racial xenos. I then turned to the global context of racial xenophobia, and an abbreviated narrative of how scientists in Europe and the US concocted a supposedly empirical recasting of the human species as a racial species, where white bodies were superior to foreign ones. Over time, the scientific (hence global) context for racial identity transformed, settling into a contemporary consensus about the chimerical quality of racial identity, and the entirely genuine character of ethnicity and culture, or ethnoculture. The questions ahead: If we are now postracial, what is the use in studying racial ideology? Furthermore, what is the relation between the emergence of the racial xenos and the sovereign's right to exclude? And perhaps most importantly, why should we care?

# 3
# Nations of Daylight, Children of the Night

The argument in Chapter 2 moved in three steps. We began with the logic of exclusion, a set of strategies for limiting certain kinds of rights and privileges to some favored groups. For many, the logic of exclusion is the central problematic of antiracist scholarly practice: identify the ways in which racism has worked to justify discriminatory exclusion, raise consciousness about it, and seek inclusive reforms. When we characterize raciality in this way, I suggested that we can see the logic of exclusion as something like a foreground rule, where modes of racial discrimination and subordination perform as a governing strategy in which a racist regime actively and explicitly denies advantages and benefits on account of race. In contrast with the foregrounded nature of racial discrimination, I then introduced the notion of racial subjection. Drawing on the work of Saidiya Hartman and Denise Ferreira da Silva, I offered racial subjection as a background rule, where racial subjection refers to the production of racial beings, racial bodies, racial subjects. Whereas the foregrounded nature of racial discrimination assumes racial beings as always already there, the backgrounded nature of racial subjection assumes the task of producing and reproducing raciality as a way to understand what human beings really are. Finally, I argued that while the foreground-background distinction makes sense for the relation between racial discrimination and racial subjection, I also suggested that it was a mistake to characterize exclusion as only implicated on the discriminatory side of the dynamic. While it is appropriate to locate sociological descriptions of exclusionary practice on the side of discrimination and subordination, I argued that the right to exclude—understood in the context of legal thought—was itself generative of the racial subject.

The second step was the introduction of Agamben's critique of liberal theory, and his argument that at the center of Hobbes' and Locke's work was a set of distinctions, that between bare human life and political life, and between a natural condition and a sphere of sovereign law. As Agamben explained, the bare life of the human being was conceptualized as foreign to the powers and protections of politicized self-determination, of *homo politicus*. The bare life of *homo sacer* was foreign in the sense that it was killable, a human being rightless in the eyes of both the sovereign and of God. The sovereign, as well as the rights-bearing individual, each possess a sanctified right to exclude *homo sacer*—an exclusion that paradoxically includes the natural condition at the very center of the liberal tradition. My purpose in rehearsing Agamben's critique was to suggest that the duality of sovereign right and *homo sacer* is the template for the making of the racial *xenos*, a

*The Right to Exclude.* Justin Desautels-Stein, Oxford University Press. © Justin Desautels-Stein 2023.
DOI: 10.1093/oso/9780198862161.003.0004

## 96  THE RIGHT TO EXCLUDE

racial production of the excludable foreign—indeed, we can see in Foucault's own treatment of biopower the effort to show how the state's turn to the management, measurement, and misuse of human life was deeply racial. And this was how I intended to frame the argument, by anticipating Agamben and Foucault's analysis of biopolitical raciality as a way to locate the right to exclude at the very center of racial subjection.

If the first step was to counter the logic of exclusion with a theory of racial subjection, and the second was to locate the right to exclude *within* that theory, the third step was to introduce the explicit effort to define the racial *xenos*. It is crucial to emphasize that this was a shift away from theological or metaphysical classification to an empirical form of modern science. Racial subjection, that is, is a scientific discourse, and as a scientific discourse it is also a global discourse, the purpose of which was to reimagine the human body as a racial body, categorize variations of the racial body as increasingly more alien, and thereby produce a continuum of racial development. The scientific discourse of racial development accomplished two things. First, it explicitly racialized the theory of biopower: the bare life of the racial *xenos* became Negro and Mongol, while the sovereign right of self-determination was named *white*. From the start, there was never anything neutral about racial development; raciality simply gave new language to a hierarchy of exclusion that preceded it. Second, racial development was a definitively *global* conceptualization of the human being. The notion of racial subjection was not conceptualized as American, or British, or European, or African. Racial subjection was a discourse about nature, a description of the human being as she existed across time and space, a global construct in the same way that zoology is a global construct. The empirical tools for classifying the physiology of the material world were never regarded as regional, but truly global, if not universal. Thus, by the time the scientific discourse of racial development had travelled through evolutionary theory and eugenics, and began its denouement by the second half of the twentieth century, what was being challenged was whether the scientific discourse about biological determinism had been *correct*. What was left entirely intact was belief in the racial subject.[1] It was not until the turn of the twenty-first century that the science of racial subjection was under fierce interrogation, but by that time, it was already too late. Racial xenophobia had become a natural feature of the sovereign's right to exclude, now sedimented in the discourses of multiculturalism and nationalism.

Throughout the remainder of this book I characterize this global discourse of racial subjection as *racial ideology*, and racial ideology as a species of legal ideology. Before turning to the articulations of racial ideology traced in the liberal structure

---

[1] DAVID HOLLINGER, POSTETHNIC AMERICA 32 (2006) ("Yet it was enlightened antiracism that led to the manufacturing of today's ethno-racial pentagon out of old, racist materials. The most immediate force behind the creation of the pentagon has been the antidiscrimination and affirmative action policies of the federal government.")

of international legal thought, I should explain what I mean by "ideology."[2] After a summary, I then explore the first manifestation of racial ideology as a style of argumentative practice in international law, what I term a *classic* style of racial ideology.

# I ON RACIAL IDEOLOGY

To be sure, a generation ago it would have been odd to even flag the issue, for the study of ideology, at least by the 1980s, was everywhere. Competing across the board were Marxist theorists arguing against the false consciousness of bourgeois ideology, neo-Marxists looking to update the out-of-fashion thinking of the *camera obscura*, social theorists eager to re-orient the study of ideology as really the study of social meaning, and social scientists ready to announce the end of ideology altogether.[3] In today's vernacular the debate is all but over, with ideology now understood to largely serve as something of an all-too-fancy synonym for words like "worldview," "mindset," or "personal politics."[4] To get a sense for what I will mean by racial ideology in legal context, we can begin with the work of Michael Freeden.[5] Freeden understands ideology as a largely unavoidable and necessary effort to make sense of and interpret our indeterminate world. It is the particular way in which this "sense-making" enterprise develops that theorists like Freeden call "ideology."[6] As Freeden describes it, this sense-making or interpretive activity begins with a basic vocabulary of political concepts, but it would be a mistake to confuse this starting point as just another strain of political philosophy.[7] Rather, to study political concepts as ideology is to situate concepts as they appear in patterns of argument. Ideology, in this view, is a linguistic structure, where

---

[2] For discussion in the context of legal ideology, *see* Justin Desautels-Stein & Akbar Rasulov, *Deep Cuts: Four Critiques of Legal Ideology*, 31 YALE J.L. & HUMAN. 435 (2021).

[3] For an overview, *see* TERRY EAGLETON, IDEOLOGY (1991). Representative texts include: RAYMOND GEUSS, THE IDEA OF A CRITICAL THEORY: HABERMAS AND THE FRANKFURT SCHOOL (1981); KARL MANNHEIM, IDEOLOGY AND UTOPIA: AN INTRODUCTION TO THE SOCIOLOGY OF KNOWLEDGE (2015); JORGE LARRAIN, IDEOLOGY & CULTURAL IDENTITY: MODERNITY AND THE THIRD WORLD PRESENCE (1994); JORGE LARRAIN, THE CONCEPT OF IDEOLOGY(1979); GEORGE LICHTHEIM, THE CONCEPT OF IDEOLOGY AND OTHER ESSAYS (1967); FREDRIC JAMESON, THE POLITICAL UNCONSCIOUS: NARRATIVE AS A SOCIALLY SYMBOLIC ACT (1982); BRUNO LATOUR, WE HAVE NEVER BEEN MODERN (1993); LOUIS ALTHUSSER, LENIN AND PHILOSOPHY AND OTHER ESSAYS (2001); ANTONIO GRAMSCI, SELECTIONS FROM THE PRISON NOTEBOOKS (1971); SLAVOJ ZIZEK, THE SUBLIME OBJECT OF IDEOLOGY (2009).

[4] This, at any rate, is what the term usually means in the wide-ranging literature of empirical legal studies. *See, e.g.*, JEFFREY SEGAL & HAROLD SPAETH, THE SUPREME COURT AND THE ATTITUDINAL MODEL REVISITED (2002).

[5] Freeden's works include, Michael Freeden, *The Morphological Analysis of Ideology, in* THE OXFORD HANDBOOK OF POLITICAL IDEOLOGIES (Michael Freeden et al. eds., 2015); MICHAEL FREEDEN, IDEOLOGIES AND POLITICAL THEORY (1998); MICHAEL FREEDEN, LIBERAL LANGUAGES: IDEOLOGICAL IMAGINATIONS AND TWENTIETH CENTURY PROGRESSIVE THOUGHT (2004).

[6] A similar view is reflected in the law and society literature. *See, e.g.*, Patricia Ewick & Susan Silbey, *Common Knowledge and Ideological Critique: The Significance of Knowing That the "Haves" Comes Out Ahead*, 33 LAW & SOC'Y REV. 1025 (1999).

[7] FREEDEN, IDEOLOGIES, *supra* note 5, at 3.

98    THE RIGHT TO EXCLUDE

open-ended concepts manifest in argumentative grooves and pathways.[8] It is less about interrogating a political concept for its meaning, and more an effort to detail its practice. In Freeden's view, this perspective is also something other than what one finds in the Marxian traditions.[9] According to Freeden, on that "critical" terrain ideology is framed as a kind of systematic distortion, an illusion separating the conscious being from the real world. As a result, ideology is "consigned to metaphysical digressions from, or interventions in, what actually happens in the world."[10] Freeden writes that it is better for the analyst of ideology to treat it as an "actual mode of political thinking,"[11] and "to categorize, elucidate, and decode the ways in which collectivities in fact think about politics, the ways they intentionally practice the art of political thinking, and unintentionally express the social patterns that that kind of thinking has developed."[12] Freeden calls this the "morphological approach" to the study of ideology.[13]

In this ostensibly acritical posture, the idea is to begin with the political concept, perhaps a concept like "sovereignty." However, rather than attempt an intellectual history of the concept, or define it philosophically, we elucidate the "ideology" of the concept when we treat that concept as something like a lens, a portal, or filter. What we want to know, on this morphological view, is how the concept is manipulated, how it functions in patterns of argument, how the necessarily open and indeterminate texture of the concept *morphs* in different contexts. For Freeden, it is precisely this functional structure of morphology that is ideology: the structure in which contested concepts change shape in order to give a *show* of closure, an *appearance* of definitive meaning. Freeden writes, "The *decontestations* proffered by ideologies are temporary stabilities carved out of fundamental semantic instability in the social and political worlds. The solutions they provide appear as apparently firm and 'final' pronouncements ... supplying charts for navigating through what would otherwise be a bewildering social environment."[14] That Freeden calls these ideological structures *temporary* stabilities highlights the morphing character of

---

[8]  *Id.* "Such patterns are most conveniently known as ideologies, those systems of political thinking, loose or rigid, deliberate or unintended, through which individuals and groups construct an understanding of the political world they, or those who occupy their thoughts, inhabit, and then act on that understanding."

[9]  Freeden, *Morphological, supra* note 5, at 116.

[10]  FREEDEN, LANGUAGES, *supra* note 5, at 238.

[11]  Freeden, *Morphological, supra* note 5, at 117.

[12]  FREEDEN, LANGUAGES, *supra* note 5, at 239.

[13]  Freeden, *Morphological, supra* note 5, at 124–25: "Ideologies possess an elaborate structure, analyzable on two main axes. First is a three-tier distinction between concepts (the middle tier), their micro-components, and their macro-conceptual concatenations. As discussed above, the arrangements among the components generate diverse conceptions of any concept; while the clusters of concepts form the specific anatomy of an ideology. Within those relatively flexible clusters lies the second axis, the distinction between core, adjacent, and peripheral concepts ... core concepts are indispensable to holding the ideology together, and are consequently accorded preponderance in shaping that ideology's ideational content."

[14]  *Id.* at 118.

the structure. "Hence another important corollary of the morphological approach is to encourage a move away from the notion that ideologies are always and only totalizing, doctrinaire, and dogmatic, locked into an unyielding configuration."[15]

Freeden's theory is intended as an alternative to those "critical" approaches associated with Marx, Althusser, Laclau, and Mouffe.[16] Rather than understand ideology as something masking the real, Freeden wants to identify ideology itself as a political and social reality.[17] There is much to gain, however, and little to lose if we consider Freeden's approach as already operating within, or at least, highly amenable with the critical tradition. What worries Freeden is Marx's notorious suggestion that ideology functions like a *camera obscura*, as a technology for making the world upside-down, confusing the true means of production for the false.[18] In this way, ideology is the opposite of true science—the empiricism of scientific discourse reveals ideology as mystification. It has been some time, however, since critical theorists adopted this "crude" version of ideology-critique.[19] A more contemporary view is illustrated in the work of John Thompson, who suggested that "We must resist [Marx's *camera obscura*] because, once we recognize that ideology operates through language and that language is a medium of social action, we must also acknowledge that ideology is partially constitutive of what, in our societies, 'is real.' Ideology is not a pale image of the social world but is part of that world, a creative and constitutive element of our social lives."[20]

Indeed, both thinkers are interested in an analysis of ideology as a sequence of concepts, expressions, and arguments operating in a shifting yet necessarily articulated linguistic structure.[21] For whereas Freeden suggests that we study the morphing structure of ideology in order to better understand how people really think, Thompson argues that the study should "help to illuminate the ideological features of discourse *by bringing out, not only their procedures of legitimation, but*

---

[15] *Id* at 124.

[16] *See, e.g.,* SLAVOJ ZIZEK, THE SUBLIME OBJECT OF IDEOLOGY (2009); ERNESTO LACLAU & CHANTAL MOUFFE, HEGEMONY AND SOCIALIST STRATEGY: TOWARDS A RADICAL DEMOCRATIC POLITICS (2014) (1985).

[17] It is a fair question as to whether Freeden's approach here is meaningfully different from much of the "critical theory" that he wishes to sidestep. For discussion, *see* Desautels-Stein & Rasulov, *supra* note 2, at 475–97.

[18] Marx wrote: "The production of ideas, of conceptions, of consciousness, is at first directly interwoven with the material activity and the material intercourse of men, the language of real life. Conceiving, thinking, the mental intercourse of men, appear at this stage as the direct efflux of their material behaviour. The same applies to mental production as expressed in the language of politics, laws, morality, religion, metaphysics, etc., of a people. Men are the producers of their conceptions, ideas, etc.—real, active men, as they are conditioned by a definite development of their productive forces and of the intercourse corresponding to these, up to its furthest forms. Consciousness can never be anything else than conscious existence, and the existence of men is their actual life-process. If in all ideology men and their circumstances appear upside-down as in a *camera obscura*, this phenomenon arises just as much from their historical life-process as the inversion of objects on the retina does from their physical life-process." *See* KARL MARX, THE GERMAN IDEOLOGY 42 (1998).

[19] For discussion, *see* SUSAN MARKS, THE RIDDLE OF ALL CONSTITUTIONS 13–15 (2000).

[20] JOHN THOMPSON, STUDIES IN THE THEORY OF IDEOLOGY 5–6 (1984).

[21] *Id.* at 136.

100   THE RIGHT TO EXCLUDE

*also their strategies of dissimulation.* To conceal the relations of domination and simultaneously to conceal the process of concealment is a risky, conflict-laden undertaking, prone to contradiction and contortion. The analysis of argumentative structure may highlight the dissimulating function of ideology by mapping out the contradictions and inconsistencies, the silences and *lapsus,* which characterize the texture of a discourse."[22] With this addition we receive a view of the ideological structure as producing a discourse serving to sustain relations of domination and subordination.[23] Ideology becomes more than only a structure of morphing patterns, but a structure in which power is relentlessly pressed into the service of the powerful.[24] Ideology therefore encompasses "procedures of legitimation," as well as the "strategies of dissimulation," those techniques for mystifying and reinforcing a state of affairs in which the winners win and the losers die. Indeed, as Stuart Hall has put it, projects of resistance are useless "without facing questions about the constitution of dominance in ideology."[25] Ideology, in this sense, concerns "the relative power distribution of different regimes of truth and social transformation at any one time—which have certain effects for the maintenance of power in the social order."[26]

In working with *racial* ideology, Hall continues, one must not mistake it for "a general theory of racism,"[27] "of extrapolating a common and universal structure to racism, which remains essentially the same, outside of its specific historical location."[28] "Racism is not dealt with as a general feature of human societies, but with historically specific racisms. Beginning with an assumption of difference, of specificity rather than of a unitary, transhistorical universal 'structure.'"[29] Putting aside these universal structures of "human nature," Hall urged the study of racism as articulated and structured practices, practices that were political, economic, and ideological.[30] To be clear, Hall's context was cultural studies, and his target was the question of whether and how racism works in tandem with capitalism. His effort, in other words, was similar in this respect to Silva's: the effort to understand the

---

[22] *Id.* at 136–37.

[23] *Id.* at 130–31.

[24] " 'Power,' at the institutional level, is a capacity which enables or empowers some agents to make decisions, pursue ends or realize interests; it empowers them in such a way that, without this institutionally endowed capacity, they would not have been able to carry out the relevant course ... When the relations of power established at the institutional level are *systematically asymmetrical,* then the situation may be described as one of *domination.* Relations of power are 'systematically asymmetrical' when particular agents or groups of agents are institutionally endowed with power in a way which excludes, and to some significant degree remains inaccessible to, other agents or groups of agents, irrespective of the basis upon which such exclusion is carried out." *Id.* at 129–30.

[25] STUART HALL, ESSENTIAL ESSAYS, VOLUME 1: FOUNDATIONS OF CULTURAL STUDIES 227 (David Morley ed., 2019).

[26] *Id.* at 228.

[27] *Id.* at 211.

[28] *Id.*

[29] *Id.* at 210.

[30] *Id.* at 213.

social world. Since it was a mistake to assume that racism had taken one single form in all capitalist formations, it was necessary "to show its articulation with the different structures of the social formation."[31] This sociocultural examination of racial ideology begins:

> [B]y investigating the different ways in which racist ideologies have been constructed and made operative under different historical conditions: the racisms of mercantilist theory and of chattel slavery; of conquest and colonialism; of trade and "high imperialism"; of popular imperialism and of so-called "post-imperialism." In each case, in specific social formations, racism as an ideological configuration has been reconstituted by the dominant class relations, and thoroughly reworked ... Here racism is particularly powerful and its imprint on popular consciousness especially deep, because in such racial characteristics as color, ethnic origin, geographical position, etc., racism discovers what other ideologies have to construct: an apparently 'natural' and universal basis in nature itself ... [Racial ideologies] also dehistoricize—translating historically specific structures into the timeless language of nature; decomposing classes into individuals and recomposing those disaggregated individuals into the reconstructed unities, the great coherences, of new ideological "subjects": it translates "classes" into "blacks" and "whites," economic groups into "peoples," solid forces into "races." This is the process of constituting new "historical subjects" for ideological discourses ... of forming new interpellative structures. It produces, as the natural and given "authors" of a spontaneous form of racial perception, the naturalized "racist subject."[32]

From Freeden to Thompson, the upshot is that we are looking at ideology as a type of language-system, as a language of dominance and interpellation. From Hall, racial ideology becomes a practice of articulation which "discovers what other ideologies have to construct: an apparently natural and universal basis in itself." At the same time, as Hall cautions, the analysis of racial ideology ought not be broadened into a general theory, as doing so falls into the very trap ideology sets for the analyst: dehistoricizing and decontextualizing the ways in which race and racism manifest over time and in different locations. Thus, we can suggest that an ideology is (1) a pattern of argumentative practice, (2) giving temporary structure to indeterminate concepts, (3) in order to justify relations of domination.

My purpose, however, is to canvass racial ideology as a *legal* ideology, and to that end, I want to merge this sense of ideology with the thesis of naturalizing juridical science I introduced in Chapter 1. As will be recalled, in the context of liberal legal thought the task of naturalizing juridical science is to harmonize the theses

---

[31] *Id.*
[32] *Id.* at 217–18.

102    THE RIGHT TO EXCLUDE

of individual right and ordered liberty. As jurists do the work of arguing through the structure's legal concepts, they are confronted with the competing demands of order and freedom. To cope with those conflicts, and as Freeden might put it, jurists rehearse certain practices of "decontesting" the rules of the legal concept, offering "necessary" forms of conclusive interpretation in a given dispute.

Since the middle decades of the nineteenth century and to the present, there have been three primary styles in which naturalizing juridical science does this work, and they are formalism, functionalism, and pragmatism. Each of these styles had its way of naturalizing the background-foreground distinction in a given legal concept. Formalism assumes a sharp distinction between subjective moral disagreement (in the political sphere) and objective legal solution (in the juridical sphere). Whereas ideological or political conflicts are irresolvable, legal conflicts must be subject to determinate resolutions. Political conflicts may be personal and open-ended, but legal conflicts are impersonal and subject to closure. The claim that legal disputes are different from political disputes because the former are open to right resolutions where the latter are not, quite obviously rests on an assumption about the availability of "right" resolutions. Roberto Unger suggested that this is liberalism leaning back in the direction of its Aristotelian enemy, for what can this belief in "right answers" possibly mean other than a belief in a universal moral order?[33] Formalism is technique of legal argument in which the jurist first poses a distinction between a natural world or individual right and a political world of social order. Next, formalism prioritizes nature over politics, for whatever exists in the natural world is good. Political life, on the other hand, is contingent. Finally, the formalist style teaches the jurist to craft legal decisions in such a way that they mimic some natural truth. Functionalism, in contrast, is a style of naturalizing juridical science in which the jurist first poses a distinction between society on the one side and law on the other. Once again, society takes precedence over law, since society is the real and law its servant. Finally, the functionalist style teaches the jurist to ask of the social problem the legal rule in question is meant to solve, turn to the best social science on the question, and fashion the rule accordingly. Pragmatism is the third style, and here the jurist has lost faith in either formalism or functionalism as a means for satisfactorily "decontesting" a legal concept. What the pragmatist jurist does have faith in, however, is that in some combination of the formalist and functionalist bags of tricks, the work of naturalizing juridical science will still be done. And done well.

Formalism, functionalism, and pragmatism are legal ideologies because they are patterns of argumentative practice giving structure to indeterminate legal concepts in order to justify relations of domination. Elsewhere I have discussed how these legal ideologies perform these tasks in the context of market relations.[34] Here,

---

[33] ROBERTO UNGER, KNOWLEDGE AND POLITICS 92–93 (1975).

[34] JUSTIN DESAUTELS-STEIN, THE JURISPRUDENCE OF STYLE: A STRUCTURALIST HISTORY OF AMERICAN PRAGMATISM AND LIBERAL LEGAL THOUGHT (2018).

I explore their performances in the context of raciality, and as such, I present three articulations of racial ideology—classic, modern, and postracial. The classic style is formalist racial ideology, the modern style is functionalist racial ideology, and the pragmatist style is postracial xenophobia. Each of these three articulations of argumentative practice can be defined in the following way: *a mode of naturalizing juridical science in which patterns of argument moving through the indeterminacy of a conceptual lexicon produce relations of racial subjection, exclusion, and discrimination.* In the remainder of this chapter, I briefly introduce international law's classic style of racial ideology, in the contexts of *imperium* and *dominium*. This discussion sets the table for the more elaborate analysis of modern racial ideology that begins in Part II, and postracial ideology in Part III.

## II CLASSIC RACIAL IDEOLOGY IN INTERNATIONAL LAW

### A Property, Sovereignty, and Territory

I should emphasize that, just as this presentation of classic racial ideology is not intended as an intellectual history of racism and imperialism, it is neither intended as an explanation for the sociological origins or existence of something called "international law." As suggested in Chapter 1's discussion of property and sovereignty, the two concepts enjoy structural similarities, particularly with respect to the right to exclude. As we saw in Locke, the natural equality of human beings bore no natural forms of ownership. That is, God gifted the world and its resources to man in common, and none had a natural claim at the expense of any other. The key to ownership, as a result, was possession, but possession couldn't be perfunctory; planting a flag or building a fence was insufficient to constitute the root of title. To mark land as one's possession required cultivation and labor, an intermixing of one's self with the world. Only then, Locke had suggested, could autonomous man carve out from the commons what the law might understand as "possession."[35]

This classic liberal demand for certain control over things, in which a natural and unified architecture is rooted in an individual's possession and rights of exclusion, is mirrored in the context of sovereignty.[36] If we again make the domestic analogy and treat the "sovereign" as a metaphor for the autonomous owner, possession is the founding move. For just as at the "domestic" level the autonomous,

---

[35] *John Locke, in* PROPERTY 14–27 (C.B. Macpherson ed., 1978).
[36] For discussion, *see* W. Schoenborn, *La Nature Juridique du Territoire, in* COLLECTED COURSES OF THE HAGUE ACADEMY OF INTERNATIONAL LAW (1929); Cara Nine, *A Lockean Theory of Territory*, 56 POL. STUD. 148 (2008); KURT BURCH, PROPERTY AND THE MAKING OF THE INTERNATIONAL SYSTEM (1998); David Miller, *Property and Territory: Locke, Kant, and Steiner*, 19 J. POL. PHIL. 90 (2011); A.J. Simmons, *On the Territorial Rights of States*, 11 PHIL. ISS. 300 (2001).

104    THE RIGHT TO EXCLUDE

rights-bearing individual enjoys a state of raw equality and must generate his *possessions* through labor, so too must the sovereign claim *territory* through tangible works.[37] Here are three ways to briefly illustrate this founding of sovereignty on territorial possession.

One way in which sovereignty requires a meaningful possessory relation with territory concerns the liberal conception of possession itself.[38] If we think of the sovereign as a natural person in an international state of nature, and we wish for that person's sovereignty to legitimately attach to a piece of land, the sovereign must persuade rivals that it has exercised a certain authority over that land, that it owns title to the realty.[39] And here the analogy to Locke's owner is most direct, as the proper form of authority at international law is the same as what we would expect at the domestic level: direct, effective control exercised by a single will, rather than a common and disaggregated plurality.[40] That is, sovereigns have gained possession of territory so long as its direct and effective exercise of authority was actual, open, and hostile.[41] As Andrew Fitzmaurice has explained, "What [writers like Locke] succeeded in creating, therefore, was a theory of property in which occupation was essential not only to the self-preservation of individuals but also to states, and as such, it was a right that could be exercised both by individuals and states. This theory provided a powerful justification of expansion."[42]

If a sovereign sent its agents into a *terra nullius*, something like a no-man's land, that sovereign could only gain this land as territory if its forces did something

[37] *See generally* Judge Huber, *Island of Palmas*, 2 RIAA 829 (1928); ROBERT YEWDALL JENNINGS, THE ACQUISITION OF TERRITORY IN INTERNATIONAL LAW (1963); Malcolm Shaw, *Territory in International Law*, 13 NETH. Y.B. INT'L L. 61 (1982); JAMES CRAWFORD, THE CREATION OF STATES IN INTERNATIONAL LAW (2007).

[38] *See, e.g.*, Justice Ammoun, *Legal Consequences for States of the Continued Existence of South Africa in Namibia*, Advisory Opinion, 1971 I.C.J Rep. 55 (June 21); Mohammad Bedjaoui, "Succession of States and Governments: Succession in Respect of Matters other than Treaties," Report to the International Law Commission A/CN.4/204, 94 (1969).

[39] Georg Schwarzenberger, *Title to Territory: Response to a Challenge*, 51 AM. J. INT'L L. 308, 320; JOSHUA CASTELLINO & STEVE ALLEN, TITLE TO TERRITORY IN INTERNATIONAL LAW (2003). For discussion of international law in the context of disagreements over title, *see* JAMES CRAWFORD, BROWNLIE'S PRINCIPLES OF INTERNATIONAL LAW 204–08 (2019).

[40] Territorial Sovereignty and Scope of the Dispute (Eritrea v. Yemen), 114 I.L.R. 1, 69 (9 Oct. 1988); *Clipperton Island Arbitration* 26 AM. J. INT'L L. 390 (1932); Legal Status of Eastern Greenland (Den. V. Nor.), 1933 P.C.I.J. (ser. A/B) No. 53 (Apr. 5) at 46. For example, just as the common form of authority exercised by American Indian tribes was regarded as "invalid" in the eyes of US property law, so too was the form of authority exercised by a Muslim sultan. *See* Johnson v. M'Intosh, 21 U.S. 543 (1823); Case Concerning the Frontier Dispute, Judgment, 1986 I.C.J. Rep. 564–70; Western Sahara, Advisory Opinion, 1975 I.C.J. Rep. 4.

[41] As in American property law, international law also has its own doctrine of prescription. For discussion, *see* Kasikili/Sedudu Island (Bots. v. Namib.), 1999 I.C.J. Rep. 1045 (Dec. 13); H. Post, *International Law Between Dominium and Imperium, in* REFLECTIONS ON PRINCIPLES AND PRACTICE OF INTERNATIONAL LAW (T.D. Gill & W.P. Heere eds., 2000).

[42] ANDREW FITZMAURICE, SOVEREIGNTY, PROPERTY, AND EMPIRE 86 (2017). *See also* CRAWFORD, BROWNLIE'S, *supra* note 39, at 217–19; Gerald Fitzmaurice, *The Law and Procedure of the International Court of Justice, 1951–1954: Points of Substantive Law, Part II*, 32 BRIT. Y.B. INT'L L. 20, 31–37 (1955–56).

beyond the planting of a flag.[43] As the jurist Georg Friedrich von Martens explained in the years after the Concert of Europe was established, if a sovereign's occupation of some foreign territory was to ripen into its property, that foreign land must have belonged to no one, and the new sovereign must *effectively* take exclusive possession.[44] This symmetry between the right of private property from exclusive possession and the sovereign's claim on new territorial holdings only deepened as the century continued toward its imperial zenith.[45] An obvious analogue here involves the wagon trains of the nineteenth century United States (US) and the claims of settlers to tracts of land in the open spaces of the American West.[46] Just as it was often insufficient for these settlers to set up a fence and claim the land as under their dominion, so too was it required of a sovereign to go beyond the perfunctory in their claims to territory.[47] Another analogue: just as the American West was a no-man's land, so too was Africa.[48] Never mind the fact that both places were already populated.[49]

If this first mode of territorial acquisition resonates with acts of first possession and occupation in property law, a second mode resembles the doctrine of adverse possession.[50] As is the case with adverse possession in property law, the new owner does not take title through the old owner's abandonment of the land. Rather than a situation in which a sovereign has relinquished control over territory, making it *terra nullius*, here the problem turns on competing claims between sovereigns to a particular parcel. In Anglo-American property law, the party claiming adverse possession must show that her use was open, notorious, hostile, exclusive, and continuous during a given period of time.[51] In international law, the use must be attributed directly to the sovereign's authorities, open and visible to the public, free of nuisance, and continuous. The use must also be exclusive, meaning, the sovereign is treating the territory as if it is the true owner.[52] However, unlike in property law, the question of whether the first sovereign has acquiesced in the claim of the

---

[43] MALCOLM SHAW, INTERNATIONAL LAW 503–20 (2009); Marcelo Kohen, *Original Title in the Light of the ICJ Judgment on Sovereignty Over Pedra Franca/Palau Batu Puteh, Middle Rocks, and South Ledge*, 15 J. HIST. INT'L L. 151 (2013). *See also* MARTTI KOSKENNIEMI, THE GENTLE CIVILIZER OF NATIONS 98–132 (2002).

[44] 1 GEORG FRIEDRICH MARTENS, PRECIS DU DROIT DES GENS MODERN DE L'EUROPE 117 (2010).

[45] HENRY MAINE, INTERNATIONAL LAW 69–75 (1888).

[46] *See* Wolf v. Baldwin, 19 Cal. 306 (1861).

[47] For a helpful critique, *see* Makua Mutua, *Why Redraw the Map of Africa? A Moral and Legal Inquiry*, 16 MICH. J. INT'L L. 1113 (1995).

[48] *See, e.g.*, FINAL ACT OF THE BERLIN CONFERENCE (1885). For discussion, *see* Matthew Craven, *Between Law and History: The Berlin Conference of 1884–1885 and the Logic of Free Trade*, 3 LON. REV. INT'L L. 31 (2015).

[49] *See generally* MATTHEW CRAVEN, THE DECOLONIZATION OF INTERNATIONAL LAW: STATE SUCCESSION AND THE LAW OF TREATIES (2009).

[50] FITZMAURICE, SOVEREIGNTY, PROPERTY, AND EMPIRE, *supra* note 42, at 43.

[51] For general discussion, *see* EDUARDO PENALVER & SONIA KATYAL, PROPERTY OUTLAWS: HOW SQUATTERS, PIRATES, AND PROTESTORS IMPROVE THE LAW OF OWNERSHIP (2010).

[52] Case Concerning Sovereignty Over Pedra Branca/Pulau Batu Puteh, Middle Rocks, and South Ledge (Malaysia v. Singapore), Judgment, 2008 I.C.J. Rep. 12; *Island of Palmas*, *supra* note 37, at 829.

106    THE RIGHT TO EXCLUDE

second will be important—as will questions going to fairness and reliance.[53] And, of course, sovereigns may come into territorial holdings through cession, or the conferral by treaty. The issue can be simple enough, either coming at the end of a boundary dispute or through a negotiated land swap. But the history of territorial cession is complex, for in many cases a sovereign's acquisition of territory through treaty was delivered in an imperial context. Often known as the system of "unequal treaties" and capitulation regimes, peoples ceded lands to colonial powers in situations of high duress.

Another connection between the sovereign and territorial right is less about a direct analogy as the sovereign as possessor, and more about the state's connection with the "nation." On this view, the sovereign ought to have an "organic" connection with the territory, typically as a byproduct of the "nation's" history with the land.[54] This history derives principally through religion, language, culture, and other ostensibly "traditional" relations.[55] It is of course possible to conceive of a sovereign's legitimate possession of territory without cultural-nationalist ties. Such an arrangement emerges in the example of the "civic nation," or what is sometimes called a multinational state.[56] The prototypical example, however, is the *nation*-state, that essentially organic relation between a nation's territory and the legal apparatus of the state.[57] In this view, the state's territorial rights are functions of the state's connection with the nation, which in turn is a natural possessor of the land.

Once the legitimate relation between man and land or ruler and territory is established through possession, we have owners and sovereigns. For sovereigns, like owners, are possessors in title.[58] And once there is possession, owners and sovereigns emerge with a right of exclusion.[59] As I have explained, in the context of

[53] CRAWFORD, BROWNLIE'S, *supra* note 39, at 220.

[54] Question Concerning the Acquisition of Polish Nationality, Advisory Opinion, 1923 P.C.I.J. 6 (Sept. 15).

[55] Robert Redslob, *The Problem of Nationalities*, GROTIUS SOC'Y 21–32 (Apr. 16, 1929); Nathaniel Berman, *But the Alternative Is Despair: European Nationalism and the Modernist Renewal of International Law*, 106 HARV. L. REV. 1792, 1794–808 (1993); ERNEST GELLNER, NATIONS AND NATIONALISM (1983); ANTHONY SMITH, NATIONAL IDENTITY (1993); ANTHONY SMITH, THE ETHNIC ORIGINS OF NATIONS (1986); ETIENNE BALIBAR & IMMANUEL WALLERSTEIN, RACE, NATION, CLASS (1991).

[56] See Arash Abizadeh, *Historical Truth, National Myths, and Liberal Democracy: On the Coherence of Liberal Nationalism*, 12 J. POL. PHIL. 291 (2004); Arash Abizadeh, *Liberal Nationalist Versus Postnational Social Integration: On the Nation's Ethno-Cultural Particularity and Concreteness*, 10 NATIONS & NATIONALISM 231 (2004).

[57] The importance of the nation is highlighted in the very nomenclature of international law, including its most critical institutions, such as the United Nations and the League of Nations. Jeremy Bentham is typically credited with the lexical transition from a *Law of Nations* to an *International Law*. *See* Mark Janis, *Jeremy Bentham and the Fashioning of "International Law,"* 78 AM. J. INT'L L. 405 (1984). For an interesting recent discussion of statehood, *see* Natasha Wheatley, *Spectral Legal Personality in Interwar International Law: On New Ways of Not Being a State*, 35 LAW & HIST. REV. 753 (2017).

[58] Case Concerning the Frontier Dispute (Burkina Faso v. Mali), 1986 I.C.J. Rep. 554, 564.

[59] In the context of state actors, the legality of a sovereign's entrance without permission on another sovereign's territory may take several forms. If there is uncertainty about the boundary line between the sovereigns, we may find ourselves in a border dispute. *See* Case Concerning the Temple of Preah Vihear (Cambodia v. Thailand), 1962 I.C.J. Rep. 6, 34; Territorial Dispute (Libyan Arab Jamahiriya v. Chad), 1964 I.C.J. Rep. 6; Land and Maritime Boundary Between Cameroon and Nigeria (Cameroon

sovereignty in liberal legal thought, the right to exclude manifests in two ways. We have already seen from the discussion above how it functions as a generative right of *imperium* over international society. In this second form, the right to exclude manifests as a territorial right of *dominium* over the national community. In doing so, the territorial face of the right to exclude the world unfolds as an impenetrable enclosure sourced in the world of natural right. The right of exclusion is a signal to the rest of the sovereign world, that this land is owned, and as it is owned, the world must keep out. As John Marshall explained in 1812, "the jurisdiction of a nation within its own territory is necessarily exclusive and absolute."[60] Violations of territorial jurisdiction therefore gave rise to a right of exclusion.[61]

Now just as the right to exclude manifests in its two background rules (*imperium* and *dominium*), the territorial right of *dominium* is itself dichotomous. First is the right of nonintervention, a distinctively Lockean view of the owner's relation to property.[62] The right of nonintervention and its demand that other sovereigns keep out of the territorial affairs of the home state is the very essence of classic liberal exclusion; without this right, sovereignty's meaning seems to drain out.[63]

---

v. Nigeria), 2002 I.C.J. Rep. 303; Decision Regarding Delimitation of the Border Between Eritrea and Ethiopia, 130 I.L.R. 2002. For discussion, *see* Steven Ratner, *Land Feuds and the Their Solutions: Finding International Law Beyond the Tribunal Chamber*, 100 AM. J. INT'L L. 808 (2006); Joseph Blocher & Mitu Gulati, *A Market for Sovereign Control*, 66 DUKE L.J. 797 (2017); Kaiyan Kaikobad, *Some Observations on the Doctrine of Continuity and Finality of Boundaries*, 54 BRIT. Y.B. INT'L L. 119 (1983). Historically, these disputes could look much like a claim of adverse possession, assuming that the two sovereigns regarded one another as equals. *See* DHN Johnson, *Consolidation as a Root of Title in International Law*, 13 CAM. L. J. 215, 219 (1955). On the related doctrines of accretion and secession, *see* Shaw, *supra* note 37, at 498–500. If an underlying presumption of sovereign equality was absent, however, the situation would revert back to the claim of first possession as *terra nullius*. If there was no question about the proper boundary, a sovereign's physical invasion on the territory of another might warrant responses either in the registers of tort or self-defense. In nuisance, for example, a sovereign can seek remedies under doctrines now associated with the Responsibility of States for Internationally Wrongful Acts. *See* Gabcikova-Nagymaros Project (Hungary v. Slovakia), Judgment, 1997 I.C.J. Rep. 38–42; LaGrand (Germany v. United States of America), Judgment, 2001 I.C.J. Rep. 489–92, 508–14. For discussion, *see* JAMES CRAWFORD, THE INTERNATIONAL LAW COMMISSION'S ARTICLES ON STATE RESPONSIBILITY (2002). These are claims, as in domestic law, based in tort. If the sovereign sees the proper response as sounding in violence, a state may use force in two situations. One involves the consent of the United Nations Security Council, and the other involves self-defense. *See* Case Concerning Military and Paramilitary Activities in and Against Nicaragua (Nicar. v. U.S.), Merits, Judgment, 1986 I.C.J. Rep. 14; Oil Platforms (Islamic Republic of Iran v. United States of America), Judgment, 2002 I.C.J. Rep. 161; Legal Consequences of the Construction of a Wall in the Occupied Palestinian Territory, Order of 30 January 2004, 2004 I.C.J. Rep. 3. For discussion, *see* CHRISTINE GRAY, INTERNATIONAL LAW AND THE USE OF FORCE (2008); YORAM DINSTEIN, WAR, AGGRESSION, AND SELF-DEFENSE (2011); Justin Desautels-Stein, *The Judge and the Drone*, 56 ARIZ. L. REV. 117 (2014). Once again, this mirrors the rights of the property owner, who might protect her right of exclusion by either calling in the police or engaging in self-defense, depending on the circumstances.

[60] Schooner Exchange v. McFaddon, 11 US 116, 135 (1812).

[61] *Id.* at 140–41.

[62] *Id. See also The Antelope*, 23 U.S. 5 (1825); LASSA OPPENHEIM, INTERNATIONAL LAW: A TREATISE 8–11, 30–35 (1912).

[63] UN Declaration on Principles of International Law concerning Friendly Relations and Cooperation among States in accordance with the Charter of the United Nations (1970), https://dig itallibrary.un.org/record/202170?ln=en; Case Concerning Military and Paramilitary Activities in and Against Nicaragua (Nicar. v. U.S.), 1986 I.C.J. Rep. 14, 109–10. *See also* JENS BARTELSON, A GENEALOGY OF SOVEREIGNTY (1995); JAMES CRAWFORD, THE CREATION OF STATES IN INTERNATIONAL LAW (2007).

108    THE RIGHT TO EXCLUDE

The right of nonintervention captures the basic thrust of autonomy and independence: every sovereign is the master of its piece of earth, and has a right to exclude every other sovereign from that national territory. The second way to frame the territorial right of *dominium* concerns the way in which territorial *dominium* grounds the sovereign's right of self-determination.[64] As is often discussed, the right of self-determination is typically broken into internal and external components.[65] Internal self-determination involves the right of the *demos*, however it has been constituted, to decide its particular form of political decision-making. Internal self-determination is essentially a commitment to some form of democracy. External self-determination, in contrast, concerns the right of a state to sovereign independence, to chart its own course as a participant in international society. The notion of external self-determination itself discloses the proximity of the two faces of the territorial right of *dominium*: when we press on the negative right of nonintervention, we find the external facet of self-determination rising to the surface.

The right of self-determination, however, is notoriously messy; is it a right belonging to a people, to a state, to individuals, or all of the above? In whichever valence you like, the right of self-determination presupposes an idea of *legal personality*.[66] This idea of a legal person exercising a right of self-determination, rooted in a claim for territorial *dominium*, is more Hegelian in its property overtones.[67] In the context of sovereign rights in international law, the entity we come to call an international legal person comes into existence through a process of territorial differentiation; the person (the *self*) of the sovereign is constituted through *dominium*. That is, rather than think about the abstract rights-bearing subject as prior to the moment of acquisition, consider the territory (and mastery over it) as itself constituting legal personality. As Margaret Jane Radin famously put it:

> Once we admit that a person can be bound up with an external "thing," in some constitutive sense, we can argue that by virtue of this connection the person should be accorded broad liberty with respect to control over that "thing." But here liberty follows from property for personhood; personhood is the basic concept, not liberty. Of course, if liberty is viewed not as freedom from interference, or "negative freedom," but rather as some positive will that by acting on the external world is constitutive of the person, then liberty comes closer to capturing the idea of the self being intimately bound up with things in the external world.[68]

---

[64] UN CHARTER (1945), art. 1, para. (2). For discussion, *see* ANTONIO CASSESE, THE RIGHT OF SELF-DETERMINATION: A LEGAL APPRAISAL (1995); Deborah Whitehall, *A Rival History of Self-Determination*, 27 EUR. J. INT'L L. 719 (2016).

[65] *See, e.g.,* HURST HANNUM, AUTONOMY, SOVEREIGNTY, AND SELF-DETERMINATION: THE ACCOMMODATION OF CONFLICTING RIGHTS (1996); KAREN KNOP, DIVERSITY AND SELF-DETERMINATION IN INTERNATIONAL LAW (2009).

[66] Alexander Wendt, *The State as a Person in International Theory*, 30 REV. INT'L STUD. 289 (2004).

[67] Dudley Knowles, *Hegel on Property and Personality*, 33 PHIL. Q. 45 (1983).

[68] Margaret Jane Radin, *Property and Personhood*, 34 STAN. L. REV. 957, 960–61 (1982); G.W.F. HEGEL, ELEMENTS OF THE PHILOSOPHY OF RIGHT (1991).

The twinned rights of nonintervention and self-determination constitute the territorial right of *dominium*, in which all sovereigns independently determine their own political, legal, economic, social, and cultural arrangements.[69] For any other entity, whether the Church, an international institution, or another sovereign, to interfere in the sovereign's choice to settle its own internal arrangements, the result is an unmistakable violation of the principle of sovereign equality shared by every sovereign deserving the name. And the territorial right of *dominium*, along with the generative right of *imperium*, constitute the sovereign's right to exclude. And in the context of classic liberal legal thought, the sovereign's right to exclude is entirely natural, either a feature of the domestic analogy on the one side, or a feature of territorial possession on the other. The upshot is that the territorial right of *dominium*, with its attendant commitments to nonintervention and self-determination, enjoys the same background status in the contexts of both property and sovereignty. Once possession is established, the right to exclude simply *becomes*. Without *dominium*, ownership and sovereignty are unrecognizable.

These structural linkages are not due to some special causal connection between international law and US law, or at least, I offer no such connections here. It is rather because liberal legal thought "happens" to operate in both the US and international contexts, and that it is the liberal language-system of law, rather than international law or American law per se, that is the vehicle for racial ideology in the sense that I'm using it here. In the US, law has long constructed race by way of the story of race science recounted in Chapter 2, in which, as thinkers from Blumenbach to Chamberlain believed, race was blood and bone.[70] Informed by what David Hollinger famously called the "ethno-racial pentagon,"[71] judges have presumed human beings to be rationally classified along the model of five primordial races, and a person's belonging to one of them was thought both natural and necessary.[72] The influence of race on international legal thought has been similarly potent, and has carried with it a similar ideological task: How to justify the limitation of the community of sovereigns—the *demos* of international legal persons—to certain favored populations?

In beginning to make this argument out, recall liberal legalism's initial encounter with its Aristotelian predecessor, articulating a baseline thesis of individual right against the theory of intelligible essences. Even in its triumph, this thesis of individual right ever yearned for something like a shadow of its Scholastic rival, and so the need for political management triggered a second liberal commitment to

---

[69] UN Declaration on Principles of International Law concerning Friendly Relations and Cooperation among States in accordance with the Charter of the United Nations (1970), https://digital library.un.org/record/202170?ln=en.

[70] *See, e.g.*, Justin Desautels-Stein, *Race as a Legal Concept*, 2 COLUM. J. RACE & L. 1 (2012).

[71] DAVID A. HOLLINGER, POSTETHNIC AMERICA: BEYOND MULTICULTURALISM (1995).

[72] The pentagon includes: Euro-American (White), Asian-American, African-American, Hispanic, and Indigenous. *Id.* at 23.

110   THE RIGHT TO EXCLUDE

political order. The problem here in the space of classic racial ideology, which was of course among the problems with Aristotelian thought, was the unavoidable place of *equality*, for in the effort to tame the thesis of individual right, no one group could naturally profit at the expense of another. The solution to this problem was a third thesis in the language of liberal legal thought: the legal ideology of the rule of law, or naturalizing juridical science.

In the classic *From Apology to Utopia*, Martti Koskenniemi addressed this problem at the level of international legal thought, in which the demands of freedom, order, and the rule of law recur.[73] Koskenniemi suggested that, as a field of technical knowledge, a paradox shrouded the legal concept of sovereignty, and this paradox was precisely the conflict between individual right and order. In the process of arguing about the meaning of sovereignty, international lawyers work to harmonize this dissonance by way of a process of mediation. So, for instance, State A will argue against State B that it deserves the freedom to act in furtherance of its self-preservation, and that it is bound by no rules to which it has not given its consent. State B will argue against State A that if there is to be any kind of meaningful international order, some rules must constrain all sovereigns, in all events. These two claims about freedom and order—what Koskenniemi calls ascending and descending patterns of argument—are mutually exclusive, so long as the whole structure is founded on an underlying premise of sovereign equality. Hence the contradiction. The way to harmonize this apparent tension between the demands of freedom and order was to suggest State A's *presumed* consent to the rule of law. Framed in the abstract, this is a non-racialized form of naturalizing juridical science. I mention Koskenniemi's important work in *From Apology to Utopia* in order to distinguish a structure of argumentative practice in which equality predominates, from a structure of argumentative practice in which it does not. Or, to put that another way, the drive toward a mediating device like tacit consent is motivated by the indispensable requirement in classic liberalism that sovereigns consent to the rules by which they are governed. Modifying consent so that it speaks at once to the contrasting theses of freedom and order gives the appearance of a harmonious rule.

Moving into the context of international law's boundary problem, however, the question is not about how to harmonize the conflict between the theses of freedom and order. It is rather about how to settle conflicts over the scope of that structure, that is, which groups participate in Koskenniemi's structure of argument, and which are left out? This, as will be recalled from Chapter 1, is the problem of closing the boundaries of the sovereign *demos*. As we will see shortly, a solution to that problem *was* a racialized form of naturalizing juridical science. Of course, the question of who's in and who's out of the global order has become a rather popular

---

[73] MARTTI KOSKENNIEMI, FROM APOLOGY TO UTOPIA: THE STRUCTURE OF INTERNATIONAL LEGAL ARGUMENT (2006).

question in postcolonial studies. In his *Imperialism, Sovereignty, and the Making of International Law*, for example, Tony Anghie agreed that the central question in international legal thought has been about how to justify the existence of rules that could bind sovereign states.[74] Anghie argued, however, that the quest to justify the limitation of that question to only certain populations served as a guarantee for the rest of the system, and that the relation between this limitation and the system's making had yet to be understood. For while it may have been true that the premise of sovereign equality made it difficult to justify a legal order, Anghie pointed out that the concept of sovereign equality came into being in a prefigured context of cultural domination and subordination. That is, the cultural character of sovereignty was itself defined by the way in which international legal thought already answered international law's boundary problem.[75] This is Anghie's well-known theory of the dynamic of difference, in which the sovereign form was defined by way of its cultural other.[76]

What is absent in so much of the international law literatures of critical and postcolonial studies, however, is an analysis of the legal ideology of racial exclusion (*imperium* and *dominium*). To analyze this structure, and yet still remain within the confines of *From Apology to Utopia's* understanding of liberal legalism, I retain the ideological focus on mediation and harmony. However, the mediating function is different when we look at international law from the vantage of its racial ideology, rather than from the traditional perspective of social contract theory. After all, if the claim from State A is that they are a people with governing power over a specified territory, and this people understands itself as subject to no higher forms of legal or political authority, it doesn't make much sense for State B to argue that State A has impliedly consented to the rule that State A ought to be excluded from the family of sovereign states. That is exactly the opposite of what they are saying. The device of presumed consent is, therefore, too narrow to justify excluding certain peoples from the structure itself. Furthermore, while I follow Anghie's lead in interrogating the cultural constitution of sovereignty, I set aside Anghie's dynamic of difference. Too broad as an explanatory device, the dynamic of difference attends us-them relations going back into antiquity, well before the invention of racial ideology. For liberals working in the nineteenth century, something else was required to solve international law's boundary problem, and it is here that race became a

---

[74] Antony Anghie, Imperialism, Sovereignty, and the Making of International Law (2007).

[75] There are many instances of the use of race as a means of exclusion throughout US law, as well as at international law. On the domestic side, critical race theory has done the most in pursuit of the point. *See, e.g.,* Ian Haney Lopez, White By Law: The Legal Construction of Race (1996); Neil Gotanda, *A Critique of "Our Constitution is Colorblind,"* 44 Stan. L. Rev. 1 (1991). For helpful discussion of the point at a broader level, *see* Thomas McCarthy, Race, Empire, and the Idea of Human Development (2009).

[76] Anghie, *supra* note 74, at 3.

## 112 THE RIGHT TO EXCLUDE

form of naturalizing juridical science, harmonizing the gap between equality and exclusion.

As was argued repeatedly by nineteenth-century jurists defending this exclusionary effort, every people enjoyed rights of nonintervention and self-determination. And every people was legally bound only by those international rules to which it had consented. Of course, in truth it wasn't "every people," and justifications were required to explain the uneven application of international law across the globe. For, as Ntina Tzouvala has recently pointed out, it was never the case that certain peoples were entirely excluded from participating in the international legal order.[77] Most notably were the presence of capitulation treaties, agreements between the colonial powers and the colonized that reflected the inclusion of the apparently "excluded" peoples. But even beyond these unequal treaties, a wide array of practices worked to assimilate the world into nineteenth-century international law. As Tzouvala persuasively explains, this uneven application functioned along the lines of a bipolar structure of argument, in which international lawyers oscillated between logics of improvement and inclusion on the one side, and a physical anthropology of human classification on the other, the effect of which was to use biological criteria as anchors for human hierarchy.

I follow Tzouvala in this approach, and concede that the practice of nineteenth-century international law actively worked to include colonized peoples in the broader logic of capitalism. But what Tzouvala and pretty much every international legal historian understands, is that there was nothing even remotely *equal* even about these "inclusive" practices. And it is here that my study of international law's racial ideology finds its port of entry. Drilling down into Tzouvala's "logic of biology," the sovereign's right to exclude was itself a rather complex structure of argument, and as I explain below, it initially relied upon justifications regarding the right of "racially developed" peoples to write the rules of the international legal order. So, for example, if a racially developed state used force on a territory "belonging" to a "racially inferior" people—the world's racial *xenos*—the rules governing the ensuing violence were purely "moral."[78] And, of course, there were exceptions, like the Russo-Japanese war of 1904 and 1905, but even these exceptions did little more than prove the rule.[79]

Inside the confines of a racialized international society, a "true" sovereign's right of *dominium* was largely to its territory. Beyond or outside of that racialized border of the sovereign *demos*, however, it was as if sovereigns crossed the *pomerium*, generating the distinction between *imperator* and barbarian—and it was the sovereign's imperial right to determine where that boundary existed. Thus, in

---

[77] Ntina Tzouvala, Civilization as Capitalism: A History of International Law (2020).
[78] Theodore Woolsey, Introduction to the Study of International Law 232–33 (1908).
[79] For discussion of Japan's engagements, see Mohammad Shahabuddin, *The 'Standard of Civilization' in International Law: Intellectual Perspectives from Pre-War Japan*, 32 Leiden J. Int'l L. 13 (2019).

the classical style of liberal legal thought, the general argument goes something along the following lines, as surveyed below. Begin with the three theses of liberal legalism: (1) freedom of right (for whom?), (2) ordered liberty (established by whom?), (3) a harmonizing rule of law (individual rights of racially superior peoples, regulated by a right of *imperium* enjoyed equally by those same peoples.) Taken together, these three theses provide the basic contours for the liberal concept of sovereignty. This construction of the racial sovereign, however, is necessarily in the *ideological background*, constituting the very idea of what counts as a full and equal participant in the international legal order.[80] In the classic liberal style, exclusion and sovereignty intertwine in the background rule: Only racially developed populations of human beings are naturally able to achieve the full and most mature legal status of sovereignty, and it is only such a sovereign state that may rightfully exclude other sovereigns from its territory (*dominium*) and from the international community (*imperium*). Hence, international law's classic racial ideology: *a pattern of argumentative practice at once giving structure to indeterminate legal concepts and justifying relations of domination through the use of seemingly natural racial classifications and on account of a naturalized foreignness.*

## B Articulating Racial Ideology in the Classic Style

Depending on your preferred starting point, the history of international legal thought predates the invention of racial ideology by a long way.[81] To be sure, international efforts to restrict political power to some chosen group of populations go back at least to the sixteenth century, if not well before.[82] The use of a distinctive racial ideology as a form of naturalizing juridical science, however, did not enter the argumentative practice of international legal thought until the 1800s. Building out from the analyses of the structure of liberal legal thought and racial ideology from above, this chapter begins the narrative with an exploration of the classical liberal style of international legal thought that launched in the nineteenth century.

As explained below, international lawyers of the time often relied upon nebulous ideas like "the Great Powers" and "the Family of Nations" as proxies for the racialization of international society. And just as the science of racial development

---

[80] Sumi Cho & Gil Gott, *The Racial Sovereign, in* SOVEREIGNTY, EMERGENCY, LEGALITY (Austin Sarat ed., 2010).

[81] *See, e.g.*, HENRY WHEATON, HISTORY OF THE LAW OF NATIONS IN EUROPE AND AMERICA (1982); WILHELM GREWE, THE EPOCHS OF INTERNATIONAL LAW 84 (2000); C.H. ALEXANDROWICZ, THE LAW OF NATIONS IN GLOBAL HISTORY (2017); STEPHEN NEFF, JUSTICE AMONG NATIONS: A HISTORY OF INTERNATIONAL LAW (2014).

[82] *see, e.g.*, ROBERT WILLIAMS, THE AMERICAN INDIAN IN WESTERN LEGAL THOUGHT: THE DISCOURSES OF CONQUEST (1992); DAVID BEDERMAN, THE SPIRIT OF INTERNATIONAL LAW (2002).

114    THE RIGHT TO EXCLUDE

emerged as a means for producing a hierarchy of human classification,[83] so too did that same "science" function to discriminate between those racially developed states enjoying the full gamut of international legal personality, and those that did not.[84] This form of racialized xenophobia was indigenous to liberal theory, grounded in empirical epistemology, rather than religion or culture. That is, racial exclusion was justifiable because it was *knowledge*, not *politics*. And if it was knowable as science, it was lawful. Indeed, this is the key to legal formalism: Wherever and whenever he can, the jurist matches legal rules and conclusions with a natural order knowable through scientific means.

One important point of reference for charting the entrance of racial xenophobia into the structure of international legal thought is the work of the Swiss theorist, Emer Vattel, canvassed earlier in Chapter 1. Vattel was widely read in the years leading up to the American and French Revolutions,[85] and his basic preoccupation was with the problem of justifying legal obligations acting upon rights-bearing sovereigns. In short, this is the problem of sovereign equality addressed in Koskenniemi's *From Apology to Utopia*: if all sovereigns are equal, how to justify the application of norms to sovereigns that have not agreed to them? The rising question of the nineteenth century was different, and the way I want to conceptualize it is by way of international law's boundary problem. Rather than focus on how to justify an impersonal law among equal sovereigns, the problem was now about how to justifiably characterize the community of these fully sovereign states. Which peoples were already sovereign, and which could never be?[86] In this new context, Vattel and other earlier writers proved of little use, as they failed to specifically address the question of the international community's scope. The hunt was on for new legal strategies that could justify a global *pomerium,* to separate the domain in which sovereigns enjoyed the rights and protections of full sovereignty from the domain of the racial *xenos*, in which there were quasi-sovereigns, states with less rights, or no rights at all.[87]

---

[83] An obvious analogue here is the problem of slavery in the US. *See, e.g.*, THOMAS DEW, THE PRO-SLAVERY ARGUMENT (1853); WINTHROP JORDAN, WHITE OVER BLACK: AMERICAN ATTITUDES TOWARD THE NEGRO, 1550–1812 (2012).

[84] TRAVERS TWISS, THE LAW OF NATIONS CONSIDERED AS INDEPENDENT POLITICAL COMMUNITIES 120 (1861). *See also* the earlier discussion of "modified natural law" in DIETRICH HEINRICH LUDWIG VON OMPTEDA, LITERATURE ON THE ENTIRETY OF INTERNATIONAL LAW, BOTH NATURAL AND POSITIVE (1785).

[85] *See, e.g.*, ANTHONY BELLIA, JR. & BRADFORD CLARK, THE LAW OF NATIONS AND THE UNITED STATES CONSTITUTION (2017).

[86] For Koskenniemi's subsequent works in this vein, *see* MARTTI KOSKENNIEMI, THE GENTLE CIVILIZER OF NATIONS: THE RISE AND FALL OF INTERNATIONAL LAW (2001); MARTTI KOSKENNIEMI, TO THE UTTERMOST PARTS OF THE EARTH: LEGAL IMAGINATION AND INTERNATIONAL POWER, 1300–1870 (2021). *See also* Matthew Craven, *The Invention of a Tradition: Westlake, the Berlin Conference and the Historicisation of International Law, in* CONSTRUCTING INTERNATIONAL LAW: THE BIRTH OF A DISCIPLINE (M. Vec et al. eds., 2012).

[87] This mode of exclusion wasn't elaborated only in terms of self-interest. Rhetorically, at least, it was often couched in terms that suggested a progressive development available to the "inferior" state. For example, Theodore Woolsey explained: "A state in the lower grade of civilization, like a savage, becomes conscious of its separate existence in the act of resistance, or of defending that existence. Such

In Chapter 2, we surveyed some of the US and European debates over the science of racial xenophobia. Despite disagreements between monogenists and polygenists, and the shifts that took place after Darwin and on the way to eugenics, there reigned a relatively stable schedule of human classification. Of course, many of our exemplars distinguished themselves with slight variations on the theme, but the theme of racial subjection was clear enough: the most developed class of human beings were whites, the intermediate class belonged to peoples from the Americas, and to some extent, from Asia, and the least developed class of human being came from parts of Asia and Africa. What's more, and what became more explicit by the century's end, was that the class of white peoples was itself indeterminate, and that certain whites—such as the Teutonic peoples—were the great ones. As a result, and if we merge some of the hierarchies populated from Blumenbach through Ripley, we can imagine the science of nineteenth century racialization in something like a set of concentric circles.

At the center of human development are those Teutonic whites. This was the very core of nature's highest achievement, and flowing outward were the progressively less developed racial beings of the world. When we map this image on the racial ideology of liberal theory, *homo politicus* emerges at the center, for all those humans descended from the Teutons. Further still, all (male) humans existing in the circle of Caucasians enjoy rights as well, though probably less rights than those at the very center. Moving further out beyond the circle of white, rights-bearing subjects, the likelihood of inclusion in liberalism's borders becomes increasingly questionable. Beyond these borders are the racialized *homo sacri*, the racial *xenoi*, a class of human bodies at once excluded but by their very nature as racial subjects working to secure the very center of the image.

Just as international theorists in the 1800s worked to do. Let us now transpose this scheme of racial subjection onto the plane of sovereign equality in the nineteenth century international legal order. Where the question in the first instance was about how to properly locate the boundaries of liberal right in a given political community, now the question is about how to generate racial subjects in the global *demos*. It is really the same question, only now analogized at the level of international society.[88] As became increasingly common among international

---

self-preservation on the part of the individual arouses, it may be, no better feeling than that of independence and self-reliance; in the state it helps the members to feel their unity and dependence, and the priceless value of the state itself. Hence war is a moral teacher: opposition to external force is an aid to the highest civic virtues." *See* WOOLSEY, *supra* note 78, at 5. *See also* LAUREN BENTON, A SEARCH FOR SOVEREIGNTY: LAW AND GEOGRAPHY IN EUROPEAN EMPIRES, 1400–1900 (2009).

[88] *See generally* JAMES LORIMER, THE INSTITUTES OF THE LAW OF NATIONS: A TREATISE OF THE JURAL RELATIONS OF SEPARATE POLITICAL COMMUNITIES 101–02 (1883): ("As a political phenomenon, humanity, in its present condition, divides itself into three concentric zones or spheres—that of civilized humanity, that of barbarous humanity, and that of savage humanity ... It is with the first of these spheres alone that the international jurist has to deal ... He is not bound to apply the positive law of nations to savages, or even to barbarians as such.") In distinguishing between the civilized, barbarous, and savage spheres of humanity, Lorimer explained that it would be helpful to "distinguish between the progressive and non-progressive races." *Id.*

116   THE RIGHT TO EXCLUDE

legal thinkers, located at the structure's bullseye were the Great Powers: the United Kingdom, Prussia, France, Austria, and Russia.[89] Repeatedly, international jurists suggested that the world would ultimately be a better place if the interests of the Great Powers were served first, since the interests of the Great Powers were themselves "global," as contrasted with the more "parochial" interests of lesser states.[90] This way of thinking about global order took off in the aftermath of the French Revolution, and as these so-called Great Powers took stock, the new organizing idea for the European system was inflected with what Gerry Simpson has aptly called legal hegemony.[91]

As the Austrian diplomat Friedrich von Gentz wrote contemporaneously, "And so Europe seems really to form a grand political family united under the auspices of a high tribunal of its own creation, whose members guarantee to themselves and to all parties concerned, the peaceful enjoyment of their respective rights."[92] This was an explicit rejection on the part of the Great Powers of a strong, Vattelian form of sovereign equality.[93] In so doing, the Great Powers erected a legal system which formalized certain rights and privileges that would accrue to superior sovereigns and be removed from the reach of other sovereigns.[94] In the context of the Concert of Europe, this effort began with the Treaty of Cheaumont of 1814[95] and culminated in the Final Act of 1815.[96] By the time of the Congress itself, the Great Powers had constituted themselves as the "Committee of Five,"[97] anticipating what would become, more than a century later and after a couple world wars, the United Nations Security Council.[98] In the context of the Great Powers themselves, a rough idea of sovereign equality was in effect, meaning, these states were analogized to *homo politicus* enjoying full liberal rights.[99]

---

[89] OPPENHEIM, INTERNATIONAL LAW, *supra* note 62, at 30–35.

[90] MARK MAZOWER, GOVERNING THE WORLD: THE HISTORY OF AN IDEA, 1815 TO THE PRESENT 5 (2013); GERRY SIMPSON, GREAT POWERS AND OUTLAW STATES: UNEQUAL SOVEREIGNS IN THE INTERNATIONAL LEGAL ORDER 68 (2004).

[91] Simpson defines legal hegemony as "the existence of with an international society of a powerful elite of states whose superior status is recognized by minor powers as a political fact giving rise to the existence of certain constitutional privileges, rights, and duties, and whose relations with each other are defined by adherence to a rough principle of sovereign equality." SIMPSON, *supra* note 90, at 68. For discussion of the Concert, *see* ROBERT MOWAT, THE CONCERT OF EUROPE (1930).

[92] Quoted in MAZOWER, *supra* note 90, at 5.

[93] SIMPSON, *supra* note 90, at 102.

[94] *Id.*

[95] SIMPSON, *supra* note 90, at 96.

[96] Immanuel Wallerstein, *The Congress of Vienna from 1763 to 1833*, 36 REVIEW 1 (2013); PHILLIP BOBBITT, THE SHIELD OF ACHILLES 540 (2002).

[97] SIMPSON, *supra* note 90, at 100–01. The Committee was composed of Britain, Prussia, France, Austria, and Russia.

[98] UN CHARTER, ch. 5. As Simpson argues, the Concert's hierarchical scheme was established as a *treaty regime*, consented to by the multitudes of European princes in attendance and manifested through a complex series of legal arrangements. *Id.* at 102–15.

[99] *See, e.g.*, JOHN WESTLAKE, CHAPTERS ON THE PRINCIPLES OF INTERNATIONAL LAW 142–43 (1894); ANGHIE, *supra* note 74, at 65.

In the next outer circle were those European states enjoying the benefits of whiteness, and thereby constituting the outer bounds of "The Family of Nations."[100] These were states with international legal personality, though due to a "weakness" or "inferiority" were not counted among the Great Powers. These were states like Portugal and Spain.[101] The US,[102] and eventually its so-called "satellites" in Central and South America, presented more difficult questions of membership,[103] but for all intents and purposes were here as well.[104]

In this group also belonged the exceptional state of Haiti.[105] In early 1825, the French monarch Charles X had flatly proclaimed that France would not recognize the sovereignty of a "black republic," but later that year the King's financial advisors prevailed.[106] But due to the racial implications of the Haitian revolution, revolutionary leaders in Spanish America tended to make the Haitian example as opaque as possible.[107] As such, the Great Powers recognized these members of the "Family" as possessing the necessary elements of statehood, as well as a kind of "civilization" necessary for the enjoyment of international legal rights, but these

---

[100] OPPENHEIM, INTERNATIONAL LAW, *supra* note 62, at 30–35.

[101] HENRY WHEATON, ELEMENTS OF INTERNATIONAL LAW 7–8 (8th ed. 1866). Wheaton covers the wide range of sovereigns and semi-sovereigns in this category at 25–74. *See also* SIMPSON, *supra* note 90, at 100.

[102] *See, e.g.*, WESTLAKE, *supra* note 99, at 95.

[103] On the question of racism and racial anxieties within the movements for colonial independence, *see* MARIXA LASSO, MYTHS OF HARMONY: RACE AND REPUBLICANISM DURING THE AGE OF REVOLUTION, COLUMBIA 1795–1831 (2007); Marixa Lasso, *Race and Nation in Caribbean Gran Columbia, Cartagena, 1810–1832*, 111 HISP. AM. HIST. REV. 336 (2006); Liliana Obregon, *Completing Civilization: Creole Consciousness and International Law in Nineteenth Century Latin America, in* INTERNATIONAL LAW AND ITS OTHERS (Anne Orford ed., 2006).

[104] OPPENHEIM, INTERNATIONAL LAW, *supra* note 62, at 32. In 1823, Metternich was ambivalent about the place of the US in the international legal order. He wrote: "Friendly relations may exist between European powers and the United States; there may be negotiations, treaties, alliances, and engagements of all kinds between them, but there does not exist a common basis upon which delegates of the United States could sit in a European congress." Quoted in William Spence Robertson, *Metternich's Attitude Toward Revolutions in Latin America*, 21 HISP. AM. HIST. REV. 538, 546 (1941). He was even more skeptical about recognizing the Spanish colonies as independent sovereigns. *See* MIKULAS FABRY, RECOGNIZING STATES: INTERNATIONAL SOCIETY AND THE MAKING OF NEW STATES SINCE 1776 (2010). On the European perspective on the independence of the Spanish colonies, *see* Ulrike Schmeider, *Spain and Spanish America in the System of the Holy Alliance: The Importance of Interconnected Historical Events on the Congresses of the Holy Alliance*, 38 REVIEW 147 (2015); William Spence Robertson, *Metternich's Attitude Toward Revolutions in Latin America*, 21 HISP. AM. HIST. REV. 538 (1941).

[105] Liliana Obregon, *Empire, Racial Capitalism, and International Law: The Case of Maunumittted Haiti and the Recognition Debt*, 31 LEIDEN J. INT'L L. 597 (2018); Michel-Rolph Trouillot, *An Unthinkable History: The Haitian Revolution as a Non-Event, in* SILENCING THE PAST: POWER AND THE PRODUCTION OF HISTORY (Michel-Rolph Trouillot ed., 1995). *See also* David Geggus, *The Caribbean in the Age of Revolution, in* THE AGE OF REVOLUTIONS IN GLOBAL CONTEXT, C. 1760–1840, (David Armitage & Sanjay Subramanyam eds., 2010); TREE OF LIBERTY: CULTURAL LEGACIES OF THE HAITIAN REVOLUTION IN THE ATLANTIC WORLD (Doris L. Garraway ed., 2008); SYBILLE FISCHER, MODERNITY DISAVOWED: HAITI AND THE CULTURE OF SLAVERY IN AGE OF REVOLUTION (2004); SUSAN BUCK-MORSS, HEGEL UND HAITI (2011); Ada Ferrer, *Haiti, Free Soil, and Antislavery in the Revolutionary Atlantic*, 117 AM. HIST. REV. 40 (2012).

[106] W.S. ROBERTSON, FRANCE AND LATIN AMERICAN INDEPENDENCE 461 (1967).

[107] Michael Zeuske, *The French Revolution in Spanish America: With Some Reflections on Manfred Kossok as Marxist Historian of Bourgeois Revolutions*, 38 REVIEW 99, 105 (2015).

118    THE RIGHT TO EXCLUDE

states (especially in Latin America and the Caribbean) were deemed too immature to yet sit with the grownups, making legal decisions that would govern the rest.[108] Thus, while full equality might not have reigned supreme in the Family of Nations, formal and procedural equality was the norm.[109]

Moving out from that sphere of states enjoying membership in the Family of Nations, international lawyers created a ring for "semi-peripheral" states like China, Persia, Japan, and the Ottoman Empire.[110] These nations tracked those intermediate racial divisions occupying the transitional space between whites and those peoples deemed closest to the animal kingdom. These were peoples that undeniably possessed civilization, but because these were nonwhite, *alien* civilizations, these were peoples that were—at best—only candidates for membership in the Family of Nations. The final and outermost circle of peripheral peoples included those with little if any chance of ever achieving the heights of civilization enjoyed at the core.[111]

When stacked together in this way, we have a strong resonance between the nineteenth-century image of racial order and the nineteenth-century image of international legal order.[112] However, I want to again emphasize that my intention here is to outline a pattern of argument within the broader structure of liberal legal thought—racial ideology as naturalizing juridical science—not an intellectual history or a general theory of racism as the ultimate explanation for imperialism. That is, mine is not the claim that had it not been for particular thinkers in the tradition of race science that nineteenth-century imperialism could never have been, or even that these images reflect the actual sociohistorical scene of the 1800s. This is not, in other words, a sociocultural study of the worldly origins and entanglements of imperialism and racism. Instead, the goal here is to elucidate the ideological structure of racial exclusion in classic liberal international legal thought, and articulate the discrete argumentative practices that morphed over time. The rationale for this emphasis is that, as liberalism has matured into the twenty-first century, so too has this structure of racial ideology transformed as well.

It is in this spirit that we consider first that at the Congress of Vienna the express question before the drafters was precisely about a legal structure determining

---

[108] MAZOWER, *supra* note 90, at 4–5.

[109] SIMPSON, *supra* note 90, at 38–39.

[110] *See, e.g.*, GERRIT GONG, THE STANDARD OF CIVILIZATION IN INTERNATIONAL SOCIETY 19 (1984). Henry Wheaton's tally of "semi-sovereign" states in the second edition (1880) of his treaties included Serbia, Monaco, Egypt, and the "savage" Indian tribes of North America. The "barbarians" of Africa apparently didn't make the cut. *See* WHEATON, ELEMENTS, *supra* note 101, at 47–50; HALL, *supra* note 25, at 52–53 (explained that despite the Treaty of Paris of 1856, Turkey had failed to meet the proper test of civilization, thus continuing to deserve unequal treatment among sovereigns. Romania and Serbia were similarly "excluded from the full enjoyment of the rights of sovereignty, because, through ignorance and evil traditions, the administrators of justice are not worthy of trust."). For further discussion, *see* ARNULF BECKER LORCA, MESTIZO INTERNATIONAL LAW (2014).

[111] OPPENHEIM, INTERNATIONAL LAW, *supra* note 62.

[112] CHARLES MILLS, THE RACIAL CONTRACT 81–89 (1997).

*which* states would take part in directing the reconstruction of Europe, and which states would be the directed.[113] As Gerry Simpson has explained, "Westphalia introduced a system of anarchy in which state sovereignty and equality supplanted the vertical authority of the Church. At Vienna, the 'democratic system' introduced after Westphalia gives way to a hegemonic or oligarchic system that was to be the mark of the Concert order."[114] And this hegemonic new order was decisively hierarchical, with the four Great Powers of Britain, Russia, Prussia, and Austria at the very center of power, surrounded by the lesser powers of the Family of Nations, and then the quasi-sovereigns and uncivilized masses. Looking back upon the nineteenth century, the international lawyer T.J. Lawrence put it this way:

> [T]he notions of classical antiquity differ immensely from those of modern Europe, and in our own day there is a great gulf fixed between the views of European and American statesmen on the one hand and those of the potentates of Central Africa on the other. But though there are several systems of international law, there is but one important system ... it grew up in Christian Europe, though some of its roots may be traced back to ancient Greece and ancient Rome. It has been adopted by all the civilized states of the earth ... We have, therefore, in our definition, spoken of it as 'the rules which determine the conduct of the general body of *civilized* states.[115]

Lawrence argued that even while certain populations might satisfy the criteria for statehood, sovereignty alone was insufficient to warrant "membership in the family of nations. For there are many communities outside the sphere of international law, though they are independent states ... It would, for instance, be absurd to expect the King of Dahomey to establish a Prize Court, or to require the dwarfs of central African forest to receive a permanent diplomatic mission."[116] Whether "a race of savages" or the more accomplished races of Turkey, China, or Japan, nonwhite peoples were presumptively inferior and were excluded from the full rights of international legal personality.[117]

Indeed, by the second half of the nineteenth century, international lawyers repeatedly sought to solve international law's boundary problem by way of racial ideology. Consider US President James Monroe's proclamation of 1823 of a right

---

[113] WHEATON, ELEMENTS, *supra* note 101, at 196–97. *See, e.g.,* W.E. HALL, A TREATISE ON INTERNATIONAL LAW 52 (6th ed. 1909) ("As has already been mentioned, international law is a product of the special civilization of modern Europe, and is intended to reflect the essential facts of that civilization so long as they are fit subjects for international rules ... If it fails to do so, either through the imperfection of its civilization, or because the ideas, upon which it is founded, are alien to those of the European peoples, other states are at liberty to render its admission to the benefits of international law dependent on [the uncivilized state's willingness to conform to European values.]").

[114] SIMPSON, *supra* note 90, at 103.

[115] T.J. LAWRENCE, THE PRINCIPLES OF INTERNATIONAL LAW 4–5 (1895).

[116] *Id.* at 58.

[117] *Id.* at 58–59.

120    THE RIGHT TO EXCLUDE

of independence enjoyed by Spain's former colonies in the Americas.[118] What precisely was this right of independence to mean? Was it an affirmation of sovereign equality, rights of legal personality and full participation in the Family of Nations? In the 1820s, the US was still itself a peripheral sovereign in the international legal order, and it remained unclear what right the US had to participate in the Family of Nations, much less what rights were due to the racially diverse (read: "foreign") and openly rebellious peoples occupying the rest of North and South America.[119]

What was very clear, however, was the US interest in preventing European conquest in the Western Hemisphere. By 1845, the US annexed Texas from Mexican control, and a few years later the Mexican–American War was in full bloom, and by the end of the conflict, Mexico had lost half of its territory to the US. Soon enough, the US found itself in a curious position with respect to the legacy of the Monroe Doctrine. With its early twentieth century imperialist adventures, could the US offer respect for an international rule of sovereign equality, with anything resembling a straight face? From the perspective of many international lawyers and politicians in South America, the results of the Spanish–American War had certainly been racially motivated. In the eyes of many, the US was no defender of sovereign equality. It was a bully and a bigot.

As the Argentine international lawyer Alejandro Alvarez would later explain, what needed clarifying was the separation between the Monroe Doctrine, as it had crystallized into a rule of customary international law, and the hegemonic and imperialist policies of the US. What the Monroe Doctrine was "really" about, according to Alvarez, was the recognition of "acquired rights to independence, to non-intervention, and to non-colonization on the American continent."[120] Nevertheless, Alvarez further suggested that the sovereign right of nonintervention could go only so far; if "civilization" demands a sovereign to abide by certain changes occurring in the international order, the fundamental right of the state to independence should give way. Alvarez explained:

[A] State may not, on the ground that it is absolutely independent, isolate itself entirely from the other States or refuse to enter into relations with them. The great Powers have compelled certain Asiatic States to open their doors to European commerce, *and this action has been approved by the whole civilized world.*[121]

---

[118] Benjamin Allen Coates, Legalist Empire: International Law and American Foreign Relations in the Early Twentieth Century (2016).

[119] A discussion of the concepts of race and racism at work in the wars of Spanish American independence is beyond the scope of this Article, but it is worth flagging just how dominant the racial ideology of the independence movements was throughout. For discussion, *see* Jeremy Adelman, Sovereignty and Revolution in the Iberian Atlantic (2006); Paul D. Naish, Slavery and Silence: Latin America and the US Slave Debate (2017).

[120] Alejandro Alvarez, *The New Monroe Doctrine and American Public Law*, 2 Minn. L. Rev. 357, 358 (1918).

[121] Alejandro Alvarez, *The State's Right of Self-Preservation*, 3 St. Louis L. Rev. 113, 124 (1919) (emphasis added).

Out of the encounter with Latin American jurists like Alvarez, a legal task before the US in the wake of new imperial control over the Philippines, Cuba, and Puerto Rico, was one of justification.[122] If Alvarez was right, and the Monroe Doctrine stood above all else for a standard of sovereign equality, what legal justifications might warrant US action everywhere from Panama to Hawai'i? Indeed, this was precisely the concern motivating President William McKinley in his decision to appoint the New York lawyer Elihu Root as his Secretary of War.[123] Later to become a President of the American Society of International Law, Theodore Roosevelt's Secretary of State and Secretary of War, as well as a Chair of several of Andrew Carnegie's corporate entities, McKinley's charge to the man that would become his international law czar was to justify the US record abroad.

In the years before World War I, and in this context of justifying US intervention abroad, Root gave an array of public lectures both in the US and throughout Latin America. Root repeatedly agreed with Alvarez that the principle underlying the Monroe Doctrine was "the right of every sovereign state to protect itself... [where] each state must judge for itself when a threatened act will create such a situation."[124] Root continued:

The fundamental principle of international law is the principle of independent sovereignty. Upon that all other rules of international law rest. That is the chief and necessary protection of the weak against the power of the strong. Observance of that is the necessary condition to the peace and order of the civilized world. By the declaration of that principle the common judgment of civilization awards to the smallest and weakest state the liberty to control its own affairs without interference from any other Power, however great.[125]

Two years later, Root addressed the American Society of International Law regarding a recently adopted declaration on the equality of nations.[126] That declaration espoused that "[e]very nation is in law and before law the equal of every other nation," and Root forcefully set this principle against the example of the warring states of Europe.[127] At the same time, however, Root cautioned that this move toward a more fulsome sense of legal equality had to be a realistic if it was to be effective.[128] Commenting approvingly of Root's "masterful" view of sovereign equality,

---

[122] For discussion of the US view of international law as relevant to the Americas, *see* CHRISTOPHER R. ROSSI, WHIGGISH INTERNATIONAL LAW: ELIHU ROOT, THE MONROE DOCTRINE, AND INTERNATIONAL LAW IN THE AMERICAS (2019).

[123] PHILIP C. JESSUP, ELIHU ROOT: 1845–1909 215–21 (1938).

[124] Elihu Root, *The Real Monroe Doctrine*, 8 AM. J. INT'L L. 427, 432 (1914).

[125] *Id.* at 434.

[126] Elihu Root, *Declaration of the Rights and Duties of Nations Adopted by the American Institute of International Law*, 10 AM. J. INT'L L. 211 (1916).

[127] *Id.* at 213.

[128] *Id.* at 216.

## 122   THE RIGHT TO EXCLUDE

Alvarez explained that what Root was talking about could not be the "absolute equality of states, subjecting the more powerful to various kinds of restraint. The equality that must be established ... is legal equality, by virtue of which no state may, merely because of its superiority, have any claim or pretention to rights which are not recognized as belonging to weaker states. All states must be equal before the law."[129]

The point that needs to be emphasized here is that while Root and Alvarez agreed on the need to consider Latin American sovereigns as equal members of the Family of Nations, they also agreed that this commitment to sovereign equality for states meant very little for the equality of the human races. Not every people, in other words, deserved a sovereign state and a legal position in the Family of Nations. In Alvarez's "Latin America and International Law," for example, he argued for the importance of understanding the racial composition of the Latin American population.[130] Unlike the "single race" of "whites" in Europe, Alvarez pointed in Latin America to the "conquering race" from Spain, the "negroes imported from Africa," and the creoles, those children born in Latin America from European-born parents.[131] Among these groups the only "thinking" part of the population was the creole: The Spanish whites and the Africans either thought of Latin America as just another piece of Europe, or didn't think at all.[132] Indeed, in the course of Spanish-American independence and the various congresses and conventions that emerged in the first third of the nineteenth century, the political construction of the new sovereigns was highly racialized.[133] The bottom line: While the new Latin American sovereigns would come to take a marginal place within the Family of Nations, this was participation only for *racially recognizable* sovereigns.

In the context of Root's work in the effort to elect Theodore Roosevelt (who would come to establish Panama's canal zone), Root argued for a racial approach to equality from a different direction. Anticipating Alvarez's criticism of US imperialism in the Western hemisphere, the Democratic Party's political platform at the turn of the century regarded the paramount issue in the presidential election to be that of "imperialism."[134] To be sure, Root argued in favor of sovereign equality for small and great states alike, but was it imperialist for the US to deny sovereign prerogatives to the Filipino people if they lacked the capacity for self-governance?

In 1898, the US and Spain fought and concluded a war that resulted in the US acquisition of several Spanish colonies, including the Philippines, Puerto Rico, Cuba, and Guam. Contemporaneously, the US took control of Hawai'i, eastern Samoa,

---

[129] Alvarez, *State's Right*, *supra* note 121, at 117.

[130] Alejandro Alvarez, *Latin America and International Law*, 3 AM. J. INT'L L. 269, 271 (1909).

[131] *Id. See also* Liliana Obregón, *Between Civilization and Barbarism: Creole Interventions in International Law*, 27 THIRD WORLD Q. 815 (2006).

[132] Alvarez, *Latin America and International Law*, *supra* note 130, at 272–73.

[133] *See generally* WALTER D. MIGNOLO, THE IDEA OF LATIN AMERICA (2005).

[134] Elihu Root, United States Secretary of War, Speech at Canton, Ohio 8 (Oct. 24, 1900) (transcript available in the Library of Congress).

the Guano Islands, the Panama canal zone, and a decade later, brought on board the US Virgin Islands. As David Immerwahr has observed, by 1940 the "Greater United States" included nearly nineteen million colonial subjects.[135] Among those territories contributing to what Aziz Rana calls America's settler empire,[136] the Philippines was a special case. Unlike in its other newly acquired territories, the Filipino people waged a war of independence as US control displaced that of the Spanish, which raised the obvious question, ought the US to have recognized the Filipino people as an independent sovereign, naturally endowed with rights of nonintervention and independence? Or, as Root framed the question, ought the US to have regarded as sovereign equals a "tribe" under the leadership of a "Chinese half-breed"?[137] "Is there anything in the circumstances of the assistance which we have received from these men which entitles them to the reward of the sovereignty of the Philippines?"[138] Root's reply: "Nothing can be more preposterous than the proposition that these men were entitled to receive from us sovereignty over the entire country which we were invading."[139] Only "Oriental treachery" might convince one otherwise.[140]

Root's suggestion was that like the American Indians, presumably not only those indigenous peoples living in the US but all throughout the Americas, the Filipino people ought to have realized that they enjoyed no entitlements over territory as against the "United States."[141] It is true, Root conceded, that democracies enjoy legitimacy from the consent of the people. But "[n]othing can be more misleading," Root cautioned, "than a principle misapplied."[142] If government arises among a people capable of making "free, intelligent and efficacious decisions," then surely the government must be by and for that people.[143] But Root asserted that the "people" of the Philippines were not of this stock, and simply "incapable of self-government."[144]

To put this another way, did the US have a right to exclude (*imperium*) the Filipino people from sovereign status in the society of international legal persons? Armed with a clear-cut ideology of racial xenophobia, Root's answer was not merely that the US was justified to exclude the Filipino people from the community of sovereigns. Rather, the US was under an international legal obligation to

---

[135] Daniel Immerwahr has recently explained the term "Greater United States" to include all of those territorial possessions belonging to the US, today including Puerto Rico, Guam, the US Virgin Islands, Alaska, Hawaii, American Samoa, the Pacific outlying islands, and the Caribbean outlying lands. *See* Daniel Immerwahr: How to Hide an Empire: A History of the Greater United States 9 (2020).

[136] Aziz Rana, The Two Faces of American Freedom (2014).

[137] Root, Canton Speech, *supra* note 134, at 9.

[138] *Id.* at 11.

[139] *Id.* at 12.

[140] *Id.*

[141] *Id.*

[142] *Id.* at 15.

[143] *Id.*

[144] *Id.* at 16.

124 THE RIGHT TO EXCLUDE

do so, given the lack of racial competence rampant in the Philippines. Of course, the point here isn't to single out Root for a racist perspective on the US war in the Philippines.[145] Rather, the purpose is to illuminate a classic form of legal justification, a racial ideology in international law which was hardly restricted to a few elite lawyers.[146] Through reliance upon a burgeoning form of race science, informing both the rising tide of eugenics as well as the borders of international society, classic racial ideology explained to the world at large both the location of these conceptual boundaries, as well as the types of human beings that belonged on the inside, as well as without.

Another example of a different sort comes from the historical work of the American jurist Henry Wheaton.[147] In Wheaton's now-classic treatment, sovereigns exist in an international society defined by equal rights of self-preservation. This international society, marked with relative differences among the various regimes of Europe, was a Family in which a "primitive" form of equality reigned. But why limit equality's reign to Europe? Why ought the imperial right to exclude be exercised in this way? In Wheaton's *History of the Law of Nations in Europe and America*, the justification turned on a matter of human nature: "As I have often said, and cannot too often repeat, there is a society which includes all mankind. Within this general society is included another composed of the same race; and within that, another still, consisting of the same state."[148] As far back as in ancient Greece, Wheaton explained, "the superiority of the Hellenic race" had been apparent in the Greeks' relations with "Barbarian" others.[149] In turn, the "great European society" of the nineteenth century inherited its "community of manners" from the Teutonic race, while the whites of the Unites States were a "race of freemen."[150] As for the various "descendants" of the Barbarians, there were those "races adhering to the religious institutions of Mohammad,"[151] along with the African peoples, "doomed to servitude from time immemorial."[152] In those territories governed by the Ottoman Empire, in Asia, and in Africa, "the indelible distinctions of race and religion remain."[153] In these nonwhite realms "the wrecks

[145] Indeed, there was plenty of racism to go around. *See, e.g.,* Theodore S. Woolsey, *The Legal Aspects of Aguinaldo's Capture,* 67 OUTLOOK 855, 855 (1901). For discussion, *see* PAUL A. KRAMER, THE BLOOD OF GOVERNMENT: RACE, EMPIRE, THE UNITED STATES, AND THE PHILIPPINES (2006).

[146] Will Smiley, *Lawless Wars of Empire? The International Law of War in the Philippines, 1898–1903,* 36 LAW & HIST. REV. 511, 511 (2018).

[147] WHEATON, HISTORY, *supra* note 81, at 27 ("There is now prevalent in Europe a desire that states should be established on the basis of nationality, so that all members of the same race may be united under the same government. The existence in their present form, of the Empire in Germany, and the Kingdom of Italy, is due in some measure to this sentiment.").

[148] *Id.* at 26–27.

[149] *Id.* at 5.

[150] *Id.* at 290. *See also* JENNIFER PITTS, BOUNDARIES OF THE INTERNATIONAL: LAW AND EMPIRE 132 (2018).

[151] WHEATON, HISTORY, *supra* note 81, at 265.

[152] *Id.* at 34.

[153] *Id.* at 555.

and fragments of the ancient world" persist, arresting the natural maturation into *nation* that has so wondrously taken place in Europe and the US.[154] Beyond these racial boundaries, it was deemed appropriate to disregard any possible legal constraints in relations between the one superior race and the inferiors, between the world of nations and the world of wrecked peoples.[155]

Perhaps, however, in looking back at these past centuries of racial distinction, Wheaton saw for international law a more unifying purpose? Wheaton pleaded that in the effort to achieve a peaceful and meaningful international order, "that nations should relinquish those absurd prejudices, which have hitherto induced them to consider differences of language, race, and religion as constituting insurmountable obstacles to a more perfect union."[156] Unfortunately, it was only *within* the borders of whiteness and the Family of Nations that Wheaton begged for tolerance, for Wheaton prayed for a more perfect union "among the members of the great European family,"[157] and not among all racial subjects. That, after all, would mistake the achievements of the white races for that of the outlaw races.

The result of these racial developments in global history was that it was in error to speak of an international law that might govern the whole human race.[158] There was an international law for the white races, gathered together in Europe and the Unites States, and within this Family of Nations the rights of sovereign equality were law.[159] In the second English edition of his textbook published in 1880, Wheaton explained that "the public law, with slight exceptions, has always been, and still is, limited to the civilized and Christian people of Europe or to those of European origin."[160] Commenting on the newly adopted Geneva Convention for the Ameliorization of the Condition of the Wounded in Armies in the Field (1864),[161] and with respect only to "sovereign states existing in a state of natural independence with respect to each other," Wheaton argued that use of force by one sovereign against another was illegal insofar as the level of violence was disproportionate to the object sought.[162] The Geneva Convention sought to flesh out this principle, "endeavoring to establish rules of international law which shall make the use of their weapons as consistent with humanity as the nature of things will

[154] *Id.*
[155] *Id.*
[156] *Id.* at 268.
[157] *Id.*
[158] *Id.* at 327.
[159] *Id.* at 758
[160] WHEATON, ELEMENTS, *supra* note 101, at 16.
[161] *See* http://www.icrc.org/ihl/INTRO/120?OpenDocument.
[162] WHEATON, HISTORY, *supra* note 81, at 404–05. Looking back at the nineteenth century, many commentators have noted a total erosion of the laws of war. In this view, wartime existed in a special lacuna, unregulated and untouched by the normal time of law and politics. *See* IAN BROWNLIE, INTERNATIONAL LAW AND THE USE OF FORCE BY STATES 19 (1963) ("The next century [the nineteenth century] was still dominated by an unrestricted right of war and the recognition of conquests, qualified by the political system of the European Concert.")

126    THE RIGHT TO EXCLUDE

permit." In short, "no use of force is lawful, except so far as it is necessary."[163] That is, the use of force was unlawful in the absence of necessity so long as we are dealing with a conflict between equal sovereigns.[164] The rules fell away once the terrain shifted away from wars between sovereign states.[165]

We see a similar pattern of justification in the work of the highly influential Swiss writer Johann Kaspar Bluntschli. In his wide-ranging *Theory of the State*, first published in 1875, Bluntschli followed the Hobbesian analogy between the human being and the sovereign state: "The state is *par excellence* a person in the sense of public law. The purpose of the whole constitution is to enable the person of the State to express and realize its will ... The personality of the state is, however, only recognized by free people, and only in the civilized nation-state has it attained its full efficacy."[166] Thus, and once again, the starting point is the idea that a sovereign is likened to a rights-bearing human being in the state of nature. The purpose of law is the promotion of individual (sovereign) will. There is no form of power, religious or secular, that stands in and of itself above the sovereign's rights of "independence" and "dignity."[167]

These are the rights belonging to all states with international legal personality, that is, sovereigns within the global *demos*. But which groups of human beings are deserving of their collective will's promotion, and which are not? Which groups achieve the status of *sovereign*? On the one side, Bluntschli seemed to follow the universalism of the Vattelian mode when he suggested that, in contrast with ancient times, "the modern state recognizes the rights of man in every one ... Man has no property in man, for man is not a thing, but always a person, i.e., a subject of rights."[168] This is so because, as Wheaton had also suggested, the sovereign state is founded upon the history of human nature.[169] And what is this history of human nature? Well, this quickly takes us to the other side: "History could not begin until a

---

[163] WHEATON, HISTORY, *supra* note 81, at 405. This may sound like we're right back to Hobbes in the state of nature. And to be sure, Wheaton does seem to have thought about drawing the analogy pretty tight: "Every state has therefore a right to resort to force, as the only means of redress for injuries inflicted upon it by others, in the same manner as individuals would be entitled to that remedy were they not subject to the laws of civil society. Each state is also entitled to judge for itself, what are the nature and extent of the injuries which will justify such a means of redress." *Id.* at 349. But this is only with respect to the *jus ad bellum*. When it came to constraints on the manner of fighting, Wheaton turned to "humanity's common interests" in much the same way as Vattel. As for the concept of "necessity," it was famously re-formulated as "instant" and "overwhelming" by Daniel Webster in his exchange with Lord Ashburton during the *Caroline* incident. For early discussions, *see* J.L. Brierly, *The Shortcomings of International Law*, 5 BRIT. Y.B. INT'L L. 4 (1924); R.Y. Jennings, *The Caroline and McLeod Cases*, 32 AM. J. INT'L L. 82 (1938). A more recent summary is available in YORAM DINSTEIN, WAR, AGGRESSION, AND SELF-DEFENSE (2005).

[164] For present purposes, it is of no matter how elastic the concept of necessity might have been. The point is that the language of territorial integrity and self-defense didn't apply *at all* outside of the Family of Nations.

[165] WOOLSEY, INTRODUCTION, *supra* note 78, at 231.

[166] JOHAN CASPAR BLUNTSCHLI, THE THEORY OF THE STATE 76 (2000).

[167] *Id.* at 389.

[168] *Id.* at 58.

[169] *Id.* at 60.

higher race showed the capacity of themselves working creatively at the perfection of mankind. It begins therefore with the appearance of the white races, the children of light, who are the bearers of the history of the world."[170] These "nations of the daylight"[171] constituted that sphere of racially superior states belonging to the Family of Nations, the common name for that group of populations that enjoyed the rights and protections of international law. The fact that the white nations could be distinguished from the nonwhite was, for Bluntschli, no small matter, since the science of racial identity was the foundation for the order of things: "The diversity of races is of the highest importance for the State and for public law: for in the State men appear in an *order*, and order cannot be imagined without difference."[172]

With respect to the nature of that order, Bluntschli followed the trends of the day, explaining that "The whole history of the world bears witness to the different endowment of races, and even to the unequal capacity of the nations that have grown out of them."[173] While Bluntschli's nations of daylight possessed the full rights of international legal personality, the world's racial *xenoi*, the "children of the night,"[174] did not. Citing Arthur Gobineau, Bluntchli explained:

> Highest in the scale stands the white race of Caucasian or Iranian nations, the "nations of the daylight," as Carus calls them in opposition to the children of the night and of the twilight ... They are preeminently the nations which determine the history of the world. All the higher religions which unite man with God were first revealed among them; almost all philosophy has issued from the works of their mind. In contact with other races they have always ended by conquering them and making them their subjects. They give the impulse to all higher political development. To their intellect and to the energy of their will, we owe, under God, all the highest achievements of the human spirit.[175]

The upshot for Bluntschli was that the rights of sovereignty belonged to nations, and nations could only come into being when the constituent human materials were of the right racial sort. Nations were historical and organic, elevated into a unity through common commitments to liberal ideals.[176] As Bluntschli put it, "Not every people is capable of creating and maintaining a State, and only a people of political capacity can claim to be an independent nation ... Strictly speaking, only those peoples in which the manly qualities, understanding and courage, predominate are fully capable of creating and maintaining a national state."[177] This was the

[170] *Id.* at 55.
[171] *Id.* at 76.
[172] *Id.* at 74.
[173] *Id.* at 75.
[174] *Id.*
[175] *Id.* at 76.
[176] *Id.* at 83.
[177] *Id.* at 93.

128    THE RIGHT TO EXCLUDE

province of those *nations* of daylight. All the rest were rightsless, killable children in the dark.

The Scottish jurist, James Lorimer, is similarly representative of this pattern of argument, in which an indeterminate concept of sovereignty is given closure by way of a core of Great Powers enjoying rights of territorial integrity and self-defense barred to the backward and nonwhite peoples of the world.[178] Writing in the context of the Crimean War (1853–1856),[179] Lorimer focused on the Ottoman Empire's position vis-à-vis the Family of Nations.[180] Throughout the eighteenth and nineteenth centuries, there had been some sense among Europeans that the Ottoman Empire was fully sovereign due its long-standing civilization, but as illustrated in a series of "unequal treaties" adopted over several centuries, many thought that the Ottoman Empire was better seen as an object of European international law, rather than a rights-bearing subject.[181] But, for late-nineteenth-century jurists like Lorimer, it mattered little whether the Ottoman Empire was properly categorized as a sovereign state or not,[182] or if by some appearances it had been gifted international legal personality after the Crimean War in the Treaty of Paris of 1856.[183] What united the Family of Nations, Lorimer explained in 1883, was far deeper than legal personality.[184] The uniting factor was rather a certain kind of natural superiority enjoyed by white Europeans—the "progressive races."[185] Looking back at the Treaty of Paris, Lorimer cringed at the possibility of having mistaken the Ottomans for a civilized race: "In the case of the Turks we have had bitter experience of extending the rights of civilization to barbarians who have proved to be incapable of performing its duties, and who possibly do not even belong to the

---

[178] For an excellent review, *see* Umut Ozsu, *The Ottoman Empire, the Origins of Extraterritoriality, and International Legal Theory, in* THE OXFORD HANDBOOK OF THE THEORY OF INTERNATIONAL LAW (Florian Hoffman & Anne Orford eds., 2015).

[179] For discussion, *see* M.S. ANDERSON, THE EASTERN QUESTION: 1774–1923 114–32 (1966).

[180] *Id.*

[181] Ozsu, *supra* note 178; PITTS, *supra* note 150.

[182] For a recent treatment of Lorimer, *see Symposium on Lorimer,* 27 EUROPEAN JOURNAL OF INTERNATIONAL LAW (2016). *See also* OPPENHEIM, INTERNATIONAL LAW, *supra* note 62, at 32–33.

[183] *See, e.g.,* H. Wood, *The Treaty of Paris and Turkey's Status in International Law,* 37 AM. J. INT'L L. 262 (1943). For a contrasting view, *see* TWISS, *supra* note 84, at 91–92 ("The Porte had already abandoned its own traditions with regard to the precedence and reception of foreign ambassadors, and had in practice conformed itself to the rules established amongst the European powers in regard to a uniform mode of reception, and a uniform scale of rank and precedence for ambassadors and other diplomatic agents ... It would thus appear, that the Ottoman Porte has for all practical purposes adopted the Common Law of Europe, as the rule of intercourse with non-Mohammadan powers.").

[184] LORIMER, THE INSTITUTES OF THE LAW OF NATIONS, *supra* note 88, at 102.

[185] *Id.* For a more moderate view, *see* TWISS, *supra* note 84, at 466–67 ("[B]etween Islam and Christendom there is no common platform, even of the simplest kind ... and the foundations of Islam are to be sought for in the legends of Judaism, or in the traditions of the Arab children of the desert. Hence, although Islam has made prodigious strides since the commencement of the present century, in order to qualify herself to participate in the benefits of the European Concert of Public Law, she can only participate in those benefits ... through the channel of Conventional Law. It is from this point of view, that the maintenance of the Capitulations is as indispensable to the Mohammedan as to the Christian race.").

progressive races of mankind."[186] But the reason for excluding the Ottomans from the Family of Nations went far beyond a few bad choices on the part of the Turks.[187] Lorimer explained that the possibility of civilizing the Turks might be:

> [M]anifested in the Semitic races only in those indefinite reaches of time which Mr. Darwin has taught us to regard as the atmosphere through which we contemplate all important changes, whether material or moral. The unspeculative character of the Semitic race, which is traceable, I am told, even in their forms of speech, warns us that ethical development from the human side, in their case, can come but very slowly. The highest forms of Semitic culture have exhibited no traces of that introspective tendency which brought the philosophy of the Greeks, on its ethical side, to the very borders of Christianity.[188]

Lorimer once again constructed an international legal order separated into a series of legal classes distinguished by race.[189] At the center was the sphere of civilized humanity, followed by barbarous humanity, and finally savage humanity.[190] "To these," Lorimer wrote, "whether arising from peculiarities of race or from various stages of development in the same race, belong, *of right*, at the hands of civilized nations, three stages of recognition—plenary political recognition, partial recognition, and natural or mere human recognition."[191] Among the Great Powers and those members of the Family of Nations—"peopled by persons of European birth or descent"[192]—a standard of sovereign equality reigned in this sphere of plenary recognition. But with respect to the "non-progressive races," who were in possession of no legal rights, the "progressive races" owed no legal obligations. Members of the Family of Nations are "not bound to apply the positive law of nations to savages, or even to barbarians as such."[193] The Ottoman Empire, Lorimer

---

[186] LORIMER, THE INSTITUTES OF THE LAW OF NATIONS, *supra* note 88, at 103.

[187] WHEATON, HISTORY, *supra* note 81, at 96 ("The Turks are not a civilizing people. They are a nation of soldiers, who care little for the peaceful pursuits of trade, literature, and science, while many of their subjects, especially the Greeks, are capable of attaining to the highest forms of civilization. The result has been that the governing race in Turkey have remained nearly stationary, while many of their subjects, and all the neighboring states, have been making great progress ... The unfortunate error underlying all attempts to improve the condition of European Turkey has been to suppose that, because this country was situated in Europe, it was therefore capable of being benefited by European institutions and the introduction of European modes of thought and action. But this is not the case. The Turks and many of their subjects are Orientals, and quite different from Europeans.").

[188] *Id.* at 121.

[189] *Id.* at 101–02 ("As a political phenomenon, humanity, in its present condition, divides itself into three concentric zones or spheres—that of civilized humanity, that of barbarous humanity, and that of savage humanity ... It is with the first of these spheres alone that the international jurist has to deal ... He is not bound to apply the positive law of nations to savages, or even to barbarians as such." In distinguishing between the civilized, barbarous, and savage spheres of humanity, Lorimer explained that it would be helpful to "distinguish between the progressive and non-progressive races.").

[190] LORIMER, THE INSTITUTES OF THE LAW OF NATIONS, *supra* note 88, at 101.

[191] *Id.*

[192] *Id.* at 101–02.

[193] *Id.* at 102.

130    THE RIGHT TO EXCLUDE

concluded, had been an object of the Great Powers in the Crimean War, and not an entity which could have meaningfully participated in the terms of the Treaty of Paris. The fulfillment of the interests of the Great Powers represented, in effect, the fulfillment of Ottoman interests. The Ottomans were, after all, barbarians.

Back in the US, and writing a few decades earlier in 1844, the same pattern of ideological justification issued from the American lawyer Caleb Cushing's racialized attempt to exclude China from the Family of Nations.[194] Following on the heels of the British opening of Chinese ports after the first Opium War (1839–1842),[195] Cushing was set on winning the same concessions for the US, and in so doing, established a treaty of extraterritorial jurisdiction for US merchants travelling in China.[196] Cushing admitted that at first blush, Chinese sovereignty might be violated by a demand to grant legal immunity for all Americans in China.[197] China, perhaps, was a member of the Family of Nations though surely not among the circle of Great Powers? Tempting, but surely mistaken.[198] Cushing argued that while China certainly possessed a "civilization," just as the Ottoman Empire did, this was still not enough to grant China entrance to the Family of Nations.[199] China may have had civilization, but civilization was only a symptom, and Cushing was after the cause. Chinese civilization was the wrong sort of civilization, *because* the Chinese were a race of "barbarians."[200]

Using the shorthand of "Christendom," Cushing explained that it would be unlawful to subject Americans to Chinese law since China failed to protect individual rights and promote other tell-tale signs of "true" civilization: a postal system, stage coaches, steamboats, and a willingness to acknowledge "the authority of certain maxims and usages received among them by common consent."[201] But could it be possible that China might have the same idea, and wish to immunize its own subjects from US law? In Cushing's mind, such a development was inconceivable.[202] It would be a violation of international law to expose Americans in China to local jurisdiction, since Chinese law was of an intellectually inferior kind. But there would be no reason to expect US law to not govern Chinese or any other

---

[194] Caleb Cushing's Abstract and Discussion of the Treaty of Wanghia, January 24, 1845.

[195] *See, e.g.*, Teemu Ruskola, *Canton is not Boston*, 57 Am. Q. 859 (2005).

[196] For discussion, *see* ARTHUR NUSSBAUM, A CONCISE HISTORY OF THE LAW OF NATIONS 194–95 (1954).

[197] Cushing, *supra* note 194, at 11.

[198] *Id.*

[199] *Id.*

[200] *Id.*

[201] *Id.* at 12.

[202] *Id.* at 9–10. According to Nussbaum, "China's resistance to contacts with foreign powers took the form of arrogance and humiliating demands; superiority of Chinese civilization, or rather non-existence of any other, was asserted; foreign negotiators were required to perform before the Emperor or his representative a definite number of ceremonial prostrations (kowtows), which, in connection with the expected gifts and tributes, were considered by the Chinese as evidence of suzerainty. It was only in the nineteenth century that the stubborn attitude of the Chinese was broken." *See* NUSSBAUM, *supra* note 196, at 123.

nationals travelling in US territory, since US law was the product of a superior race.[203] Equal terms only made sense when international lawyers were dealing with what they understood to be equal peoples.[204] And for the "Mohammadan" and "pagan" races of China, Cushing explained, they were dominated by "phrenzied bigotry" and "barbarism."[205] The Chinese people were simply ill-equipped to govern disputes involving Americans; the US, in contrast, represented the model from which the Chinese should be learning.[206] As Cushing flatly put it, "I do not admit as my equals either the red man of America, or the yellow man of Asia, or the black man of Africa."[207]

To sum up, international law's classic liberal style of racial ideology functions along the following lines. Nineteenth-century international lawyers like Root, Alvarez, Wheaton, Bluntchli, Lorimer, and Cushing, along with so many (but certainly not all) of their contemporaries, approached the concept of sovereign equality from a basically Hobbesian-Vattelian premise known as the domestic analogy: Like human beings in a state of nature, all sovereigns enjoy equal rights of *dominium* (nonintervention and self-determination), which is to say that all sovereigns possess a right to exclude the world from its internal affairs and life-decisions. At the same time, however, international law's boundary problem posed questions about how to determine the society of international persons possessing these rights of *dominium*. This limiting effort lacked an obvious source of justification, given the apparently universal nature of sovereignty itself, and the gap was quickly filled with a new racial ideology. As the formalist argument went, if it was *natural* for the peoples of the world to rank in empirically guaranteed systems of racial development and classification, then it would be *lawful* for those systems to serve as means for limiting the boundaries of international society. Indeed, it would be *illiberal* to grant the lower forms of humanity the fullest rights of sovereign states. Classic racial ideology secures a harmonious result to an apparently insurmountable problem for classic liberals, since there is no hypocrisy in a "liberal nation" colonizing, enslaving, raping, exploiting—so long, that is, everyone retained faith in the natural science of racial xenophobia—a global science of racial subjection, generating a separation between rights-bearing bodies, and the bare life of the racial *xenoi*. The stage was set for international law's empire, with its nations of daylight and children of the night.

It is sometimes a commonplace to treat the foregoing as all there really is to the history of racism in international law. Once we get past World War I, so the story goes, international law becomes increasingly egalitarian and antiracist. That is true, to an extent. But if the treatment of international law's racial ideology were

---

[203] Cushing, *supra* note 194, at 9–10.
[204] *Id.*
[205] *Id.* at 11.
[206] *Id.*
[207] 2 CLAUDE FEUSS, THE LIFE OF CALEB CUSHING 230–31 (1923).

## 132 THE RIGHT TO EXCLUDE

to end with a statement of its classic phase, the shifting patterns of argument found among the moderns might very well come off as the progressive denouement of an ugly period in international legal history. As I argue in Part II, however, it is precisely in the context of a receding *imperium* that a newly racialized *dominium* came into view. Or, to put that another way, it was the arrival of a more inclusive racial ideology that helped transform international law in the middle decades of the twentieth century, some for the good, some for the not-so-good.

I call this more inclusive articulation, international law's *modern* racial ideology. At the level of the law of sovereigns, race slowly receded as a means for excluding other peoples from the realm of international legal personality. But while the gradual eclipse of racialized *imperium* actively foregrounded the prohibitive work of the antidiscrimination principle, the racialization of *dominium* was now underway. Which is to say that I am fully sympathetic with the concern that the study of racial exclusion might lead to a dead end, especially if we consider classic racial ideology, the imperial right to exclude, and international law's boundary problem as the full measure of its race problem. International law's encounter with classic racial ideology was, however, only the beginning of an affair in which we are still very much entangled. In the pages that follow, we trace how that affair transformed.

# PART II
# MODERN RACIAL IDEOLOGY IN INTERNATIONAL LEGAL THOUGHT

# 4

# Modern Racial Ideology as Naturalizing Juridical Science

This classic liberal style of racial ideology dominated international legal thought throughout much of the nineteenth century and into the early decades of the twentieth. By that time, however, much was changing in international law, along with its racial ideology. In contrast with its classic sibling, international law's *modern* racial ideology would interpret the legal concept of sovereignty as universal, justify its expanding application by the lights of a social science understanding of racial classification, and gently propose a logic of inclusion. It would be a mistake, however, to understand the arrival of modern racial ideology as replacing the classic style. The relation between the two is far more complex than ideology by substitution. First, ideologies are never mutually exclusive in operation, even when their terms are irreconcilable. Indeed, it was common then, and it is increasingly the case today, to find modern arguments sitting side-by-side with classic arguments, no matter the incoherence. Second, modern racial ideology's colonization of international legal thought advanced unevenly. Most visibly, modern racial ideology first emerged in the context of *imperium*, the space of international law's boundary problem. In doing so, however, this visibility of the modern logic of inclusion distracted attention away from racial ideology's simultaneous colonization of another borderland, that between members of a national community and outsiders. That is, the arrival of a logic of inclusion at the level of international society moved in tandem with the arrival of a new racialization of territorial borders. Modern racial ideology, as a result, gives with one hand while it takes with the other, beginning a process of deracializing *imperium* while allowing for classic forms of racial development to dig in at the space of *dominium*.

The morphing from a classic style of racial ideology to the modern is marked by three transformations, discussed here and in Chapters 5 and 6. One transformation in the morphing from classic racial ideology to the modern concerned the new correlation between racial justice and decolonization. At the level of *imperium*, modern racial ideology's logic of inclusion came to offer a more expansive view of the global *demos*. Race lost pride of place as an answer to international law's boundary problem, and instead the conversation eventually—though briefly—became about the right of *imperium* as a key to global antiracism. For if the right of *imperium* in classic racial ideology was a form of exclusion, in decolonization the sovereign's right to write the rules of a "New International Economic Order" was

---

*The Right to Exclude.* Justin Desautels-Stein, Oxford University Press. © Justin Desautels-Stein 2023.
DOI: 10.1093/oso/9780198862161.003.0005

136   THE RIGHT TO EXCLUDE

also the means for achieving racial justice. On the other hand, anticolonial thinkers believed that the right of *dominium* was similarly essential to antiracist strategy just as well. In this context, antiracism meant that once peoples of color achieved independence, these new sovereigns consequently enjoyed the rights of nonintervention and self-determination—and it is was through the exercise of these rights of exclusion that racial justice would be achieved on a global scale. This is the story of Chapter 6.

Another transformation involves the displacement of the imperial right of boundary-making from the plane of sovereigns vs. *peoples* to the plane of sovereign vs. *individuals*. This is the shift from a concern with policing the imperial borders of the Family of Nations to the territorial borders of the nation-state. That is, while the racialized right of *imperium* was losing steam as an answer to international law's boundary problem, it was reappearing as the right of *dominium* and an answer to the nation-state's migration problem. In the United States (US), Australia, Canada, South Africa, and elsewhere, this displacement occurred during the last decades of the nineteenth century and the first decades of the twentieth. Peaking in the 1920s, domestic immigration laws would enact regimes of racial hierarchy ideologically consistent with the modes of justification examined in Chapter 3's discussion of classic racial ideology. The result was the naturalization of the sovereign's territorial right to exclude. These developments are the topic of Chapter 5.

If two of the transformations in the morphing in international law from a classic style of racial ideology to a modern one included the racialization of *dominium* on the one side and the deracialization of *imperium* on the other, a third phase governing each of the other two was the development of a new form of naturalizing juridical science called legal functionalism. Inspired by currents of thought moving through Europe, especially those of the German philosopher Rudolph von Jhering and the French jurist Francois Geny, legal formalism was increasingly sidelined in favor of a view of international law that was more "realistic," "effective," and "functional." Section I of this chapter surveys the rise of this new form of legal ideology in the exemplary works of Jhering and Geny. The discussion then moves on to the influence of functionalism in international legal thought. The impact was dramatic, and in the course of the discussion I only touch upon a couple of the most relevant developments. First, functionalism opened the door to thinking about non-state actors as having international legal personality. This would come to include cognizability for the rights of international organizations, national groups, and eventually, individual human beings. This "unbundling" of the sovereign tie to international legal personality would prove crucial as a baseline condition for the new modern racial ideology. Second, functionalism counseled in favor of discarding natural law and abstract logic as orienting discourses for the international legal order. This included a rejection of the idea that certain peoples could never be truly sovereign, or a part of the international community, on the basis of inferior racial identity. According to the new logic of inclusion, excluding peoples from the international legal order on the basis of race was simply "bad science." What was needed was a savvy international law that understood the real problems of the international world, and answered those problems with legal solutions sourced in the social sciences. The key to implementing such solutions was the rise of the international institution. If these new international institutions, like the League of Nations and its successor the United Nations (UN), would harness the power of social science to meet the needs of international society, international law would finally matter.

To restate, modern racial ideology is functionalist. Functionalism is a form of naturalizing juridical science which discards the formalist effort to match legal rules and conclusions with *natural* science, and replaces it with an effort to match legal rules and conclusions with the dictates of *social* science. It is a legal ideology of purpose and realism. Modern racial ideology is also committed to a logic of inclusion, which manifests separately in the domains of *imperium* and *dominium*. At the level of *imperium*, and in the context of decolonization, racial categories increasingly lost their capacity to solve international law's boundary problem, as "Third World" peoples formerly excluded from international society very slowly made their way in. At the level of *dominium*, and in the context of global migration, however, sovereigns discover in racial ideology an answer to national border problems, initially relying upon eugenics as a justification for racialized exclusion. This racialization of *dominium*, however, was still seen as facially in keeping with the logic of inclusion since every sovereign, no matter their racial identity, should enjoy the right to exclude the world from their territory.

Looking ahead to the survey of postracial ideology in Part III of the book, modern racial ideology's logic of inclusion did eventually seep into the sovereign's right of *dominium*, emptying immigration controls of racial content in a way similar to what it had done to the right of *imperium* earlier in the century. By the 1950s and 1960s, immigration law increasingly conformed to the antidiscrimination principle and the attendant notion of colorblindness that later shaped much of US civil rights law, as well as a nascent international human rights law.[1] A few decades later, the concept of self-determination—so central to the decolonization movement—was similarly engulfed by the antidiscrimination principle and the human rights frame. Further, by the time that the sovereign's right to exclude went colorblind, functionalism was increasingly sidelined by a new mode of naturalizing juridical science called neoformalism. We will see in this moment when the rights of *imperium* and *dominium* are governed by a neoformalist antidiscrimination principle, how international law's structure of racial ideology hits a threshold, ready to tip into the postracial.

---

[1] ERIKA LEE, AMERICA FOR AMERICANS: A HISTORY OF XENOPHOBIA IN THE UNITED STATES 225 (2019).

138    THE RIGHT TO EXCLUDE

Before we can get to the transformation of modern racial ideology into the pragmatist structure of postracial xenophobia, however, we must turn first to the transformation of the classic into the modern. And to do that, we begin with functionalism.

## I  THE RISE OF LEGAL FUNCTIONALISM

The combined effects of the two world wars and the economic catastrophes of the period in-between helped consolidate a consensus about the appropriate route for political, social, and legal change.[2] This consensus was two-sided. On the one hand, there developed a particular view about how to define the specter of "ideology." On the other hand, there emerged a program for what to do after ideology had been properly abandoned.

To the first hand, first. In the postwar years of the US, there was the increasingly popular idea among intellectuals that the hortatory powers of the grand ideologies, writ large, had gone out of fashion. On this view, an ideology was considered something like a broad blueprint for social engineering, a set of interconnected ideas that necessarily led to particular forms of political action.[3] This purportedly neutral construction of ideology could manifest in any political program, left, right, and center.[4] An ideology, on this view, was like the dinosaur—Classic Liberalism, Capitalism, Socialism, Fascism, Anarchism—these were the sorts of master narratives that had once dominated the political imagination, but whose time had come and gone.[5] These ideologies, these programmatic and totalizing if not totalitarian visions for political and social action, had characteristically taken the form of rigid formulas and doctrinaire plans, and in the context of this postwar consensus, grand ideologies were disfavored for exactly this reason.

By the 1950s and 1960s, many American scholars were suggesting that, rather than rely on totalizing ideologies, what was needed instead were more realistic, more flexible, more functional, more empirical assessments of real people's needs. And it was this latter prescription for a more *realistic* understanding of society that reflects the second side of the postwar consensus. The dogma of ideology, in this consensus view, stood in poor contrast against the rich and supple postures of interdisciplinary expertise. Or to put that another way, whereas totalizing ideologies had been the currency of the long nineteenth century, a postwar *End of Ideology*

---

[2] *See* HOWARD BRICK, TRANSCENDING CAPITALISM: VISIONS OF A NEW SOCIETY IN MODERN AMERICAN THOUGHT (2015); RAYMOND ARON, THE OPIUM OF THE INTELLECTUALS (1955); Michael Polanyi, *On Liberalism and Liberty*, 4 ENCOUNTER 29 (1955).

[3] DANIEL BELL, THE END OF IDEOLOGY 402 (1962).

[4] MARTIN SELIGER, IDEOLOGY AND POLITICS (1976).

[5] FELIKS GROSS, EUROPEAN IDEOLOGIES: A SURVEY OF TWENTIETH CENTURY POLITICAL IDEAS (1948).

RACIAL IDEOLOGY AND FUNCTIONALISM   139

program suggested a turn to real, material needs and interests.[6] What had gone wrong? Ideology in the sense of grand political narrative. What to do? Pursue a program grounded in the empirical expertise of the social sciences that rejected ideological dogma. Here, ideology comes to be defined precisely as the opposite of a naturalizing empiricism.[7]

For sociologists associated with the "End of Ideology" program like Daniel Bell, blueprint ideology was a problem less deserving of a solution than of just being avoided altogether. As Bell explained it, nineteenth-century visions of capitalism simply failed to meet the needs of modern industrial society.[8] Here had been the:

> [I]mage of capitalism in the early forties: the capitalist was an old miser sitting on his pile of sterile bullion, which weighed down the economy. Since *he* found it impossible to inject the money into an economy which needed it, if that economy was to provide jobs and the standard of living it was technologically capable of producing, the government would have to force him to disgorge it—or tax it away and spend it on useful projects.[9]

The traditional ideological emphasis on private property and freedom of contract as the engines for *laissez-faire*, Bell assured, had finally lapsed. The ideology of traditional capitalism was, here in the middle of the twentieth century, exhausted.[10]

If so, perhaps, the ideology of socialism was the preferred alternative? Nope. Like the doctrinaire vision of *laissez-faire* capitalism, the doctrinaire ideology of a socialist world order was also too disconnected from the real world of social needs and interests. "The socialist movement," Bell explained:

> [B]y the way in which it rejected the capitalist order as a whole, could not relate itself to the specific problems of social action in the here-and-now, give-and-take political world. In sum, it was trapped by the unhappy problem of living *in* but not *of* the world ... It could never resolve, but only straddle, the basic issue of either accepting capitalist society and seeking to transform it from within, as the labor movement did, or becoming the sworn enemy of that society, like the Communists. A religious movement can split its allegiances and (like Lutheranism) live *in* but not *of* the world ... a political movement cannot.[11]

---

[6] Howard Brick, *The End of Ideology Thesis*, in THE OXFORD HANDBOOK OF POLITICAL IDEOLOGIES (Michael Freeden & Marc Steers eds., 2013).
[7] *See, e.g.*, GEORGES CANGUILHEM, A VITAL RATIONALIST: SELECTED WRITINGS (2000); BRUNO LATOUR, WE HAVE NEVER BEEN MODERN (1993).
[8] BELL, *supra* note 50, at 85.
[9] *Id.* at 80.
[10] *Id.*
[11] *Id.* at 278–79.

140   THE RIGHT TO EXCLUDE

All in all, Bell claimed in what came to be the call-sign of the new post-ideological consensus, the "End of Ideology" had arrived.[12] In its place would come a social-democratic compromise, a mixed economy, the Welfare state, decentralized power, and above all, an understanding of the necessity of an anti-ideological, utterly *realistic* view of politics, the market, and civil society.[13] The program for political science, economics, and sociology was up and running.[14] But what of law? Ought judges, lawyers, and legal theorists make a similar turn?[15] If so, what would the "End of Ideology" mean for the postwar world of law? Interestingly, in Europe an examination of the legal context for these questions was already well under way, and had been for decades.[16]

In Chapter 1, we saw how, in the eighteenth century, thinkers like Pufendorf and Vattel developed a system of sovereign equality on the basis of Hobbes' theory of individual right. While Hobbes' influence was real enough, another powerful influence on Vattel was the German philosopher Christian Wolff. Indeed, much of Vattel's particular understanding of sovereign right and obligation traced to Wolff's global philosophy of natural law. Vattel's intervention was precisely in the effort to harden that natural vision with a proto-positivist understanding of the international legal order. The result was the bedrock against which a classical form of racial ideology would emerge.

International lawyers like Vattel, however, were not the only thinkers looking to rebel against Wolff's naturalism. Wolff's philosophy, in some ways more akin with medieval Scholastic efforts than Hobbesian ones, began with a study of human nature and proceeded to find in that nature a set of universal fixtures. From these universals Wolff believed he could logically deduce increasingly particular rules of international behavior. The result, for Wolff and his followers, was a comprehensive, gapless, enduring system of natural rules for the international world. Among the major critics of this German approach was Immanuel Kant. It is beyond the scope of our interest here to follow Kant's rationalist critique of natural law, but suffice it to say that after Kantian philosophy took flight, there emerged a need to develop a post-Wolffian approach to a more "serious," and truly positivist, German legal science. In the years following the French Revolution and the Napoleonic Wars, that need was filled by the work of Friedrich Carl von Savigny.[17]

---

[12] *See, e.g.*, SEYMOUR MARTIN LIPSET, POLITICAL MAN 404–05 (1960)

[13] *Id.* at 402.

[14] *See* DOROTHY ROSS, THE ORIGINS OF AMERICAN SOCIAL SCIENCE (1990).

[15] *See* David Trubek, *Toward a Social Theory of Law: An Essay on the Study of Law and Development*, 82 YALE L.J. 1 (1972).

[16] STEPHEN STEINBERG, TURNING BACK: THE RETREAT FROM RACIAL JUSTICE IN AMERICAN THOUGHT AND POLICY (1995); GUNNAR MYRDAL, AN AMERICAN DILEMMA: THE NEGRO PROBLEM AND MODERN DEMOCRACY (1962).

[17] Savigny was, of course, hardly alone. *See* Mathias Reimann, *The Historical School Against Codification: Savigny, Carter, and the Defeat of the New York Civil Code*, 37 AM. J. COMP. L. 95 (1989); M. JOHN, POLITICS AND LAW IN NINETEENTH CENTURY GERMANY (1989).

Savigny's so-called historical school of German legal science rested, as the name implies, on a view of the historical nature of law. Savigny believed that a legal system's roots were in the core customs, beliefs, and attitudes of a people. These customs were not the stuff of rational debate; they were characteristics defining the very essence of a people, of what later came to be called the *volkgeist*, the spirit of the community. A nation's legal system was therefore derived from the essence of racial subjection, and not as Wolff had suggested, from a universal vision of human nature. Over time, however, the racial essence of a people, or their "genius," would evolve and develop into a system of legal customs. As a nation's legal system matured organically over time, lawyers and judges would increasingly systematize the people's custom.

In other words, for Savigny a nation's system of positive law had to be analyzed as national history. The purpose was not for jurists to become historians; it was for jurists to become legal scientists, surveying the history of a people in order to build a comprehensive system of legal concepts immanent in the people's spirit. Although the provenance of the concepts was thoroughly racial, the contemporary relation between legal concepts was—for Savigny—supremely rational. Born in the sweat and blood of folk history, these customs were destined for transformations in legal science: a heaven of legal concepts and logical operations, interlocking in pure, rational harmony. In Savigny's case, the nascent nation of Germany's *volkgeist* was traceable to Rome, linking ancient Roman law to German legal science though a bond that was at once as historically organic as it was logically systematic.

In a nutshell, this was the very formal mode of legal science reigning in Germany throughout much of the nineteenth century.[18] And it is this "classic" mode of legal science which set the scene for the arrival of a new and contrasting "modern" mode of legal science: functionalism. Functionalist legal science was hardly a German affair; it spread across Europe and into the US, and across the globe, eventually finding its way to the legal realists and scholars like Daniel Bell.[19] In these early moments, however, and on the continent, at the epicenter of the revolt were the German Rudolph von Jhering and the French Francois Geny.[20]

Jhering was trained in the traditions of Savigny and the historical school of legal science, and in the first half of his career Jhering continued the work of studying the abstractions of Roman law as the true source of the German spirit. In the years before the Franco-Prussian war, however, Jhering's scholarship took a sharp turn

---

[18] *See* Mathias Reimann, *Historical Jurisprudence, in* THE OXFORD HANDBOOK OF LEGAL HISTORY (Markus Dubber & Christopher Tomlins eds., 2018).

[19] On the "spread," *see* ARNULF BECKER LORCA, MESTIZO INTERNATIONAL LAW (2014).

[20] William Seagle, *Rudolf von Jhering: Or Law as a Means to an End*, 13 U. CHI. L. REV. 71 (1945); Mathias Reimann, *Nineteenth Century German Legal Science*, 31 B.C. L. REV. 837 (1990); James E. Herget & Stephen Wallace, *The German Free Law Movement as the Source of American Legal Realism*, 73 VA. L. REV. 399 (1987); Neil Duxbury, *Jhering's Philosophy of Authority*, 27 OXFORD J. LEG. STUD. 23 (2007).

142    THE RIGHT TO EXCLUDE

against his former masters.[21] By the 1870s and 1880s, Jhering had published what would become a foundational text for a new mode of legal science, his *Law as a Means to an End*.[22] In outright opposition with the conceptual abstractions of the Historical School, Jhering argued that law was no heaven of legal concepts, but a site of ongoing and constant struggle. The content of individual right in any given place was only and always a frozen snapshot of a battle in time; a battle over whatever the contestants believed to be law's end. As Jhering put it, "Everything found on the ground of law was called into life by a purpose, and exists to realize some purpose ... It is a matter of science, in the history of the formation of law as well as in the formation of the earth's crust, to reconstruct the actual processes, and the means are found in the idea of purpose."[23]

Indeed, whereas classical legal science saw law as a racial essence crystallized in logical form, what was becoming modern legal science saw law as a way of serving certain purposes, and of reconciling competing visions of those purposes. The German fascination with deduction and derivation from Roman legal concepts was more than a wild goose chase—it was a mystifyingly deadening conservatism. In one of Jhering's last publications, he satirized the classical view of the legal concept in the following:

> They are absolute truths-they have been from time immemorial-they will be eternally. To ask about reality and to ask why is no better than asking why two times two are four. It is four. With this IS, everything is said. There is no reason for it. Just so is the case with the concepts. They are based on absolute truths in themselves. There is no reason for them. The only thing incumbent upon the thinking intellect with respect to the concepts is to become engrossed in them with complete, unreserved devotion and to bring about the understanding of the depth of content locked up inside them. What can be brought to light in this way is truth, and as every truth, it is entitled to absolute respect ... Established on the unshakable principle of theory, liberated from every consideration of practical life, like the naturalist who seeks to penetrate the mysteries of nature, the legal investigator has no other goal than to unlock the wondrous mysteries of the world of law and to expose the delicate blood vessels of the logical organism of the law. And it is astonishing what he achieves simply with the assistance of logical thought-the most elegant filigree work, true miracles of human ingenuity, monuments to nineteenth century brain power, which, like those of the scholastics, still elicit the admiration of remote generations and will stimulate imitation. However, all this has only been possible since theory has been completely emancipated from

---

[21] Jhering's functionalist turn began with the publication of six letters published in a German law journal between 1860 and 1866.

[22] RUDOLPH VON JHERING, LAW AS A MEANS TO AN END (1913) (1873).

[23] *Id.* at 330.

practice and has finally become independent. For the condition of this free dialectical, reative activity is the prevention of every contact with practical life, which exerts the same pernicious influence on theoreticians that in the judgment of an expert, war exerts on soldiers.[24]

For Jhering, the cure was to rid the jurist of the fantasy that this heaven of legal concepts was a meaningful and productive locus for work, as if jurists were like mathematicians, zoologists, or theologians.[25] What was needed was a view of law's practical reality, its life in the real world, law's "social mechanics." "This is," said Jhering, "the picture of society as life presents it daily to our eyes. Thousands of rollers, wheels, knives, as in a mighty machine, move restlessly, some in one direction, some in another, apparently quite independent of one another as if they existed only for themselves, nay in apparent conflict, as if they wanted mutually to annihilate each other—and yet all work ultimately together harmoniously."[26] The vehicle for this harmonization—the ultimate source of compulsion in the social mechanism—was the law of the state.[27]

The idea that law harmoniously realizes social purpose seems at odds, however, with the other basic plank in Jhering's functionalism. And this is the idea that social purposes are always changing, and that law is a constant *struggle* for and between warring purposes. As Jhering further observed:

> The standard of law is not the absolute one of truth, but the relative one of purpose. Hence it follows that the content of law not only *may* but *must* be infinitely various. As the physician does not prescribe the same medicine to all sick people, but fits his prescription to the condition of the patient, so the law cannot always make the same regulations, it must likewise adapt them to the conditions of the people, to their degree of civilization, to the needs of the time ... A universal law for all nations and times stands on the same line with a universal remedy for all sick people. It is the long sought for philosopher's stone, for which in reality not philosophers but only the fools can afford to search.[28]

It would seem, then, that as the new modern legal science was emerging it quickly found itself in a pickle. On the one side Jhering taught to see law as a servant of social need, ever-ready for adaptation to the changing and diverse purposes of various peoples in different times. Here, the judge begins to look very much like the legislator, and the wall between law and politics seems to fade. On the other side,

---

[24] Rudolph von Jhering, *In the Heaven for Legal Concepts: A Fantasy*, 58 TEMPLE L.Q. 799, 825 (1985).
[25] FRANCOIS GENY, METHOD OF INTERPRETATION AND SOURCES OF PRIVATE POSITIVE LAW 60–81 (1963).
[26] JHERING, LAW AS A MEANS TO AN END, *supra* note 22, at 71–72.
[27] *Id.* at 230–31.
[28] *Id.* at 328.

144    THE RIGHT TO EXCLUDE

however, Jhering was emphatic about law's harmony, about how the much-needed freedom of the judge to move away from codes and legal concepts was *not* a descent into subjectivism and chaos. What is the basis for law's harmony, for calling this new approach a form of *legal science*, and not just politics by other means?

Let us turn here to one of Jhering's most influential disciples, the French jurist Francois Geny.[29] In 1899, Geny published his classic *Method of Interpretation and Sources of Private Positive Law*.[30] Geny largely followed Jhering in proposing a purposive or functional approach to law, rather than a strictly formalist approach to statutes and legal concepts. It was not, however, that the functionalist approach would displace statutory and conceptual analysis entirely. It was simply that thinkers like Jhering and Geny had concluded that the formal sources of law were hardly capable of resolving every kind of contemporary dispute that might arise. There were gaps in statutes that couldn't be ignored, ambiguities in legislative texts that proved immune to exegesis, and a dramatic distance between the real needs of contemporary society and the chimerical distinctions of ancient Roman concepts like *dominium* and *imperium*. To be sure, when a statute, a live custom, or a meaningful analogy helpfully governed a dispute, the jurist should begin with these formal sources.[31] But all too often, they didn't.

When the jurist found that the formal sources had run out, what would the functionalist mode of legal science suggest in their place? What should he do? As controversial as it sounds, Geny suggested that the jurist begin with an equivalence between judicial decision and legislative act. In both contexts, the actor governs in the names of justice and welfare. Unlike the politician, however, Geny explained that the jurist "eliminate as much as possible any personal influence or influence related to the specific case, and base his decision on objective elements."[32] But how could this be done? How to keep law from dissolving into politics, once the "mathematical precision" of the classical mode had been abandoned?[33] As Geny said, "I am aware in advance that the results which my point of departure predetermines will completely lack any dogmatic tendencies and the quasi-mathematical rigidity which the traditional method *seems* to have."[34]

---

[29] *See* Jean-Pascal Chazal, *Leon Duguit and Francois Geny, Controversy on the Renovation of Legal Science*, 65 Revue Interdisciplinaire d'études Juridiques 85 (2010).

[30] *See, e.g.*, Wolfgang Friedman, *Legal Philosophy and Judicial Lawmaking*, 61 Colum. L. Rev. 821 (1961).

[31] Geny, *supra* note 25, at 399 ("Whenever the statute or the custom are silent or insufficient, the activity of the courts must change in nature: beginning with the interpretation of human will and intent, it becomes the interpretation of that complex nature of things which conditions all human relations. From then on, it is not enough for the lawyer to know how to infer the binding rule from an obscure or ambiguous statutory formula. If this source fails, he must know how to address himself to a higher level and to draw directly on the great social source where the statute itself finds its more secure inspiration. But this common social source can reveal itself to him objectively only with the help of social sciences, each of which this becomes an auxiliary of legal interpretation.").

[32] *Id.* at 355.

[33] *Id.* at 148.

[34] *Id.* at 142.

The jurist ought to freely search the political and social landscape for ways to resolve the dispute, but this "free search," Geny advised, must be constrained by the techniques of science.[35] "Within the sphere of free search, legal method should be predominantly concerned with discovering autonomously, without support by formal sources, the objective elements which will determine all the rules required by legal practice."[36] As Jhering too had believed, once the formal sources had run out, the jurist was tasked with developing an understanding of law's purpose, its various functions.[37] Once these functions were identified, the jurist could then search out how the rules served larger social needs. The functions of rules ought, as a consequence, be shaped in ways that realized these needs as they changed in context. In other words, the jurist must adapt law to changing conditions, always with an eye on law's function and its service to social need. But now we find ourselves back at the question we'd posed for Jhering: How can this search be objective and "satisfy the needs of life without any possible reproach of arbitrariness"?[38] The key here is the phrase, "the needs of life," and how that phrase connects to "the nature of things." The nature of things, and the needs of life, were most certainly *not* the province of natural law or human nature, in either the register of Wolff's philosophy or Savigny's historical transcendentalism.[39] The key to understanding the nature of things and the needs of life was a new and intimate relationship between jurisprudence and social science.

At the turn of the twentieth century, Geny believed that the social sciences had much to offer, even if they had yet to achieve a certain level of maturity. It was in these growing social sciences that law could understand both its role in the larger society, and the changing conditions that generated an evolving sense of the "needs of life." Geny explained that "the judicial practice, in all its manifestations, has the duty to inquire into the social organization of which it is itself only one element ... it must look at all the elements of contemporary culture and civilization inasmuch as they reveal a state of order and equilibrium within which the main contemporaneous legal needs originate."[40] "If we are to penetrate to the very foundations of the nature of things, and open to the judicial practice a broader and objectively free field of inquiry" we must go beyond appearances and general tendencies. "We must address ourselves to social sciences, in which we have both the highest and the most practical instrument, and draw from them the essential pattern permitting us to order pertinent human relations in detail for the purpose of legal interpretation."[41]

---

[35] "[It is a] free search, because it is outside the reach of any positive authority; objective search, because it can be solidly based only upon objective elements which systematic-scientific jurisprudence alone can reveal." *Id.* at 355.

[36] *Id.*

[37] "[The jurist] ought to scrutinize the needs that result from the nature of the matters and the conditions of life in all cases where he is not restricted by [statutes or custom]." *Id.* at 142.

[38] *Id.* at 356.

[39] *Id.* at 365–67.

[40] *Id.* at 393.

[41] *Id.* at 394.

146    THE RIGHT TO EXCLUDE

This leads us to sociology, psychology, political theory, political economy, and history.[42] This also leads us away from a static view of statute and decision, and toward a "detailed study of our contemporary living law,"[43] which is the full gamut of the legal process.

> All of this should be considered and thoroughly searched with a view of finding in the facts of legal practice the elements of harmony which positive law has the mission to realize. Once this harmony is sensed or discovered, the norms will follow automatically. They must not be articulated in a conceptual and ideal form, in which they would be powerless to direct the operation of positive law. Rather we should draw from them objective realities, carefully defined and analyzed, and true principles which express ethical, social, political, and economic needs and which should dominate any legal system concerned with its proper objective.[44]

We can only find the "necessary objective support" in "the nature of the subject matter of its inquiry and in a logical systematization which makes it fruitful and develops it."[45] Systematizing is not logic! Systematizing is about technique—"legal technique, as it sets out the characteristic facts susceptible of legal consequences and defines these consequences, orders the actual facts of social life into general schemes, if not hierarchical categories, where these facts find their place and shape."[46] It is the jurist's task "to fortify the system by an ingenious systematization of its parts and to facilitate its function by an application constantly adapted to the purpose."[47] The "law of their harmony" resides outside and above the facts.[48]

We now have the basic elements of legal functionalism: a view of law's purpose as the servant of social need, as understood in the matrix of social science. When functionalism is understood in the context of liberal legal thought, we arrive at the modern mode of naturalizing juridical science. As Geny explained, "In our present social organization, each of these three spheres is governed by a general and essential principle which is in harmony with its proper objective, of which it is merely a development ... These principles can simply be formulated as (1) the principle of private autonomy; (2) the principle of public order and higher interest; (3) the principle of balancing the private interests. These three principles, which are combined and interwoven in practice, animate our whole legal system."[49] Indeed, it is with the arrival of a functionalist version of Geny's "third principle," that effort to balance the antinomies between the demands of private autonomy and public order,

[42] *Id.* at 395–96.
[43] *Id.* at 397.
[44] *Id.* at 398.
[45] *Id.* at 357.
[46] *Id.* at 358–59.
[47] *Id.* at 359.
[48] *Id.* at 362
[49] *Id.* at 404.

that functionalism performs as naturalizing juridical science. It is simply that the "nature of things" is no longer an artifact of natural law or a frozen image of human nature. And it is no longer the natural sciences to which the realm of jurisprudence is meant to turn for instruction. The "nature of things" is now the social, wild and complex. And "science" is now the science of that social. Mathematics, physics, physiology, zoology, and the like, have been traded in for sociology, economics, and political science. It is in these disciplines that the jurist may find an objective guide toward the "right" rules, and "the law of their harmony."

As we saw in Chapter 3, naturalizing juridical science had a special role to play in providing justification for a heightened restriction on the exercise of the sovereign's imperial right to exclude. Only those racially superior sovereigns enjoyed the right as members of the Family of Nations. This was the work of a classic style of racial ideology, explaining and guaranteeing racial exclusion in the register of natural science. We are not ready to properly introduce a full picture of modern racial ideology, but the problem of equality was already front and center in the minds of the early functionalists.

The issue was this: thinkers like Jhering and Geny were unhappy with *laissez-faire* capitalism, but they were similarly uninterested in socialism. As with the "End of Ideology" program that emerged later, the direction was toward social democracy, and what eventually came to be known as the social-democratic compromise. Thus, rather than dispense with the classic liberal preoccupation with individual right, the move involved the placement of individual right in the context of social need and purpose. Or to put this another way, Jhering and Geny helped usher in a functionalist perspective on individual rights, and of special interest here, a functionalist perspective on *equal* rights. What would follow was a general emphasis on the practical benefits of social inclusion, and not the launch of what we would now recognize as the familiar language of human rights.

Jhering and Geny both identified justice as a central purpose for any legal system. From the functionalist angle, however, the point is to ask of the *purpose* of justice—not of whether justice is good for its own sake, or taken as a given. Perhaps, Jhering suggested, the purpose of justice is the guarantee of equality among a nation's citizens. But if this is so, "what is there so great in equality that we measure the highest concept of right—for this is what justice is—by it? Why should law strive for equality, when all nature denies it? And what value has equality independently of any particular content? Equality may be as much as anything else equality of misery . . . The desire for equality seems to have its ultimate ground in an ugly trait of the human heart; in ill-will and envy."[50]

Whatever reason might motivate the individual's hunger for equality, Jhering argued, the social desire for equality concerns the role of equality is supplying "the

---

[50] JHERING, MEANS, *supra* note 22, at 276.

148   THE RIGHT TO EXCLUDE

condition of the welfare of society."[51] If certain segments of society shoulder too heavy a burden, the needs of society as a whole will go unmet. In order to effectively meet these needs, every group ought to carry its share of the load. This did not, however, lead Jhering to make a claim for the equal rights of various nationalities or racial groups in a given social order. Once again, the guiding light here is the *telos*. From an ancient, Aristotelian view of equality, the goal was not "an external, absolute, arithmetical equality, which would assign every participant exactly the same share as the next one."[52] Rather than take a view of equality as symmetry, take the geometrical view of equality, whereby the equality to be realized is always relative, a function of the relation between the capacity of a group to perform and the problem to be solved.[53] Jhering argued:

> It is therefore the practical interest in the continuance and success of society which dictates the principle of equality in this sense, and not the *a priori* categorical imperative of an equality to be realized in all human relations. If experience showed that society could exist better with inequality, such would deserve the preference. The very same thing is true also of civil society, no matter what the species of equality which the law has to maintain in order to realize the practical interest of that society. The determining standpoint in this matter is not that of the individual, but of society. From the former we arrive at an external, mechanical equality which measures all by the same standard ... and which, by treating the unequal as equal, in reality brings about the greatest inequality ("summum jus summa injuria"). Under such conditions society cannot exist. It would mean practically to deny the differences which actually are and must be within it.[54]

To put a finer point on it, it is not merely that functionalism didn't bear any predictable relationships with equality. It is that functionalism easily allowed for its adherents to abide by a vulgar racism—so long as that racism was borne out in social science. Jhering himself published *The Evolution of the Aryan* in 1897,[55] an extensive racial history that he was only able to begin in the years before his death. But in the introduction to the part that he did complete, Jhering explained that the question to which his study of the Aryans was moving was the issue of *difference* between "the five nations of Europe," the Greeks, Latins, Celts, Teutons, and Slavs.

---

[51] *Id.*

[52] *Id.* at 277.

[53] *Id.* at 278–79.

[54] *Id.* at 278.

[55] To be sure, the term "aryan" did not emerge with the racist overtones that it came to possess during the Nazi era. On the relation between aryan and the proto-Indo-European language system, *see, e.g.,* Karel Werner, *The Indo-Europeans and the Indo-Aryans: The Philological, Archeological, and Historical Context*, 68 ANN. BHANDARKAR ORIENT. RES. INST. 491 (1987); DAVID ANTHONY, THE HORSE, THE WHEEL, AND LANGUAGE: HOW BRONZE-AGE RIDERS FROM THE EURASIAN STEPPES SHAPED THE MODERN WORLD (2010).

As I discuss in Chapter 5, by the turn of the twentieth century, this was precisely where so much of the scientific study of race was moving: into the separation of the "progressive" races of Northern Europe from the "lazy and dim-witted" races in the South.

Before moving on, it is worth mentioning at this point that Jhering was hardly alone in this initial wave of functionalists to show a keen interest in the science of racial xenophobia.[56] Over in the US, progressive economists like Richard Ely, who are most popularly known for their left-leaning critiques of *laissez-faire*, regularly deployed their craft in the service of excluding "racially inferior" immigrants.[57] Another example is that of John Commons, an institutional economist and author of the well-known *Legal Foundations of Capitalism*, who published in 1907 *Races and Immigrants in America*. In this lesser-known work, Commons complained of the "peasants of Catholic Europe, who constitute the bulk of our immigration of the past thirty years, have become almost a distinct race, drained of those superior qualities which are the foundation of democratic institutions."[58] The influx of Southern Europeans, compounded by the presence of African-Americans and Asians, was bringing the US to a point of no return. "This question of the 'race suicide' of the American or colonial stock should be regarded as the most fundamental of our social problems, or rather, as the most fundamental consequence of our social and industrial institutions."[59] This most pressing of social problems warranted a functional response. For social scientists like Commons, that response was best marshaled forward in the work of groups like the infamous Immigration Restriction League,[60] of which Commons was a member. The answer, for these functionalists, would eventually emerge in a total overhaul of international migration law.

Before moving to the arrival of legal functionalism in international legal thought, let me sum up what we've seen thus far in the inchoate style of modern racial ideology. First, a rejection of the formal sources of law as being able to provide a comprehensive and gapless system of rules and concepts from which jurists could logically derive the answers to every conceivable legal controversy. Second, a turn away from the *nature of legal concepts* and toward the *nature of things*. This is the turn in jurisprudence away from philosophy and theology and toward the science of society. What do legal rules *do*, and *why*? What is the function of law in the social? How can rules better serve the real needs of the society in which we live today? How can they adapt? Third, the free search of the jurist for better rules needed to

---

[56] Robert Cherry, *Racial Thought and the Early Economics Profession*, 34 Rev. Soc. Econ. 147 (1976).

[57] Richard Ely, *Pauperism and Poverty*, 152 N. Atl. Rev. 393 (1891).

[58] John Commons, Races and Immigrants in America 11–13 (1907). Commons was here citing to Ripley.

[59] *Id.* at 200–01.

[60] *See generally* Daniel Tichenor, Dividing Lines: The Politics of Immigration Control in America (2002).

150   THE RIGHT TO EXCLUDE

be constrained and distinguished from raw, political action. Yes, judicial decision making and legislative enactment were largely the same thing. Nevertheless, the jurist's work ought to be impersonal, objective, and harmonious. The way to do this was through a form of naturalizing juridical science. Legal rules ought to be harmonious with the needs of social life, and that harmony was only available in the hard-won expertise of the nascent social sciences.

And what of equality? Already we can see the requisites of a modern form of racial ideology: Inequality in law might or might not be justifiable in terms of racial identity. But what was already clear was the fact that in functionalist legal science, social justice and broader forms of inclusion would find no support in a theory of equal rights. They would find support to the extent that equality made for a better world, but *only* to that extent. This could mean, and very often did mean, that "progressive" social scientists were battling economic hierarchies in the name of social welfare, and at the same time entrenching racial hierarchies, *also* in the name of social welfare. As Rogers Smith has said of this frequent juxtaposition among the early functionalists:

> [They] could all support racial hierarchies at home and abroad while believing that they were sincerely attached to democratic republicanism and to individual rights—*if those doctrines were properly understood in light of evolutionary theory and scientific evidence of racial capacities.* Hence their various fusions of ongoing liberal democratic idealism with ascriptive Americanism promised to satisfy middle-class white Protestant's desires for social control and continued cultural hegemony. The revised intellectual outlooks of the day argued that the best in traditional American ideals had been race-specific all along. That is why many passages by these writers appear to exhibit allegiance to Myrdal's American Creed of equal rights and justice for all races. But to read those statements as implying that all races should have equal rights at present, as Reconstruction radicals held, is to reject their self-understandings without warrant.[61]

## II  FUNCTIONALISM IN INTERNATIONAL LEGAL THOUGHT

Enough has been written on the reception of Jhering and Geny in the early works of sociological jurisprudence and legal realism in the US.[62] Roscoe Pound, Benjamin Cardozo, Jerome Frank, Karl Llewellyn, Arthur von Mehren, and others were all

---

[61]  ROGERS SMITH, CIVIC IDEALS 418 (1997).

[62]  *See, e.g.,* Duncan Kennedy, *Three Globalizations of Law and Legal Thought, in* THE NEW LAW AND DEVELOPMENT: A CRITICAL REAPPRAISAL (David Trubek & Alvaro Santos eds., 2006); Martin Gelter, *The Influence of Rudolf von Jhering on Karl Llewellyn,* 48 TULSA L. REV. 93 (2012).

RACIAL IDEOLOGY AND FUNCTIONALISM    151

disciples of the new functionalism.[63] What has been less discussed, however, is the impact of functionalism on early twentieth-century international legal thought. Or rather, while functionalism is regularly pointed to for the specific origins of international institutions,[64] or as somehow related to a broader sociology of international law,[65] it is less frequently studied as a distinctive mode of legal thought, and certainly less so as an articulation of legal ideology.[66] As Jan Klabbers has suggested, functionalism is really a family of approaches, rather than a single concept. There is the broad functionalism of legal thought that is my target, and the more specific forms of functionalism working in the domain of international organizations, either from the perspective of international lawyers like Klabbers, or political scientists like David Mitrany.[67] My approach is to focus on the deeper style of functionalist legal thought initiated by thinkers like Jhering and Geny.[68]

The impact was immense. The arrival of functionalism provided the conditions for a new mode of racial ideology in international law, and in particular, the beginnings of a great bait-and-switch. As Jhering had already realized, while the classic liberal style of legal thought had enjoyed a formal and unrealized belief in legal equality, the new modern functionalism harbored no such commitments. Commitments to social justice, greater welfare, and scientific expertise in the interpretation of law—yes. Equality—well, that depended on the circumstances. What was coming was a general acceptance of equality at the level of sovereign states, including equal sovereign rights to exclude less desirable persons from immigrating into home territory. But we're getting ahead of ourselves.

While it may very well have emerged earlier, international legal functionalism is apparent in the writings of international lawyers from at least the beginnings of World War I.[69] Elihu Root, a figure we have already encountered in Chapter 3,

---

[63] See generally JOHN HENRY SCHLEGEL, AMERICAN LEGAL REALISM AND EMPIRICAL SOCIAL SCIENCE (1995).

[64] See, e.g., Jan Klabbers, International Institutions, in THE CAMBRIDGE COMPANION TO INTERNATIONAL LAW (James Crawford & Martti Koskenniemi eds., 2012); Jan Klabbers, The Emergence of Functionalism in International Institutional Law: Colonial Inspirations, 25 EUR. J. INT'L L. 645 (2014).

[65] See MARTTI KOSKENNIEMI, THE GENTLE CIVILIZER OF NATIONS: THE RISE AND FALL OF INTERNATIONAL LAW: 1870–1960 266–352 (2001).

[66] Martin Loughlin, The Functionalist Style in Public Law, 55 U. TORONTO L.J. 361 (2005).

[67] FUNCTIONALISM (A.J. Groom & P. Taylor eds., 1975); DAVID MITRANY, THE PROGRESS OF INTERNATIONAL GOVERNMENT (1933); David Mitrany, The Functional Approach to World Organization, 24 INT'L AFF. 350 (1948). In an attempt to revamp the older functionalism, Joel Trachtman has argued that functionalism "made the mistake of moving directly from cooperation problems to organizational solutions. They elided a critical intermediate, and perhaps final, step: the utility of international law separate from the establishment of additional international organizational structures ... A positive social scientific functionalist theory would seek to link certain causes to the establishment of rules for the organizations, in order to predict the circumstances under which particular rules or institutions might arise." See JOEL TRACHTMAN, THE FUTURE OF INTERNATIONAL LAW 14–15 (2013).

[68] For a discussion of Geny's influence in the separate domain of customary international law, see, e.g., Emily Kadens, Custom's Past, in CUSTOM'S FUTURE 12–13 (Curtis Bradley ed., 2016); ANTHONY D'AMATO, THE CONCEPT OF CUSTOM IN INTERNATIONAL LAW 49 (1971).

[69] I tend to distinguish between legal realism and legal functionalism along a critical/reconstructive axis. See Justin Desautels-Stein, The Realist and the Visionary: Property, Sovereignty, and the Problem of

152   THE RIGHT TO EXCLUDE

was a significant voice in the years leading up to and beyond the creation of the League of Nations. Root's essay from 1916, "The Outlook for International Law," is exemplary of the functionalist attitude that would come to sweep the field.[70] When the leaders of the world emerged from the war, Root predicted they would find it irresistible but to reconsider the "fundamental basis of obligation upon which all rules depend."[71] Just as the individual in political society requires definite and enforceable rules promulgated by a sovereign, so do sovereigns in the international world require clear and constraining norms. But how to justify such hard obligations? And more to the point, how could they be made more effective? How could their function be best fulfilled?[72] Root found the answer in a jurisprudential turn from away from the formalism they associated with the old debates about naturalism and positivism, and into a modern functionalism. As Root discussed, it was only on a theory of collective action and a generalized self-interest that the real purposes of international law, and the "general opinion of mankind," might be made "effective."[73]

Root's associate Alejandro Alvarez, who we also have already met, was of a similar mind.[74] Like Root, Alvarez was eager to erect a new architecture of international administration, and believed in the need for a more effective international law. International law could realize these aims by aligning itself with the "social facts of which it is only the reflection."[75] These social facts pointed away from a classical individualism and toward social solidarity.[76] And while social solidarity was what the international world now needed, administrative effectiveness would always be dependent on context. Alvarez explained, "The scope of law, at least of its rules, is greater or less dependent on its environment. It is universal in its tendency toward solidarity because in all countries the productive social phenomena are impressing on the law this new doctrine."[77] Thus, whereas in the past international society's *pomerium* was guarded by an individualist and racial ethos of exclusion, the "new international law" was all about global solidarity. Nevertheless, Alvarez added, "in other matters [international law] differs according to the conditions of the country, racial aptitude, etc."[78]

---

*Social Change, in* Contingency in International Law: On the Possibility of Different Legal Histories (Ingo Venzke & Kevin Jon Heller eds., 2021).

[70] Elihu Root, *The Outlook for International Law*, 10 Am. J. Int'l L. 1 (1916).

[71] *Id.* at 3.

[72] *Id.* at 4.

[73] *Id.*

[74] *See, e.g., Symposium: Alejandro Alvarez and the Launch of the Periphery Series*, 19 Leiden J. Int'l L. 825 (2006)

[75] Alejandro Alvarez, *New Conception and New Bases of Legal Philosophy*, 13 Ill. L. Rev. 167, 179 (1919).

[76] Solidarity was the watchword, particularly in the rising work of French functionalists working in the shadow of Emile Durkheim.

[77] Alvarez, *supra* note 75, at 180.

[78] *Id.*

With respect to the method for aligning international law with the social facts, Alvarez relied upon the characteristic tendency to find guidance in "the fundamental notions of the political and social sciences."[79] The world of theory and of natural law had passed, and a new epistemology had begun: "This reconstruction [of international law] must be accomplished with the aid of factors that are essentially scientific and positive. To this end, not only must politics be considered together with juridical rules, but also a much vaster inquiry must be undertaken: a thorough study of international life in its entirety; that is to say, there must be created the science of international relations."[80] With a tenor that would eventually come to sound much like that of the New Haven School popularized by Myres McDougal and Harold Lasswell, Alvarez explained that this new science would incorporate the objective study of pretty much everything: not merely the customary and conventional rules regulating the behavior of sovereigns, but all international phenomena, properly contextualized in time and space.[81] The goal: "The establishment of this harmony between politics and legal rules is the greatest step which can be accomplished in international law."[82] Not justice, not equality, not fairness of distribution of wealth and resources, not the alleviation of human suffering. The greatest step for international law was to find that missing harmony, a harmony between legal rule and social fact.

A contemporary of Root and Alvarez was the British international lawyer, J.L. Brierly, who similarly surfaced the obvious and oft-stated issue of international law's lack of enforcement.[83] Like Root and Alvarez, Brierly pointed to bigger fish, "deeper causes" that had been obscured by the obsession with the "enforcement problem."[84] The real problem was that international law was not well-suited to the "needs" of international society.[85] Until the creation and application of international rules operated from a functional perspective regarding the constantly shifting interests of the community of states, international law would remain wedded to a mechanical, lifeless, and useless set of metaphysical fairy tales.[86] The supremely influential and future judge on the International Court of Justice (ICJ), Hersch Lauterpacht, abided by the same platform, encouraging international lawyers against the specter of formalism, positivism, and the fascination with "mechanical jurisprudence"[87]—all impediments in the wellness program

---

[79] *Id.* at 181. The quote is from Alejandro Alvarez, *A New International Law*, 15 Trans. Grotius Soc'y 35, 41 (1929).

[80] *Id.* at 40.

[81] *Id.* at 40–41.

[82] *Id.* at 47.

[83] J.L. Brierly, *The Shortcomings of International Law*, 5 Brit. Y.B. Int'l L. 4 (1924).

[84] *Id.* at 7. *See also* Carl Landauer, *J.L. Brierly and the Modernization of International Law*, 25 Vand. J. Transnat'l L. 881 (1993).

[85] Brierly, *supra* note 83, at 8.

[86] *Id.* at 8–12.

[87] Roscoe Pound, *Mechanical Jurisprudence*, 8 Colum. L. Rev. 605 (1908). Brierly, for example, cited Pound for support, *supra* note 83, at 8.

154    THE RIGHT TO EXCLUDE

for international law.[88] This perspective on the needs of international society led Lauterpacht to argue for seeing non-state actors, and particularly individuals, as the real subjects of the international legal order.[89]

Indeed, this last point is well worth emphasizing in this little sketch of international legal functionalism. While functionalism certainly led a number of international lawyers to argue against the primacy of the sovereign state as the frame for international legal personality, and develop international institutional designs as the answer to international society's most pressing challenges, functionalism wasn't limited to the supranational. Well before Lauterpacht published his *International Law and Human Rights*, the French jurist Georges Scelle wrote *Precis de Droit des Gens* in 1932.[90] In his *Precis*, Scelle explained that international society was, in fact if not law, composed of individual human beings, and that a law in service of formal abstractions like "the state" was fantasy, best sequestered to Jhering's heaven of legal concepts. From a sociological perspective similar in spirit to that of Alvarez, Scelle argued that human beings were bonded through a myriad of solidarities. These solidarities were biologically founded, objective, and social facts.[91] The function of international law was to conform to these objective solidarities emanating out from the various societies spanning the globe, eventually coalescing into an overarching, planetary society. The idea for Scelle was less that this view of international law paid respect to an idea of human *rights*, so much as this was the view that necessarily followed from a view of social needs— social needs predicated on the immutable place of the individual human being as the only real subject of the global order. With reference to Scelle's earlier work, but still consistent with the functionalist theme running throughout his *oeuvre*, Anne-Charlotte Martinou has commented, "[Scelle's] thesis rests on the assumption that one can properly grasp the legal evolution of *asientos de negros* only if one studies the socio-economic and political context in which they were negotiated and implemented. This implies that the legal scholar must move beyond formal law and carry on an anti-formalist assessment."[92]

These two veins in early international legal functionalism—(1) the need to go beyond formal law and search for the sociological context in which to realize an objective law; and (2) the effort to unbundle the sovereign concept and emphasize the priority of non-state actors—continued into the next several decades. As for the first vein, writing in the middle of the twentieth century, Julius Stone carried

---

[88] For further discussion, *see* Martti Koskenniemi, *Hersch Lauterpacht and the Development of International Criminal Law*, 2 J. INT'L CRIM. JUST. 810 (2004).

[89] HERSCH LAUTERPACHT, INTERNATIONAL LAW AND HUMAN RIGHTS (1950).

[90] Hubert Thierry, *The Thought of Georges Scelle*, 1 EUR. J. INT'L L. 193 (1990); Rene-Jean Dupuy, *Images de Georges Scelle*, 1 EUR. J. INT'L L. 235 (1990); Nicholas Kasirer, *A Reading of Georges Scelle's Precis de Droit des Gens*, 24 CAN. Y.B. INT'L L. 372 (1986).

[91] *See* Leon Duguit, *Objective Law*, 20 COLUM. L. REV. 817 (1920).

[92] Anne-Charlotte Martineau, *Georges Scelle's Study of the Slave Trade: French Solidarism Revisited*, 27 EUR. J. INT'L L. 1131, 1135 (2016).

the torch for a sociological view of international law's function,[93] and Georg Schwarzenberger announced an "inductive" approach to international law that was meant as a corrective for the fallacies of logical deduction, in either its naturalist or positivist guise.[94] Schwarzenberger explained: "[T]he inductive treatment of international law is not intended as an exercise in logic. It is an empirical device [which will] safeguard international law against the subjectivism of deductive speculation and eclectic caprice, and the vested interests prone to use—and abuse—both. On the level of social studies, inductive legal analysis is supplemented by the study of the history of international law, with particular emphasis on ... the sociological exploration of the place of international law in world society."[95] The fascination with the sociological context for international law may not be as intense today as it was in the postwar decades, but it certainly remains.[96]

In terms of the newly emerging cognizance of non-state actors, international law bore witness to an uneven appreciation for legal rights operating beyond the bounds of the sovereign state. Functionalist arguments raised by the ICJ helped reinforce the idea that international organizations could have limited forms of international legal personality, while the idea that subnational entities—like minority groups—could bear rights steadily fell off the table. Later, in the slow transition from debates about minority rights and national self-determination to debates about human rights, functionalism eventually gave way to a resurgence of formalist legal reasoning. This transition from a functionalist justification for giving legal personality to non-state actors to a formalist justification for human rights is an important threshold moment in the transition from modern racial ideology to our own postracial xenophobia, discussed in Chapter 7.

---

[93] JULIUS STONE, THE PROVINCE AND FUNCTION OF LAW (1946). *See also* Edward McWhinney, *Julius Stone and the Sociological Approach to International Law*, 9 U. NEW S.W. L.J. 14 (1986).

[94] GEORG SCHWARZENBERGER, THE INDUCTIVE APPROACH TO INTERNATIONAL LAW 8–19 (1965). *See also* Georg Schwarzenberger, *Jus Pacis ac Belli? Prolegomena to a Sociology of International Law*, 37 AM. J. INT'L L. 460 (1943).

[95] SCHWARZENBERGER, INDUCTIVE, *supra* note 94, at 6–7.

[96] *See, e.g.*, MOSHE HIRSCH, INVITATION TO THE SOCIOLOGY OF LAW (2015); RYAN GOODMAN & DEREK JENKS, SOCIALIZING STATES: PROMOTING HUMAN RIGHTS THROUGH INTERNATIONAL LAW (2013). To be sure, I should not be understood to be suggesting that everyone from Root and Alvarez to Stone and Schwarzenburger and beyond were all in happy agreement about the right direction for every international legal dispute. There was contest and contention every which way. My purpose here is rather to show, at the level of international legal thought, how the functionalist ethos of Jhering and Geny was operating among international lawyers in the first half of the twentieth century. Similarly, I do not mean to suggest that what I am offering here is anything like a quick intellectual history; I leave for others to argue over whether Leon Duguit and Francois Geny were "really" at odds with one another over the proper place of sociology, or the extent to which Antoine Pillet's scholarship offers the most direct "influence" on Alvarez, or whether Roscoe Pound is the better vehicle to understand Stone. *See, e.g.*, KOSKENNIEMI, *supra* note 65; Jean-Pascal Chazal, *Leon Duguit et Francois Geny, Controverse sur la Renovation de la Science Juridique*, 65 REVUE INTERDISCIPLINAIRE D'ETUDES JURIDIQUES 85 (2010). My point is rather that, in the works of Jhering and Geny we see a particular structure of legal justification, and in the works of many twentieth century international lawyers we see that same structure of legal justification suggesting broad orientations to the international legal order. And the reason I'm interested in demonstrating these structural connections is because of the impact functionalism has on the right to exclude.

# III THE LOGIC OF INCLUSION

As twentieth-century functionalism spread into modern international legal thought, the reasons for the shift were certainly diverse. J.L. Brierly and Hersch Lauterpacht, for example, pushed back against Jhering and Geny's anti-naturalism, believing in the necessity of natural law as a supplement to "realistic" prescriptions for world order. That said, both Lauterpacht and Brierly were keen to qualify that their use of "natural law" wasn't exactly old-fashioned.[97] True, they wanted a tele-ological approach to international law, but they remained committed to the classic principle of sovereign equality.[98] This commitment to equality was less about a formal and abstract appreciation of the principle; it was more about the devel-oping idea that sovereign equality was worth pursuing, because it was practically *necessary*.

To put the point more in line with the language of Jhering or Geny, for many of these international lawyers the international law of equality would need to be in keeping with the fundamental facts of international life.[99] Among these "fun-damental facts" were the existence of sovereign states, including peoples that a generation earlier a classic racial ideology had banned from an international society of full equals. "It would seem ludicrous," the international law scholar

---

[97] Brierly, *supra* note 83, at 10. "And yet, as M. Alvarz points out, apart from treaties international law is a customary law not only in its origin and development, but also in the inspiration that it draws from the political situation of the age, and its rules are (or at any rate, they ought to be) constantly changing and modeling themselves on the ever-changing needs of international life. It was a disaster that the [re-jection of natural law] should have coincided with the beginning of a century which has to be one of un-precedented growth in the society of states." *Id.* LAUTERPACHT, *supra* note 89, at 24. "The law of nature has been rightly exposed to the charge of vagueness and arbitrariness. But the uncertainty of the higher law is preferable to the arbitrariness of naked force." *Id.*

[98] Hersch Lauterpacht, a forceful proponent of the new functionalist approach, was also a strong advocate of sovereign equality. In the context of the debate over which states might properly enter the Family of Nations and obtain international legal personality, for example, Lauterpacht supported the idea that sovereigns were under a legal duty to recognize a people sovereign, regardless of their cul-tural or racial heritage, so long as that people met the criteria of statehood. *See* HERSCH LAUTERPACHT, RECOGNITION IN INTERNATIONAL LAW 26–36 (1947). Lauterpacht's focus on equality is also apparent in his work on human rights law, and the notion that human beings are fundamentally equal. In his de-fense of human rights law, Lauterpacht makes direct analogies between states and individuals, affirming the long-standing domestic analogy. *See* HERSCH LAUTERPACHT, INTERNATIONAL LAW AND HUMAN RIGHTS (1950). This tendency to think of equality between individuals and equality between states as operating in tandem is also illustrated in the preamble of the UN Charter itself: "We the peoples of the United Nations determined ... to reaffirm faith in fundamental human rights, in the dignity and worth of the human person, in the equal rights of men and women and of nations large and small." Nevertheless, it bears emphasis that a commitment to sovereign equality should not be attributed to all scholars working in the mode of functionalist jurisprudence. *See, e.g.,* EDWIN DICKINSON, THE EQUALITY OF STATES IN INTERNATIONAL LAW 336 (1920): "Insistence upon complete political equality in the constitution and functioning of an international union, tribunal, or concert is simply another way of denying the possibility of an effective international organization." *Id.* Indeed, the point here is that there is no *logical* connection between functionalism and equality at all, in the same way that there is a logical connection between sovereign equality and positivism. *See also* Benedict Kingsbury, *Sovereignty and Inequality,* 9 EUR. J. INT'L L. 599 (1998).

[99] Phillip Marshall Brown, 9 AM. J. INT'L L. 305, 310 (1915); Frederick Charles Hicks, *Equality of States and the Hague Conferences,* 2 AM. J. INT'L L. 530 (1908).

RACIAL IDEOLOGY AND FUNCTIONALISM    157

Phillip Marshall Brown explained, "to assert that states do not exist and are subject to no rights under international law simply because [they lack] proper social standing."[100] Brown continued, "Nothing could be more unjust as well as arrogant than the claim that the nations possessing European civilization were the sole arbiters of the rights and obligations of other nations under international law. A recognition of this important fact is essential to a comprehensive understanding of the real nature of international law and of its evolution as a science."[101] This is the functionalist chastening of racial development as a schedule for international society: science was losing its capacity to legitimize an imperial right of certain sovereigns to exclude other would-be sovereigns from the global legal order. At the same time, scholars like Brown argued that the reality of international relations similarly knew nothing of a "perfect equality of nations." Thus, it was a mistake to see a functionalist critique of *imperium* as necessarily leading to the conclusion that all nations and states were equal in capacity or influence, or really anything at all except their right to international legal personality. Just because race science may have been bad science, this didn't mean that everyone was equal. So while the white races may not justifiably exercise a right to exclude nonwhite peoples from international society, Brown concluded, "it would seem not only impossible, but grotesque, to conceive a world organization in which England and Liberia would be treated as having an equal status."[102] Quite clearly, functionalism had left the door wide open for some other form of justification, and before long, the ideology of racial development would be replaced by an ideology of economic development.

After the end of World War I, it was this hedged and functionalist sense of equality formalized in the Covenant of the League of Nations, and which formally marked the end of the Family of Nations model.[103] Scholars like Edwin Dickinson and S.W. Armstrong, writing at the end of the War, tried to distinguish different types of legal equality that would help fashion the new international law. Moving forward there would be what Dickinson termed "equality before the law," where states were "equally protected in the enjoyment of their rights and equally compelled to fulfill their obligation."[104] But equality of participation didn't mean

---

[100] Brown, *supra* note 99, at 310. *But see* DICKINSON, *supra* note 98, at 223.

[101] Brown, *supra* note 99, at 311. It is a basic feature of functionalist legal thought that claims like Brown's are typically vulnerable to reversal, so long as the claimant has the "facts" on his side. Dickinson argued, for example, "Other have urged that in theory recognition need not be essential to normal membership in the international society. Yet it hardly seems likely that the problem could have been solved by such dialectical sleight of hand. The theories suggested were significant *only if they were in some measure relevant to the facts of international life.* It was indispensable that there should be in fact a right to recognition, that it should be possible to establish that right in some kind of impartial proceeding, and that the right once established should be effective in all international relationships." *See* Edwin Dickinson, *The New Law of Nations,* 32 W. VA. L.Q. 4, 9 (1925)

[102] Brown, *supra* note 99, at 332.

[103] *See, e.g.,* PIETER HENDRIK KOOIJMANS, THE DOCTRINE OF THE LEGAL EQUALITY OF STATES: AN INQUIRY INTO THE FOUNDATIONS OF INTERNATIONAL LAW (1964).

[104] Brown, *supra* note 99, at 334–35.

158   THE RIGHT TO EXCLUDE

equality of capacity or contribution. Hence, the Covenant of the League could at once espouse an equality of membership and the collapse of colonial power, and the rise of new and legal hierarchies. Formal equality was overtaking racial exclusion as an orienting idea for the global *demos*—but it was equality modified. The League was governed by an executive-styled Council, with Britain, France, Italy, and Japan enjoying permanent membership in that body. The Council, in other words, was quite exclusive—though as we can see in Japan's position here, international law's racial ideology was morphing. All members of the League did however have a representative in the League's Assembly, acting somewhat like a congressional body (though with very little actual power, beyond determining new membership in the Assembly and the Council). But who could be members of the League? Could the colonial powers exclude anyone they wished? With the dissolution of the German, Hapsburg, and Ottoman Empires, and the entrenchment of the British and French empires, the question of membership in this new international organization was fairly open, or at least, much more open than it had been.[105] While the age of racialized *imperium* was coming to an end, it was nevertheless still a moment in which international society was surely not for *everyone*, and certainly not for everyone in the same way.[106]

As famously articulated in Article 22 of the Covenant, many formerly colonized peoples entered the new international order as "Mandates" rather than as independent sovereign states.[107] Article 22 refers to those "peoples not yet able to stand by themselves," an idea of infancy that certainly echoes the inequalities of the Family of Nations model. But rather than justify this inequality through racial ideology, the new distinction between "Mandates" and "sovereigns" gained support with arguments about the "practical" needs of international administration, increasingly economic in nature.[108] From this functionalist perspective, Armstong explained, an abstract "doctrine of equality must give way."[109] All the same, the Mandate system included many of the former colonies within the scope of the new international legal order, pairing certain "immature" peoples with "big brother"

---

[105] The founding members of the League, entering on Jan. 10, 1920: in Africa (Liberia); Asia (China, Japan, Siam); Europe (Belgium, the British Empire (Australia, Belgium, Canada, India, New Zealand, and South Africa), Czechoslovakia, Denmark, France, Greece, Italy, the Netherlands, Norway, Poland, Portugal, Romania, Spain, Sweden, Switzerland, Yugoslavia); Central & South America and the Caribbean (Argentina, Bolivia, Brazil, Chile, Columbia, Cuba, El Salvador, Guatemala, Haiti, Honduras, Nicaragua, Panama, Paraguay, Peru, and Uruguay); the Middle East (Persia). Ethiopia joined the League in 1923, Germany in 1926, Mexico in 1931, Turkey and Iraq in 1932, the Soviet Union in 1934, and Egypt in 1937.

[106] *See generally* JAN JANSEN & JURGEN OSTERHAMMEL, DECOLONIZATION 37 (2017).

[107] For discussion, *see* GEORG SCHWARZENBERGER, THE LEAGUE OF NATIONS: A TREATISE ON THE PRINCIPLE OF UNIVERSALITY IN THE THEORY AND PRACTICE OF THE LEAGUE OF NATIONS (1936); David Kennedy, *The Move to Institutions*, 8 CARDOZO L. REV. 841 (1986).

[108] *See, e.g.*, Anthony Anghie, *Nationalism, Development, and the Postcolonial State: The Legacies of the League of Nations*, 41 TEX. J. INT'L L. 447 (2006).

[109] S.W. Armstrong, *Doctrine of the Equality of Nations in International Law and the Relation of the Doctrine to the Treaty of Versailles*, 14 AM. J. INT'L L. 540, 563 (1920).

nations responsible for helping the previously colonized come into their sovereign powers. These big brother states—the erstwhile colonial powers—were renamed the Mandatory Powers. In the view of the League, some peoples would experience the Mandate system as a bridge toward independence. For others, the road to "real equality" would be a long one, possibly without end.[110]

Peoples formerly under the authority of the Ottoman Empire, with the exception of Persia, which became a founding member of the League, were classed as "A" Mandates. Class A Mandates were peoples believed to "have reached a stage of development where their existence as independent nations can be provisionally recognized subject to the rendering of administrative advice and assistance by a Mandatory until such time as they are able to stand alone. The wishes of these communities must be a principal consideration in the selection of the Mandatory."[111] These included Syria, Lebanon, Israel, Jordan, and Iraq, and were governed by the French and British as the "mandatory" imperial powers. Class B Mandates were created out of the remains of the German colonies in Africa, and included Rwanda, Burundi, Tanzania, Cameroon, Nigeria, Volta, Ghana, and Togo. Class C Mandates were former German holdings in Southwest Africa and the South Pacific, including Papua New Guinea, Nauru, Paula, the Marshall Islands, and Namibia. Overall, France and Britain remained the Mandatory powers.

These "weaker" peoples were deemed inferior, but the League understood itself as having a duty to raise them up and into the new global order. Despite this ideological transition in which race was losing its pride of place, as scholars like Sundhya Pahuja have explained, the League's functionalist conception of sovereign equality didn't change all that much between the First and Second World Wars.[112] Various commitments to a "formal" or "juridical" equality would deepen as the Family's transition to the League was fortified in the destination that became the UN. The distinction between the Council and the Assembly was strengthened in the move to the UN Security Council and its permanent veto powers. As for the Mandate system, it changed names and became the Trust system, eventually absorbed into the process we have come to call decolonization, and then later, the human rights movement. This deracialization of *imperium* reflects international law's logic of inclusion, a steady strand in modern racial ideology.

As Jan Jansen and Jurgen Osterhammel have explained, "The First World War did not shine a beacon illuminating a universal pathway to decolonization. It did, however, allow the first signs of a fundamental legitimation crisis in colonial rule to surface, a crisis that erupted openly in the decades to follow."[113] Indeed, the League

---

[110] *See* ROSE PARFITT, THE PROCESS OF INTERNATIONAL LEGAL PRODUCTION: INEQUALITY, HISTORIOGRAPHY, RESISTANCE (2019).

[111] Covenant of the League of Nations, art. 22 (1924), available at https://avalon.law.yale.edu/20th_century/leagcov.asp.

[112] SUNDHYA PAHUJA, DECOLONIZING INTERNATIONAL LAW: DEVELOPMENT, ECONOMIC GROWTH, AND THE POLITICS OF UNIVERSALITY (2011).

[113] JANSEN & OSTERHAMMEL, *supra* note 106, at 42.

## 160 THE RIGHT TO EXCLUDE

of Nations was hardly paradigmatic for its commitments to sovereign equality, much less global antiracism. But it is true that even before the War, cracks in the edifice of international law's classic racial ideology were already beginning to show. In 1898, Tsar Nicholas II of Russia suggested the idea for an international peace conference with the aim of deescalating the rush for developing ever-more sophisticated weaponry. The Netherlands hosted the peace conferences that came as a result, held in 1899 and 1907. Although the 1899 conference hosted only a few representatives beyond the traditional confines of the Family of Nations, 1907 was a different matter. In addition to China, Japan, and Siam, much of South and Central America was represented at The Hague. As Gerry Simpson has explained, it was at these meetings that lawyers and politicians from Europe and the Americas debated how to frame equal rights for sovereigns. Nevertheless, while much greater representation from the racially "undeveloped" world was in attendance, it would be mistaken to see the Hague conferences as conferences about racial progress as such. After all, while Nicholas II had been the instigator for the peace conferences, it was Nicholas and his cousin Kaiser Wilhelm II of Germany who both so worried over the "yellow peril" in the coming "race war" with Japan.[114]

---

[114] Rosamund Bartlett, *Japonisme and Japanophobia: The Russo-Japanese War in Russian Cultural Consciousness*, 67 RUSSIAN REV. 8 (2008).

# 5

# The Promise of International Migration Law

Perhaps more than any other twentieth-century document, the preamble of the United Nations (UN) stands as a monument to the ostensible undoing of the classic mode of racial ideology in international legal thought. The opening line of the preamble reads:

> We the peoples of the United Nations determined to save succeeding generations from the scourge of war, which twice in our lifetime has brought untold sorrow to mankind, and to reaffirm faith in fundamental human rights, in the dignity and worth of the human person, in the equal rights of men and women of nations large and small.[1]

But, just as it endlessly ironic to ponder the example of the slaveowner Thomas Jefferson's role in the drafting of the United States (US) Declaration of Independence, so too is that of the South African politician Jan Smuts, who penned the Charter's preamble.[2] In his study of the ideological origins of the UN, Mark Mazower has appropriately focused attention on Smuts, an architect of both South African segregation and the systems of international egalitarianism and order that followed the Family of Nations.[3] In the League and the UN, thinkers like Smuts "sought to prolong the life of an empire of white rule through international cooperation."[4] In his highly influential *The League of Nations: A Practical Suggestion*, Smuts designed what came to be the League's Mandate system, regarding it the "sacred duty" of the "white race in Africa" to act as the "trustees of the coloured races."[5] In Smuts' view, one could allow for a formal degree of equality of participation in exchange for a prolonged form of hierarchy, entrenched in the divisions between Council and Assembly, Mandatory Power and Mandate, League Member and Colony. An equality any deeper would run afoul not only of the racism still so vital in the hearts of men like Smuts; it ran afoul of the basic functionalism marching the new internationalists toward a "real and effective" international system.

---

[1] United Nations, Charter of the United Nations, Oct. 24, 1945, 1 UNTS XVI.
[2] Adam McKeown, Melancholy Order: Asian Migration and the Globalization of Borders 210 (2011).
[3] Mark Mazower, No Enchanted Palace: The End of Empire and Ideological Origins of the United Nations 30 (2013).
[4] *Id.* at 30.
[5] *Id.* at 48.

*The Right to Exclude.* Justin Desautels-Stein, Oxford University Press. © Justin Desautels-Stein 2023.
DOI: 10.1093/oso/9780198862161.003.0006

## 162 THE RIGHT TO EXCLUDE

What is going on when characters like Smuts could author such inspirational texts and at the very same time have been the intellectual force behind South African apartheid? In this chapter, I introduce a second piece in the puzzle that became international law's modern racial ideology, and with this piece in place, figures like Smuts become all the more comprehensible. Detestable, for sure. But more comprehensible too.

Along with functionalism, this second element in the transition to modern racial ideology concerns the rise of racialized *dominium*, and with it, international migration law's failure to launch. As I elaborate in Chapter 6 on decolonization, between the making of the Mandates system and the 1970s, classic racial ideology slowly faded as a justification for the sovereign's right of *imperium*. But as I discuss below, it wasn't that classic racial ideology vanished. Rather, it's strategies and articulations shifted from one plane of legalized exclusion to another. Whereas international law's racial ideology of exclusion had previously worked to guarantee the border between the Family of white, civilized nations and the nonwhite, outsider world, it was now moving to guarantee the right of sovereigns to exclude from its borders the arrival of individual migrants.

This right of sovereigns to exclude foreigners was new to the international legal order. As international lawyers had explained for centuries, a sign of fluency with the Law of Nations was an open border between states. Nominally, and certainly by the nineteenth century, the status of international legal personality in the Family of Nations signaled an appreciation of open migration as commercial intercourse. In this respect, migration was merely a facet in the *laissez-faire* world of civilized legal relations.[6] In much of Europe at the turn of the twentieth century, debates were heating up around whether the old *laissez-faire* approach to migration still made sense, and international lawyers tended to veer toward the elaboration of a new and modern "international migration law." Like any other field of international law, this terrain would involve concepts and interpretive directions aimed at both constituting and regulating the movement of persons through territorial borders. At stake was a version of the more traditional boundary problem known to democratic theory (as opposed to international law's boundary problem, discussed above): How should international law respond to social questions about the closure of political communities? Or to put that another way, ought international law develop a field of foreground rules for migration, immigration, deportation, naturalization, and the like? Or should these questions be solved by a background rule, left to the sovereign's *dominium*, the sovereign's territorial right of exclusion? The answer that would emerge in the context of modern racial ideology was that, whatever international migration law had been in the nineteenth century, in the

---

[6] JOHN TORPEY, THE INVENTION OF THE PASSPORT: SURVEILLANCE, CITIZENSHIP, AND THE STATE 71 (2018).

twentieth it would be consumed by the right to exclude. Immigration questions would not be international questions but national questions.

In the US, the issue of how and whether international migration law might realize itself came to the same conclusion, but by way of a different path. As common as it was, the open-borders system (for individual migrants) had never been universal. Likely, the most vivid counter-example to the long-standing "free movement" regime was the situation for free African-Americans in the antebellum US. As Kunal Parker has explained, for whatever the reality of other international pressures that might have pushed against a sovereign's desire to adopt national immigration controls, at least in the US the arrival of a national immigration law was held in abeyance for as long as individual states feared a loss in the rights to exclude African-Americans from their territories. It was only after the Civil War and the adoption of the Fourteenth Amendment that slavery's block on a national immigration law finally caved in. However, rather than the inclusionary ethos of radical reconstruction, it was precisely the slave states' racialized right to exclude that rose to prominence in the now-national context of migrant exclusion. Thus, while the Fourteenth Amendment of 1868 had cleared domestic obstacles for a national immigration law, it was only 14 years later that Congress adopted the Chinese Exclusion Law of 1882.

As the name suggests, Chinese Exclusion was a classic example of racial xenophobia. What has been less studied is how that law mirrored the ideology of racial exclusion supporting sovereigns in their rights of *imperium*. As US Supreme Court Justices regularly explained, international law was a major source for the emergence of US immigration control. After World War I, the movement toward a national immigration regime encountered the international legal functionalism common to the architects of the new League of Nations. Immigration was increasingly viewed as a social problem demanding application of the best available, cutting-edge social science. How should the US approach the tremendous influx of persons moving in to the territory? Thinking about migration as free commercial intercourse didn't make sense; it hadn't really ever made sense, at least in the US, considering the situation first for freed slaves and then Chinese immigrants. But now, with such an increase in migration from southeastern Europe, how could a new migration law best meet the country's social needs? The answer was supplied by racial ideology, this time in the form of eugenics.

Through the Johnson–Reed Act of 1924, and inspired by a congressionally sponsored commission tasked with studying the science of race and migration, the US established a domestic form of border control that bore all the marks of classic racial ideology. It was hierarchical, exclusionary, and rooted in a science of race. As Mai Ngai has written, "In a sense, demographic data was to twentieth century racists what craniometric data had been to race scientists during the nineteenth. Like the phrenologists who preceded them, the eugenicists worked backward from classifications they defined a priori and declared a causal relationship

164    THE RIGHT TO EXCLUDE

between the data and race."[7] Sadly, the Act of 1924 quickly went global, inspiring sovereigns around the world to racialize a new right of *dominium*, forged as a right to exclude individuals from national territory. As Adam McKeown has argued, "Institutions that had their origins in exceptional methods necessary to preserve the ideals of self-government from the threats of an uncivilized world had now become indispensable technologies of population management. Their adoption became a prerequisite for recognition as a self-determining state in the international system."[8] The 1924 law became the international gold standard for migration regulation,[9] and it was "the potent mix of race and self-rule that built a world of border control."[10]

In the shadow of the American example, international law's brief affair with a nascent migration law came to an end. To be sure, it might not have been this way. An international law of migration might have arisen, preventing a racialized right to exclude from naturalizing into the background of the international legal order. But it didn't. The remains, now regarded as exceptions to the general rule of sovereign prerogative, were given to the new field of refugee law, and eventually, over to human rights law. That, however, is a story for Chapter 7. For now, on to the racialization of *dominium*, and the stillborn arrival of international migration law.

## I  MIGRATION LAW IN THE FAMILY OF NATIONS AND THE UNITED STATES

In Chapter 3, we examined the nineteenth-century right of *imperium*, and how the ideology of racial xenophobia justified the closure of international law's boundary problem. The focus there was on relations between *peoples*: the so-called nations of daylight, and then everyone else, the bare life of the racial *xenos*. Generally speaking, and from the perspective of international law, the global color line was the one drawn around the Family of Nations, not around individual sovereign states. It was at the end of the nineteenth century that this all started to change. The fact that it wasn't until quite late in the day that sovereign states started claiming a right of *dominium* that could bar individual migrants from the sovereign's territory might come as something of a surprise. Today, it seems both normal and natural that sovereign states can exclude "outsiders" from their borders as they please. In a sense, it feels as natural as it does because of how deeply embedded the domestic analogy has become in our everyday thinking: the structural similarity between an individual's property right of exclusion and the sovereign's control of its territory

---

[7] Mae Ngai, Impossible Subjects: Illegal Aliens and the Making of Modern America 31–32 (2004).

[8] McKeown, *supra* note 2, at 319–20.

[9] *Id.* at 334.

[10] *Id.* at 213.

THE PROMISE OF INTERNATIONAL MIGRATION LAW    165

just seems *unavoidable*. Given today's general tendency to regard the sovereign's territorial right to exclude as so important, it's natural to imagine that it has been around for a very long time. But it hasn't.

At least since Vitoria, international lawyers had counseled for open territorial borders.[11] Sovereigns keeping sovereigns out of their lands was one thing, but sovereigns excluding foreign nationals was the exception, not the rule. And since the beginnings of international law's alliance with racial ideology, the color line was rarely used to justify territorial borders; international law's color line was for the global *imperium*, not territorial *dominium*. Frédéric Mégret explains that "the absolute and unfettered power to exclude foreigners, if it ever existed, would have appeared as a historical anomaly to international lawyers writing before the nineteenth century. As late as the second half of the nineteenth century and even into the first half of the twentieth, a number of international lawyers, notably operating through the *Institut de droit international*, advocated vigorously for a presumptive right to immigrate."[12] And as Vincent Chetail has similarly argued, "Indeed, assuming the power to exclude aliens as the earliest prerogative of the state is inaccurate and highly disputable. On the contrary, free movement of persons has long been the rule, rather than the exception, in the history of humanity ... the admission of foreigners was traditionally viewed as a means of strengthening the power of host states (primarily for demographic and economic reasons)."[13] Thus, it was not so much that international lawyers believed that sovereigns could never be justified in excluding individual migrants from their territories. It was rather that these jurists thought of the right to exclude as unnecessary and at times inconsistent with the demands of commercial progress.[14]

For example, among the thinkers canvassed in Chapter 3 was Johann Caspar Bluntschli.[15] It will be recalled that for this Swiss jurist, racial ideology was an important and explicit criterion in fashioning the Family of Nations and its hierarchical structure. Drawing on thinkers like Count Arthur de Gobineau, Bluntschli argued for an international law that divided the Nations of Daylight from the Children of the Night. The racial *pomerium* between the white Family of Nations and the nonwhite peoples of the earth required a vigilant guardian in international law.[16] When it came to the borders between individual sovereign territories, however, Bluntschli was singing a different tune. As Chetail explains:

[11] Francisco Vitoria, *On the American Indians, in* POLITICAL WRITINGS 277–92 (Anthony Pagden & J. Lawrance eds., 2008 [1539]).

[12] Frederic Megret, *The Contingency of International Migration Law, in* CONTINGENCY IN INTERNATIONAL LAW: ON THE POSSIBILITY OF DIFFERENT LEGAL HISTORIES (Ingo Venzke & Kevin Jon Heller eds., 2021).

[13] VINCENT CHETAIL, INTERNATIONAL MIGRATION LAW 38–39 (2019).

[14] *Id.* at 40. *See also* G.F. MARTENS, THE LAW OF NATIONS 83 (4th ed. 1829); MICHAEL FISHER, MIGRATION: A WORLD HISTORY (2014); GLOBAL HISTORY AND MIGRATIONS (Wand Gungwu ed., 1997).

[15] CHETAIL, *supra* note 13, at 43–44; MCKEOWN, *supra* note 2, at 93–94.

[16] MCKEOWN, *supra* note 2, at 211.

## 166 THE RIGHT TO EXCLUDE

The Professor of Heidelberg University first observed that freedom of emigration was recognized by most European states and, as a result, both nationals and foreigners were free to leave their state of residence. When discussing admission, he further added that: "no state has the right to prohibit in an absolute way the entry of foreigners onto its territory." Such a rule is grounded in "civilized international law which is bound to protect the peaceful relations between men."[17]

What deserves emphasis, however, was that "the free movement of persons" jurists like Bluntschli were talking about was very specifically a free movement of migrants departing from nations and entering nations all of which belonged to his category of so-called white sovereigns. This was a free movement of persons primarily for peoples that were already racially "developed," citizens of the global *demos*, the *homo politicus*, operating within the legal boundaries of the Family of Nations. Throughout the nineteenth century, massive migration flows moved from Europe and into the US. Millions of German and Irish freely passed American borders, though to be sure, the process of integrating would prove more tortuous, especially for the Irish. For people like Bluntschli, such movements helped build commercial connections between racially developed nations. It was not about "migration" as we think of the concept today—about the rights of individuals to determine their future life stories.

The migration of racially "inferior" peoples from beyond the Family of Nations and into "developed" nations was a different story all together.[18] A common distinction is drawn between the rights of states to regulate travel among its inhabitants, and the rights of states to exclude foreigners. Some argue that the former right had a more mature pedigree than the latter, but this distinction between individuals subject to the sovereign's authority on the one side, and foreigners subject to an external power on the other, is not quite as obvious as we might think. What happened, for instance, when a sovereign was a member of the Family of Nations and therefore participated in the free flow of commercial migration, but only to the extent that this "free movement of persons" excluded the free movement of nonwhites?

## II CLASSICAL RACIAL IDEOLOGY FROM BELOW

An often-overlooked example of this is the right of migration in the context of American slavery. As Kunal Parker has recently observed, it is a mistake to look at

---

[17] CHETAIL, *supra* note 13, at 42.

[18] MCKEOWN, *supra* note 2, at 95. Limitation on the right to exclude foreigners were applicable only within the boundaries of the Family of Nations. As Adam McKeown has observed, "Beginning in the 1850s, white settlers around the Pacific worked to keep Chinese at the margins of their communities, if not entirely excluded." *Id.* at 121.

THE PROMISE OF INTERNATIONAL MIGRATION LAW    167

the transition to twentieth-century immigration control without seeing that transition through the lens of the US Civil War. To be sure, throughout the eighteenth and early nineteenth centuries, the US did largely follow the international rule of free movement. At the same time, however, slave states exercised considerable control over their territorial borders, and no issue was more salient in the early 1800s than that of the free movement of persons between states. More specifically, this was a concern about the free movement of former slaves, and the need to racialize territorial borders.[19]

Resembling the debates surrounding entry into the Family of Nations, in the decades before the Civil War the question increasingly surfaced whether white citizens had a right to exclude freed blacks from taking up residence in their communities. Here Parker recounts a typical response from the white south: "It is not every person who is born in a State, and born free, that becomes a member of the political community. The Indians born in the States continue to be aliens, and so, I contend, do the free negroes ... *[N]ature seems to have made the negro a perpetual alien to the white man.*"[20] True, no state could exclude American citizens from its territory. But the issue wasn't whether a person carried the prerequisites for citizenship, namely native birth. The issue was whether racial underdevelopment served as a natural bar to the political community. And as Justice Taney famously explained in the *Dred Scott* decision from 1857, it most certainly did. Due to the racial inferiority of freed slaves, Taney claimed that descendants of the African race were never understood to be a part of the American political community, and because of their racial status, never could be. Among many results was the consolidation of a class of native-born foreigners—insider-outsiders—human beings living in the US but subject to exclusions in much the same way as the undocumented persons of today.[21] As Parker explains:

> The panoply of restrictions on free blacks' residence and movement in both North and South makes clear that, from the perspective of many, there was to be no place for blacks in the United States once they were not slaves. At the point of freedom, blacks became aliens of a sort, excludable and removable. The Tennessee Supreme Court put it thus in 1834: "All the slaveholding states, it is believed, as well as many of the non-slaveholding, like ourselves, have adopted the policy of exclusion."[22]

It was with the Civil War that this "policy of exclusion" went under for some changes. Until that time the rise of a federal immigration control had been politically swamped; if a federal immigration law was adopted, slave states would

---

[19] KUNAL PARKER, MAKING FOREIGNERS: IMMIGRATION AND CITIZENSHIP LAW IN AMERICA, 1600–2000 83 (2015).
[20] *Id.* at 93.
[21] *Id.* at 95.
[22] *Id.* at 97.

168    THE RIGHT TO EXCLUDE

lose the right to exclude freed blacks and whoever else might be deemed a poor fit for the political community. After the War, however, and with the eventual passage of the Fourteenth Amendment, freed blacks became citizens and states lost the right to exclude, since no state could exclude from its territory a US citizen. Citizens could freely move within the territory of the US, just as "citizens" of the Family of Nations enjoyed free movement within the global *demos*. Of course, this right to exclude, long-cherished by the states and guaranteed in numerous Court decisions,[23] didn't just go away. With the slavery block now out of the way, a federal approach to immigration could finally take shape. And as it did, two features are of special importance for our story: it would become heavily racialized, and it would become influential on a global scale.

With respect to the racial nature of the coming immigration controls, Parker comments how as "the old exclusion laws barring blacks from entering states and territories fell away, racial segregation and violence took their place."[24] Indeed, in the wake of the postwar settlement Reconstruction at once provided new rights to African-Americans and helped usher in a reactionary period of Jim Crow segregation.[25] The community of freed blacks bore the strange arrival of citizenship rights on the one side, and the Ku Klux Klan on the other. Or to put this another way, as the new immigration regime would take shape in the next generation, the central question would no longer be about refusing African-Americans citizenship or figuring out how to exclude freed blacks from racialized borders. Nevertheless, it was the South's defeat which helped relocate a racial ideology of exclusion at the level of local and regional boundaries to a new *national* right to exclude. The slave-owner's ideology of racial borders seeped into the emerging immigration regime, and at this early moment, the ideology of racial xenophobia had a different target: the so-called "Asian."

The backdrop was not only the lapse of states' rights to exclude; it was also the arrival of about 25 million immigrants by the beginning of World War I. On the whole, there had been little in the way of excluding migrants travelling from within the Family of Nations. Or, if migrants from within the international community were not quite "white," they would become so.[26] Things were otherwise for the 250,000 Chinese that had flocked to the West Coast of the US before 1882, and the 120,000 Japanese that were in residence by the 1920s, for just as freed slaves had been excluded at the border on the basis of race, so too would the citizenry of

---

[23]   New York v. Miln, 36 U.S. 102 (1837); Passenger Cases, 48 U.S. 283 (1849).

[24]   PARKER, *supra* note 19, at 137. Nevertheless, After the Civil War, strategies for rendering the native-born foreign were various: formal denials of birthright citizenship; subjection to plenary power free of constitutional constraints just as immigrants were; the opening of a gulf between formal and substantive citizenship; subjection to surveillance, suspicion, and border controls like immigrants of the same racial background; involuntary expatriation, and controlling movement and presence through territorial controls, discrimination, and violence. *Id.* at 131.

[25]   Plessy v. Ferguson, 163 U.S. 537 (1896).

[26]   *Cf.* ROBERT DIVINE, AMERICAN IMMIGRATION POLICY: 1924–1952 18 (1957).

China, and later, that of Japan.[27] Considerable work has already documented the rise and fall of anti-Asian immigration law and ideology, not only in the US, but around the globe. And the racial ideology at work here truly was operating on an international scale, for as Adam McKeown has commented, "Although particular formations could assume infinite nuances, the general framework and vocabulary varied remarkably little around the Pacific."[28]

In 1868, the same year that the Fourteenth Amendment was adopted, the US and China negotiated the Burlingame Treaty of Friendship and Commerce. On its face, the treaty was consistent with the *laissez-faire* view of migration as commerce holding sway in the Family of Nations, guaranteeing free movement from China to the US, and vice versa. This view of China's relation with the US, however, was short-lived. Before long a new Congress was preparing for a new Chinese treaty, and by 1882, Congress passed its first exclusionary immigration law. Under the racial premises of the law, extended in 1892 by the Geary Act and again a decade later, Chinese "laborers" were prohibited from entry.[29] In 1888, the Scott Act barred Chinese from returning to the US, despite having already been lawful residents. As President Grover Cleveland explained, already beginning to conflate rights of *imperium* and *dominium*, "The admitted and paramount right and duty of every government to exclude from its borders all elements of foreign population ... must be regarded as a recognized canon of international law and intercourse."[30] In the effort to effectuate these new restrictions, federal agencies were created to formally take responsibility from the states. In 1891, an Office of Superintendent of Immigration was created in the Treasury Department, the responsibility of which was to oversee an immigration service tasked with constituting the nation's newly legalized racial contours. A few years later, it was renamed the Bureau of Immigration and shifted its administrative home over to the Department of Commerce and Labor.

## III CLASSICAL RACIAL IDEOLOGY FROM ABOVE

Thus far I have been suggesting that, in the rise of US immigration and law and its spread around the world, the racial ideology of territorial exclusion common to slave states relocated to the national border. By the end of the nineteenth century, as Parker has recounted, space had opened up for the arrival of a federal immigration regime—but it was a space that was immediately racialized as white anger spread from Reconstruction to Asian immigration. To be sure, this is an important thread in the constitution of US immigration law's racial ideology. What I want to

---

[27] PARKER, *supra* note 19, at 123.
[28] *Id.*
[29] Although, of course, many Chinese laborers made it in anyway. For discussion, *see* McKEOWN, *supra* note 2, at 137–48.
[30] *Id.* at 171.

170 THE RIGHT TO EXCLUDE

return to, however, is the making of international law's modern racial ideology, and how the emergence of US immigration law fits in.

As I will argue, two sources contribute to the racialization of the sovereign's right of territorial exclusion. On one side is that of the US Civil War and the relocation of *slave-state* border ideology to a *national* regime of border ideology. On the other is the ideological articulation of the sovereign's right to exclude at the level of *international law's* boundary problem, to the sovereign's right to exclude at the level of the *nation's* migration problem. That is, even while international law's modern racial ideology empties race out from the discussion of international legal personality (discussed further in Chapter 6), it paradoxically begins with a deeply racist and xenophobic account of national political community and migration control. The sovereign's racialized right of exclusion didn't simply weaken and die in the confrontation with decolonization. It moved to another part of town.

In their wonderful history of an emerging global migration regime in the late nineteenth and early twentieth centuries, Marilyn Lake and Harold Reynolds provide a helpful illustration of the transition from classic to modern racial ideology with the well-known plight of the Japanese in the Versailles negotiations.[31] As the First World War came to an end, and so many of the world's leaders saw in the nascent League of Nations a moment to fashion a new form of international life, Japan sought to include in the League's founding Covenant a clause establishing the racial equality of humankind—but an idea about racial equality something other than the functionalist opening of international institutions. The Japanese claim wasn't coming out of nowhere. Since 1913, several US states had passed alien land laws excluding Japanese and other persons ineligible for citizenship land. Japan's reaction was as loud as it was logical: in diplomatic correspondence and newspaper editorials, Japan condemned the US land laws as white supremacy and as they argued at the Universal Races Congress of 1911, an affront to emerging norms of racial justice.[32] Many at that Congress, and around the world, predicted a coming race war that would engulf the globe, pitting East against West. Of course, what happened rather than a war between whites and Asians was a war between Europeans and Europeans, and when that war concluded, Japan had high hopes for Woodrow Wilson's rhetoric of self-determination and universal brotherhood in the "new world order." What Japan wanted was the inclusion of an article in the League Covenant proclaiming the racial equality of humankind.

The stakes were high. Well before the days of Bandung and the rise of the tricontinental bloc, Japan carried itself as the global representative for the non-white world. And here was the definitive moment to transform an international

---

[31] MARILYN LAKE & HAROLD REYNOLDS, DRAWING THE GLOBAL COLOUR LINE: WHITE MEN'S COUNTRIES AND THE INTERNATIONAL CHALLENGE OF RACIAL EQUALITY (2008).

[32] For discussion, *see* ANDREW GEIGER, SUBVERTING EXCLUSION: TRANSPACIFIC ENCOUNTERS WITH RACE, CASTE, AND BORDERS, 1885–1928 (2011).

law of racial hierarchy into a global law that might end the "usurpation of rights and interests on the part of the white race," and "check the unbridled selfishness and domination of the white people."[33] It wasn't enough to gradually leech race out of the membership problem for the new international institutions. That was important, sure, but it wasn't enough. And at first blush, one might imagine that including a racial equality clause in the Covenant wouldn't have been a very hard sell for the Japanese delegates. One draft of the clause intended to remove the "badge of shame"[34] worn everywhere by the nonwhite peoples was the following:

> The equality of nations being a basic principle of the League of Nations, the High Contracting Parties agree that concerning the treatment and rights to be accorded to aliens in their territories, they will not discriminate, either in law or in fact, against any person or persons on account of his or their race or nationality.

The trouble with the clause and for the Japanese was its conflation of *imperium* and *dominium*. At the level of *imperium*, as the Family of Nations model gave way to the new League of Nations, sovereigns slowly lost the right to exclude other peoples from international society on grounds of racial underdevelopment. At the level of *dominium*, as the colonial powers tread the path toward functionalism and the new international institutions, racial exclusion was slowly becoming more important to these sovereigns, in terms of protecting their territorial boundaries. There was racial equality between sovereigns, and there was racial equality between sovereigns and individual migrants. The former was becoming familiar. The latter was increasingly alien. Japan's effort to supply the Covenant with a racial equality clause was offered and received as moving beyond the functionalist deracialization of *imperium*, and toward a limitation on how sovereigns could regulate their territorial borders. And that simply wouldn't do.

International lawyers generally agreed about how ineffective the new international institutions would be if they remained caught up in the old racial hierarchies of the nineteenth century. Whatever their racial inferiorities, all sovereigns were expected to join the League, either as full members or as members in training. But did this same reliance on "realism" and "effectiveness" suggest a similar approach to the sovereign's territorial right to exclude? Did social science support Japan's case for the racial equality clause?

In response to a request for input on the League from the Republican National Committee, Elihu Root told the American delegates in Versailles to oppose any language that pushed the idea of racial equality beyond the level of international

---

[33] LAKE & REYNOLDS, *supra* note 31, at 286.

[34] Paul G. Lauren, *Human Rights in History: Diplomacy and Racial Equality at the Paris Peace Conference, in* RACE AND US FOREIGN POLICY FROM 1900 THROUGH WORLD WAR II 265 (1998).

172    THE RIGHT TO EXCLUDE

society.[35] To do otherwise, Root counseled, would suggest a "plan for unlimited yellow immigration."[36] As Root had written earlier, "With the great varieties of race and custom and conceptions of social morality in the human family the right of each nation to conduct its own internal affairs according to its own ideas is the essence of liberty."[37] Racism should not bar a sovereign state from being left alone to organize its own affairs—this was a bland version of the principle of self-determination Wilson was promoting, and which would eventually catch fire. At the same time, notions of racial equality could not tell sovereigns how to do the organizing. In a passage quite out of place from the perspective of today's Republicans in the US, Root believed that it was essential for all sovereigns to abide by the procedures and decisions of international arbitrations and adjudications. Importantly, this included the US, for it was every nation, regardless of its economic, military, or cultural achievements, which was bound to submit its claims to international law and its attendant mechanisms for conflict resolution. This was essential if future wars were to be avoided, and Root thought that the League Covenant didn't go far enough in making the rules for international dispute resolution more effective.[38] In this sense, Root continued, all sovereign peoples were equals in the eyes of international law.

However, while the US shared an interest with all other sovereigns in promoting a more effective and functional international law, it shared no interests at all in regulating a sovereign's territorial right of exclusion. True, choices about how to constitute and police the membership and boundaries of the new *international community* was a question for the League leadership. Questions about the membership of a sovereign's *own political and national community*, however, were "purely American affairs," to be determined solely by domestic policy.[39] As Root put it, "The nations of Europe in general are nations from which emigrants go. The United States is a nation to which immigrants come ... Europe and America are bound to look at questions of emigration and immigration from different points of view."[40] There was simply no connection between the willingness of the US to participate in a new international legal order, in the service of fostering world peace and the end of war, and allowing the League to intervene in questions related to the US right to exclude certain kinds of people from its borders.[41] As a result, Root suggested that the US qualify its entrance into the League with an amendment

[35] Elihu Root, *The Proposed Convention for a League of Nations: Letter to the Chair of the Republican National Committee, March 29, 1919*, 5 INT'L CONCILIATION 694 (1919).

[36] LAKE & REYNOLDS, *supra* note 31, at 292–93.

[37] Elihu Root, *The Declaration of the Rights and Duties of Nations Adopted by the American Institute of International Law*, 10 AM. J. INT'L L. 211, 216 (1916). For discussion of Root's "imperialist" vision for international law, *see* Erik Moore, *Imperial International Law: Elihu Root and the Legalist Approach to American Empire*, 47 ESSAYS IN HIST. 1 (2013).

[38] Root, *Proposed Convention*, *supra* note 35, at 706–07.

[39] *Id.* at 709.

[40] *Id.* at 710.

[41] *Id.*

THE PROMISE OF INTERNATIONAL MIGRATION LAW    173

reading in part, "the representatives of the United States of America sign this convention with the understanding that nothing contained therein contained shall be
construed to imply a relinquishment by the United States of America of its traditional attitude toward purely American questions ... (including therein the admission of immigrants), to the decision or recommendation of other powers."[42]

For American international lawyers like Root, migration was increasingly seen
as an issue best left to sovereign *dominium*, rather than regulation by treaty.[43]
Indeed, this was a view regularly promulgated by the powerful Immigration
Restriction League ("IRL"), of which Root—and many of the early functionalists—
was a member. Since its establishment in 1894, the IRL had been a constant advocate for the use of eugenics in the making of social policy, racial borders, and
new regimes of exclusion.[44] For architects of the new international, was there a tension, or at least some ambivalence, between membership in groups like the IRL and
commitments to norms of inclusion becoming visible in the new functionalism of
international organizations? Indeed, Root was an advocate not only for the League,
but for the creation of the new Permanent Court of International Justice as well. We
could ask the same question of figures like Smuts, Wilson, Colonel House, and so
many other dead celebrity hypocrites.

With respect to anyone's personal psychology, I remain agnostic. The method
here is not, after all, that of intellectual history. I am rather in pursuit of the structural history of racial ideology, and at least at that level, what is coming into view
is a clean separation of foreground and background. In the foreground, racial ideology is becoming more modern, more inclusive, more open. In the background,
the sovereign's territorial right to exclude the world—not just other sovereigns,
but foreigners as well—is naturalizing. There is also nothing inconsistent at all in
the functionalist support of a modern racial ideology of inclusion in one sphere
of international law, and its support of a classic racial ideology of exclusion in another. Recall that in the work of Jhering and Geny, as well as Americans like John
Commons (also a member of the Immigration Restriction League), functionalism
never emerges as anything like an ally of egalitarian jurisprudence. As a mode of
naturalizing juridical science, functionalism instructs the jurist to analyze law's
social purpose. In doing so, the jurist seeks out the social problems law is meant
to solve, and the social science that will enable law to fashion itself accordingly.
Among such social sciences was eugenics.

Thus, if the social problem is migration and the national community, and the scientific study of racial development shows not only that Africans, Indians, Asians,
and southeastern Europeans generally refuse to assimilate to the "American race,"

---

[42] *Id.* at 716.

[43] McKeown, *supra* note 2, at 318.

[44] For discussion, *see, e.g.*, Daniel Tichenor, Dividing Lines: The Politics of Immigration
Control in America (2002).

174   THE RIGHT TO EXCLUDE

but that due to their intellectual inferiority these peoples would also diminish the stock of the American race even if they did assimilate, then the policy path is clear: a racialized and exclusionary policy of border control. In the space of *dominium*, international law's racial ideology underwent a strange morphing: the use of race science combined now with functionalism, rather than formalism, yielding a new territorial right to exclude the world. If we shift gears, however, and identify the relevant social problem as "international order," take as a given that the scientific study of racial development shows that nonwhite races are at least potentially able to govern themselves as sovereigns, then the path is clear for a more open approach to international legal personality. In the space of *imperium*, international law's modern racial ideology rejects the use of race science—precisely on functionalist grounds.

As a result, functionalist jurisprudence cares little for the substantive debate between eugenicists like Harry Laughlin who argued hard for the hereditary aspects of racial identity, and anthropologists like Franz Boas, who argued for ethnicity over race as the more valid frame of analysis. In other words, functionalists could be happily on board with eugenics, given its technical demands for demographic and genetic research, and regulations that would serve the findings of that research. But functionalism could be just as satisfied with a social science platform that rejected the eugenicist commitment to racial difference. And it is precisely in this direction that functionalism was headed, in both spheres of migration law and international organization.

To come back to the Japanese campaign at Versailles, the reasons for rejecting the racial equality clause had little to do with the racial ideology of exclusion that had guarded the Family of Nations during the nineteenth century. On the contrary, in the atmosphere of the League and the UN, the ascending view was that all peoples ought to be included in the new world order—and if they couldn't be included right away, then soon. Or, sort of soon. In any case, the reasons for rejecting the racial equality clause, and why it was characters like Jan Smuts who steered the course of the new international institutions, was that "modern" international law guaranteed for sovereigns a racialized right of *dominium*—the sovereign's new right to exclude racially underdeveloped people from the national community.[45] Of course, Japan lost this particular fight, and the racial equality clause failed to find a way into the Covenant. In its effort to embed a strong commitment to racial equality in the new international law, Japan inadvertently helped mark the frontiers of international law's modern racial ideology: (1) Divest international legal hierarchy of its overt racism in reliance on nineteenth century theories of racial xenophobia; (2) Justify a new sovereign right to racialize its borders on a twentieth century theory of eugenics.

---

[45] Lothar Stoddard, The Rising Tide of Color Against White World Supremacy (1922).

## IV RACIAL IDEOLOGY AND *DOMINIUM* IN THE SUPREME COURT

As Chetail has pointed out, by the turn of the twentieth century there was considerable debate among international lawyers over the sovereign's emerging territorial right to exclude. Illustrative of this "period of transition," in the same year that the US passed its first exclusion law the Institute of International Law adopted its "International Rules on the Admission and Expulsion of Aliens." These rules straddled a pronouncement in favor of free movement and "exceptional circumstances" in which sovereigns could exclude migrants on racial or cultural grounds.[46] Some jurists like Lassa Oppenheim argued for a strong sovereign right to exclude, while many more such as Paul Fachille emphasized the primacy of the free movement of persons.[47]

American international lawyers like Root joined the debate as well, but the more enduring impact came from the US Supreme Court. *Chae Chan Ping*,[48] widely known as The Chinese Exclusion Case, was profoundly influential on the development of immigration law in the US. Together with cases like *Fong Yu Ting*,[49] these decisions round out what is sometimes called the "classical" phase of immigration control.[50] What I want to emphasize, however, is that in laying the foundations for US immigration law, the Chinese Exclusion case was entirely rooted in *international law*. It is a feature of just how quickly the sovereign's territorial right of exclusion was turning into a background rule—natural, neutral, necessary—that in the decades to come the fact that international law had been the source was fading out of sight. As Kunal Parker has observed: "As a matter of international law, as a [Know-Nothing-dominated House of Representatives report] observed, it was clear that every community had a right to protect itself against the evils associated with the influx of outsiders. But in the context of the US, where exactly did that power to regulate immigration lie? The report's equivocal response reveals a great deal: 'The power exists somewhere, either in the States, or in the general government, or in both of them.' The locus of the power to regulate immigration was 'not well settled even to the present time.' "[51] It wasn't well-settled then, and it isn't well-settled now. Why? The Supreme Court's use of international law's racial ideology gives us some clues.

Justice Stephen Field offered an early and paradigmatic argument for the legal justification for the racialization of *dominium*, and in particular, for Chinese

---

[46] Chetail, *supra* note 13, at 44.
[47] *Id.* at 51; McKeown, *supra* note 2, at 342.
[48] 130 U.S. 581 (1889).
[49] 149 U.S. 698 (1893).
[50] Peter Schuck, *The Transformation of Immigration Law*, 84 Colum. L. Rev. 1 (1984).
[51] Parker, *supra* note 19, at 108.

176 THE RIGHT TO EXCLUDE

exclusion.[52] In the well-known 1889 case of *Chae Chan Ping v. U.S.*, Field wrote the Supreme Court's majority opinion in the context of the Chinese Exclusion Law of 1882. The plaintiff in the case was a Chinese citizen who had resided and worked in San Francisco between 1875 and 1887. In 1887, Chae journeyed to China, but brought with him a certificate entitling him a return to the US, which he did in 1888. The certificate was valid under the exclusion law of 1882, but unfortunately for Chae, in his absence Congress had amended the 1882 law, nullifying all certificates of return. The question before the Court was whether Congress was within its legal powers, either under US law or international law, when it amended the 1882 Act to effectively exclude all Chinese workers.

Field began with a look at the relevant treaty law, beginning with the Treaty of Wanghia, negotiated by Caleb Cushing (who you will recall from Chapter 3's rogue's gallery), "a gentleman of large experience in public affairs. He found the government ready to concede by treaty to the United States all that had been reluctantly yielded to England through compulsion."[53] As Field saw it, Cushing's embrace of the Chinese opened the door to a "perfect, permanent, and universal peace" between the two nations.[54] And while Cushing's treaty made no stipulation for immigration from China to the US, the Burlingame treaty explicitly did.[55] That is, while the Wanghia treaty gave the US extraterritorial jurisdiction in China, and "universal peace" to boot, it seemed fair to interpret the Burlingame treaty as actually characterizing China as a member of the Family of Nations, insofar as the rule of free migration was operating in the white world. According to Field, the trouble, which Cushing himself would have seen easily enough, was that in having extended the rule of free migration to China the US jeopardized "the preservation of our civilization."[56]

As Field saw it, it was mistaken to think that the shift to the Burlingame treaty's view of commercial migration had presumed China's membership in the Family of Nations. That treaty instead rested on the domestic need for cheap labor. After the discovery of gold in California, news made it across the Pacific that there was plenty of work, and Chinese began taking the voyage east to the US. The Burlingame treaty was meant to assist in the migration flow, but by the 1870s, the arrival of Chinese workers posed an "Oriental invasion," threatening a "menace to our civilization."[57] "Differences in race," as Field explained, made the Chinese

---

[52] For broader discussion of Field, *see, e.g.*, Charles McCurdy, *Justice Field and the Jurisprudence of Government-Business Relations: Some Parameters of Laissez-Faire Constitutionalism, 1863–1897*, J. AM. HIST. 970 (1975); RALPH GABRIEL, THE COURSE OF AMERICAN DEMOCRATIC THOUGHT: AN INTELLECTUAL HISTORY SINCE 1815 216–27 (1940).

[53] *Chae*, 130 U.S., at 590.

[54] *Id.* at 590.

[55] *Id.* at 594.

[56] *Id.*

[57] *Id.* at 595.

THE PROMISE OF INTERNATIONAL MIGRATION LAW    177

> [S]trangers in the land, residing apart by themselves, and adhering to the cus-
> toms and usages of their own country. It seemed impossible for them to assimilate
> with our people, or to make any change in their habits or modes of living. As they
> grew in numbers each year the people of the coast saw, or believed they saw, in
> the facility of immigration, and in the crowded millions of China, where popu-
> lation presses upon the means of subsistence, great danger that at no distant day
> that portion of our country would be overrun by them, unless prompt action was
> taken to restrict their immigration. The people there accordingly petitioned ear-
> nestly for protective legislation.[58]

But was the coming of these "strangers in the land" with their stubborn racial ways, as Field infamously designated the Chinese, sufficient to justify a new rule of im-migration control? The question was two-sided. On the one hand was a question of whether prior treaty commitments with China precluded the exclusion regimes of the 1880s. On the other hand the question was about whether Chinese residents had a vested right of entry that trumped the sovereign's right to exclude them.

Field's analysis began with the traditional outline of legal formalism: it drew a sharp line between law and politics, and Field's argument would work to ensure that line. Field explained that the international law of treaties was *political*, and that an adjudication of whether the US had violated its treaty obligations would push the judiciary beyond its legal competence (which was law, not politics). Determining the international legal validity of the 1882 Act was a political deci-sion, not a legal decision—or, at least, it was a legal decision that couldn't be made by the courts. It belonged to the field of "diplomacy and legislation."[59] For if the ex-ecutive and legislative branches have the power to determine US treaty obligations, it is simply not a judicial task to "inquire whether [the political branches have], by the statute complained of, departed from the treaty or not ...."[60] Field continued, "the province of the courts is to pass upon the validity of the laws, not to make them, and, when their validity is established, to declare their meaning and apply their provisions. All else lies beyond their domain."[61]

This opening move is more formidable than it might seem at first glance. In carving the field into a political space on the one side where treaty law exists, and a legal space where the US judiciary is able to perform its task, the latter necessarily emerges as apolitical—*natural*. And the first thing naturalized is what Field has already accomplished in this initial gambit. According to Field, what he is doing is simply passing upon the validity of rules that *precede* him—not the making of new

---

[58] *Id.*
[59] *Id.* at 602.
[60] *Id.*
[61] *Id.* at 603.

178  THE RIGHT TO EXCLUDE

rules that had never been. And yet, that is *exactly* what is about to happen. Without any clear constitutional or statutory rule on point, Field offered the new rule:

> [Chinese] laborers are not citizens of the United States; they are aliens. *That the government of the United States, through the action of the legislative department, can exclude aliens from its territory is a proposition which we do not think open to controversy.* Jurisdiction over its own territory to that extent is an incident of every independent nation. It is a part of its independence. If it could not exclude aliens it would be to that extent subject to the control of another power.[62]

Later coming to be known as "the plenary power doctrine,"[63] Field would draw explicitly on the international law of sovereign right to justify the new right to exclude, citing John Marshall's discussion from *The Schooner Exchange*, decided in 1812.[64] In that older case, the US Supreme Court adjudicated a seemingly ordinary claim from a pair of American sailors against the French government for the confiscation of their ship on the high seas. When the French ported in Philadelphia due to stormy weather, the Americans sued for the return of their ship. Writing for the Court, Chief Justice Marshall set out the structure of international legal argument that would influence Field and so much of the later "plenary power" jurisprudence. But keep in mind: the right of sovereigns to exclude foreigners was not the question in *The Schooner Exchange*. To answer that question, Field would have to make some hay.

Field quoted Marshall's now-famous foundational view of sovereignty: "The jurisdiction of the nation within its own territory is necessarily exclusive and absolute. It is susceptible to no limitation not imposed by itself ... All exceptions, therefore, to the full and complete power of the nation within its own territories, must be traced up to the consent of the nation itself. They can flow from no other legitimate source."[65] Of course, if Marshall's decision had ended here, there would have been little reason for it to evolve into a canonical text in international law. What Marshall pointed to next was the juridical task of identifying precisely those legal exceptions to the nation's right of jurisdiction. And Field followed suit, explaining that rights of exclusive jurisdiction are not truly absolute, restricted in US law by the constitution, but more generally by "considerations of public policy and justice which control, more or less, the conduct of all civilized nations."[66] This is just as Marshall had put it, more than 70 years earlier:

---

[62] *Id.* (Emphasis added).

[63] *See, e.g.,* Hiroshi Motomura, *Immigration After a Century of Plenary Power: Phantom Constitutional Norms and Statutory Interpretation*, 545 YALE L.J. 100 (1990); Sarah Cleveland, *Powers Inherent in Sovereignty: Indians, Aliens, Territories, and the Nineteenth Century Origins of Plenary Power over Foreign Affairs*, TEX. L. REV. 81 (2002).

[64] 11 U.S. 116 (1812).

[65] *Chae, supra* note 53, at 604.

[66] *Id.* at 604.

The world being composed of distinct sovereignties, possessing equal rights and equal independence, whose mutual benefit is promoted by intercourse with each other, and by an interchange of those good offices which humanity dictates and its wants require, *all sovereigns have consented to a relaxation in practice*, in cases under certain peculiar circumstances, *of that absolute and complete jurisdiction within their respective territories which sovereignty confers ... A nation would justly be considered as violating its faith, although that faith might not be expressly plighted, which should suddenly and without previous notice, exercise its territorial powers in a manner not consonant to the usages and received obligations of the civilized world.*[67]

The question for Field was whether in exercising the sovereign's territorial right to exclude foreigners, the US would be violating its faith, exercising its territorial powers inconsistently with the norms of the Family of Nations.[68] In *The Schooner Exchange*, Marshall concluded that if the US were to grant the Americans' claim to the ship, the Court would effectively be exercising its own law on the person of a foreign sovereign. Of course, Marshall conceded that the US could exercise its local law on French citizens residing in its territory. But to exercise US law over *public* representatives of the French sovereign was inconsistent with international law:

This full and absolute territorial jurisdiction being alike the attribute of every sovereign, and being incapable of conferring extra-territorial power, would not seem to contemplate foreign sovereigns nor their sovereign rights as its objects. One sovereign being in no respect amenable to another; and being bound by obligations of the highest character not to degrade the dignity of his nation, by placing himself or its sovereign rights within the jurisdiction of another, can be supposed to enter a foreign territory only under an express license, or in the confidence that the immunities belonging to his independent sovereign station, though not expressly stipulated, are reserved by implication, and will be extended to him ... This perfect equality and absolute independence of sovereigns, and this common interest impelling them to mutual intercourse, and an interchange of good offices with each other, have given rise to a class of cases in which every sovereign is understood to wave the exercise of a part of that complete exclusive territorial jurisdiction, which has been stated to be the attribute of every nation.[69]

According to Marshall, "the whole civilized world," including the US, had "concurred" in the legal limitation of a sovereign's right to exercise jurisdiction over the public manifestations of a foreign government. Why? Because all sovereigns

---

[67] *Schooner, supra* note 64, at 137.
[68] *Chae, supra* note 53, at 596.
[69] *Schooner, supra* note 64, at 137.

180   THE RIGHT TO EXCLUDE

had consented to the restriction of rights when their exercise might violate "the dignity of the nation."[70]

For Field, the "whole civilized world" had apparently now concurred in the racialization of *dominium*, as Field now characterized it precisely as incidental to the very identity of any nation. And it is here that Field extended Marshall's earlier argument, since in 1812 the question of a nation's racial development hadn't been on the table. For Field, however, this was precisely the question. Citing to Marshall's opinion in *Cohens v. Virginia*, decided in 1821, Field again quoted the late, and great, Chief Justice: "That the United States form, for many, and for most important purposes, a single nation, has not yet been denied. In war, we are one people. In making peace, we are one people. In all commercial regulations, we are one and the same people."[71] Preserving the independence and dignity of a people, Field echoed, "is the highest duty of every nation, and to attain these ends nearly all other considerations are to be subordinated."[72] And this self-preservation of the nation was paramount, regardless of whether a sovereign was at war or at peace; what mattered was the duty of every sovereign to protect its national dignity. Field concluded:

> If, therefore, the government of the United States, through its legislative depart-
> ment, considers the presence of foreigners of a different race in this country, who
> will not assimilate with us, to be dangerous to its peace and security, their exclu-
> sion is not to be stayed because at the time there are no actual hostilities with the
> nation of which the foreigners are subjects.[73]

If we pause for a brief restatement, we can say that Field articulated a classic liberal defense of the right to exclude under international law. The articulation began with a separation between the political province of legislative action, and the apolitical task of the judiciary in its application of the rule of law. To wade into the particulars of whether the US decision to depart from the rule in favor of free migration was "immoral" would take the Court into an out-of-bounds political territory. For Field, the jurist's work could only be about the application of law, not the making of it. This maneuver had the effect of rendering apolitical the decision to come, which was to lie precisely in the justification of a new rule of international law: the right (and indeed, the *duty*) to enforce racial borders on sovereign territory. As Field explained, the starting point was international law, and the sovereign's right of absolute and exclusive territorial jurisdiction. This right could only be limited to the extent that a sovereign consented to a restriction. And had the US or any other

---

[70] *Id.*
[71] *Chae, supra* note 53, at 604.
[72] *Id.* at 606.
[73] *Id.*

civilized states decided to limit the right of exclusive jurisdiction in the case of alien entry? On the contrary, limitations on sovereign right result from violations of a nation's dignity, and in this case, it would violate American dignity to prolong the Chinese "menace." What's more, this wasn't a rule of American constitutional law Field was discovering, since no such rule existed. It was an international rule, derived precisely from those "considerations of justice" which constitute the "highest duty of *every* nation."

Although we are working to build *modern* racial ideology, what Field is doing here is utilizing the classic form of racial ideology explored in Chapter 3, but pressing it to work at a very different sort of borderland. The difference is that whereas those nineteenth-century international lawyers were working to justify the exclusion of racially inferior peoples from the international legal order (*imperium*), here an American judge was working to justify the exclusion of racially inferior people from American society (*dominium*). In either case, the ideology of racial xenophobia was key to the naturalizing effect of the legal argument. After all, if it was the highest duty of every nation to protect itself from racial contamination, what could be more natural than a Chinese Exclusion Act? Thus, a key feature of international law's modern racial ideology is the emergence and defense of classical modes of racial subjection at the boundaries of national communities. Or, we can say that modern racial ideology involves the racialization of *dominium*.

If we return to the question with which the analysis of *Chae Chan Ping* begun, we can now see more easily why the legal source of the sovereign's territorial right to exclude seemed so nebulous. The power of Field's decision was its ideological effect of transitioning a right of *dominium* as nonintervention into *dominium* as a right to racial purity. Before the Chinese Exclusion Act, the question was entirely open as to whether under international law a sovereign had the right to exclude foreign nationals from its territory. The possibility of something meaningfully called "international migration law" was real. But after *Chae Chan Ping*, this new and more restrictive version of the right to exclude was fast on its way to becoming a background rule, a rule almost not a rule at all, and yet somehow as overwhelming as the midday sun.

# V THE TRANSFORMATION OF MIGRATION LAW AFTER WORLD WAR I

By the first decade of the twentieth century, a new set of immigration concerns supplemented preexisting anxieties about Chinese influence along the Pacific, and as Aristide Zolberg has put it, "in the aftermath of World War I, the United States loudly proclaimed to the world its determination to cease being a nation of immigrants."[74] And although decisions like *Chae* were specifically targeted

---

[74] Aristide Zolberg, A Nation By Design: Immigration Policy in the Fashioning of America 243 (2006)

182    THE RIGHT TO EXCLUDE

at China, for groups like the Immigration Restriction League, Japan was a similarly worrisome "menace." With the Chinese Exclusion laws largely irrelevant to Japanese and Indian immigrants, and in the absence of a political will to enact a similar law, in 1907 the US negotiated with Japan a "Gentlemen's Agreement." Accordingly, Japan agreed to restrict its emigres to the US, but unappeased with Japan's efforts, in the Immigration Act of 1917 Congress created an "Asiatic Barred Zone" for potential emigrants seeking their way to the US, stretching from the Middle East to the Polynesian islands.[75]

What proved game-changing, however, was an intensifying concern about the rapidly increasing influx of southern and eastern Europeans. Bolstered by racist views of the Far East, it was this worry about a breed of "illiterate," "stagnant and downtrodden" Europeans that spurred on a new phase in the science of race development. Unlike the "hardworking and intelligent" Europeans from the north and west, these Europeans posed a potentially even greater threat to the purity of the white race than did all of Asia. The whole idea of "whiteness" was in danger. By the time of the Gentlemen's Agreement with Japan, more than 80 percent of the more than a million European immigrants were coming from countries like Greece, Italy, Poland, Russia, Spain, and Turkey. As the restrictionists saw it, these immigrants were unlike the German, English, and Scandinavian peoples, but also unlike Africans and Asians. Were they even "white" at all? The question mattered for all sorts of reasons, none more immediate than the application of US naturalization law. Since its first years, the US had enacted a law barring naturalization to nonwhites. Exceptions were made after the Civil War for African-Americans, but the white bar remained. The question of naturalization, however, only came into view once an immigrant had already arrived in the US. The prior issue that was steadily heating up was whether to push the Chinese Exclusion laws, and the new concept of an "Asiatic barred zone," right into Europe. But, if Europe was entering the calculation, where precisely should the new lines of immigrant exclusion be drawn? And how to draw them?

With works like Ripley's *The Races of Europe* in mind, answering this question became the task of a nine-member commission headed by Senator William Dillingham, chair of the Senate Immigration Committee. As Desmond King has explained, the Dillingham Commission's work between 1907 and 1911 was immense. The Commission examined "patterns of immigration from Europe; conditions in the European countries from which the immigrants were drawn; the position and economic status of recent immigrants in the United States, including their occupations, residential patterns, levels of assimilation, and incidences of incarceration for pauperism, insanity, or criminality; the fecundity of immigrant women; and conditions in cities."[76] Over the course of four years, in a report that

[75] McKeown, *supra* note 2.
[76] Desmond King, Making Americans: Immigration, Race, and the Origins of Diverse Democracy 59 (2000).

consisted of 42 volumes, the Dillingham Commission obtained data on about three million individuals. The Commission, in other words, exercised the very best of social science available at the time.

What the data showed, as presented by the Commission, was a decisive hierarchy of racist development. What was coming into view in the Commission's voluminous study was a separation between America's "old immigrants" and the new. For whereas the racial identity of the older immigrants from the northern and western regions of Europe easily receded in the assimilation to the local population, newer immigrants remained isolated. Whether Chinese, Japanese, Italian, Greek, Russian, or whatever, the new groups sequestered themselves, retaining their language and customs. These "colonies" were essentially "foreign quarters, which cut the immigrant off from American influences and this constitutes a serious menace to the community."[77] However, and just as if not even more troubling than the persistence of racial identity, was the low intelligence demonstrated in these isolated communities. This intellectual inferiority, rather predictably, was calculated on the extent to which new immigrants were literate, could speak English, and demonstrated a tendency to "abandon native customs."[78] In the effort to classify the racial diversity of the "new immigrants," the Commission produced a racial dictionary. Among the dictionary's contributions was the inclusion of the Irish in the Anglo-Saxon category, a national group that had previously been considered nonwhite due to the association of the Irish with the "Celtic race."[79] Otherwise, the dictionary followed the increasingly common classification of five races: Caucasian, Mongolian, Malay, Ethiopian, and American Indian.

The Dillingham Commission's recommendations were unambiguously racial and xenophobic. Immigration from Asia and throughout southeastern Europe posed a substantial threat to the unity and coherence of what restrictionists were starting to call the "American race."[80] As the eugenicist Harry Laughlin would suggest a decade later:

> If the American race is comprised, first, of descendants of immigrants from the British Isles; then immigrants coming from Germany, Scandinavia, from the Netherlands, from France, then the Jewish group, then from Spain, then, possibly, Hungary, Russia, and the group from other countries, if that is the stuff out of which the American race is made, and if we maintain those proportions, I think we would make a great step in advance.[81]

---

[77] *Id.* at 60.

[78] *Id.* at 64.

[79] REPORTS OF THE IMMIGRATION COMMISSION, DICTIONARY OF RACES OR PEOPLES (1911).

[80] *Id.*

[81] Quoted in KING, *supra* note 76, at 135.

184    THE RIGHT TO EXCLUDE

The fact of their unassimilable character distinguished the new immigrants from the older generations, who had easily "melted" into an American race of primarily Teutonic stock. The other races were intellectually inferior, and so there was little reason, given the social science on the subject, to expect these inferior races to do anything but remain a threat to America's national identity. As a result, the Commission recommended that Asian exclusion continue; that immigrants pass a literacy test; that racial groups immigrate along fixed quotas; that unskilled laborers stay out; that there be annual limits for ports of entry; that there be increases in head taxes. All in all, the Commission's report was a decisively functionalist/eugenicist approach to immigration: With a view of the intellectual difference of racial identity, immigration law ought to follow the dictates of a powerful social need with a regulatory design informed by social science. The social need was the protection of the American race from racial contamination. The scientific solution was to restrict, if not exclude, the entry of those racial groups that threatened national dignity.

The report was published in 1911, and in the next 15 years, the efforts of eugenicists helped solidify the new racialization of *dominium*. Congress' approach to the immigration landscape culminated in the Johnson–Reed Act of 1924. As Kunal Parker has said, it was with the 1924 Act that "for the first time in the history of immigration restriction, the basic theory of exclusion shifted from a matter of the shortcomings of the individual immigrant ... to a matter of numerical restriction ... The presumption of open borders became a presumption of closed ones."[82] Similarly, Mai Ngai observes that the Act "marked both the end of one era, that of open immigration from Europe, and the beginning of a new one, the era of immigration restriction ... The new regime had two major consequences: it remapped the ethno-racial contours of the nation and generated illegal immigration as the central problem of immigration law."[83]

Senator Albert Johnson's basic idea for the Act of 1924, which would eventually emerge as a model for immigration control the world over, was to cap the number of new arrivals relative to a baseline population.[84] For example, if the new Act had designated 1850 as the baseline, then the US would admit some percentage of the number of Chinese, or Japanese, or Italians, or Polish, or what-have-you. If, in 1850, there were 100 Italians living in the US, and the new Act designated a quota of 2 percent of the 1850 number, then, in 1924, the US would admit a whopping two Italian immigrants. In the 1920s, the actual debate was whether to use 1890 as the baseline, and whether to allow 2 or 3 percent of a given racial group new entry. For those eager to further restrict the entry of southern Europeans, not

---

[82] PARKER, *supra* note 19, at 155.
[83] NGAI, *supra* note 7, at 17.
[84]    ROGER DANIELS & OTIS GRAHAM, DEBATING AMERICAN IMMIGRATION, 1882–PRESENT 198 (2001)

to mention those coming from the Asia, 1890 was a great baseline year to choose since it predated the largest waves of "undesirable" immigrants. The trouble was how to justify choosing the census data from 30 years ago—1920 seemed the much more logical choice, except for the fact that choosing 1920 would undermine the very purpose of the Act in allowing for larger numbers of southern Europeans and Asians.

Senator David Reed offered a view of the American *polis* that could at once clamp down on the entry of "racially inferior" migrants and do so in the name of social science. This was the eugenicist theory of national origins: an understanding of the world community in the light of a scientifically rooted racial hierarchy. First, rather than base the quotas only on the numbers of the target population, the new immigration plan should follow the "entire" US population as it was measured in the 1920 census. Thus, 16 percent of the population were the "new" immigrants from southern and eastern European nations, while 84 percent was constituted by the "old" immigrants from northern and western Europe.[85]

Congress passed the Johnson–Reed Act of 1924 along precisely these lines, marrying the new idea of quotas with national origins. The Act restricted the total of annual immigration to 155,000 persons, establishing temporary quotas based on 2 percent of the foreign-born population as it stood in 1890, waiting on the work of a new committee to formulate the relevant quotas by 1927. In 1929, Congress approved a table of national origins devised by the newly created Quota Board. It might seem at first that the Quota Board's work was simply a matter of demographics: Figure out the total US population, filter by national origin, calculate the proportion of each group to the population, and allocate the new quotas relative to the proportions of the national groupings. Of course, there was little that was straightforward about any of it. For one thing, there was never any intention to use the "entire" American population as the baseline. There were no numerical restrictions at all for immigrants coming from the Western hemisphere. The legacy of the Monroe Doctrine was still in effect. Further, the Act excluded all persons ineligible for citizenship, which now included Japanese and Indians with the already-excluded Chinese. Further, when it came to defining a given American's nationality, "the law excluded nonwhite people residing in the United States in the 1920s from the population universe governing the quotas."[86] The US population that counted for constituting the national origins quota system did not include immigrants from the Western hemisphere or their descendants, aliens ineligible for citizenship or their descendants, the descendants of slave immigrants, the descendants of American Indians, and US citizens residing in Hawaii, Alaska, and Puerto Rico.[87] As Ngai explained, "to the extent that the inhabitants of the continental United

---

[85] NGAI, *supra* note 7, at 22.
[86] *Id.*
[87] *Id.* at 26.

186   THE RIGHT TO EXCLUDE

States in 1920 constituted a legal representation of the American nation, the law excised all nonwhite, non-European peoples from that vision, erasing them from the American nationality."[88]

> Thus, while the national origins quota system intended principally to restrict immigration from southern and eastern Europe and used the notion of national origins to justify discrimination against immigrations from those nations, it did more than divide Europe. It also divided Europe from the non-European world. It defined the world formally in terms of country and nationality but also in terms of race ... In this presentation, white Americans and immigrants from Europe have national origins, that is, they may be identified by the country of their birth or their ancestors' birth. But the "colored races" were imagined as having no country of origin. They lay outside the concept of nationality, and therefore, citizenship. They were not even bona fide immigrants.[89]

The direct intellectual influence behind the Act of 1924 was the Eugenics Record Office, funded by the Carnegie Institution. In an effort led by Charles Davenport and Harry Laughlin, the findings of the Dillingham Commission were boosted by reports on the threats posed by the "feeble-minded races" and the necessary regulations for restricting and excluding their further entry. Laughlin argued that "racially, the American people, if we are to remain American, and to purge our people of degeneracy, and to encourage a high rate of reproduction by the best endowed portions of our population, can assimilate in the future many hundreds of thousands of northwestern Europeans, but even these only if carefully selected as to inborn family qualities superior to the average of our own people ... we can assimilate only a small fraction of this number of other white races; and of the colored races practically none."[90] This way of looking at the American nation as an American race primarily constituted by certain peoples, and essentially threatened by the contamination of others, inspired the idea of the quota system. Laughlin continued:

> The quota law is trying to include the proportion, not connected with any one race, that has an integral part here. [The 1924 Act has] attempted to exclude races that are not subject to naturalization, because they are not integrals in the American race. I feel, after we determine what the American race is, and the biological components of it in the proper proportion, then our immigration policy should be to recruit each element of these races, and only to bring in such individuals of personal qualities and good family stock qualities whose progeny

[88] *Id.*
[89] *Id.* at 27.
[90] KING, *supra* note 76, at 134–35.

## THE PROMISE OF INTERNATIONAL MIGRATION LAW 187

will improve the natural talents, the emotions, instinct, intellect, quality of the American people. We ought to breed up the American people by immigration.[91]

Unlike the race scientists of the nineteenth century, eugenicists often claimed that their studies of heredity and demographics highlighted a natural and unavoidable system of racial difference, and not a system of racial superiority. Of course, we needn't gesture at the continued oppression of American Indians, Jim Crow segregation, mass prejudice against Chinese, Japanese, and Indians, or antisemitism everywhere, including the rise of Nazi Germany, to see what eugenics really was—an ideology of racial subjection. We can just look at the 1924 Act itself. In keeping with the eugenicist view of an American race, and the belief that the peoples "core" to that American race ought to be bred through a new immigration law, the racial borders of the new exclusions were certainly about protecting a "master race" of Americans. Indeed, when we consider the structure of exclusion operating in the nineteenth-century international legal order, and the structure of exclusion now coming into view with the new immigration regime of the early twentieth century, the hierarchies of racial development are strikingly similar.

The Immigration Act of 1924, along with its racial ideology, became the template for migration control across the globe,[92] and as Adam McKeown has argued, an immigration regime of racial borders became necessary for international recognition as a modern nation state.[93] Indeed, just as the right to exclude nonwhite peoples had been a marker of international legal personality in the Family of Nations, reproduced at the territorial boundaries of sovereign states was a new marker of international belonging: racial quotas.[94] McKeown continued:

The techniques designed to control Asians became the template for practical workings of general immigration laws in white settler nations, and ultimately around the world. By the 1920s, appropriation of these laws were driven less by practical needs than by the need to produce the documentation expected by other nations and live up to international standards of a well-governed nation-state. *States often claimed that immigration law was a domestic concern, not subject to international regulation. But this very assertion of a unilateral prerogative was part of a broader diffusion and standardization of principles about what it meant to be a sovereign state within an international system.*[95]

---

[91] *Id.* at 135.
[92] McKEOWN, *supra* note 2, at 123. *See also* DAVID SCOTT FITZGERALD & DAVID COOK-MARTIN, CULLING THE MASSES: THE DEMOCRATIC ORIGINS OF RACIST IMMIGRATION POLICY IN THE AMERICAS (2014); Gabriel Vhin, *Regulating Race: Asian Exclusion and the Administrative State*, 37 HARV. CIV. RTS. CIV. LIB. REV. 1 (2002); LUCY SALYER, LAWS HARSH AS TIGERS (1995).
[93] McKEOWN, *supra* note 2, at 321.
[94] *Id.* at 322.
[95] *Id.* at 13.

## 188  THE RIGHT TO EXCLUDE

The result: By the end of the first third of the twentieth century, democratic theory's boundary problem was a problem for national communities, not for international law. Who was properly a part of the *demos*, the nation, the political community? When could the sovereign exclude particular types of human beings, and why? International law's modern racial ideology had answers: Matters of migration and immigration were best left to background rules like the sovereign's right to exclude. Its functionalism counseled that, if these questions demanded solutions from the field of eugenics, so be it. A separate field of international migration law was a non-starter. And as for racial justice, that was a project for *imperium*, not *dominium*. It was impractical to discriminate against sovereign peoples on the basis of race, when it came to formal participation in the global order. But it was similarly impractical to force sovereigns to abide by an antidiscrimination principle when it came to territorial frontiers. Racial borders might have gone out of fashion as a global *pomerium*, but they were all the rage in the rise of modern immigration law. The sovereign's right to exclude, its *dominium*, had been thoroughly racialized.

# 6

# Decolonization and the Ambivalence of Self-Determination

In Chapter 5, we saw how functionalism helped justify a eugenicist approach to national border controls. As discussed, however, it is a mistake to understand functionalism as necessarily racist, or necessarily *anything*, beyond its teleological mission in the service of sociolegal jurisprudence. For even while functionalism proved a ready handmaiden in the effort to racialize *dominium*, at the very same time international lawyers were also raising functionalist arguments to deracialize *imperium* through a new logic of inclusion.

On the side of *imperium*, and by the end of World War II, a functionalist logic of inclusion helped condition an international space in which it became gradually less and less common to hear international lawyers argue for a racialized vision of international society. That is, by the middle decades of the twentieth century, the sovereign's right of *imperium* was losing *race* as an ideological justification for solving international law's boundary problem. In terms of bounding international society, classic racial ideology was suffering a loss of legitimation due to a logic of inclusion: if peoples were to be excluded from the plane of international legal personality, race, and racism were becoming less and less fashionable for doing so. But this weakening of classic racial ideology at the level of *imperium* should not be mistaken for the disappearance of *imperium* altogether. There were other functionalist hierarchies entering the scene—economic development for racial development, for example. But the idea that formal participation in international society should be open to all peoples, regardless of race, was a form of inclusionary ideology that was becoming more and more popular.[1] As discussed below, this trend had some of its beginnings in events like the Universal Races Congress of 1911 (URC), the Pan-African-Movement that began in 1900, and the emergence of the Tricontinental bloc at the United Nations (UN). However, in the eyes of some anticolonial critics, the logic of inclusion's diminishing of the racialization of *imperium* was insufficient. It wasn't enough to say that international law's hierarchies could no longer enjoy justification through reference to nineteenth and early twentieth century race science. Because in truth, the right of *imperium* hadn't itself diminished; it was only that racial xenophobia had lost its luster as an official form of justification. By

[1] *See, e.g.,* Benedict Anderson, The Age of Globalization: Anarchists and the Anticolonial Imagination (2013).

*The Right to Exclude.* Justin Desautels-Stein, Oxford University Press. © Justin Desautels-Stein 2023.
DOI: 10.1093/oso/9780198862161.003.0007

190    THE RIGHT TO EXCLUDE

the very end of the decolonization period, it was increasingly believed that global justice required more than divesting *imperium* of racial ideology; global justice required giving rights of *imperium* to the newly independent, decolonized world. With efforts like the "New International Economic Order" (NIEO), postcolonial states sought to determine the boundaries of the global *demos*, but now in explicitly economic terms. Where was the line marking those economic equals from everyone else? Who would decide? The NIEO project meant to let the postcolonial states answer those questions.

On the side of *dominium*, however, and as we saw in Chapter 5, the sovereign's right to exclude became, in the early years of the twentieth century, a powerful contributor to structures of racial hierarchy through the domestication of migration law. The sovereign's rights to self-determination and nonintervention *justified* the turn to eugenics as a policy tool for border control. What we will see in this chapter, however, was the development of the idea that the sovereign's territorial right to exclude could also *challenge* the racial status quo. Indeed, for many early anticolonial thinkers, antiracism entailed national self-determination for those people living under the "fetters of alien domination."[2] Peoples should have the right to "master their house," and it was precisely racial discrimination against the *house* that was problematic. Or, as the UN's Decolonization Declaration (1960) would put it, "the subjection of peoples to alien subjugation, domination, and exploitation constitutes a denial of fundamental human rights."[3] That is, rather than understand the sovereign's right of *dominium* as a part of the architecture of racial hierarchy, territorial *dominium* (now connected up with the inchoate language of "human rights") was precisely the way to tear it down. That was the idea, at any rate.

As we can see from this well-known quotation from the UN Decolonization Declaration, part of the discourse that would emerge around self-determination as a challenge to global structures of racial hierarchy was human rights. It is important to emphasize, however, that the anticolonial use of human rights discourse was a different thing than would develop later in the colorblind context of the antidiscrimination principle, discussed in Chapter 7. In the anticolonial register, third world international lawyers spoke of self-determination as the *prerequisite* for the exercise of human rights, which is to say that collective emancipation from racial hierarchy and the achievement of sovereign rights of exclusion were at the heart of anticolonial human rights discourse. Or to put that another way, global racial justice itself was a precondition for the exercise of human rights. Human rights wasn't the means for undoing racial hierarchy; undoing racial hierarchy was a baseline to be achieved *before* human rights could be meaningfully protected. Antiracism, self-determination, nonintervention, and human rights all coalesced

---

[2]    IMANUEL GEISS, THE PAN-AFRICAN MOVEMENT 396 (1974).

[3]    UN General Assembly Resolution 1514(XV), *Declaration on the Granting of Independence to Colonial Countries and Peoples*, A/RES/1514(XV) (Dec. 14, 1960), para. 1.

in a single, anticolonial strategy for what Adom Getachew calls "worldmaking after empire."[4] This is, of course, a radically different sensibility than the one with which we are more familiar today: the right of self-determination is (arguably) meaningful for indigenous peoples, but not for anyone else,[5] and the protection of human rights is the means for realizing racial justice—not the other way around.

If, by 1960, events like the Bandung Conference and the UN's Decolonization Declaration were regularly uniting the right of self-determination with human rights, this was certainly something other than what Woodrow Wilson had envisioned several decades earlier. In the years immediately leading to the creation of the League of Nations, Wilson famously elaborated an idea of self-determination in the classic liberal sense, appropriately exercised by members of international society. This was an idea about self-determination as self-government by the racially "developed" peoples of the world.[6] Lenin had offered a more radical and universal view of self-determination, and it was Lenin's rather than Wilson's that served as the impetus for what self-determination would become by the 1960s. In the context of the Decolonization Declaration, Getachew observes how self-determination emerged as an assault on global imperialism and racial hierarchy: "between the 1930s and 1960s, anticolonial nationalists increasingly framed empire as enslavement and conceived the right of self-determination as the response to this problem. In this pairing of question and answer, the anticolonial account of self-determination was invented."[7] What this amounts to, in the context of the right to exclude, was a reversal of what we saw in Chapter 5, and the potential for envisioning *dominium* as *antiracism*.

The result was a modern racial ideology that at once espoused a functionalist logic of inclusion regarding membership in international society, and yet remained entirely agnostic about the relations of raciality and national self-determination. What mattered was that sovereigns—*all sovereigns*—enjoyed the right of *dominium*, which meant that they had natural rights to determine and sustain the boundaries of their national communities. Whether, or when, these sovereign rights might deepen structures of racial hierarchy and exclusion operating through insider/outsider regimes produced through border controls—well, that just wasn't a question for international law. Looking at the right of *dominium* from the twinned perspective of migration and decolonization, we get a glimpse of modern racial ideology's double image of self-determination. On the one side is a view of self-determination as a means for unravelling the sovereign's right of *imperium*, as "worldmaking."

---

[4] Adom Getachew, Worldmaking After Empire: The Rise and Fall of Self-Determination (2019)

[5] , Accordance with International Law of the Unilateral Declaration of Independence in Respect of Kosovo, Advisory Opinion, 2010 I.C.J. Rep. 403 (July 22)

[6] *See, e.g.*, Rayford Logan, The Betrayal of the Negro: From Rutherford B. Hayes to Woodrow Wilson (1997).

[7] Getachew, *supra* note 4, at 77.

## 192 THE RIGHT TO EXCLUDE

Self-determination is freedom, is antiracism, is anticolonialism, it is the black radical tradition of W.E.B. Du Bois, George Padmore, and C.L.R. James. On the other side, the right of self-determination beckons classic racial ideology, shifted from the borders of international society to the borders of the nation. Self-determination, from this side of things, is racist, is neocolonial, and a fixture of international law's enduring racial xenophobia. It reproduces raciality and racial subjection by naturalizing the borders of new states, and guaranteeing the rights of these states to exclude foreign peoples as they wish. It is a lens through which we see the interplay of racial subjection via the rights to exclude individual migrants and the rights to exclude peoples.

Here at the end of modern racial ideology's dominance, that fight is now a fight against individual acts of racial discrimination. The problem of structural racism, and the deep and complex relation between race and the right to exclude, is simply out of sight. In framing the situation this way, it might seem that we are ready to move on to the third phase in this history of international law's racial ideology. But not yet. What we have seen thus far is the rise of legal functionalism, a purposive style of juridical science intended to give legal concepts closure through a matching of legal rules with social science. We have seen the nascent deracialization of the sovereign's right of *imperium*, and we will see below the failure to turn the tables on *imperium* in the context of the NIEO. We have seen the rise of the postcolonial state's right of *dominium*, and we will see below how the right of self-determination transformed from an antiracist strategy and into a functionalist justification for the status quo. Global antiracism, once connected at the hip to the sovereign's right to exclude, eventually detaches itself from this decolonizing idea and lands in the territory of the antidiscrimination principle.

To sum up as we move forward: First, modern racial ideology deploys a logic of inclusion at the level of international society, where more of the previously excluded are allowed to participate in international institutions. This is the gradual deracialization of *imperium*, the move from the Family of Nations to the UN, brought on by developments in functionalism and physical anthropology. Second, the sovereign's right of *dominium* has a doubled character with respect to its relation to structures of racial hierarchy and subjection. On the one side, as we have seen in the discussion of the failed launch of international migration law, *dominium* turns out to be a powerful vehicle for racial subjection and the sovereign's right to exclude migrants. As discussed in this chapter, however, anticolonial thinkers characterized *dominium* as a critical weapon in the fight *for* racial justice. Nevertheless, the connection between the sovereign's right of self-determination and the campaign for racial justice was short-lived. Before long, it would become less and less clear why or how borders might be the repositories of racial content, or what the exercise of the right of *dominium* might suggest for racial hierarchy at an international level. I trace this trajectory first in the context of the early international race conferences, then to the rise of the decolonization project in the UN, and finally, into the status quo settlement of the self-determination cases from the International Court of Justice (ICJ).

## I THE INTERWAR ALLIANCE BETWEEN ANTIRACIST AND ANTICOLONIAL STRATEGY

### A The Universal Races Congress

While race was clearly a dominant variable in the Hague meetings at the turn of the twentieth century, these were not conferences *about* race. The first of such meetings was motivated by deepening concerns about an incipient "war of the races."[8] Columbia University Professor, Felix Adler, and Secretary of the International Society of Ethical Culture, Gustav Spiller, together headed up an executive council that, in 1911, would launch the first and last "Universal Races Congress," held at the University of London. With two thousand academics from around the world in attendance, Adler and Du Bois served as co-secretaries for the delegation from the United States (US).[9] The Congress was preceded by a one-day conference focused on race and international law, and among the Congress' honorary officers were a number of scholars we have already encountered, including Antoine Pillet, Alberic Roulin, Leon Duguit, Paul Fachille, Georg Jellinek, Lassa Oppenheim, and T.S. Woolsey. Perhaps predictably, Elihu Root sent his apologies for missing the event.[10]

The conference invitation stated that the purpose of the gathering was to discuss, "in the light of modern knowledge and the modern conscience," the nature of relations between the peoples of the East and West, the "so-called white and so-called colored peoples."[11] Of note in the call for papers were two ideas worth further exploration: the state of "modern knowledge and modern conscience" in those years before and after the Great War, and the "apolitical" relation between race and imperialism.[12] Indeed, in the context of the URC we can get a glimpse of

---

[8] The history of the abolition of the international slave trade is a related development here, but only partially. I do not understand the British impulse toward abolition as motivated by a rejection of the science of racial development, but rather as a feature of the anti-slavery mission of British abolitionism. *See* G. Heuman, *Slavery, the Slave Trade, and Abolition, in* 5 THE OXFORD HISTORY OF THE BRITISH EMPIRE 32 (1999). For the argument that abolition was really about Britain's pursuit of market advantage in the new economy of the nineteenth century, *see* ERIC WILLIAMS, CAPITALISM AND SLAVERY (1944). On the trade more generally, *see* George Scelle, *The Slave Trade in the Spanish Colonies of America: The Assiento*, 4 AM. J. INT'L L. 617 (1910); JEAN ALLAIN, SLAVERY IN INTERNATIONAL LAW (2012); JENNY MARTINEZ, THE SLAVE TRADE AND THE ORIGINS OF INTERNATIONAL HUMAN RIGHTS LAW (2012); HUGH THOMAS, THE SLAVE TRADE: THE STORY OF THE ATLANTIC SLAVE TRADE: 1440–1870 (1997).

[9] Robert John Holton, *Cosmopolitanism or Cosmopolitanisms? The Universal Races Congress of 1911*, 2 GLOBAL NETWORKS 153, 161 (2002); Elliott Rudwick, *WEB Dubois and the Universal Races Congress of 1911*, 20 PHYLON Q. 372 (1959).

[10] Record of the Proceedings of the First Universal Races Congress, July 26–29, 1911, available at https://babel.hathitrust.org/cgi/pt?id=uiug.30112069959390&view=1up&seq=27.

[11] *First Universal Races Congress*, 21 INT'L J. ETHICS 248 (1911).

[12] Political issues were intended to stay separate from the URC deliberations. They didn't.

194    THE RIGHT TO EXCLUDE

two important tracks in the establishment of modern racial ideology—the critique of nineteenth-century race science and a belief in decolonization as an antiracist strategy for international law.

As we have seen in previous chapters, the early years of the twentieth century were rife with new thinking about the biological foundations of racial identity. In some quarters the debate had moved to eugenics, largely concerned as it was with social science prescriptions for race relations. In others, however, and as pointedly elaborated at the Congress, the connection between biology and race was becoming increasingly ambiguous. To be sure, the argument that race was a social construction was yet to come.[13] John Gray, President of the Royal Anthropological Institute, for example, presented a paper at the Congress ranking the "natural capacities for intelligence" among the world's races, with the whites of the US ranking first, the "negroes" of the US ranking last.[14] But even among the more "modern" statements, the biological reality of racial classification tended to ground the discussion, even while a more egalitarian perspective took to the surface. As Oxford Professor Charles Myers suggested in his paper, "if only the environment can be gradually changed, perhaps with sufficient slowness and certainly in the appropriate direction, both the mental and the physical characters of the lowest races may ultimately attain those of the highest, and vice versa."[15]

The famed German anthropologist Felix von Luschan concurred, explaining to the audience how so many physical attributes are products of the environment, and how very little should be gleaned from particular colors of skin and hair. Further, he reminded that "beauty is very relative," and the line between the savage and the civilized to be very much in the eye of the beholder.[16] Nevertheless, von Luschan maintained that races were still real enough, and that anthropology ought to outline the "separate evolution of the 'so-called white and the so-called coloured peoples,'" since "racial barriers will never cease to exist."[17] But this was admittedly a moral or political imperative for anthropology, given that the "three chief varieties of mankind—the old Indo-European, the African, and the East-Asiatic ... all three

---

[13] Indeed, there remained plenty of the older, nineteenth century visions of racial classification, even at the moment of the Congress. H.H. Johnston, for example, in his review of the Congress explained that there were four human divisions: "The white, or Caucasian; the Yellow, or Mongolian ... the Brown mixed races ... and the Negro, or black sub-species." *See* H.H. Johnston, *Racial Problems and the Congress of Races*, 100 CONTEMP. REV. 149, 155 (1911). For Johnston, these were not equal races. Rather, "the White Man of Europe" was the "redeemer of the world." *Id.* This racial superiority was ostensibly evidenced by larger brain size, greater physical development, a trend in which females are more beautiful than males (females in the nonwhite races were "invariably ugly and ill-formed"), and culture, read to mean art, language, manufacturing, agriculture, "and the taming of the wild." *Id.*

[14] PAPERS ON INTER-RACIAL PROBLEMS, COMMUNICATED TO THE FIRST UNIVERSAL RACES CONGRESS, HELD AT THE UNIVERSITY OF LONDON, JULY 26–29, 1911 83 (Gustav Spiller ed., 1911).

[15] *Id.* at 78.

[16] *Id.* at 14.

[17] *Id.* at 23.

forming a complete unity, intermarrying in all directions without the slightest decrease of fertility."[18]

The Congress was certainly dominated by scientific views more in keeping with von Luschan's presentation than Gray's,[19] but what of the "modern conscience" with which to pursue the study of the instability of human type, as the founder of modern anthropology, Franz Boas, had put it? The emerging view, in a phrase, was a logic of inclusion. To take two quite divergent presentations with very similar end-points, Felix Adler understood the fundamental problem to be racial animosity on the global scale, an "international situation full of menace and cause for the greatest anxiety."[20] Fueled by false beliefs about racial superiority and cultural arrogance, the Occidental and Oriental peoples were speeding down a blind alley, and without a change in course, a race war was the unavoidable result. We wouldn't find a way out with more sympathy, more moral feeling, or abstract visions of "world peace." Rather, the peoples of the world needed to recognize a basic social fact: the human species is a unified organization, and racial diversity can pose threats to the health of that organization, just as it holds the secret of its success. "The garden of humanity should present the spectacle of flowers infinitely varied in hue and fragrance," Alder explained. "The human orchard should include trees bearing the most diverse fruit."[21] However, just as elements of any ecosystem might turn hostile, undermining the stability of the system (as Occidental races have tended to do to the Oriental peoples), so too will the diversity of a system prove a great strength and cure. For Adler, a scientific understanding of the interconnected interests of the world's races was the only way to find a "new direction," a way out of the coming conflict.

A similar presentation but from a different perspective came from Abdu'l-Baha, a leader of the Baha'i religious movement that had begun in Persia and spread into Europe and the US, and which eventually came to include thinkers like Alain Locke and Nina Du Bois.[22] Indeed, Adler's language shared much with Abdu'l-Baha's, who explained that God had made all people as "drops of one sea and leaves of one tree," exemplifying a "unity in diversity":

The world is in a warlike condition, and its races are hostile one to the other. The darkness of difference surrounds them, and the light of kindness grows dim. The foundations of society are destroyed and the banners of life and

---

[18] *Id.* at 17.

[19] Von Luschan's political views, however, were generally regarded as alien to the spirit of the Congress. *See* George Cutter, *Race Prejudice*, 73 ADVOCATE OF PEACE 233, 233 (1911).

[20] *Id.* at 262.

[21] *Id.* at 264.

[22] *See* RICHARD THOMAS, RACIAL UNITY: AN IMPERATIVE FOR SOCIAL PROGRESS (1993); Guy Emerson Mount, *A Troubled Modernity: W.E.B. Du Bois, "The Black Church," and the Problem of Causality, in* ABDU'L BAHA'S JOURNEY WEST: THE COURSE OF HUMAN SOLIDARITY (Negar Mottahedeh ed., 2013).

196   THE RIGHT TO EXCLUDE

joy are overthrown. The leaders of the world seem to glory in the shedding of blood ... [The way forward is to embrace the Reality of all things] ... Consider the varieties of flowers in a garden. They seem but to enhance the loveliness of each other. When differences of color, ideas, and character are found in the human kingdom, and come under the control of the power of Unity, they too show their essential beauty and perfection.[23]

Alfred Haddon echoed the point, arguing against the view that all of humanity might merge into a single, "common" race. The strength of the human species was its diversity, as it constantly bettered itself not through assimilation but through the progressive encounter with difference.[24] Haddon continued with the botanical metaphor: "There are differences in mankind. You do not say that the rose is better than the lily—you say they are different. So with mankind: there are differences, and we want to learn the lesson that each *nationality* can teach us."[25]

If modern knowledge was increasingly pointing toward the instability of racial classifications, and modern conscience was increasingly pointing toward multicultural inclusiveness,[26] what of the geographical context? What was the site for the fight for racial equality? For many participants at the Congress the site for antiracist strategy was unquestionably global, and a fight that would take place on the terrain of international law.[27] The question was how to square modern knowledge and the modern conscience with the nineteenth-century's conception of sovereignty. Two paths would emerge, one in the direction of the functionalist logic of exclusion/inclusion, the other more heterodox. The first was reflected in many of the views expressed by European thinkers. The second was best represented by the Chinese delegation.

Dedicated to the discussion of this issue was the seventh session of the Congress. Walter Schucking of the University of Marburg, and member of the Institute of International Law, began his presentation with a functionalist credo: "There has always been a reciprocal relation between facts and law, and the development of the law has ever proceeded in such a way that every change in the facts has given rise to new laws, which must answer the new needs."[28] And what were the facts staring everyone in the face? Nineteenth-century race science could no longer support a sovereign's right to exclude so-called racial inferiors from the Family of Nations. The Family of Nations must increasingly become multiracial, allowing for a gradual

---

[23] INTER-RACIAL PROBLEMS, *supra* note 16, at 156.
[24] Proceedings of the URC, *supra* note 12, at 26.
[25] *Id.* at 27.
[26] It should be emphasized that even at the Congress, there were plenty of opposing views. *See, e.g.,* Charles Bruce, *The Modern Conscience in Relation to the Treatment of Dependent Peoples, in* PAPERS ON INTER-RACIAL PROBLEMS (Gustave Spiller ed., 1911); Harry Johnston, "The World Position of the Negro," *in* PAPERS ON INTER-RACIAL PROBLEMS (Gustave Spiller ed., 1911).
[27] Ulysses Weatherly, *The First Universal Races Congress*, 17 AM. J. SOC. 315, 323 (1911).
[28] INTER-RACIAL PROBLEMS, *supra* note 16, at 387.

inclusion of every race, every people, every nation. That is, the Family of Nations would become ever more inclusive where the "expansion proceeds by the advance of some of the non-European States to the rank of equal members in the sphere of international law, *by the progressive Europeanization of the non-European parts of the world.*"[29] Some states were assimilating in the "civilizing work" more quickly than others, which was a good thing. As international organizations slowly developed, "the States of all races would thus find themselves interconnected, and we should in the end be led to elaborate a law for the whole commerce of the world."[30]

John McDonnell of the University of London pushed the ball forward, asking, if we assume the eventual expansion of international society to include the "subject races," what else can international law do in the service of racial equality? Racial questions about the prospects of "Negroes" in the US, Jews in Russia, Macedonians in Turkey, Indians in South Africa, and more, all seem to cash out with the same answer: "Today each State says, and will long continue to say, 'I must be master in my house.' That position must be accepted—at all events for the time."[31] Beyond this, the thrust of the matter really did lie at the level of international community, and the need to push beyond racial hierarchy as a justification for excluding "the unpromising races"[32] from the Family of Nations. Citing Bluntschli, Gobineau, and Chamberlain, among others, McDonnell anticipated the coming idea that every people ought to find a place in the governing shade of international law, even if it meant sub-sovereign forms—which would, in the space of a few years time, become Mandates.

Indeed, as already articulated in the Berlin Conference of 1885, and as it was to be codified in the League Covenant a few years later, the civilized states owed the "inferior or backward" races a "sacred duty," a trust that the backward races would be given every opportunity to mature.[33] As McDonnell explained, "If certain races are in the position of minors, not fit in their present condition to be their own masters, those who claim superiority and control ought to justify their position as guardians."[34] And if the biology of racial development could no longer serve such justifications, what could? McDonnell was skeptical, for not only was the concept of "civilization" unmanageable as a test, the truth was that a distinction between civilized and backward did very little in terms of specifying the varying characteristics of the many races unjustifiably clumped together in this way. Peoples "radically different from one another" are found in both the "civilized" and "uncivilized" worlds, and the better standard for measuring the justness of relations between the races is modern knowledge sitting on the shoulders of modern conscience.

[29] *Id.* at 389.
[30] *Id.* at 392–93.
[31] *Id.* at 398–99.
[32] *Id.* at 401.
[33] *Id.* at 402.
[34] *Id.*

198  THE RIGHT TO EXCLUDE

Together, Schucking and McDonnell's presentations suggested agreement on the need to push beyond the outdated racial hierarchies of nineteenth-century international law, as well as mutual understanding about the duties owed to the subordinated races by the dominant ones. The nature of these duties, however, were pretty much up for grabs—was the question one of assimilation to a capitalist mode of economic development, or a broader understanding of "Western Culture"? Or rather, was the sacred trust owed to the "backward races" a more multicultural one? In any event, the two scholars from Germany and England seemed of apiece with respect to the terrain on which these improvements were to be made: the terrain of international society, and the functionalist inclusion of various races in international law. The quest for racial equality seemed to end at this particular frontier.

On the other hand, a rather different sense for the interplay between international law and racial equality was forming—not in the context of *imperium* but in that of *dominium*, and it is here that we can see glimpses of a deeper critique. Henri La Fontaine of Belgium, for example, seemed to anticipate a decolonization argument in favor of self-determination when he argued for "the extension to all races forming parts of nations the rights at present accorded to each nation collectively."[35] Presentations from representatives from Haiti, Japan, India, Iran, and Egypt were suggestive of a similar view, largely arguing for the strengths of their respectively distinctive but "civilized" racial cultures.[36] The Chinese presentation, however, differed in its emphasis on the need to understand the claim for racial equality in the context of the newly emerging right of racialized *dominium*. Bemoaning the rise of a "white policy" of racialized exclusion of Chinese and other nonwhite migrants, Wu Ting-Fang argued that there was no better example of "uncivilized behavior."[37] At least for participants like Fontaine and Wu, an antiracist approach to international law might mean something *other* than the sovereign's right to master his house, as McDonnell had put it. "Mastering one's house" was certainly a way of expressing the right to exclude in the register of *dominium*, but rights of self-determination and nonintervention could also serve as structures of exclusion (as we saw in Chapter 5, in the context of migration law). An antiracist international law might, in this view, challenge this racialization of the sovereign's emerging right of *dominium*, in addition to its rethinking of *imperium*.

It is largely true that the racialization of *dominium* that occurred in the space of a nascent international migration law, and that we can see on the minds of the Chinese delegation at the URC, never really made it onto the decolonization radar. The modern form of racial ideology that was emerging at this point combined a new ideology of inclusion at the level of *imperium*, largely masking a new ideology

[35] INTER-RACIAL PROBLEMS, *supra* note 16, at 69.
[36] For an analysis of a distinctive approach on the part of the Turkish representative, *see* Mansour Bonakdarian, *Negotiating Universal Values and Cultural and National Parameters at the First Universal Races Congress*, 92 RAD. HIST. REV. 118 (2005).
[37] INTER-RACIAL PROBLEMS, *supra* note 16, at 132.

of exclusion emerging at the level of *dominium*. And at the Congress, there was certainly plenty of functionalist talk of inclusion, and a bit of rhetoric about *dominium* as antiracism for the colonized world. But there were glimpses of more; glimpses of what could have been a structural assault on raciality that took international law to account for bounding not just international society, but national societies as well. As Susan Pennybacker has put it, "in the congress' interstices lay fodder for a militant challenge to the global order right alongside imperialism's most ardent defenders."[38] But more to the present point, the URC is an illustration of international law's modern racial ideology at an early moment, including both the modern approach to race science and an inclusive multiculturalism.[39] Indeed, perhaps while it was diplomats like Wu who best embodied the URC's more radical potential, it was probably Haddon that best summed up the attitudes that would dominate in the years after the War: "What so many ardent spirits cannot appreciate is that safe progress is slow progress and that compromises have to be made."[40]

## B  Pan-Africanism, The League Against Imperialism, and the Black Radical Tradition

The Universal Races Congress was intended as the first in a series of consultations about global antiracism. Rather than another URC, what followed instead was the outbreak of the Great War.[41] And so, it wasn't the tradition of the URC that would carry forward an international view of race, but rather another global project with which Du Bois was involved. A decade before the URC landed in London, that city hosted the first Pan-African Conference of 1900.[42] The Conference was the brainchild of a Trinidadian lawyer, Henry Sylvester Williams.[43] Williams hoped to bring together representatives from the African diaspora, without a geographical limit to those living on the African continent, and the idea of "Pan-Africanism" seems to have been a synonym for Du Bois' earlier term, "Pan-Negroism."[44] An animating idea was that the problems of racism and colonialism were deeply intertwined, and a focus on one without the other was unproductive.[45] Hence the perceived need

[38] Susan Pennybacker, *The Universal Races Congress, London, Political Culture, and Imperial Dissent, 1900–1939,* 92 RAD. HIST. REV. 103, 106 (2005); Helen Tilley, *Racial Science, Geopolitics, and Empires,* 105 ISIS 773 (2014).

[39] MARILYN LAKE & HAROLD REYNOLDS, DRAWING THE GLOBAL COLOUR LINE: WHITE MEN'S COUNTRIES AND THE INTERNATIONAL CHALLENGE OF RACIAL EQUALITY (2008).

[40] A.C. Haddon, *The First Universal Races Congress,* 34 SCIENCE 304, 306 (1911).

[41] W.E.B. DU BOIS, DUSK OF DAWN: AN ESSAY TOWARD AN AUTOBIOGRAPHY OF A RACE CONCEPT 230 (1940).

[42] Paul Harris, *Racial Identity and the Civilizing Mission: Double-Consciousness at the 1895 Congress on Africa,* 18 REL. & AM. CULT. 145 (2008).

[43] GEISS, *supra* note 2, at 176.

[44] W.E.B. DU BOIS, THE CONSERVATION OF RACES (1897).

[45] GEISS, *supra* note 2, at 185–86.

200    THE RIGHT TO EXCLUDE

to unite antiracist and anticolonial practice across the continents. The Conference was attended by around 30 speakers, with almost half coming from the US, including Du Bois and Anna Julia Cooper, a handful from African nations, and a few from Canada, Haiti, and the United Kingdom.

The mission and the stakes are evident in the Conference's famous declaration to "The Nations of the World." With Du Bois at the pen, the document left little question about the motivation for this first Pan-African gathering:

> In the metropolis of the modern world, in this the closing year of the nineteenth century, there has been assembled a congress of men and women of African blood, to deliberate solemnly upon the present situation and outlook of the darker races of mankind. The problem of the twentieth century is the problem of the color line, the question as to how far differences of race-which show themselves chiefly in the color of the skin and the texture of the hair-will hereafter be made the basis of denying to over half the world the right of sharing to utmost ability the opportunities and privileges of modern civilization.[46]

As the participants of this first Conference saw it, the world order that was coming to a close with the end of the nineteenth century had come to a crossroads. On the one side was a path toward a world order of racial justice. "Let the world take no backward step in that slow but sure progress which has successively refused to let the spirit of class, of caste, of privilege, or of birth, debar from life, liberty and the pursuit of happiness a striving human soul. Let no color or race be a feature of distinction between white and black men, regardless of worth or ability."[47] This was a path that seemed open, yet entirely unknown in its particulars. On the other side was a way that was all too familiar: "But if, by reason of carelessness, prejudice, greed and injustice, the black world is to be exploited and ravished and degraded," not to mention "the brown and yellow myriads elsewhere,"[48] the world as a whole would suffer for it.

Despite the clarion call of this first Pan-African gathering, plans for subsequent conferences fell through, and the Pan-African Association that had been born in the Conference's wake ceased thereafter. And it was the URC of 1911, rather than this first Pan-African Conference of 1900, that would enjoy Du Bois' loudest laudations. Nevertheless, Du Bois would eventually return to the Pan-African concept, and at the end of World War I he travelled to Paris to take part in the Peace Conference at Versailles. The result was the first of five Pan-African Congresses.[49] Despite resistance from Woodrow Wilson, and a US block on visas

---

[46] W.E.B. Du Bois, *To the Nations of the World* (July 25, 1900), available at https://www.blackpast.org/african-american-history/1900-w-e-b-du-bois-nations-world/.

[47] *Id.*

[48] *Id.*

[49] Geiss, *supra* note 2, at 235. The Second Congress was held in 1921 (London, Brussels, and Paris), the Third in 1923 (London and Lisbon), and the Fourth in 1927 (New York).

to African-Americans wishing to attend the Pan-African Congress in Paris, on February 19, 1919, 57 representatives from the US, the French West Indies, Haiti, Liberia, South America, Algeria, Egypt, and the Belgian Congo were in attendance.[50] The Congress' final resolution was much in keeping with the plan of the League of Nations, developing the mandates system under the guiding principle that, when the "darker races" were mature enough, they could emerge from League supervision and take the sovereign mantle.[51] Later resolutions from Pan-African Congresses in the 1920s included demands for "absolute racial equality" and increasingly more aggressive critiques of the League's mandate system and apparent failure to understand race as a question of international importance.[52]

Representative of the critical view of the League shared by many African-American writers of the time,[53] Rayford Logan of Howard University joined the Pan-African Congress' view of the global connection between racism and colonialism.[54] As Logan saw it, "practically all persons interested in the Negro as a whole are beginning to realize that the solution of his problem in any part of the world is dependent upon and affected by general world movements."[55] And these general world movements, typified by the League's international control of the mandate system, offered mixed blessings. Logan agreed with the basic thrust of functionalist inclusion, holding the superiority of a world order of international administration and adjudication over the nineteenth century's mode of colonial possession. But the mandate system was riddled with terrible difficulties, from inadequate means for the League to effectively guide the mandatory powers in their rule over the former colonies, to the sense in which the Class C mandates—with special emphasis on South West Africa—looked forever destined for subjugation. The trouble with the mandate system was a trouble with raciality—a focus that both Logan and the organizers of the Pan-African Congress saw as inadequately appreciated at the level of League governance.

In the midst of looming financial and organizational difficulties, including the coming depression, the Pan-African Congresses stalled after a fourth iteration in 1927. In that same year, however, the ball passed to Brussels with the founding of the League Against Imperialism and for National Independence.[56] Organized by the German communist Willi Munzenberg, about 180 participants were in attendance, coming from Europe, North and South America, the Caribbean, Africa,

---

[50] *Id.* at 238.

[51] *Id.* at 239.

[52] *See, e.g.*, Ida Hunt, "The Coloured Races and the League of Nations," Third Pan-African Congress, November 25, 1923.

[53] For discussion, *see* Penny Von Eschen, Race Against Empire: Black Americans and Anticolonialism, 1937–1957 (1997). On the New Negro Movement, of which writers like Logan might be considered a part, *see* The New Negro: An Interpretation (Alain Locke ed., 1925).

[54] Rayford Logan, *The Operation of the Mandate System in Africa*, 13 J. Negro Hist. 423 (1928).

[55] *Id.* at 423.

[56] *See generally* Fredrik Petersson, *Hub of the Anti-Imperialist Movement: The League Against Imperialism and Berlin, 1927–1933*, 16 Int'l J. Postcolonial Stud. 49 (2013).

202    THE RIGHT TO EXCLUDE

and Asia. In many ways, the League Against Imperialism more resembled the URC than the Pan-African Congress. More broadly conceived, the League took direct aim at the League of Nations itself, positioning itself as a critic of racism, colonialism, and capitalism—and the issue of Pan-Africanism became an element of the program.[57] Indeed, in the texts of the League Congress these problems were once again inseparable. As Lamine Senghor, the chair of the League's commission dedicated to the "Negro Question," had explained, "Imperialist oppression ... springs from capitalism. It is this that engenders imperialism among the peoples of the principal countries ... It must be destroyed and replaced by the union of free peoples and then there will no longer be any slavery."[58] And as the African-American radical Richard Moore argued, in the encounter with "the monster of world imperialism," the human races must unite "against fascism, against the Ku Klux Klan movement, against chauvinism and against the doctrine of white superiority ... as long as European workers are still infected with these unfortunate ideas it will be impossible to free the world from the burden of imperialism."[59]

In speeches like these, the equality of peoples was a principle about racial, national, and economic equality. To "liberate the Negro race throughout the world," the League's resolution on the Negro Question demanded, among other things, possession by Africans of African lands and administration, immediate abolition of forced labor and indirect taxes, and abolition of all racial and class distinctions in economic and political matters.[60] James Ford, an African-American Marxist, reported to the League in 1929 that "the toiling masses of the Negroes throughout the world can see no hope for rectifying their conditions under imperialism, indeed there is no hope, not the slightest chance. The Negro toiling masses must look forward mobilizing their forces for a joint struggle against imperialism, for independence, and self-rule."[61] A year earlier, the World Congress of the Communist International released its "Theses on the Revolutionary Movement in the Colonies and Semi-Colonies," similarly emphasizing the importance of self-determination—for colonized peoples the world over, including African-Americans.[62] Known as the "Black Belt" thesis, as Cheryl Higadisha explains, "Black liberation was predicated on the right of African Americans in the Black Belt region of the South, where they formed a majority, to secede as their own nation under the correct historical

---

[57] See also The League of Coloured Peoples, in THE OXFORD COMPANION TO BLACK BRITISH HISTORY (David Dabydeen et al. eds., 2007).

[58] GEISS, supra note 2, at 328.

[59] Id. at 329.

[60] Id. at 330.

[61] James Ford, The Negro Question: Report to the 2nd World Congress of the League Against Imperialism, THE NEGRO WORKER 7–8 (Aug. 1929). See also James Ford, The Communist's Way Out for the Negro, 5 J. NEGRO ED. 88 (1936).

[62] See CEDRIC ROBINSON, BLACK MARXISM: THE MAKING OF THE BLACK RADICAL TRADITION 222–25 (1983).

conditions."[63] Claudia Jones put it this way: "It is only by helping to interconnect the partial demands with the right of self-determination, that we Communists, in concert with other progressive forces, can contribute guidance to the struggle for complete equality for the Negro people."[64]

Along with Du Bois' monumental work, *Black Reconstruction in America*, perhaps the most well-known thinker of the period engaging raciality through a much debated Marxist lens (from today's perspective, not James'), was the Trinidadian journalist and historian C.L.R. James.[65] As Cedric Robinson has famously argued, James is a key figure in the elaboration of the Black Radical Tradition for his insistence that colonized peoples liberate themselves, rather than wait on the eventual maturation of trusteeship. In his famed history of the Haitian Revolution, James

> had made a singular contribution to radical Black historiography when he and his comrades in the [International African Service Bureau] were mapping out their contending positions in the last years of the third, and during the fourth decade of the century. It was then that [George Padmore] had written *How Britain Rules Africa*, Eric Williams his *The Negro in the Caribbean*, Kenyatta his *Kenya: Land of Conflict*, and James *The Black Jacobins*. The first three had proposed national independence for African peoples but were addressed to the colonial powers. The fourth had not appealed. Instead it was a declaration of war for liberation.[66]

Indeed, James was after something much deeper than inclusion in the world's new international institutions:

> Today 150 million Negroes, knit into world economy infinitely more tightly than their ancestors of a hundred years ago, will far surpass the work of that San Domingo half-million in the work of social transformation. The continuous risings in Africa, the refusal of Ethiopian warriors to submit to Mussolini; the American Negroes who volunteered to fight in Spain in the Abraham Lincoln Brigade, as Rigaud and Beauvais had volunteered to fight in America, tempering their swords against the enemy abroad for use against the enemy at home—these lightnings announce the thunder. The racial prejudice that now stands in the way will bow before the tremendous impact of the proletarian revolution.[67]

---

[63] Cheryl Higashida, Black Internationalist Feminism: Women Writers of the Black Left, 1945–1995 18 (2013); Robinson, *supra* note 64, at 222.

[64] Claudia Jones, *On the Right to Self-Determination for the Negro People in the Black Belt, in* Words of Fire: An Anthology of African American Feminist Thought 74 (Beverly Guy-Sheftal ed., 1995). On earlier versions of Black nationalism, directed more toward emigration than secession, *see* Roderick Bush, We Are Not What We Seem: Black Nationalism and Class Struggle in the American Century (2000).

[65] Robin D.G. Kelley, *The World the Diaspora Made: C.L.R. James and the Politics of History, in* Rethinking C.L.R. James (Grant Farrad ed., 1996).

[66] Robinson, *supra* note 64, at 274.

[67] C.L.R. James and Revolutionary Marxism 86 (Scott McLemee & Paul Le Blanc eds., 2018).

204 THE RIGHT TO EXCLUDE

A fellow Trinidadian and longtime associate of James, George Padmore is similarly well-known as an originary figure for Black Internationalism. Also, and like James (and also Du Bois), Padmore had a complex relationship with Marxism. As Roderick Bush observes, "Padmore moved to embrace a form of Black Internationalism that called for the unity of Blacks from Africa, the United States, the West Indies, and other lands."[68] After his break with the Communist International, however, in 1934 Padmore allied with Du Bois in the effort to find an alternate intellectual source for an international approach to race.[69] What turned out to be the impetus for the new shift was Italy's invasion of Ethiopia in 1935, for what that event illuminated for both Padmore and James was the uselessness of international institutions like the League, and the ultimate unreliability of the Comintern. Colonialism, Padmore argued, *was* fascism, and while Mussolini and Hitler were its most visible representatives, the fascist domination of the world's "darker" bodies was a foundational feature of a new colonialism, a "neocolonialism."[70] This argument led Padmore to believe in the necessity of making further alliances across national and continental lines. As Leslie James has written, Padmore believed that "whether officially under imperialism or not, the condition of all black workers was the same. This was a crucial articulation of black transnationalism that placed imperialism at the center of the black experience. Padmore used the language of enslavement to describe black labor wherever it might be: in Africa, the West Indies, Latin America, and the United States."[71] And as Padmore would later explain in his *Pan-Africanism or Communism*, "In our struggle for national freedom, human dignity, and social redemption, Pan-Africanism offers an ideological alternative to Communism on the one side and Tribalism on the other. It rejects both white racialism and black chauvinism. It stands for racial co-existence on the basis of absolute equality and respect for human personality."[72]

As with the Pan-African congress movement, by the 1930s, the League Against Imperialism faced increasing challenges with the rise of Nazism in Germany, the Soviet Union's joining with the League of Nations, and a general tightening of the financial screws. Of course, many worldwide stirrings were relevant to international engagements with the problem of racial imperialism in the years before the onset of World War II,[73] but it was the combined effect of Mussolini and Hitler that marked a new phase in Pan-Africanism.[74] By 1944, many of the groups that had

---

[68] RODERICK BUSH, THE END OF WHITE WORLD SUPREMACY: BLACK INTERNATIONALISM AND THE PROBLEM OF THE COLOR LINE 124 (2009).

[69] Padmore later published PAN AFRICANISM OR COMMUNISM? THE COMING STRUGGLE FOR AFRICA (1956).

[70] *See* KWAME NKRUMAH, NEOCOLONIALISM: THE LAST STAGE OF IMPERIALISM (1965); BUSH, THE END OF WHITE WORLD SUPREMACY, *supra* note 68, at 122–26.

[71] LESLIE JAMES, GEORGE PADMORE AND DECOLONIZATION FROM BELOW: PAN-AFRICANISM, THE COLD WAR, AND THE END OF EMPIRE 37 (2015).

[72] GEORGE PADMORE, PAN AFRICANISM OR COMMUNISM? THE COMING STRUGGLE FOR AFRICA 355 (1972).

[73] Perhaps nothing was more prominent than the Second Italo–Ethiopian War.

[74] ROBINSON, *supra* note 64, at 271.

emerged during the 1930s came together in the new Pan-African Federation, the entity that would form the fifth Pan-African Congress of 1945 in Manchester, with Padmore, Du Bois, James, and a young Kwame Nkrumah at the helm.[75]

Despite (or perhaps in part because of) the lack of an African-American presence (with the exception of Du Bois, attending in a private capacity), Nkrumah and Padmore were the Congress' joint secretaries and together held the nucleus of the new leadership. Ranging over questions of racial discrimination in Britain, the South Africa problem, and the Italian invasion of Ethiopia, the Congress passed two general resolutions: "The Challenge to the Colonial Powers" and "Declaration to the Colonial Workers, Farmers, and Intellectuals."[76] Interestingly, "The Challenge to the Colonial Powers" spoke in terms of national independence, cultural autonomy, and "economic democracy as the only real democracy."[77] The Declaration to Colonial Workers registered a similar appeal, demanding freedom from "imperialist control" as the prerequisite to "complete social, economic, and political emancipation."[78] Without reference to race and racism, both the Challenge and the Declaration wanted independence, sovereignty, and autonomous culture. In its final resolutions, the Congress rejected the idea of "trust" and "mandate" associated with the League, and while it demanded "the immediate abolition" of all "racial and other discriminatory laws," in South Africa and elsewhere, the focus remained on national self-determination.

## C Decolonizing the United Nations

If the decolonizing focus of the Fifth Pan-African Congress was increasingly coming to the right of *dominium* (rights of national self-determination and non-intervention) as the most fundamental challenge to global racism, this was certainly not the emphasis over in San Francisco. A few months before the Congress, delegates from 50 nations met in that city to debate and finalize the UN Charter. In addition to the Colonial Powers, among those peoples from the Global South that had already achieved independence and that counted among the UN's founding members, were: Argentina, Bolivia, Brazil, Chile, Colombia, Costa Rica, Cuba, the Dominican Republic, El Salvador, Ecuador, Haiti, Mexico, Nicaragua, Paraguay, Panama, Peru, Uruguay, Venezuela, Egypt, India, Iran, Iraq, Lebanon, Saudi Arabia, Syria, Turkey, China, Philippines, Ethiopia, Liberia, and South Africa. These member states pushed for the new world organization to take the problem of colonialism head-on and, in the San Francisco debates, they urged for an end to

---

[75] GEISS, *supra* note 2, at 388.
[76] *Id.* at 407.
[77] Available at https://www.marxists.org/archive/padmore/1947/pan-african-congress/ch02.htm.
[78] Available at https://www.marxists.org/archive/padmore/1947/pan-african-congress/ch03.htm

206　THE RIGHT TO EXCLUDE

the colonial mandate relationships that had so powerfully endured between World War I and World War II. The colonial powers were receptive to the need for some sort of transition in French, British, and Dutch colonial relations, but the question was about how to do it.[79] The metropoles knew that time had run out on the classic form, but was the moment ripe for tearing down the global *pomerium*, once and for all?

As the Egyptian scholar Yassin El-Ayouty recounted, "The war had destroyed the myth of white supremacy and revealed the hitherto unpublicized defects of the colonial regimes."[80] The emerging Afro-Asia bloc's position was "enacted on the strong premise that colonialism meant foreign exploitation and represented the worst form of racial discrimination."[81] And what did this "worst form" of racism entail? It essentially turned on the exclusion of peoples from the international community of equal sovereigns—the sovereign's right of *imperium*. This was "the intense and burning desire to be equal—not only as individuals, but as nations— bred of the history of Africa, but still more grievances, real or imagined grievances, against the colonial system."[82] The compromise solution that came out of the San Francisco meeting was the development of a dual-strategy, in some ways reminiscent of the League's much-criticized partition between those peoples entitled to the minority rights system, and those relegated to the mandates system. For those peoples liberated from enemy colonies, they entered what came to be called the Trusteeship system, outlined in Chapter 12 of the UN Charter.[83] The territories governed by the British and French fell into the nebulous space of the Declaration Regarding Non-Self-Governing Territories (NSGT), which became Chapter 11.[84] The division between Chapters 11 and 12 was itself a division in the UN's basic approach to postwar colonialism—an approach that increasingly antagonized the Global South and which helped give rise to a new and powerful chorus of anticolonial voices within the UN. From this "Third World" perspective, the UN ought to be wholly supportive of a right of self-determination for all peoples living under colonial rule, regardless of whether labeled a Trust territory or a territory "whose people have not yet attained a full measure of self-government."[85]

---

[79] Philip Bell, *Colonialism as a Problem in American Foreign Policy*, 5 WORLD POL. 95 (1952); ANNUAL REVIEW OF UNITED NATIONS AFFAIRS, 1960–1961 132 (R. Swift ed., 1961); Annette Baker Fox, *The United Nations and Colonial Development*, 4 INT'L ORG. 201 (1950).

[80] YASSIN EL-AYOUTY, THE UNITED NATIONS AND DECOLONIZATION: THE ROLE OF AFRO-ASIA 5 (1971).

[81] *Id.* at 5–6.

[82] *Id.* at 6.

[83] Duncan Hall, *The Trusteeship System*, 24 BRIT. Y.B. INT'L L. 33 (1947).

[84] The Charter's text left it open as to which territories would be included. The original listing contributed by Australia, Belgium, Denmark, France, the Netherlands, New Zealand, the United Kingdom (UK), and the US, included 74 territories.

[85] This division was partly premised on the idea that, while the Trust territories required international supervision, NSGTs actually existed under the umbrella sovereignty of the colonial powers. Thus, art. 2(7) functioned as a powerful antidote to Chapter 11, since international intervention in the NSGTs could easily implicate a violation of the sovereign's right to exclude.

DECOLONIZATION AND SELF-DETERMINATION    207

It is in the years following 1945 that the process of decolonization is generally thought to reach high gear, beginning with Gandhi's successful battle for Indian independence in 1947. Of course, with the collapse of the Russian, Ottoman, and Habsburg Empires several decades earlier, a number of colonial territories had already achieved independence, like Egypt, Greece, Turkey, Romania, Serbia, Finland, Estonia, Poland, and Czechoslovakia. It was in the 1950s, however, that the last formal remnants of colonial rule really started to unravel. Sukarno's Indonesia won independence from the Dutch in 1949, Nkrumah's Ghana became independent in 1957, and by 1960, much of what was being termed the Third World had joined the UN.[86]

As the international process of decolonization started taking off in the 1950s and 1960s, the discourses of human rights and the rights of peoples were of one voice. The push against racial discrimination was really a push for sovereign independence—the idea that the protection of individuals against racism might prove a separate and even conflictual issue was still a ways off in the distance. Take, for example, the much discussed Bandung Conference of 1955. By this time, the group of Third World nations that had first stormed the UN was now larger and led by a handful of new world leaders. Participants at Bandung included representatives from Egypt, Ethiopia, Ghana (still the Gold Coast), Liberia, Sudan, and most of Asia. Emerging leaders included Nkrumah, John Kotelawala, Gamal Abdel Nasser, Jawaharlal Nehru, Ahmed Sukarno, Zhou Enlai, and Carlos Pena Romulo. Decades later, Bandung is now something of a Rorschach Test for historians of the period. As Luis Eslava, Michael Fakhri, and Vesuki Nesiah have suggested, Bandung offered a "unique" contribution to an understanding of how "racism and political, legal, and economic structures of racial difference were an inextricable part of international law and the genealogy of the nation-state."[87] Bandung offered this contribution despite a wholesale lack of consensus at the Conference about the meaning of race or even its relevance to anticolonial struggle.[88] While some speakers lamented the global presence of racial hierarchy, the Philippines' Romulo had argued that the only place in the world in which "the evil of racialism" continued was Africa. It is with this plurality of viewpoints in mind that Eslava, Fakhri, and Nesiah write, "Bandung also has a life in the global history of antiracism."[89] But

---

[86] States that joined between the initial founding and 1960 included: Afghanistan, Thailand, Pakistan, Yemen, Burma, Israel, Indonesia, Albania, Austria, Bulgaria, Cambodia, Ceylon, Finland, Hungary, Ireland, Italy, Jordan, Laos, Libya, Nepal, Portugal, Romania, Spain, Japan, Morocco, Sudan, Tunisia, Ghana, Federation of Malaya, Guinea, Cameroun, Central African Republic, Chad, Congo (Brazzaville), Congo (Leopoldville), Cyprus, Dahomey, Gabon, Ivory Coast, Malagasy Republic, Mali, Niger, Nigeria, Senegal, Somalia, Togo, and Upper Volta.

[87] El-Ayouty, *supra* note 82, at 17. *See* VIJAY PRASHAD, THE DARKER NATIONS: A PEOPLE'S HISTORY OF THE THIRD WORLD (2007).

[88] El-Ayouty, *supra* note 82, at 17.

[89] *Id.*

## 208 THE RIGHT TO EXCLUDE

why? Was Bandung doing something other than marching to the drum of international law's increasingly muscular modern racial ideology?

In his opening remarks, Sukarno put the Conference in the context of the League Against Imperialism, initiated 30 years earlier. What so distinguished the current moment of 1955 from events like that one, however, was that "Our nations and countries are colonies no more. Now we are free, sovereign, and independent. We are again masters in our own house."[90] With its echoes from London of 1911, this mantra of mastering one's house, the right of peoples throughout Africa and Asia to decide what was going on in there, and the right to be left alone in doing so, was certainly a (if not the) unifying theme in Bandung. This theme directly implicated, of course, the sovereign's rights of self-determination and of nonintervention: the right to exclude (*dominium*).

After highlighting the importance of developing means of economic and cultural communication across Asia and Africa, the Conference's Final Communiqué characterized self-determination as a human right belonging to "peoples and nations," and the "prerequisite" for the exercise "of the full enjoyment of all fundamental Human Rights."[91] The Communique also emphasized that colonialism, in all its manifestations, must end immediately. The document's support of both human rights and anticolonialism were each connected with concerns about the persistence of racism in Africa, and indeed, the three ideas were mutually constitutive, all directed at the same thing: mastery over the house as the answer to global racism.

For scholars like Roland Burke, however, this connection between human rights and decolonization would prove to be problematic. Bandung, Burke observed, "served as a key point of origin for the human rights agenda that would be pursued by the decolonized states in the General Assembly."[92] Burke suggested that the interest in human rights was always secondary in the Bandung texts to the interest in independence from colonial rule. But this might not be the most helpful way of parsing it; for Burke, there were those participants whose demand for independence was really a demand for *liberal* democracy (and along with it, its attendant suite of individual rights), while others were merely interested in mastery over the house—sovereign independence and the right to exclude.[93] This distinction tracks a familiar duality in the literature on self-determination. On the one side is "external" self-determination, which refers to the national right to independence and an equal place in the global order. On the other is "internal" self-determination,

---

[90] President Sukarno of Indonesia, Bandung Conference: Opening Address, Apr. 18, 1955, available at https://www.cvce.eu/content/publication/2001/9/5/88d3f71c-c9f9-415a-b397-b27b8581a4f5/publishable_en.pdf.

[91] Final Communiqué of the Asian-African Conference of Bandung, Apr. 24, 1955, available at https://www.cvce.eu/en/obj/final_communique_of_the_asian_african_conference_of_bandung_24_april_1955-en-676237bd-72f7-471f-949a-88b6ae513585.html.

[92] ROLAND BURKE, DECOLONIZATION AND THE EVOLUTION OF HUMAN RIGHTS 13 (2013).

[93] *Id.* at 38–39.

which refers to the right of a people to democratically choose its representatives and legal arrangements. For Burke, the internal form of self-determination made only a minor showing at Bandung, but it was the dominating external perspective that hogged the limelight, threatening to undermine a true and uniform acceptance of the Universal Declaration of Human Rights. Failing to appreciate this difference, Burke argued, contributed to the failure to truly develop decolonization into a human rights movement.[94] He continued:

> The competitive nature of sovereignty and the protection of individual rights were conveniently avoided in the Bandung rhetoric, so deeply removed from the practicalities of securing those rights ... National rights and human rights were typically presented as parallel and mutually supportive projects, a proposition that would be advanced in session after session of the UN in the 1950s. Several speakers simply conflated the pursuit of self-determination and human rights, making the struggle for one coterminous with the struggle for the other.[95]

The complaint is that there was wasted potential here in the heady beginnings of decolonization, and that it was a mistake to assume that the protection of human rights would inevitably follow from the protection of sovereign rights.[96] Give a people its sovereignty, and human rights would be the result? Nope. To be sure, it is no doubt a mistake to assume that in guaranteeing the sovereign's right to exclude, the protection of human rights will follow. Nevertheless, the sort of reasoning on display among many of the Bandung participants is only "mistaken" if we already have in mind our own contemporary meaning of "human rights." Is there a conflict if we consider the drive for sovereign independence and autonomy in tandem with a view of individual rights that takes analytical priority over sovereignty? Sure. But if we take seriously the idea that national self-determination was itself the "prerequisite" human right, and that sovereign rights and human rights were "mutually supportive projects," then decolonization emerges less as a problem of conflation and more of just a very different understanding of what "human rights" might have been all about.[97] At this point in international legal history, human rights *meant* people's rights.

---

[94] *Id.* at 36. Burke suggests that the Colonial Declaration was the high point of universalist view of self-determination made prominent in the Bandung Final Communiqué. *Id.* at 55.

[95] *Id.* at 26.

[96] Christian Reus-Smit, Individual Rights and the Making of the International System (2013).

[97] If we examine this "holistic" approach in which sovereign and individual rights coalesce, essentially doing away with the domestic analogy, it may very well be possible that the result is something other than today's individualist vision of human rights. Nehru's suggestion that the international world be conceived in light of Panscheel, a constellation of principles of coexistence: (1) mutual respect for sovereignty and territorial integrity, (2) nonaggression, (3) noninterference in internal affairs, (4) equality and mutual benefit, and (5) peaceful coexistence. From this direction, the very ideas of "sovereignty" and "right" simply take on meanings other than what they have in the context of liberal legal thought. *See* Antony Anghie, *Bandung and the Origins of Third World Sovereignty, in* Bandung,

210   THE RIGHT TO EXCLUDE

Through the 1960s, the issue of how to interpret concepts like "sovereignty" and "right" was fundamental to the ultimate trajectory of decolonization in international law. Many of the participants in Bandung had now joined the UN and, in 1960, the General Assembly adopted its Declaration on the Granting of Independence to Colonial Countries and Peoples.[98] The Declaration echoed much from the Bandung Communiqué, decrying the subjection of peoples to alien subjugation, domination, and exploitation, demanding a right of self-determination for all peoples, and uniting claims for the Universal Declaration of Human Rights, non-interference with territorial integrity, and sovereign right. It was a tremendous moment for the global legal order: up from the world of Mandates and Mandatory Powers, the UN now boasted a collection of sovereigns truly invested in the dismantling of colonialism. And the dismantling of colonialism was about rectifying the "denial of fundamental human rights," which in turn was about the denial of self-determination. Anticolonialism, antiracism, and fighting for human rights were all about the same thing: giving the new independent peoples the rights to master their houses, to self-determination, to the right of *dominium*.

## II  FROM ANTICOLONIAL SELF-DETERMINATION TO HUMAN RIGHTS

Whatever the right of *dominium* might have become, as I explore through a survey of cases from the ICJ,[99] the earlier connection between global antiracism and self-determination would come apart as the actual self-determination of peoples gave way to international law's interest in guaranteeing the borders of newly independent states. In a spate of decisions about the legacies of colonialism in the Third World, what seemed to matter most for the Court was functionalism: how to make decolonization practically effective, more realistic. The way for international law to best serve anticolonial and antiracist ends was to make the former colonies independent, treat these new states like real sovereigns, and then generate a system of sovereign equality. If doing so meant sanctifying a regime of inherited colonial borders, then so be it.

What fell out of the picture was the relation between *dominium* and racism. Once this functionalist interpretation of self-determination gained prominence, and the borders of international society were no longer guarded by a science of

---

GLOBAL HISTORY, AND INTERNATIONAL LAW: CRITICAL PASTS AND PENDING FUTURES 538 (Luis Eslava et al. eds., 2018).

[98] *Declaration on the Granting of Independence to Colonial Countries and Peoples*, GA Res 1514 (XV), UN Docs A/PV.927, 933, 937, 939 (Dec. 14, 1960).

[99] For discussion, *see* JAMIE TRINIDAD, SELF-DETERMINATION IN DISPUTED COLONIAL TERRITORIES (2018); ANDREW COLEMAN, RESOLVING CLAIMS TO SELF-DETERMINATION: IS THERE A ROLE FOR THE INTERNATIONAL COURT OF JUSTICE? (2013).

racial xenophobia, the international challenge to racism simply came down to the international manifestation of the US civil rights movement: international human rights law. Or to put that another way, if in 1960 the suppression of self-determination was a violation of human rights, a generation later the antiracist right of self-determination was almost entirely disconnected from the new machinery of the human rights era. Indeed, by the 1990s, human rights law had pushed the anticolonial right of self-determination out of sight. And along with it, so too the idea of *dominium* as relevant to the problem of global racism. What had emerged by that time was the view that the antidiscrimination principle was the only answer international law would need. The problem of structural racism, and the deep and complex relation between race and the right to exclude, was fading from view. This would be true as well in the space of the indigenous rights movement, a field in which the concept of the rights of peoples would be funneled *through* the human rights lens of the antidiscrimination principle.[100]

## A  *Western Sahara*

In its 1975 decision in the *Western Sahara* case, the ICJ included judges from the Ivory Coast (Alphonse Boni, an ad hoc judge chosen by Morocco), Lebanon, Senegal, India, Argentina, the Philippines, Nigeria, and Benin. The decision was almost unanimous, with the only dissenting opinion from Jose Ruda of Argentina. *Western Sahara* provides a square look at what the sovereign right of *dominium* had become at this mature stage of decolonization. The background involved a question about how to distribute territory in the wake of Mauritania's independence from France, and Morocco's independence from both France and Spain. Both Mauritania and Morocco claimed sovereignty over the Western Sahara, a Non-Self-Governing Territory (NSGT) administered by Spain. In its request for an Advisory Opinion from the ICJ, the General Assembly sought clarification on the legal status of the Western Sahara, and about how to think that status in relation to newly independent successor states.

As the Court saw it, the primary task was to provide the General Assembly with assistance in its "proper exercise of its functions concerning the decolonization of territory."[101] The point of departure was the UN's Decolonization Declaration (1960) and its enunciation of a right of self-determination belonging to all peoples, as well as its demand that all Trusts and NSGTs gain independence without delay.[102] As the General Assembly had expressed in its Guiding Principles for implementing Article 73 of the UN Charter, the Court cited three means by which

---

[100]  *See infra* Chapters 7 and 8.
[101]  Western Sahara, Advisory Opinion, 1975 I.C.J. Rep. 12 (Oct. 16).
[102]  *Id.* at 31.

212   THE RIGHT TO EXCLUDE

the right of self-determination might be effectuated. A people might emerge as a sovereign state in the international legal order, they might "freely associate with an independent state," or "integrate" into a previously existing state.[103] Whichever modality might arise, the Court emphasized that self-determination required a baseline of freedom and equality: the people "freely" decide their political fate, and the right of that people to so decide is the equal of every peoples' right, everywhere.[104]

It was in the light of this anticolonial imperative that the Court moved to the General Assembly's questions. The first was whether it was appropriate to consider the Western Sahara, at the time it was colonized by the Spanish in the late nineteenth century, as a "no-man's land," a *terra nullius* without legal status in international law. The second question was, if the Western Sahara was not *terra nullius* but rather a territory legally belonging to a people, what was the legal connection between that territory and the Moroccan and Mauritanian peoples?

To the first question the Court explicitly invoked *dominium*, explaining that in order for a sovereign to acquire new territory through "occupation," the territory must first belong to no one. Of course, this doctrine of ownership presupposes an idea of the owner—who can own at all, and how owners are regarded as against one another. The Court explained that, in the 1880s, regular state practice suggested that the European powers did not colonize by means of "occupation," but rather through treaty with local rulers. As a result, the Court concluded that the colonial powers could not have regarded African and Asian territories as *terra nullius*, since it was the establishment of treaty which proved the root of title.[105] This was both a general approach of the colonial powers, as well as the particular form in which the Spanish took control of the Rio de Oro.[106]

Nevertheless, with its affirmative answer to the General Assembly's first question in hand, the Court moved to the second. That is, if the first question went to whether there was a legally cognizable "self" in the Western Sahara, the next was about how to determine what that self ought to become. For Spain, this was a case about the Saharan people's right to exercise self-determination.[107] For Morocco and Mauritania, however, the relevant "self" was broader, and so the Court should ask whether Western Sahara should become a full sovereign in international society, or assimilate in some way with its neighbors? Before allowing that "self" to

---

[103]  *Id* at 32.
[104]  *Id.* at 33.
[105]  *Id.* at 39.
[106]  To be clear, the Court was not suggesting that the Spanish regarded the locals of Western Sahara as their equals, or that the Saharan chiefs were sovereigns with rights in international society. Of course, if we pushed a little harder we could ask, "Did the Spanish believe that the Western Sahara was governed by a sovereign's right of *dominium*?" "Did the Spanish regard these agreements with local chiefs as anything other than evidence of domination to be shared with Spain's colonial neighbors?" "Did Spain 'occupy' Western Sahara in a way that it would never have done in a land of whiteness?" The answers would all suggest that, from the perspective of the colonizer in the 1880s, of course the Western Sahara belonged to "no one." It belonged to no one that mattered, at any rate.
[107]  *Id.* at 62.

express itself in a vote, the Court was tasked with answering whether, perhaps, there was no independent self at all, but rather a group of people that had been artificially separated through Spanish colonization from its home community. Indeed, this was precisely the argument of the two newly independent states. For Morocco's part, the Court explained that "it is urged that Western Sahara has always been linked to the interior of Morocco by common ethnological, cultural, and religious ties, and that the Sakiet El Hamra was artificially separated from Moroccan territory of the Noun by colonization."[108] Mauritania argued that "the colonial powers ... in drawing frontiers took no account of these human factors and in particular of the tribal territories and migration routes, which were as a result, bisected and even trisected by those artificial frontiers."[109]

Though the conception dates back much further, the elements of statehood were crystalized in the Montevideo Convention on the Rights and Duties of States of 1933.[110] Now the Court was not trying to determine whether the Western Sahara was a state, but the Convention's listed elements of permanent population, defined territory, government, and sovereignty were certainly in the background of the Court's assessment of the Western Sahara territory. It began by pointing out that Western Sahara had "special characteristics," first and foremost having to do with the population, which was anything but permanent. As the Court explained, at the time of colonization the territory hosted "a sparse population that, for the most part, consisted of nomadic tribes the members of which traversed the desert on more or less regular routes dictated by the seasons and the wells or waterholes available to them."[111] Further, these nomads generally enjoyed communal or group rights of ownership, frequently travelled through territories now belonging to Morocco and Mauritania, and all were members of the Muslim faith. The whole region lay within the Dar al-Islam, a term used to denote a territory in which a predominance of Muslim practice ensures religious security.

While the Court confidently proclaimed a "self" that was present for purposes of its analysis in Question 1, that confidence seeped away in Question 2 as the Court analyzed whether there was ever a display of effective governmental authority on the Western Saharan territory. Were these Muslim nomads a "permanent population" related to a "defined territory"? Morocco argued that indeed they were, assuming that these international law concepts could be functionally adapted to different contexts. Further, Morocco claimed that since the Arab conquest of North Africa, Moroccan authorities exercised sovereign control over the Western Sahara territory. But what evidence of an actual display of sovereign authority was available at the time of Spanish colonization? Morocco claimed

[108] *Id.* at 45.
[109] *Id.* at 60.
[110] Montevideo Convention on the Rights and Duties of States (1933), available at https://www.jus. uio.no/english/services/library/treaties/01/1-02/rights-duties-states.xml.
[111] *Western Sahara, supra* note 103, at 41.

214    THE RIGHT TO EXCLUDE

that its sovereign authority dated at least as far back as to the rule of Ismail Ibn Sharif, the Sultan of Morocco from 1672–1727. Under a regime of Islamic governance, the Court conceded, there is "a common religious bond of Islam existing among the peoples," but "the allegiance of various tribes [is] to the Sultan, through their caids or sheiks, rather than on the notion of territory."[112] Beyond this, Morocco argued that the tribes of Western Sahara showed allegiance to the Sultan through the payment of taxes. The Court, however, was more inclined to follow Spain's claim that, for whatever the relationship between Morocco and Western Sahara, it always remained purely religious and cultural and had rarely, if ever, been political and territorial. The connections between the "self" of the Western Sahara and the governmental authority of the Sultan in Morocco "must clearly be real,"[113] and as the former colonizer explained, Morocco's authority had never been as "real" as the authority exercised by the Spanish.[114] The Court agreed. Unsurprisingly, the Court was similarly unpersuaded that, at the turn of the twentieth century, Europe had at that time regarded Morocco as sovereign over Western Sahara.[115]

With respect to Mauritania's claim that "the concepts of 'nation' and of 'people' would be the most appropriate to explain the position of the Shinguitti people at the time of colonization," and that this nation's territory extended through to the south of the Wad Sakiet El Hamra, Spain was not persuaded. "In the view of Spain," the Court explained, "the idea of an entity must express not only a belonging but also the idea that the component parts are homogenous. The Mauritian entity, however, is said to have been formed of heterogeneous components, some being mere tribes and others having a more complex degree of integration, such as an emirate."[116] Once again, the Court agreed with Spain, concluding that despite the "racial, linguistic, religious, cultural, and economic"[117] ties between the peoples of Western Sahara and Mauritania, there was insufficient evidence to support the claim that, at the time of Spanish colonization, the Mauritanian people exercised any sovereignty in Western Sahara.[118] The Court concluded that, with respect to both Morocco and Mauritania's claims, Spain had the right of it, and that the people of Western Sahara was a separate self with its own life-story to tell. The right of self-determination would follow the contours of Spanish colonization.

[112] *Id.* at 44.
[113] *Id.*
[114] *Id.* at 48–49.
[115] *Id.* at 56.
[116] *Id.* at 61.
[117] *Id.* at 63.
[118] The Court did conclude, however, that some degree of "legal tie" existed between Western Sahara and Mauritania, just not legal ties sufficient to constitute an effective display of governmental authority. *Id.* at 64.

## B Case Concerning the Frontier Dispute

A similar issue was raised a decade later in the *Frontier Dispute Case*.[119] Here, however, the question concerned the residue of French colonial rule in what had been French West Africa, and what after 1960 became the independent states of Mali and Burkina Faso. A special chamber of the Court was constituted to hear the case, with Mohammad Bedjaoui, Manfred Lachs, and Jose Ruda presiding, and Luchaire and Abi-Saab serving as ad hoc judges. The disagreement between Mali and Burkina Faso was about a stretch of land including "the largest of the temporary watercourses in the region,"[120] not far from the point at which the two countries meet at the Niger border. The Court noted at the outset that the parties wished for the dispute to be guided by "the principle of the intangibility of frontiers inherited from colonization,"[121] which led to an encounter with the principle of *uti possidetis juris*.[122]

The principle of *uti possidetis* is a doctrine of possession, and it literally means, "as you possess, so you may possess." Dating back to Roman Law, the rule originally referred to the immovability of private property. Its prominence in international law gained momentum as a way of regulating Spanish American Independence, and hit its high point in the context of decolonization.[123] Though the principle of *uti possidetis* originally signaled a view of giving legal title to an owner with effective possession and certain control (i.e., *dominium*), it came to embody a preference for consolidating the status quo.[124] As the Court recognized, the application of *uti possidetis* in the context of decolonization was not without its challenges. In the African context *uti possidetis* came to mean a respect for the colonial demarcations arbitrarily established in the height of classic racial ideology. As discussed earlier, by the 1880s it became a customary practice of the colonial powers to regard Africa as outside of what Oppenheim called the "dominion" of the Family of Nations, a space in which human beings certainly lived, but not humans or peoples with international rights of *dominium*. How, then, was one to square the idea that these borders born in a crucible of vulgar racism were now to constitute the contours of

---

[119] Frontier Dispute (Burk. Faso v. Mali), Judgment, 1986 I.C.J. Rep. 554 (Dec. 22).

[120] *Id.* at 562.

[121] *Id.* at 564. The Court referenced a Resolution from the African Heads of State, adopted in Cairo in 1964, stressing the relevance of *udi possidetis* for African decolonization.

[122] For discussion, *see, e.g.*, Tiyanjana Maluwa, *Oil Under Troubled Waters? Some Legal Aspects of the Boundary Dispute Between Malawi and Tanzania Over Lake Malawi*, 37 MICH. J. INT'L L. 351 (2016); Brian T. Sumner, *Territorial Disputes at the International Court of Justice*, 53 DUKE L.J. 1779 (2004); Steven R. Ratner, *Drawing a Better Line: Uti Possidetis and the Borders of New States*, 90 AM. J. INT'L L. 590, 600 (1996).

[123] MIKULAS FABRY, RECOGNIZING STATES: INTERNATIONAL SOCIETY AND THE ESTABLISHMENT OF NEW STATES SINCE 1776 (2010).

[124] Malcolm Shaw, *The Heritage of States: The Principle of Uti Possidetis Today*, 67 BRIT. Y.B. INT'L L. 75 (1996).

216    THE RIGHT TO EXCLUDE

new and independent African states? As Judge ad hoc Bola Ajibola of Nigeria put it in his Separate Opinion in the *Libya/Chad* case:

> The colonial penchant for geometric lines (as exemplified by Lord Salisbury's "horseshoe"-shaped Tripolitanian hinterland), has left Africa with a high concentration of States whose frontiers are drawn with little or no consideration for those factors of geography, ethnicity, economic convenience or reasonable means of communication that have played a part in boundary determinations elsewhere.[125]

In the dispute between Burkina Faso and Mali, the Court explained that *uti possidetis* "confirmed the maintenance of the territorial status quo at the time of independence."[126] *Uti possidetis*:

> [I]s a general principle, which is logically connected with the phenomenon of the obtaining of independence, wherever it occurs. Its obvious purpose is to prevent the independence and stability of new States being endangered by fratricidal struggles provoked by the challenging of frontiers following the withdrawal of the administering power.[127]

This being the "obvious purpose" of the property rule, how to reconcile its conservatism with the right of peoples to self-determination? If it was right that the boundaries of new states were relics of a colonial racism, should antiracism simply give way in the encounter with the more fundamental value of *uti possidetis*? As the Court explained:

> [T]he maintenance of the territorial status quo in Africa is often seen as the wisest course, to preserve what has been achieved by peoples who have struggled for their independence, and to avoid a disruption which would deprive the continent of the gains achieved by much sacrifice. The essential requirement of stability in order to survive, to develop and gradually to consolidate their independence in all fields, has induced African States judiciously to consent to the respecting of colonial frontiers, and to take account of it in the interpretation of the principle of self-determination of peoples. Thus the principle of *uti possidetis* has kept its place among the most important legal principles, despite the apparent contradiction which explained its coexistence alongside the new norms implied. Indeed it was by deliberate choice that African States selected, among all the classic principles, that of *uti possidetis*. This remains an undeniable fact.[128]

---

[125] Territorial Dispute (Libya v. Chad), Judgment, 1994 I.C.J. Rep. 52–53 (Feb. 3).
[126] *Frontier Dispute, supra* note 121, at 565.
[127] *Id.* at 565.
[128] *Id.* at 567.

## DECOLONIZATION AND SELF-DETERMINATION 217

This understanding of *uti possidetis* as something of a prerequisite for the exercise of self-determination led the Court to conclude that French colonial law would determine the proper boundaries between the new sovereigns.[129] That is, as the Court explained, Burkina Faso and Mali needn't follow the dictates of French legislation; they were sovereign states and enjoyed the full rights of *dominium*. However, with respect to the geographic limits of these sovereign territories, French law was controlling.

> By becoming independent, a new State acquires sovereignty with the territorial base and boundaries left to it by the colonial power. This is part of the ordinary operation of the machinery of State succession. International law—and consequently the principle of uti possidetis—applies to the new State (as a State) not with retroactive effect, but immediately and from that moment onwards. It applies to the State as it is, i.e., to the "photograph" of the territorial situation then existing. The principle of *uti possidetis* freezes the territorial title; it stops the clock, but does not put back the hands.[130]

At this point in the analysis of international law's modern racial ideology, what is worth emphasizing about the *Western Sahara* and *Frontier Dispute* cases is what was already happening in the Court's "border" jurisprudence. In each case there simply was no question about how a classic racial ideology had helped justify the colonial imposition of territorial borders. Did France or Spain regard the peoples of Africa as organic communities, peoples united by certain historical connections? Did it matter where the colonial lines were drawn, or what effect they might have on the civilizations that had grown up in these lands? Neither the Justices of the Court (many of whom were nationals of these newly independent states) nor the lawyers for Spain, Morocco, Mauritania, Burkina Faso, or Mali had any doubts about it. The colonial "scramble for Africa" was drenched in racism. But what is so notable about the international legal response in these cases was the Court's unwillingness to treat territorial borders as a site for antiracist strategy. It was as if, for whatever had been the unfortunate history of these frontiers—these *pomeria*—the way to think about racial justice now was through a functionalist emphasis on the political self-determination of a people. As for the borders that came along, racial justice had little to do with it.

What mattered here, as the Court explained it, was what would make decolonization practically effective; what would make self-determination *functional*. Did Islamic governance provide an "effective display of authority"? The Court didn't really seem to think so—but what seemed to count for the Court was that the most practical exercise of self-determination in the case was to avoid the

---

[129] *Id.* at 568.
[130] *Id.*

218    THE RIGHT TO EXCLUDE

troublesome implications of re-writing the borders of newly independent states like Morocco, and simply give the people of Western Sahara the vote. Was the fortification of these colonial boundaries in the interest of global antiracism? Certainly, if fortifying those borders meant keeping the project of decolonization afloat. And the same functionalist view of self-determination was working through the *Frontier Dispute* case.

## C   The Acquired Rights Debate

Writing for the Court, Justice Mohammed Bedjaoui, an Algerian diplomat and lawyer with extensive experience in the UN,[131] made the point explicitly: the way for international law to best serve anticolonial and antiracist ends was to make the former colonies independent, treat these new states like real sovereigns, and then generate a system of sovereign equality. If doing so meant sanctifying a regime of colonial borders, then so be it.

Before joining the ICJ in 1982, Bedjaoui had served as the UN Special Rapporteur on State Succession resulting from Sources other than Treaties. In his first report to the International Law Commission (ILC), Bedjaoui had already signaled his preference for *uti possidetis*, suggesting that a status quo approach to colonial borders was inspired by "realism and political wisdom."[132] True, there were exceptions to the rule, and perhaps ways in which the right of self-determination should counter the rule of *uti possidetis*, but on the whole, decolonization was better off avoiding such "dangerous developments."[133] Not to beat a dead horse, but once again, doctrines like *terra nullius* and *uti possidetis* highlight the way in which the discourse on sovereignty was so deeply linked to property. Indeed, the central question in Bedjaoui's second report to the ILC considered the question of how to reconcile the new state's right to exclude as against that of the private property owner. When the independent state succeeds the colonial or administrating power, would the new state be required to respect the property rights already in existence? And if so, to what degree? Bedjaoui's approach was explicitly functionalist. Whether an individual's acquired property rights in a decolonized territory should continue would depend on the social function of property in the effort to rid the world of colonial domination and exploitation.[134]

Bedjaoui began by pointing out how the traditional Roman distinction between *imperium* and *dominium* had entrenched a view of private property as transcending

---

[131] Mohammed Bedjaoui, *Expediency in the Decisions of the International Court of Justice*, 71 BRIT. Y.B. INT'L L. 1 (2000).

[132] Mohammad Bedjaoui, *Second Report on Succession of States in Respect of Matters other than Treaties*, *in* 2 YEARBOOK OF THE INTERNATIONAL LAW COMMISSION 112 (1969).

[133] *Id.* at 113.

[134] *Id.* at 75.

DECOLONIZATION AND SELF-DETERMINATION 219

the will of the sovereign. When new states succeeded older states, *imperium* changed hands between the colonial power and the newly independent state. *Dominium*, however, remained in the power of the individual property owner.[135] Bedjaoui explained that this individualized right of *dominium* constituted an "acquired right."[136] The sovereign's right to exclude, in other words, was a natural feature of state succession. The individual's right to exclude, in contrast, was entirely dependent on the law of the state—hence, the individual's rights were *acquired* rights. And acquired from whom, from where? From the prior sovereign. As a result, Bedjaoui observed, that just as all of liberalism itself was coming under fire for being out of line with the social trends of decolonization, so too would its attendant relation with private property.[137] "A whole new—or rather reanimated— philosophy has come into play in the debate on acquired rights. As the product of the purest liberalism, those rights must share the latter's vicissitudes and pass away with it altogether if it is true—as seems obvious to some—that liberalism's historic function is drawing to an end."[138] Thus, in rejecting the idea that *dominium* was a human right that might continue independently of the contemporary sovereign power, Bedjaoui gave a positivist rejoinder: rights are claimed only from the sovereigns that have created them.[139]

This led to the emphasis on the new successor state as a sovereign equal in the international legal order. The new state was under no obligation to respect individual property rights, since the imposition of such an obligation would constitute an impairment of the state's own rights of nonintervention and self-determination. And if it were believed that, because the predecessor state was under an obligation to respect individual property rights, so too should the successor state exist under the same obligation, the question then goes to the source of these individual rights. Are they protected by international law, hence their continuing viability in the face of changing sovereigns? For Bedjaoui, to suggest as much would do more than distort the nature of the obligations of the predecessor state—as it would have been clear enough that every state has the right to alter its laws of property. It would place the new, decolonized state in a position of subordination: "By some mysterious phenomenon of legal transmutation ... these acquired rights, which derived from an obligation under municipal law from the predecessor state, become rights derived

---

[135] *Id.* at 73.

[136] *Id.*

[137] *Id.* at 72 ("The jurist must possess an unerring skill in interpreting the trends in society in order to perform his function, which is to help that society to produce new forms needed for social progress. Progress means a change for the better, but a change nonetheless; in other words, it usually rejects acquired rights. If such rights were maintained, all human societies would be paralysed. Sociology demolishes the concept of acquired rights, for it teaches us that no social group and no State can indefinitely retain its privileges, which are constantly called into question. How could the law fully endorse a concept which is unknown in sociology?").

[138] *Id.* at 73.

[139] *Id.* at 74.

220   THE RIGHT TO EXCLUDE

from an international obligation for the successor state."[140] Bedjaoui, like so many of the modern functionalists, had little patience for transcendental and mysterious forms of legal transmutation. New states gained their sovereign rights from international law—not from the colonial power—thus achieving for themselves both the rights of *dominium* as subjects of international society, and the rights of *imperium* in their claims to enter as equal members of that society. Thus, "the independence of the juridical order of the successor State leads *a priori* to the assumption that the new authority will not be bound by rights of individuals, which it had no part in creating."[141]

Indeed, from the perspective of a decolonizing attitude toward world order, the protection of individual property rights and the assertion of sovereign right stand in fundamental tension. As Bedjaoui put it, decolonization raised the formerly colonized peoples of the world into a community of political equality by giving them sovereign status. What it did not do—yet—was provide anything like economic equality.

> Rather than the "renewing function" of decolonization, it is its "reversing function" that necessarily takes precedence, in order to put an end to the relationships based on domination. And these relationships are not just political; indeed, it may be said that they are primarily economic. Consequently, the process of decolonization is inevitably a process of gradual destruction of certain types of economic and financial relationships which helped to maintain those relationships based on subordination ... Thus it is clear that that decolonization and the renewal of acquired rights are contradictory. Either decolonization or acquired rights must be sacrificed.[142]

### D   *Imperium* and the New International Economic Order

And it wasn't decolonization that would be sacrificed. As the Third World or Tricontinental bloc in the UN continued to gain strength, the idea that decolonization could easily prove political equality through grants of independence, and yet struggle with the "primary" forces of domination and exploitation that were economic, a movement toward a "New International Economic Order" (NIEO) gained momentum.[143] In some ways the NIEO brought together a number of themes that had been developing since conferences like the URC, and began to

---

[140] *Id.* at 77.
[141] *Id.* at 80.
[142] *Id.* at 91.
[143] For perspective on the trajectory of economic development in Latin America, *see, e.g.,* Margarita Fajardo, The World That Latin America Created: The United Nations Economic Commission for Latin America in the Development Era (2022).

DECOLONIZATION AND SELF-DETERMINATION   221

crystallize in Bandung. With clear connections to Bedjaoui's reports to the UN,[144] by the early 1970s the General Assembly had rallied around the idea that neocolonialism required an economic response, a rejoinder to the way in which formal colonial domination had shifted into an informal structure of global inequalities.[145] As Umut Ozsu has noted:

> At the heart of the [NIEO] project lay a demand for greater aid, debt relief, technology transfer, and respect for permanent sovereignty in regard to natural resources, as well as the establishment of a specific right to development, the normalization of preferential and nonreciprocal treatment for developing countries, the tight regulation of foreign investors and multinational corporations, and the stabilization of raw materials and primary commodities.[146]

The NIEO project shared much of the intellectual orientation already on display in Bedjaoui's reports.[147] On the one side was a powerful functionalism, arguing for a new interpretation of international law guided by a sociological and economic preference for the general welfare, social solidarity, and all in all, the elevation of a global New Deal. On the other side was a strict commitment to sovereign equality, and the rights of states as the fundamental architecture of international development. The focus was on inequality between states, not inequality between peoples; the rights of states to exclude the world from their territories, not the rights of individuals to economic justice.[148]

What is interesting to note here is what was happening to the right of *imperium* in the context of decolonization. As we saw earlier, challenging global racism meant opening up the new international institutions to greater participation. This was the falling away of classic racial ideology as a means for solving international law's boundary problem. However, what was becoming clear by the time of the NIEO project was that it just wasn't enough to diminish the right of *imperium*. It wasn't enough to say that international law's hierarchies could no longer enjoy justification through nineteenth- and early twentieth-century race science. Because the right of *imperium* hadn't itself diminished; it was only that classic racial ideology had ceased to perform as its primary justification. Now an economic ideology was doing the same work, empowering a sovereign right of *imperium* to once

---

[144] MOHAMMAD BEDJAOUI, TOWARDS A NEW INTERNATIONAL ECONOMIC ORDER (1979).

[145] *Declaration on Permanent Sovereignty over Natural Resources*, GA Res 1803 (XVII) (Dec. 14, 1962); *Declaration on the Establishment of a New International Economic Order*, GA Res 3201 (S-VI) (May 1, 1974).

[146] Umut Ozsu, *Neoliberalism and the New International Economic Order: A History of Contemporary Legal Thought*, in SEARCHING FOR CONTEMPORARY LEGAL THOUGHT 333–34 (Justin Desautels-Stein & Christopher Tomlins eds., 2017).

[147] DOREEN LUSTIG, VEILED POWER: INTERNATIONAL LAW AND THE PRIVATE CORPORATION, 1886–1981 183–84 (2020).

[148] Ozsu, *supra* note 148, at 342.

222    THE RIGHT TO EXCLUDE

again solve international law's boundary problem, this time replacing a hierarchy of racial development with a hierarchy of economic development. Of course, these hierarchies were virtually identical in terms of which people enjoyed greater and lesser advantages. But the classic mode of racial ideology had drained out.

Realizing this, the NIEO project sought to push the ball forward, doing more than discipline a racialized right of *imperium*. Now was the time for the newly independent states to seize the sovereign right of *imperium* as well. Thus far, international law's antiracist strategy involved the attack on racial development as a justification for *imperium*, the participation of formerly colonized peopled in the new international institutions, and the giving to these new states the rights of *dominium* (nonintervention and self-determination). What was lifting off, just before it crashed, was the idea that the postcolonial states could themselves gain the right to determine the boundaries of the global demos, but now in explicitly economic terms. Where was the line marking those economic equals from everyone else? Who would decide? The NIEO project meant to let the postcolonial states answer those questions.

## E  After Apartheid

Of course, by the 1980s, the NIEO project was all but undone, yielding in favor to the Washington Consensus and an attendant "neoliberal colorblindness."[149] International law's modern racial ideology was certainly able to justify giving postcolonial states their seats in the UN General Assembly or at the World Trade Organization (WTO), but what it was never positioned to explain was a postcolonial use of the right of *imperium*. And so, as decolonization's short-lived experiment with an economized right of *imperium* was coming to a close, so too was its use for a right of self-determination. But not before apartheid came to an end.

As for how the problem looked from the vantage of the ICJ, South African segregation came to the surface shortly after the creation of the UN when the General Assembly asked for an Advisory Opinion on the status of a former German colony, now known as Namibia.[150] In the League system, Namibia had been designated a C class Mandate, Britain took authority as the Mandatory power, and the Union of South Africa exercised that power on behalf of the UK. In 1950, the General Assembly sought clarification on whether South Africa was responsible as a Mandatory power now in the context of the Trusteeship system, and the Court concluded that it was. South Africa, however, refused to internationalize its Mandate under the Trust system, propelling a number of cases through the world court.[151] In 1966, the Court addressed complaints from Liberia and Ethiopia,

---

[149]  *See infra* Chapter 7.
[150]  International Status of South West Africa, Advisory Opinion, 1950 I.C.J. Rep. 128 (July 11).
[151]  Iterations of the controversy surfaced in the years 1950, 1956, 1962, 1966, 1971.

claiming that in South Africa's failure to fulfill its obligations as a Mandatory power, and in its application of apartheid to the people of South West Africa, South Africa was in violation of international law. In what was regarded by many observers as a surprising result (8 to 7, with the President of the Court casting the deciding vote), the ICJ ruled in favor of South Africa, finding that Ethiopia and Liberia had failed to prove the existence of a right or interest in the subject matter.[152]

The Court returned to the issue in 1971.[153] Not long after the Court's ill-received judgment from 1966, the General Assembly passed a Resolution terminating South Africa's status as a Mandatory power over Namibia, and the Security Council ordered South Africa to withdraw from the territory. Subsequently, the Security Council requested an Advisory Opinion from the ICJ regarding the continued presence of South Africa in Namibia. Drafting the majority opinion was Zarafulla Khan, a jurist forcibly recused during the 1966 proceedings, and who had a long history as an anticolonial diplomat and believer in self-determination. The Court's opinion began by rejecting South Africa's contention that the South West Africa Mandate had lapsed along with the termination of the League, and that in any event, C class Mandates were never intended to become independent states. It explained that the Mandate system required interpretation in the context of the current climate of decolonization and the UN Declaration on Colonial Peoples, and that all Mandates and NSGTs were governed by the principle of self-determination.[154] Continuing in this functionalist mode of reasoning, the Court wrote:

> It would have been contrary to the overriding purpose of the mandates system to assume that difficulties in the way of the replacement of one regime by another designed to improve international supervision should have been permitted to bring about, on the dissolution of the League, a complete disappearance of international supervision. To accept the contention of the Government of South Africa on this point would have entailed the reversion of mandated territories to colonial status, and the virtual replacement of the mandates regime by annexation, so determinedly excluded in 1920.[155]

However debatable it might have been that in 1920 there was consensus about C class Mandates like South West Africa enjoying an inchoate right of self-determination, the Court in 1970 was simply uninterested in the "true" intentions of the framers; the question was about how to understand Namibia's legal status in the contemporary social climate, not the climate of a postwar world in which

---

[152] Wolfgang Friedman, *The Jurisprudential Implications of the South West Africa Case*, 6 COLUM. J. TRANSNAT'L L. 1 (1967); ROSALYN HIGGINS, THEMES AND THEORIES (2009).
[153] Legal Consequences for States of the Continued Existence of South Africa in Namibia, Advisory Opinion, 1971 I.C.J. Rep. 16 (June 21).
[154] *Id.* at 30–31.
[155] *Id.* at 33.

224    THE RIGHT TO EXCLUDE

Britain and France still enjoyed the imperial stage. And as the contemporary climate was governed by the UN Trusteeship system, it would further frustrate the purpose of the Mandates to exclude Namibia from international administration. With respect to the international status of Namibia in 1970, the General Assembly had already declared the Mandate's termination, therefore relieving South Africa of any rights of administration. South Africa's claim of title by occupation, or in the alternative, title through annexation of mandate, was null.[156] As a consequence, the Court concluded that the UN's members were "under obligation to recognize the illegality and invalidity of South Africa's continued presence in Namibia,"[157] which effectively meant that all states were barred from entering legal arrangements with South Africa when the matter concerned Namibia.

With respect to South Africa's defense of its performance in fulfilling the sacred trust of civilization owed by a Mandatory power to a Mandate, South Africa sought to provide a functional account of apartheid. The question, South Africa explained, was about whether and how apartheid actually enhanced the welfare of the people; but the Court disagreed. "No factual evidence is needed" to determine the legality of apartheid. It is enough to know that to "enforce distinctions, exclusions, restrictions, and limitations exclusively based on race, color, descent, or national or ethnic origin which constitute a denial of fundamental human rights is a flagrant violation of the purposes and principles of the Charter."[158] This statement summed up the Court's brief foray into race—stating pretty much whatever the Court's majority felt needed to be said. Racial discrimination was wrong, period.

The Court's Vice President, Justice Fouad Ammoun of Lebanon, felt that the Court hadn't gone far enough, given the weighty matter before it. What the Court was facing here in 1970, Ammoun explained, was "the outward expression of an irreversible social and political evolution of the modern world," and because the Court's opinion was too muted in properly developing an account of international law in the context of decolonization, self-determination, and racism, Ammoun would do it separately.[159]

Ammoun began by postulating Namibia's legal personality as a subject of international law—a legal personality that had always existed, despite its suppression by the colonial powers.[160] Like so much of the rest of Africa, what was now Namibia had been regarded as the colonial powers as merely a "geographical concept," a *terrae nullius* devoid of right.[161] But Namibia had been and continued to be a subject of the international legal order, since "sovereignty, which is inherent

---

[156] *Id.* at 50–51.
[157] *Id.* at 54.
[158] *Id.* at 57.
[159] *Id.* at 67. For further analysis of Ammoun's opinion, see Nathaniel Berman, *Sovereignty in Abeyance: Self-Determination and International Law*, 7 WIS. INT'L L.J. 51 (1988).
[160] *Namibia, supra* note 155, at 68.
[161] *Id.* at 86.

in every people, just as liberty is inherent in every human being, ... did not cease to belong to the people subject to mandate."[162] The appropriate way to understand Namibia's sovereignty was to place it in historical perspective, and in particular, the notion that peoples' rights were less a feature of positive texts like constitutions and charters, but rather were the produce of human progress itself.[163] What Ammoun was referring to was an alternative way of thinking about the development of customary international law. Referencing everything from the Atlantic Charter to Bandung to the General Assembly Declarations, Ammoun explained:

> Would these international or universal instruments have seen the light of day if it had not been for the heroic fight of peoples aspiring with all their hearts after freedom and independence? If there is any "general practice" which might be held, beyond dispute, to constitute [customary international law], it must surely be made up of the conscious action of the peoples themselves, engaged in determined struggle. This struggle continues for the purpose of asserting, yet once more, the right of self-determination, more particularly in southern Africa, and specifically, in Namibia. Indeed one is bound to recognize that the right of peoples to self-determination, before being written into charters that were not granted but won in bitter struggle, had first been written painfully with the blood of the peoples, in the finally awakened conscience of humanity.

To ignore these historic developments was to fall prey to outdated postulates of classic international law and "servitudes of a past through which we have ourselves lived and from traditions we have always respected."[164] To look in vain for the foundations of self-determination in the positive law of a colonial international law was cowardice: international law had changed, and international lawyers needed the courage to see it.

What, precisely, had changed? Ammoun believed that the right of self-determination was a right to equality, "the foundation of other human rights which are no more than its corollaries."[165] Of course, we have already seen this view of self-determination in the context of Pan-Africanism and the Bandung conference, where a people's right to self-determination was placed as the "prerequisite right," the *a priori* of all other human rights. Here's how, as this idea was coming to its historical terminus, it was articulated in Ammoun's opinion. The right of equality dated back to the Stoics, Ammoun explained, and while it found disfavor in Platonic and Aristotelian theory, the notion of equal rights slowly but surely spread across both sides of the Mediterranean (a Greco-Roman stream

[162] *Id.* at 68.
[163] *Id.* at 73.
[164] *Id.* at 75.
[165] *Id.* at 76.

226    THE RIGHT TO EXCLUDE

and an Afro-Asian stream), sowing "the seeds of equality between men and nations ... "[166] The right of equality emerged in the age of revolutions, found its way to Latin America in the nineteenth century, and as codified in the international instruments of the twentieth, finally landed in Asia and Africa.[167] And when the right of equality emerged on the international plane at the height of decolonization, it was *equality* and not self-determination as such, that was truly crowned King. It wasn't quite right to say that a people's right of self-determination was the prerequisite for the enjoyment of individual human rights. Rather, it was the right of equality that was the fountainhead for all forms of self-determination, whether exercised by peoples or individual human beings. It was this view of a right to equality, slowly marching through time, and bloodied with the human wreckage of rebellion, that belonged to the people of Namibia and the human objects of South African apartheid in equal measure, "for individuals and peoples alike."[168] The mark of the "new modern" international law would lie in the recognition of equal rights, both for peoples that had for so long been held in abeyance, and for human beings to be free of racial discrimination.

What was decolonization about? If we look at it through the lens of the Universal Races Congress (URC), to the Pan-African movement, and into Bandung and the UN Declaration on the Granting of Independence to Colonial Peoples, it is tempting to conclude that decolonization was an international movement directed at ending colonial legacies of racial, gendered, and economic oppression. Further, notions like oppression, human rights, and colonial independence all seemed to work together in the global context of self-determination. Self-determination was the means for ending a global narrative in which the white peoples of the world dominated the rest, and as such, self-determination was a *people's* right and the prerequisite for the exercise of *human* rights. What I'd like to emphasize, however, and as we transition in Chapter 7 to the discussion of self-determination and decolonization in the context of neoliberalism, is that this particular vision of decolonization is just that—one vision among many. One could argue that decolonization was never about promoting the rights of peoples—a people is not a legal concept, after all—it was about guaranteeing the rights of *states*. And as it was about the rights of states, it was also about the boundaries of states, the maintenance of borders, of structures of exclusion. Or, one could argue instead that decolonization was never about the rights of peoples or states, it was always about the rights of individual human beings—it's only that many of the movement's leaders just never realized the truth of it. And on this view, decolonization never really matured until self-determination dropped out of the picture: the protection of human rights has no prerequisites other than the living mind and body of the human being. To suggest

[166] *Id.* at 78.
[167] *Id.*
[168] *Id.* at 80.

anything else is to misunderstand the proper relation between the humans and the world in which they live.

I'd like to suggest that our tendency to prioritize one or another of these visions of decolonization—through the lens of peoples' rights, states' rights, and human rights—has much to do with the grip of modern racial ideology. The tighter the grip, the more all of this looks like a story about reducing the racial exclusion of formerly colonized peoples through the promotion of the rights of new states and individual rights to be free from racial discrimination. Self-determination, on this view, is a twilight kind of right. It is a means to an end, a crutch on the way toward the making of a more inclusive international legal order. We need it, but only until decolonization matures in the person of the newly arrived sovereign state, and the sovereign's newly arrived, rights-bearing citizens. Raciality can neither exclude sovereigns nor citizens from these rights, and indeed, racial discrimination is fast becoming an issue of domesticated, individual harm. After decolonization, it becomes increasingly unclear just what sort of problems race and racism will continue to pose for international society and its law.

What must be emphasized, however, is that at this decolonizing moment in the history of international law's modern racial ideology, the sovereign's right to exclude has become terribly ambiguous. At the level of international society, the sovereign's right to exclude the global outlaw, the racial *xenos*, has become increasingly deracialized. It is simply out of favor—initially for functionalist reasons, and later, for neoformalist ones (as we will discuss more in Chapter 7)—to use any science of racial classification to mark a borderland between the international community of sovereigns and the rightsless. To be sure, other ideological justifications would emerge in the gap but, by the 1950s and 1960s, raciality was off-trend.

At the level of national societies, however, the sovereign's rights of self-determination and nonintervention existed in a strangely enigmatic posture. On the one side, and in the context of migration, the sovereign's right of *dominium* had emerged in the first half of the twentieth century as intensely racialized. *Dominium* was a powerful agent in the erection of global racial hierarchy, justifying the rights of sovereigns to exclude individual migrants on eugenicist grounds. As recounted in Chapter 5, these developments were hardly limited to the US, as a racialized right of *dominium* became a common currency for standing in the global *demos*. On the other side, we have *dominium* as it was developing in the lateral context of decolonization. Here, *dominium* was equally associated with raciality, but now from the opposite direction. Rather than understand the sovereign's territorial right to exclude as *promoting* racial hierarchy, anticolonial thinkers claimed the right of *dominium* as decisively antiracist. By allowing the new sovereigns the right to master their houses, to determine their own fates, anticolonialism and antiracism went hand in glove.

Of course, the trouble (at least as I see it) with the right of *dominium* here in the two contexts of migration and decolonization is that we can see how the territorial

## 228 THE RIGHT TO EXCLUDE

rights of self-determination and nonintervention coalesce in the space of international law's modern racial ideology. In the field of migration law, the right of *dominium* came to mean that sovereigns had a natural right to determine for themselves the boundaries of their national communities. Even as raciality eventually fell away as a justifiable criterion for excluding migrants, the backgrounded nature of *dominium* stayed firmly in place. So much so that even today it remains difficult to challenge the "natural and necessary" sensibility that sovereigns can decide immigration questions as they see fit. International law has no role to play here, besides undergirding the very notion of *dominium* itself. In the space of decolonization, the right of *dominium* was similarly naturalized as an inevitable feature of true sovereignty, the right of the sovereign to determine its social, political, and cultural boundaries. And even while this right of *dominium* was characterized as antiracist, the notion of racial hierarchy targeted by the anticolonialists was—in large part—racial hierarchy at the level of *imperium*, of international society. There was little in the way of resurrecting the views of the Japanese at Versailles or the Chinese delegation from the URC, that what was needed was a deracialization of *imperium* on the one side, to be sure, but also a racialization of *dominium* on the other that explicitly focused on national boundaries as productive engines of racial hierarchy. And this never happened, neither in the context of migration law nor the law of decolonization.

# 7
# On the Ideological Threshold

This chapter explores the passageway between two structures of racial ideology in international legal thought, that of the modern and that of what I will be calling postracial xenophobia. Let me begin first, however, with a summary of the transition between the classic and modern structures with which we have thus far been occupied. In Chapter 3, I outlined a process of racial subjection in which international lawyers in the eighteenth and nineteenth centuries increasingly turned to scientific discourses about the human being as a means for conceptualizing international society as a racialized structure of—to use Agamben's phrasing—"inclusive exclusion." The result was a productive distinction between *homo politicus*, the rational, rights-bearing sovereign, and the nonwhite bodies of the homo *sacri*, the racial *xenoi*, which in itself generated a schedule of racial development. Constitutive of this classic structure of racial ideology was the sovereign's right to exclude, and in this classic structure the sovereign's right of *imperium* was the means for solving international law's boundary problem, manifesting as the right to determine the borders of a white supremacist international society. Heavily featured in the classic style was a particular understanding of the natural world, from its reliance on physical anthropology and biology to its formalist implementation. As a mode of naturalizing juridical science, it was the function of this vision of nature to provide the jurist with a family of justifications for producing a racialized outsider, a *xenos*, enacting and maintaining an international law by and for the "anglosphere."

The morph of the classic into the modern goes by a number of turns, and on the whole, it is largely unhelpful to try and pin the origins of modern racial ideology in a given decade. Indeed, the modern and classic forms have often worked in tandem, and it is certainly a mistake to think of them too sequentially. That said, the modern style didn't really exist in the 1850s, and was close to fully formed by the 1950s. Classic racial ideology, in contrast, was barely visible in the sphere of *imperium* by the time of the UN Decolonization Declaration of 1960, and was beginning its recession in the sphere of *dominium*.

As for what we have seen as the elements of modern racial ideology, the first was a shift in naturalizing juridical science, from legal formalism to legal functionalism. As we saw in Chapter 4, in the wake of thinkers like Rudolph von Jhering and Francois Geny, by the turn of the twentieth century, jurists across the globe were increasingly thinking about law in functionalist terms: rejecting the idea of law's nature and preferring to identify law's purpose, finding an empirical study

*The Right to Exclude*. Justin Desautels-Stein, Oxford University Press. © Justin Desautels-Stein 2023.
DOI: 10.1093/oso/9780198862161.003.0008

230  THE RIGHT TO EXCLUDE

of law's purpose as social need, and deciding concrete legal controversies in the light of this functionalist understanding. Further, functionalism had its own view of legal equality: rather than stake equality on a natural view of justice, one wanted to know the use of equality and its value in social context. This, of course, was an inherently problematic view, as became clear in Jhering's own xenophobic interest in the Aryans, and eventually, the functionalist tendency toward eugenics. In the context of international legal thought, the functionalist turn helped generate modern racial ideology through its focus on the production of non-state actors as a solution to international society's "real" problems. Nationalism, national groups, and the rights of minorities were primal forces that required international regulation, and the invention of international institutions like the League of Nations and the Mandate system became the preferred way for doing so. What's more, international legal functionalism promoted a view of these new institutions as much more racially inclusive than the Family of Nations model they were meant to replace. Unfortunately, it wasn't that functionalist international lawyers were necessarily any less racist. It was rather that the racial hierarchy of the Family of Nations had become impractical, unprofitable, and bad science.

It is in this sense that functionalism helped usher in a logic of inclusion for international lawyers of the early decades of the twentieth century. Cognizant of nineteenth-century tactics for excluding the colonized world from the rights of international society, functionalist lawyers sought to include these peoples—very slowly—in the new international legal order. This ideology of inclusion defined a modern transformation in the sovereign's right of *imperium*. For whereas in the classic style the sovereign's right to exclude entailed the power to determine the racial boundaries of the international world, this right was gradually deracialized. The right of *imperium* didn't vanish, or even weaken. But raciality did eventually fade away as its justification, yielding theories of racial development to theories of economic development, from a logic of exclusion to a logic of improvement.

The arrival of legal functionalism—and its attendant affiliation with twentieth-century theories of race science—had its effects on the sovereign's right of *dominium* as well. In this register, the sovereign's right to exclude was as racialized as the right of *imperium*, but the process of racial subjection was more complex. In a word, that process was doubled. On the one hand, and as we saw in Chapter 5, up until the end of the nineteenth century, the sovereign's right of *dominium* was primarily a right to exclude others sovereigns from a nation's territory. It was with shifts in migration patterns that, by the 1880s, sovereign members of the Family of Nations were flirting with a right to exclude individual human beings—*darker* human beings, particularly from Europe and Asia. Thus, just as the modern ideology of inclusion began its work on the sovereign's right of *imperium*, the classic ideology of exclusion was relocating to the borders of national territories. Instead of a formalistic embrace of evolutionary theories of racial development, however, the process of racial subjection occurring in the space of *dominium* relied upon a functionalist use of twentieth-century race science. During the interwar years the result was at once a deep racialization of the sovereign's territorial right to exclude, as well as an evacuation of migration out of international law's developing concerns with racial discrimination.

On the other hand, and as we saw in Chapter 6, anticolonial movements of the twentieth century tended to think of the sovereign's right of *dominium* as exactly the opposite of what I recounted in Chapter 5. Rather than see the sovereign's territorial right to exclude as a retrenchment of global racial hierarchy, participants spread across the Pan-African congresses to the Universal Races Congress (URC) to Bandung and to the "new" United Nations (UN) of the 1960s, all believed in rights of self-determination and nonintervention as the *cure* to racial hierarchy— or, at the very least, the beginnings of a cure. On this view, the self-determination of peoples was hardly reactionary but *radical*, uniting the rhetoric of human rights, decolonization, and antiracism; it would allow for a planetary *xenoi* to reinvent the world, remaking *imperium* and *dominium* in one fell swoop.

Whether and how this radical vision of *dominium* might have undone international law's racial ideology in the 1970s, we'll never know. But what was and remains clear is how the characterization of the sovereign's right of *dominium* shifted from a means for entrenching racial hierarchy in the context of migration, and into a means for assaulting racial hierarchy in the context of decolonization. For many of the thinkers associated with twentieth-century decolonization, the right of self-determination was the tip of the spear in the battle against a global economy that was fundamentally racist, but that's all that it was—the tip. And after 1960, as it matured in the machinery of the UN, and then in the International Court of Justice (ICJ), this generative and tension-filled understanding of self-determination first worked to liberate Trust and Non-Self-Governing Territories (NSGT), hit turbulence in the movement for a New International Economic Order (NIEO), and as I discuss in Chapter 8, was later sequestered in the liminal space of the movement for indigenous rights, and largely demobilized in the ideological quarters of the human rights movement. What began as a view of self-determination as a prerequisite for human rights, and *dominium* as an argument against structures of racial hierarchy and economic exploitation, eventually shrank into a cabined caveat in the lexicon of international human rights law.[1] Illustrative of the process is a comment from T.O. Elias in 1983, a Nigerian President of the ICJ, in which he referred to the human rights of "self-determination of peoples for peoples under colonial domination" and "the elimination of racial discrimination" as having signaled the "emergence of the legal personality of the *human being* as a significant feature of contemporary international law."[2] After apartheid, self-determination had little to

---

[1] ADOM GETACHEW, WORLDMAKING AFTER EMPIRE: THE RISE AND FALL OF SELF-DETERMINATION 91 (2019).

[2] TASLIM ELIAS, THE INTERNATIONAL COURT OF JUSTICE AND SOME CONTEMPORARY PROBLEMS 150 (1983).

232   THE RIGHT TO EXCLUDE

do with the struggle against racism, shifting almost entirely over into a rhetorical proxy for cultural integrity and diversity. When faced with future questions about race and racism, now funded by the antidiscrimination principle, human rights was the only answer international law could (or should) muster.

In this chapter, I explore this ideological threshold in the context of naturalizing juridical science, that is, the weakening of functionalism and the rise of a pair of neos: *neoformalism* and *neoliberalism*. There are many explanations for the lapse of functionalism at the end of the twentieth century, but the one I focus on here is the rise of a retro view of classic liberal legalism. It isn't that classic liberalism was back in style, as if 1980 was 1880. The structure of liberal legal thought was transforming, morphing, moving from a relatively stable structure of modern racial ideology and into what I call later on, *pragmatic liberalism*. The beginnings of that transformation are relevant here, for it was in the contexts of neoformalism and neoliberalism that the antidiscrimination principle took the form that would so dominate the agenda for human rights law, self-determination, and international law's twenty-first-century approach to racism. Eduardo Bonilla-Silva has observed that the hallmark of this neoliberal racialism was a new kind of "racism without racists."[3] It was a phenomenon that began in the 1960s with the United States (US) civil rights movement, and while it initially began with a progressive agenda, ultimately replaced Jim Crow racism with the mantra of colorblindness.[4] It is in the wake of this commitment to colorblind antidiscrimination law that Bonilla-Silva speaks of an era of racism without racists—a new "color-blind racism."[5] Colorblind racism, Bonilla-Silva observes, "explains contemporary racial inequality as the outcome of nonracial dynamics. Whereas Jim Crow racism explained blacks' social standing as the result of their biological and moral inferiority, color-blind racism ... rationalize[s] minorities' contemporary status as the product of market dynamics, naturally occurring phenomena," and cultural differences.[6]

I recount this development first in the American context of the antidiscrimination principle, and its eventual capture by a general theory of colorblindness. I then turn to a survey of the structural transition from functionalism into neoformalism. This discussion sets the scene for an analysis of the antidiscrimination principle in international law, first in the context of the International Convention on the Elimination of Racial Discrimination (ICERD), and then in refugee law. The chapter concludes by underlining the full maturation of international law's modern ideology of racial xenophobia. It is here, in the maturation of late modern racial ideology, that we

---

[3] Eduardo Bonilla-Silva, Racism without Racists: Color-blind Racism and the Persistence of Racial Inequality in America (2018).

[4] For general discussion, *see* Christopher Schmidt, Civil Rights in America: A History (2020). Critical accounts include Ian Haney Lopez, White By Law: The Legal Construction of Race (1996); Neil Gotanda, *A Critique of Our Constitution is Colorblind*, 44 Stan. L. Rev. 1 (1991).

[5] Bonilla-Silva, *supra* note 3, at 2.

[6] *Id.*

arrive at a tipping point in the story of international legal thought and racial xenophobia. It is the tipping over into the postracial.

## I THE ANTICLASSIFICATION/
## ANTISUBORDINATION DEBATE

In 1948, the UN promulgated its Universal Declaration of Human Rights (UDHR). Nowhere in that document is there mention of a national right of self-determination. True, Article 21 states that "The will of the people shall be the basis of the authority of government; this will shall be expressed in periodic and genuine elections which shall be by universal and equal suffrage and shall be held by secret vote or by equivalent free voting procedures." But Article 21, like the rest of the UDHR, is often read alongside various references in the UN Charter to faith in fundamental human rights. A question of some significance has gone to whether, here in the late 1940s and early 1950s, this understanding of human rights is the same as our understanding of the phrase today, and what relation it had to the right of self-determination. Contemporary views of human rights law associate that body of norms with an individualist antidiscrimination principle, and on the whole, today's human rights activism has little to do with the rights of *peoples*.[7] In this section, I detail a shift between what we might term "early" and "late" modern racial ideology. The former, as we have seen, is occupied with concerns about nineteenth-century race science, decolonization as antiracism, the right of *dominium* as "mastery over one's house," and national self-determination as a prerequisite for the exercise of human rights. "Late" modern racial ideology, however, began a movement away from many of these ideas, or if not quite "away," we could say that these concerns were slowly muted. Decolonization drifted into a functionalist effort to protect the new borders of formerly colonized peoples (as we saw in the discussion of the ICJ in Chapter 6), self-determination became a human right, and antiracism became the province for a colorblind antidiscrimination principle. It is to these latter developments that we should now give attention, and I want to start by jumping over to the civil rights tradition of the US.

In 1976, Paul Brest and Owen Fiss provided two visions of what the civil rights jurisprudence of the US had come to mean in the wake of *Brown v. Bd. of Educ.* and the Civil Rights Acts.[8] In Brest's "In Defense of the Antidiscrimination Principle," he explained that the principle disfavored classifications made on the basis of race, and that this was an idea animating the equal protection clause of

---

[7] That is, with the major exception of the international movement for the rights of Indigenous Peoples (discussed *infra* Chapter 8). *See Declaration on the Rights of Indigenous Peoples*, General Assembly Resolution A/RES/61/295 (Sept. 13, 2007).

[8] Paul Brest, *In Defense of the Antidiscrimination Principle*, 90 HARV. L. REV. 1 (1976); Owen Fiss, *Groups and the Equal Protection Clause*, 5 PHIL. & PUB. AFF. 107, 130 (1976).

# 234 THE RIGHT TO EXCLUDE

the Fourteenth Amendment and the desegregation policy of *Brown*, and lying at the core of the Civil Rights Act of 1964, the Voting Rights Act of 1965, and the Fair Housing Act of 1968. The question that had emerged by the 1970s was whether the antidiscrimination principle was colorblind. Was the idea that classifications based on racial identity were presumptively unconstitutional, regardless of their purpose? Or was the idea that this "colorblind" approach to antidiscrimination law was flawed precisely because it failed to see how "benign" race-conscious law and policy was key to remedying the historical inequities afflicting racial minorities? As Fiss explained:

> The antidiscrimination principle does not formally acknowledge social groups ... it only knows criteria or classifications; and the color black is as much a racial criterion as the color white. The regime it introduces is a symmetrical one of "color blindness," making the criterion of color, any color, presumptively impermissible. Reverse discrimination, so the argument is made, is a form of discrimination and is equally arbitrary since it is based on race.[9]

What had emerged in US constitutional doctrine was the view that the state's race-dependent decisions could survive the antidiscrimination principle's commitment to colorblindness only when the decision was necessary to promote some compelling objective. But, as Brest pointed out, this approach seemed oblivious to the "heart" of the antidiscrimination principle, which was the effort to ameliorate the conditions of historically disadvantaged groups. Thus, if the "objective and immediate effect" were to benefit a racial minority, Brest believed that the "strict scrutiny" standard should be replaced by a more lax assessment of whether the benefits outweighed the harms.[10] The antidiscrimination principle was designed, after all, to prevent irrational and unfair injuries.[11] Unequal treatment could be justified if one group was actually more deserving of another, but since this wasn't the case, policies that treated peoples differently on the basis of race were unfair and irrational. The harder question, as Brest saw it, was whether the antidiscrimination principle afforded any protections against race-neutral decisions that had a racially disproportionate impact.[12]

Brest believed that the answer was yes, but only insofar as those racially disparate impacts were traceable to some past violation of the antidiscrimination principle itself. Brest argued, "Discrimination often works its injuries through practices, not

---

[9] Fiss, *Equal Protection*, *supra* note 8, at 130.

[10] Brest, *supra* note 8, at 19.

[11] *Id.* at 6.

[12] Fiss has repeatedly argued that disparate impact analysis cannot be derived from the antidiscrimination principle. *See* Owen Fiss, *The Accumulation of Disadvantages*, 106 Cal. L. Rev. 1945, 1948–49 (2018). After the Supreme Court's decision in Washington v. Davis, race-neutral decisions from the state that have racially disparate impacts are considered constitutionally permissible. Disparate impact analysis under US statutory law, however, is a different story.

themselves race-dependent, implemented by institutions that have not themselves discriminated. Past and remote discrimination often manifest themselves in racially disproportionate impact, and the antidiscrimination principle may therefore support its amelioration or elimination."[13] If this anchor—the identification of "remote" violations of the antidiscrimination principle—was lost, the judiciary would find itself adrift in a sea of ad hoc entanglements.[14] It could also lead away from the most basic premise of the antidiscrimination principle of all: "remedies for race-specific harms recognize the sociological consequences of group identification and affiliation only to assure justice for individual members."[15]

It was precisely this focus on individualism that led Fiss to his well-known argument for a connection between equal protection doctrine and "specially disadvantaged groups." Rather than focus unnecessarily on equal protection as about discriminatory treatment, Fiss' "group disadvantaging principle" was intended to protect against the aggravation or perpetuation of the subordinate status of a specially disadvantaged group.[16] In Fiss' formulation, the antidiscrimination principle and its colorblind approach to racial classifications stood on one side, and his own group disadvantaging principle with its race-conscious approach stood on the other. Fiss clearly backed the latter, while Brest defended the former: "If a society can be said to have an underlying political theory, ours has not been a theory of organic groups but of liberalism, focusing on the rights of individuals, including rights of distributive justice."[17] What's more, Brest concluded, states that have in fact opted to allocate power among "racial and national groups are strikingly oppressive, unequal, and unstable."[18] This view was likely underscored with a point with which Brest began, and that it would be mistaken to forget, most poignantly here in the Black Panther years of the 1970s: Racial justice and economic justice were separate matters.[19]

About 25 years later, Jack Balkin and Reva Siegel suggested that Fiss was right on the merits but wrong on the analysis.[20] What was wrong was the way in which Fiss appeared to be struggling over the appropriateness of relying upon the antidiscrimination principle, or something else, as the best way to interpret the Fourteenth Amendment. Rather than see Fiss' approach as set against the antidiscrimination principle, Balkin and Siegel suggested that the group disadvantaging principle was simply one interpretation of antidiscrimination—not

[13] Brest, *supra* note 8, at 31.
[14] *Id.* at 48.
[15] *Id.*
[16] Fiss, *Equal Protection, supra* note 8, at 157.
[17] Brest, *supra* note 8, at 49.
[18] *Id.* at 50.
[19] *Id.* at 5. For an overview, *see* CHRISTOPHER SCHMIDT, CIVIL RIGHTS IN AMERICA: A HISTORY 90 (2020).
[20] Jack Balkin & Reva Siegel, *The American Civil Rights Tradition: Anticlassification or Antisubordination?* 58 U. MIAMI L. REV. 9, 10 (2003).

236  THE RIGHT TO EXCLUDE

an alternative to it. By the twenty-first century, it had become a commonplace to view the antidiscrimination principle from two warring perspectives: antisubordination and anticlassification. The former approach, Balkin and Siegel explained, had its roots in Fiss' theory of groups, and suggested that legal equality depends on the reform of legal structures that discriminate against historically oppressed groups. The latter approach, that of anticlassification, is mostly what Brest was defending, prohibiting the state from classifying citizens on the basis of a protected category, such as race or sex. From the perspective of the antisubordination approach, the antidiscrimination principle would forbid facially neutral policies with racially discriminatory impacts and allow affirmative action programs, while from the perspective of the latter, it was the reverse. Balkin and Siegel thought that Fiss had it right, just as others did in preferring what came to be labeled the antisubordination approach.[21] The anticlassification approach, in contrast, has typically been considered the terrain of the Rehnquist Court, alert to and wary of the state's use of race-conscious policy regardless of its social purpose.[22]

In his article "A Critique of 'Our Constitution is Color-Blind,'" Neil Gotanda argued that in *Brown's* wake, the anticlassification effort to make law and policy oblivious to race had the counterintuitive effect of fostering a new kind of white supremacy.[23] To be sure, Gotanda wasn't suggesting that the notion of a colorblind constitution was birthed in the era of civil rights; the tradition went at least as far back as Justice Harlan's debate in *Plessy* itself, in which equal protection of the law was based on common citizenship, regardless of the way in which "separate but equal" actually manifested in society.[24] But it wasn't until the last decades of the twentieth century that the racial ideology of colorblindness took its mature formation, when racial categories were crafted as "formal" classifications, "neutral, apolitical descriptions, reflecting merely 'skin color' or country of ancestral origin. Formal-race is unrelated to ability, disadvantage, or moral culpability. Moreover, formal- race categories are unconnected to social attributes such as culture, education, wealth, or language. This 'unconnectedness' is the defining characteristic of formal-race."[25]

The primary feature of contemporary colorblindness, Gotanda explained, was precisely this idea of "unconnectedness," a sharp separation between abstract classifications of racial identity—which may or may not have their origins in biological truths—and the social realities of race. As the Supreme Court put it in *Croson*, if claims of large-scale social forms of racial discrimination could justify the use remedial racial preferences, "the dream of a Nation of equal citizens in a

---

[21] Including folks like Owen Fiss, Catherine Mackinnon, Lawrence Tribe, and Derrick Bell.
[22] *See* Richard Primus, *Equal Protection and Disparate Impact: Round Three*, 117 HARV. L. REV. 494 (2003).
[23] Gotanda, *supra* note 4, at 1.
[24] *Id.* at 38.
[25] *Id.* at 4.

ON THE IDEOLOGICAL THRESHOLD    237

society where race is irrelevant to personal opportunity and achievement would be lost in a mosaic of shifting preferences based on inherently unmeasurable claims of past wrongs."[26] This formal disconnect between a new jurisprudence anchored in a background structure of racial classifications, and a socio-political context in which racial hierarchies continued unabated, Gotanda argued, helped sustain a new form of white supremacy. The essential mechanism was the way in which this formal gloss on race now framed racism as "irrational personal prejudice." Racism was "irrational," as Brest explained decades earlier, because race had become an abstraction best left unrecognized, a meaningless descriptor of a person's physical appearance.[27] And racism was personal, a problem of individual prejudices and psychological dispositions, since the whole point here was to decontextualize race and racism from those social realities "beyond" law's proper domain.[28] "In short," Gotanda concluded, "color-blind constitutionalists live in an ideological world where racial subordination is ubiquitous yet disregarded—unless it takes the form of individual, intended, and irrational prejudice."[29]

While Gotanda didn't frame it this way, a point worth emphasizing on the road to postracial xenophobia, was how the transition toward a colorblind kind of racism was facilitated by the lapse of legal functionalism. Whereas in the functionalist style a jurist ought to ask of the social functions of racial classification, it was precisely such questions Gotanda found "unconnected" from the new formalism, or neoformalism, of race law. And while Fiss didn't frame it this way either, what was largely motivating both his group disadvantaging theory as well as Brest's concerns about a too-much expanded version of the antidiscrimination principle, was precisely a functionalist view of equal protection doctrine. Reva Siegel has persuasively argued that it was this effort to disconnect *Brown* in particular from its social science rationales that in the 1960s and 1970s led to the rise of the anticlassification approach, and with it, these newly formalistic and colorblind conceptions of race and racism.[30]

Indeed, by the 1970s and 1980s, functionalism was a hot mess. If the rationale for prohibiting racial segregation turned on scientific data regarding the harms to racial minorities, what would be the result if social science suggested the harms of integration? Even Richard Posner, a scholar more in tune with the advantages of purposive analysis than most, was cited by Brest for the argument that the antidiscrimination principle be "divorced from empirical inquiries into the effects of discrimination on the affected groups."[31] As we have seen in earlier chapters,

---

[26] City of Richmond v. J.A. Croson Co., 109 S.Ct. 706, 727 (1989) (quoting *Bakke*).
[27] Gotanda, *supra* note 4, at 43.
[28] *Id.* at 44.
[29] *Id.* at 46.
[30] Reva Siegel, *Equality Talk: Antisubordination and Anticlassification Values in Constitutional Struggles Over Brown*, 117 HARV. L. REV. 1470, 1499 (2004).
[31] Brest, *supra* note 8, at 21. To be sure, Brest thought Posner was exaggerating the difficulties.

238    THE RIGHT TO EXCLUDE

this is part and parcel of the functionalist style; it is as open to equality discourse as much as it is closed, for it all depends on the manner in which the functionality of progress is characterized. In contrast, as more formalistic defenses of *Brown* began to emerge, the judicial edifice for the new Civil Rights Acts seemed more secure. Turning away from the "social realities" of racial hierarchy and toward the presumption of constitutional illegality when the state relied upon racial classifications, courts were relieved of "the burden of analyzing the racial logic of the regulation, in any but the most abstract form."[32]

While functionalism had increasingly turned out to be undependable as antiracist strategy, so too did this return to formalism, and it was this "return" that gave rise to Gotanda's critique of colorblindness. It is worth pausing at this point to ask, when we talk here of a new "formalism" of race, are we referring to the old mimetic techniques of the nineteenth and early twentieth centuries that we canvassed in Part I, or to something different? Derrick Bell believed that "despite the Realist challenge that demolished its premises, the basic formalist model of law survives, although in bankrupt form."[33] I agree that legal formalism survives, here in the 2020s as it did in the 1990s, but it is important to see how it has transformed. Furthermore, we must inquire into the relation between this new formalism and another contemporaneous neo—neo*liberalism*.

## II  TOWARD NEOLIBERALISM AND NEOFORMALISM

Duncan Kennedy and Samuel Moyn have each recently suggested how the 1970s and 1980s bore witness to the rise of neoliberalism and an attendant return to legal formalism.[34] In Kennedy's analysis, which is similar to Bell's, the story is about the techniques of legal argument, and it begins with the classical, nineteenth-century mode of formalism. This, as we saw in the likes of Root, Bluntschli, Lorimer, and Cushing surveyed in Chapter 3, and from John Marshall and Stephen Field in Chapter 5, is an argumentative technique for negotiating a choice between the theses of competition and order, between two legitimate but incompatible guides for shaping a legal concept.[35] The jurist might resort to formalism if he wants to suggest the availability of a principled, logical, *a priori* means for harmonizing the interpretive conflict, and conclude with a "natural" and "necessary" legal resolution. In what Kennedy calls "classical legal thought," the use of formalism

---

[32]  Siegel, *supra* note 30, at 1503.

[33]  Derrick Bell, *Racial Realism*, 24 CONN. L. REV. 363, 376 (1992).

[34]  DUNCAN KENNEDY, A CRITIQUE OF ADJUDICATION (2000); Duncan Kennedy, *Three Globalizations in Law and Legal Thought, in* THE NEW LAW AND DEVELOPMENT (David Trubek & Alvaro Santos eds., 2006); SAMUEL MOYN, THE LAST UTOPIA: HUMAN RIGHTS IN HISTORY (2010); SAMUEL MOYN, NOT ENOUGH: HUMAN RIGHTS IN AN UNEQUAL WORLD (2018).

[35]  What follows is my own rendition of formalism. While similar to Kennedy's, it should not be confused for a restatement.

was intensely individualistic and defined by a reliance upon property rights and freedom of contract. The reason for doing so was a belief in an immanent world of natural law, and the task of the judge was to align positive law with the natural blueprint. With the natural science of rights, judges could resolve most legal tensions from the vantage of first principles.

Eventually, and as we saw in Chapter 4, formalism was joined by a rival type of naturalizing juridical science, legal functionalism. Functionalism was far less concerned with individual rights, and more interested in the larger social project of making law more realistic, better at serving social needs and solving social problems, and helping realize the design of the welfare state. It would be a mistake to consider functionalism as anti-rights exactly; but in this view rights were a means for realizing some other social purpose, and not an end in their own right.

Kennedy argues that in the context of American legal thought, by the last decades of the twentieth century, the functionalism of the moderns was losing traction. Whereas the social contexts of law had for a generation been the holy grail of legal professionals the world over, an exhaustion with social needs, social purposes, social interdependence—an exhaustion with *society* was setting in. In the place of this functionalist approach to law and society, jurists rekindled a love affair with abstractions, namely, *individual rights* and the *synergies of free market competition*.[36] Of course, concepts of individual right and free competition were hardly new. What *was* new, however, was the manner in which these older types of rights claims were now joined by the center-left, hard-charging for individualized rights to be free from torture, rights of political expression, rights to be free from racial discrimination, and more. What else was new was the belief that it was up to the state to enforce these rights, whether the rights were oriented from the left or the right. The last time rights had been all the rage in legal thought, back in the late 1800s, it was the market-oriented claim for property rights and freedom of contract that blazed the trail. A hundred years later, rights were now making a center-stage comeback. But it was not only the civil and political rights claimed from the human rights movement—rights were now claimed by the Left *and* the Right: the human rights movement and a retro appreciation for classic liberal ideas (i.e., neo-liberalism), strange—yet entirely natural—bedfellows.

In a structuralist register, we can say that neoliberalism offered a return to a grammatical preference for the liberal thesis of right and competition, and against the thesis of social control and ordered liberty. Thus, everything from Reagan and Thatcher to the World Bank's structural adjustment programs, to the Rehnquist Court, to the 1980s image of Wall Street appeared to reflect a return to the classic liberal orientations toward property and contract, but with a renewed appreciation for the role of the state in promulgating a free market society. Wendy Brown argues

---

[36] Kennedy, *Three Globalizations, supra* note 34, at 63–73.

## 240 THE RIGHT TO EXCLUDE

in this vein that neoliberalism is not about the state leaving the economy alone. Rather, neoliberalism activates the state on behalf of the economy, *not* to undertake economic functions or to intervene in economic *effects*, but rather to facilitate economic competition and growth and to economize the social, or, as Foucault puts it, to "regulate society by the market."[37] Brown continues, "nature is the province of classical liberalism, hence the importance of *laissez-faire* to its theorists. By contrast, convention, intervention, and even subvention are key to neoliberalism."[38]

Consider in this regard the emblematic economist-philosopher Friedrich Hayek, and as he described his project in *The Constitution of Liberty*:

> The conception of freedom under the law that is the chief concern of this book rests on the contention that when we obey laws, in the sense of general abstract rules laid down irrespective of their application to us, we are not subject to another man's will and are therefore free. It is because ... *the judge who applies them has no choice in drawing the conclusions that follow from the existing body of rules and the particular facts of the case, that it can be said that laws and not men rule* ... This, however, is true only if by "law" we mean the general rules that apply equally to everybody. This generality is probably the most important aspect of that attribute of law which we have called its 'abstractness.' "[39]

In crafting this naturalizing understanding of law, Hayek reinforced the classic liberal distinction between the Rule of Law (rules that apply equally and generally) and legislation (rules that are partisan). The former concept—the Rule of Law—is what gives the human subject its freedom. This freedom-enhancing quality is a result of several factors, one of which is its provenance. For Hayek, the Rule of Law is not the product of deliberate human consideration, but is rather a natural evolution, a material to be discovered in the world rather than produced. "Most of these rules have never been deliberately invented but have grown through a gradual process of trial and error in which the experience of successive generations has helped to make them what they are. In most instances, therefore, nobody knows or has ever known the reasons and considerations that have led to a rule being given a particular form. We must thus often endeavor to *discover* the functions that a rule actually serves."[40] These naturally evolving common law rules were neutral, general, and abstract, only to be discovered and applied by the judiciary, without any preference for a particular class or party. Hayek continued, "For here no human decision will be required in the great majority of cases to which the rules apply; and even when a court has to determine how the general rules may be applied to a

---

[37] WENDY BROWN, UNDOING THE DEMOS: NEOLIBERALISM'S STEALTH REVOLUTION 62 (2015).
[38] *Id.* at 63.
[39] FRIEDRICH HAYEK, THE CONSTITUTION OF LIBERTY 221–22 (1978) (emphasis added).
[40] *Id.* at 225.

ON THE IDEOLOGICAL THRESHOLD 241

particular case, it is the implications of the whole system of accepted rules that decide, not the will of the court."[41] Citing John Marshall, Hayek intoned, "Courts are
the mere instruments of the law, and can will nothing."[42]

In contrast with this vision of the Rule of Law, Hayek identified legislation
as a rival way of formulating legal prescriptions. Whereas the Rule of Law gives
freedom, legislation and regulation take it away. As a political act of intervention,
legislation "emanates from the legislative authority [and] is the chief instrument of
oppression."[43] This oppressive form of law is outcome-determinative and focused
precisely on partisan interests, whereas the Rule of Law is general and neutral.
Citing Oliver Wendell Holmes, Jr., in support of the prevalence of this politically
oriented view of legislation, Hayek warned, "To say that laws rule and not men may
consequently signify that the fact is to be hidden that men rule over men ... The
confusion of these two conceptions of law and the loss of belief that laws can rule,"
Hayek explained, "that men in laying down and enforcing laws in the former sense
are not enforcing their will, are among the chief causes of the decline in liberty."[44]

Hayek's was a vision that assigned marching orders for judges and lawyers,
tasking them with the completion of a legal order that properly mirrored the naturally evolved norms of property and contract, and the separation of judges from
so-called political points of view. It was this emphasis on the natural power of
the market—a power harnessed through the courts of the sovereign—and on the
ways in which the market was a guide for shaping everything else, that led critics
like David Theo Goldberg to characterize neoliberalism as a worldmaking ideology: "Far from dismantling the state, or drowning it, then, neoliberalism would
remake it."[45] Whereas in the classic liberal mode, individuals were characterized
in the Hobessian/Lockean imaginary as white men competing in a natural market
society, here in the colorblind apparatus of the neoliberal mode, as Brown argued,
"To speak of the relentless and ubiquitous economization of all features of life by
neoliberalism is thus not to claim that neoliberalism literally *marketizes* all spheres
even as such marketization is certainly one important effect of neoliberalism.
Rather, the point is that neoliberal rationality disseminates the model of the market
to all domains and activities—even where money is not at issue—and configures
human beings exhaustively as market actors, always, only, and everywhere as *homo
oeconomicus*."[46]

Neoformalism, as opposed to neoliberalism, is a bit of a different fish. For while
neoliberalism suggests a reorientation in the grammar of liberal legal thought

[41] *Id.*
[42] *Id.* at 224.
[43] *Id.*
[44] *Id.*
[45] David Theo Goldberg, The Threat of Race: Reflections on Racial Neoliberalism 333 (2009).
[46] Brown, *supra* note 37, at 31.

242   THE RIGHT TO EXCLUDE

by way of a return to private law rights and the benefits of free competition over and against the welfare state, neoformalism is what I have termed a mode of naturalizing juridical science. Or to put that in the language of Chapter 1, whereas neoliberalism is a grammatical structure operating in the space of the *langue*, neoformalism is a manifestation of liberal legalism's third thesis—it is a style of argumentative practice aspiring to juridical moments of legal necessity. As will be recalled from earlier chapters, legal formalism is a mimetic technique whereby the jurist first posits a sharp distinction between nature and politics, between private and public, allocates context to these separate spheres, and then attempts to match positive law with an organic and historically driven set of natural orders. As a result, legal formalism inevitably pushes in a conservative trajectory, given its "scientific" aspirations for "making law great again."

As a mode of naturalizing juridical science, neoformalism, however, is much more ambiguous with respect to its normative credentials. Indeed, it is precisely this politically equivocal aspect of late twentieth-century rights claims that leads Kennedy to identify neoformalism in contemporary legal thought. Whereas in classical formalism legal thinkers resorted to a narrow script of individual rights in the effort to resolve legal tensions, in contemporary legal thought rights play the same mediating task—only now, the script has flipped to the extent that individual rights have at once enlarged and diminished. They have enlarged in the sense that property rights and freedom of contract are now in a contest with rights of free expression and freedom from torture: rights of market competition coalesce with rights of civil society. They have diminished in the sense that it is only rarely believed that individual rights of any kind might offer a programmatic vision for how to rearrange the world.[47] In the nineteenth century, individual rights were decisively about the right to compete in the market, and were seen as the keys for unlocking a natural and invisible set of political and economic arrangements. Today, individual rights might serve as trumps, or naturalizing techniques for navigating interpretive blockades. But individual rights are rarely suggested as a platform for social reorganization. Hence, it is a "new" rights formalism.

Samuel Moyn's account arrives at a very similar destination as Kennedy's, but rather than take the structuralist route through legal thought, Moyn's explanation moves through intellectual history.[48] By the late 1970s, a rights zeitgeist

---

[47] It is true that the human rights movement was later enlisted in the larger broadside of democracy promotion. To the extent that thinkers really saw the elaboration of human rights—as opposed to say, the neoliberal rule of law—as an engine for the spread of liberal democracy, perhaps we can see here the way in which human rights itself underwent an ideological shift. For discussion of what Gerry Simpson has called "liberal anti-pluralism" in this context, *see* GERRY SIMPSON, GREAT POWERS AND OUTLAW STATES (2004).

[48] The two narratives are complementary not only in the fact that the conclusions are similar; methodologically, Kennedy's account of the structure of legal thought pairs well with Moyn's account of the political and social contexts for that structure. There is now a sizable literature surrounding Moyn's claims for the novelty of the human rights movement, though I am unaware of any efforts to link Moyn's argument with Kennedy's.

was swirling throughout the rich, industrialized countries of the north. And yet, Moyn suggested that the new spirit of human rights was without meaningful precursors: The language of rights known to liberal theory and the Revolutions of the eighteenth century were entirely different creatures. Rather than offer a vision of rights capable of penetrating the sovereign exterior of the state, these older traditions were essentially about the *constitution* of the sovereign state. The postwar UN system, including the adoption of the UDHR, were similarly unrelated to the rights revolution that came later. Without any real impact as a system of *individualized* rights, human rights were primarily understood after World War II as the rights of formerly colonized peoples to be free from a racially discriminatory world order. That is, human rights were set against the classical ideology of racial xenophobia described above, but *that* conception of human rights was not the conception that emerged in the neoformalism of the human rights movement. As both a social movement and a conception of law, human rights between 1945 and 1975 were simply something other than the ethos of individualism that caught on later.

Like Kennedy, Moyn suggests that what enabled the rise of neoformalism was not the slow evolution of rights-based thinking from the revolutionary wars and up until Vietnam, but rather the collapse of a prior vision for world order.[49] Once again, while Kennedy's focus is on the structure of legal thought, Moyn's is on the intellectual context of non-governmental organizations, political dissidents, and perhaps most crucially, the decline of earlier, more fulsome "utopias." Related though ultimately distinct, it was the decline of the decolonization movement and the principle of national self-determination on the one side, and the decline of socialism on the other, that paved the way for a new utopia of individual rights to fill the vacuum. And again like Kennedy, Moyn points to the catholic nature of rights discourse that flowered in the 1970s and 1980s, moving all across the political spectrum. Indeed, the international human rights movement and the neoliberal "Washington Consensus" were twins.[50]

What caught on by 1980 was a language of human rights that triumphed as a utopia of minimalism. Defined more by its distance from debates about national self-determination and racial justice, than from any commitments about reforming the global order, human rights individualism emerged along the Amnesty International model of an "apolitical" approach to protecting threatened individuals. This minimalism was therefore defined by a morality of individualism

---

[49] While Moyn does not use the phrase "neoformalism," I take his argument to amount to the same thing.

[50] Moyn and Kennedy agree on another point as well: it is fruitless to search for a causal explanation with respect to the international human rights movement giving rise to neoliberalism. For Kennedy, the two factions belong to the same *langue*. For Moyn, the human rights movement didn't cause neoliberalism; the end of socialism did. "After its participation in the creation of welfare states, socialism had become and long remained the most identifiable language of material equality, and its departure explains more than any other factor why the age of human rights was also the age of neoliberalism: it was no longer the age of the socialist left." *See* MOYN, NOT ENOUGH, *supra* note 34, at 180.

## 244 THE RIGHT TO EXCLUDE

over programmatic views of social justice, legal rights over political theory, and universalism over national identity.

If we jump back to the discussion of antidiscrimination in constitutional law, we can see how the analyses of Kennedy, Moyn, and Brown explain what Balkin and Siegel were suggesting about the then-current state of equal protection doctrine. In their argument for the apparent triumph of the antidiscrimination principle—the question was no longer whether but how it would apply to equal protection doctrine—they also argued that, rather than concede the apparent victory of anticlassification over antisubordination, the two approaches tended toward overlapping scenes of struggle and mutual constitution. Anticlassification theorists defended the rights of everyone to be protected against race-dependent decisions, while antisubordination theorists defended the rights of disadvantaged groups to be protected against decisions with disparate impacts. While the two approaches are certainly different, and while the stakes are clearly high in choosing between them, Balkin and Siegel explained that "both antisubordination and anticlassification might be understood as possible ways of fleshing out the meaning of the antidiscrimination principle, and thus as candidates for the 'true' principle underlying antidiscrimination law."[51] Or in other words, the debate here was largely a matter of formalism versus functionalism—formalism carried the antidiscrimination principle into colorblindness and an anticlassification stance, whereas functionalism tended to move more in the direction of antisubordination and disparate impact. Nevertheless, and as Balkin, Siegel, and so many scholars have conceded, these two approaches are not equals. By the turn of the twenty-first century, the antidiscrimination principle had gone predominantly colorblind—in the neoformalist sense described by Gotanda. It had gone colorblind in a neoliberal sense as well, for as Goldberg put it, for neoliberals committed to "privatizing individualization, the standard racism—rewarding people for no reason other than their membership in a racial group—came to be affirmative action (or 'positive discrimination' in Europe). Liberalism's very instrument for undoing the effects of racism became neoliberalism's poster child for the condition of racism itself."[52]

I return to neoliberalism and its relation with postraciality in the next chapters, but in the remainder of this one, the question moving forward is this. Through the 1960s and into the 1970s, Malcolm X, Martin Luther King, Jr., and then the Black Panthers all criticized the shortcomings of the US civil rights movement and the limits of the antidiscrimination principle. Perhaps a better alternative, they wondered, was available elsewhere? Malcolm X had argued in his famous "The Ballot or the Bullet" speech of 1964 that a much-needed broader interpretation of the freedom struggle was available in the lesser-known fields of international

---

[51] Balkin & Siegel, *supra* note 20, at 10.

[52] DAVID THEO GOLDBERG, THE THREAT OF RACE: REFLECTIONS ON RACIAL NEOLIBERALISM 337 (2008).

human rights. Three years later, King similarly looked for the turn to human rights as the obvious "next step." Below, we will continue with our look at colorblindness and antidiscrimination, but shift back into international law and where we left off in the framing of self-determination as an antiracist and anticolonial "prerequisite" for the exercise of human rights. And so the question is this: Were antiracist activists disenchanted with the US civil rights movement right to hope for something more than formal colorblindness in the field of international law? Not to spoil it for you, but the answer is no.[53]

## III TOWARD THE UN'S DISCRIMINATION CONVENTION

Our trajectory toward that unfortunate answer begins in the wake of the Universal Races Congress of 1911 (URC), when Du Bois proclaimed the event as among the most important developments in the coming war against racism, and chief among these armaments was a clarification about the science of race. As we have seen, the early decades of the twentieth century reflected something of a Manichean moment for the science of racial identity: on the one side was the eugenicist movement, and on the other was the attack on racial biology that was only just beginning at the time of the URC. Perhaps the most popular instance of the latter was the work of Jean Finot, both in his widely read *Race Prejudice* of 1907, and the summary of the work published in 1911 under the name *The Death Agony of the Science of Race*. Indeed, *Death Agony* was prepared specifically for the URC, and in the main, detailed the follies of eugenics. Back in Chapter 3, I discussed some of the developments in antirace science taking place in the interwar years, most notably in the work of Boas, Haddon, Huxley, and Montagu.[54] This was the moment when, in the context of racial theory, "nation," "culture," and "ethnicity" began a slow leakage out of the race concept. The effort, of course, was to neutralize race, turning it into an apolitical classification system, divorced from claims about intellectual, moral, physical or aesthetic capacity.

In the context of international law, what was emerging was the slow effort to empty raciality of its moral content and embed it in a new scheme of antidiscrimination law.[55] As is well known, the preamble of the UN Charter

---

[53] For an argument moving in the other direction, *see, e.g.*, Berta Esperanza Hernandez-Truyol, *Building Bridges: Bringing International Human Rights Home*, 9 LA RAZA L.J. 69 (1996).

[54] *See also* TRACY TESLOW, CONSTRUCTING RACE: THE SCIENCE OF BODIES AND CULTURES IN AMERICAN ANTHROPOLOGY (2014); GEORGE STOCKING, RACE, CULTURE, AND EVOLUTION (1982); ELAZAR BARKAN, THE RETREAT OF SCIENTIFIC RACISM: CHANGING CONCEPTS OF RACE IN BRITAIN AND THE UNITED STATES BETWEEN THE WORLD WARS (1992); Paul Weindling, *Julian Huxley and the Continuity of Eugenics in Twentieth Century Britain*, 10 J. MOD. EUR. HIST. 480 (2012).

[55] WARWICK MCKEAN, EQUALITY AND DISCRIMINATION UNDER INTERNATIONAL LAW (1983); E.W. VIERDAG, THE CONCEPT OF DISCRIMINATION IN INTERNATIONAL LAW (1973). On the early surge in Latin America to tie human rights to racial equality, *see* DAVID SCOTT FITZGERALD & DAVID

246    THE RIGHT TO EXCLUDE

states that the UN's constituent parties determined "to reaffirm faith in fundamental human rights, in the dignity and worth of the human person, in the equal
rights of men and women and of nations large and small ... "[56] As with the League
Covenant, the Charter does not include a "racial equality" clause, though as we
have seen, this wasn't for lack of trying.[57] Instead, the drafters went with the language of Article 2(7), reserving to the states' domestic jurisdiction over "internal"
affairs, presumably including the racial equality of peoples.[58] Similarly, the UDHR
of 1948 proclaims in its Article 2 that "Everyone is entitled to all the rights and freedoms set forth in this Declaration, without distinction of any kind, such as race,
colour, sex, language, religion, political or other opinion, national or social origin,
property, birth or other status." Article 7 goes on to hold that "All are equal before
the law and are entitled without any discrimination to equal protection of the law.
All are entitled to equal protection against any discrimination in violation of this
Declaration and against any incitement to such discrimination."

In 1949, and at the request of the Economic and Social Council, the UN Sub-
Commission on Prevention of Discrimination and Protection of Minorities prepared a report for the Secretary-General, meant to explore "the main types of
discrimination which impede the equal enjoyment by all of human rights and fundamental freedoms and the causes of such discrimination ... "[59] In its elucidation,
the Sub-Commission relied upon a number of studies in anthropology, sociology,
psychology, and history, among other things, "as an attempt to place in systematic
order the findings and various suggestions of various scientists."[60] In framing these
findings, however, the Sub-Commission articulated a distinction between the
elimination of discrimination and the affirmative protection of "non-dominant"
groups[61]—a distinction that foreshadowed the sorts of disagreement forthcoming
from the likes of Brest and Fiss, twenty five years later. The latter reference would
persist, to be sure, but the initial connection between the antidiscrimination principle and group-oriented racism wouldn't last.[62] The former, however, would
prove to be the province of the Commission's task in fleshing out the Charter and

---

COOK-MARTIN, CULLING THE MASSES: THE DEMOCRATIC ORIGINS OF RACIST IMMIGRATION POLICY
IN THE AMERICAS 76 (2014).

[56] *See also* UN Charter, art. 55: "With a view to the creation of conditions of stability and well-being
which are necessary for peaceful and friendly relations among nations based on respect for the principle
of equal rights and self-determination of peoples, the UN shall promote: a. higher standards of living,
full employment, and conditions of economic and social progress and development; b. solutions of international economic, social, health, and related problems; and international cultural and educational
cooperation; and c. universal respect for, and observance of, human rights and fundamental freedoms
for all without distinction as to race, sex, language, or religion."

[57] MICHAEL BANTON, INTERNATIONAL ACTION AGAINST RACIAL DISCRIMINATION 22 (1996).

[58] *Id.*

[59] The report was titled "The Main Types and Causes of Discrimination."

[60] *Id.* at 1.

[61] *Id.* at 2–3.

[62] *See, e.g.,* Peter Jones, *Human Rights, Group Rights, and Peoples' Rights,* 21 HUM. RTS. Q. 80 (1999).

UDHR's provisions related to equality and freedom: "any action which denies to individuals or groups of people equality of treatment,"[63] or distinctions made on grounds of natural or social categories, which have no relation either to individual capacities or merits, or to the concrete behavior of the individual person."[64] These discriminatory acts originated in "prejudice which creates an unfavorable attitude of mind."[65] Among the "most important pretexts for prejudice" was race.

Echoing much of the reporting made almost forty years earlier at the URC, the Sub-Commission explained that while racial classifications were both real and pernicious, there was little scientific support for the idea that races existed as distinctive human groups with particular physical or intellectual capabilities. "While the concept of race as a definite human group appears illegitimate from the scientific standpoint, the concept of people or nation expresses a historical and sociological reality. This concept, however, is not based on natural factors, but rather on culture."[66] What was different, however, was the Sub-Commission's explanation of this cultural background—a background motivated by a "racial ideology" arousing a false consciousness, tending "to distort everything that may fall within its sphere. The member of the disliked racial group must be repressed and made a non-entity, and the idea of assimilation made repulsive; therefore the out-group is portrayed as physically and morally unclean."[67] The report concluded with a survey of the main types of discrimination and the legal and educational measures best situated to eliminate prejudice and its legal manifestations.

A year later, in 1950, and also as a result of the Economic and Social Council's interest in elaborating the meaning of racial discrimination, a series of documents were promulgated by the United Nations Educational, Science, and Cultural Organization (UNESCO), a new branch of the UN system initially headed up by Huxley.[68] In some ways the "Statements on Race" that UNESCO would issue here and in later phases were in keeping with what we have already seen in international law's early modern racial ideology,[69] but in others we can already detect in the

---

[63] Main Types, *supra* note 59, at 2.

[64] *Id.* at 9.

[65] *Id.* at 10.

[66] *Id.* at 18.

[67] *Id.* at 18–19.

[68] Sarah Brouillette, UNESCO and the Fate of the Literary (2019); Banton, Action, *supra* note 57, at 24; Michael Banton, The International Politics of Race (2002).

[69] Bioethical and Ethical Issues Surrounding the Trials and Code of Nuremburg (Jacques Rozenberg ed., 2003); Jenny Reardon, Race to the Finish: Identity and Governance in an Age of Genomics (2015); Penny von Eschen, Race Against Empire: Black Americans and Anticolonialism, 1937–1957 (1997); Race and Other Misadventures: Essays in Honor of Ashley Montagu in his Ninetieth Year (Larry Reynolds & Leonard Lieberman eds., 1996); Robert Proctor, *Three Roots of Human Recency*, 44 Current Anth. 213 (2003); Jenny Bangham, *What is Race? UNESCO, Mass Communication, and Human Genetics in the Early 1950s*, 28 Hist. Hum. Sci. 80 (2015); Perrin Selcer, *Beyond the Cephalic Index: Negotiating Politics to Produce UNESCO's Scientific Statements on Race*, 53 Current Anth. S173 (2012); Michelle Brattain, *Race, Racism, and Antiracism: UNESCO and the Power of Presenting Science to the Postwar Public*, 112 Am. Hist. Rev. 1386, 1390 (2007).

248   THE RIGHT TO EXCLUDE

UNESCO documents a shifting of the winds.[70] As Michelle Brattain has argued, UNESCO's "epistemological dynamic reproduced the limitations of the collective scientific imagination at that moment, precluded a more profound reassessment of the race concept, and inadvertently reconstructed an intellectual space for thinking of race as a legitimate and determinist category of human variation."[71]

The immediate impetus for the UNESCO race project, as Ashley Montagu put it, was that "in the decade just passed more than six million human beings lost their lives because it was alleged they belonged to an inferior race."[72] Indeed, it was neither in the context of the anticolonial race congresses, nor that of the recent racialization of global migration policies the world over, but rather that of the Holocaust, that in 1949 that the United Nations Economic and Social Council asked UNESCO to produce a report on the contemporary state of race science. Soon a committee of ten experts was convened in Paris,[73] and the first "Statement on Race" of 1950 adamantly distinguished between concentrations of gene frequencies in certain human populations—these populations were what might sensibly be called "races"—and "national, religious, geographic, linguistic, and cultural groups."[74] That is, the experts found no scientific connections between a so-called racial group and any other label in the second category. In order to help clarify this separation, the UNESCO report suggested doing away with the label of "race" and replacing it with "ethnic group," an idea already suggested several decades earlier, as we saw in Chapter 3. Underlining the point, the report explained that "wherever it has been possible to make allowances for differences in environmental opportunities, the tests have shown essential similarity in mental characteristics of all human groups. In short, given similar degrees of cultural opportunity to realize their potentialities, the average achievement of each ethnic group is about the same."[75]

With the 1950 report squarely in Montagu's shadow, it was immediately criticized as too much of an exercise in anthropology, with insufficient input from the biologists. As a result a second Statement was issued, this time with less emphasis on the sociological critique of race and more of a defense of relatively neutral racial classifications.[76] I say "relatively" here, because, while the second Statement defended "the primary conclusion that there were no scientific grounds whatever for the racialist position regarding purity of race and the hierarchy of inferior and

---

[70] Sebastian Gil-Riano, *Relocating Anti-Racist Science: The 1950 UNESCO Statement on Race and Economic Development in the South*, 51 Brit. J. Hist. Sci. 281 (2018).

[71] Brattain, *supra* note 69, at 1390.

[72] Ashley Montagu, Statement on Race: An Extended Discussion in Plain Language of the UNESCO Statement by Experts on Race Problems ix (1951).

[73] *Id.* at 4.

[74] *Id.* at 13.

[75] *Id.* at 14.

[76] *See* Jean Hierneaux, *Biological Aspects of the Racial Question, in* Four Statements on the Race Question (1969).

superior races to which this leads,"[77] it nevertheless helped further reify beliefs in racial culture. Echoing the faith-based beliefs of the eugenicists, the Statement explained that "the physical anthropologist as well as the man in the street both know that races exist." Perhaps this so-called "man in the street" was none other than the ghost of Houston Stewart Chamberlain, who had been so sure that even a child could pick a Jew out from a crowd of Teutonic Germans. In any case, the second UNESCO Statement assured that the everyday man knows another's race "from the immediate evidence of his senses when he sees an African, an Asiatic, and an American Indian together."[78]

The first UNESCO Statement had wished to do away with "race" altogether and replace it with "ethnic group." The second Statement, in contrast, put the race back in race science, conceding many of the criticisms of older modes of physical anthropology, but retaining "race" as an appropriately empirical concept.[79] While the second Statement certainly reflected a consensus about the wrongheadedness of Nazism, eugenics and schedules of racial development, it ultimately reflected little else. Like the race science of the nineteenth century, mid-twentieth-century race science still seemed largely under the spell of a theory of racial difference (if not development) that was more a product of faith than fact.[80] As Sebastian Gil-Riano has argued, UNESCO's work on race from the 1950s:

> [R]elied upon conceptions of race that theorized human biological variation as subject to continual change through cultural and environmental forces and focused on immaterial objects such as social institutions, cultural patterns, family structures and personality types as crucial sites for studying the historical formation and evolution of racial consciousness. Within this anti-racist racial regime, the apparent alterability of social institutions, cultural patterns and the physical body was upheld as evidence that "simpler peoples" could and should escape their hapless state of cultural and even biological inferiority. For these antiracist scientists, typological conceptions of race thus opposed the purposive conceptions of social change in which they were so invested, and denied backward "races" their rightful incorporation into an imagined industrial and urban modernity.[81]

By the 1960s, the modern racial ideology of racial inclusion and human equality, as now espoused in international law, was beginning to settle into a broad

---

[77] UNESCO, "Statement on the Nature of Race and Race Differences," 36, available at https://unesdoc.unesco.org/ark:/48223/pf0000122962.

[78] *Id.*

[79] THE RACE CONCEPT: RESULTS OF AN INQUIRY (1952).

[80] Brattain, *supra* note 69, at 1404. Claude Levi-Strauss, *Race and History, in* THE RACE QUESTION IN MODERN SCIENCE (1961).

[81] Gil-Riano, *supra* note 70, at 297.

250  THE RIGHT TO EXCLUDE

consensus.[82] UNESCO issued two further "refinements" of its Statements from the 1950s in 1964 and 1967, as well as a "Declaration on Race and Racial Prejudice" in 1978, and the UN moved forward with the first human rights covenant, the International Convention on the Elimination of All Forms of Racial Discrimination (ICERD).[83] Adopted in 1965, and entering into force in 1969, ICERD crystallized much of the international momentum from the last two decades, as exemplified by the UNESCO statements and the Sub-Commission's report on discrimination. The Convention was preceded by a Declaration from the General Assembly a few years earlier. The immediate trigger for the Declaration was an uptick in anti-Semitism throughout Europe and the US, while the looming background impetus was the problem of apartheid in South Africa. In both cases, the Sub-Commission on Prevention of Discrimination and Protection of Minorities viewed the issue less as anticolonial and more as a "human rights" problem—which made sense, given that this was a Sub-Commission of what was then called the Commission on Human Rights—and recommended the preparation of a new human rights treaty on racial discrimination. The General Assembly's Third Committee took up the task, initially drafting a Declaration that focused solely on racial discrimination, leaving the religious aspects of anti-Semitism for another day.[84] This Draft laid the template for the Sub-Commission in its drafting of what would become the ICERD, and when the Sub-Commission's Draft came before the General Assembly for debate and adoption, a recurring point concerned the relation between the elimination of racial discrimination and anticolonialism.[85] I will return to this cleavage momentarily, but first, let us take a look at what emerged in the Convention itself.

If we recall the basic distinction between a logic of exclusion/inclusion and racial subjection explored in Chapter 2, the ICERD was unmistakably a product of the former orientation. Largely divorced from views of antiracism as anticolonialism, the key to the document was the citizen's right to be free from racial discrimination. The ICERD was also buoyed by a scientific approach to race that was busily emptying it of all that was "real," that is, ethnoculture. While there was talk in the preparatory discussions of whether UNESCO hadn't already proved the races to be scientifically false, there wasn't agreement on the issue. The result was a decision to avoid language directed at the "unreality" of race and treat it instead as an empirically plausible, but morally vacant classification.[86] These two aspects were united in

---

[82] International Convention on Civil and Political Rights, art. 2 (1966). Other efforts between the articulation of the first two Statements and the work begun on the Racial Discrimination Declaration include those of the UN Committee on Information from NSGTs. *See* https://research.un.org/en/docs/ga/quick/regular/7. *See also* ILO Discrimination Convention No 111 (1958).

[83] NATAN LERNER, THE UN CONVENTION ON THE ELIMINATION OF ALL FORMS OF RACIAL DISCRIMINATION (1970).

[84] *See* PATRICK THORNBERRY, THE INTERNATIONAL CONVENTION ON THE ELIMINATION OF ALL FORMS OF RACIAL DISCRIMINATION: A COMMENTARY (2016).

[85] BANTON, INTERNATIONAL ACTION, *supra* note 57, at 58.

[86] E/CN.4/Sub.2SR.410, p. 11.

the idea that individual discrimination was grounded in prejudices concerning irrational and unfair beliefs about the meaning of racial classifications. Theoretically, one could "eliminate" discrimination if people were sufficiently educated about the misbegotten origins of racial type.

Article 1 begins with a definition of racial discrimination, borrowing from prior articulations from the Sub-Commission, UNESCO, and the International Labour Organization (ILO): "racial discrimination shall mean any distinction, exclusion, restriction or preference based on race, colour, descent, or national or ethnic origin which has the purpose or effect of nullifying or impairing the recognition, enjoyment or exercise, on an equal footing, of human rights and fundamental freedoms in the political, economic, social, cultural or any other field of public life." This anticlassification version of the antidiscrimination principle is now the standard, having since been included in the International Covenant of Civil and Political Rights of 1966 (ICCPR), and many other instruments.[87] The UN's Human Rights Committee has explained that the antidiscrimination principle, "together with equality before the law and equal protection of the law without any discrimination, constitute a basic and general principle relating to the protection of human rights."[88] Further, the Committee emphasized that while many instruments fail to define "discrimination" per se, the ICERD's "purpose or effect" language should be read into the ICCPR as well.[89]

This reference to a prohibition on distinctions that are "based on race" and which have discriminatory "effects" might suggest the antisubordination stance of disparate impact doctrine.[90] The trouble here is the same as the trouble in the US context: the "based on" language seems to suggest an intentionality requirement. For regardless of whether we are looking at purpose or effect, if the discriminatory conduct must be "based on race," it seems difficult to see how race-neutral decisions with a discriminatory impact would fall within the ambit of Article 1.[91] In his exhaustive commentary on the ICERD, however, Patrick Thornberry has emphasized that the Convention's governing committee has typically characterized Article 1 as providing for disparate impact analysis, though this isn't the Committee's preferred language.[92] As Thornberry explains, the Committee, known as CERD, has tended

---

[87] *See, e.g.*, Convention on the Elimination of Discrimination Against Women (1981); African Charter on Human and Peoples Rights (1986); American Convention on Human Rights (1978); Arab Charter on Human Rights (2008); Convention for the Protection of Human Rights and Fundamental Freedoms (1953); Inter-American Convention against All Forms of Discrimination and Intolerance (2020).

[88] CCPR General Comment No. 18: Non-Discrimination, para. 1 (Nov. 10, 1989).

[89] *Id.* at para. 7.

[90] Theodor Meron, *The Meaning and Reach of the International Convention on the Elimination of All Forms of Racial Discrimination*, 79 Am. J. Int'l L. 283 (1985).

[91] *See* Vill. of Arlington Heights v. Metro. Hous. Dev. Corp., 429 U.S. 252 (1977).

[92] Thornberry, *supra* note 84, at 114. The Committee has used disparate language, however: "In seeking to determine whether an action has an effect contrary to the Convention, it will look to see whether that action has an unjustifiable disparate impact upon a group distinguished by race, colour, descent, or national or ethnic origin." *See* General Recommendation XIV on Article 1, Paragraph 1, of

## 252 THE RIGHT TO EXCLUDE

to characterize measures "that are not discriminatory at face value but are discriminatory in fact and effect" as "structural discrimination."[93]

> The use of the term by the Committee frequently relates to discrimination as a product of historical processes that have marginalized populations from the institutions of the State and the enjoyment of basic rights. The larger story in many cases, notably that of indigenous peoples, is that structures of State and society were crafted around models that offered little sense of ownership or participation on the part of non-dominant populations.[94]

Article 2 sets out the duties on states, exhorting them to ensure that all public authorities and institutions are in conformity with the Convention; to review existing laws and policies that have the effect of creating or perpetuating racial discrimination; to end racial discrimination by any persons, groups, or organizations through the implementation of new regulations; to encourage multiracial and integrationist movements and policies. To the extent it is necessary, states should take concrete and affirmative measures to ensure the protection of racial groups in the equal enjoyment of their fundamental freedoms and human rights. These affirmative measures will not be regarded as, in themselves, acts of racial discrimination. Article 3 condemns apartheid and "racial segregation," Article 4 prohibits the propagation of race science and theories of racial superiority, and Article 5 outlines the fundamental freedoms and rights that are the object of protection.[95] Article 6 assures individuals that states will provide effective remedies for violations, and Article 7 encourages states to undertake educational efforts to combat and eliminate racial prejudice. Part II of the ICERD, beginning with Article 8, outlines

---

the Convention (Forty-Second Session, 1993). *See also* LR v. Slovakia, UN Doc CERD/C/66/D/31/2003, para. 10.4.

[93] THORNBERRY, *supra* note 84, at 116.

[94] *Id.* at 116–17.

[95] "(a) The right to equal treatment before the tribunals and all other organs administering justice; (b) The right to security of person and protection by the State against violence or bodily harm, whether inflicted by government officials or by any individual group or institution; (c) Political rights, in particular the right to participate in elections-to vote and to stand for election-on the basis of universal and equal suffrage, to take part in the Government as well as in the conduct of public affairs at any level and to have equal access to public service; (d) Other civil rights, in particular: (i) The right to freedom of movement and residence within the border of the State; (ii) The right to leave any country, including one's own, and to return to one's country; (iii) The right to nationality; (iv) The right to marriage and choice of spouse; (v) The right to own property alone as well as in association with others; (vi) The right to inherit; (vii) The right to freedom of thought, conscience and religion; (viii) The right to freedom of opinion and expression; (ix) The right to freedom of peaceful assembly and association; (e) Economic, social and cultural rights, in particular: (i) The rights to work, to free choice of employment, to just and favourable conditions of work, to protection against unemployment, to equal pay for equal work, to just and favourable remuneration; (ii) The right to form and join trade unions; (iii) The right to housing; (iv) The right to public health, medical care, social security and social services; (v) The right to education and training; (vi) The right to equal participation in cultural activities; (f) The right of access to any place or service intended for use by the general public, such as transport hotels, restaurants, cafes, theatres and parks."

the nature and function of the Committee of Experts tasked with overseeing the Convention. This governing Committee (CERD) would hear reports from states, as well as offer commentaries on the various Articles. Under Article 14, the CERD is empowered to hear individual complaints from those living in states that have acceded to the CERD's jurisdiction.

In the discussion that follows, I want to return to Article 1.[96] Article 1(2) states that the Convention's prohibition on racial discrimination shall not extend to the rights of states to distinguish or exclude non-citizens. Article 1(3) reads: "Nothing in this Convention may be interpreted as affecting in any way the legal provisions of States Parties concerning nationality, citizenship or naturalization, provided that such provisions do not discriminate against any particular nationality." At first glance, these limitations on the Convention's scope present a bewildering manifestation of racial xenophobia, right in the first article of international law's chief weapon against racism. In contrast with the universalizing language of Article 1(1), and much of the remainder of the Convention, paragraphs 2 and 3 appear to offer states substantial allowances in the right to exclude migrants characterized as existing beyond the frontiers of the sovereign's territorial jurisdiction. True, paragraph 3 prohibits the state from targeting particular "nationalities" in their respective citizenship regimes. But all in all, as Thornberry puts it, Article 1's non-citizen exemptions are "particularly striking."[97]

## IV RACIAL EQUALITY, REFUGEES, AND THE RIGHT TO EXCLUDE

In its General Recommendation 30 on "Discrimination against Non-Citizens" from 2005, CERD explained that Article 1(2) "must be construed so as to avoid undermining the basic prohibition of discrimination; hence, it should not be interpreted to detract in any way from the rights and freedoms recognized and enunciated in particular in the Universal Declaration of Human Rights, the International Covenant on Economic, Social and Cultural Rights and the International Covenant on Civil and Political Rights."[98] Furthermore, "Under the Convention, differential treatment based on citizenship or immigration status will constitute discrimination if the criteria for such differentiation, judged in the light of the objectives and purposes of the Convention, are not applied pursuant

---

[96] Article 1(4) states that when states take "special measures" to protect racial and ethnic groups in the exercise of their "human rights and fundamental freedoms," these measures will not constitute racial discrimination. This latter issue has been simple enough, in which the CERD has rejected notions of "reverse discrimination," opting against a hardcore version of colorblindness.

[97] THORNBERRY, *supra* note 84, at 140.

[98] UN Committee on the Elimination of Racial Discrimination (CERD), *CERD General Recommendation XXX on Discrimination Against Non Citizens*, August 5, 2004, available at https://www.refworld.org/docid/45139e084.html, accessed August 23, 2022.

254  THE RIGHT TO EXCLUDE

to a legitimate aim, and are not proportional to the achievement of this aim."[99] These statements were boosted with general recommendations for states to ensure against racial discrimination against non-citizens, "regardless of their immigration status."[100]

In the decades since the adoption of the ICERD, these sorts of interpretive comments from human rights bodies have been the norm.[101] It is worth pausing momentarily, however, to ask why such limitations were so easily included in the first place, and what they suggest about this transitional moment in international law's racial ideology.

Recall that in Chapter 5 we discussed the failure of what might have been the launch of an interwar international immigration law. Throughout the nineteenth century, sovereigns characteristically enjoyed a right to exclude other sovereigns from their respective territories. In contrast, there was little in the way of justification for a sovereign's right to exclude individual migrants. The right to exclude operated along a single plane: individual property owners could exclude other individuals, but not the state, and sovereigns could exclude other sovereigns, but generally not individuals. This rough consensus started to shift with the acceleration of global migration in the last third of the nineteenth century, and new conversations about the racialization of national frontiers had intensified by the time of World War I. This was a moment in which a classic mode of racial ideology was beginning its slow displacement from the sphere of *imperium*, and newly emerging in the space of *dominium*. As modern racial ideology began operations at the borders of international society, racial xenophobia colonized the borders of the national frontier.

An important feature of the manner in which international migration law gave way to the racialization of *dominium* was the adoption of eugenicist systems of migration control, both in the US and across the globe. The US, as Adam McKeown has argued, set the bar.[102] As we have seen, the Immigration Act of 1924 was the first permanent quota law and a piece of classic racial xenophobia, making aliens ineligible for citizenship due to race also excludable from entry. Even after the establishment of the UN in 1945 and into the 1950s, the US, Canada, Australia, South Africa, and New Zealand continued to chafe at the inclusion of human rights language in international instruments out of fear that claims for racial equality could be interpreted to undermine the sovereign's right to exclude.[103] But even after the link between racial equality and border control had finally dissolved, what had already

---

[99] *Id.* at para. 4.

[100] *Id.* at para. 7.

[101] THORNBERRY, *supra* note 84, at 144–59. *See also* E. Tendayi Achiume, *Race, Refugees, and International Law, in* THE OXFORD HANDBOOK OF INTERNATIONAL REFUGEE LAW (Catherine Costello et al. eds., 2021).

[102] *See generally* ADAM MCKEOWN, MELANCHOLY ORDER: ASIAN MIGRATION AND THE GLOBALIZATION OF BORDERS 210 (2011).

[103] FITZGERALD & COOK-MARTIN, *supra* note 55.

calcified was the deep naturalization of the sovereign's right to exclude, an idea of *dominium* as self-determination and nonintervention. Initially, *dominium* was exercised in the language of classic racial ideology, but even as self-determination was increasingly argued as a logic of inclusion/exclusion by anticolonial activists, modern racial ideology nevertheless reinscribed self-determination as a means for naturalizing systems of borders that were still latently racial. And it is this feature of sovereignty that was bequeathed to the newly independent states—those same states that helped author the UN Decolonization Declaration of 1960, as well as the ICERD itself just a few years later. In a discussion of the UN's Third Committee, including representatives from Ethiopia, the Democratic Republic of Congo, India, Sudan, Chile, Jamaica, Nigeria, Zambia, Sierra Leone, Turkey, and Greece, the representative from Uganda commented that, with respect to the view that the ICERD would not apply to "distinctions made by a State Party between citizens and noncitizens ... it was natural that a country which had just become independent" would wish to prioritize the needs and interests of its own national community over those of outsiders.[104]

What paragraphs 2 and 3 of Article 1 seem to suggest is that by the 1960s, the anticolonial view of self-determination and antiracism had absorbed the idea that sovereigns enjoyed a right of *dominium* which included a highly discretionary and "plenary" right to exclude individual migrants from newly independent national communities. Is this the view of *dominium* espoused by Japan in its demands for the Covenant forming the League of Nations, or what the Chinese delegate Wu Ting-Fang had argued for at the URC of 1911? Probably not, for in those earlier moments the quest for racial equality in international law was still entangled with the contemporaneous regulation of migration. By the time the UN adopted the ICERD, however, migration questions had been peeled away from international law's modern racial ideology. Hence, the "natural" sense for xenophobic distinctions between citizens and noncitizens in the chief instrument in international law for the elimination of racial discrimination.

It is beyond the scope of our inquiry into international law's racial ideology to follow too closely the ins and outs of why, for example, the Chinese Exclusion Act was finally repealed in 1943, or why the US McCarran–Walter Act of 1952 finally eliminated racial restrictions for naturalization,[105] but what is clear enough is that by 1965, US immigration law had made the transition away from eugenics and into the kind of modern race science populated by UNESCO's Statements on Race project. As Gabriel Chin has argued, the 1965 Act's "revolutionary feature was its race-neutrality: For the first time since the United States started regulating immigration, race was not a factor."[106] The Act limited visas or persons travelling

[104] A./C.3/SR.1305, para. 30.
[105] Gabriel Chin, *The Civil Rights Revolution Comes to Immigration Law: A New Look at the Immigration and Nationality Act of 1965*, 75 N.C. L. REV. 273 273 (1996).
[106] *Id* at 298.

256   THE RIGHT TO EXCLUDE

from the Eastern hemisphere to 170,000, and migrants from the western hemisphere to 120,000, and included preference categories for employment skills and family connections to the US. But unlike any migration control adopted in the US for more than 150 years, the 1965 Act was colorblind. As one congressman put it, "Just as we sought to eliminate discrimination in our land through the Civil Rights Act, today we seek by phasing out the national origins quota system to eliminate discrimination in immigration to this Nation composed of the descendants of immigrants."[107] By the 1970s, and despite the first limitations on Latin American immigration after the end of the Bracero program, the 1965 Act was now doing its work, opening the gates to people of color in numbers that many claim were entirely unforeseen.[108] Today, and with Supreme Court decisions like *Graham v. Richardson* and *Plyler v. Doe* as a legal foundation, noncitizens in the US regularly claim nondiscrimination rights in the broader context of US civil rights.[109]

The shift toward a logic of inclusion in immigration control was hardly unique to the US. By the 1980s, much of Europe, Australia, and the Western hemisphere had consolidated around the view that race was an inappropriate criterion for national immigration policy.[110] As David Cook-Martin and David Fitzgerald have observed, "While immigration policies continue to have a differential impact on particular national-origin groups, and discriminatory practices persist, the history of [North and South American immigration policy] plainly shows that policies have dramatically moved in the direction of non-racial selection."[111] The question they attempt to answer is an important one: Why? Did the US and much of the rest of the world slowly shift away from a classic racial ideology of hierarchy to the modern racial ideology of inclusion because, well, inclusion is simply better than exclusion? Their argument largely proceeds on the terrain of the geopolitical, in the vein of Mary Dudziak and Peggy Von Eschen's respective Cold War histories.[112] And while these explanations may very well be on the money, what I want to

---

[107] Laurence Berton, quoted in Chin, *supra* note 105, at 302.

[108] *See, e.g.*, ROGER DANIELS, COMING TO AMERICA: A HISTORY OF IMMIGRATION AND ETHNICITY IN AMERICAN LIFE 338 (1990).

[109] Hiroshi Motomura, *The New Migration Law: Migrants, Refugees, and Citizens in an Anxious Age*, 105 CORNELL L. REV. 457, 466 (2020). These four examples do not suggest that civil rights arguments have usually won. They often have not, as the Muslim/travel ban litigation has made clear so far. More generally, the persistence of the plenary power doctrine explains why civil rights arguments often lose traction. But these examples show that what matters is whether civil rights arguments are apt. Why are civil rights concepts so dominant as terms of debate? One reason is the long association of immigration law and immigrants' rights with antidiscrimination and the rule of law. But another reason—subtle but basic—is closely tied to justifications for national borders. *Id.* at 471. These, then, are three limits of a civil rights framework—neglect of economic justice inside the US, inability to assess the larger context for international migration, and the incomplete fit of any system of nation-based justice for assessing migration across national borders. *Id.* at 477.

[110] CHRISTIAN JOPPKE, SELECTING BY ORIGIN: ETHNIC MIGRATION IN THE LIBERAL STATE (2005).

[111] FITZGERALD & COOK-MARTIN, *supra* note 55, at 2.

[112] MARY DUDZIAK, COLD WAR CIVIL RIGHTS: RACE AND THE IMAGE OF AMERICAN DEMOCRACY (2000); PENNY VON ESCHEN, RACE AGAINST EMPIRE: BLACK AMERICANS AND ANTICOLONIALISM, 1937–1957 (1997).

emphasize is less the explanation for why domestic immigration controls the world over shifted into a more antiracist register, and more of the idea that when this progressive transition took place, it also signaled the final demise of the possibility of seeing an international approach to racial equality as including an assault on self-determination and the "natural" right of sovereigns to exclude foreigners from their borders.

This dynamic has a parallel in the space of international refugee law. As we have seen, in the wake of World War II there was little appetite for adopting rules that might conceptualize racial hierarchy as entrenched in border control. If anything it was the opposite: the emerging anticolonial right of self-determination was the key for antiracist strategy, and the right of *dominium* would give old and new states alike carte-blanche for determining the frontiers of their national communities. Consequently, to the extent that international law was concerned at all with migration, the target was the exceptional character of the refugee.[113] As Vincent Chetail has argued, it's a mistake to think of the Geneva Convention Relating to the Status of Refugees, adopted in 1951, without the context of domestic immigration control that emerged after World War I. "It is not by coincidence that the emergence of modern refugee law occurred with the generalization of migration controls during the interwar period. International refugee law constitutes an exception to the migration control paradigm and, as such, the former legitimates the latter within a self-referential logic."[114] Indeed, the Refugee Convention is an *exceptional* area of legal obligation, focused not on the migrant per se, but a very specialized class of human: the refugee.[115] Thus, the crux of the Convention are its definition of refugee status and guarantee of *nonrefoulement*, the duty not to return a refugee to persecution on account of some protected status, such as race, religion, or nationality. As for what counts as a refugee, the Convention (as amended by the 1967 Protocol) counts a person as such who:

> [O]wing to well-founded fear of persecution for reasons of race, religion, nationality, membership of a particular social group or political opinion, is outside the country of his nationality and is unable or, owing to such fear, is unwilling to avail himself of the protection of that country; or who, not having a nationality and being outside the country of his former habitual residence as a result of such events, is unable or, owing to such fear, is unwilling to return to it.[116]

---

[113] James Hathaway, *The Evolution of Refugee Status in International Law: 1920–1950*, 33 INT'L & COMP. L.Q. 348 (1984); James Hathaway, *A Reconsideration of the Underlying Premise of Refugee Law*, 31 HARV. INT'L L.J. 129 (1990).

[114] VINCENT CHETAIL, INTERNATIONAL MIGRATION LAW 169 (2019); JAMES HATHWAY, LAW OF REFUGEE STATUS 231 (1991).

[115] C.M. SKRAN, REFUGEES IN INTER-WAR EUROPE: THE EMERGENCE OF A REGIME (1995).

[116] Convention Relating to the Status of Refugees, July 28, 1951, 189 UNTS 2545 and Protocol, GA Res 2198(XXI), Dec. 16, 1966, available at https://cms.emergency.unhcr.org/documents/11982/55726/Convention+relating+to+the+Status+of+Refugees+%28signed+28+July+1951%2C+entered+into+force+22+April+1954%29+189+UNTS+150+and+Protocol+relating+to+the+Status+of+Refugees+

## 258 THE RIGHT TO EXCLUDE

On its face, the refugee definition appears as a manifestation of the antidiscrimination principle. If a person has a relatively objective fear of persecution on account of a protected status, they may be eligible for refugee protections from a host sovereign. And certainly in the US, asylum jurisprudence as it developed after the 1980 Refugee Act matured in context of civil rights litigation. But this was largely a later development; the idea was less about promoting the rights of certain individuals against the state, as much as it was about assigning duties to sovereigns in exceptional circumstances. And when we consider the general trend in international legal thought with respect to a nascent international migration law, this cabined way of conceptualizing the refugee makes perfect sense.[117]

In the decades since, however, the thrust in much of these cases has turned on the intentional motive of state actors so crucial to the constitutional side of the antidiscrimination principle: Was the asylum seeker persecuted by the state on the basis of their race, or some other protected class?[118] Further, "persecution" was left undefined in the Convention, and as stated in a report from the United Nations High Commissioner for Refugees, over the decades it became increasingly necessary to fill this gap with content borrowed from human rights law.[119] As Paul Weiss has commented, "Clearly, the concept of persecution cannot have remained unaffected by subsequent developments in the law relating to human rights. Any meaning that has to be given to the concept of persecution must take into account the existing general human rights standards. Principles of human rights have considerably widened the ambit of protection afforded to persons generally."[120] Thus, what began as very much an exceptional situation for international law with respect to international obligations dealing with noncitizens, over the course of the twentieth century, refugee law became more and more a part of the human rights system. The inadequacies of the 1951 Refugee framework go far beyond the initially barren sense of persecution; as many scholars have argued, international refugee law relies upon a very limited distinction between refugees—who will garner sovereign protection—and migrants seeking a new home destination for economic reasons.[121] The latter group is shuttled through a state's immigration system,

%28signed+31+January+1967%2C+entered+into+force+4+October+1967%29+606+UNTS+267/0bf3248a-cfa8-4a60-864d-65cdfece1d47.

[117] B.S. Chimni, *The Geopolitics of Refugee Studies: A View from the South*, 11 J. Ref. Stud. 350 (1998); Lucy Mayblin & Joe Turner, Migration Studies and Colonialism (2021). *See also* Peter Spiro, *A New International Law of Citizenship*, 105 Am. J. Int'l L. 694 (2011).

[118] For a helpful overview, *see* AILA's Asylum Primer: A Practical Guide to US Asylum Law and Procedure (2019).

[119] Guy Goodwin-Gill, The Refugee in International Law (1983).

[120] The Refugee Convention, 1951: The Travaux Preparatoires with a Commentary by Paul Weiss, available at https://www.unhcr.org/en-us/protection/travaux/4ca34be29/refugee-convention-1951-travaux-preparatoires-analysed-commentary-dr-paul.html; Paul Weiss, *Refugees and Human Rights*, 1 Israel Y.B. Hum. Rts. 35 (1971).

[121] David Scott Fitzgerald, Refuge Beyond Reach: How Rich Democracies Repel Asylum Seekers (2019); Erika Feller, *The Evolution of the International Refugee Protection Regime*, 5 Wash. U. J.L. & Pol'y 129 (2001); Elizabeth Keyes, *Unconventional Refugees*, 67 Am. U. L. Rev. 89 (2017);

while the former merits participation in the international regime. The criticism is that there are many deserving seekers of refuge, and that the binary between refugee and economic migrant is far too narrow, unnecessarily excluding a great deal of people who have *rights* to resettle.[122] As Hiroshi Motomura suggests, "the core problem is a protection regime that is ill-suited to migration realities that are shaped by unsettled political conditions, civil wars, environment degradation, and other causes of large-scale forced migration."[123]

This sort of contemporary thinking in international law about migration and race has converged in relatively recent concerns about the rise of xenophobia. As the UN High Commissioner for Refugees (UNHCR) has explained, xenophobic harm is cognizable on the basis of race, nationality, national or ethnic origin, color, or descent.[124] What distinguishes a harm as particularly related to xenophobia, however, is the status of "foreignness."[125] According to the United Nations Special Rapporteur on Contemporary Forms of Racism, Racial Discrimination, Xenophobia, and Related Intolerance, E. Tendayi Achiume, foreignness is the status of being an actual or perceived outsider to a given political community.[126] When a community brands a person as an outsider, it is often on account of national origin, but any number of factors, including race, often intersect in the construction of the status. Indeed, as Achiume suggests, "race is a fundamental determinant of who among those of foreign national origin or nationality are deemed deserving of xenophobic harm."[127] The primary entity in international law responsible for regulating xenophobic discrimination, beyond the office of the Special Rapporteur, has been the UNHCR. Notably, and in keeping with the general trajectory in which human rights law has commandeered refugee law, however, UNHCR has tended to emphasize the ICERD as the main vehicle for tackling xenophobic discrimination.[128] The defining feature of UNHCR's approach, according to Achiume, is its

---

Andrew I. Schoenholtz, *The New Refugees and the Old Treaty: Persecutors and Persecuted in the Twenty-First Century*, 16 CHI. J. INT'L L. 81, 85, 93–94 (2015); Joan Fitzpatrick, *Revitalizing the 1951 Refugee Convention*, 9 HARV. HUM. RTS. J. 229, 231 (1996); Jaya Ramji-Nogales, *Migration Emergencies*, 68 HASTINGS L.J. 609, 611 (2017); Arthur C. Helton & Eliana Jacobs, *What Is Forced Migration?*, 13 GEO. IMMIGR. L.J. 521, 528 (1999)

[122] James Hathaway, *Reconceiving Refugee Law as Human Rights Protection*, 4 J. REF. STUD. 113 (1991); *UNHCR and Human Rights*, UNHCR 1 (1997), available at http://www.refworld.org/ docid/ 3ae6b332c.html; Jacqueline Bhabha, *Internationalist Gatekeepers?: The Tension Between Asylum Advocacy and Human Rights*, 15 HARV. HUM. RTS. J. 155, 168 (2002); Brian Gorlick, *Human Rights and Refugees: Enhancing Protection Through International Human Rights Law*, 69 NORDIC J. INT'L L. 117, 119 (2000).

[123] Motomura, *supra* note 109, at 491.

[124] UN High Commissioner for Refugees (UNHCR), *Combating Racism, Racial Discrimination, Xenophobia and Related Intolerance through a Strategic Approach* (2009), available at https://www.refwo rld.org/docid/4b30931d2.html.

[125] E. Tendayi Achiume, *Beyond Prejudice: Structural Xenophobic Discrimination Against* Refugees, 45 GEO. J. INT'L L. 331 (2014).

[126] *Id.* at 331.

[127] *Id.* at 332.

[128] Combating Racism, *supra* note 124, at para. 11.

260 THE RIGHT TO EXCLUDE

focus on punishing individuals for explicit discrimination against foreigners, and education campaigns to promote tolerance and inclusion for refugees. Taken together, these initiatives revolve around the problem of individual prejudice, and the need to highlight xenophobic discrimination as irrational and unfair. The UNHCR's approach to racial inequality here in the context of refugee protection is, in a word, the approach defended by Paul Brest almost 50 years ago: a colorblind antidiscrimination principle.

Contemporary reforms in international law have tended to move in a more race-conscious direction, as illustrated in the New York Declaration of 2016 and the UN's Global Compact on Migration from 2018. But, as Achiume has argued, there's very little "new" about these new reforms. She notes, "a review of [international law's migration] Framework and its constitutive elements reveals an approach to the problem of xenophobia that treats it primarily as a problem of individuals engaging in apolitical, prejudice-motivated acts against foreigners, especially involuntary migrants. Put differently, the problem of xenophobia currently commanding the attention of international actors is that of *explicitly prejudice-based* anti-foreigner actions and attitudes of *individuals* against non-nationals."[129] The international law framework for dealing with xenophobia, such that it is, is firmly in the grip of the antidiscrimination principle, leading Achiume to argue that since "xenophobia goes to the very foundation of the global nation-state system," there is very little in the current framework that could make a structural difference. "Such a difference," Achiume writes, "would require a radical reimagining of international law and nation-state sovereignty to align it with the world at hand, which is characterized by deep historical, economical, and even territorial interconnection and interdependence."[130] What international law has to offer with respect to racial xenophobia is certainly race-conscious, but once again it is a consciousness that marshals the antidiscrimination norm pragmatically, confidant about the direction of international law's general trajectory, leaving questions about the sovereign's right to exclude both unasked and unanswered.

In this chapter, I have laid out the contours of an ideological tipping point, between a late modern racial ideology and the emergence for international law's postracial xenophobia discussed in the next chapters. The discussion has also worked to answer to the question posed earlier about whether thinkers like Malcolm X were right to hope for something more than the colorblind antidiscrimination principle in the field of international human rights law. In the contexts of the run-up toward the UN's Racial Discrimination Convention, in the development of a framework for thinking about international xenophobia, and in the maturation of decolonization and self-decolonization from a status quo oriented functionalism and into an individualism as comfortable with neoliberalism as human rights,

---

[129] E. Tendayi Achiume, *Governing Xenophobia*, 51 VAND. J. TRANSNAT'L L. 333, 365 (2018).
[130] *Id.* at 393.

international antiracism coalesced in the same grooves marked out in the domestic context: a colorblind norm of antidiscrimination. We have seen how a formalistic antidiscrimination principle arose in international human rights law, and how that principle has tended to dominate international law's capacity for antiracist strategy. It features as the conceptual core for the UN's Convention on Racial Discrimination, as well as for the human rights conventions that followed in its wake. What's more, while distinctions between citizens and noncitizens were initially understood to be beyond the parameters of an international response to racism, both refugee law more generally and the jurisprudence of the UN's Discrimination Committee in particular have gravitated toward colorblindness at the border. Or to put that another way, while the rights of *dominium* as rights of border control were initially conceived by anticolonial thinkers as a part of the struggle against global racism, that struggle was about the self-determination of a people, which included the right to exclude outsiders. To be clear, however, I should restate that the dominance of colorblind antidiscrimination law should not be confused for postracial xenophobia. It is rather a tipping point or a threshold between a fully mature modern ideology of inclusion, and the beginnings of something else. *Our* something else.

# PART III
# POSTRACIAL XENOPHOBIA

# 8

# Multiculturalism, Nationalism, Pragmatism

An ideology of racial xenophobia colonized international law throughout the nineteenth century, leading to the racialization of a sovereign's right to exclude—first in the context of fixing the boundaries of international society, and then later in the early decades of the twentieth century, into the racial borders of national territories as well. Slowly, this classic form of racial xenophobia was joined by a modern, antiracist, anticolonial logic of inclusion. This ideological transformation deracialized the sovereign's right to exclude, first with respect to the enlargement of the international community of sovereigns, and then in the context of a people's right of self-determination as itself a cure for racial hierarchy. By the last decades of the twentieth century, and as international law's modern racial ideology achieved its maturity, racism was dropping off the radar as a problem for international law per se, and with it, the right of self-determination as a mode of decolonization had become exhausted. One result was the dislocation between the right of self-determination and racial justice. Another was the rise of the human rights paradigm as the paramount approach in international law for remedying claims of racial injustice and territorial (mis)rule.

These results mark the point of passage from the modern to the postracial, for when the modern logic of inclusion has captured the sovereign's right to exclude, the means by which that right continue to function as a generator for racial borderlands have become opaque. In the fields of domestic immigration law, refugee law, the law of state borders, the law of international institutions, the law of international legal personality, the law of territories, and so much else—we no longer perceive these fields as *generative* of racial hierarchy, and to the extent we find racism to have infiltrated these increasingly neutral spaces, human rights law is the answer for dealing with these prejudices. To anticipate the argument a bit, the ideal has shifted into inclusion as a colorblind *diversity*, where we promote ethnic and cultural difference in ways that are as oblivious to racial xenophobia as possible, while at the same time we characterize national identity as functionally necessary for a socially integrated political community. Racial xenophobia still exists, but it is unclear now how international law could possibly participate in its propagation, or in the absence of the antidiscrimination principle, offer any remedies. This is the condition of postracial xenophobia.

My portrayal of international law's structure of postracial xenophobia is tripartite, unpacking it as a confluence of three developments: postracial multiculturalism, postracial nationalism, and postracial pragmatism. The analysis of postracial

*The Right to Exclude.* Justin Desautels-Stein, Oxford University Press. © Justin Desautels-Stein 2023.
DOI: 10.1093/oso/9780198862161.003.0009

266   THE RIGHT TO EXCLUDE

multiculturalism begins by recalling the discussion from the end of Chapter 2, and with a colorblind demand that late twentieth-century developments in race science, proving the imaginary aspects of racial biology, push analysis in the direction of better understanding the sociolegal construction of race—if not abandoning race altogether for the more "real" study of ethnoculture. This basic premise of multicultural theory offered analysts a means for at once continuing the fight against subordination and exclusion, but now in an explicitly "postracial" posture. The turn to culture over race found an analogue in several currents of international legal thought. Among them was the indigenous rights movement, which, and despite its progressive agenda, underscored the power of human rights formalism in its cooptation of self-determination and the erasure of race from the legal imagination. Second, the interest in protecting the autonomy and integrity of cultural entities pushes up against countervailing tendencies in postracial nationalism. Whereas in the space of multiculturalism there is a strong tendency toward neoformalism, human rights, and the antidiscrimination principle, arguments for the use of national identity tend to highlight their roots in more "realistic" assessments of global dynamics. It would be mistaken to assume, however, that there is any direct relation between realism and nationalism, just as it is a mistake to assume a special affinity between neoformalism and multiculturalism. As I discuss, the so-called functional necessity of sovereign control over national boundaries and territorial borders comes in a variety of flavors, from the ultranationalist to the moderate and beyond. Nevertheless, while neither the antidiscrimination principle nor the norm of multicultural diversity prove to be of much use in preventing the ratcheting up of xenophobic discourse, functionalist arguments for postracial nationalism are only exacerbating these insider/outsider dynamics. In the third step of the analysis, I return to the structure of liberal legal thought. In each instance, it is important to emphasize that what I term postracial multiculturalism and postracial nationalism are also *liberal* theories of multiculturalism and nationalism, as explicitly developed by thinkers like Will Kymlicka and David Miller, respectively. And as liberal theories operating in the context of international law, they are shaped by the grammar of liberal legal thought. The third thesis in that grammar is that of naturalizing juridical science, and it is here that I argue that in the oscillations between functionalism and neoformalism, a contemporary style of legal argument has come into view, what I call postracial pragmatism.

These three intellectual developments—the rise of postracial multiculturalism, postracial nationalism, and postracial pragmatism—set the frame for developing what international law's modern racial ideology has become. The task of this chapter is to elaborate this ideological structure of postracial xenophobia. As I argue more conclusively in Chapter 9, international law's postracial xenophobia not only fails indigenous peoples, (post)colonial subjects, migrants, and racial subjects by way of its impoverished toolkit for addressing today's racial hierarchies. It actively and affirmatively works to blind us from the way in which the sovereign's

# MULTICULTURALISM, NATIONALISM, PRAGMATISM 267

right to exclude continues—now in its *postracial* configuration—to produce racial borders, racial outsiders, and racial xenophobia.

## I THE CRITIQUE OF NEOFORMALISM: POSTRACIAL MULTICULTURALISM

As a result of work among physical anthropologists and biologists, by the turn of the century substantial doubts emerged about the reality of race as an object of the natural sciences. A question for many analysts of race thus became whether it was high time to abolish the very concept of raciality, turning instead to the "real" terrain of culture. Of course, racism had persisted, even if the science of race had not, and norms of racial equality and antidiscrimination would continue as legal principles. But as social science and political theory, ground zero for the idea of postracial ideology begins with the abandonment of race science as natural science. We are literally "after race" in the sense that scientific discourse has moved beyond the older notions of racial classification which posited the genetic continuity of racialized blood and bone. But we ought not interpret, as Stuart Hall cautions, this interest in "moving on" from race to mean that racial problematics "have been re-solved or replaced by some conflict-free era. Rather, [the idea of 'post'] marks the passage from one historical power configuration or conjuncture to another."[1]

It is now a commonplace to conceive race entirely in sociohistorical terms.[2] As explained by David Hollinger, "Fewer and fewer Americans believe in the bi-ological reality of races, but they are remarkably willing to live with an officially sanctioned system of demographic classification that replicates precisely the crude, colloquial categories, black, yellow, white, red, and brown."[3] As Ian Haney Lopez has put it, this is racial thinking about a "process of social differentiation rooted in culturally contingent beliefs in the biological divisions of humans."[4] The concept of raciality, as Anthony Appiah observes, holds that "there are heritable character-istics, possessed by members of our species, which allow us to divide them into a small set of races, in such a way that all the members of these races share certain traits and tendencies with each other that they do not share with members of any other race. These traits and tendencies characteristic of a race constitute ... a sort of racial essence."[5] A question that has figured into much of cultural theory over

---

[1] STUART HALL, ESSENTIAL ESSAYS, VOLUME 2: IDENTITY AND DIASPORA 99 (David Morley ed., 2019).

[2] *See, e.g.*, ANTHONY APPIAH, IN MY FATHER'S HOUSE: AFRICA IN THE PHILOSOPHY OF CULTURE 35–36 (1993).

[3] DAVID HOLLINGER, POSTETHNIC AMERICA: BEYOND MULTICULTURALISM 8 (1995).

[4] Ian Haney Lopez, *Race, Ethnicity, Erasure: The Salience of Race to LatCrit Theory*, 10 LA RAZA L.J. 57, 66 (1997). *See also* MICHAEL OMI & HOWARD WINANT, RACIAL FORMATION IN THE UNITED STATES (2d ed. 1994).

[5] APPIAH, *supra* note 2, at 13.

268    THE RIGHT TO EXCLUDE

the last decades concerns the issue of how to square these apparently conflictual notions, about the apparent (un)reality of racial "essences" and the fact that human races are social configurations. If race isn't really *real* in a biological sense, and if raciality actually unpacks as a process of social meaning, then perhaps—and here is one of the explanations for the turn toward ethnocultures as the *real*—the way forward is to leave raciality behind. As Appiah argued 30 years ago, "Talk of 'race' is particularly distressing for those of us who take culture seriously. For, where race works ... it works as an attempt at metonym for culture, and it does so only at the price of biologizing what *is* culture, ideology."[6] We know today that there aren't races in the world, but rather "communities of meaning, shading variously into each other in the rich structure of the social world."[7] Walter Benn Michaels put the point more colorfully: "Treating race as a social fact amounts to nothing more than acknowledging that we were mistaken to think of it as a biological fact and then insisting that we ought to keep making that mistake. Maybe we ought to stop making the mistake."[8]

For Appiah, and other influential scholars like Hollinger, Robert Miles, Henry Louis Gates, Jr., and Paul Gilroy, the best bet is to discard race an analytical concept. "There is no need for a distinct (critical) theory of 'race,'" Antonio Darder and Rodolfo Torres representatively suggest. As they argued in their influential *After Race*, "It is high time we disrupt the continued use of a dubious concept that cannot help but render our theorizing ambiguous and problematic. In its simplest terms, this ambiguity is most visible in the inconsistency with which the term 'race' is applied—sometimes meaning ethnicity, at other times referring to culture or ethnicity."[9] Among the most prominent alternative sites for the interrogation of power and domination has been that of culture. Illustrative concepts like "cultural citizenship," they argued, "attempt to engage difficult and often conflicting questions of citizenship with respect to culture, identity, and political participation ... Key to the concept is a critical universalism that fundamentally respects the particularities of populations while working to dismantle structures of inequality that interfere with the exercise of human rights."[10]

When postracial discourse of this sort joined forces with increasingly popular concepts like cultural difference, cultural integrity, cultural rights, and multicultural theory, a kind of postracial multiculturalism was the result. Now, according to theorists like David Theo Goldberg, the phase of the postracial doesn't really kick in until multiculturalism has come and gone. That is, for Goldberg, multiculturalism

---

[6] *Id.* at 45.

[7] *Id.*

[8] WALTER BENN MICHAELS, THE TROUBLE WITH DIVERSITY: HOW WE LEARNED TO LOVE IDENTITY AND IGNORE EQUALITY 39 (2006).

[9] ANTONIO DARDER & RODOLFO TORRES, AFTER RACE: RACISM AFTER MULTICULTURALISM 12 (2004).

[10] *Id.* at 23.

was a step on the way to postracial ideology.[11] This might very well be true, that a sort of fully mature postracialism requires a *departure* from multicultural theory. As I argue, however, I think the better view is to see multiculturalism as essential in the elaboration of postracial xenophobia. That is, postraciality is certainly not synonymous with multiculturalism, but multiculturalism is an important constituent in postracialism's argumentative style.

The notion that culture, and cultural difference, might prove to be the true battleground for equality, has been debated over the years in a myriad of contexts. Without attempting to even remotely cover the many literatures, from one angle is a political theory of multiculturalism that aspires for a place in the space of liberal democracy.[12] As Iris Marion Young argued in the late 1980s, the logic of inclusion surveyed through much of this book had extended the rights of citizenship to all groups in liberal democratic societies, whereby previously excluded and oppressed peoples were on a footing of formal equality.[13] And yet, many members of these groups continued to experience themselves as second-class citizens. Rather than push harder on a universal form of citizenship which implicated a movement for the oppressed group to ultimately assimilate with the majority culture, Young offered the idea of differentiated citizenship as way of recharging the logic of inclusion.[14] If cultural differences existed among the various groups in a democracy (which they did), and if certain groups are privileged (which they are), then norms of equal citizenship and participation would inevitably disadvantage the non-dominant cultures. Young's prescription was a regime of different kinds of rights that could both protect the integrity of these cultures, and also give them a voice in the broader national community. These ideas led to what increasingly became known as a politics of recognition, a political theory of cultural difference.[15] It was also one of many currents that led to the broader notion of multiculturalism, an umbrella term for the promotion of cultural diversity, cultural flourishing, and cultural rights. As Nancy Fraser explained, a multicultural politics of recognition is anchored in the analysis of cultural injustice, in which certain cultures are subject to the representative and interpretive practices of more dominant ones, and a remedial approach where disrespected cultural identities are given greater forms of recognition, visibility, and autonomy.

Since the 1980s, multiculturalism has become something of a flashpoint in the struggle against racism. Was multiculturalism an impediment for antiracist activism, or what antiracism had become? Like any heavy concept, it came to mean

---

[11] David Theo Goldberg, Are We All Postracial Yet? 26 (2015).

[12] For an overview, *see* Multiculturalism (Amy Gutmann ed., 1994).

[13] Iris Marion Young, *Polity and Group Difference: A Critique of the Ideal of Universal Citizenship*, 99 Ethics 250 (1989).

[14] *Id.* at 251.

[15] Nancy Fraser, *Rethinking Recognition*, 3 New Left Rev. 107 (2000); Nancy Fraser & Axel Honneth, Redistribution or Recognition? A Political-Philosophical Exchange (2003).

270  THE RIGHT TO EXCLUDE

a number of things to different constituencies, but some consensus settled around the idea that multiculturalism had to mean something more than the civil rights agenda of integration and the protection of individual rights, and that in this context the antidiscrimination principle should evolve beyond the race relations paradigm and adapt itself to the unavoidable differences of "ethnocultural" groups.[16] According to philosophers like Will Kymlicka, this relation between multiculturalism and antidiscrimination was initially seen as suggesting a push against liberal democracy in favor of communitarian or democratic socialism, but quickly enough the issue demanded resolution within liberalism, rather than outside of it.[17] For thinkers like Kymlicka, Joseph Raz, Yael Tamir, and others, what surfaced was the liberal culturalist view of multiculturalism: "each of us, in our own way, argues that there are compelling interests related to culture and identity which are fully consistent with liberal principles of freedom and equality, and which justify granting special rights to minorities."[18] Given its orientation in liberal theory, this perspective on cultural rights depends on some tricky but unavoidable decisions about "bad" minority rights that restrict individual rights of expression, and how they are to be distinguished from the "good" ones that protect the group from external, assimilating pressures.

As Kymlicka has argued, one important reason for the necessity of affirmative measures in the protection of cultural integrity is the tendency for liberal states to promote a particular "societal culture," a "territorially concentrated culture, centered on a shared language which is used in a wide range of societal institutions, in both public and private life." Kymlicka continued:

> Virtually all liberal democracies have, at one point or another, attempted to diffuse a single societal culture throughout all of its territory ... So states have engaged in this process of "nation-building"—that is, a process of promoting a common language, and a sense of common membership in, and equal access to, the social institutions operating in that language. Decisions regarding official languages, core curriculum in education, and the requirements for acquiring citizenship, all have been made with the intention of diffusing a particular culture throughout society, and of promoting a national identity based on participation in that societal culture.[19]

The effects of state-sponsored nation-building on ethnocultural minorities are entirely dependent on particular contexts in particular moments, but as Kymlicka suggests, every one of them negotiates a logic of inclusion and exclusion, "choosing"

---

[16] WILL KYMLICKA, CONTEMPORARY POLITICAL PHILOSOPHY 335 (1990).
[17] Id. at 338–39.
[18] Id. at 339.
[19] Id. at 347.

MULTICULTURALISM, NATIONALISM, PRAGMATISM 271

either a path toward assimilation or one of autonomy and self-determination. For present purposes, four of his ethnocultural case-studies are of special relevance: "substate nations," "indigenous peoples," "immigrant groups," and "African-Americans."

In the context of the history of United States (US) imperial holdings, substate nations like Puerto Ricans, Filipinos, and Hawaiians reflect three different modes in the inclusion/exclusion dynamic. In each case, the peoples of these territories resisted liberal nation-building through the persistence of self-governing institutions, and the maintenance of linguistic independence in schools, courts, media, and elsewhere throughout the "culture." These national minorities were effectively seeking the sovereign's right of *dominium*, a right to exclude the world from their territories, as well as the development of their life-stories—albeit a right to exclude highly limited by the presence of an imperial authority. Of course, the ethnocultural minority inhabiting the Philippines was given a right to exclude of the sort demanded by the colonial world, bestowed by the US in 1946. Hawaii achieved a type of autonomy and self-determination through its admission as a state of the US in 1959, and the Puerto Rican people remain neither a sovereign state nor a state of the union, but instead an "unincorporated territory" with partial rights of self-determination. The status of indigenous peoples living within the territorial boundaries of the US are slightly more analogous to the situation of Puerto Ricans, since American Indians are neither sovereign under international law in the way enjoyed by the Philippines, nor do they rule in the way that state governments like Hawaii do. The question, then, for ethnocultures denied the traditional forms of a right to exclude, is how are these national minorities nevertheless able to exercise the kind of autonomy that the right to exclude is typically meant to deliver?

This multicultural bestowal of a right to exclude has less purchase in the context of immigrant groups. Here, as Kymlicka observes, the rights of foreign-born citizens to integrate into the national culture turn less on arguments about autonomy and exclusion and more about a process of national assimilation that better accommodates the cultural norms of the immigrant group. This could mean everything from provisions of services in the language of the immigrant group, to "the need to examine dress codes, public holidays, even height and weight restrictions, to see whether they are biased against certain immigrant groups. We also need to examine the portrayal of minorities in school curricula or the media to see if they are stereotypical, or fail to recognize the contributions of immigrants to national history or world culture."[20] As we have seen in previous chapters, the ways in which immigrants have been excluded and then integrated along a civil rights model are par for the course, with respect to the traditional form of the antidiscrimination

---

[20] *Id.* at 355.

272   THE RIGHT TO EXCLUDE

principle. In the context of multiculturalism, however, an individualized rights regime just won't cut it—group rights aimed at various degrees of cultural autonomy, even understood in a larger process of assimilation, are the way to go.

Beyond the discussion of ethnocultural minorities like Puerto Ricans, indigenous American Indian tribes, or immigrant groups, Kymlicka singled out the case of African-Americans as a *sui generis* problem for liberal multiculturalism.[21] Unlike other ethnocultural minorities, African-Americans are descended from peoples who were involuntarily brought into the US, so they don't fit well into the "immigrant" pattern. They are also ill fit for the national minorities pattern, since African-Americans are a diasporic community without a homeland within the US or a common historical language. The result is a situation in which neither the inclusionary "immigrant path toward integration" nor the exclusionary concept of black nationalism has ever really made good sense, despite so much of the history of antiracism being entangled with one of these two directions.[22] This unusual situation, Kymlicka noted, suggests that "the long-term aim is to promote the integration of African-Americans into the American nation, but it is recognized that this is a long-term process that can only work if existing black communities and institutions are strengthened. A degree of short-term separateness and colour-consciousness is needed to achieve the long-term goal of an integrated and colour-blind society."[23]

## A  LatCrit and TWAIL

In the 1990s, this increasingly powerful focus on ethnocultural integrity and diversity found a fruitful base of operations in international law. The movement known as TWAIL (Third World Approaches to International Law), for example, was deeply focused on the rights of formerly colonized *peoples*, where "people" was largely synonymous with ethnoculture. About a decade after a group of Harvard students and scholars were forming around the nascent pillars of what would become critical race theory, another Harvard group was embarking on a similar journey. With thinkers like Antony Anghie, Bhupinder Chimni, James Gathii, David Kennedy, Makau Mutua, and Vasuki Nesiah in the initial core, what would become TWAIL was at once a critical and emancipatory project aimed at the promises and failures of anticolonial activism.[24] As Anghie and Chimni

---

[21]  *Id.* at 361.

[22]  *Id.* at 360–61.

[23]  *Id.* at 361.

[24]  James Thuo Gathii, *TWAIL: A Brief History of Its Origins, It Decentralized Network, and a Tentative Biography*, 3 Trade L. & Dev. 26 (2011); Makau Mutua, *What is TWAIL?* 94 Proc. Ann. Meet. Am. Soc. Int'l L. 31 (2000); B.S. Chimni, *Third World Approaches to International Law: A Manifesto*, 8 Int'l Comm. L. Rev. 3 (2006); Antony Anghie & B.S. Chimni, *Third World Approaches to International Law and Individual Responsibility in Internal Conflicts*, 2 Chi. J. Int'l L. 77 (2003); Luis Eslava & Sundhya

famously suggested, a "Third World" approach to international law could be categorized in two ways. First, there were the anticolonial international lawyers working in the last third of the twentieth century, like Bedjaoui, Ammoun, and Elias. These "TWAIL I" scholars criticized what I have been calling the sovereign's imperial right to exclude, and by the lights of a logic of inclusion, saw the United Nations (UN) system and the right of self-determination as the proper vehicles for bringing an end to global forms of subordination.[25] TWAIL I was, I'd like to suggest, entirely demonstrative of international law's late modern racial ideology. The second round of TWAIL (TWAIL II) positioned itself as an effort to expand upon but substantially alter the basic approaches of anticolonial, Third World, international legal thought.

An important plank in the TWAIL overhaul was considerable skepticism around the heavy focus that anticolonialism had come to place on sovereign rights and sovereign equality. At the same time, there developed within TWAIL a concern about the trajectory of human rights as well.[26] What was paramount, Anghie and Chimni explained, was shifting away from perspectives that were too hung up sovereign/individual rights arguments, and toward a renewed emphasis on the "lived histories" of "the peoples within Third World states—women, peasants, workers, minorities"—peoples that had ended up largely excluded by the first wave of anticolonial activism.[27] It was surely a return to this older notion of an international law of "peoples"[28] that signaled a new direction for Third World scholarship, but even more, so too a renewed interest in challenging the twentieth century's sociohistoric logic of inclusion. The trouble with imperialism and international law, these new scholars argued, went far beyond the notion that if international law was cleansed of its irrational prejudices and expanded to include the formerly excluded, the international legal order could finally find its way home. The problem was much more fundamental, and it concerned the manner in which international law's "civilizing mission has endured over time, and how its essential structure is preserved in certain contemporary initiatives, for example, of 'development,' democractization, human rights, and good governance, which posit a Third World that is lacking and deficient and in need of international intervention for its salvation."[29]

In a LatCrit symposium from 2007, Anghie highlighted the powerful symmetries between TWAIL and the LatCrit movement—a branch of critical theory focused

---

Pahuja, *Beyond the Postcolonial: TWAIL and the Everyday Life of International Law*, 45 L. & POL'Y IN AFR. ASIA & LAT. AM. 195 (2012).

[25] Anghie & Chimni, *supra* note 24, at 81.

[26] Makau Mutua, *The Ideology of Human Rights*, 36 VA. J. INT'L L. 589 (1996); Anghie & Chimni, *supra* note 24, at 83; UPENDRA BAXI, THE FUTURE OF HUMAN RIGHTS (2002); RATNA KAPUR, GENDER, ALTERITY AND HUMAN RIGHTS: FREEDOM IN A FISHBOWL (2018).

[27] Anghie & Chimni, *supra* note 24, at 83.

[28] This is not intended as a reference to JOHN RAWLS, THE LAW OF PEOPLES (1993).

[29] Anghie & Chimni, *supra* note 24, at 86.

274    THE RIGHT TO EXCLUDE

on questions around ethnocultural dominance and postmodernism.[30] Among these symmetries was the shared emphasis on the lived experiences of the world's many subordinated peoples:

> We—LatCrit and TWAIL—need to make the experiences and perspectives of the disadvantaged (who are the subject of our concerns) the basis of our inquiry. It is out of this experience that we may fashion a vocabulary, set of principles, methodology, and even an epistemology that may be adequate for the purposes of contesting and undermining traditional narratives and structures.[31]

Quoting Kieth Aoki, Anghie concluded with a plea for what LatCrit scholars have since come to call the "glocal."[32] As Francisco Valdes has more recently put it, this is a methodological posture that works "toward increasingly globalized and localized contexts. This commitment to globalized contextualism aims to connect the legal and the social both at the micro/local level and at the macro/global through OutCrit scholarship that conjoins the interrogation of legal, cultural, and material realities."[33] Luis Eslava has similarly emphasized TWAIL themes in keeping with the LatCrit approach, including ideas about the global in the local and the local in the global, the north in the south and the south in the north, multiple and morphing points of entry, and the usefulness of a decentralized and practical approach to a landscape of moving targets.[34]

What, however, of the analytics of raciality? Like the LatCrits, TWAIL scholars have tended to treat imperialism and subordination through the vehicles of culture and ethnicity rather than race.[35] To be sure, a symposium from 2000 suggested the potential for linkages between TWAIL and the critique of global racism,[36] and in that same year Makau Mutua wrote that "the first objective" of TWAIL was to "understand, deconstruct, and unpack the uses of international law as a medium for the creation and perpetuation of a racialized hierarchy of international norms and institutions that subordinate non-Europeans to Europeans."[37] Without a doubt, LatCrit and TWAIL scholarship has certainly considered raciality as an important feature of their research agenda, but it is also true that over the last 20 years the

---

[30] Antony Anghie, *LatCrit and TWAIL*, 42 CAL. WEST. INT'L L.J. 311 (2012).

[31] *Id.* at 318.

[32] FRANCISCO VALDES & STEVEN BENDER, LATCRIT: FROM CRITICAL LEGAL THEORY TO ACADEMIC ACTIVISM 70 (2021).

[33] Francisco Valdez, *Theorizing and Building Critical Coalitions: Outsider Society and Academic Praxis in Local/Global Justice Struggles*, 12 SEATTLE J. SOC. JUS. 983, 1020 (2014).

[34] Luis Eslava, *TWAIL Coordinates* (Apr. 2, 2019), available at https://criticallegalthinking.com/2019/04/02/twail-coordinates/.

[35] For discussion, *see, e.g.*, Keith Aoki & Kevin Johnson, *As Assessment of LatCrit Theory Ten Years After*, 83 IND. L.J. 1151 (2008); Robert Chang & Neil Gotanda, *The Race Question in LatCrit Theory and Asian American Jurisprudence*, 7 NEVADA L.J. 1012 (2007).

[36] *Symposium: Critical Race Theory and International Law*, 45 VILL. L. REV. (2000).

[37] Mutua, *supra* note 26, at 31.

terrains of culture and ethnicity have very often been considered the *real* killing floor. This tendency has its roots in anxieties over the Black/White paradigm and over-inclusive claims of structure, but is also rooted in developments in race science and the rise of multicultural theory that was becoming increasingly prominent at the turn of the century.[38]

## B Postracial Self-Determination

This postracial dynamic in the LatCrit/TWAIL literatures had a parallel in the simultaneous rise of the indigenous rights movement in international law,[39] the most prominent space in which we might identify a kind of postcolonial afterlife for the right of self-determination.[40] In 1994, Palau became the last of the UN's Trust territories to achieve independence,[41] and by 2023, there remained 17 Non-Self-Governing Territories (NSGT).[42] With respect to the US, among these included Guam, American Samoa, and the US Virgin Islands. Puerto Rico was removed from the UN's list in 1952, after the US reported to the UN that it would cease its reporting due to Puerto Rico's change in status to a Commonwealth.[43] The intervening 70 years have not, however, reinforced the wisdom in displacing Puerto Rico from the UN's decolonization framework. In 2021, the UN's Special Committee on Decolonization approved a draft resolution referencing Puerto Rico's continued colonization by the US.[44] The resolution pointed to Puerto Rico's lack of meaningful autonomy, underlined by the US's recent establishment of a powerful financial oversight board for Puerto Rico (without Puerto Rican advice or consent), and the US Supreme Court's decision in *Puerto Rico v. Sanchez Valle*, affirming that the rights of sovereignty over the territories are located in the US government.[45] The Committee reaffirmed "the inalienable right of the people of Puerto Rico to self-determination,"[46] and the notion that the people of Puerto Rico

---

[38] Juan Perea, *The Black/White Binary Paradigm of Race: The 'Normal Science' of American Racial Thought*, 85 CAL. L. REV. 1213 (1997); Kevin Johnson, *The Ring of Fire: Assimilation and the Mexican-American Experience*, 85 CAL. L. REV. 1259 (1997).

[39] For discussion, *see* Amar Bhatia, *The South of the North: Building on Critical Approaches to International Law with Lessons from the Fourth World*, 14 OR. REV. INT'L L. 131 (2012).

[40] For a recent overview of the large literature, *see*, *e.g.*, RESEARCH HANDBOOK ON THE LAW OF INDIGENOUS RIGHTS (Dwight Newman ed., 2022).

[41] *See* UN, INTERNATIONAL TRUSTEESHIP SYSTEM, available at https://www.un.org/dppa/decolonizat ion/en/history/international-trusteeship-system-and-trust-territories (last visited May 12, 2022).

[42] *See* UN, NON-SELF-GOVERNING TERRITORIES, available at https://www.un.org/dppa/decolonizat ion/en/nsgt (last visited May 12, 2022).

[43] *See* UN, LIST OF FORMER TRUST AND NON-SELF-GOVERNING TERRITORIES, available at https:// www.un.org/dppa/decolonization/en/history/former-trust-and-nsgts#_ednref11 (last visited May 12, 2022).

[44] UNGAOR, *Decision of the Special Committee concerning Puerto Rico*, UN Doc A/AC.109/2021/L.7 (June 16, 2021), available at https://undocs.org/en/A/AC.109/2021/L.7 (last visited May 12, 2022).

[45] *Id.*

[46] *Id.*

## 276 THE RIGHT TO EXCLUDE

constitute a Latin American and Caribbean nation that has its own distinct national identity."[47] It concluded by calling upon the US "to assume its responsibility to promote a process that will enable the Puerto Rican people to fully exercise their inalienable right to self-determination and independence, in accordance and in full compliance with" the UN's Decolonization Declaration of 1960.[48]

From the perspective of international law's postracial xenophobia, an unfortunate but expected reaction to all of this is the tired refrain, "too little, too late." Some of the trouble for territories like Puerto Rico, Guam, and others still on the UN list concerns the development of the right of self-determination after the desuetude of decolonization. From one angle, it would appear that along with the lapse of decolonization by the 1980s and 1990s, so too had the right of self-determination gone the way of the dodo. Or if the right hadn't gone extinct, it was certainly unclear from the International Court of Justice's (ICJ) jurisprudence what applicability it enjoyed beyond the second half of the twentieth century.[49] It wasn't clear, that is, from the vantage point of the international legal effort to respond to colonialism that surfaced between the 1950s and 1970s. From the position of the emerging Indigenous Peoples movement of the 1990s, however, it was a very different story.[50]

The disjuncture is a result of an important distinction between "exploitation" modes of colonial control, of the sorts rallied against throughout Africa, the Middle East, and Asia during twentieth-century decolonization, and the distinct phenomenon known as settler colonialism.[51] International law's anticolonial imperative, most visibly illustrated in the UN's Decolonization Declaration, was directed at the former and governed by what is often called the "blue water thesis," the restriction of self-determination and sovereign right to those entities deemed by the UN to be holdovers from the League of Nations' mandate system, as well as the NSGTs.[52] Without an ocean separating the colonizer from the colony, so went the idea, the right of self-determination didn't apply.[53] The idea here, however untenable, was that decolonization was the cure for exploitation modes of colonial control—those

---

[47] *Id.*

[48] *Id.*

[49] Accordance with International Law of the Unilateral Declaration of Independence in Respect of Kosovo, Advisory Opinion, 2010 ICJ Rep 436 (July 22).

[50] *See, e.g.,* Kristen Carpenter & Angela Riley, *Indigenous Peoples and the Jurisgenerative Moment in Human Rights,* 102 Cal. L. Rev. 173 (2014).

[51] Natsu Taylor Saito provides a helpful exploration of the distinction and its stakes in Settler Colonialism, Race, and the Law: Why Structuralism Racism Persists (2020). *See generally* Audra Simpson, Mohawk Interruptus (2014); Robert Williams, The American Indian in Western Legal Thought: The Discourses of Conquest (1992).

[52] Saito, Settler Colonialism, *supra* note 51, at 190.

[53] For critical assessments, *see generally* Anna Stilz, Territorial Sovereignty: A Philosophical Exploration (2019); Karen Knop, Diversity and Self-Determination in International Law (2009); Elizabeth Chadwick, Self-Determination in the Post-9/11 Era (2011); James Hofbauer, Sovereignty in the Exercise of the Right to Self-Determination (2016); Jorg Fisch, The Right of Self-Determination of Peoples: The Domestication of an Illusion (2015).

scenarios in which a foreign population subjugated a given territory, squeezed it for its natural and human resources, and returned home to make a fortune. Settler colonialism, in contrast, referred to a process of eliminating the indigenous population, since the foreign invader was less interested in returning home. They were there to stay. The upshot was that the UN's decolonization effort was entirely focused on colonialism of the first sort, the sort in which an ocean separated the metropolitan colonial power from its colonial holdings. Settler situations in which the conquering people continued to live among the indigenous was simply off the table. This distinction wasn't an issue so much for the anticolonial effort that matured throughout the twentieth century, since the imperial powers were geographically separate from their colonies. Left out of the picture, quite intentionally, were the settler states—and of course, the indigenous peoples who lived there.[54] In those territories, like that of the US, Canada, New Zealand, and Australia, for example, talk of liberating "colonized" peoples required scare quotes, since colonization and its unwinding was regarded a matter for where white people were (arguably) not in the majority.

From the perspective of these settler territories, as well as the indigenous rights movement that was subsequent to decolonization, the entire decolonization movement (i.e., TWAIL I) had ignored the interests of those subordinated peoples who continued to live amongst their conquerors.[55] As James Anaya has observed:

> Liberation movements in Africa promoted decolonization through the establishment of new political orders organized on the basis of the territorial boundaries imposed by the colonial powers, despite the arbitrary character of most such boundaries in relation to precolonial political and social organization ... In its focus on the colonial territorial unit, this model of decolonization bypassed spheres of community—that is, *tribal and ethnic groupings*—that existed prior to colonialism; but it also largely ignored the ethnic and tribal identities that continued to exist and hold meaning in the lives of people. Hence, as to some enclave groups or groups divided by colonial frontiers, decolonization procedures alone may not have allowed for a sufficient range of choice or otherwise may not have constituted a complete remedy.[56]

It is true that there were earlier glimmerings of a movement that would focus on indigenous peoples, and it is typical to look, for example, at postwar Conventions from the International Labor Organization (ILO) as a first start. But on the whole, international law's concern with settler colonialism really didn't launch

---

[54] Patrick Wolfe, *Settler Colonialism and the Elimination of the Native*, 8 J. GEN. RES. 387 (2006).

[55] For a recent overview of the history, *see* STEPHEN YOUNG, INDIGENOUS PEOPLES, CONSENT, AND RIGHTS: TROUBLING SUBJECTS (2021).

[56] S. JAMES ANAYA, INDIGENOUS PEOPLES IN INTERNATIONAL LAW 84–85 (1996) (emphasis added).

## 278 THE RIGHT TO EXCLUDE

until decolonization had ended, starting in earnest with the establishment of a UN Working Group on Indigenous Populations in 1982, and culminating in the UN's Declaration on the Rights of Indigenous Peoples (2007).[57] The Declaration, as has been roundly recognized, is first and foremost a human rights instrument in the contemporary sense—not in the anticolonial sense discussed above. It is also deeply committed to self-determination, but again, this is a different self-determination as well. Of course, on the face of the UN's Indigenous Rights Declaration—as well as in documents like the Decolonization Committee's recent resolution on Puerto Rico—the language all seems pretty much the same. After its provisions on human rights, equality, and antidiscrimination in its first two articles, the Declaration announces in Article 3 that "indigenous peoples have the right of self-determination. By virtue of that right they freely determine their political status and freely pursue their economic, social, and cultural development." Article 4 continues, "Indigenous peoples, in exercising their right to self-determination, have the right to autonomy or self-government in matters relating to their internal and local affairs, as well as ways and means for financing their autonomous functions." But as Kristen Carpenter and Angela Riley have argued, this "jurisgenerative" discourse of self-determination, human rights, and the assault on settler colonialism in the context of indigenous rights are all relatively alien to the sort of anticolonial "worldmaking" launched in the middle decades of the twentieth century.[58]

As we conceptualize international law's postracial ideology, there are a few points to emphasize here when situating, in this post-decolonization moment, the rights of peoples as human rights.[59] First, the right of self-determination is prominent, clearly a pivotal idea in the matrix of indigenous rights. But this prominence is undermined by a point already alluded to: As the ICJ very briefly explained in its *Kosovo* decision, decided three years *after* the UN's adoption of the Indigenous Rights Declaration, "whether, outside the context of non-self-governing territories and peoples subject to alien subjugation, domination, and exploitation, the international law of self-determination confers upon part of the population of an existing State a right to separate from that State is" a question without any semblance of consensus.[60] One might object that, after the adoption of the Indigenous Rights Declaration, there was certainly consensus about the applicability of self-determination beyond the sphere of NSGTs. But a critical cleavage here, as noted by Natsu Taylor Saito,[61] is the tendency for non-Indigenous writers to assume that

---

[57] *Id.* at 45–58.

[58] Carpenter & Riley, *supra* note 50.

[59] Peter Jones, *Collective and Group-Specific: Can the Rights of Ethno-Cultural Minorities be Human Rights? in* ETHNO-CULTURAL DIVERSITY AND HUMAN RIGHTS (Gaetano Pentassuglia ed., 2018).

[60] *Kosovo, supra* note 49, at para. 82. For discussion, *see* ELIZABETH CHADWICK, SELF-DETERMINATION IN THE POST 9/11 ERA (2011).

[61] Natsu Taylor Saito, *Why Xenophobia?* BERKELEY LA RAZA L. REV. 1 (2021).

self-determination must manifest in the light of something like the ICJ's *Western Sahara* case, and which will mean most of the time conflating the right of self-determination with a claim for statehood.[62] Both the situations for indigenous peoples and those peoples residing in the territories exemplify the effort to provide self-determination without statehood through various measures of local autonomy—an effort that has been stymied, time and time again.

What then, does the contemporary right of self-determination offer American Indians, Puerto Ricans, and so many others, if not the promise of a sovereign right to exclude? Before the Indigenous Rights Declaration was adopted, Anaya—who also went on to serve as the UN Special Rapporteur on the Rights of Indigenous Peoples—provided an influential explanation. Anaya's theory of self-determination "arises within international law's human rights frame and hence benefits human beings *as human beings* and not sovereign entities as such."[63] Further, he continued, "self-determination is not separate from other human rights norms; rather, self-determination is a configurative principle or framework complemented by the more specific human rights norms that in their totality enjoin the governing institutional order."[64]

Notice that a people's right of self-determination is no longer a "prerequisite" for the exercise of human rights, as it was in anticolonial discourse. It is now rather a kind of atmosphere in which human rights breathe and grow. But even this metaphor doesn't seem quite right, for Anaya goes on to say that there is a specific human rights norm which actually serves as the "minimum condition" for the exercise of self-determination, and it is the antidiscrimination principle.[65] The "point of departure" for UN activity that led to the adoption of the Indigenous Rights Declaration, the antidiscrimination principle has "special implications for indigenous groups which, practically as a matter of definition, have been treated adversely on the basis of their immutable or cultural differences."[66]

This vision of self-determination is not, however, solely about the protection of individual members of indigenous groups. It is also concerned with individuals in their capacities "as social creatures engaged in the constitution and functioning of communities."[67] These "communities," however, are not "mutually exclusive 'sovereign' territorial communities."[68] They should not, it would seem, be understood as possessing sovereign rights to exclude—which makes perfect sense, given the different sense of exclusion often offered, for example, in the context of American Indian property law.[69] What Anaya envisions here is a right of self-determination

---

[62] Western Sahara, Advisory Opinion, 1975 I.C.J. Rep.
[63] ANAYA, *supra* note 56, at 76.
[64] *Id.* at 77.
[65] *Id.* at 97.
[66] *Id.* at 98.
[67] *Id.* at 77.
[68] *Id.* at 78.
[69] Kristen Carpenter et al., *In Defense of Property*, 118 YALE L.J. 1022 (2009).

280    THE RIGHT TO EXCLUDE

belonging to individual human beings, but also to the intersecting cultural entities to which we belong as peoples.[70] Anaya explains:

> Any conception of self-determination that does not take into account the multiple patterns of human association and interdependency is at best incomplete and more likely distorted. The values of freedom and equality implicit in the concept of self-determination have meaning for the multiple and overlapping spheres of human association and political ordering that characterize humanity. Properly understood, the principle of self-determination, commensurate with the values it incorporates, benefits groups—that is, "peoples" in the ordinary sense of the term—throughout the spectrum of humanity's complex web of interrelationships and loyalties, and not just peoples defined by existing or perceived sovereign boundaries.[71]

This demand for the right of self-determination to track the sociological "reality" of cultural mixture, of integration and disintegration, allowing at once for protections against individual and group discrimination, Anaya concluded, required little in the way of interpretive complexity. The rights of "peoples," like so many terms in international instruments, should be interpreted in the light of its "plain meaning."[72] Like a cigar is sometimes just a cigar, so too—apparently—a people is just a people. According to Anaya, the trick lies in understanding that even in the midst of intense cultural dispersion, peoples nevertheless have rights to cultural integrity. As pronounced in the Declaration, peoples have the right to "practice and revitalize their cultural traditions and customs," "to manifest, practice, develop, and teach their spiritual and religious traditions," "to transmit to future generations their histories, languages, oral traditions, philosophies," "the right to dignity and diversity of their cultures, traditions, histories, and aspirations." Like the human being, peoples with cultural integrity enjoy the human right of self-determination. Questions about who counts as a people, or whether such a people's right of self-determination as cultural integrity turns out to be a right to exclude in disguise, are best left to vernacular sociology—we know cultures when we see them.

If, in this particular vision, the right of self-determination was divorced from the right to exclude (though we have to wonder to what extent the notion of "cultural integrity" isn't also about exclusion, or if this isn't *exactly* what the Special Committee on Decolonization envisions for Puerto Rico), it was also largely divorced from race. The Declaration repeats from the International Convention on the Elimination of Racial Discrimination (ICERD) in its preamble a condemnation of race science, and in its Article 8 demands that states prevent the use of racial or

---

[70] ANAYA, *supra* note 56, at 79.
[71] *Id.*
[72] *Id.* at 80.

MULTICULTURALISM, NATIONALISM, PRAGMATISM 281

ethnic propaganda. But on the whole, the Indigenous Rights Declaration—along with so much of the literature on indigenous rights as well as that of TWAIL—avoids the language of race, emphasizing instead tribal, ethnic, and cultural groupings. And it is this point which gets us up to speed on postracial multiculturalism in international legal thought.

If we take twenty-first-century international legal discourse about the rights of peoples as indicative of the current moment, self-determination has been detached from twentieth-century strategies for interlocking colonialism and racism, detached from concerns about migration and border controls, and detached from questions about racial hierarchy in the international legal order. Instead,—and here more so in the space of the indigenous rights movement than TWAIL—self-determination is now a human rights concept, through and through. It is guided by a colorblind antidiscrimation principle, a sociological emphasis on cultural intermixture and "webs of complexity," and formalistic demands for both individualized and group rights. As Taylor has correctly argued, an indispensable move in the yet-to-be developed critique of racism in international law is precisely an analysis of settler colonialism—the mode of colonial aggrandizement that continues to plague so many of the planet's subordinated populations.[73] In the space of settler colonialism we see patterns of domination and oppression that, deplorably, have yet to witness "worldmaking" efforts to transform the status quo of racial hierarchy and neocolonial territoriality. The question is whether, despite its critical mission, the mantra of cultural integrity has helped fuel a new ideology of postracial xenophobia. Given its deep alliance with the antidiscrimination principle so dear to human rights law, it is worth asking whether postracial multiculturalism might itself be a part of the problem.[74]

## C  An Analytics of Raciality

This first plank in postracial ideology is powerfully effective as a progress narrative. On the one side, racism has been sequestered as a form of irrational and largely anomalous behavior, a function of individual prejudice chastened by the regimes of antidiscrimination law. On the other, the social production of hierarchy has been revealed as a contest between practices and figurations that were really there all along, but hidden beneath the deceiving veneer of race: ethnoculture. And the means for reducing these hierarchies is about the provision of rights to these cultures, rights that will guarantee their differences and, in one way or another, the right of a culture to exclude external threats of interference. These practices and

---

[73] SAITO, SETTLER COLONIALISM, *supra* note 51, at 45.
[74] *See generally* DAVID KENNEDY, THE DARK SIDES OF VIRTUE: REASSESSING INTERNATIONAL HUMANITARIANISM (2004).

## 282  THE RIGHT TO EXCLUDE

figurations—the stuff of culture itself—are both good and bad, from this multicultural perspective. They are laudable when they suggest tolerance and the celebration of difference, and bad when they don't.

Among the many challenges here is what is sometimes called the critique of anti-essentialism, a challenge to conceptualize what the "integrity" of a given ethnoculture could even mean, much less whether a practice associated with such an entity is "good or bad."[75] As appealing as it sounds, and at least from the perspective of cultural studies, it could be that just as a cigar might *not* be a cigar, so too, the "common sense" of cultural integrity is more slippery than it seems. Homi Bhaba suggests that cultures demand translation, and not in the sense that one language be converted into another. Cultural translation is:

> A process through which cultures are required to revise their own systems of reference, norms and values by departing from their habitual or "inbred" rules of transformation. Ambivalence and antagonism accompany any act of cultural translation because negotiating with the "difference of the other" reveals the radical insufficiency of our own systems of meaning and signification.[76]

If cultural translation is unavoidable, it is useful to think of cultural "hybridity."[77] Stuart Hall argued that "colonized traditional cultures" "are no longer (if they ever were) organic, fixed, self-sustaining, self-sufficient entities."[78] As hybrids, cultures are constantly fluctuating, dialogic and diasporic, "repertoires of meaning" that must be convened, deployed, and enforced.[79] Some who identify with "ethnic minority communities" "remain deeply committed to 'traditional' practices and values, though rarely without diasporic inflection," while others find themselves deeply ambivalent or disassociated. " 'Hybridity' marks the place of this incommensurability."[80] Hall continued:

> Ethnic minority communities are not integrated collective actors, such as would allow them to become the legal subjects of all-encompassing community rights. The temptation to essentialize "community" has to be resisted—it is a fantasy of plenitude in circumstances of imagined loss ... In making the move toward greater cultural diversity at the heart of modernity, therefore, we must take care lest we simply reverse into new forms of ethnic closure ... The pure assertion of

---

[75] On the reification of cultural rights in this context, *see* KAREN ENGLE, THE ELUSIVE PROMISE OF INDIGENOUS DEVELOPMENT: RIGHTS, CULTURE, STRATEGY (2010).

[76] Homi Bhaba, *The Vernacular Cosmopolitan, in* VOICES OF THE CROSSING 141 (Ferdinand Dennis & Naseem Khan eds., 2000).

[77] ROBERT J.C. YOUNG, COLONIAL DESIRE: HYBRIDITY IN THEORY, CULTURE, AND RACE (1995); LEELA GANDHI, POSTCOLONIAL THEORY 122 (2019).

[78] HALL, *supra* note 1, at 113.

[79] *Id.*

[80] *Id.* at 114.

MULTICULTURALISM, NATIONALISM, PRAGMATISM    283

difference is only viable in a rigidly segregated society. Its ultimate logic is that of *apartheid*.[81]

Like Bhaba and Hall, Richard Ford has argued that multiculturalism and its discourse of cultural integrity and difference is certainly many things, some of which are undoubtedly progressive. But multiculturalism, and the attendant idea that racism bottoms out as a consequence of cultural difference, can be mystifying when it comes to racial justice.

> The focus on difference diverts attention from racism—a social institution based on a formal status hierarchy and a set of ideologies that justify that status hierarchy—and instead misleadingly suggests that racial justice is primarily the result of objective and intrinsic difference among natural racial groups ... Worst of all, by insisting that socially imposed statuses are defined by real differences in cultural characteristics, the difference focus encourages members of minority groups to define themselves in terms of group stereotypes.[82]

Following Foucault's analysis of sexuality, Ford argued that the urge to celebrate authentic cultural differences against an assimilative state apparatus is less about opposing a repressive societal culture, and more consistent with a social production of "canonical identity groups."[83] And these identity groups do indeed aspire toward a "canon," a set of beliefs, practices, and institutions which are not merely "real" but require regulation and maintenance from within the group. "Conformity to these recognizable types is a prerequisite to acceptance in many social circles,"[84] and this demand for conformity to a cultural essence, to "cultural integrity," inevitably ends up circling back to "the fact of intrinsic racial difference"[85]—the very idea the rejection of which sits at the center of the postracial style. Curiously, the attempted escape from cultural assimilation leads to the multicultural right to difference, which "delivers us all the more firmly in the grasp of a racism that always includes both."[86] For it is in the turn away from race to the "reality" of cultural difference, Ford suggests, that *racial* differences are endlessly reproduced in the social affirmation of cultural integrity. The result is a postracial ideology that oddly reinforces "the idea of distinctive and unassimilable, if not opaque, racial cultures." Ford continues:

---

[81] *Id.* at 120–21.
[82] RICHARD FORD, RACIAL CULTURE 31 (2005).
[83] *Id.* at 39.
[84] *Id.* at 40.
[85] *Id.*
[86] *Id.* at 42.

284   THE RIGHT TO EXCLUDE

This orthodoxy sends a pernicious message: The status distinctions that divide society (such as distinctions of race, gender, ethnicity and sexual orientation) are defined (and perhaps justified) by real and profound differences in lifestyle, morality, temperament, norms, and aesthetic sensibility. This message not only provides ready justification for continued bigotry and aversion on the part of those outside the group in question; perhaps worse yet, it also encourages group members themselves to emphasize their differences from outsiders, to exaggerate the degree, importance, and antiquity of those differences (every trait becomes a cultural practice, every practice a tradition and every tradition hails from the misty domicile of 'time immemorial') and even to invent traditions ... that never were.[87]

Perhaps the most visible way in which multicultural theory has helped produce a new postracial ideology is through the rise of the term "diversity." At least in the US, since the Supreme Court's *Bakke* decision, the diversity norm has increasingly achieved a kind of hegemonic status in the quest for racial justice. But like the discourse of cultural difference with which "racial diversity" bears a deep familial connection, demands for diversity tend to both naturalize ideas about the essential characteristics of racial cultures and neutralize efforts to think racial justice beyond these affirmations of cultural difference. The *Bakke* case itself helped propagate this particular catch-22, with its easy transitions between "racial" and "ethnic" diversity, where, like in Kymlicka's own analysis of African-Americans, and Anaya's theory of a people's right of self-determination, raciality drops out as an independent variable. What's more, the diversity rationale goes beyond eclipsing raciality from the discussion; it actively incentivizes litigants to emphasize cultural distinctions that might put meat on the bare bones of whatever it is "diversity" was meant to signify—people of color would need to "prove" their cultural bona fides. The raw fact of racial otherness—and the history of racial hierarchy—doesn't really compute here, and it is for this reason that Ford says that "In this light it would appear that a central function of 'diversity' is to finesse, if not obscure the salience of contemporary racism."[88]

To be sure, it is entirely possible for racial diversity to mean something other than a reduction to cultural essence. Illustratively, Ford offers the example of the well-known slogan, "It's a black thing, you wouldn't understand." On the one side, this phrase suggests raciality as ideology: there are formal and informal designations of racial status known to Black Americans and known so thoroughly that they structure the perceptions and beliefs of Black people in a way that they become incomprehensible to non-black people. Blacks differ from others in terms

---

[87]  *Id.* at 41.
[88]  *Id.* at 52.

of a racial status, but that is the only relevant difference—in all other respects, the categories of "Black," "White," and so on are meaningless. This is status difference without cultural difference. To say that "this is a black thing, and that you don't understand," is a way of signaling an enlivened awareness of racial ideology—perhaps Black Lives Matter is a good, contemporary illustration. On the other hand, Ford explains, one could use the phrase in the register of cultural difference and cultural integrity. As a non-black person, you simply don't understand, but your lack of knowing isn't a result of your inexperience with racial ideology. It is rather that the cultural achievements of "blacks are only fully intelligible to other blacks, and our culture is mysterious and opaque to the outsider."[89] Today, the diversity rationale is primarily, if not exclusively, about race as culture. Raciality as an ideology of domination, exclusion, style, and structure—this is just not what postracial multiculturalism teaches.

As Walter Benn Michaels has argued, "the general principle here is that our commitment to diversity has redefined the opposition to discrimination as the appreciation (rather than the elimination) of difference. So with respect to race, the idea is not just that racism is a bad thing (which of course it is) but that [difference] itself is a good thing."[90] This really does reflect an interesting turn in the history of raciality, for in its origins raciality was invented as a way of justifying unequal treatment and status among the world's human beings. A world where certain peoples were clearly excludable, but others were not, presented a problem—and racial xenophobia was a solution. In postracial ideology, the tables have turned. If the problem now is raciality itself, the solution is the celebration of difference, the demand for diversity. Like Ford, however, Michaels suggests that for all of its appeal, "our current notion of cultural diversity—trumpeted as the repudiation of racism and biological essentialism— in fact grew out of and perpetuates the very concepts it congratulates itself on having escaped."[91] The norm of multicultural diversity teaches that cultures are different but essentially equal, that it is mistaken to judge any one culture's practices against another. The implication is that actual inequalities in social life, as a result, can't be the result of cultural difference, but are instead due to individual failings. And it is here that we can see, once again, the antidiscrimination principle as the one and only cure. In the multicultural context, the possibility that racism is operating at a level beyond that of the antidiscrimination principle just doesn't come into view.

---

[89] *Id.* at 92.
[90] MICHAELS, *supra* note 8, at 5.
[91] *Id.* at 7.

# II THE CRITIQUE OF FUNCTIONALISM: POSTRACIAL NATIONALISM

It is easy to point a finger at the past decade as the site for a new form of racist, ultranationalist xenophobia. It is easy, because, there was in fact quite a lot of that.[92] As Jayashri Srikantiah and Shirin Sinnar have suggested, the motivation for much of the Trump Administration's approach to immigration was a return to the idea that America is, was, and should always be a white nation first.[93] This commitment to white supremacy, they suggest, represented the "most wide-ranging Executive Branch attempt to restrict immigration policy in generations."[94] Among such policies were the effort to build a wall along the southern border of the US, issue travel bans barring noncitizens from Muslim-majority countries, proposals to end birthright citizenship, terminate temporary protected status for noncitizens from certain states, eliminate Deferred Action for Childhood Arrivals, and escalate law enforcement, detention, and deportation.[95] Similarly, Rose Cuison Villazor and Kevin Johnson argued that "the immigration policies that the Trump Administration has adopted or seeks to deploy reveal the executive branch's war on immigration diversity in both admissions and deportations." "When situated within the history of immigration laws and policies in the United States," they continued, "the current war against immigration diversity exhibits the Administration's broader goal of returning to pre-1965 immigration policies designed to maintain a 'white nation.'"[96] Seen in the context of this history of blatant racial xenophobia, Michelle Goodwin and Erwin Chemerinsky agreed that, at least in the US, immigration policy is witnessing a return to its vulgar roots:

> [O]ur concerns and observations stem from the fact that racist symbolism profoundly impacts law to during, poisonous effect. American legal history demonstrates the lingering, institutional effects of racial symbolism and how it hampers the pursuit and achievement of equality in schooling, housing, serving on juries, voting, and criminal justice and social equality generally. When rally-goers and pundits urged in 2016 to "take Trump seriously, not literally," sadly they misunderstood the power behind racist rhetoric and the ways that it could be weaponized by any political leader, let alone a President.[97]

---

[92] For recent discussion, *see* E. Tendayi Achiume, *Migration as Decolonization*, 71 STAN. L. REV. 1509 (2019).

[93] Jayashri Srikantiah & Shirin Sinnar, *White Nationalism as Immigration Policy*, 71 STAN. L. REV. ONLINE 197, 198 (2019).

[94] *Id.* at 200.

[95] *Id.* at 201.

[96] Rose Cuison Villazor & Kevin Johnson, *The Trump Administration and the War on Immigration Diversity*, 54 WAKE FOREST L. REV. 575 (2019).

[97] Michelle Goodwin & Erwin Chemerinsky, *The Trump Administration: Immigration, Racism, and Covid-19*, 169 U. PA. L. REV. 313, 348–49 (2021).

There is no shortage of speculation about what might explain these recent retro-outbursts of racial xenophobia. And while there's little in the way of consensus about it, what no one disputes is the proffered justification for all of the aggression: borders must be defended, walls must be built, nations must be purified—all in the name of realism. These, we are assured, are the measures necessitated by hardheaded studies of global problems, no more, no less. At the same time, however, that these forms of racist race consciousness have been rearing their heads in the name of a political realism, the approach in international law has been far more in keeping with twenty-first-century norms about race—even while also committed to a "realism" just the same.

To take one prominent example, consider a sample of work from the immigration law scholar David Martin. In a chapter from the turn of the century titled "The Authority and Responsibility of States," Martin argued for a classic liberal understanding of the sovereign's right to exclude.[98] As Martin explained at the outset, "the starting point" is "broad state authority" in "setting the standards for admission to and exclusion from national territory."[99] This starting point is a "basic assumption" of our "international system,"[100] and all restrictions on and attempts to regulate this fundamental right to exclude are exceptional.[101] Nevertheless, Martin explained that "it has been exceedingly rare for any state to exercise the maximum of its theoretical power by halting virtually all migration."[102] Why do states not exercise the full extent of this power, and just close down their borders altogether? Today's answer from international lawyers is that, in this "realistic" approach to the problem, it would be impractical to do so. Closing down national borders would cause problems; perhaps not as many problems as a policy of open borders would create. But neither approach makes sense in light of the need to mitigate the sovereign's right to exclude in the light of practical considerations.

For example, Martin suggests that states actually end up constrained in their decisions about admission and exclusion on a problem-by-problem, field-by-field basis. As international law relates to national security, international trade, development, investment, employment and labor, education policies, public health concerns, forced migrants, and the threat of returning would-be refugees to hostile territory, international legal rules may affect and regulate sovereign rights of exclusion in the form of bilateral treaties, like consular treaties, investment treaties, friendship, navigation, and commerce treaties, and the like. International law

---

[98] David Martin, *The Authority and Responsibility of States, in* Migration and International Legal Norms (T. Alexander Aleinikoff & Vincet Chetail eds., 2003).

[99] *Id.* at 33.

[100] *Id.* at 31.

[101] *Id.* at 32. The most obvious and yet still relatively weak such restriction is the antidiscrimination principle.

[102] *Id.* at 33.

288 THE RIGHT TO EXCLUDE

may also pose restrictions in the form of regional agreements and multinational conventions, like NAFTA on the one side or the Refugees Convention on the other.

From this point of view, broad statements about the state's "plenary power" are too generalized when analyzed beyond the context of some particular problem. As Martin recently argued, there is no longer a popular consensus for the broad authority of the state to fashion its own immigration controls based on an unwavering faith in the sovereign's right to exclude, per se. Rather, the plenary power *persuades* because the plenary power *works*. In a treatment of *Chae Chan Ping* and *Fong Yu Ting*, Martin observed that the Court had never intended to raise a sovereignty claim in order to trump competing visions of social justice and human rights. Rather, these decisions helped articulate the relation between federal and state power in the distinctive context of the American constitutional system. If the Supreme Court had deemed the US unable to decide matters concerning migration control, then the role would have fallen to the states in their exercise of the police power. Not finding a natural home in any of the constitution's enumerated powers, the US would have only been able to speak to border controls with the plural voices of the individual states. However, as Martin explained, without a unified voice about how or who to exclude from the national political community, the very coherence of a national *polis* might dissolve. Thus, Martin concluded, "Asserting jurisdiction over a territory, which includes authority to choose which noncitizens to admit or exclude, is simply part of what it means to be a sovereign nation."[103]

Perhaps, however, the problems of the late nineteenth century are not the problems of the early twenty-first? Maybe the need to immunize the federal government's decisions about migration and exclusion are no longer necessary due to the pressing needs of national coherence—needs that "made sense" earlier in the nation's life, but make less sense for today? For Martin, the problem has indeed changed, but its solution presses in the same direction:

> Failed states are more common, and well-armed insurgencies have proliferated. The march of democracy has slowed and, in several countries, reversed. Climate change and even plague-like diseases presage more complicated foreign policy challenges, many of which will have a migration dimension ... I do not foresee the Supreme Court retreating significantly from the strong deference doctrines derived from *Chae Chan Ping*.[104]

The upshot: privileging the sovereign's right to exclude provides concrete solutions to real problems, both domestic and international. To understand why, or in what ways the right to exclude ought to be extended or diminished, we need to look at the problem at hand and the expertise we will need to solve it.

[103] *Id.* at 36.
[104] *Id.* at 49–50.

Of course, and as we have seen, "realism" and "practical considerations" are argumentative spaces in which the jurist can find any number of pathways. Consider one more example, that of the postwar literature of the New Haven School.[105] Like many others of their generation,[106] Harold Lasswell and Myres McDougal were post-realists in the sense that they were deeply informed by early twentieth-century attacks on the classic conception of the sovereign's right to exclude. Lasswell and McDougal's "Policy Perspective" steadily developed in parallel with the work of Henry Hart, Jr. and Albert Sacks, producing what is probably best understood as an international variant of the legal process school.[107] This new institutionalism would be guided by the freshest of cutting edge thinking about the functional nature of law, an understanding of the deeply political nature of law, and a process-oriented program in which a legal regime was best considered in its social contexts—much of what we surveyed back in Chapter 4.[108] The basic goals of the New Haven regime were very broad—in their case, it was "human dignity"—and the actual meaning of the goal could only be discovered in practice, and not before it. The goal values were targeted through "continuous reappraisal of the circumstances in which specific institutional combinations can make the greatest net contribution to the overarching goal."[109] To the extent that the goal might find itself manifested differently in the specifics of various local contexts, these "varying detailed practices by which the overriding goals are sought need not necessarily be fatal ... but can be made creative in promoting [our goals]."[110]

In the immigration context, Lasswell and McDougal's study of the "contemporary emerging world society, with its ever-increasing personal mobility and transnational interactions,"[111] was the analytical starting point—not a classic defense of the right to exclude, as was the case in Martin's alternate functionalist approach. Rather, Lasswell and McDougal began with a concession to the relativity of rights between sovereigns and non-state actors, and in particular, the rights of individuals. On their view, the traditional distinction between citizen and alien was already a mistake, since "every individual is a potential alien in relation to all the states of which he is not a national."[112] To be clear, Lasswell and McDougal had no interest

[105] See, e.g., Harold Koh, Is There a New New Haven School in International Law? 32 YALE J. INT'L L. 559 (2007).
[106] See generally MORTON HORWITZ, THE TRANSFORMATION OF AMERICAN LAW, 1870–1960: THE CRISIS OF LEGAL ORTHODOXY (1979).
[107] On legal process in the US, see Charles Barzun, The Forgotten Foundations of Hart and Sacks, 99 VA. L. REV. 1 (2013).
[108] See Justin Desautels-Stein, At War with the Eclectics: Mapping Pragmatism in Contemporary Legal Analysis, 2007 MICH. ST. L. REV. 565 (2007).
[109] Myres S. McDougal & Harold D. Lasswell, The Identification and Appraisal of Diverse Systems of Public Order, 53 AM. J. INT'L L. 1, 5 (1959).
[110] Id. at 6.
[111] Myres McDougal et al., The Protection of Aliens from Discrimination and World Public Order: Responsibility of States Conjoined with Human Rights, 70 AM. J. INT'L L. 432, 433 (1976).
[112] Id. at 437.

## 290  THE RIGHT TO EXCLUDE

in making an argument for open borders; there will, they conceded, always be rational forms of exclusion.[113] But the rationality of the regime intended to keep certain individuals out of a sovereign's territory ought to be guided by two pillars: the common interests of international society in servicing the principle of human dignity, and the complexity of a world system in which concepts like "sovereigns" and "owners" are best analyzed as bundles of rights and relationships,[114] rather than "reified pseudoabsolutes."[115] As Lasswell and McDougal concluded the essay:

> The fact of alienage does not change the fundamental demands and interests of the individual as a human being; its only relevance must be to the organized interests of a territorial community, which, in various contexts, his activities may affect. It is widely recognized today that many, if not most, "national" boundaries are highly artificial and anachronistic from any functional perspective, impeding a rational regional organization of the world, and, as suggested above, that the grounds commonly employed by states in making their characterizations of "nationality" may bear only an accidental relation to the facts of community membership. In this context, the necessities of an aggregate common interest in a global community and society, requiring a more rational relation of peoples to resources, should be made to yield as little as possible to the demands and practices of an outmoded and destructive nationalism. A clear consciousness of interdependence offers more hope even for shared exclusive interests than the amnesia of parochialism.[116]

Ultimately, it was simply unrealistic to adhere to a rigid and mechanical view of the sovereign's right to exclude through the implementation of xenophobic and increasingly militarized immigration regimes. It was unrealistic on the one hand for its prioritization of a sovereign's rights over other rights in the system, and it was unrealistic on the other as a matter of capturing the complexities of international society.

In the context of liberal legal thought, we will expect the language of a legal concept to be shaped by the theses of free competition (i.e., the sovereign's right to exclude) and social control (i.e., the applicability of certain restrictions on the right to exclude). We will also expect the thesis of naturalizing juridical science to mediate that relation, *legally*. This means that we hope for the availability of legal arguments intended to "make sense" of that tension, resolving dissonance into consonance. For Martin, the argument began by securing the sovereign's right to exclude the world. This securing, however, was due less to a metaphysical belief in the sanctity of sovereign equality than it was due to a belief in the reality of sovereign right.

---

[113] *Id.*
[114] *Id.* at 439.
[115] *Id.* at 432.
[116] *Id.* at 439.

Sovereigns have the right to admit and reject economic migrants, not because it is just, but because it makes sense. What's more, sovereigns nevertheless allow migration, and take part in various treaty regimes that restrict their choices. Why? What justifies limits on the right to exclude foreigners? Sovereigns participate in these architectures of social control because it makes sense to do so. It works. If sovereigns are to realize their many goals, they have to work with the cards they have been dealt. To do otherwise is simply impractical, and all "modern" nations at least aspire toward a degree of rationality, of making "it work." Ultimately, the concept of international migration is legal and consistent with the rule of law because its argumentative claims are not arbitrary or so politically malleable as to make the concept into a farce. The concept is shaped by the practical reality of sovereign right, and the practical reality of real-world problems that *demand* the technical expertise of legal professionals, yielding objective legal conclusions. Pragmatic problem-solving resolves the tension between free competition and social control on an ad hoc, case-by-case basis.

In contrast, Lasswell and McDougal began the argument with the necessity of international interdependence, moving out first from the thesis of social control. This necessity, however, had less to do with a natural view of a global community than it did with a belief in the reality of a global social process in which both sovereigns and economic migrants make their way. True, sovereigns retain a right to admit and reject these migrants, but it is no longer a right that orients the system because it somehow "makes sense to do so." Rather, the sociolegal counsel for the field of international migration law is motivated by a concern for functionality and effectiveness. The questions that matter are about the international reality of migration, who is coming from where, in what numbers, when, and why. These are empirical questions, and international migration law must track the empirical data, both in terms of the world's most pressing needs, and in terms of the best answers social science can provide. To do otherwise is to relegate international law to an irrelevant morality out of touch with the real needs of international society. Ultimately, the concept of international migration is legal and consistent with the rule of law because its argumentative claims are not arbitrary and so ethically malleable as to make the concept into a politically impotent cluster of beliefs. The concept of international migration is shaped by the reality of rights—both those of sovereigns and individuals—but also and probably more importantly, by an empirical understanding of the global social system, with its various problems, needs, and interests. These problems, needs, and interests *demand* the application of social science expertise, yielding objective legal conclusions. A functionalist, sociolegal view of global social process in which international migration takes place resolves the tension between free competition and social control at the level of the international system.

These, at any rate, are the means by which functionalism *aspires* to achieve coherence, and a mediation between the theses of free competition and social control

292   THE RIGHT TO EXCLUDE

that appears *legal* and not merely political. I want to emphasize a few points as we transition from this structural argument to the idea that what we are looking at is an underlying theory of postracial nationalism. Functionalism is an argumentative practice in international law that can cut in multiple directions—just like every well-developed legal style. But what must be noted in the diverging works of Lasswell, McDougal, and Martin—as well as in the policy choices defining international law's "antixenophobia framework" mentioned in Chapter 7—is its postraciality. International law's contemporary approach to questions pertaining to national boundaries—in the immigration context—is largely postracial in the sense that race has fallen out of the conversation in ways very similar to what we saw above in the context of multiculturalism. Is race a visible element in global discourses about migration? Of course. Was the Trump Administration regularly accused of racism in its use of nationality bans? Definitely. But so much of these current—and horrible—examples are illustrative of an older, classic racial ideology. They remind us of formal exclusions rooted in outdated racial hierarchies, and as a result, invite all of the opprobrium they deserve. But the *postracial* element isn't lurking in these hot spots. Instead, we find the reigning form of international law's contemporary racial ideology in the far more subtle works of neoformalist and functionalist modes of jurisprudence, claiming practical necessity for the focus on national security, human dignity, or whatever. And what is left unfocused is just as critical: the sovereign's right to exclude, and the domain of culture and cultural difference as the "real" site for questions of autonomy and justice.

As we have seen in the discussion above, postracial multiculturalism indicates a commitment to rights formalism. This isn't the formalism of international law's classic racial ideology, but rather the neoformalist tendencies of the antidiscrimination principle. We've also seen, in the context of the indigenous rights movement, how neoformalism leaves quite a lot off the table, not only in achieving racial justice, but justice for the world's many victims of settler colonialism. An assault on international law's postracial ideology is not, however, only a matter of unwinding the neoformalism of the multicultural knot. Postracial ideology is also deeply nationalist, which I characterize as a functionalist defense of the sovereign's right to set the boundaries for the nation. This functionalism, as we have seen, moves in a number of directions, from ultranationalist concerns about walling up borders, to more moderate and "realistic" defenses of national exclusion, as we saw in the examples of Martin, Lasswell, and McDougal. While postracial multiculturalism often moves by the lights of a neoformalism, international law's typical defenses of a national right to exclude migrants are more often informed by a family of functionalist arguments.

What is it, however, that makes this functionalist nationalism *postracial*? Functionalist nationalism is typically characterized as *after race*, unless, that is, we are encountering examples of the Trumpian sort. More characteristically, however, the vast majority of contemporary claims about national identity and exclusion avoid references to race altogether while nevertheless reconfiguring the racial problematic—and not merely in ignoring race, but rather in having adopted a triumphant and weirdly quasi-colorblind commitment to cultural diversity. We saw this plainly in the discussion of Kymlicka and Anaya above, as well as with Martin, Lasswell, and McDougal. Anxieties about foreigners, about the racial *xenos*, are powerfully vibrant in this discourse, but they have been relentlessly deracialized.

Consider here the highly influential work of the philosopher David Miller, and in particular, his theory of liberal nationalism—a theory of national identity that fits particularly well with the underlying negotiation of the theses of free competition and social control operative in contemporary international legal thought.[117] Notice as well that Miller's argument for liberal nationalism, when contrasted with the postracial multiculturalism I associated with Kymlicka and Anaya, moves in the opposite direction. For whereas Kymlicka and Anaya were anxious about the ways in which national cultures suppress the authentic differences of ethnocultures, Miller's effort is to justify the practical necessity of national identity. Further, where the multicultural argument is often neoformalist, the nationalist argument is often functionalist.

Among Miller's basic premises is the functionalist one that liberal democratic states require a national identity in order to secure effective and meaningful forms of political community. The artificiality of the political state, in other words, requires "grounding" by the organic quality of a state's national identity. This national identity, in turn, is a function of a publicly shared culture.[118] The state's *political* power, as a result, is justifiable because of its confluence with the nation's *cultural* power. With respect to the proper boundary for the state's political community, it extends to those people that share in the constitution of that cultural power.

Miller argued that this liberal type of national identity emerges in the presence of five characteristics.[119] First, co-nationals must believe that they are members of a nation. When there is mutual recognition among members, all (or most, many?) of whom believe in the existence of a common, national bond, then we have satisfied an initial prerequisite: shared beliefs that members belong together in a national community. Second, a nation enjoys a history. In this history contemporary members must see in their ancestors a dedication to the nation that becomes an obligation on the present. For just as prior generations have died for national honors, so too must contemporary generations be willing to sacrifice in the name of that shared past. Third, acts like sacrifice reflect the need for an ongoing, active relation between members and the nation. Rather than allow the past to merely reflect what one's national identity once was, liberal nationalism requires an on-going engagement with the national culture, sustaining it with regular contributions, choices,

---

[117] Achiume, *supra* note 92, at 1516.
[118] KYMLICKA, *supra* note 16, at 327.
[119] DAVID MILLER, ON NATIONALITY 22 (1995).

294 THE RIGHT TO EXCLUDE

and decisions. Fourth, this ongoing and active engagement with a national culture, in which co-nationals believe in a shared history, community, and experience, must be rooted in a territorial location. The nation must have its property, the place it calls home. Finally, the common public culture to which I have been alluding, must be of a certain sort. For Miller, it isn't that this national culture ought to be "based on biological descent, that our fellow-nationals must be our 'kith and kin,' a view that leads directly to racism."[120] And if the base of that national culture needn't be ethnicity, it is neither necessary that it turn on whether aspiring nationals were born on the national territory. Foreigners are welcome.[121]

What, then, is the meaning of this fifth requisite in the search for national identity? Miller explains, "A public culture may be seen as a set of understandings about how a group of people is to conduct its life together."[122] These "understandings" may very well be rather loose: beliefs in democracy and the rule of law, how to queue when waiting for a bus, what language to speak at a given restaurant, the sorts of things that Hall and Bhaba critiqued as unavoidably hybrid. But what Miller is clear about is the idea that while a national public culture is essential for national identity, it isn't necessary for anyone to share the same understandings in the same degree, and indeed, there may be such substantial divergences as to constitute many private subcultures within the broader one. What must exist, however, is enough of an overlap between these subcultures as to constitute a national identity that has boundaries. If the boundaries are unclear, insiders and outsiders are indistinguishable, and if that's the case, national identity remains ambiguous, and if *that's* the case, political community isn't functional. Miller's account of liberal nationalism has certainly proven influential, but the problem of closure is undeniable: if it is necessary to prove the existence of a shared public culture, and if that culture is prohibited—on liberal grounds—from collapsing into an *ethnic* culture, it very quickly becomes rather difficult to understand how the *nation* will be able to set the boundaries for the liberal state.[123] Miller put the question this way: "If we value national allegiances and want them to continue to serve as the basis for political association, what stance should we adopt towards subnational group identities, especially perhaps ethnic identities whose substance may be at odds with the national identity itself?"[124]

Miller's Goldilocks approach to the "liberal" relation between national identity and the claims of outsider ethnicities tracks much of the discussion I've already laid out in this chapter. On the one side, Miller explained, is the view of a "radical multiculturalism."[125] Miller's rendition is close to the views of Young, Kymlicka,

[120] *Id.* at 25.
[121] *Id.* at 26.
[122] *Id.*
[123] Arash Abizadeh, *Does Liberal Democracy Pressupose a Cultural Nation? Four Arguments*, 96 AM. POL. SCI. REV. 495 (2002).
[124] MILLER, *supra* note 119, at 119.
[125] *Id.* at 131.

MULTICULTURALISM, NATIONALISM, PRAGMATISM 295

and Anaya summarized above, in which the state carries the burden of allowing ethnocultures to formulate their own "authentic set of claims and demands, reflecting its particular circumstances."[126] The state must do more than merely respect these claims on an equal basis, but rather promote a politics of difference, subsidizing activities the ethnoculture regards as essential to its identity. "Radical multiculturalism reaches far beyond mutual tolerance and the belief that each person should have equal political opportunities regardless of sex, class, race, etc., to the view that the very purpose of politics is to affirm group difference."[127]

If a multicultural politics of difference naturally leads away from the promotion of a national culture and identity, a conservative ultranationalism pushes in the opposite direction. Miller explained that on this view, national identity requires more than a family of continuities between members, both past and present; it requires a vertical relationship between the community and the sovereign. This vertical relation is authoritative in the sense that the national community must see in the sovereign a father figure, where "junior members" must show "not merely loyalty but piety"—the true marker of patriotism.[128] In this context of conservative nationalism, the "sovereign" needn't be personalized, for it can just as easily manifest in national institutions that deserve the same respect and reverence. These national institutions, perhaps manifested in religion and language, are not merely a reflection of one set of cultural practices among many—they are *the* cultural practices of the nation.[129] Quoting Roger Scruton, Miller explained that on this view, liberals were not "prepared to accept the real price of community: which is sanctity, intolerance, exclusion, and a sense that life's meaning depends on obedience, and also on vigilance against the enemy."[130] Miller notes that this type of conservatism is often chalked up as racism, in just the way many commentators today view Trumpism. This is a mistake, however, if what these conservative nationalists are really worried about is the inclusion of foreigners who lack reverence for cultural manifestations of sovereign authority, precisely because this lack of reverence and allegiance is destabilizing for a common national identity which is functionally necessary for political stability. It isn't racism, necessarily. It may be realism—practical anxieties about national security.

Miller finds both the conservative and multicultural approaches inadequate for a liberal theory of national identity. On the one hand, the conservative approach, Miller argues, is simply misconceived. It fails to appreciate the postmodern commonplace that national identities are social constructions, imagined communities that are in "constant flux."[131] These brute facts of contingency and change suggest

[126] *Id.*
[127] *Id.* at 132.
[128] *Id.* at 124.
[129] *Id.* at 125.
[130] *Id.*
[131] *Id.* at 126.

296   THE RIGHT TO EXCLUDE

that the nation's dominant ethnocultures enjoy no pride of place, and certainly no degree of piety—they participate in the formation of national identities on an equal footing with any other ethnocultural claims. The conservative hostility to immigration is also misconceived, at least to the extent that the rate of migration never reaches a point where it becomes impractical for citizens and new arrivals to find "mutual adjustment."[132] The multiculturalist position, on the other hand, commits a similar type of error. For where the conservative nationalist (mistakenly) characterizes the nation as authoritative and natural, so too does the multiculturalist do the same for ethnocultures. If national identities are imagined communities, Miller argues, cultural groups are just as imaginary.[133] Or if not imaginary in just the same way, certainly they are imagined in conceptually similar ways, where what must be avoided is:

> [T]hinking of the ethnic identities we wish to support as "genuine" or "authentic" in contrast to other identities which are "manufactured" or "imposed" ... What we find, in all cases, is a complicated picture in which the ambitions and interests of particular subgroups jostle with cultural beliefs and values to create identities that are always impure when measured against the hypothetical standard of a group of people sitting down together to think out what it means to them to be Jewish or black.[134]

Multiculturalism not only mistakes one type of identity as "real" and another as "manufactured," rather than seeing them all as socially constructed; it also misconceives the functional necessity of national identity in terms of its psychological role in social integration, and in turn, the role social integration plays in the liberal dispensation of rights and justice.[135]

If both conservative ultranationalism and radical multiculturalism are illconceived in terms of grounding a national identity, Miller's liberal—or what I'm calling here postracial—approach is intended to thread the needle. As mentioned above, Miller does believe in the functional necessity of national identity, and this type of identity must be something more than a "civic" commitment to certain ideals and abstractions. If this were sufficient, Miller concedes, there would be little conflict between the claims of difference coming from ethnocultures, and such a "thin" veneer of national identity. But it's not. What it requires instead is a national identity that is at once "as far as possible from group-specific cultural values," and at the same time, not culturally neutral either. Meaningful national identities will unavoidably bear certain cultural residues, in national languages, forms of education,

---

[132] *Id.* at 128.
[133] *Id.* at 133.
[134] *Id.* at 135.
[135] *Id.* at 139–40.

national myths, and more. But this "common identity" must evolve so it is "accessible to all cultural groups, an identity that is expressed partly through allegiance to a body of principles embedded in the Constitution, but also includes the more concrete ideas of common membership and shared history that are essential to nationality."[136] Ultimately, what Miller was after was a pragmatic give-and-take, where the social construction of national identity morphs as it strips away those cultural elements repugnant to the minority ethnocultures, and where the ethnocultures do the same, divorcing themselves from those features anathema to national identity.[137] The result: a shared national culture at once consistent with liberal democratic ideals and the claims of minority ethnocultures.

In the last analysis what is unavoidable for liberal nationalism is the idea that national identity is necessary for social integration, and that what is core to that national identity is a shared culture that cannot be neutral, no matter how hard it tries. This inability for the cultural core to achieve neutrality is another way of saying that the liberal nation cannot simply be what Anthony Smith termed the "civic nation," a kind of national identity constituted by rational commitments to ideals and practices. The nation must have a shared culture that is itself the product of one particular culture, albeit subject to much alteration. And when we find, having dug down into the nation's shared culture one *particular* culture, if we dig further still we find that at the bottom of the cultural institutions, norms, and practices there is the idea that what *truly* motivates social integration is the *ethnic* basis for that shared, national culture. As Arash Abizadeh has put it, "Behind the cultural nation lurks an ethnos, eager to cover its next of kin with a warm and rather constricting embrace. A constructing embrace."[138] Abizadeh continues:

> [In liberal nationalism] the functionalist argument ... is the following: it is ethnicity, and not the nation per se, that provides motivational power, and the nation can mobilise its citizens only in so far as it draws upon ethnicity. Nations functionally need an ethnic core for social integration. So any nation that lacks an overarching myth of shared descent must emulate shared ethnicity by creating some sort of myth of origin to do the job.[139]

Everything about twenty-first-century liberal nationalism, as was similarly the case for twenty-first-century multiculturalism, is postracial. There is the sense that national identity is both highly inclusive and quiasi-colorblind, as well as deeply attached to norms of antidiscrimination. At the same time, national identity is posited

---

[136] *Id.* at 141–42.

[137] *Id.* at 142–43.

[138] Arash Abizadeh, *On the Demos and Its Kin: Nationalism, Democracy, and the Boundary Problem*, 106 AM. POL. SCI. REV. 867, 873 (2012).

[139] Arash Abizadeh, *Liberal Nationalist Versus Postnational Social Integration: On the Nation's Ethno-Cultural Particularity and Concreteness*, 10 NATIONS & NATIONALISM 231, 237 (2004).

as a cultural identity—where culture is most certainly *not* racial but turns out to be unavoidably ethnic. And perhaps most importantly, for all of the claims for inclusion and colorblindness, postracial nationalism remains what nationalisms have always been—defined by a separation between insiders and outsiders. As is plain in any survey of the news here in the early 2020s, xenophobia isn't simply alive and well. In its postracial life, xenophobia is thriving.

## III THE CRITIQUE OF STRUCTURE: POSTRACIAL PRAGMATISM

As I explained early on, the structuralist approach to racial ideology is semiotic, offering a view of legal thought as a language-system. Let me offer a brief recap. In this book, I have focused on the language-system of liberal legalism, and as I discussed in Chapter 1, the legal context of liberal legal thought begins with a grammar of three master theses. These are (1) the thesis of free competition, (2) the thesis of social control, and (3) the thesis of naturalizing juridical science. If we focus in on the dialects of international law, and burrow deeper into the legal concepts that constitute its lexicon, we find the concepts riddled with tensions between the theses of free competition and social control, as well as the availability of naturalizing juridical science for resolving that tension. Racial ideology is one form of naturalizing juridical science, offering racial subjection as a means for creating cognitive consonance.

In the liberal structure of international legal thought, the thesis of free competition holds that international society is entirely artificial, and that the true supports of the international architecture are sovereign states. These sovereigns are autonomous and rights-bearing, and if international society happens at all, it happens as a result of the exercise of sovereign will. There is no a priori definition of international society that might precede the exercise of sovereign will. It is only through the contest of these sovereign wills that borders come into being, and individual human beings decide to remain domiciled where they are or take their chances in the global migration market. Thus, in the light of this first thesis, we would expect sovereigns to exercise full authority over the question of which persons are allowed to migrate, which are excluded, and what counts as the appropriate characterization of national identity. The extent to which migrants are able to select new residences in this global marketplace of sovereign prerogatives is left to individual abilities to compete and prove their worth as potential citizens/residents. While citizens might potentially exert political influence on the sovereign's decisions regarding its right to exclude, foreign participants in the global migration marketplace remain objects of consumption.

In the liberal structure of international legal thought, the thesis of social control holds that if left unchecked, the thesis of free competition yields an anarchical society. Not only will the thesis of free competition make it ultimately impossible for sovereigns to freely exercise their own wills, the potential goods we expect from competition and cooperation remain unrealized in the absence of meaningful regulation. As a result, the second thesis of social control holds that some form of international police power must exist, defining the proper scope of sovereign right and obligation. International society remains artificial, but if we are to realize the goods we expect from a world in which sovereigns freely exercise their rights, sovereigns must be subject to social control. Thus, in the light of this second thesis, we would expect a legal regime for regulating and protecting the passage of citizens across borders—a legal regime irreducible to the mere exercise of sovereign caprice. In this view, it is unacceptable to leave the question of successful migration entirely in the hands of sovereign choices about which kinds of migrants make "successful" citizens. Nevertheless, migrants in the global marketplace remain objects, not subjects.

There is an ongoing dissonance in the contesting demands of the first two master theses in liberal legal thought—here it is the tension between the sovereign's right to exclude the world from its territory, and the sovereign's duty to yield in favor of certain rules regulating the sovereign's right to exclude. These contrasting theses govern the forms in which legal concepts like property, sovereignty, and migration take shape in their various doctrinal manifestations. What we have thus far, however, is only tension and paradox without consonance and coherence: sovereigns have the authority to exclude all migrants in the name of national identity, and yet, if the rights of sovereigns writ large are to be guaranteed, we need international controls that limit what sovereigns can and cannot do. It is this dissonance between the demands of the first two theses which gives rise to the third thesis in liberal legal thought. This is the harmonizing task of naturalizing juridical science.

The task of naturalizing juridical science is to ensure that the tension between the theses of free competition and social control is resolved harmoniously, objectively, in *law*. The resolution must be "legal," it cannot be merely political, and it cannot be merely moral. That is, the task of naturalizing juridical science is about both law's identity as something other than politics or morality, and law's fidelity to an order that is justifiable in "objective" registers. If naturalizing juridical science fails in its task, the international law of migration fades into raw politics, therefore failing to be law, or consistent with the rule of law, which in liberalism now amounts to the same thing. For example, if the field of international migration law does nothing other than codify the rights of sovereigns to enjoy a plenary power of exclusion in the reserved domain of domestic jurisdiction, we fail in the effort to talk of an international *legal* concept of migration: we have tipped passed the space of law and are just talking about national politics. In the other direction, if the field of international migration law does nothing other than talk of a cosmopolitan human right to migrate across open borders, we have tipped passed the space of law and now seem to be just talking about a free-floating morality. In the

300  THE RIGHT TO EXCLUDE

context of liberal legal thought, what we need to justify the rule of law—migration as a *legal* concept—is naturalizing juridical science.

What is notable about the use of naturalizing juridical science as racial ideology, here in the contemporary context of migration and nation, is precisely how deeply xenophobic and *post*racial this use has turned out to be. Furthermore, naturalizing juridical science as postracial xenophobia not only works to reconcile tensions between the theses of free competition and social control; it also actively works toward its own disguise. In prior chapters, I have detailed two modes of naturalizing juridical science, that of legal formalism and legal functionalism. Furthermore, I have elaborated the ways in which these modes are articulated as racial ideologies in international law, in the classic and modern styles. We are now ready introduce a third mode of naturalizing juridical science, pragmatic liberalism. And as articulated as racial ideology, pragmatic liberalism yields postracial xenophobia. As in the cases of postracial multiculturalism and postracial nationalism, what I have been calling a "quasi-colorblindness" is a key ingredient in the third plank of the postracial—postracial pragmatism.[140] Here, however, it is the neoliberal brand of colorblindness that merits our attention. This is so because, as I discuss below, it was neoliberalism which morphed into a pragmatist sensibility so characteristic of today's postracial ideology.

Wendy Brown has argued that neoliberalism has become something quite other than what its founding architects ever envisioned, and I think she is exactly right—through its various encounters with a reigning postmodernism, neoliberal ideas eventually merged into a pragmatist mindset at once comfortable with neoliberal preferences along with their opposites. Thus, when Brown writes that "Neoliberalism as economic policy, modality of governance, and order of reason is at once a global phenomenon, yet inconsistent, morphing, differentiated, unsystematic, contradictory, and impure,"[141] I take this detection of the "impure" to suggest the appearance of what I defined in *The Jurisprudence of Style* as "Pragmatic Liberalism."[142] As I explored it there, pragmatic liberalism is a structure of legal thought in which the third thesis of naturalizing juridical science has transformed along the lines of a pragmatic shifting between neoformalist and functionalist patterns of justification, sometimes highlighting the necessity of free market ideas, sometimes the effectiveness of the welfare state, but in all cases demonstrating a lack of faith in either the classic or modern structures as any longer affording its agents with a coherent view of the world. Instead, the pragmatic liberal only

---

[140] The following discussion should be understood as separate from questions about the connection between *philosophical* pragmatism and race. *See* Terrance MacMullan, Habits of Whiteness: A Pragmatist Reconstruction (2009).

[141] Wendy Brown, Undoing the Demos: Neoliberalism's Stealth Revolution 48 (2015).

[142] Justin Desautels-Stein, The Jurisprudence of Style: A Structuralist History of American Pragmatism and Liberal Legal Thought (2018).

has faith in the tools, operating in small-scale, trial-by-error, ad hoc problem-by-problem minimalism.

In this chapter, we have already seen how both liberal nationalism and multicultural theory tended to exacerbate the ambiguities of quasi-colorblindness, offering arguments for cultural diversity and integrity that more "realistically" move beyond the fabrications of race and racial identity. And these arguments, whether from the progressive left or the conservative right, tend to either deploy a rights formalism or a capacious functionalism—abstract and principled arguments about the natural justice of their rights claims, or realistically motivated claims about national security, practical problem-solving, and sovereign right. As I see it, on the one side, postracial ideology in the contexts of human rights, multiculturalism, and neoliberalism testify to the catholic terrain of neoformalism. On the other hand, postracial ideology is warm to functionalism as well. And just as neoformalism runs the gamut from left to right, so too does functionalism: Recall that functionalism was the mode of naturalizing juridical science affiliated with *modern* racial ideology, both with its logic of inclusion in the space of *imperium* and eugenicist bordering in the space of *dominium*. In the postracial context, however, functionalism has lost sight of race as an analytical space, abandoning racialism to more primitive times. Indeed, postracial ideology is not only about a turn to culture over race, the rise of a culture of racelessness, and the power of neoformalist rights claims. It is also about a functionalist realism giving rise to varying degrees of xenophobic nationalism.

This dynamic might at first suggest a kind of incoherence or contradiction sitting at the bottom of the postracial mode of naturalizing juridical science. After all, functionalism arose precisely as a means for disciplining the errant ways of the formalist enterprise. If neoformalism in the context of multicultural and neoliberal rights claims now allies itself with a functionalist nationalism, is the result a peculiar form of Hegelian synthesis? I think the better answer is no. Pragmatic liberalism is the mode of naturalizing juridical science that marks the emergence of a juridical hamster wheel, turning from formalism to functionalism and back again. This is the distinctive mode of postracial ideology, a "field of oscillations,"[143] to borrow Stuart Hall's frame for neoliberalism, shifting between formalist and functionalist patterns of argument, without any attempt whatsoever at synthesis or reconciliation. In the context of raciality, the result is not really a *quasi*-colorblindness so much as a *pragmatic* colorblindness,[144] an approach to race and racism that foregrounds ideas like particularity, locality, minimalism, globalism, networks, and trial-by-error problem-solving—much of what we have already seen in international law's cultural turn, discussed above. From this vantage point, while

[143] Stuart Hall, *The Neoliberal Revolution*, 48 SOUNDINGS 9 (2011).
[144] Kimberle Crenshaw, *Twenty Years of Critical Race Theory: Looking Back to Move Forward*, 43 CONN. L. REV. 1253, 1314 (2011).

302   THE RIGHT TO EXCLUDE

the very idea of race had become *passe*, racism was to be studied—if studied at all—in bits and pieces, the smaller the better. Generalized and totalizing visions of racial domination necessarily misunderstood the specific materiality of ethnocultural dominance and subordination, or in the alternative, had entirely missed the boat with respect to the increased flows of goods and services across national boundaries. The pragmatist tendency is precisely to forge ahead, rotating between postracial deployments of formalism and functionalism in a patchwork effort to use what works in whatever contexts. This pragmatic minimalism isn't random, but rather what became of neoliberalism, and what now serves as the final piece in the pie that is international law's ideology of postracial xenophobia.

As I discussed in Chapter 7, neoliberalism is typically framed as an ideology of individualism, economic supremacy, and a view of the rule of law oriented toward property, contract, and the competitive marketplace as the model for social life. In her *Undoing the Demos* from 2015, Wendy Brown argued that neoliberalism was something much more than this, and the concept of "governance" was emblematic of her point. Brown explained that governance—as opposed to government—"signifies a transformation from governing through hierarchically organized command and control—in corporations, states, and nonprofit agencies alike—to governing that is networked, integrated, cooperative, partnered, disseminated, and at least partly self-organized."[145] Governance is focused on tools and techniques for problem-solving, rather than programmatic visions; Governance is collaborative and cooperative, rather than adversarial; Governance is horizontal and transboundary, rather than vertical and authoritarian; Governance is savvy, pragmatic, and context-driven, rather than totalizing and rooted in the past. This mode of exercising power, Brown noted, is not "only or by nature neoliberal, but neoliberalism has both mobilized and increasingly saturated its formulations and development."[146] As I have already suggested, this type of description is precisely what I take to be emblematic of the turn from neoliberalism to pragmatic liberalism.

At its core, the governance mentality of pragmatic liberalism dissolves the line between political and business practice, interchanging the tactics of government with the tactics of managerial expertise, wherever and whenever the need suggests itself. Indeed, the confluence of governing and managing might suggest a deep politicization of governance, in whichever contexts it takes place. The turn to governance from government might, we could say, suggest an enlargement of the political. But the erasure of these traditional borders between public and private forms of authority has moved in the opposite direction—not yielding an expansion of political discourse about the distribution of wealth and resources, about the yawning gaps in global inequality, but rather, its dramatic reduction. Brown observes, in its emphases on the privatization of public industries, the decentering of traditional

[145] BROWN, UNDOING, *supra* note 141.
[146] *Id.* at 122.

MULTICULTURALISM, NATIONALISM, PRAGMATISM    303

modes of authority, "and above all, increasing reliance on partnerships, networks, and novel forms of connection and communication about policy design and delivery,"[147] governance refers to a mode of control that is deeply *depoliticized*, "evacuated of agents and institutionalized in process, norms, and practices."[148]

In her most recent book, *In the Ruins of Neoliberalism*, Brown suggests the orientation I'd like to suggest we take toward neoliberalism, governance, and the problem with the problem-solving approach.[149] It is certainly plausible to characterize problem-solving regimes as going hand-in-glove with neoliberal rationality. But the better view, as Brown intimates, is that in the turn to governance and its ilk, neoliberalism became something else. Brown concedes that neoliberals like Hayek would have been "horrified by the contemporary phenomenon of leaders at once authoritarian and reckless riding to power."[150] Indeed, Brown suggests that although "the constellation of principles, policies, practices, and forms of governing reason that may be gathered under the sign of neoliberalism has importantly constituted the catastrophic present, this was not neoliberalism's intended spawn, but its Frankensteinian creation."[151]

In a similar space, Goldberg has pointed to the neoliberal push for globalization and global governance, and the related commitment to conceptualize raciality as a phenomenon with little place in the hypersophisticated world of transnational networks.[152] Neoliberal colorblindness yielded a culture of racelessness that only came into effect once the logic of inclusion associated with modern racial ideology had run its course. The racelessness of postracial ideology, Goldberg observed, "marks the moment that a society is accepted into (or even as a momentary moral leader of) the world. It marks, in a word, the moment of globalization's relative (and repeated) triumph. To be of the world, in the world, in worldly society, racism nominally has been rejected. Now the category of race must be erased. But we are being asked to give up on race before and without addressing the legacy, the roots, the scars of racisms' histories, the weights of race."[153] Neoliberalism helped push a view of antiracialism—not because of a commitment to white supremacy—but instead because there wasn't any longer a point to arguing about racial supremacy at all. In reaction against the modern emphases on welfare, inclusion, and equality, Goldberg suggests:

---

[147] *Id.* at 125.

[148] *Id.* at 124.

[149] WENDY BROWN, IN THE RUINS OF NEOLIBERALISM: THE RISE OF ANTIDEMOCRATIC POLITICS IN THE WEST (2019).

[150] *Id.* at 9.

[151] *Id.* at 9–10.

[152] DAVID THEO GOLDBERG, THE THREAT OF RACE: REFLECTIONS ON RACIAL NEOLIBERALISM 333 (2008).

[153] *Id.* at 21.

# 304 THE RIGHT TO EXCLUDE

[T]he force(s) of racial order reached for the formalism of the law. In the face of instabilities and insecurities, state recourse in each instance quickly reduced to an insistence upon formal equality ... Formalism "saved" racism in each case by abandoning (or at least threatening to abandon) race ... [This] is racism without race, racism gone private, racism without the categories to name it as such. It is racism shorn of the charge, a racism that cannot be named because nothing abounds with which to name it. It is a racism purged of historical roots, of its groundedness, a racism whose history is lost.[154]

My claim is that what Brown and Goldberg were diagnosing in the dislocations of neoliberal reason was a wrenched shifting of neoliberalism into pragmatic liberalism. An important midwife in this transition, curiously enough, was the parallel intellectual universe we have come to know as postmodernism.[155] I think it unnecessary to launch a full-scale assault here on the concept of the postmodern, and I'm certainly not offering an intellectual history tying together theorists of postmodernism with the architects of the Washington Consensus. My interest is rather in suggesting how much of what thinkers like Brown and Goldberg were witnessing in the warped arena of neoliberal rationality is rather easily identifiable with the currents of postmodernism, and how the result, in the context of legal thought, was postracial pragmatism. To that end, I summarize below five of these postmodern currents.

A first is an argument about temporality, and more specifically, a weighty skepticism about the availability of apodictic stories, "grand," "master," or "meta" narratives, historical explanations and periodizations reaching across space and time. The postmodern suggestion that we worry about meta-explanations is broader than the typical concern about neoliberal narratives as developed by, let's say, a Walt Whitman Rostow.[156] Just as much on the hook is Giovanni Arrighi's leftist story of capitalism; a story of capital and its historical modes of material production as the central drivers in the history of what might be called modernism and the turn to the postmodern, and an idea that seems to posit a fundamental anchor in the center of five hundred years or more of Western history.[157] Like Rostow's manifesto, this is a history of continuities and consistencies, though instead of a history of victories we see a history of exploitation and domination.

---

[154] *Id.* at 23.

[155] In the pages that follow, many readers will wonder at certain absences, among them Jacque Derrida, Jurgen Habermas, Slavoj Zizek, and so many others. These absences are generally strategic, and due to the limits of space more than anything else. For a recent overview, *see* BRIAN McHALE, THE CAMBRIDGE INTRODUCTION TO POSTMODERNISM (2015). *See also* PERRY ANDERSON, THE ORIGINS OF POSTMODERNITY (1999); TERRY EAGLETON, THE ILLUSIONS OF POSTMODERNISM (1996).

[156] W.W. ROSTOW, THE STAGES OF ECONOMIC GROWTH: A NON-COMMUNIST MANIFESTO (1991).

[157] GIOVANNI ARRIGHI, THE LONG TWENTIETH CENTURY: MONEY, POWER, AND THE ORIGINS OF OUR TIMES (2010). *See also* IMMANUEL WALLERSTEIN, HISTORICAL CAPITALISM WITH CAPITALIST CIVILIZATION (2011).

When we encounter deep explanations such as these, we know the postmodern is in the air if we sense that the articulation of a homogenizing grand narrative of capital, whether in its conservative or emancipatory registers, is simply naïve. Where totalizing continuities once were, postmodernism suggests breaks, ruptures, gaps.

A second current concerns the notion of "totality." The "war on totality,"[158] as Fredric Jameson says, is about a number of interrelated anxieties. Chief among them is the work of Friedrich Nietzsche's "knights of totality" and their ostensible production of integrated, coherent, and unified concepts aimed to pass beyond the bounds of immediate experience, tracing the contours of the universal and the true.[159] True, the postmodern assault initially took these Knights to be Marxists, and it was the Marxist usage of totality that came under fire.[160] But liberal totalities are just as vulnerable, and to take a quintessential illustration, postmoderns have worried much about the totality of the autonomous, independent, intentional subject. The suggestion is that we regard the totality of the individual as myth. As Judith Butler has recently put it:

[W]hen we speak about subject formation, we invariably presume a threshold of susceptibility or impressionability that may be said to precede the formation of a conscious and deliberate "I." That means only that this this creature that I am is affected by something outside of itself, understood as prior, that activates and informs the subject that I am. When I make use of the first-person pronoun in this context, I am not exactly telling you about myself.[161]

What we are dealing with here, instead of the so-called sovereign individual, is an infinite play of interpretative possibilities and language games,[162] a schizophrenia of desire rather than a fixed order of the personal.[163]

A third current is hostility towards philosophical realism, flowing over Descartes, Bacon, Locke, Hume, Kant and the analytic tradition, and seeping even into continental modes as well.[164] The problem, in every case, is the problem in laying empirical and/or naturalizing claims about how the world really is. Instead, postmoderns suggest a world of radical indeterminacy, endless heterogeneity and plurality, wanton randomness, multiple multiples, simulacra, copies without originals. As Maurice Merleau-Ponty suggested, in step with the Cartesian tradition was the

---

[158] FREDRIC JAMESON, POSTMODERNISM, OR THE CULTURAL LOGIC OF LATE CAPITALISM 400 (1992).
[159] MARTIN JAY, MARXISM AND TOTALITY: THE ADVENTURES OF A CONCEPT FROM LUKACS TO HABERMAS 12–13 (1986).
[160] Id. at 512–13.
[161] JUDITH BUTLER, SENSES OF THE SUBJECT 1 (2015).
[162] See, e.g., JEAN-FRANCOIS LYOTARD, THE POSTMODERN CONDITION: A REPORT ON KNOWLEDGE 33 (1984).
[163] See, e.g., GILLES DELEUZE & FELIX GUATTARI, ANTI-OEDIPUS: CAPITALISM AND SCHIZOPHRENIA (2009).
[164] See, e.g., RICHARD RORTY, PHILOSOPHY AND THE MIRROR OF NATURE (1981).

306    THE RIGHT TO EXCLUDE

fantasy of "Objective Thought," which in its various ways "build[s] up all knowledge out of determinate qualities, offers us objects purged of all ambiguity, pure and absolute, the ideal rather than the real themes of knowledge."[165] This purging and the belief in the freestanding object was "based on the foreshadowing of an imminent order which is about to spring upon us a reply to questions merely latent in the landscape."[166] But Objective Thought was mistaken in its presentation of a world awaiting rational analysis, a world kept distant from the perceiving subject. To move away from this representational view of knowledge, and enter the chiasm of consciousness in world and world in consciousness, was therefore to accept "the indeterminate as a positive phenomenon."[167] Standing against this understanding of an empirical pursuit of an objective world was therefore a prioritization of experience with radical indeterminacy. "The world," said Merleau-Ponty, "does not hold for us a set of outlines which some consciousness within us binds together into a unity."[168]

Fourth, we should see the world as endlessly dedifferentiated, its boundaries with economics, culture, politics, and nature as ultimately indiscernible. And the idea here, as Bruno Latour has explained, is really something more than the argument that the borders are messy and bleeding. It is rather that there are no borders, and the world is in fact a matrix of networks. For the agent-network theory (AT) associated with science and technology studies:

> [M]odern societies cannot be described without recognizing them as having a fibrous, thread-like, wiry, stringy, ropy, capillary character that is never captured by the notions of levels, layers, territories, spheres, categories, structure, systems. It aims at explaining the effects accounted for by those traditional words without having to buy the ontology, topology and politics that goes with them. AT has been developed by students of science and technology and their claim is that it is utterly impossible to understand what holds the society together without reinjecting in its fabric the facts manufactured by natural and social sciences and the artefacts designed by engineers. As a second approximation, AT is thus the claim that the only way to achieve this reinjection of the things into our understanding of the social fabrics is through a network-like ontology and social theory.[169]

If postmodern concerns about the erosion of disciplinary boundaries and a relentless free play between the so-called sphere of the natural and the social is right,

---

[165] MAURICE MERLEAU-PONTY, PHENOMENOLOGY OF PERCEPTION 11 (1962).
[166] *Id.* at 17.
[167] *Id.* at 320.
[168] *Id.* at 328–29.
[169] Bruno Latour, *On Actor-Network Theory: A Few Clarifications Plus More than a Few Complications*, 25 SOZIALE WELT 369, 372 (1996).

MULTICULTURALISM, NATIONALISM, PRAGMATISM    307

Latour has suggested that the implications are all for the good. The modern pro-clivity for separating out the human world of culture from the nonhuman world of nature never *really* took place, and at least one sort of "postmodernism" assists in getting at this final, porous, truth.[170] As Latour has explained:

> Our intellectual life is out of kilter. Epistemology, the social sciences, the science of texts—all have their privileged vantage point, provided they remain separate. If the creatures [i.e., hybrids] we are pursuing cross all three spaces, we are no longer understood. Offer the established disciplines some fine sociotechnical network, some lovely translations, and the first group will extract our concepts and pull out the roots that might connect them to society or to rhetoric; the second group will erase social and political dimensions, and purify our network of any object; the third group, finally, will retain our discourse and rhetoric but purge our work of any undue adherence to reality—*horresco referens*—or to power plays ... That a delicate shuttle should have woven together the heavens, industry, texts, souls, and moral law—this remains uncanny, unthinkable, unseemly.[171]

A fifth current in the postmodern milieu is what Jameson called pastiche.[172] A spectacle with its emergence in the US of the 1970s,[173] and to blend the terms of Guy Debord and Perry Anderson, postmodern pastiche reflects a neolib-eral society in which its every pore been saturated "in the serum of capital."[174] Postmodern pastiche offers up a "new kind of flatlessness or depthlessness, a new kind of superficiality in the most literal sense, perhaps the supreme formal feature of all the postmodernisms."[175] For Jameson, this surface sensibility is a byproduct of postmodern anxiety, a situation in which we are forever divorced from every-thing with depth: history, individuality, reality.[176] Pastiche, as a result, involves a blank and blind "imitation of dead styles, speech through all the masks and voices stored up in the imaginary museum of a now global culture."[177] It is a practice, once more, "which randomly and without principle but with gusto cannibalizes ... styles of the past and combines them in overstimulating ensembles."[178] Hall adds, and which could easily be attributed to neoliberalism just as well: "What [postmod-ernism] says is: this is the end of the world. History stops with us and there is no place to go after this. But whenever it is said that *this* is the last thing that will ever

---

[170] For a recent take, *see* BRUNO LATOUR, AN INQUIRY INTO MODES OF EXISTENCE: AN ANTHROPOLOGY OF THE MODERNS (2013).

[171] BRUNO LATOUR, WE HAVE NEVER BEEN MODERN 5 (1993).

[172] JAMESON, *supra* note 158, at 9.

[173] ANDERSON, *supra* note 155, at 84–85.

[174] *Id.* at 55.

[175] JAMESON, *supra* note 158, at 9.

[176] *Id.* at 185, 250.

[177] *Id.* at 18.

[178] *Id.* at 19.

308   THE RIGHT TO EXCLUDE

happen in history, that is the sign of the functioning, in the narrow sense, of the ideological."[179]

These five currents in the movement of what came to be called postmodernism—the critique of grand historical narrative, the critique of the totalizing concept, the argument for indeterminacy, the claim for networks, and the claim for pastiche—demonstrate some readily discernable synergies with what Brown and Goldberg have recently identified in the "ruins" of neoliberalism. Neoliberalism became another sort of liberalism, precisely as it was funneled through an increasingly prevalent postmodern sieve. As Brown observes, we have journeyed beyond the space of neoliberal rationality, but to where? Contemporary thought conjoins:

> [F]amiliar elements of neoliberalism (licensing capital, leashing labor, demonizing the social state and the political, attacking equality, promulgating freedom) with their seeming opposites (nationalism, enforcement of traditional morality, populist antielitism, and demands for state solutions to economic and social problems). They conjoin moral righteousness with nearly celebratory amoral and uncivil conduct. They endorse authority while featuring unprecedented public social disinhibition and aggression. They rage against relativism, but also against science and reason, and spurn evidence-based claims, rational argumentation, credibility, and accountability. They disdain politicians and politics while evincing a ferocious will to power and political ambition. Where are we?[180]

In the land of postracial pragmatism, that's where.[181] Goldberg put his finger on it when he argued that it was only in the waning hours of what I have been calling modern racial ideology—those moments in which human rights minimalism, neoliberalism, and postmodernism were coming to the surface—that the broad effort to get past race, to get beyond it, to get after it, to go *postracial*, was really coming into its own. An ethos of anti*racism* was replaced with an ethos of anti*racialism*, where what was more important than identifying global structures of racial domination, subjection, and exclusion, was being against race itself. And however inadvertently, neoliberalism, human rights discourse, and postmodernism were all saying the same thing, albeit in different registers. Goldberg wrote:

---

[179] STUART HALL, ESSENTIAL ESSAYS, VOLUME 1: FOUNDATIONS OF CULTURAL STUDIES 226 (David Morley ed., 2019)

[180] BROWN, RUINS, *supra* note 149, at 2.

[181] "If neoliberalism is conceived only as a political rationality featuring the ubiquity of markets and *homo oeconomicus* ... we cannot grasp the affective investments in privileges of whiteness and First World existence in the nation and national culture or in traditional morality. We also cannot grasp the ways that the hierarchies and exclusions of 'tradition' legitimately challenged democratic equality in the name of both family values and freedom. This means that we cannot grasp the new formations of subjectivity and politics that are, in good part, neoliberal effects. At the same time, we cannot grasp what the forces are that neoliberalism accidentally intersects or instigates and this what its produces inadvertently and even against its own aims." *Id.* at 182.

## MULTICULTURALISM, NATIONALISM, PRAGMATISM    309

I am suggesting that in the wake of whatever nominal success, antiracist struggle gave way in each instance to antiracial commitments at the expense of antiracist effects and ongoing struggle ... Antiracism requires historical memory, recalling the conditions of racial degradation and relating contemporary to historical and local to global conditions. If antiracist commitment requires remembering and recalling, antiracialism suggests forgetting, getting over, moving on, wiping away the terms of reference, at best (or worst) a commercial memorializing rather than a recounting and redressing of the terms of humiliation and devaluation. Indeed, antiracialism seeks to wipe out the terms of reference, to wipe away the every vocabulary necessary to recall and recollect, to make a case, to make a claim.[182]

What Goldberg was here calling antiracialism in 2008, he later dubbed the postracial in 2015. What, however, makes this postracial attitude necessarily pragmatic? Certainly in the context of legal thought, the transformation of neoliberalism through postmodernism couldn't come along without some marching orders for jurists. After all, it is one thing for social theorists to delight in the free play of hybrids, networks, and the end of objective thought. It is another for judges and regulators. In the legal context, neoliberalism morphed into pragmatic liberalism as it settled into an "everyday" pragmatist sensibility that was entirely hospitable toward the hodgepodge of techniques that had preceded it. Pragmatic liberalism was, as a structure of legal thought, pastiche. And to repeat from Jameson, we can think of pragmatic liberalism as a structure of legal thought as the "imitation of dead styles, speech through all the masks and voices stored up in the imaginary museum of a now global culture," a style of legal argument "which randomly and without principle but with gusto cannibalizes . . styles of the past and combines them in overstimulating ensembles."[183]

Indeed, by the first decades of the twenty-first century, the main faith traditions that had kept the candle burning for either formalism or functionalism as "truly" believable techniques for the production of legally necessitated outcomes, had largely petered out. What remained as the mainstream view was not, however, a wholesale effort to replace these modes of naturalizing juridical science with a completely new legal style. Rather, the dominant ethos became a status quo complacency, content with the use of small-scale, trial-and-error, serial borrowing. Use a bit of functionalism here, some formalism there, whatever might work in the effort to solve this problem, here and now. Anything grander, anything more totalizing, anything more objective, anything more *structural*, was a fool's errand. At the same time, what counted as a problem, what counted as a benchmark, what counted as good governance—everything that counted at all—was measured in terms of return on investment, in terms of a market lexicon for effective outcomes.

---

[182] GOLDBERG, THREAT, *supra* note 152, at 21.
[183] JAMESON, *supra* note 158, at 19.

310    THE RIGHT TO EXCLUDE

This, at any rate, is a glimpse of the type of postmodern pragmatism that entered liberal legal thought by the end of the twentieth century. This pragmatist style is notable for its ideological emphasis on doing "what works" with the available resources, and in the context of liberal legalism, this suggests an open attitude toward various manifestations and combinations of formalist and functionalist arguments alike. It is a legal pastiche that, in the context of raciality, explains what, in 2011, Kimberle Crenshaw had already labeled postracial pragmatism.[184] In its nebulous and ever-oscillating character, postracial pragmatism, Crenshaw explained:

> [J]ettisons the liberal ambivalence about race consciousness to embrace a colorblind stance even as it foregrounds and celebrates the achievement of particular racial outcomes. In the new post-racial moment, the pragmatist may be agnostic about the conservative erasure of race as a contemporary phenomenon but may still march under the same premise that significant progress can be made without race consciousness. This realignment brings liberals and some civil rights activists on board so that a variety of individuals and groups who may have been staunch opponents of colorblindness can be loosely allied in post-racialism.[185]

Crenshaw emphasized the case of Barack Obama's election as highly illustrative. When viewed in the light of US racism over the centuries, the appointment of a Black man to the nation's most powerful position was epoch-making. And the reason, of course, for the ubiquity of this language was precisely that the racial identity of the President of the US mattered a great deal. And yet, what so many took Obama's election to mean was that the President's racial identity didn't actually matter at all, that "the chapter on race could at last be closed."[186] What did matter was that Americans had enough race consciousness to understand that the history of racism was over, because a Black man had been elected President. As Crenshaw put it, "contrary to the thrust of colorblind proscriptions against noticing race, Obama's blackness was harnessed to prove that the remaining markers of racial subordination ... are no longer indicators of exclusion but merely opportunities yet to be realized by individuals disinclined to take advantage of them."[187] As for Obama's own approach, as opposed to how racial conservatives tended to situate his success, the Obama campaign's insistent avoidance of race-talk "masked an intensely race-conscious campaign to counter his racial deficit where necessary and to bolster his racial capital where advantageous. This was anything but an avoidance of race; it was, instead, a direct encounter with it."[188] The counterintuitive upshot of the Obama example is well described by Michael Tesler, in that the

---

[184] Crenshaw, *Twenty Years, supra* note 144, at 1314.
[185] *Id.*
[186] *Id.* at 1318.
[187] *Id.*
[188] *Id.* at 1319.

"post-racial" becomes the "most-racial,"[189] and as Crenshaw noted, "post-racial defined in terms of the Obama campaign cannot be taken to mean 'beyond race' or even colorblind, but instead, to symbolize a particular kind of approach toward dominant racial sensibilities."[190]

Crenshaw's point, however, was not that postracial pragmatism somehow displaced colorblindness. It is, as I have been suggesting, that from within the new frame of postraciality, colorblindness transformed. The concept of colorblindness began its career as a radical plank in the emerging architecture of modern racial ideology, and by the 1970s, a colorblind approach to racial integration was well on its way into the mainstream. This functionalist brand of colorblindness—forgetting about race in the program for social transformation—was coopted by the right, merging into a neoformalist and neoliberal colorblindness made famous by the US Supreme Court. Despite the ways in which multiculturalism additionally assisted in the displacement of race consciousness, neoliberal colorblindness—like the larger enterprise of neoliberalism itself—was losing ideological dominance, largely because the center-left had never gotten on board. The advent of postracialism, Crenshaw suggests, was exactly what the colorblind doctor ordered:

> One might characterize colorblindness as a reasonably popular act that played well to specialized audiences, but one that never enjoyed the bandwidth of a truly crossover phenomenon. Today's post-racialism brings rock star marketability to colorblindness's legitimizing project, rebranding it with an internationally recognized symbol attached to its conservative rhetorical content. While the celebratory dimension of the "Obama phenomenon" pulls countless people into its orbit, the colorblind rhetoric of racial denial strips ongoing efforts to name and contest racial power of both legitimacy and audience. The still emerging elements of post-racial rhetoric appear to be both grounded in and extensions of colorblindness... While colorblindness declared racism as a closed chapter in our history, post-racialism now provides reassurance to those who weren't fully convinced that this history had ceased to cast its long shadow over contemporary affairs. Post-racialism offers a gentler escape, an appeal to the possibility that racial power can be side-stepped, finessed and ultimately overcome by regarding dominance as merely circumstance that need not get in the way of social progress.[191]

While I have characterized postracial pragmatism as a discrete element in the makeup of the ideology of postracial xenophobia, I have also tried to weave its effects throughout the entirety of this chapter. It is true that postracial multiculturalism

---

[189] Michael Tesler, Post-Racial or Most-Racial? Race and Politics in the Obama Era (2016).
[190] Crenshaw, Twenty Years, supra note 144, at 1320.
[191] Id. at 1326–27.

312   THE RIGHT TO EXCLUDE

drinks heartily at the well of neoformalist practice. Its deployment of the right of self-determination is thoroughly individualized, much more an adjunct to the antidiscrimination principle than an anticolonial war machine. At the same time, indigenous rights scholarship tends to display much of the postracial pragmatist mindset, from the focus on minimalism and localism to the blurring of cultural boundaries and apologies for cultural integrity that at once demand and deny the necessity of insider/outsider regimes. When we hear claims that cultures are complex networks of human interdependence and, at the same time, that they are as plain as the nose on your face, it's a good bet that we've stumbled into the topsy-turvy world of postracial pragmatism. A similar story attends the rise of postracial nationalism. Functionalism surely justifies much of the current discourse on national identity, both in international law and in political theory. There is also more than just a splash of pragmatism in the rise of nationalist xenophobia, both in its racial (Trumpian) and postracial forms. When Martin argues for a realistic approach to sovereign rights to exclude intended to harmonize conflicts between the demands for free competition and social control, or when Miller expects an iterative process of give-and-take between national cultures and the demands of "sub-national" groups, left behind are both the classic forms of racial xenophobia and the modern logics of inclusion. We have arrived instead in the neoliberal-cum-pragmatist world of minimalist postracialism.

# 9
# On the Inevitability of Racial Borders

In the context of liberal legalism, the ideology of racial xenophobia is a mode of naturalizing juridical science in which patterns of argument moving through the indeterminacy of a conceptual lexicon produce relations of racial subjection, exclusion, and discrimination, on account of a naturalized foreignness. As discussed in Chapter 8, the ideology of postracial xenophobia relies upon patterns of argument that include antiracialism, the priority of ethnocultural difference, the reproduction of xenophobic discourse, pragmatism, and antistructural minimalism. This is particularly the case in the context of the contemporary situation for international human rights and self-determination, and more specifically, the evaporation of race and racism from the general terrain of international legal thought. The discussion began with the emergence of the "politics of recognition," a phrase made famous by scholars like Nancy Fraser, Iris Marion Young, and Charles Taylor. In this multiculturalist milieu, it became increasingly common to talk of the rights of cultures and ethnic groups to autonomy and integrity—rights to language, to religion, to education, the rights that defined the boundaries of who they were, as against what something else was. More often than not, that "something else" was a culturally oppressive state apparatus, and the claim here was for rights of autonomy (exclusion) against that state-sponsored culture. In international law, multiculturalism had its clearest analogue in the movement for the rights of Indigenous Peoples that had been gaining steam in the twentieth century's last decades, and culminated in the United Nations Declaration on the Rights of Indigenous Peoples (2007). For all of its strengths, and as much as the rights of Indigenous Peoples and minority cultures have been so terribly neglected through the sequestered state of settler colonialism in United Nations (UN) practice, the movement for indigenous rights was largely coopted by a phase of international human rights law that had become thoroughly postracial. That is, by the first decades of the twenty-first century, human rights law was in the grip of a colorblind antidiscrimination principle which worked to not only erase race as a structural problematic for international law and reduce racism to low-level instances of personal prejudice—it also foregrounded the idea that a human right to ethnocultural diversity (including a right to exclude) was what the right of self-determination had become.

If from the one side a postracial multiculturalism was offering a colorblind and neoformalist argument for the right to exclude, from the other there came a postracial nationalism. In contrast with the popularity of rights claims on the multicultural side, however, postracial nationalism is typically more functionalist in orientation.

*The Right to Exclude*. Justin Desautels-Stein, Oxford University Press. © Justin Desautels-Stein 2023.
DOI: 10.1093/oso/9780198862161.003.0010

314   THE RIGHT TO EXCLUDE

To be sure, postracial nationalism bottoms out in a defense of the sovereign's *right* to secure its boundaries and exclude the world from its cultural frontiers. But the argument here is functionalist in the sense that the sovereign necessity to produce and protect a national identity is a prerequisite for the sort of social integration conducive to a properly functioning liberal democracy. Thus, just as the focus was on multiculturalism's grounding in liberal theory, so too is this brand of nationalism, what thinkers like David Miller have called "liberal nationalism." The content of liberal nationalist theory, which does much in terms of supporting the current posture of international legal arguments for the sovereign's continued right to unilaterally secure its borders, has nothing to say of race. Liberal nationalism instead speak of national identity as a national "culture," race talk at all costs, explaining national identity instead as a national "culture," a culture that "must be defended" against and defined by its differences with other, national cultures. Without cultural foreignness as a "constitutive outside," without a *xenos*, liberal democracy fails.

Chapter 8 concluded by situating postracial multiculturalism and postracial nationalism in the argumentative context of what I have elsewhere defined as "pragmatic liberalism."[1] As legal ideology in the space of argumentative practice, pragmatic liberalism encourages precisely the kind of oscillation we see between neoformalism and functionalism in the debates over multiculturalism and nationalism. It isn't that functionalism is thesis to the antithesis of neoformalism, yielding a synthesis in legal pragmatism. It is rather that, having lost faith in either the functionalist or neoformalist imaginaries as capable of securing that "harmonious display of essences," pragmatism instead counsels in favor of small steps, ad hoc problem-solving, and the use of liberalism's old harmonies wherever and whenever it makes practical sense to use them. Furthermore, legal pragmatism reflects the strange fruit borne out of the intellectual congress between neoliberalism and postmodernism. The result was not only a default preference for networked pastiche—it was a general hostility toward structural analysis and programmatic perspectives that might violate the ethos of the minimalist, grassroots priority of local experience.

In most respects, this discussion of postracial xenophobia has been limited to the plane of the sovereign's right of *dominium*. In these final pages I conclude with a return to the sovereign's *imperial* right to exclude, but here in the context of postracial xenophobia. What, that is, of postracial *imperium*? Was the lapse of the New International Economic Order (NIEO) project the last word, as *imperium* bore witness to a final surrender of racial development to the Washington Consensus? How should we characterize the sovereign's right of *imperium* in international law's current structure of postracial xenophobia, and perhaps more importantly, what might it become? In the discussion that follows, I continue from where the

---

[1] Justin Desautels-Stein, The Jurisprudence of Style: A Structuralist History of American Pragmatism and Liberal Legal Thought (2018).

narrative left off in Chapter 8, in the transition from neoliberalism to pragmatic liberalism, but push forward into the contexts of globalization and global governance. After a brief survey, I turn to the common complaint about democratic deficits and the erosion of sovereign right. My argument is that these complaints are generally unresponsive to the foundational problem of the right of *imperium* and, in particular, what we can call international law's boundary problem.

It is a commonplace to assume that in order for democracy to be viable, it must be attached to a discrete community. Democracy depends, that is, on insiders and outsiders—in order for there to be a "we" there must also be a "them." As explored below, however, liberal defenses of nationalism and multiculturalism of the sort offered by David Miller and Will Kymlicka tend to collapse into demands for ethnic cores. At the end of the day, these theories delineate a "we" and a "them" as *ethnoi*, and what lies beneath the façade of the *ethnos* is race. The argument for the necessity of bounding the *demos*, it turns out, is an argument for racial borders. It isn't that nationalism or multiculturalism or liberal democracy are intrinsically committed to the constitution of a racial *xenos*. It is rather that, in this liberal register, the act of *boundary-making* is racial.[2]

The chapter concludes with a suggestion that, if the imposition of racial borders appears unavoidable, it is only because of our deep dependencies on the apparatus of naturalizing juridical science in liberal legal thought—and our sense that for however unfortunate these boundaries might be, they are *realistic*. A potential antidote here is a body of literature that has been relatively secluded from international legal theory, and that has informed much of the entirety of this book: the critical race tradition. Postracial xenophobia's production of an unavoidable realism, as well as its domestication of global antiracist strategy, is a victory for international law's racial ideology, and in particular, its see-saw logic of inclusion/exclusion. It is a victory over a great many things, and a great many people, including the formerly colonized, migrants, national minorities, indigenous communities, and every other type of racial *xenos* leveraged in the ideological fulcrum. It has also been a victory over and against the rise of the critical race tradition in international law. More than a hundred years ago, and beginning with W.E.B. Du Bois' theory of double consciousness, and moving through engagements with the likes of C.L.R. James and George Padmore, the critical race tradition produced a global view of raciality that was deeply intertwined with problems of colonial and neocolonial domination and subjection, and above all, understood this global context as a structural one. And yet it remains nearly unheard of in international legal thought, crowded out first by modern racial ideology's emphases on international institutions and self-determination, inclusion and exclusion, and later, through postracial ideology's focus on human

---

[2] For a terrific analysis of the problem, *see* E. Tendayi Achiume, *Racial Borders*, 110 Geo. L.J. 445 (2022).

316  THE RIGHT TO EXCLUDE

rights, antidiscrimination, and cultural diversity. To be sure, there were glimpses of the critical race approach to international law at the Universal Races Congress, at the Pan-African Congresses, at Bandung, in Fanon, in Cabral, in James and Padmore, in Robinson and Silva, and more recently, and more explicitly, in the pathbreaking work of scholars like Tendayi Achiume, Joel Modiri, Natsu Taylor Saito, and Chantal Thomas. The question moving forward is, what's next?

## I GLOBAL GOVERNANCE AND DEMOCRATIC DEFICITS

This book's overarching premise concerns the role of the sovereign's right to exclude in the maintenance and propagation of international law's many structures of racial ideology. But what if sovereignty has now lapsed? Or if it is merely a fiction? Indeed, a characteristic trend of the late twentieth century was the prediction of sovereignty's demise.[3] The idea wasn't so much that sovereignty was fictitious— it was rather that, as a result of social transformations the world over, sovereignty just wasn't what it used to be. This argument about sovereign erosion was most common in discussions of globalization, or what scholars like Anne-Marie Slaughter called the "New World Order." A first notion in this setting was the escalation of globalism, which Robert Keohane and Joseph Nye defined as networks of connections operating at multicontinental distances.[4] These networks were varied, ranging in their military, environmental, economic, and sociocultural dimensions, and while the existence of these global connections was ancient, the globalizing trend in terms of intensity and extensity was new. From the global economy to the spread of climate and health challenges to McWorld,[5] the connective tissue of the global order had congealed in such a way that "small events in one place can have catalytic effects, so that their consequences later and elsewhere are vast."[6]

A second and related idea with globalism was governance. "By governance," Keohane and Nye explained, "we mean the process and institutions, both formal and informal, that guide and restrain the collective activities of a group."[7] These formal and informal processes and institutions were multilayered and resulted in the diffusion of political authority across borders and between various types of actors. Governance, unlike government with its authority to obligate, happens

---

[3] SUSAN STRANGE, THE RETREAT OF THE STATE (1996); RICHARD FALK, PREDATORY GLOBALIZATION: A CRITIQUE (1999); Louis Henkin, *That S Word: Sovereignty, Globalization, and Human Rights, etc*, 68 FORDHAM L. REV. 1 (1999); Harold Koh, *Why Do Nations Obey International Law?* 106 YALE L.J. 2599, 2630 (1997).

[4] Joseph Nye & Robert Keohane, *Introduction, in* GOVERNANCE IN A GLOBALIZING WORLD 2 (Joseph Nye & John Donahue eds., 2000).

[5] BENJAMIN BARBER, JIHAD VS. MCWORLD: HOW GLOBALISM AND TRIBALISM ARE RESHAPING THE WORLD (1995).

[6] Nye & Keohane, *supra* note 4, at 11.

[7] *Id.* at 12.

within and beyond state boundaries, and operates at subnational, national, and supranational levels. What's more, it isn't merely the actors that have multiplied, supplementing formal government with governance by the private sector, transnational nongovernmental organizations, and private individuals. The means of governance were different as well, through the multiplication of norms, markets, and architectures. Keohane and Nye, citing Lawrence Lessig, suggested the arrival of an "Internet world in which governance is shifting from law made by governments to architecture created by companies. 'Effective regulation then shifts from lawmakers to code writers.' At the same time, private firms press governments for favorable legal regimes domestically and internationally, as do actors from the third sector. The result is not obsolescence of the nation-state but its transformation and the creation of politics in new contested spaces."[8] The key to a properly balanced system of global governance—"networked minimalism" is what they called it—was the identification of a "set of practices for governance that improve coordination and create safety valves for political and social pressures, consistent with the maintenance of nation-states as the fundamental form of political organization. Such arrangements will, we argue, involve a heterogenous array of agents— from the private sector and the third sector as well as from governments ... The efficacy of these agents will depend on the networks in which they are embedded and their positions in those networks. And no hierarchy is likely to be acceptable or effective in governing networks."[9]

If globalism and globalization were genuinely impactful phenomena, and if these new social forces had called forth a new type of means for their governance, one question among many was about how to make global governance legitimate in terms of democratic accountability. This is what Slaughter called the "governance trilemma: we need global rules without centralized power but with government actors who can be held to account through a variety of political mechanisms."[10] Slaughter agreed with Keohane and Nye that the solution could be found in the transnational space of networked governance, though rather than emphasize the efficacy of public-private hybrids, Slaughter preferred the transgovernmental network. She argued that "government networks can help address the governance trilemma, offering a flexible and relatively fast way to conduct the business of global governance, coordinating and even harmonizing national government action while initiating and monitoring different solutions to global problems. Yet they are decentralized and dispersed, incapable of exercising centralized coercive authority."[11] The arrival of networked governance, Slaughter explained, signaled an important development in international law: the fiction of the domestic analogy

---

[8] *Id.* at 12–13.
[9] *Id.* at 14.
[10] ANNE-MARIE SLAUGHTER, A NEW WORLD ORDER 10 (2004).
[11] *Id.* at 11.

318   THE RIGHT TO EXCLUDE

and its attendant view of a unitary sovereign had outlived its usefulness. Sovereign states did not act on the international stage with rights and interests, but rather acted as bits and pieces, agencies, bureaus, departments, courts, and individuals. The state had become "disaggregated, parceled into a system of global governance that institutionalizes cooperation and sufficiently contains conflict such that all nations and their peoples may achieve greater peace and prosperity, improve their stewardship of the earth, and reach minimum standards of human dignity."[12]

Parallel responses to the governance dilemma, or trilemma or whatever, have been many. There is the popular proposal to see the new international legal order less as a system of networks and more in the light of administrative law, as popularized by scholars like Benedict Kingsbury.[13] There is Paul Schiff Berman's effort to conceptualize global governance as "global legal pluralism,"[14] there are neofunctionalist theories of "international constitutionalization,"[15] there are arguments for "cosmopolitan democracy,"[16] and much more. In any case, Martti Koskenniemi has suggested that "being 'contemporary' today is precisely to engage with the jargon of 'globalization' and 'governance' that imagines a sovereign-independent, neutral system of managerial techniques through which 'development' and 'welfare' are brought to the world."[17] This "neutral" and "natural" system of problem-solving, Koskenniemi observed, spanned the entire range of international law's fragmented surface. Managerial technique had, in this context of global governance, become the model for everything from the public to the private and everything in between. "Human rights are a global governance tool, on a par with investment arbitration or scrutiny of market distortions in a WTO panel. They make contestable choices about matters on which domestic political audiences disagree. As with governance generally, the point often turns into one of jurisdiction—who should decide?"[18]

Who should decide, or perhaps better, who *can* decide? Questions such as these often lead into what is commonly called the problem of globalization's democratic deficits.[19] In a word, the worry was (and remains) that decision-makers in the networked minimalism of global governance are unaccountable, or at least, they are unaccountable along the traditional measures, that their decisions are

---

[12] *Id.* at 15.

[13] Benedict Kingsbury et al., *The Emergence of Global Administrative Law*, 68 LAW & CONTEMP. PROBS. 5 (2005).

[14] THE OXFORD HANDBOOK OF GLOBAL LEGAL PLURALISM (Paul Schiff Berman ed., 2020).

[15] *See, e.g.,* RULING THE WORLD? CONSTITUTIONALISM, INTERNATIONAL LAW, AND GLOBAL GOVERNANCE (Jeffrey Dunoff & Joel Trachtman eds., 2009).

[16] David Held, *Cosmopolitan Democracy and the Global Order: Reflections on the 200th Anniversary of Kant's Perpetual Peace*, 20 ALTERNATIVES 415 (1995).

[17] Martti Koskenniemi, *International Law as "Global Governance,"* in SEARCHING FOR CONTEMPORARY LEGAL THOUGHT 201 (Justin Desautels-Stein & Christopher Tomlins eds., 2017).

[18] *Id.* at 214.

[19] Eric Stein, *International Integration and Democracy: No Love at First Sight*, 95 AM. J. INT'L L. 489 (2001).

opaque and that electorates have no say. Notably, these concerns about globalization and its effects on democracy were politically plural. In 2001, Richard Falk and Andrew Strauss pointed to the lack of citizen participation in global institutions and transnational modes of governance as the key problematic that had become known as globalization. Their solution was the establishment of "some type of popularly elected global body," what they termed a "Global Parliament."[20] On the other side of the spectrum, and writing a year earlier, when he was Assistant Secretary of State, John Bolton claimed that in the confrontation with the effects of global governance, the "Americanist party has awakened," and warned of "the harm and costs to the United States of belittling our popular sovereignty and constitutionalism."[21] Somewhere between or hovering over these diverging pleas for global democracy and to Make America Great Again was the popular unrest boiling over in protests against global financial institutions, such as the famed "Battle for Seattle."[22]

As I hope is clear, scholars like Keohane, Nye, Slaughter, and others were describing the paradigm that, in Chapter 8, I called pragmatic liberalism. From its focus on problem-solving, to governance over government, to networks, to blurred boundaries, to minimalism, to private-public partnerships more private than public, the diagnosis of late twentieth-century international theory, and the general prescriptions, all indicate the transition from neoliberalism to pragmatic liberalism. It is in this sense that Wendy Brown has argued that the governance model's threat to democracy has moved beyond questions about *who* decides. Pragmatic liberalism's problem-solving approach to governance makes it difficult to know why anyone would even *want* to decide anything. The accountability demanded by cosmopolitan writers, Brown argued, only does so much in the context of a deliberative terrain that has been so relentlessly depoliticized. And for Brown, this is the real trouble, for it isn't at all that there has been a proliferation of the political, out there and in reach, as Keohane, Nye, and others were suggesting in the century's early years. It is rather that, in the ideological space of pragmatic liberalism, "governance fundamentally reconceptualizes democracy as distinct or divorced from politics and economics: democracy becomes purely procedural and is detached from the powers that would give it substance and meaning as a form of rule."[23] Brown continues:

> It is a short step from this reorientation of democracy into problem solving and consensus to a set of additional replacements fundamental to the meaning and operation of governance today: "stakeholders" replace interest groups or classes,

---

[20] Richard Falk & Andrew Strauss, *Toward Global Parliament*, 80 FOREIGN AFF. 212 (2001); RICHARD FALK & ANDREW STRAUSS, A GLOBAL PARLIAMENT: ESSAYS AND ARTICLES (2011).

[21] John Bolton, *Should We Take Global Governance Seriously?* 1 U. CHI. J. INT'L L. 205, 206 (2000).

[22] David Sanger, *The Shipwreck in Seattle*, N.Y. TIMES (Dec. 5, 1999).

[23] WENDY BROWN, IN THE RUINS OF NEOLIBERALISM: THE RISE OF ANTIDEMOCRATIC POLITICS IN THE WEST 128 (2019).

320  THE RIGHT TO EXCLUDE

"guidelines" replace law, "facilitation" replaces regulation, "standards" and "codes of conduct" disseminated by a range of agencies and institutions replace overt policing and other forms of coercion. Together, these replacements also vanquish a vocabulary of power, and hence power's visibility, from the lives and venues that governance organizes and directs.[24]

Democracy defined as inclusion, participation, partnership, and teamwork in problem solving is also absent all concern with justice and the designation of purposes, along with particularistic struggles over all these things. As power vanishes and ends become givens in the way problems are specified, democracy becomes divested of politics, defined either as the handling of power or as struggle over common fundamentals or goals.[25]

If, as Brown implies, pragmatic liberalism presents an existential threat to democracy—in whatever shape democracy might take—what to do? Her mission is to rescue the possibility of political equality, which in itself requires the resuscitation of the political animal, *homo politicus*.

> This subject, *homo politicus*, forms the substance and legitimacy of whatever democracy might mean beyond securing the individual provisioning of individual ends; this "beyond" includes political equality and freedom, representation, popular sovereignty, and deliberation and judgment about the public good and the common. Only toward the end of the twentieth century did *homo oeconomicus* (in its distinctly neoliberal iteration) finally get the better of *homo politicus*, usurping its territory, terms, and objects both in the figure of the human and the polity. If this process were to become complete, if *homo politicus* were really vanquished, it would darken the globe against all possibilities of democratic or other just futures.[26]

Another political theorist, Yael Tamir, agrees with Brown about the dangers currently facing democracies, and that the regimes of global governance are largely responsible. She also agrees that the key is to invigorate the democratic citizen, the *homo politicus*. Their normative directives, however, move in opposite directions. While Brown seeks to repoliticize everything pragmatic liberalism has marketized, for Tamir, invigorating citizenship is a *prepolitical* operation. "Democratic regimes require a pre-political partnership that turns citizens into a collective entity that has a common past and a common future. In the absence of a political *we*, states disintegrate, and the political structure that allows them to turn into democratic

[24]  *Id.* at 128.
[25]  *Id.*
[26]  WENDY BROWN, UNDOING THE DEMOS: NEOLIBERALISM'S STEALTH REVOLUTION 87 (2015)

ON THE INEVITABILITY OF RACIAL BORDERS    321

and decent entities dissolves. A political *we* had never been a natural phenomenon; it must be created, and then constantly nurtured, supported, and reinvented."[27]

The "prepolitical" prerequisite to the "political we" of a fully functioning democracy, Tamir explains, can be nothing less than the nation. Without the nation, there is no political community, and without properly integrated political communities, there isn't legitimate government. And without that, we have no rights. Yes, the demand for national identity creates insiders and outsiders, and yes, it threatens a revival of racial xenophobia.[28] But this is the price of democracy, the price of our liberty. Like David Miller, Tamir's proposal for liberal nationalism as the cure for democratic deficits is largely pragmatic. She writes of the need to "rebuild societies on the basis of mélange of values and ideas borrowing from different schools of thought in order to create an untidy but decent and workable compromise."[29] If it makes sense to fight fire with fire, maybe fighting pragmatism with pragmatism works, too.

While it's hard to imagine Brown agreeing with much of Tamir's prescription, she nevertheless seems in agreement about the importance of national boundaries to the reawakening of democratic politics. Referring again to Carl Schmitt's *Nomos of the World*, Brown observed, "Schmitt's etymology of nomos may be contested ... but his appreciation of enclosure as a prerequisite of political order and law is difficult to set aside. This prerequisite could even constitute a fundamental challenge for advocates of global citizenship or democracy without borders: How is an unbounded polity even possible? The line is the basis of constitution, of *pouvoir constitue* within what it encloses, as well as the threshold beyond which the law does not hold."[30] Similarly, Chantal Mouffe has argued—also in Schmitt's wake—for the necessity of linking the *demos* to a discrete people: "The liberal conception of equality postulates that every person is, as a person, automatically equal to every other person. The democratic conception, however, requires the possibility of distinguishing who belongs to the demos and who is exterior to it; for that reason, it cannot exist without the necessary correlate of inequality."[31]

To recap, the question before us is how the advent of phenomena like globalization and global governance in the late twentieth century might have rendered irrelevant the sovereign's imperial right to exclude. After all, if sovereignty had diminished, eroded, shrunk, or something like that, one would think that so too would a sovereign's right (or ability) to determine the boundaries (and therefore the identity) of the international legal order. And this has been exactly the claim from international relations theorists and international lawyers for more than a quarter century; in the tightening of global ties and interdependencies, the traditional

---

[27] YAEL TAMIR, WHY NATIONALISM? 6 (2019).
[28] *Id.* at 130.
[29] *Id.* at 180.
[30] WENDY BROWN, WALLED STATES, WANING SOVEREIGNTY 57 (2010).
[31] CHANTAL MOUFFE, THE DEMOCRATIC PARADOX 39 (2005).

## 322 THE RIGHT TO EXCLUDE

forms of sovereign authority have stepped aside in favor of novel modes of global governance. As the story goes, the pragmatic managerialism of global governance might have had its benefits, but it had its costs as well. First among them has been the disintegrating effect on democratic rule. The result seems to be something of a rock and a hard place, Scylla and Charybdis sort of deal: We either ascend into the labyrinth of global governance, where, in Wendy Brown's words, "distinctly political meanings of 'equality,' 'autonomy,' and 'freedom' are giving way to economic valences of these terms, and the distinctive value of popular sovereignty is receding as governance through expertise, market metrics, and best practices replaces justice-framed contestations over who we are, what we should be or become, what we should or should not do as a people. Democracies are conceived as requiring technically skilled human capital, not educated participants in public life and common rule."[32] Or, following Tamir, we marshal the prepolitical power of the nation, invoking the *xenos* as the natural boundary-maker, and therefore *source* for, a revitalized democratic life. It certainly appears to be an unfortunate set of options, either into the jaws of Frankenstein's neoliberalism, or a Trumpian xenophobia.

## II THE *DEMOS* UNBOUND

The sense that here, in the second decade of the twenty-first century, we face a Hobson's choice between an eviscerated democratic existence and democracy founded upon the racial *xenos* is, I believe, in no small way attributable to the ideology of postracial xenophobia. Postracial xenophobia at once pushes the human rights/multicultural ideal of the antidiscrimination norm, advocates for a pragmatic liberal agenda (i.e., global governance), and encourages national and cultural identities as collective modes of association that are at once postracial and dependent on the availability of a racial *xenos*. Why do these options so powerfully crowd the field? Is it because, as Brown says, "It is nearly impossible to reconcile the classical features of sovereignty ... with the requisites of rule by the *demos*"?[33] Or is it something else?

My argument is for the "something else," and we can see as much by way of a different trajectory, if we follow the trace of international law's racial ideology. Consider where the narrative began in Part I, with the development of *homo sacer* and the *racial xenos*. This was a maneuver indigenous to liberalism itself, where the universalism of *homo politicus*, the rights-bearing, rational subject, was reimagined in the eighteenth and nineteenth centuries through processes of racial subjection. From there, the problem of exclusion was resolvable through a new family of

---

[32] BROWN, UNDOING, *supra* note 26, at 177.
[33] BROWN, WALLED, *supra* note 30, at 61.

solutions: through the production and inclusion of the racial *xenos* in the liberal imagination, everything *other* than the *xenos* was what belonged to the insides, to the world of rights and powers. This was the conceptual background for the claim that, in international law, the sovereign's right to exclude was central to the role of racial ideology as naturalizing juridical science, as a mediating technology in the grammar of liberal legal thought.

To expand on this a bit more, and recalling the discussion from early on, the classic liberal structure of international legal thought begins with the domestic analogy. In this metaphor, sovereign states are imagined as liberal individuals competing in a global state of nature. Just as the *homo politicus* had a right of self-determination, so too did the sovereign, for there was no higher authority with a natural right to determine the good life, to make law and order, without the sovereign's consent. But it was here that the domestic analogy broke down. For whereas on the domestic plane the rights-bearing individual is expected, through the device of the social contract, to surrender much of his natural rights in exchange for the protection of the sovereign, sovereigns were not expected to renounce anything at all. And it this absence of surrender which leads to the premise that sovereignty makes the whole notion of a global *demos* incoherent. The trick, at least for thinkers like Pufendorf and Vattel, was that there could nevertheless still be something called international *law*, a binding sphere of rules that determined the rights and duties for those subjects of the global order—*even when they no longer consented to be bound*. In international legal thought, sovereigns were at once conceptualized as the citizens of an international legal order which they also and at the same time governed. In the liberal structure of international legal thought, there is a strict identity between sovereigns as *rulers* and sovereigns as the *ruled*. International law is legitimated, on this view, due to its provenance: it is sourced in the consent of the community of the ruled.

This doubled sense of the sovereign as ruled/ruler suggests a deep and underlying commitment in the liberal structure of international legal thought to the availability of some form of global *demos*. As Mouffe has noted, the identity between rulers and ruled is fundamental to the democratic project.[34] Of course there has never been in liberal legal thought a global leviathan, a world parliament in which sovereign states vote and deliberate and all the rest. Nevertheless, the fact that lawyers, politicians, and philosophers have for centuries believed in the reality of an international rule of law that is both sourced for its legitimacy in the will of individual sovereigns, and that objectively governs the will of individual sovereigns, reflects the underlying premise of liberal international law—that sovereigns are members of a global *demos*, however loosely defined. This is, to be sure, an old and perhaps very outdated understanding of sovereignty. At the same

---

[34] MOUFFE, *supra* note 31, at 43.

324    THE RIGHT TO EXCLUDE

time, I'm not sure how outdated it really is—even in the midst of their constant commentaries on the advent of the "global," thinkers like Keohane, Nye, Slaughter, and so many others never tired of reminding about the remaining centrality of the sovereign state. But even conceding an "evolution" away from international law's domestic analogy, it is surely a mistake to think that because the international legal order has become more complex, that the underlying premise of the global *demos* ought to be discarded. It is a mistake because, even if we throw into the mix of "law-making" actors those of international institutions, non-governmental organizations, corporations, transgovernmental networks, and the private individual to boot, the international legal order remains committed to a self-referential theory of legitimacy. International actors, whether they are sovereigns or something else, must abide by the same identity-structure of ruled/ruler, so long as the domestic analogy remains in play.

And it is this point that moves us to the next step in the analysis: If it is right that international legal thought presupposes a kind of global *demos*, what of the common complaint about democracy necessarily entailing exclusion, requiring a discrete people? Does international law's presumption of a global *demos* betray its own incoherence, precisely because a global *demos* is an impossibility? Though not working in the context of international law, Arash Abizadeh's work helps illuminate what is wrong about the assumption that a theory of democracy ought to require a right to exclude.

As we have seen, the classic liberal structure of international legal thought conceptualizes sovereigns as simultaneously the authors of a legal system which also makes them its subjects. This is sometimes called the self-referential aspect of democratic theory.[35] As Abizadeh has explained, in a liberal democracy the justification for the exercise of political power over the *demos* is that it is the *demos* itself which is doing the ruling. Collective self-rule legitimizes the exercise of coercive authority, but in a self-referential way, since the "principle of legitimacy refers right back to the very persons over whom political power is exercised."[36] The reason that this argument about democratic theory is of interest here, is that Abizadeh points out how all self-referential theories of rule—and I would argue that this includes the way in which sovereignty functions in international society via the domestic analogy—end up hiding the ball. And the "ball" is the problem of establishing borders for the political community. Self-referential theories of political legitimacy demand:

> [T]hat the human object of power, those persons over whom it is exercised, also be the subject of power, those who (in some sense) author its exercise. The striking

---

[35] Arash Abizadeh, *On the Demos and Its Kin: Nationalism, Democracy, and the Boundary Problem*, 106 AM. POL. SCI. REV. 867 (2012).

[36] *Id.* at 867.

feature of self-referential theories is that a second question must consequently be addressed before the question of legitimacy can be determinately answered. This is the question of *boundaries*: To have determinate content, a principle of legitimacy referring to a collective self requires specifying who that collective self is.[37]

The trouble is that there is nothing internal to democratic theory that explains where its borders ought to be drawn, and as a result of this lacunae, Abizadeh claims that the choice to mark an inside from an outside must be justified to insiders *and* outsiders alike. His argument rests on two premises. First, in democratic theory it is necessary that the exercise of coercive power be justified to everyone that is subjected to that power. This is a normative claim with which there is little controversy: if you are coerced, there ought to be a good justification for it. The second premise is that when the sovereign exercises its right to exclude and sets boundaries for the *demos*, the very act of boundary-making, of inclusion/exclusion, necessarily coerces both insiders and outsiders. And since outsiders are coerced—interpellated as "outsiders," subjected as *xenoi*—the sovereign must justify its right to exclude *to them*. The result is that, in having exercised its right to exclude, the sovereign has in fact demonstrated the unbounded character of the *demos*, for if subjection is unbounded, and the *demos* comprises the subjected, the *demos* is unbounded, too.

At least two theories support this argument for an unbounded *demos*, known as the "all-affected" principle and the "all-subjected" principle.[38] As the name suggests, the former principle would constitute the *demos* with reference to every interest affected by a decision from that community. The proper bounds of the "people" would generally be in flux, alternating with respect to a given decision. The underlying principle of inclusion, however, would be that every person potentially affected by a sovereign decision would have the right to vote in that community's elections, or at least participate in some meaningful way. Obviously, the all-affected-interests principle cares little for territorial or cultural-national borders, and the relevant community for any given decision might very well be global. The all-subjected principle shares with its counterpart a disdain for the traditional means for excluding potential members from the *demos*. Territorial lines and cultural frontiers are of little use; rather, what counts here is whether a person has been subjected to the coercive power of the sovereign. It is irrelevant whether a person has an "interest" in the rule or decision. What matters is whether a person has been subjected to the sovereign's coercive power, and if so, as a matter

---

[37] *Id.* at 867–68.

[38] *See* Robert Goodin, *Enfranchising All Subjected, Worldwide*, 8 INT'L THEORY 365 (2016); Archon Fung, *The Principle of Affected Interests: An Interpretation and Defense*, in REPRESENTATION: ELECTIONS AND BEYOND (Jack Nagel & Rogers Smith eds., 2013); Arash Abizadeh, *Democratic Theory and Border Coercion: No Right to Unilaterally Control Your Borders*, 36 POL. THEORY 37 (2008); Claudio Lopez-Guerra, *Should Expatriates Vote?* 11 J. POL. PHIL. 216 (2005).

326    THE RIGHT TO EXCLUDE

of respecting the liberal commitments to autonomy and equality, every person so subjected ought to have (at least) a right to vote.

Regardless of whether we follow the all-affected principle or the all-subjected principle, the underlying assumption is the same: "the *demos* to whom justification is owed is in principle unbounded."[39] Abizadeh suggests that the tendency for political theorists to deny the unbounded *demos* argument and presume the linkage between democracy and a bounded people is caught up in what Frederick Whelan has called democratic theory's "boundary problem,"[40] As Whelan put it:

> Whatever form a democracy takes, collectively binding decisions are made, laws and policies are enacted, and these things are done for and in one way or another by a particular group or *people* that is set apart—and bound together—for the purposes of self-government from other people or peoples, who are correspondingly excluded.[41]

The question then is about how to justify from within the limits of democratic theory some criterion for "constituting the demos," that "people" bound together and set apart.[42] It isn't about what legitimizes the exercise of political power for one political community, but rather, it is about what legitimizes the constitution of a political community at all. Compounding democratic theory's inability to justify the boundaries constituting a particular *demos*, is that the requirements of democratic theory demand that it do so anyway. Abizadeh observed, "the act of constituting civic borders is always an exercise of power over both insiders and outsiders that intrinsically, by the very act of constituting the border, disenfranchises the outsiders over whom power is exercised. It is this conceptual feature of civic borders that confronts democratic theory with an externality problem."[43]

Abizadeh's critique is not that democratic theory is itself incoherent, since it poses no answers to questions about how to justify its boundaries or count its members. The incoherence, rather, is due to the interpretation of democratic theory which demands a bounded *demos*. It is incoherent because it presupposes a prepolitically constituted people in order for democracy to be legitimate, even though there is nothing within democratic theory capable of answering the question of who or where or what that prepolitically constituted people might be.[44]

---

[39] Abizadeh, *Unilateral, supra* note 38, at 45.

[40] Frederick Whelan, *Prologue: Democratic Theory and the Boundary Problem*, 25 NOMOS 13 (1983). *See also* Camil Parvu, *The Boundary Problem in Democratic Theory: Cosmopolitan Implications, in* COSMOPOLITANISM WITHOUT FOUNDATIONS (Tamara Caraus & Dan Lazea eds., 2015); A.J. SIMMONS, BOUNDARIES OF AUTHORITY (2016).

[41] Whelan, *supra* note 40, at 15.

[42] Robert Goodin, *Enfranchising All Affected Interests, and its Alternatives*, 35 PHIL. & PUB. AFF. 40 (2007).

[43] Abizadeh, *Unilateral, supra* note 38, at 46.

[44] *Id.* at 47.

Unsurprisingly, two responses to Abizadeh's unbounded *demos* thesis are rooted in territorialism and nationalism, and they are the same sources for concerns about globalization's democratic deficits—(1) global power unresponsive to a territorial *demos* reflects transparency and accountability concerns; and (2) global power reflecting an array of alien cultures is, well, alien.

One response, and this is the response seemingly assumed by Brown and Mouffe, has been to gesture in the direction of a theory of a territorially bounded *demos* as presumptively efficacious.[45] The idea is that the contingency of the state is made up for the fact that it is only within the context of a bounded, territorial *demos* that democratic principles of equality and deliberation can be effectively protected. If the political community isn't strictly bounded, and a deterritorialized or "unbounded" *demos* is constituted every time a new decision is handed down, there is little chance for the sort of trust that binds a political community together to form between members, or between members and their representatives.[46] Sarah Song has argued that the *demos* should be bounded by the state because the state provides the requisites for democratic operability, and serves as the primary site of solidarity conducive to democratic participation.[47] Anna Stilz has similarly claimed that the all-affected and all-subjected principles are mistaken for doing away with the traditional confines of territorial borders—not only because they are "politically unviable."[48] More importantly, they are mistaken because they fail to realize that the principle of political autonomy is most effectively guaranteed by the sovereign state. In consequence, Stilz notes, "I argue that our natural duty to respect and protect the autonomy of others is best fulfilled through a pluralistic and decentralized order of self-governing territorial units."[49]

The trouble is that these sorts of claims are not especially satisfying. To offer in response to the question of how to justifiably identify the "people" from within democratic theory, that the "people" must be the population bounded by the territorial state because it is only then that freedom and equality are best protected, is to move in circles. Who are the "people" that are best protected in this case? Insiders? And if so, why only these and not those on the other side of the line? Perhaps a realism or functionalism is what is actually shouldering the lift here, but if so, that only underscores the failure to develop a justification from within democratic theory for bounding the *demos* here and not there. Abizadeh suggests that as a result of these failures from the vantage of the territorial state, there has been a characteristic tendency to look to nationalism for an answer.[50] In this effort to

---

[45] Sarah Song, *The Boundary Problem in Democratic Theory: Why the Demos Should be Bounded by the State*, 4 INT'L THEORY 39 (2012).

[46] *See also* SEYLA BENHABIB, THE RIGHTS OF OTHERS: ALIENS, RESIDENTS, AND CITIZENS (2004); JURGEN HABERMAS, THE POSTNATIONAL CONSTELLATION: POLITICAL ESSAYS (2000).

[47] Song, *supra* note 45.

[48] ANNA STILZ, TERRITORIAL SOVEREIGNTY: A PHILOSOPHICAL EXPLORATION 8 (2019).

[49] *Id.* at 12.

[50] Abizadeh, *Demos*, *supra* note 35, at 875.

328    THE RIGHT TO EXCLUDE

identify a prepolitical membership, the *demos* has been in search of a public culture, of the sort imagined by David Miller and Yael Tamir. As we have seen earlier
in the discussion, Miller and Tamir have argued that democratic authority is legitimate when it is traceable to a prepolitical nation and its culture. The proper
boundaries of the *demos* as a result, are the prepolitical boundaries of precisely
that national culture. This all presumes, of course, that we can solve the problem
of democratic closure by illuminating cultural closure—the missing boundaries at
one level are provided in the found boundaries of another. And this is what, in one
way or another, Kymlicka, Anaya, Miller, and Tamir have sought to accomplish in
their respective discussions of cultural and national identity.[51] As we have seen in
Chapter 8, however, and as explained by thinkers like Homi Bhaba and Stuart Hall,
cultural closure of the sort required to ground a prepolitical national community is
just not going to happen.

It is in this context of cultural indeterminacy that Abizadeh likens the plight
of the social contract theorist's search for an anchor in the nation, that the cultural nationalist too ends up descending into ethnicity. That is, we see here in the
assumption of a bounded *demos* a double descent: since the traditional orientation of territorial efficacy fails to offer a non-tautological answer to the boundary
problem, it seeks refuge in the prepolitical ground of the nation—but here too, the
concept of a national culture inevitably suffers from a fatal indeterminacy, leading
toward refuge in the prepolitical ground of the *ethnos*. Abizadeh explains, "So the
cultural nation must go casting about for an extracultural supplement to anchor its
boundaries in space and time. And this is precisely what ethnicity, constituted by a
myth of common descent, purports to supply: An extracultural basis for the continuity of the cultural nation through time—a natural, prepolitical anchor."[52] What is
it that ethnicity can do for the boundary problem that culture cannot? As discussed
back in Chapter 3, culture draws into ethnicity when it requires the hard, objective
qualities that race had once supplied but—in the lexical space of modern racial
ideology—no longer can. Of course, ethnicity appears subjective when countered
against race, but it looks objective when joined with culture—hence the appeal of
the hybrid term, ethnoculture. Here in the context of a prepolitical community,
cultural boundaries turn out to be unavoidably porous, too subjective, generated
at least in part through appeals to experience, which accounts for the necessarily

---

[51] Abizadeh writes: "Hence the elusiveness of any satisfactory answer to the problem of closure: because there are an infinite number of features on which different individuals can be similar and different
in cross-cutting ways, because the selection of some subset of features as decisive for individuating cultural groups begs the question of why other features are irrelevant, and because any candidate set for
what essentially differentiates cultures is itself subject to the problem of closure, the problem of closure
remains intractable. Any attempt to specify once and for all the members of a distinct cultural group,
and the set of features that constitute its boundaries, faces the insurmountable problem that further difference can always be found within, and similarity across, the collective boundaries that were supposed
to mark off difference." *Id.* at 871.

[52] *Id.* at 873.

ON THE INEVITABILITY OF RACIAL BORDERS 329

slippery boundaries and constant bleeding between cultural entities. Is "ethnicity" really any more secure? After all, it is a deeply plastic term as well, though the meanings of the *ethnos* are more referential. Contrasted with race, ethnicity looks like culture. Contrasted with culture, ethnicity looks like race. Only the *ethnos* is superior to race, since whatever ethnicity is, its *xenos* is definitively postracial.

This final point delivers us at the destination to which we have been driving. If the premise of territoriality is tautological in terms of defining the necessary boundaries of a *demos*, and if nationalism works to close its cultural boundaries by way of a turn to a myth of ethnic descent, the effort is racial but without all the trappings of modern racial ideology, it is, *postracial*. This critique of an ethnic discourse as mystifying the underlying presence of a racial problematic is now a commonplace in critical race theory, as analyzed above in the work of Richard Ford. In a response to an effort to erase race from ethnic discourse, in 1997, Ian Haney Lopez explained how the turn to the *ethnos* can inadvertently reproduce racial hierarchies.[53] Lopez recognized that much of the current that he saw in the late 1990s, and that we can now say only continued through the first decades of the twenty-first century, was not a rejection of the idea that human populations had been repeatedly racialized for centuries. It was rather that "although attention should be given to processes of racial differentiation and their consequences, racialized groups should no longer be discussed in racial terms."[54] But it was a mistake, Lopez believed, to think of racial analyses of race as redundant with ethnocultural studies, since "the language of race may well constitute the single most indispensable tool for combating and ameliorating the deleterious effects of racism."[55] Why?

Since its popular inception in the early years of the twentieth century (and as discussed in Chapter 3), ethnicity has regularly been used as a marker for the cultural content of a population, while race has been the marker for biological descent. After it turned out that racial science was fake news, and that ethnocultures were the real deal, the turn away from race as a language of subordination made perfect sense. The trouble was that even while the chimerical nature of race as biology has come to light, the ideology of racial hierarchy remained entirely wedded to beliefs in biological—and consequently, immutable—imaginaries. Lopez continued:

> Utilizing ethnicity as the sole lens through which to view socially constituted groups can be used to hide the extent to which harms and benefits have been conferred on the basis of presumed racial differences. Embracing an exclusively ethnic focus allows one to effectively abjure at the level of vocabulary the role of race in structuring opportunities in the United States. "Ethnicity" under this

---

[53] Juan Perea, *The Black/White Binary Paradigm of Race: The "Normal Science" of American Racial Thought*, 85 CAL. L. REV. 1213 (1997); Kevin Johnson, *The Ring of Fire: Assimilation and the Mexican-American Experience*, 85 CAL. L. REV. 1259 (1997).

[54] Lopez, *supra* note 38, at 94.

[55] *Id.* at 101.

approach becomes a way to focus attention on the surface, on the word, and to forestall attention to the underlying social relations of domination and subordination that do not observe such neat word-boundaries. In this way, it facilitates the politically charged belief that every ethnic group that has come to the United States has found the same possibilities, and encountered the same hurdles. Under such an approach, group differences in social standing and economic success must be explained as a function of group attributes or failings, not as a result of social prejudices or structural advantages and disadvantage.[56]

In her recent book, *Inventing Latinos: A New Story of American Racism*, Laura Gomez doubles down on the point. Acknowledging that more than twenty years after Lopez worried over the displacement of race by ethnoculture, Gomez states that "conventional wisdom portrays Latinos as an ethnic rather than a racial group."[57] "The very fact of our collective unwillingness to name as racism," Gomez observes, "and instead classify as 'Hispanophobia,' 'xenophobia,' or 'ethnic prejudice,' racist attacks and institutional racism targeting Latinos is itself a reflection of the nature of Latino racialization."[58] What's more, swapping ethnicity for race silently reinforces the prevalence of white supremacy, both as it manifests in the contexts of phenotypical hierarchies within racial groups themselves,[59] as well as in the perpetuation of a Black/White paradigm which inevitably characterizes Latinos in an intermediate category—not yet white, but better than Black. As Gomez remarks, "the refusal to see and name anti-Latino racism *qua* racism serves to enlist Latinos in policing the White-over-Black color line."[60] Ideologically, ethnicity *is* race by another, more palatable, postracial name.

The result is that rather than a double descent, justifications for a bounded *demos* fail in triplicate: (1) as the territorial argument fails and looks for solace in a national culture, (2) and as the cultural nationalist argument fails and looks for solace in a prepolitical *ethnos*, (3) the ideological content of otherness associated with the *ethnos* becomes virtually indistinguishable from that of the racial *xenos*. That is, from territory we turn to the nation, from the nation we turn to the *ethnos*, and from ethnicity we bottom out in race. Abizadeh's claim that beliefs in the unavoidable character of the bounded *demos*—that democratic theory's boundary problem necessitates a discretely bordered people—rest on an ethnic core can go one step further: the demand to bound the *demos* rests on the availability of a racial *xenos*. The upshot: in liberal theory, a bounded *demos* is a racialized *demos*.

---

[56] *Id.* at 118.
[57] LAURA GOMEZ, INVENTING LATINOS: A NEW STORY OF AMERICAN RACISM 13 (2020).
[58] *Id.* at 13.
[59] *Id.* at 14.
[60] *Id.* at 15.

## III  ARE RACIAL BORDERS AN IRON CAGE?

In the discussion above, I surfaced the question of whether the analysis of international law's racial ideology has been rendered irrelevant by the advent of globalization. Globalization has ushered in a corresponding paradigm of global governance, which in itself triggered concerns about democratic accountability, cultural imperialism, and depoliticization. At the root of the issue is a view that the viability of liberal democracy requires a territorially grounded people—hence, the challenges of globalization require solutions that, in the end, are beholden to a sovereign's right to exclude. The trouble, however, is that these solutions, from territorial fiat to cultural nationalism, ultimately reproduce a foundational commitment to drawing the line between insiders and outsiders in racial terms. The liberal claim that a *demos* must be territorially bound, it turns out, requires a regime of racial borders.

As I have argued throughout this book, for close to two centuries the sovereign's right to exclude has been justified in international law through various articulations of racial ideology. And what we have just seen, in this very brief run of democratic theory, is that—and to translate Abizadeh's phrasing—"Behind the [ethnic] nation lurks a [racial *xenos*], eager to cover its next of kin with a warm and rather constricting embrace. A constructing embrace." As racial ideology justifies the sovereign's right to exclude in the structure of international legal thought, so too does it shoulder the same task in the discourse of global governance and democratic deficits. So has the emergence of globalization and the global governance paradigm rendered the sovereign's right to exclude irrelevant? Hardly. If anything, the ideology of postracial xenophobia generates its own reinforcements. Its role in international law is as foundational as it is obscure, and the same can be said for its place in debates about the viability of a global *demos*. Over and over and over again, the figure of the racial outsider is generated in the effort to produce a society of insiders, the society of sovereigns, the society of white supremacy. Of course, the ideological contours have transformed over the years, but in the transition from classic to modern to postracial, the racial *xenos* remains constitutive—it remains constitutive, that is, when liberalism works to secure its boundaries. This was so in the context of the Family of Nations, in the context of the UN, and remains so in the context of a globalizing world, a global *demos*. Must this always be so? Are the borders of communities, whether they are national or global, inevitably racialized?

The answer must surely be no. Recall that this book has offered an analysis of a structure of thought, a series of articulations, styles of argumentative practice. The racial ideology of international legal thought is no iron cage, no prison house without exit. Liberal legalism is a language of dominance and subjection, or perhaps, it is *like* a language. But it is surely no law of nature that human beings must interpellate one another as racial beings, as rational sovereigns and racial *xenoi*. What does seem extraordinarily challenging in the contemporary conjuncture, however, is avoiding a right to exclude that is also and at the same time a right to

## 332 THE RIGHT TO EXCLUDE

racialize. The demand for borders—at least for the moment—is a demand for *racial* borders. But if this process of subjection is not inevitable, is the only escape from our postracial xenophobia something like a postnational, all-subjected principle? I'm unwilling to say that this is the *only* escape, but what seems fairly evident is this: the sovereign's right to exclude must be rethought in the register of *unboundedness*, in *both* the dimensions of *dominium* and *imperium*. To be sure, relinquishing the bounds of the *demos* won't solve every problem. But it *would* reorient the purpose of the racial *xenos*, and that is at least a start.

The inevitable question is, *but how?* Realism blocks the way, as does functionalism, neoformalism, and the pragmatic apparatus of naturalizing juridical science as it presently stands.[61] It isn't enough to recommend the view that there is nothing natural or necessary at all about these structures of exclusion, though this is a necessary beginning. We require tools for reenvisioning property and sovereignty, opening the door to structures of inclusion we have yet to discover.[62] This cannot happen out of whole cloth, of course. The routes toward doctrinal and institutional imagination emerge in a space of becoming: in order to see what sovereignty and property might *become*, we must first understand where they have been and what they currently are. In a word, to imagine what they might become, we must first inhabit their structure. This is what Roberto Unger meant in the cryptic, final paragraph of his *What Should Legal Analysis Become?*

> Our interests and ideals remain nailed to the cross of our arrangements. We cannot realise our interests and ideals more fully, nor redefine them more deeply, until we have learned to remake and to reimagine our arrangements more freely. History will not give us this freedom. We must win it in the here and now of legal detail, economic constraint, and deadening preconception. We shall not win it if we continue to profess a science of society reducing the possible to the actual and a discourse about law anointing power with piety. *It is true that we cannot be visionaries until we become realists. It is also true that to become realists we must make ourselves into visionaries.*[63]

I believe that this "chiastic" approach—an approach in which realism becomes the property of the visionary, where the real is a function of will—has a long pedigree in the critical race tradition, and what might become a critical race approach to international law. As Nahum Demetri Chandler has explored, the generative tradition of *chiasmus*, of the *X*, finds its traces in the work of W.E.B. Du Bois.[64] In his

---

[61] PARTHA CHATTERJEE, THE NATION AND ITS FRAGMENTS: COLONIAL AND POSTCOLONIAL HISTORIES 5 (1993) ("Even our imaginations must remain forever colonized").

[62] ROBERTO UNGER, DEMOCRACY REALIZED: THE PROGRESSIVE ALTERNATIVE (2000).

[63] ROBERTO UNGER, WHAT SHOULD LEGAL ANALYSIS BECOME? 189–90 (1996).

[64] NAHUM DEMETRI CHANDLER, X: THE PROBLEM OF THE NEGRO AS A PROBLEM FOR THOUGHT 23 (2013). *See also* Justin Desautels-Stein, *Chiastic Law in the Crystal Ball: Exploring Legal Formalism and Its Alternative Futures*, 2 LON. REV. INT'L L. 263 (2014). Eve Kosefsky Sedgwick provides a typical

*The Souls of Black Folk* and *The Souls of White Folk*, published in 1903 and 1920, respectively, Du Bois argued from the outset that the problem of race was much more than a question of bad apples, prejudiced individuals poisoning what was otherwise a pretty good haul.[65] The problem of race was a problem of structure, a problem in the very way human society produced racial beings, and at the end of the day, these beings were of two types. Society produced human beings that had been raised to believe they were the natural rulers of the universe, and then there were human bodies to be ruled—the dark skins of the *homo sacri*, the racial *xenoi*. In the first group were the white folk. "This theory of human culture and its aims," Du Bois explained, "has worked itself through warp and woof of our daily thought with a thoroughness that few realize. Everything great, good, efficient, fair, and honorable is 'white'; everything mean, bad, blundering, cheating, and dishonorable is 'yellow'; a bad taste is 'brown'; and the devil is 'black.' The changes of this theme are continually run in picture and story, in newspaper heading and moving-picture, in sermon and school book."[66] Du Bois continued:

This assumption that of all the hues of God whiteness alone is inherently and obviously better than brownness or tan leads to curious acts; even the sweeter souls of the dominant world ... are continually playing above their actual words an obligate of tune and tone, saying: "My poor, un-white thing! Weep not nor rage. I know, too well, that the curse of God lies heavy on you. Why? That is not for me to say, but be brave! Do your work in your lowly sphere, praying the good Lord that into heaven above, where all is love, you may, one day, be born—white!" But what on earth is whiteness that one should come to desire it? Then always ... I am given to understand that whiteness is the ownership of the earth forever and ever, Amen! Now what is the effect on a man or a nation when it comes passionately to believe such an extraordinary dictum as this? That nations are coming to believe

---

definition of chiasmus in the context of rhetoric: "chiasmus: ki-AZ-mus. Gr. "a placing crosswise, a diagonal arrangement." " Repetition of ideas or grammatical structures in inverted order (AB–BA). "It is boring to eat; to sleep is fulfilling"; "Ask not what your country can do for you; ask rather what you can do for your country." Like anacoluthon, it generally presumes a context of parallel structure. Because of its criss-cross relation to temporality, a looser, narrative notion of chiasmus is often associated with the psychoanalytic notion of *Nachträglichkeit* or deferred action (what Silvan Tomkins calls posticipation), in which experiences, impressions, and memory traces may be revised at a later date to fit in with fresh experiences or with the attainment of a new stage of development. *See* JEAN LAPLANCHE & JEAN-BERTRAND PONTALIS, THE LANGUAGE OF PSYCHO-ANALYSIS 111 (Donald Nicholson-Smith trans., 1973); Eve Kosefsky Sedgwick, *Rhetorical Devices*, EVEKOSOFSKYSEDGWICK.NET (2001), *available at* https://evekosofskysedgwick.net/teaching/rhetorical-devices.html (last visited April 18, 2022). *See also* Anthony Paul & Boris Wiseman, *Chiasmus in the Drama of Life*, *in* CHIASMUS AND CULTURE (Boris Wiseman & Anthony Paul eds., 2014).

[65] W.E.B. DU BOIS, THE SOULS OF BLACK FOLK (1961); W.E.B. DU BOIS, BLACK RECONSTRUCTION IN AMERICA, 1860–1880 [1935] (1998); W.E.B. DU BOIS, SELECTIONS FROM HIS WRITINGS (2014); W.E.B. DU BOIS, DARKWATER: VOICES FROM WITHIN THE VEIL (2021).

[66] DU BOIS, SOULS, *supra* note 65, at 174.

334    THE RIGHT TO EXCLUDE

it is manifest daily. Wave on wave, each with increasing virulence, is dashing this
new religion of whiteness on the shores of our time.[67]

The natural outcome of white supremacy, Du Bois continued, was of course a fundamentally racial society shaped by a global color line. But it was more. Looking
upon the wreckage of World War I, "we darker men said: This is not Europe gone
mad; this is not aberration nor insanity; this *is* Europe; this seeming Terrible is
the real soul of white culture—back of all culture;–stripped and visible today. This
is where the world has arrived—these dark and awful depths and not the shining
and ineffable heights of which it boasted. Here is whither the might and energy
of modern humanity has really gone."[68] And, Du Bois suggested, the ideology of
whiteness was only expanding. "[I]t is colonial aggrandizement which explains,
and alone adequately explains, the World War. How many of us today fully realize the current theory of colonial expansion, of the relation of Europe which is
white, to the world which is black and brown and yellow? Bluntly put, the theory is
this: It is the duty of white Europe to divide up the darker world and administer it
for Europe's good."[69] Indeed, this is what whiteness *is*: "the chance to levy endless
tribute on the darker world—on coolies in China, on starving peasants in India, on
black savages in Africa, on dying South Sea islanders, on Indians of the Amazon."[70]

What then of the "darker world," that majority of the human species never destined for sovereignty, for self-determination, for goodness? It became, in Chandler's
phrasing, "an exorbitance for thought: an instance outside of all forms of being
that truly matter."[71] Du Bois famously characterized this notion of a strangely ex-
orbitant liminality for the world's racial *xenoi* as "double-consciousness."[72] Du Bois
explained:

After the Egyptian and Indian, the Greek and Roman, the Teuton and Mongolian,
the Negro is a sort of seventh son, born with a veil, and gifted with a second-sight
in this American world,—a world which yields him no true self-consciousness,
but only lets him see himself through the revelation of the other world. It is a peculiar sensation, this double-consciousness, this sense of always looking at one's
self through the eyes of others, of measuring one's soul by the tape of a world that
looks on in amused contempt and pity. One ever feels his twoness—an American,

---

[67]   DU BOIS, SELECTIONS, *supra* note 65, at 165.
[68]   *Id.* at 170.
[69]   *Id.* at 172.
[70]   *Id.* at 175.
[71]   CHANDLER, *supra* note 65, at 23.
[72]   PAUL GILROY, THE BLACK ATLANTIC: MODERNITY AND DOUBLE CONSCIOUSNESS 126 (1993) ("Du
Bois produced this concept at the junction point of his philosophical and psychological interests not
just to express the distinctive standpoint of black Americans but also to illuminate the experience of
post-slave populations in general.").

a Negro; two souls, two thoughts, two unreconciled strivings; two warring ideals in one dark body, whose dogged strength alone keeps it from being torn asunder.[73]

As Paul Gilroy has observed, the concept of double consciousness operates on three levels. The first implicates racial particularity, wherein the racial *xenos* knows at once that she is indeed human, and in being human possessive of all rational self-determination, but also that her racial identity places her in a paradoxical position of existing at once inside the human sphere and yet somehow placed beyond it. The second level concerns membership in the national community, wherein the operation of the veil reproduces itself: the racial *xenos* bears witness to the political society in which she is a member (she is no slave) and yet she is an alien at the same time. Third, double consciousness operates at the global level, instituting the "color curtain" between the world's racial *xenoi* and the universalism of international society.[74] At each level of analysis we see the specter of a distinction waiting to collapse on itself: (1) a body *can* be raced *and* human, but *cannot*; (2) a body *can* be foreign and American, but *cannot*; and (3) a body *can* be a racial *xenos* and sovereign, but *cannot*. It is the phenomenology of this "two-ness" that is, for Du Bois, double consciousness. As Chandler puts it, Du Bois' figure of the double involves "the necessity to both mark or name a difference while simultaneously inhabiting the necessity of elaborating an understanding of this difference as other than pure or simple." This necessity, it turns out, is for the racial subject "*both to be and not to be.*"[75]

The idea of double consciousness has always been pregnant with various possibilities. For example, Du Bois penned in the very next paragraph that the history of the American Negro was the history of a longing "to attain self-conscious manhood, to merge his double self into a better and truer self."[76] Here, double consciousness and the image of the veil appear in solidarity with the functionalist logic of inclusion, and indeed, Denise Ferreira da Silva questions the emancipatory potential of double consciousness for just this reason, as I recounted in Chapter 2. And there is certainly something persuasive about this sort of criticism.[77] Consider Du Bois' claim that, from the perspective of the colonized world, World War I signaled only the beginning and hardly the end of white supremacy: "[World War I] is nothing to compare with that fight for freedom which black and brown and yellow men must and will make unless their oppression and humiliation and insult at the hands of the White World cease. The Dark World is going to submit to

---

[73] DU BOIS, SOULS, *supra* note 65, at 16–17.

[74] GILROY, *supra* note 72, at 127. *See also* RICHARD WRIGHT, THE COLOR CURTAIN: A REPORT ON THE BANDUNG CONFERENCE (1956).

[75] CHANDLER, *supra* note 65, at 60.

[76] *Id.* at 17.

[77] *See, e.g.*, Anthony Appiah, *The Uncompleted Argument: Du Bois and the Illusion of Race*, 12 CRIT. INQ. 21 (1985).

336 THE RIGHT TO EXCLUDE

its present treatment just as long as it must and not one moment longer."[78] Double consciousness, in this trajectory, seems little more than a logic for inverting exclusion into inclusion: With its perennial separation between the worlds of rational man and abandoned bodies, the mind that is doubly conscious knows that it is only a matter of time before the doors open. This is double consciousness as emblematic of what would become international law's modern racial ideology, with its logic of inclusion, its functionalism, and prohibition on discrimination.

At the same time, Du Bois also believed that this merging of the two selves meant neither an assimilation of the *xenos* into whiteness, nor some blended hybrid. The purpose was to inhabit the conflict, to be both and neither, both racial *xenos* and *homo politicus*, living in the world as an insider-outsider in which insides and outsides lose their meaning. Riding shotgun with double consciousness into the middle decades of the twentieth century, it is this Kierkegaardian sensibility that we find in Ralph Ellison's *Invisible Man*.[79] For Ellison's nameless protagonist, the defining characteristic of double consciousness is the *chiasmus*, the paradox, the criss-crossed *X*. It is in the understanding of and commitment to this relation between visible and invisible, structure and surface, freedom and control—between the visionary and the realist—that Ellison illuminates "the blackness of my invisibility."[80] For those invisible bodies doubly conscious,[81] "you're constantly being bumped against by those of poor vision ... you often doubt if you really exist."[82] Ellison wrote:

> Invisibility, let me explain, gives one a slightly different sense of time, you're never quite on the beat. Sometime you're ahead and sometimes you're behind. Instead of the swift and imperceptible flowing of time, you are aware of its nodes, those points where time stands still or from which it leads ahead. And you slip into the breaks and look around ... The unheard sounds [of the music] came through, and each melodic line existed of itself, stood out clearly from the rest ... That night I found myself hearing not only in time, but in space as well. I not only entered the music but descended, like Dante, into its depths ... and beneath the surface ... I found a lower level ... and I heard someone shout: "Brothers and sisters, my text this morning is the 'Blackness of Blackness.' In the beginning ... there was blackness ... and the sun ... was bloody red ... Now black is ... and an' black

---

[78] Du Bois, Selections, *supra* note 65, at 177.

[79] Ralph Ellison, Invisible Man (1995). On Richard Wright and Soren Kierkegaard, *see* Gilroy, *supra* note 72, at 159.

[80] Ellison, *supra* note 79, at 13.

[81] Ellison was explicit in the claim that having a certain shade of skin color is insufficient in itself. It is probably worth emphasizing again, what were are constructing as *black legal thought* is not an account of a lived experience, or an identity, or a cultural dominant, or any related thing. When Frantz Fanon wrote, for example, "My blackness was there, dense and undeniable," he was speaking of precisely that identitarian idea of blackness that we are trying to avoid. *See* Frantz Fanon, Black Skin, White Masks 96 (2008).

[82] Ellison, *supra* note 79, at 4.

ON THE INEVITABILITY OF RACIAL BORDERS 337

ain't ... Black will git you ... an' black won't ... Black will make you ... or will black will unmake you ... "[83]

My [underground home] is warm and light. Yes, *full* of light. I doubt if there is a brighter spot in all New York than this hole of mine, and I do not exclude Broadway. Or the Empire State Building on a photographer's dream night. But that is taking advantage of you. Those two spots are among the darkest of our whole civilization ... which might sound like a hoax or a contradiction, but that (by contradiction, I mean) is how the world moves: Not like an arrow, but a boomerang ... I know; *I have boomeranged across my head so much that I now can see the darkness of lightness.* And I love light. Perhaps you'll think it strange than an invisible man should need light, desire light, love light. But maybe it is exactly because I *am* invisible. Light confirms my reality, gives birth to my form ... Without light I am not only invisible, but formless as well; and to be unaware of one's form is to live a death. *I myself, after existing some twenty years, did not become alive until I discovered my invisibility.*[84]

More recently, Chandler has underscored the radical potential of concepts like double consciousness and invisibility, as making "possible the opening for a powerful critical reflection upon the scene of its own historical production,"[85] and opening a "passageway of irruption [leading] ... to another world, beyond the possible as a given horizon."[86] Du Bois' chiastic practice, "of becoming other, of becoming oneself as even an encompassment of the other ... is a referral to a constitutive order of the possibility of sensibility, being, and existence." "Du Bois' practice solicits *us*—whomever might be such—to look at ourselves in a radically *other* way. This is the figure of the X ... this remains *the* [color] *line* for contemporary thought in our time."[87]

And it is here, in this chiastic rendering of double consciousness made manifest in the figure of the X, that perhaps we can reimagine the right to exclude. Perhaps this is one among many of the critical race tradition's offerings in the effort to become visionaries of the real, reimagining the *unbounded demos*, reimagining the meaning of the racial *xenos*, the foreigner at home. Perhaps.

[83] *Id.* at 8–10.
[84] *Id.* at 6–7.
[85] CHANDLER, *supra* note 65, at 37.
[86] *Id.* at 36–37.
[87] *Id.* at 111.

# Index

*For the benefit of digital users, indexed terms that span two pages (e.g., 52–53) may, on occasion, appear on only one of those pages.*

Abdu'l- Baha 195
Abizadeh, Arash 297, 315, 324–25, 326–29, 330, 331
Achiume, E. Tendayi 259–60, 315–16
Acquired Rights debate 218–20
Agamben, Giorgio 29, 62–63, 68–72, 73–74, 93–94, 95–96, 229
Alvarez, Alejandro 120–22, 152–53, 154
anthropology 246–47
 cultural 91
 ethnicity 88–89
 modern anthropology 195
 physical *see* physical anthropology
 UNESCO race project 248–49
anticlassification/antisubordination debate 233–38
anticolonialism
 anticolonial nationalists 191
 anticolonial self-determination to human rights 210–28
 antiracism, and 227, 250–51
 *dominium* 255
antidiscrimination principle 2, 3–5
 ameliorating conditions of historically disadvantaged groups 234
 anticlassification/antisubordination debate 233–38
 antiracism, and 192, 233, 260–61
 colorblindness 232–34, 238
 cultural difference 279
 group disadvantaging principle 235–36, 237
 indigenous groups 279
 multiculturalism, and 269–70
 neoformalism and neoliberalism 232
 preventing irrational and unfair injuries 234
 race-neutral decisions with racially disproportionate impact 234–35
 unconnectedness 236–37
 unequal treatment, justifying 234
anti-essentialism 7, 282
antiracialism 11, 313
 antiracism, replacing 308–9
 neoliberalism, and 303

postracialism's antiracialism 12, 309
antiracism 231, 308–9
 anticolonialism, and 227, 250–51
 antidiscrimination principle, and 192, 233, 260–61
 antiracialism, replaced by 308–9
 black nationalism, and 272
 decolonization as 233
 *dominium* as antiracism 191, 198–99, 210
 global antiracism 135–36, 159–60, 192, 199–200, 207–8, 210, 217–18, 260–61
 integration, and 272
 postracialism, and 9–10, 309
 right of *imperium* as a key to global antiracism 135–36
 self-determination, and 18, 19, 135–36, 190–91, 210
 *uti possidetis*, and 216
apartheid 3–4, 17–18, 162, 249–50
 after apartheid 222–28
Aristotle 31–32, 34, 36, 38, 51–52, 71–72, 76–77, 109–10, 147–48
 finding happiness as purpose of man 31–32
 function of ethics 31–32
 humans as innately political 31–32
 medieval Aristotelianism 30–33
 natural scale 78

Bandung Conference 207–10, 220–21, 226–27, 231
Barthes, Roland 14–15, 20
Bell, Daniel 139–40
Bernier, Francois 76–78
 characterizing humans as racial beings 76–78
 four basic *especes ou races* 76–77
biological determinism 80–81, 90, 96
biopower 71–73, 74–75
 benefits of 72
 dark sides of 72
 emergence of 73, 74–75
 meaning of 71–72
 population management and control 71–72, 73, 95–96

340  INDEX

biopower (*cont.*)
 raciality, and  74–75, 96
 racism as biopower reconceptualizing idea
  of war  72
 scientific discourse of racial development
  racializing theory of  96
Black Internationalism  204
Black Lives Matter  8–9, 284–85
black nationalism  272
Black Radical Tradition  202–4
Blumenbach, Johann Friedrich  78, 79–80
 differences between humans a matter of
  environmental pressure  78
 *On the Natural Variety of Mankind*  78
 sub-division of the human species into five
  groups  78, 81, 109
 Caucasian race  78, 85
Bluntschli, Johann Kaspar  126–28
 free movement of persons  165, 166
 *Theory of the State*  126
Boas, Franz  174, 195, 245
border controls *see* exclusion
borders *see* racial borders
Brierly, J.L.  153–54, 156
Brown, Wendy  7–9, 19–20, 239–40, 241, 244,
  300–1, 302–3, 304, 308, 319–22, 327
Buffon, Georges- Louis Leclerc, Comte de  77–78
 characterizing humans as racial beings  77
 differences between humans a matter of
  environmental pressure  78
 white raciality as the 'norm' of racial
  development  77, 78

Caucasian race  78, 81–82, 83–84, 85, 115–16,
  127, 183
Chamberlain, Houston Stewart  86–88, 109
Chandler, Nahum  332–33, 334, 335, 337
Chetail, Vincent  165–66, 175, 257
China
 Family of Nations, and  118, 130–31, 176
 US, and  169
 migration to US *see under* migration law
classic racial ideology  102–32
 articulating racial ideology in the classic
  style  113–32
  international law's boundary problem,
   racial ideology and  119–32
  racial subjects in the global *demos*  115–19
  racialization in 19th century  115
  racialized xenophobia indigenous to liberal
   theory  113–14
  sovereign equality, domestic analogy
   approach and  119–32
  property, sovereignty, and territory  103–13

 I acts of first possession and
  occupation  104–5
 adverse possession, resemblance to  105–6
 international law's boundary problem  110–
  13, 131
 legal ideology of the rule of law  109–10
 right to exclude  106–9
 sovereign's 'organic' connection with the
  territory  106
 sovereigns as possessors in title  106–7
colonialism/colonization
 decolonization *see* decolonization
 foreign exploitation, colonialism as  206
 lapse of  2
 racial discrimination, colonialism as worst
  form of  206
 racism developing with colonization  72
 UN approach to  207
colorblindness
 antidiscrimination principle  232–34, 238
 colorblind diversity  265
 colorblind racism  7–8, 232
 critical race theory  7–8
 cultural diversity  292–93, 301
 emergence of formalistic and colorblind
  conceptions of race and racism  237
 ineffective performance in a competitive
  marketplace, pointing to  7–8
 national identity  297–98
 neoliberalism, and  7–8
 postracial pragmatism  260–61, 283, 301
 racial ideology, and  7–8, 236
 racial integration  311
 unconnectedness  236–37
 value of seeing race without history  8–9
Congress of Vienna  118–19
critical race theory  1–2, 21–22
 antidiscrimination principle  3–4
 colorblind racism  7–8
 development of  7, 272–73
 racism, and  6–7, 329
 Trumpian attack on  65
cultural assimilation  283
cultural autonomy  205, 271–72
cultural difference  79, 232, 268–69, 291–92
 antidiscrimination principle, and  279, 285
 celebration of  3–4
 collisions of  7
 cultural diversity promoting  9–10
 ineffective performance in a competitive
  marketplace  7–8
 multicultural right to difference  283
 multiculturalism, and  283
 political theory of  269

postraciality, and 9–10
priority of ethnocultural difference 11, 313
racial diversity 284–85
racism, and 14–15
'reality' of 283
self-determination, as vehicle for 10
true battleground for equality, as 269
cultural diversity 282–83
colorblind diversity 265
colorblindness, and 292–93, 301
cultural diversity over racial justice 10–11
ethnic and cultural difference, promotion
of 9–10
inclusion, as 9–10
multiculturalism, and 269–70, 283, 284–85
postraciality, and 9–10
self-determination, as vehicle
for 10, 231–32
cultural identity 4–5
liberal theory of 10
national identity, as 298
cultural integrity 268–69
affirmative measures in protection of 270
demand for conformity to a cultural
essence 283
exclusion, and 280–81
international law protecting 281
racial differences, reproduction of 283
rights to 280
self-determination, and 231–32, 280
cultural nationalism 63, 106, 328–29, 330, 331
cultural rights 268–69
cultural diversity, rights to 280
cultural integrity, protection of 270
ICERD *see* International Covenant on
Economic, Social and Cultural
Rights (ICERD)
minority rights 269–70
multicultural right to difference 283
multiculturalism, and 269
cultural studies 91–92, 282
cultural translation 282
Cushing, Caleb 130–31, 176, 238–39

Darwin, Charles 83, 115
natural selection 82, 83–84
*On the Origin of the Species* 82, 83–84
Social Darwinism 83–85
decolonization 137, 189–228
anticolonial self-determination to human
rights 210–28
Acquired Rights debate 218–20
apartheid, after 222–28
*Frontier Dispute* case 215–18

*imperium* and New International Economic
Order 220–22
*Western Sahara* 211–14, 278–79
*dominium* as necessary condition for 17–18
end of 2–3
human rights as effect of national
self-determination 18–19
interwar alliance between antiracist and
anticolonial strategy 193–210
Bandung Conference 207–10, 220–21,
226–27, 231
Black Radical Tradition 202–4
decolonizing the UN 205–7
League against Imperialism 201–3, 204–5
Pan-African Movement/Pan-
Africanism 189–90, 199–202, 204–6,
226–27, 231
Universal Races Congress 1911 (URC) 170,
189–90, 200–1, 220–21, 226–27,
231, 245
UN Decolonization Declaration 190–91
DNA 90
*dominium*
anticolonialism, and 255
antiracism, as 191, 198–99, 210
racial hierarchy, eliminating 17–19, 231
decolonization, as necessary
condition for 17–18
decolonization nonintervention,
right of 18, 62, 107, 109, 131
eugenics, and 190
nature of 107–8, 109, 112
new states 222
private owners 46, 107–8
property rights 219–20
racial subjection, and 18
sovereign's right of 27–28, 107–8, 120, 135–
36, 190, 208
racial justice, and 192–93
right to exclude, as 15–16, 47
sovereign's right *see dominium*: sovereign's
right to exclude
rights of *imperium* and *dominium* conflating in
the sovereign 48
Roman law 45, 46–47
root of title in property law, as 46–47
self-determination, right of 62, 107–8, 109
cultural difference as vehicle for 10
cultural diversity as vehicle for 10, 231–32
cultural integrity, and 231–32, 280
eugenics, and 190
external self-determination 107–8
human rights as effect of 18–19
internal self-determination 107–8

342  INDEX

*dominium (cont.)*
  nature of  17–18, 107–8, 109, 112
  new states  222
  presupposing idea of legal personality  108
  property rights  219–20
  racial hierarchy, as cure to  231
  racial subjection, and  18
  sovereign's right of  27–28, 107–8, 135–36,
    190, 208
  sovereignty and *dominium*, connection
    between  48–49
  territorial right of  106–8, 109
*dominium*: sovereign's right to exclude  6, 15–18,
    41–61, 107–8, 174
  coercive nature of right to exclude  5–6
  *demos*  17, 49–61
  domestic analogy and the global *demos*  49–
    61, 119–32
    global *demos* of free and equal
      sovereigns  49–50
    Pufendorf *see* Pufendorf, Samuel
    recognition  60–61
    sovereign in an international state of
      nature  49–50
    Vattel *see* Vattel, Emerich
  generative dimension of see *imperium*
  global antiracism, and  192
  *imperium*, right of see *imperium*
  international law, right to exclude in  47–49
  liberal legal thought  29
  logic of exclusion and its limits *see under*
    exclusion
  migration  28
  national and cultural identity, enforcing  4–5
  nature of  28
  *pomerium, dominium*, and *imperium*  43–49
  possession leading to  106–7
  racial subjection, and *see* racial subjection
  raciality *see* postracial xenophobia; racial
    xenophobia; raciality
  right of *dominium*, as  15–16, 47
  sovereign exclusion as right against all other
    sovereigns  28
  territorial dimension, *dominium* as  27–28, 106–8
  US Supreme Court, *dominium* in  175–81
  xenology as means for distinguishing between
    human collectivities  5–6
  *see also* individual right to exclude
Du Bois, W.E.B.  70, 191–2, 193, 195, 199–201,
    203, 204–5, 245, 315–16, 332–211, 335–
    36, 337

Ellison, Ralph  336–37
'End of Ideology' program  138–39, 140

environmentalism  80–81, 82
ethnicity
  meaning of  22, 92–93
  physical anthropology, and  88–89, 174
  racialized and non-racialized ethnicity  92
ethnocultural difference  9–11
eugenics  4, 17–18, 115, 188, 245
  biopower  72
  functionalism, and  174
  ideology of racial subjection, as  187
  key assumptions of the eugenics
    movement  84–85
  policy tool for border control, as  190
  raciality/theory of racial identity  84–87
  social science prescriptions for race
    relations  194
  US migration control *see* migration law:
    United States
  white supremacy, disaggregating  85–86
Eurocentrism  2–3
exclusion
  logic of exclusion and its limits  68–76
    governing and generative power of raciality,
      underestimating  65–66
    liberalism, criticisms of  64–65
    racial discrimination and racial
      subjection  66–68
    racial hierarchy as feature of
      liberalism  64–65
    sociohistorical logic of exclusion  65–
      68, 74–75
  right to exclude
    individuals, of *see* individual right to
      exclude
    racial equality, and *see* racial equality,
    refugees, and the right to exclude
    sovereigns, of see *dominium*: sovereign's
      right to exclude

Family of Nations  125, 159–60, 167, 179, 331
  China  118, 130–31, 176
  Dominion of  215–16
  end of Family of Nations model  157–58
    giving way to new League of Nations  171
    move from Family of Nations to UN  192–93
  equality of the human races, and  122
  formal and procedural equality as the
    norm  117–18
  free movement within the global
    demos  167–68
  Great Powers, and  117–19
  imperial borders of, policing  136
  inequalities of Family of Nations
    model  158–59

**INDEX** 343

international legal personality in 117, 162–63, 187
Latin American sovereigns 122
lesser powers of 118–19
migration law in 164–66
  free movement of persons as the rule 165–66
  migrants travelling from beyond Family of Nations 166
  migrants travelling from within Family of Nations 168–69
  view of migration as commerce in Family of Nations 166, 169
multiracial, becoming 196–97
natural superiority of white Europeans as uniting factor 128–29
Ottoman Empire 118, 128–30
outer bounds of 117
proxy for racialization of international society, as 113–14
racial hierarchy
  becoming impractical and unprofitable 229–30
  justification for exclusion, as 197
racial ideology of exclusion 174
racially superior states belonging to 126–27, 147
right to exclude individual human beings 230–31
semi-peripheral states 118
sovereign equality 119, 125–26, 129–30
sovereignty alone insufficient to warrant membership 119
systems of international egalitarianism and order following 161
United States 119–20
Field, Stephen 175–79, 180–81, 238–39
formalism 238–39
  formalist racial ideology *see* classic racial ideology
  legal formalism *see* legal formalism
  legal ideology as 102–3
  nature of 102
formalist racial ideology 102–3
Foucault, Michel 63, 71–73, 74–75, 93–94, 95–96, 239–40, 283
  biopower *see* biopower
free competition *see* individual right and free competition
Freeden, Michael 97–100, 101–2
*Frontier Dispute* case 215–18
functionalism 102, 136–37, 239
  functionalist racial ideology *see* modern racial ideology

legal functionalism *see* legal functionalism
legal ideology as 102–3
nature of 102, 137
neoformalism, into 232–33
postracial ideology 301
problems with 237–38
rights as an end to be realized 239
weakening of 232
functionalist nationalism 292–93, 301–2
functionalist racial ideology 102–3

Galton, Francis
  *Hereditary Genius* 84–85
genetic variation 90–91
Geneva Convention 125–26
Geny, Francois 144–47, 150–51, 156, 173, 229–30
  *Method of Interpretation and Sources of Private Positive Law* 144
globalization
  continued relevance of sovereignty 21–22
  democracy, and 21–22
  global governance
    response to globalization, as 20
    unavailability of a global *demos* 21
Gobineau, Count Arthur de 87–88, 127, 165
  polygenist thinking, as apogee of 82
  *The Inequality of Races* 81–82
Great Chain of Being 78, 83
Great Powers 120, 130
  Committee of Five 116
  Family of Nations, and 117–19
  global interests of 115–16
  membership 115–16, 118–19
  proxy for racialization of international society 113–14
  rights of territorial integrity and self-defense 128–29
  sovereign equality, nature of 116, 129–30
Grotius, Hugo 29, 60

Haddon, A.C. 87–89, 91–92, 245
  *We Europeans* 87–88
Hall, Stuart 12–13, 92–93, 99–100,
Hartman, Saidiya 63, 67, 68, 73, 74–75, 93–94, 95
Herder, Johann Gottfied von
  cultural nation, concept of 79
  hierarchy of racial subjects 79–80
  unified but differentiated human species 79–80
Hobbes, Thomas 16–17, 34–37, 38, 48, 50–51, 54–55, 61, 65, 71–72, 131, 140
  features of human personality 36
  *Leviathan* 50–51, 56, 76–77

## 344    INDEX

Hobbes, Thomas (*cont.*)
  state of nature
    individualism and equality  34–36, 49–50,
      57–58, 68–69
    meaning of  34–35
    warring state of nature  54–55, 57
  subordination of individual freedoms to the
    sovereign  36, 40–41, 52, 54–55, 63–64
  transition to a political community through
    social contract  35–36, 63–64
*homo politicus*  320–21
  alone and self- interested, as  49–50
  central position in racial ideology  115
  citizens of global *demos*, as  166
  citizens of political society, as  68–69
  human being as inherently sociable  31–32
  'possessive individual', as  34–35
  rational, reasoning, self- determining, as  74,
    95–96, 322–23
  rights-bearing  75, 229, 322–23
  self-determination, right of  323
  universalism of  322–23
  white humans, as  83
  *xenoi/xenos*, and  68–69, 73, 75, 80–81, 83,
    229, 336
*homo sacer*  70–72, 73, 74
human rights
  antidiscrimination principle *see*
    antidiscrimination principle
  apolitical approach to protecting
    individuals  243–44
  effect of self-determination, as  18–19
  individualism  239, 243–44
  minimalism  243–44
  national identities  4–5
  neoliberal colorblindness  19
  racial justice reform  4
    means for realizing racial justice, as  190–91
    racial justice as precondition for exercise
      of  190–91
  refugees *see* racial equality, refugees and right
    to exclude
  rise of human rights framework  2
  self-determination, and *see* self-determination
  UDHR  233, 242–43, 245–47, 253–54
Huxley, Julian  87–89, 91–92, 245
  *We Europeans*  87–88
  UNESCO  247–48

ideology
  meaning of  96–103
    ideology as political and social reality  97–100
    ideology as type of language system  101
  postracial *see* postracial ideology

  racial *see* racial ideology
*imperium*
  generative dimension of right to exclude,
    as  27–28, 106–7
  global antiracism, as key to  135–36
  nature of  75–76
  NIEO, and  220–22
  province of the sovereign state, as  59
  racial justice  188
  right to determine the bounds of the
    collectivity  59
  rights of *imperium* and *dominium* conflating in
    the sovereign  48
  Roman law  43–44, 45–46
  sovereign's right to exclude  15–16
  sovereign's right to set rules for the
    international system  27–28, 29, 48
  sovereign's rule-making power  59
  statehood  60–61
  state's authority to make rules, as  47
inclusion
  cultural diversity, as  9–10
  logic of inclusion  156–60
Indigenous Peoples, rights of
  antidiscrimination principle  279
  Indigenous Rights Declaration  279
  Indigenous Rights movement  265, 275–81
  multiculturalism, and  313
  UN Declaration on Rights of Indigenous
    Peoples 2007  277–79, 280–81
individual right and free competition  25–26, 27,
  34–35, 36–37, 241–42
  liberal legalism  25–26, 27, 34–35, 36–37, 239–
    40, 241–42
  Locke  39–41
individual right to exclude  28
  debate about primacy of right to exclude  43
  property rights  41–42, 48, 219–20
    *dominium* as root of title in property
      law  46–47
  right to exclude happening
    naturally  42–43
  territorial right of *dominium*  28
integration  237–38, 269–70, 280
  antiracism, and  272
  colorblind approach to racial integration  311
  ICERD  252–53
  national identity, psychological role in social
    integration of  296
  social integration
    ethnic basis for shared, national
      culture  297
    national identity, importance of  314
    role of  296

INDEX    345

International Covenant on Civil and Political
    Rights of 1966 (CCPR)  251, 253–54
International Covenant on Economic, Social and
    Cultural Rights  253–54
International Convention on the Elimination of
    Racial Discrimination (ICERD)  1–3, 19,
    232–33, 245–53, 254–55
  adoption of  249–50
  background  246–50
  CERD General Recommendations  253–54
  citizen's right to be free of racial
    discrimination  250–51
  integration movements and policies,
    encouraging  252–53
  provisions of  251–54, 255, 280–81
International Labor Organization (ILO)  277–78
international law
  boundary problem  110–13, 119–20, 131
  classic style of racial ideology *see* classic racial
    ideology
  cultural integrity  281
  influence of race on international legal
    thought  109
  *jus gentium*  33, 51–52
  natural law, deriving from  33
  necessary, arbitrary, and voluntary law of
    nations, as  55–57
  product of a global authority, as  54–55
  recognition  60–61
  right to exclude see *dominium*: sovereign's
    right to exclude
  teaching rights as the derivative of duties  55
  Third World Approaches to International
    Law  272–75
  white races in Europe and US, international
    law for  125–26

Japan
  migration to US *see under* migration law
  proposed racial equality clause in League of
    Nations  170–73, 174
Jhering, Rudolph von  141–44, 147–49, 150–51,
  156, 173, 229–30
  *Law as a Means to an End*  141–42
  *The Evolution of the Aryan*  148–49

Kant, Immanuel  86, 140
Kennedy, Duncan  238–39, 242, 243, 244, 272–73

LatCrit movement  273–75
Latin America  122
Laughlin, Harry  174, 183, 186–87
Lauterpacht, Hersch  153–54, 156
  *International Law and Human Rights*  154

recognition  60
League against Imperialism and for National
  Independence  201–3, 204–5
League of Nations  4, 136–37, 151–52, 191
  African-American writers criticizing  201
  Covenant  4, 157–58, 170–71, 245–46
  Family of Nations transition to  159, 171
  governance  157–58
  Japan's proposed racial equality clause  170–
    73, 174
  League against Imperialism criticizing  201–2
  legal functionalism  163
  Mandate system  2–3, 158–59, 161, 162, 201,
    223–24, 276–77
    Class A Mandates  159
    Class B Mandates  159
    Class C Mandates  159, 201, 222–23
  Namibia  222–23
  raciality, and  201
  sovereign equality  159–60
  Soviet Union joining  204–5
legal formalism  136–37, 238–39, 300
  legal formalism to legal functionalism, shift
    to  229–30
  naturalizing juridical science, as new form
    of  136–37
legal functionalism  230–31, 239, 300
  lapse of  237
  legal formalism to legal functionalism, shift
    to  229–30
  rise of  138–50, 192
liberal legal thought  12–15, 25–27
  background and foreground
    rules  26–27
  global context of  29–30
  grammar of  13–14, 25–26
  language- system, as  26
  sovereign's right to exclude  29
  sovereignty, concept of  15–16
  structure of  15
  theses of *see* liberal legalism, three theses of
liberal legalism, three theses of  27, 30–41
  Hobbes *see* Hobbes, Thomas
  individual right and free competition  25–26,
    27, 34–35, 36–37, 241–42
  Locke *see* Locke, John
  medieval Aristotelianism *see under* Aristotle
  naturalizing juridical science  25–26,
    27, 36–37
  ordered liberty and social control  25–26,
    27, 35–37
liberal nationalism  10, 21–22, 267–68, 293–98,
  301, 313–14, 321
liberalism, criticisms of  64–65

346 INDEX

Locke, John 37–41, 65
  individual right and free competition 39–41
  natural condition of humans/state of
    nature 37–38, 39–40, 49–50
  natural economic practices 39, 40–41
  right of ownership 38–39, 40–41, 49–50, 53
  ownership of own physical bodies 38–39, 41–42
  Rule of Reason 37–38
  *Second Treatise* 76–77

Marshall, John 106–7, 178–80, 238–39, 240–41
Marx, Karl/Marxism 97–98, 99, 203, 204, 305
McKeown, Adam 164, 168–69, 187, 254–55
migration law, international
  American *see* migration law: United States
  Family of Nations *see under* Family of Nations
migration law: United States 163–66, 169–74
  American slavery, and 163, 166–69
    free movement of persons between
      states 166–68
    insider-outsiders 167
    international rule of free movement, US
      following 166–67
    Jim Crow segregation 168, 187
    Ku Klux Klan 168, 201–2
  Asian immigration 85, 168–70, 173–74, 181–
    82, 183, 184, 187
  border control 163–64, 187
  Chinese immigration 168–69
    Chinese Exclusion case 175–81, 182, 288
    Chinese Exclusion Laws 163, 182, 255–56
    Chinese immigration 168–69, 175–81, 288
  *dominium* in Supreme Court 175–81
  eugenics 181, 184
    eugenicist theory of national origins 185
    Eugenics Record Office 186
    quota law 186–87
    transition of immigration law from eugenics
      to modern race science 255–56
  Immigration Restriction League 149,
    173, 181–82
  Japan
    Japanese immigration 168–69,
      170, 181–82
    proposed racial equality clause at League of
      Nations 170–73, 174
  Johnson–Reed Act 1924 163–64, 184–86, 187
  land laws 170
  massive migration flows into US 166, 168–69
  national right to exclude 168–70, 175
  open-borders system for individual
    migrants 163, 184
  race neutrality in immigration law, move
    to 255–57

transformation of migration law after World
  War I 181–88
  capping new arrivals relative to baseline
    population 184–87, 254–55
  Dillingham Commission 182–84, 186
  hierarchy of racial development, data
    showing 183
  Immigration Act 1924 as template for global
    migration control 187, 254–55
  intensifying concern about southern and
    eastern European immigration 182
  naturalization law 182, 255–56
  protection of American race from racial
    contamination 184, 186
  unassimilable character of new
    immigrants 183, 184
modern racial ideology 102–3, 135–60
  early and late modern racial ideology 233
  functionalism in international legal
    thought 150–55
  functionalist nature of 137
  logic of inclusion 156–60
  rise of legal functionalism rise of 138–50
Montagu, Ashley 88–89, 91–92, 245, 248–49
  *Man's Most Dangerous Myth: The Fallacy of
    Race* 88
  racial development, challenging 88–89
  'ethnic group' preference for 88–89
  *The Concept of Race* 88
  UNESCO's 1951 'Statement on Race' 88
Montevideo Convention on Rights and Duties of
  States 1933 60
Morton, Samuel George 81
Moyn, Samuel 91, 93, 230, 238–39, 242–43,
  314, 315
  African-Americans 272
  antidiscrimination, and 269–70
  cultural difference 283, 294–95
  cultural diversity 269–70, 283, 284–85
  cultural integrity 283
  group rights aimed at cultural
    autonomy 271–72
  Indigenous peoples, rights of 313
  liberal culturalist view of 269–70
  liberal theory, and 10, 313–14
  neoformalism, and 265–66
  political theory of multiculturalism 269
  postracial ideology, and 268–69, 301
  postracial multiculturalism *see* postracial
    multiculturalism
  race consciousness,
    displacing 311
  racial justice reform 4
  radical multiculturalism 295, 296–97

umbrella term for promotion of cultural
diversity and rights, as 269
URC illustrating inclusive
multiculturalism 198–99

Namibia *see* South West Africa/Namibia
national identity 265–66
American 184
exclusion, and 292–93
functionalism, and 311–12
functionally necessary for socially integrated
political community 265, 293–98, 321
common national identity necessary for
political stability 295
cultural identity, national identity
as 297–98
inclusive and colorblind, national identity
as 297–98
meaningful national identities 296–97
psychological role of national identity in
social integration 296
shared culture that cannot be
neutral 297, 313–14
social integration, national identity
necessary for 297, 313–14
liberal theory of 10, 21–22, 293–98
characteristics in which national identity
emerges 293–94
function of publicly shared culture, national
identity as 293–94
participation in societal culture, national
identity based on 270
social constructions, as 295–96
sovereign's right to exclude, and 10, 299
sovereign's right to produce and enforce 4–
5, 298
universalism 243–44
vertical relationship between community
and sovereign, national identity
requiring 295
nationalism 10–11, 93, 290, 315, 326–28
black nationalism, and 272
conservative ultranationalism 265–
66, 295–97
cultural nationalism 63, 106, 328–29, 330, 331
functionalist nationalism 292–93, 301–2
international regulation 230
liberal nationalism 10, 21–22, 267–68, 293–
98, 301, 313–14, 321
liberal theory defending 10
postracial nationalism *see* postracial nationalism
self-determination *see* self- determination
xenophobic nationalism 301, 311–12
ultranationalist xenophobia 286, 292

natural law 153, 156, 238–39
citizens' rights and duties 51–52
functionalism, and 136–37
global philosophy of 140
human law subject to 31
international law deriving from 33
law of nations, as 51–52, 55–56
nature of theory 30–31, 35–36
nature of things, and 145, 146–47
universal and perpetual, natural law as 30–
31, 52
'Rule of Reason' 38
source for 53–54
states and individuals, applying to 55–56
naturalizing juridical science 25–26, 27, 137,
232, 298, 300–2, 332
dependency on 315–16
formalism *see* formalism
functionalism *see* functionalism
harmonizing demands of freedom and
order 37, 101–2, 110, 299–300
neoformalism *see* neoformalism
race as form of 111–12
racial ideology *see* racial ideology
racial xenophobia *see* racial xenophobia
right to exclude 27, 68, 147, 322–23
rule of law 36–37, 110
styles of 102–3
nature/state of nature
critical to distinction between humans and
rights-bearing citizens 68–69
culture, and 91
exclusion of state of nature from political
society 69
generating owner's right to exclude 42–43
Hobbes *see* Hobbes, Thomas
human being as a rights-bearing individual in
a state of nature 15
justifying racialized exclusion in genetic and
biological differences 14–15
law of nature 30–31, 37–38, 56–57
Locke *see* Locke, John
sovereigns as rights-bearing individuals in a
global state of nature 15, 16–17, 49–50,
55, 58–59
Nazism 72, 81–82, 87–88, 187, 204–5, 249
neoformalism 10–11, 19, 241–44, 301, 314, 332
antidiscrimination principle 232–33
critique of neoformalism: postracial
multiculturalism 267–85
functionalism transitioning into *see under*
functionalism
multiculturalism, and 265–66, 292, 301–2
naturalizing juridical science, as new form of 137

348 INDEX

neoliberalism 238–41
  colorblindness, and 7–8
  criticisms of 19–20
  ideology of the market, as 7–8
    liberal thesis of right and
      competition 239–40
  neoliberal colorblindness see neoliberal
    colorblindness
  pragmatic liberalism, and see under pragmatic
    liberalism
neoliberal colorblindness 2, 7–8, 10–11
  ideological dominance, reasons for losing 311
  international human rights law, and 19
  meaning 7–8
  NIEO project, and 222
  postracial xenophobia, and see under
    postracial xenophobia
  `racial categories crafted as 'formal'
    classifications 236
New Haven School 289
New International Economic Order
      (NIEO) 189–90, 192, 231–32, 314–15
  imperium, and 220–22
  intellectual orientation 221
  movement towards 220–21
  objectives 221
  racial justice, means for achieving 135–36
  Washington Consensus, yielding to 222
Ngai, Mai 163–64, 184, 185–86
nonintervention, right of see under dominium

othering 7, 66
Ottoman Empire
  Family of Nations, and 118, 128–30

Pan-African Movement/Pan-Africanism 189–
    90, 199–202, 204–6, 226–27, 231
Parker, Kunal 163, 166–68, 169–70, 175, 184
phrenology 80–81, 163–64
physical anthropology 77–78, 79, 192–93
  Blumenbach, and 78, 79
  criticisms of older modes of 249
  ethnicity 88–89, 174
  genetic variation 90–91
  human classification 112
  human DNA, focus on 90
  modern anthropology 195
  natural world, reliance on 229
  nature and purpose of 77–78
  phrenology 80–81
  race and racial identity
    biological criteria for human hierarchy,
      use of 112
    ethnicity 88–89, 174

  genetic variation 90–91
  race rarely considered as meaningful term 9
  race science as natural science, doubts
    about 267
  racial barriers, existence of 194–95
  racial formation occurring in distant
    past 82–83
  racial identity 9, 63, 88
  racial ideology 29–30
  white race functioning as original standard,
    erroneous nature of 89–90
  UNESCO race project 88, 248–49
polygenism 81, 82
pomerium 43–49, 62–63, 90–91
postracial ideology 8–9, 11
  abandonment of race science as natural
    science 267
  colorblindness, and 283, 301
    antidiscrimination law 260–61
  diversity 284, 285
  'field of oscillations', as 301–2
  functionalism 301
  minimalism to address racism 9–10
  multiculturalism, and 268–69, 301
  nationalist nature of 292
  pragmatism 11, 300
  racelessness, culture of 301, 303
  racial ideology transforming into 61
  self-determination see self-determination,
    right of
postracial multiculturalism 20, 265–66, 267–
    85, 293
  affirmative measures to protect cultural
    integrity, need for 270–72
      African- Americans 272
    immigrant groups 271–72
    indigenous peoples 271
    substate nations 271
  colorblindness 300
  culture/cultural difference as battleground for
    equality 269
  LatCrit movement 273–75
  liberal theory of multiculturalism, as 265–66
  multiculturalism as flashpoint in struggle
    against racism 269–70
  postracial self-determination 275–81
  raciality, analytics of 281–85
    cultural translation 282
    diversity 284–85
  rights formalism 292
  TWAIL movement 272–75
postracial nationalism 20, 286–98, 313–14
  colorblindness 300, 313–14
  functionalism 313–14

liberal theory of multiculturalism, as 265–66
neoformalism 292
pragmatic liberalism, and 314
racial ideology, and 266–67
postracial pragmatism 10–11, 20, 265–67,
298–312
colorblindness 11
cultural diversity over racial justice 10–11
postracial xenophobia 102–3
colorblindness, and 300
contemporary form of racial ideology, as 12
meaning 8–9
neoliberal colorblindness morphing into 8–9,
11–12, 311
ethnic and cultural difference, promotion
of 9–10
ethnocultural integrity as engine for
self-determination 10
postracial pragmatism 10–11
race as fictive nonfiction 9
pragmatic liberalism, and 11, 300
pragmatic colorblindness 301–2
pragmatic liberalism 11–12, 232, 320–21
colorblindness 300
governance 302–3, 319
meaning of 300–1, 309, 314
neoliberalism morphing into 11–12, 19–20,
302, 304, 309, 314–15, 319
pragmatism
legal ideology as 102–3
nature of 102
pragmatic liberalism *see* pragmatic
liberalism
racial ideology, pragmatist style of *see*
postracial xenophobia
Pufendorf, Samuel 54, 55
*Law of Nature and Nations* 50–51
natural law, dictate of right reason as source
for 53–54
natural state of peace, nature of 53
sovereign state holding supreme
authority 51–52
sovereign's natural right of *dominium* over its
territory 52–53
sovereigns not coming together in a social
contract. 54
state as a moral *person* with rights and
duties 50–52

racelessness
neoliberal colorblindness yielding to 303
postracial ideology 303
rise of culture of 301
racial borders 313–37

global governance and democratic
deficits 316–22
unbounded *demos*, argument for 322–30
whether borders of communities inevitably
racialized 331–37
racial discrimination
colonialism as worst form of 206
fight against individual acts of 192
racial subjection, and 66–68
subordination and exclusion 66
*see also* antiracism; antiracialism
racial equality, refugees, and the right to
exclude 253–61
non-discrimination requirement 253–54
refugees 257–60
definition of refugee 258
duty of nonrefoulement 257
economic migrants 258–59
foreignness and xenophobic harm 259–60
Geneva Convention Relating to the Status of
Refugees 257
human rights, and 258–59
persecution, concept of 258–59
UN High Commissioner for Refugees
(UNHCR) 259–60
xenophobic discrimination 259–60
shift toward logic of inclusion in immigration
control 255–57
UN Global Compact on Migration 260
racial hierarchy
antiracism eliminating 17–19, 231
Family of Nations, and 197, 229–30
feature of liberalism, as 64–65
racism, as 72
self-determination, as cure to 231
social realities of 237–38
white supremacy, and 237
racial ideology 1–2, 7, 62–63
antistructural racial ideology,
emergence of 12
boundary problem, solving 119–20
classic style of *see* classic racial ideology
colorblindness as form of 7–8, 236
pointing to ineffective performance in a
competitive marketplace 7–8
empirical and anthropological nature
of 29–30
Family of Nations *see* Family of Nations
formalist racial ideology *see* classic racial
ideology
functionalist racial ideology *see* modern racial
ideology
global structure of 2
growing influence 2

350 INDEX

racial ideology (*cont.*)
  manifestation of the liberal *pomerium*,
    as 62–63
  meaning of 97–103
    ideology as a political and social
      reality 97–100
    ideology as type of language system 101
  modern style of *see* modern racial ideology
  naturalizing juridical science, as form of 113,
    118, 135–60
  postracial *see* postracial xenophobia
  pragmatist style of *see* postracial xenophobia
  racial xenophobia as *see* racial xenophobia
  species of legal ideology, as 96–97
racial justice
  cultural diversity, and 10–11, 284
  decolonization, and 135–36
  *dominium* as weapon in fight for 192–93
  economic justice, and 235
  global migration 4
  human rights 4
    means for realizing racial justice, as 190–91
    racial justice as precondition for exercise
      of 190–91
  *imperium*, and 188
  multiculturalism, and 4, 283
  neoformalism, and 292
  NIEO as means for achieving 135–36
  right of self- determination, and 192–93, 217,
    243–44, 265
  URC 200
  US land laws 170
racial subjection 66–67
  biopolitics of 68–76
    biopower *see* biopower
    distinction between 'bare life' and
      'politicized life' 68–69, 70, 71–72, 73–
      74, 95–96
    *homo sacer* 70–72, 73, 74, 95–96
    inclusive exclusion 68–71, 73–74
    sovereign's right to declare situations of
      exception 69–71
  discourse about nature, as 96
  eugenics as ideology of racial subjection 187
  human classification 115
  radical critique of 67
  racial discrimination, and 66–68
  racial ideology, as 96–97
racial xenophobia 8–9, 11–12
  global context of 76–94
    Bernier and Buffon's characterization of
      human beings as racial beings 76–77
    Blumenbach's subdivision of human species
      into five groups 78

    environment to evolution 80–84
    eugenics 84–87
    physical anthropology, emergence of 77–78
    proto-racial ideas of Blumenbach and
      Herder, dominance of 79–80
    raciality to ethnocultures 87–94
    scientific views 79–80
  ideology of othering 7
  racial ideology 7
raciality 281–85
  emergence as background rule 74–75
  ethnocultures, raciality to 87–94
  eugenics *see* eugenics
  governing and generative power of raciality,
    underestimating 65–66
  Mandate system 201
  racial discrimination *see* racial discrimination
  racial subjection *see* racial subjection
racism 2–3, 6, 9–10
  anti-essentialism, and 7
  antiracism *see* antiracism
  biopower, as 72
  colorblind racism 7–8, 232
  colonization, developing with 72
  fragment and debris, as 12
  irrational personal prejudice, as 236–37
  legitimizing racialized exclusion in genetic and
    biological differences 14–15
  liberal racism, conceptualizing 66–68
  local problem, as 7
  racial hierarchy, as 72
  South African apartheid 3–4
  structural racism 12, 192, 210–11
  xenophobia, and 2
refugees *see under* racial equality, refugees, and
  right to exclude
Rehnquist Court 235–36, 239–40
right to exclude *see* exclusion
Ripley William Z. 85–86
  *The Races of Europe* 85, 182–83
  three primary European races 85
Root, Elihu 121–24, 151–52
  Japan's proposed racial equality clause 171–
    73, 174
  right to exclude 175
rule of law 36–37, 110, 240–41
  legal ideology of 109–10
  nature of 37
  resolving tensions between theses of individual
    right and ordered liberty 36–37

Savigny, Friedrich Carl von 140–42
Scelle, Georges 154
  *Precis de Droit des Gens* 154

INDEX    351

self-determination, right of
   decolonization, and *see under* decolonization
   *dominium*, and *see under dominium*
   human right, as 233
   meaning of 191, 192
   people's right, as 226–27
   prerequisite for exercise of human rights 226–27
Schmitt, Carl 5–6, 321
Silva, Denise Ferreira da 63, 65–67, 68, 70–71,
   73, 74–75, 77–78, 83, 93–94, 95, 100–1,
   315–16, 335–36
Smuts, Jan 161, 162, 173, 174
social integration *see under* integration
societal culture 270, 283
South West Africa/Namibia
   Advisory Opinion on International Status of
     South West Africa 222–23
   Advisory Opinion on legal consequences of
     continued existence of South Africa in
     Namibia 223–26
   termination of South Africa's status as
     Mandatory Power over Namibia 223
sovereigns/sovereignty
   concept of sovereignty 15–16
   *dominium* see *dominium*
   each sovereign enjoying same rights of
     *dominium* and *imperium* 58–59
   Family of Nations
     sovereign equality 125–26, 129–30
     sovereignty alone insufficient to warrant
       membership 119
   globalization, continued relevance of
     sovereignty in 21–22
   Great Powers 116, 129–30
   *imperium* see *imperium*
   national and cultural identity, and *see* national
     and cultural identity
   nonintervention, right of *see under dominium*
   racial ideology *see* racial ideology
   retaining natural rights of self-preservation 55
   right to declare situations of exception 69–71
   right to exclude see *dominium*: sovereign's
     right to exclude
   rights-bearing individuals in a global state of
     nature, sovereigns as 15, 16–17, 49–50,
     55, 58–59, 75–76
   self-determination, right of *see under*
     *dominium*
   sovereign equality 114, 125–26, 129–30
     domestic analogy approach, and 119–32
   sovereign states living together in the state of
     nature 55
   subjects and objects of the international legal
     order, sovereigns as 17

voluntary law of the great society 17
structuralism
   definition of 12–13
   structural racism *see under* racism

Teutonic peoples 85, 115, 124–25, 184, 248–49
Third World Approaches to International
   Law 272–75

ultranationalism
   conservative ultranationalism 265–
     66, 295–97
   ultranationalist xenophobia 286, 292
UN Special Rapporteur on Contemporary Forms
   of Racism 1–2
UNESCO 250–51
   Declaration on Race and Racial
     Prejudice 249–50
   Huxley, and 247–48
   'Statement on Race' 1951 88, 247–51, 255–56
     criticisms of 248–49
     impetus for project 248
     refinements of 249–50
     Second Statement 248–49
United Nations (UN)
   Afro-Asia block 206
   Charter 161, 205–6, 233, 245–46
   Declarations
     Decolonization Declaration 190–91, 254–
       55, 276–77
     Granting of Independence to Colonial
       Peoples 226–27
     Rights of Indigenous Peoples (2007) 277–
       79, 280–81
   decolonizing the UUN 205–7
   establishment of 254–55
   Family of Nations moving to UN 192–93
   Founding members 205–6
   Global Compact on Migration 260
   ICERD *see* International Convention on the
     Elimination of All Forms of Racial
     Discrimination (ICERD)
   refugees *see* racial equality, refugees and right
     to exclude
   Security Council 117, 159
   South West Africa *see* South West Africa
   Tricontinental bloc 189–90
   Trusteeship and Non-Self-Governing
     Territories (NSGT) systems 2–3, 159,
     206, 231–32, 276–77
   UN Sub-Commission on Prevention
     of Discrimination report into
     discrimination 246–47, 249–50
   UNESCO Statements on Race *see* UNESCO

352  INDEX

United States (US)
  antidiscrimination principle 233–38
    ameliorating conditions of historically
      disadvantaged groups 234
    anticlassification/antisubordination
      debate 233–38
    *Brown v. Bd. of Educ.*, disaggregation policy
      of 233–34, 236, 237
    Civil Rights Acts 233–34, 237–38
    civil rights movement, criticisms
      of 231–32
    colorblindness, and 232–34, 238
    cultural difference 279
    disfavoring classifications made on basis of
      race 233–34
    equal protection clause of Fourteenth
      Amendment 233–34
    Fair Housing Act 1965 233–34
    group disadvantaging principle 235–
      36, 237
    preventing irrational and unfair
      injuries 234
    race-neutral decisions with racially
      disproportionate impact 234–35
    unconnectedness 236–37
    Voting Rights Act 1965 233–34
  asylum and refugees 258
  China, and 169
    Chinese migration *see under*
      migration law
  Civil War 74–75, 163, 166–68, 170, 182
  cultural diversity 284–85
  Declaration of Independence 161
    Fourteenth Amendment 163, 167–68, 169,
      233–34, 235–36
  eugenics in migration control *see under*
    migration law: United States
  Family of Nations, and 97–98, 117
  human beings rationally classified along five
    primordial races 109
  indigenous peoples, right of self-
    determination and 279–81
  justifying US intervention abroad 121–24
  migration law *see* migration law:
    United States
  Monroe Doctrine 120–21
  polygenism 81
  postracial nationalism 286–98
  racial ideology and *dominium* in Supreme
    Court 175–81
    Chinese Exclusion case 175–81, 182, 288
    *Fong Yu Ting* 175, 288
    *The Schooner Exchange* 178, 179

  racial xenophobia 85
  Reconstruction 67, 150, 163, 168, 169–70
  sovereign equality 120
Universal Declaration of Human Rights
  (UDHR) 233, 242–43, 245–47, 253–54
Universal Races Congress 1911 (URC) 170,
  189–90, 200–1, 220–21, 226–27, 231, 245
  illustrating inclusive
    multiculturalism 198–99
  racial justice 200
*uti possidetis*
  antiracism, and 216

Vattel, Emerich 53, 54–59, 126–27, 131, 140
  international law, nature of 55–56
  natural law applying to states 55–56
  necessary, arbitrary, and voluntary law of
    nations 55–56
  sovereign equality 114
  sovereign states living together in the state of
    nature 55
  sovereigns each enjoying same rights of
    *dominium* and *imperium* 58–59
  sovereigns retaining natural rights of
    self- preservation 55
  use of force/war 57–58
    'offensive' wars 57–58
    self-defence 57
Vitoria, Francisco 32–33, 60

Washington Consensus 49
  NIEO yielding to 222
*Western Sahara* case 211–14, 278–79
Wheaton, Henry 124–26
  *History of the Law of Nations in Europe and
    America* 124–25
white supremacy 3–4, 10–11, 74–75
  colorblindness fostering new form
    of 236–37
  environmentalism as explanation for white
    supremacy, rebuttal of 80–81
  eugenics 84–85
    disaggregating white supremacy 85
  myth of 206
  race as explanation for 82
  rebuttal of environmentalism as coherent
    explanation for 80–81
  US land laws 170
Wolff, Christian 54–55, 140
  *civitatis maximae* 54–55, 56
Woodrow Wilson, President 170, 191, 200–1
World Bank 239–40
World Trade Organization 222

## INDEX 353

xenology 5–6
xenophobia
ethnocultural 6–7
global problem, as 7
natural occurrence, as 7

postracial *see* postracial xenophobia C
racial *see* racial xenophobia
racism, and *see under* racism
ultranationalist xenophobia 286, 292
xenophobic nationalism 286, 292, 301, 311–12